COME HOME, INDIO

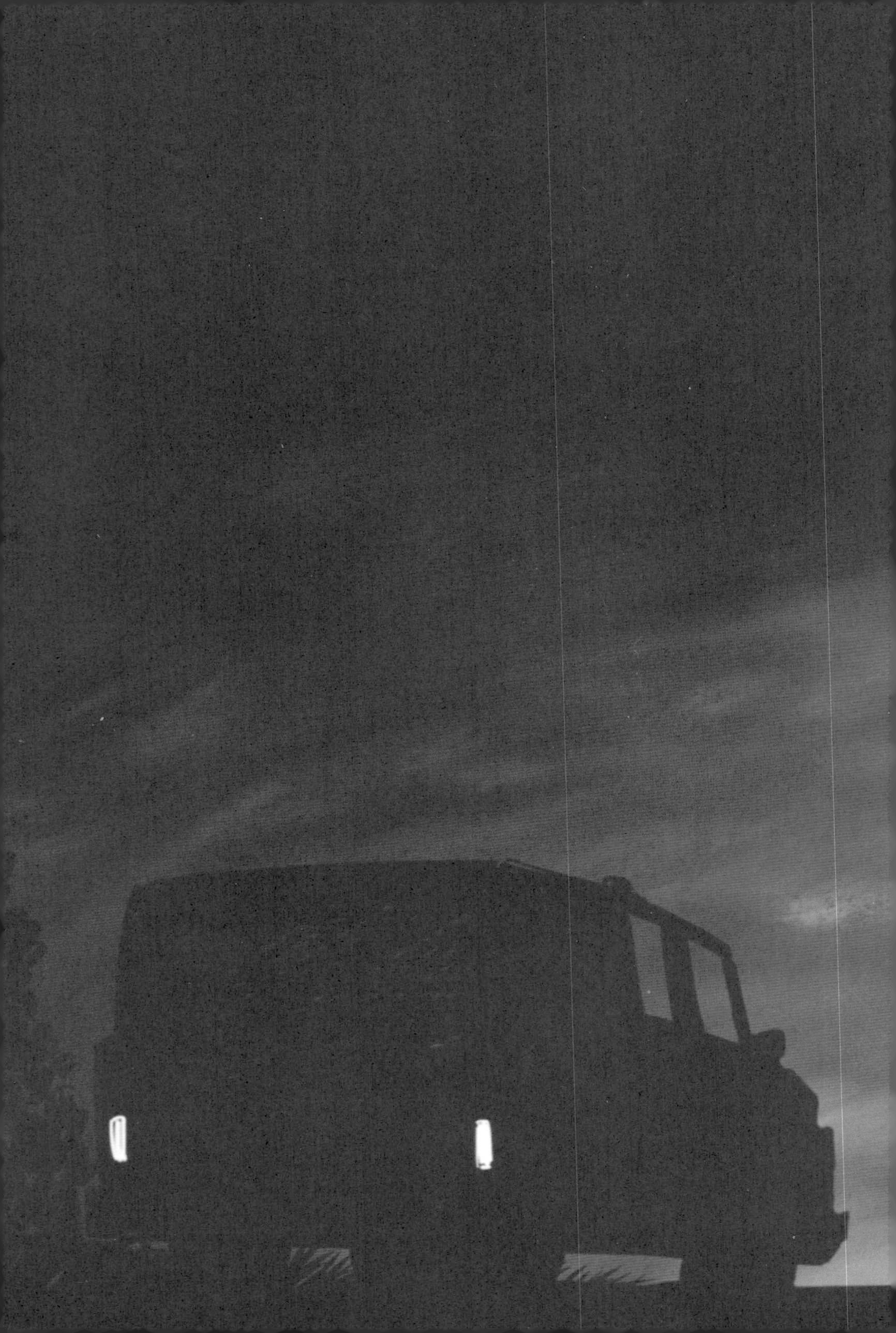

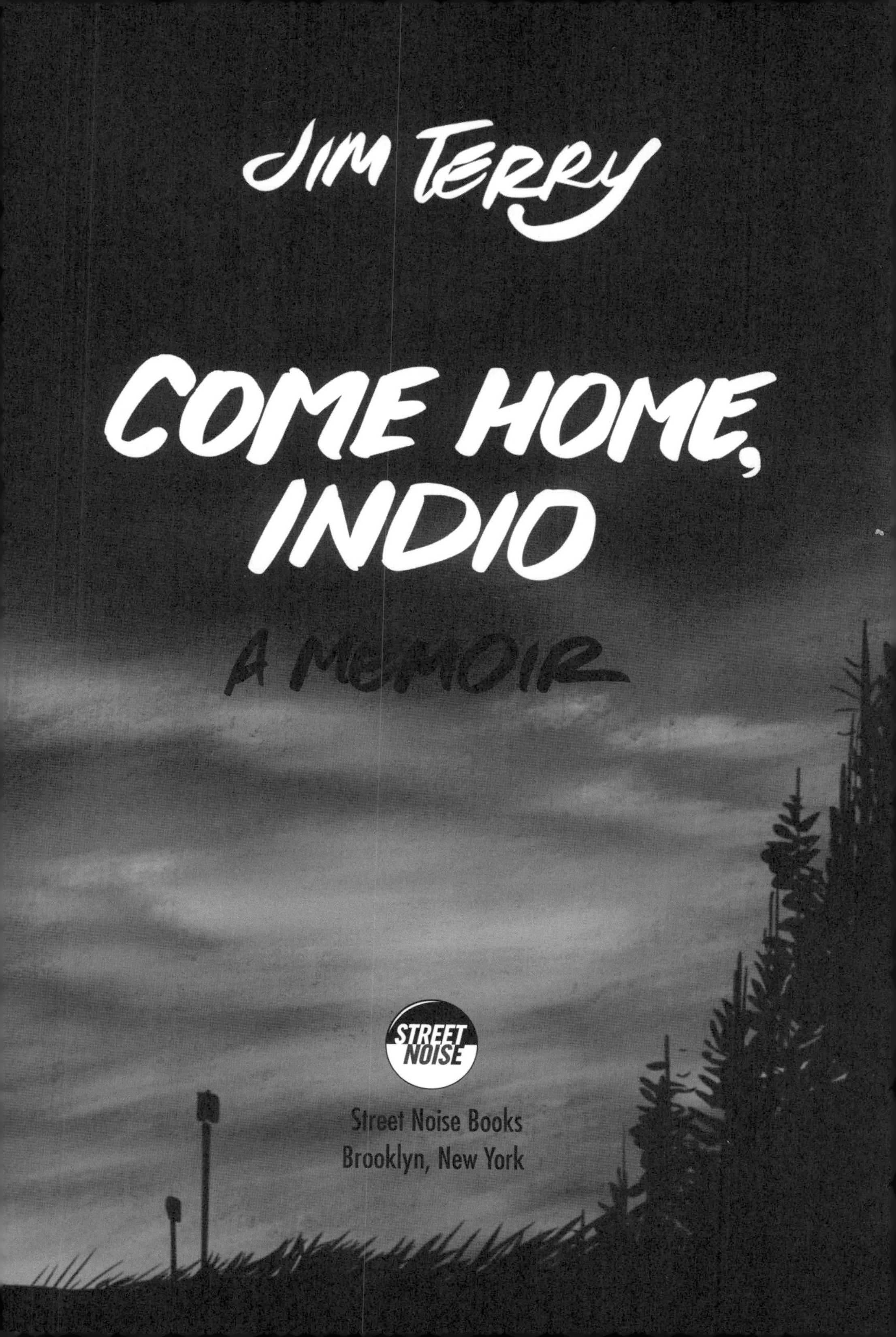

JIM TERRY

COME HOME, INDIO

A MEMOIR

Street Noise Books
Brooklyn, New York

Copyright © 2020 by Jim Terry

All rights reserved.

No part of this publication may be reproduced or transmitted
in any form or by any means, electronic or mechanical,
including photocopy, recording, or any information storage and retrieval system
now known or to be invented, without permission in writing from the publisher,
except by a reviewer who wishes to quote brief passages
in connection with a print, online, or broadcast review.

Library of Congress CIP data available.

ISBN 978-1-951-491-04-8

Edited by Whit Taylor
Book design by Liz Frances

Printed in South Korea

9 8 7 6 5 4 3 2 1

First Edition

For those who are still here.

PART 1

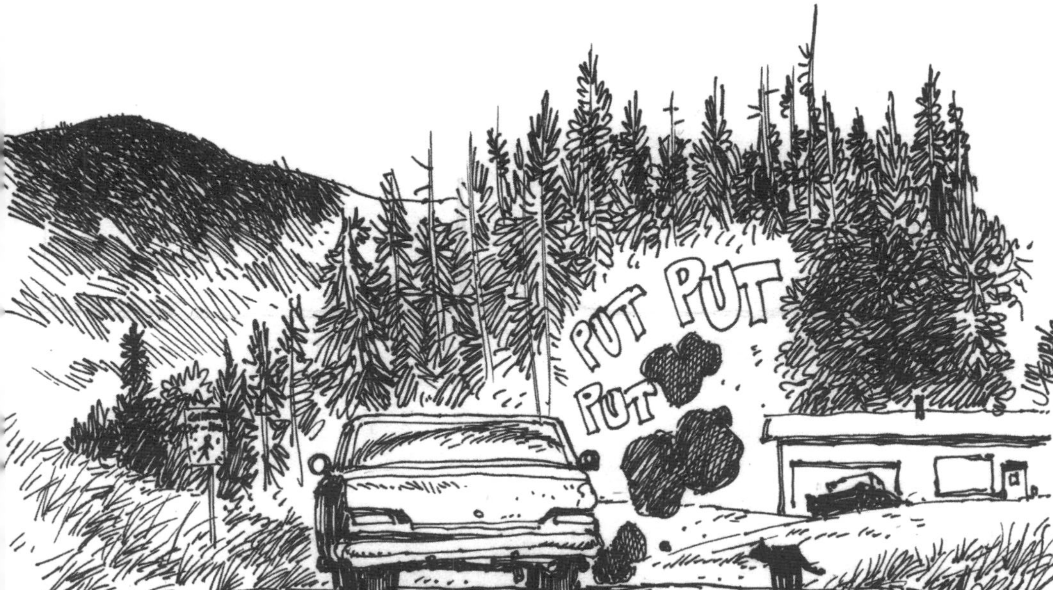
PUT PUT
PUT

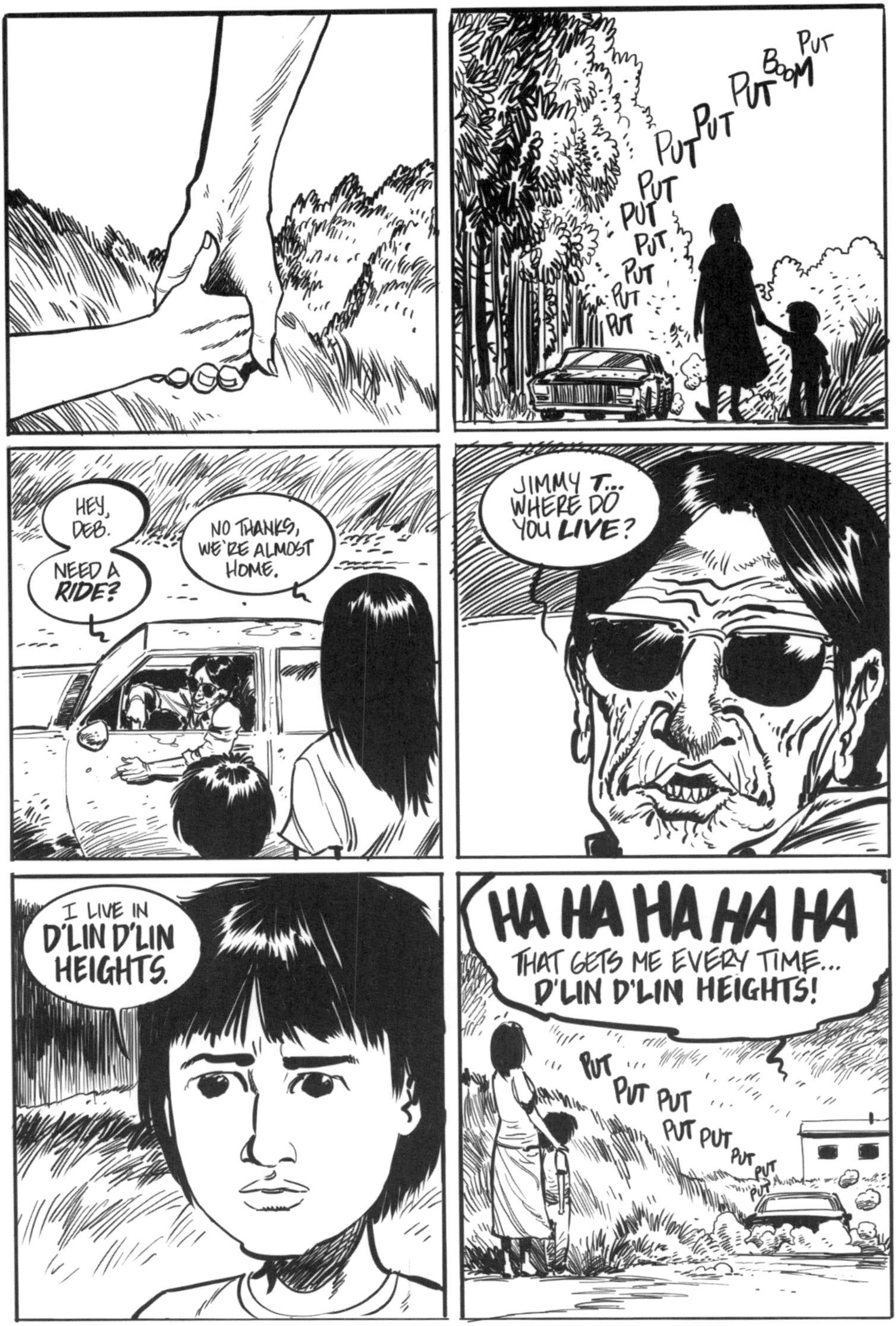
PUT PUT PUT PUT PUT PUT PUT PUT PUT BOOM PUT
HEY, DEB.
NEED A RIDE?
NO THANKS, WE'RE ALMOST HOME.
JIMMY T... WHERE DO YOU LIVE?
I LIVE IN D'LIN D'LIN HEIGHTS.
HA HA HA HA HA
THAT GETS ME EVERY TIME... D'LIN D'LIN HEIGHTS!
PUT PUT PUT PUT PUT PUT PUT PUT

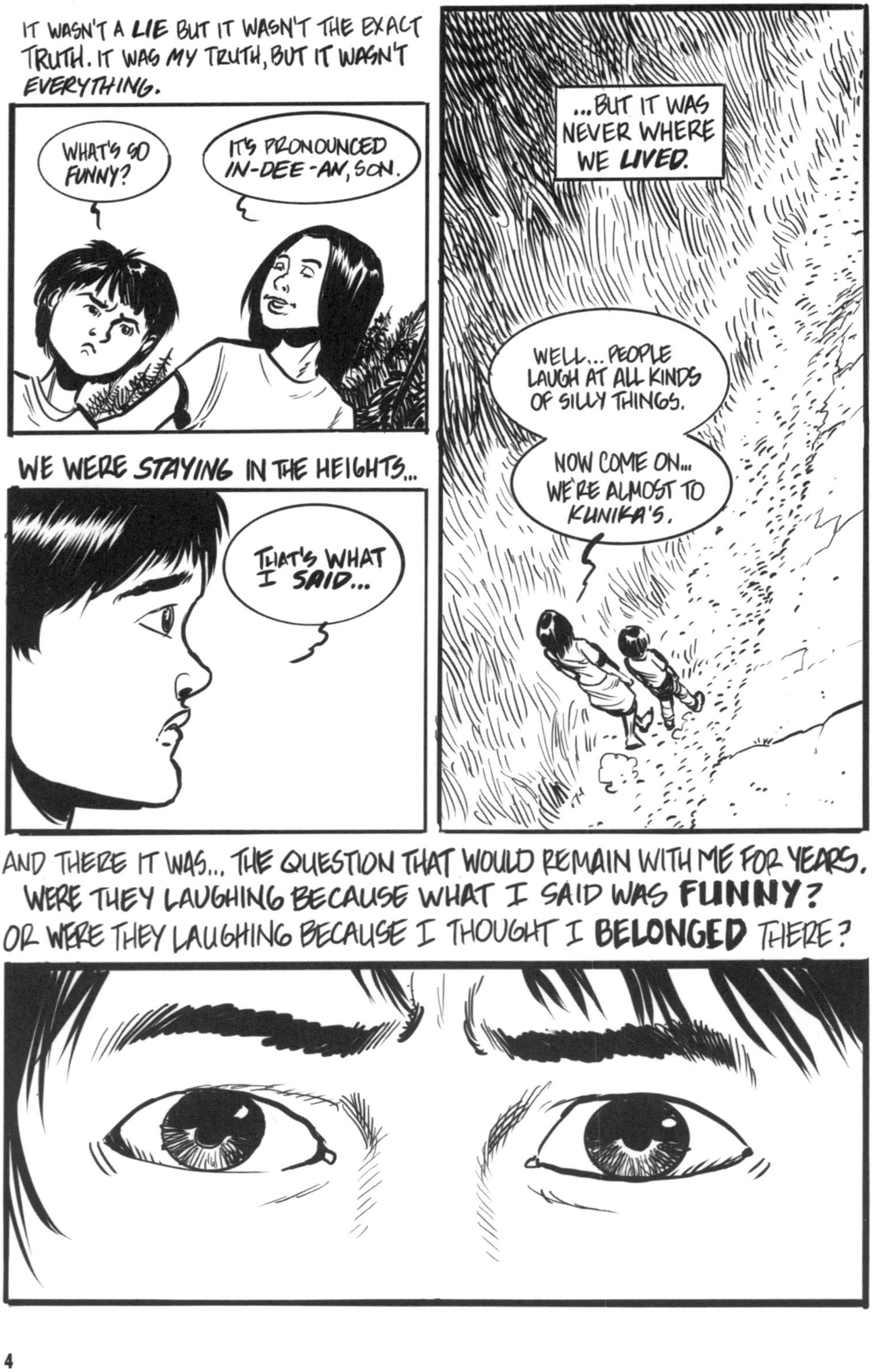
IT WASN'T A LIE BUT IT WASN'T THE EXACT TRUTH. IT WAS MY TRUTH, BUT IT WASN'T EVERYTHING.
WHAT'S SO FUNNY?
IT'S PRONOUNCED IN-DEE-AN, SON.
WE WERE STAYING IN THE HEIGHTS...
THAT'S WHAT I SAID...
...BUT IT WAS NEVER WHERE WE LIVED.
WELL... PEOPLE LAUGH AT ALL KINDS OF SILLY THINGS.
NOW COME ON... WE'RE ALMOST TO KUNIKA'S.
AND THERE IT WAS... THE QUESTION THAT WOULD REMAIN WITH ME FOR YEARS.
WERE THEY LAUGHING BECAUSE WHAT I SAID WAS FUNNY?
OR WERE THEY LAUGHING BECAUSE I THOUGHT I BELONGED THERE?

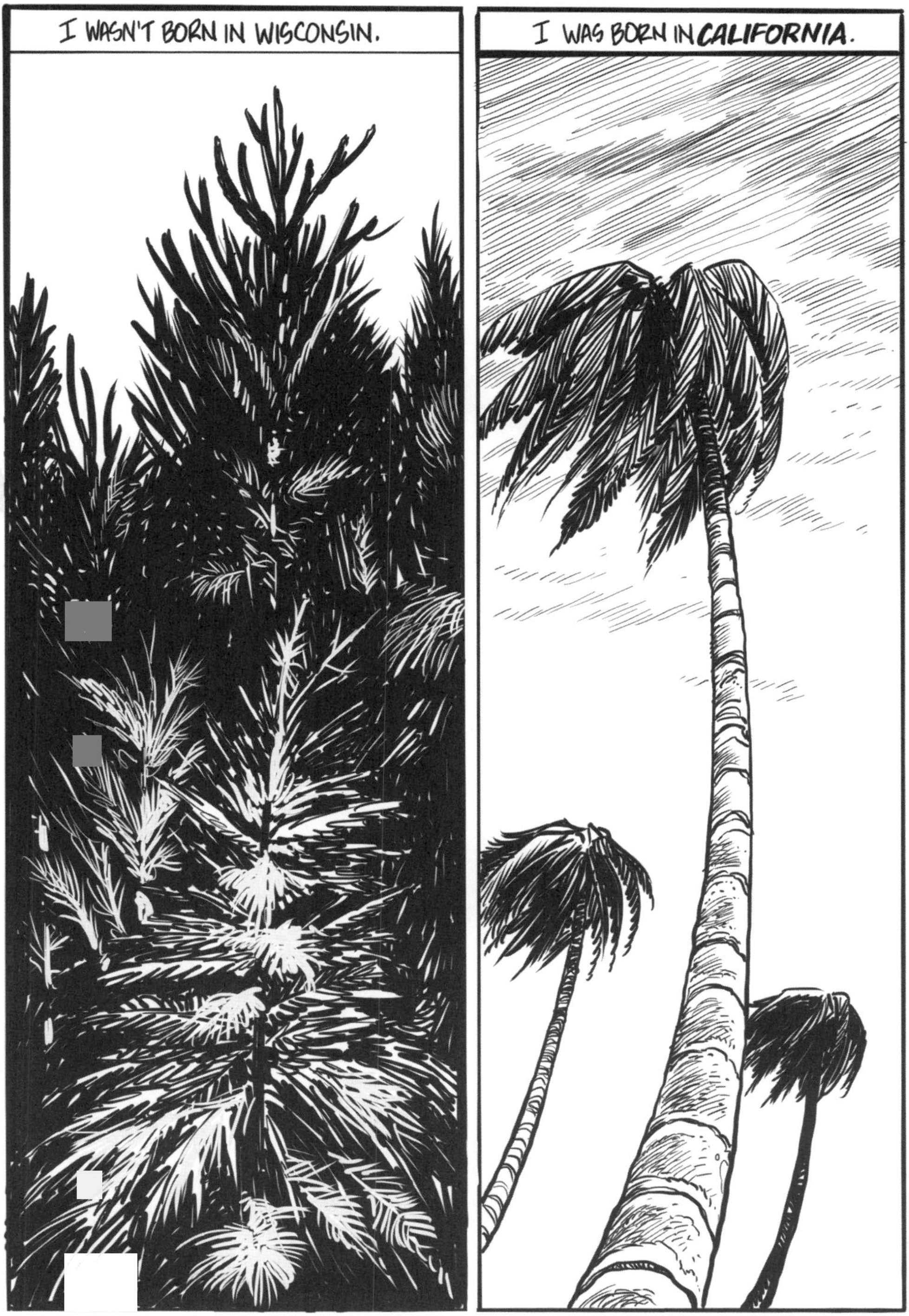
I WASN'T BORN IN WISCONSIN.
I WAS BORN IN CALIFORNIA.

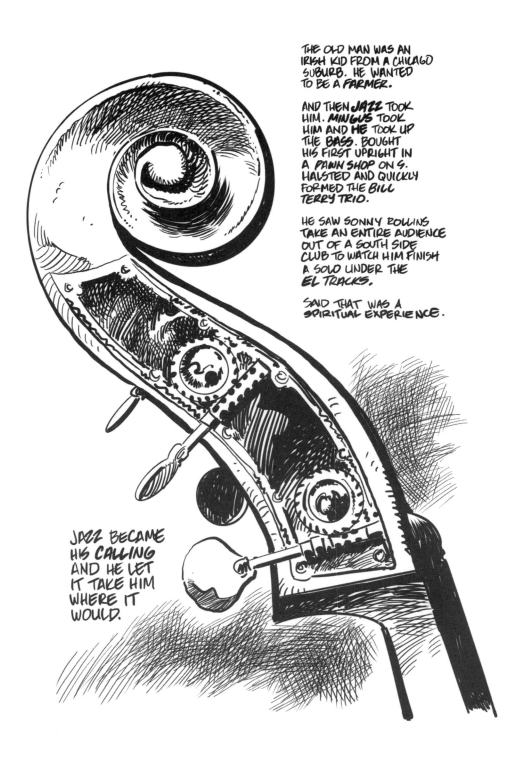

THE OLD MAN WAS AN IRISH KID FROM A CHICAGO SUBURB. HE WANTED TO BE A *FARMER*.

AND THEN *JAZZ* TOOK HIM. *MINGUS* TOOK HIM AND **HE** TOOK UP THE **BASS**. BOUGHT HIS FIRST UPRIGHT IN A *PAWN SHOP* ON S. HALSTED AND QUICKLY FORMED THE *BILL TERRY TRIO*.

HE SAW SONNY ROLLINS TAKE AN ENTIRE AUDIENCE OUT OF A SOUTH SIDE CLUB TO WATCH HIM FINISH A SOLO UNDER THE EL TRACKS.

SAID THAT WAS A SPIRITUAL EXPERIENCE.

JAZZ BECAME HIS *CALLING* AND HE LET IT TAKE HIM WHERE IT WOULD.

IT TOOK HIM TO NEW YORK, FLORIDA, ARIZONA ...ZIG ZAGGING UNTIL HE HIT *CALIFORNIA*. HIS ***SERIOUS LOOK*** WAS ***PERFECTED*** BY THEN AND HE WAS READY TO PLAY SOME MUSIC.

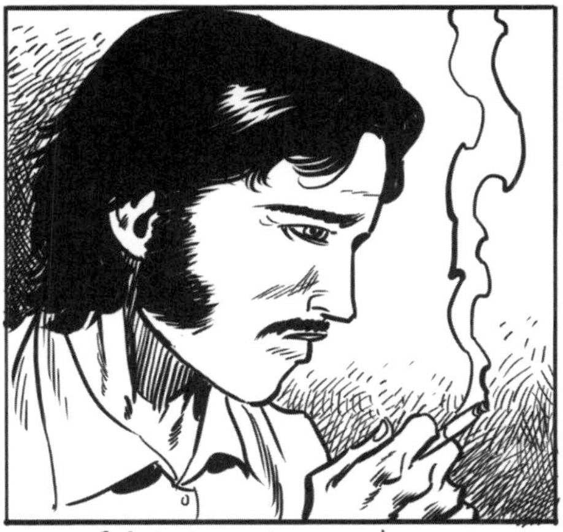

POP WAS THE ONLY SURVIVOR OF *FOUR SONS*. ONE DIED OF PNEUMONIA, ONE WAS HIT BY A *TRAIN*, AND ***TOMMY*** - THE YOUNGEST AND HIS *BEST FRIEND* - WAS KILLED BY A *HIT-AND-RUN DRIVER*.

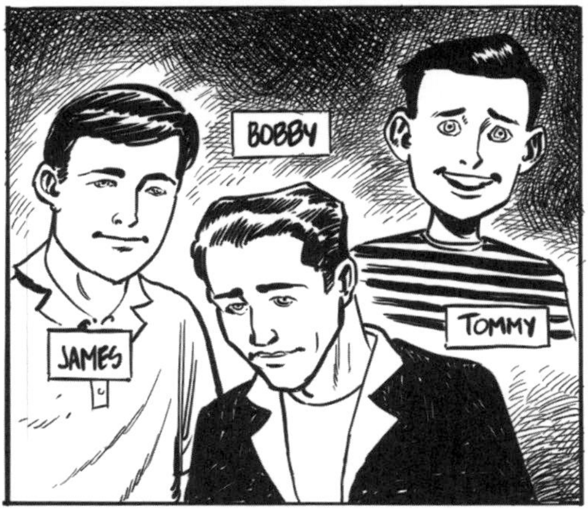
BOBBY
JAMES
TOMMY

HE GOT TO **L.A.** AND COULDN'T HAVE *CARED LESS* ABOUT ***ROCK AND ROLL*** OR THE *HIPPIE SCENE*... HE WAS **ALL** ABOUT ***JAZZ*** AND THE NEW *LATIN MUSIC* THAT WAS EXPLODING OUT OF ***PUERTO RICO*** AND ***NEW YORK CITY***... **SALSA.**

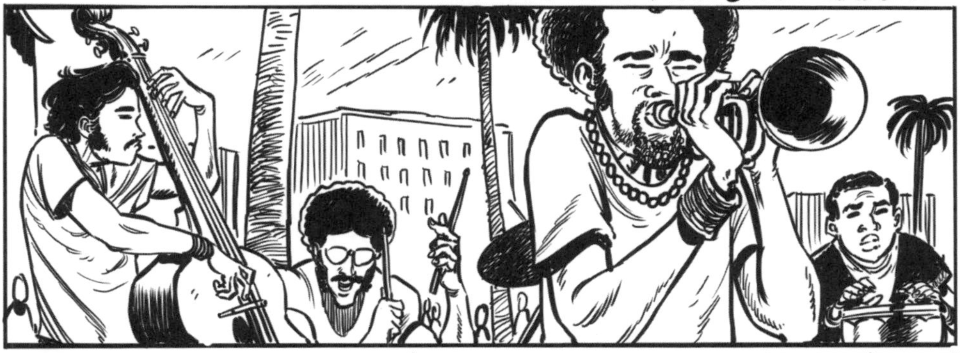

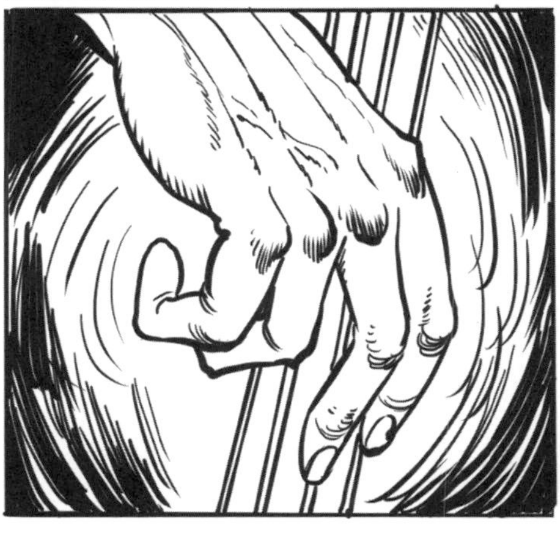

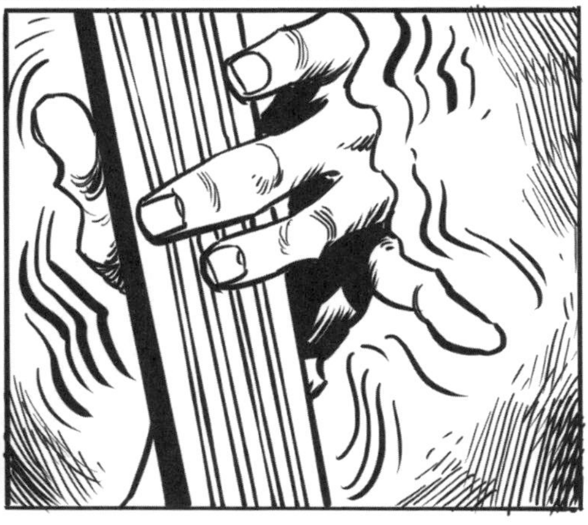

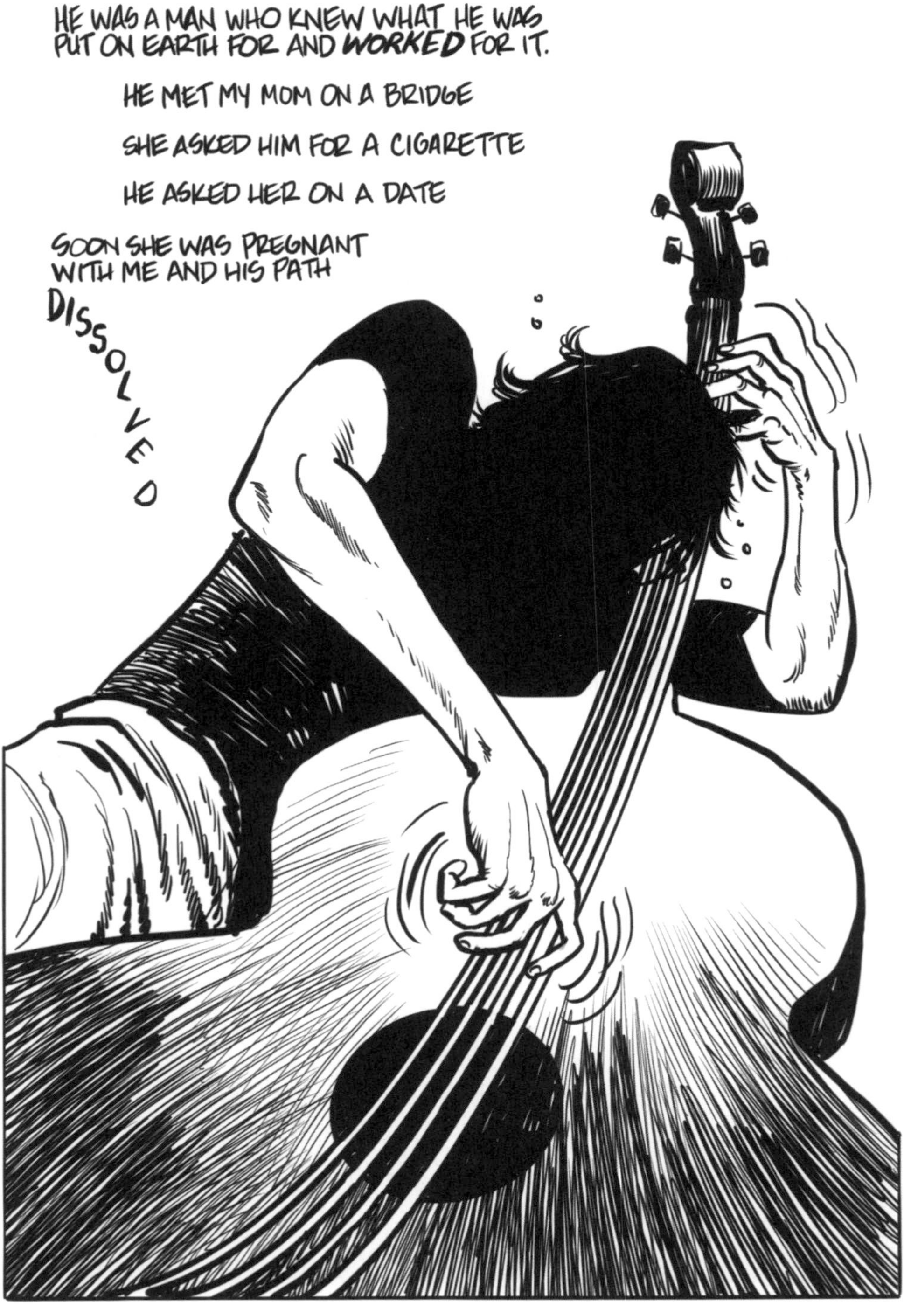
HE WAS A MAN WHO KNEW WHAT HE WAS PUT ON EARTH FOR AND ***WORKED*** FOR IT.
HE MET MY MOM ON A BRIDGE
SHE ASKED HIM FOR A CIGARETTE
HE ASKED HER ON A DATE
SOON SHE WAS PREGNANT WITH ME AND HIS PATH
DISSOLVED

THAT'S HOW *SHE* TOLD IT, ANWAY, THO SHE WAS NEVER ONE TO SHY AWAY FROM A BIT OF *DRAMATIC* **EMBELLISHMENT.**

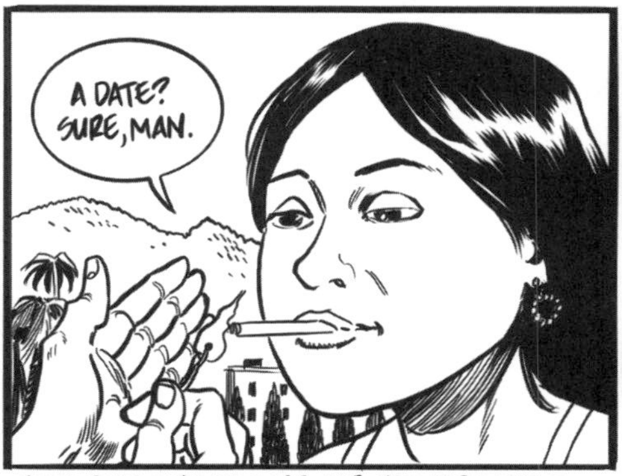
A DATE? SURE, MAN.

SHE WAS FROM A DIFFERENT *WORLD* THAN HE WAS. THE FIRST BORN OF EIGHT, SHE COULD RECALL LIVING IN A *CIIPÓROKÉ* - A MUD-AND-WOOD SHELTER.

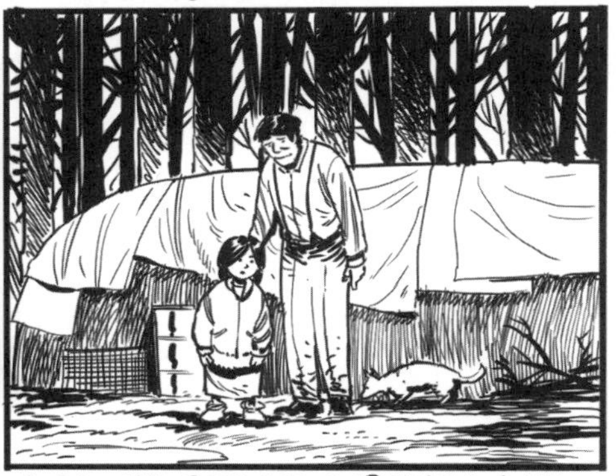

HER CHILDHOOD WASN'T THE *EASIEST* - KUNIKA WAS AN ACTIVIST AND MOM WAS OFTEN LEFT TO TEND THE HOUSE AND KIDS.

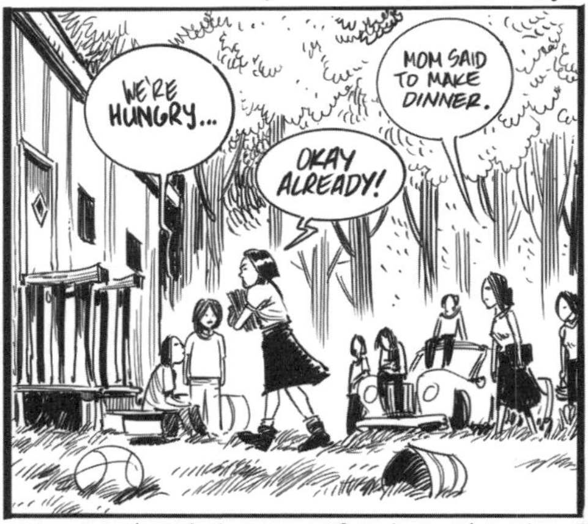
WE'RE HUNGRY...
MOM SAID TO MAKE DINNER.
OKAY ALREADY!

SHE LOVED READING AND MUSIC AND HAD A BEAUTIFUL SINGING VOICE. YEARS LATER SHE SANG THE *NATIONAL ANTHEM* AT A **WHITE SOX GAME.**

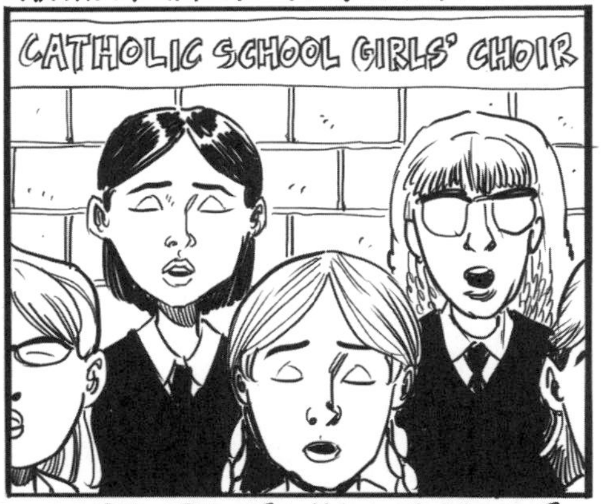
CATHOLIC SCHOOL GIRLS' CHOIR

IN COLLEGE SHE MET A GUY WHO PROMISED HER IT WAS *IMPOSSIBLE* TO GET PREGNANT THE FIRST TIME... HE MUST HAVE *LIED*, BECAUSE NINE MONTHS LATER ***TONY*** WAS BORN. SHE NEVER SAID MUCH ABOUT HIS DAD.

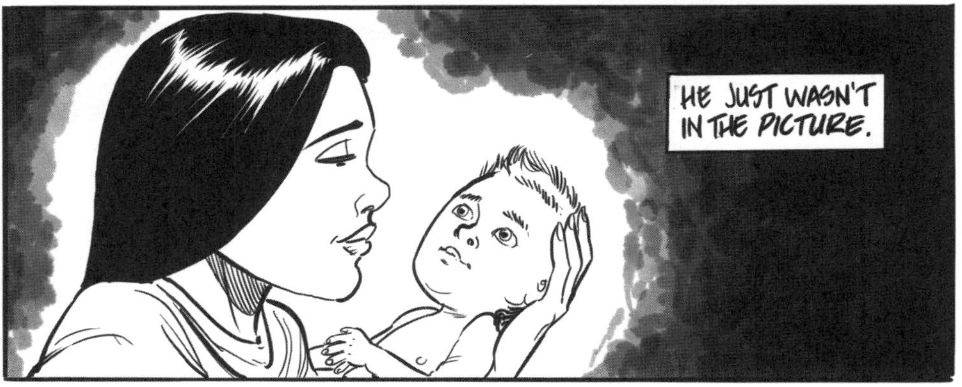
HE JUST WASN'T IN THE *PICTURE*.

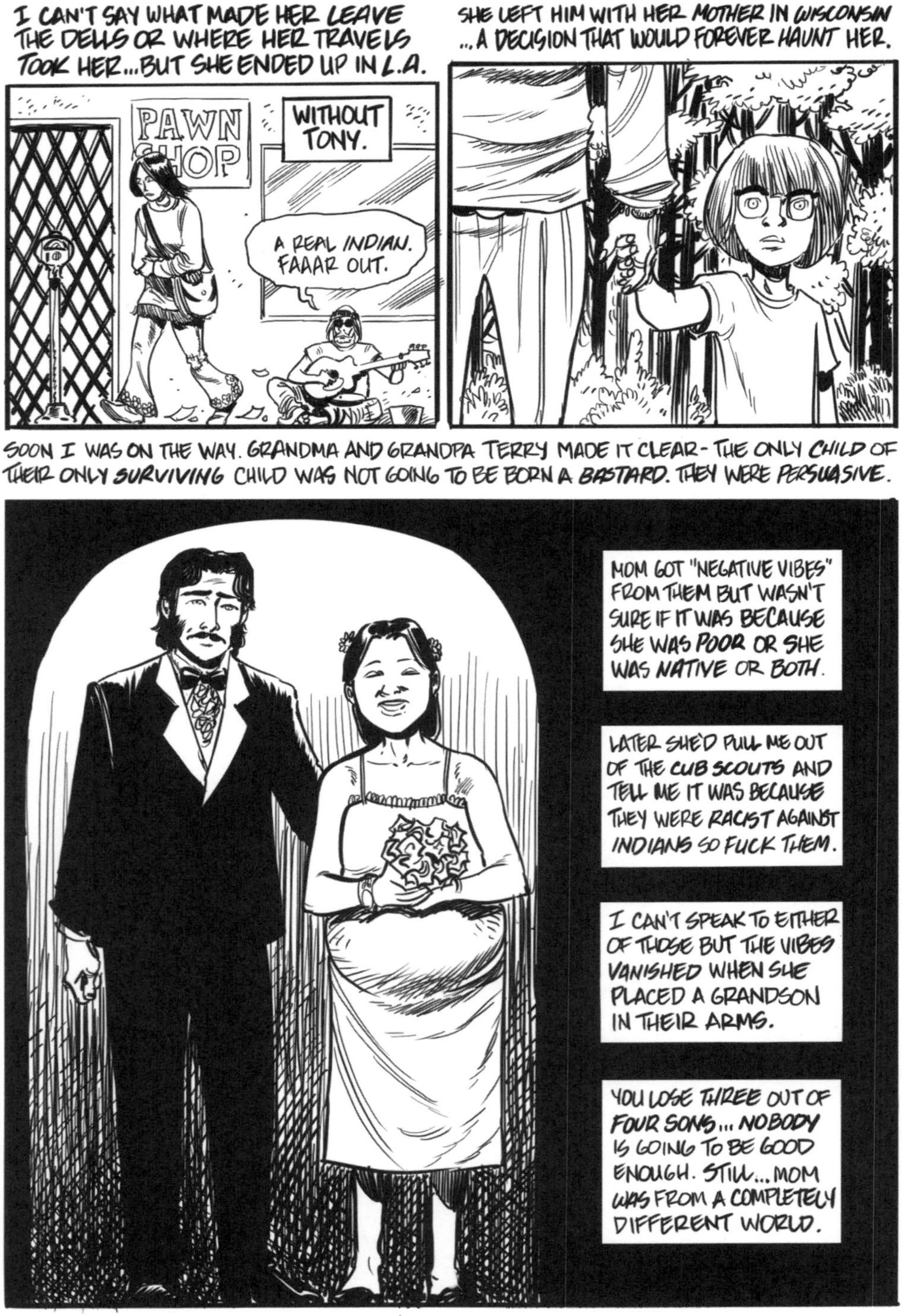
I CAN'T SAY WHAT MADE HER LEAVE THE DELLS OR WHERE HER TRAVELS TOOK HER... BUT SHE ENDED UP IN L.A.
PAWN SHOP
WITHOUT TONY.
A REAL INDIAN. FAAAR OUT.
SHE LEFT HIM WITH HER MOTHER IN WISCONSIN ...A DECISION THAT WOULD FOREVER HAUNT HER.
SOON I WAS ON THE WAY. GRANDMA AND GRANDPA TERRY MADE IT CLEAR- THE ONLY CHILD OF THEIR ONLY SURVIVING CHILD WAS NOT GOING TO BE BORN A BASTARD. THEY WERE PERSUASIVE.
MOM GOT "NEGATIVE VIBES" FROM THEM BUT WASN'T SURE IF IT WAS BECAUSE SHE WAS POOR OR SHE WAS NATIVE OR BOTH.
LATER SHE'D PULL ME OUT OF THE CUB SCOUTS AND TELL ME IT WAS BECAUSE THEY WERE RACIST AGAINST INDIANS SO FUCK THEM.
I CAN'T SPEAK TO EITHER OF THOSE BUT THE VIBES VANISHED WHEN SHE PLACED A GRANDSON IN THEIR ARMS.
YOU LOSE THREE OUT OF FOUR SONS... NOBODY IS GOING TO BE GOOD ENOUGH. STILL... MOM WAS FROM A COMPLETELY DIFFERENT WORLD.

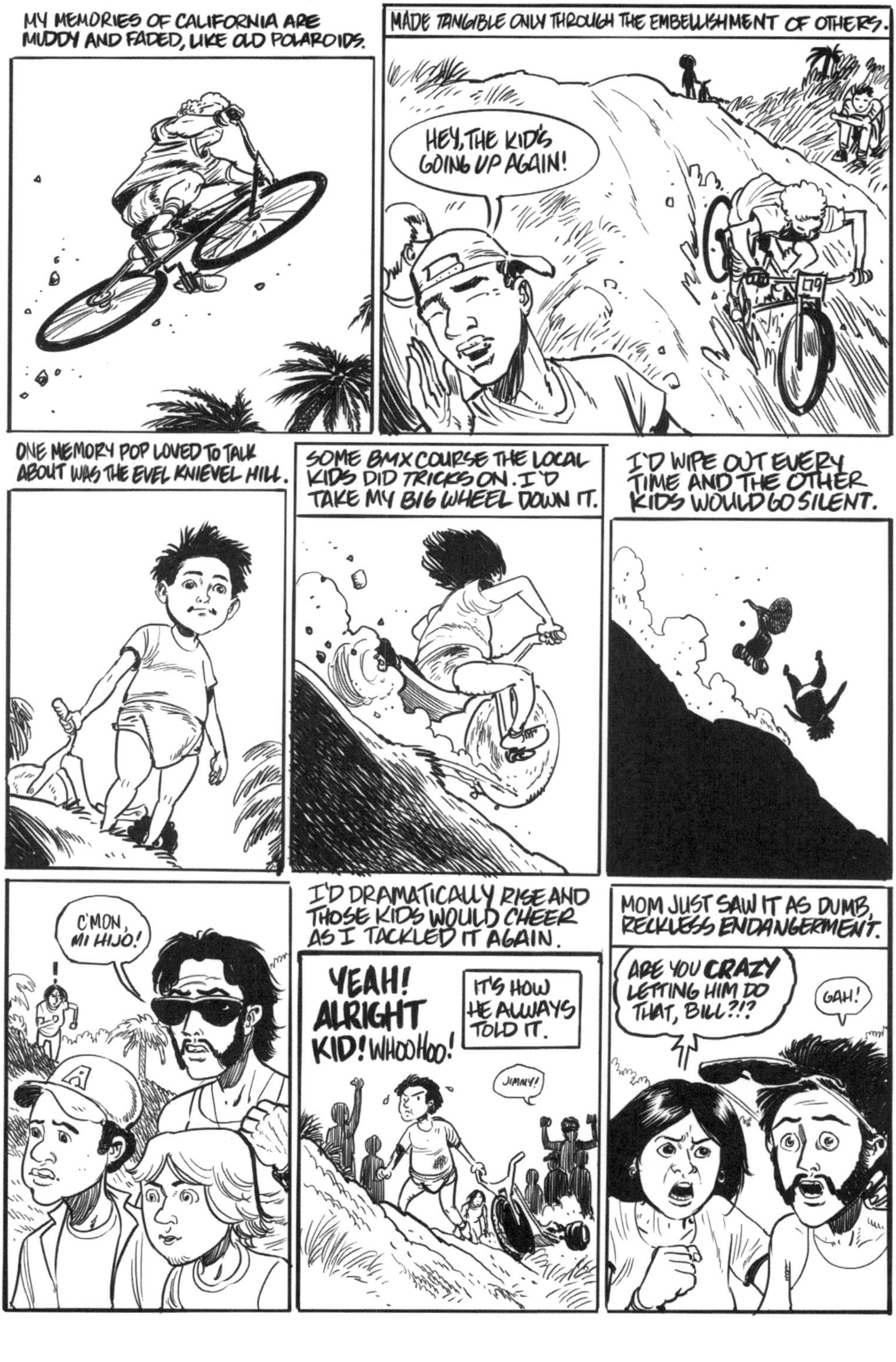

MY MEMORIES OF CALIFORNIA ARE MUDDY AND FADED, LIKE OLD POLAROIDS.
MADE TANGIBLE ONLY THROUGH THE EMBELLISHMENT OF OTHERS.
HEY, THE KID'S GOING UP AGAIN!
ONE MEMORY POP LOVED TO TALK ABOUT WAS THE EVEL KNIEVEL HILL.
SOME BMX COURSE THE LOCAL KIDS DID TRICKS ON. I'D TAKE MY BIG WHEEL DOWN IT.
I'D WIPE OUT EVERY TIME AND THE OTHER KIDS WOULD GO SILENT.
C'MON, MI HIJO!
!
I'D DRAMATICALLY RISE AND THOSE KIDS WOULD CHEER AS I TACKLED IT AGAIN.
YEAH! ALRIGHT KID! WHOOHOO!
IT'S HOW HE ALWAYS TOLD IT.
JIMMY!
MOM JUST SAW IT AS DUMB, RECKLESS ENDANGERMENT.
ARE YOU CRAZY LETTING HIM DO THAT, BILL?!?
GAH!

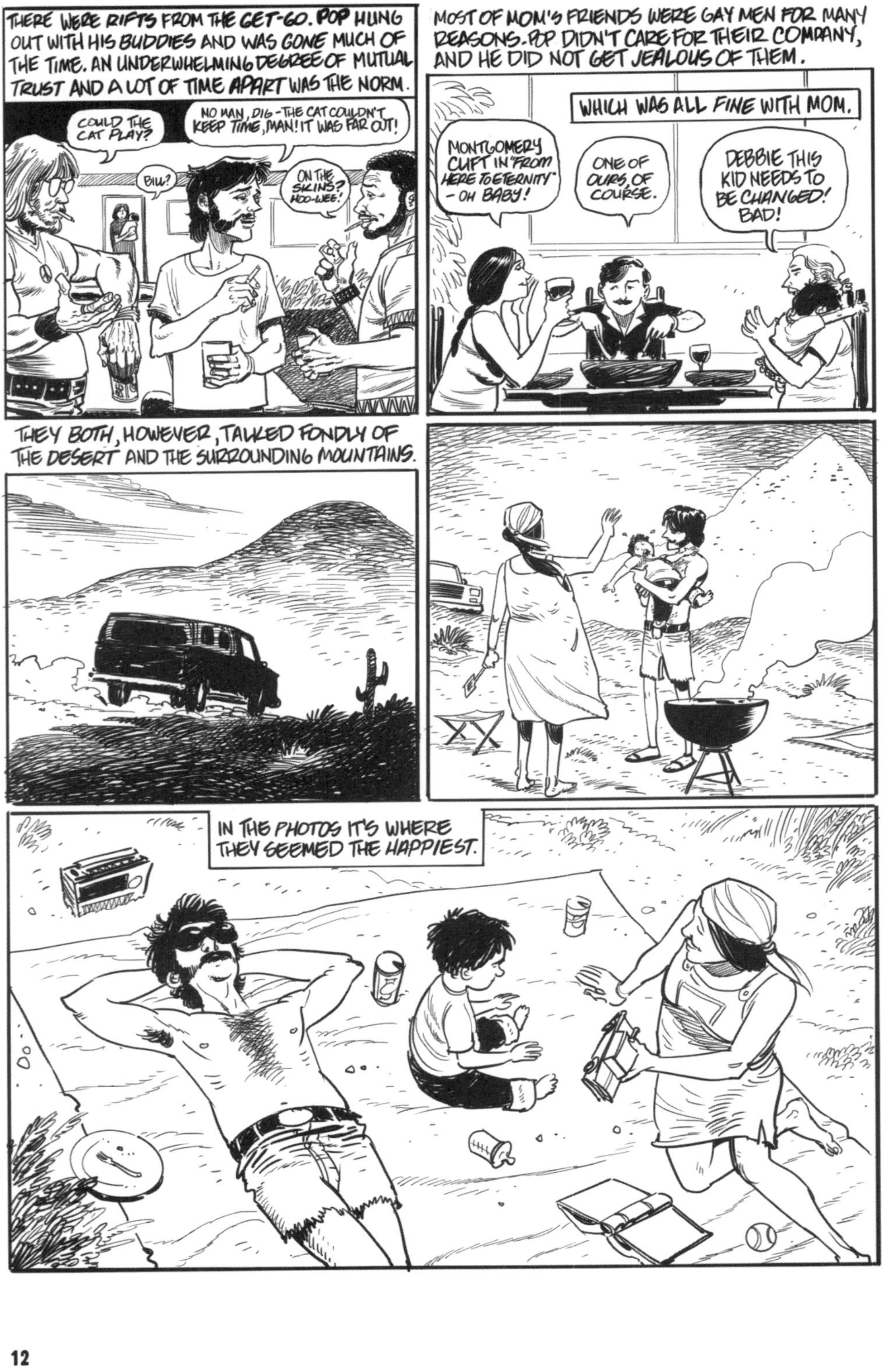
THERE WERE RIFTS FROM THE GET-GO. POP HUNG OUT WITH HIS BUDDIES AND WAS GONE MUCH OF THE TIME. AN UNDERWHELMING DEGREE OF MUTUAL TRUST AND A LOT OF TIME APART WAS THE NORM.
COULD THE CAT PLAY?
NO MAN, DIG - THE CAT COULDN'T KEEP TIME, MAN! IT WAS FAR OUT!
BILL?
ON THE SKINS? HOO-WEE!
MOST OF MOM'S FRIENDS WERE GAY MEN FOR MANY REASONS. POP DIDN'T CARE FOR THEIR COMPANY, AND HE DID NOT GET JEALOUS OF THEM.
WHICH WAS ALL FINE WITH MOM.
MONTGOMERY CLIFT IN "FROM HERE TO ETERNITY" - OH BABY!
ONE OF OURS, OF COURSE.
DEBBIE THIS KID NEEDS TO BE CHANGED! BAD!
THEY BOTH, HOWEVER, TALKED FONDLY OF THE DESERT AND THE SURROUNDING MOUNTAINS.
IN THE PHOTOS IT'S WHERE THEY SEEMED THE HAPPIEST.

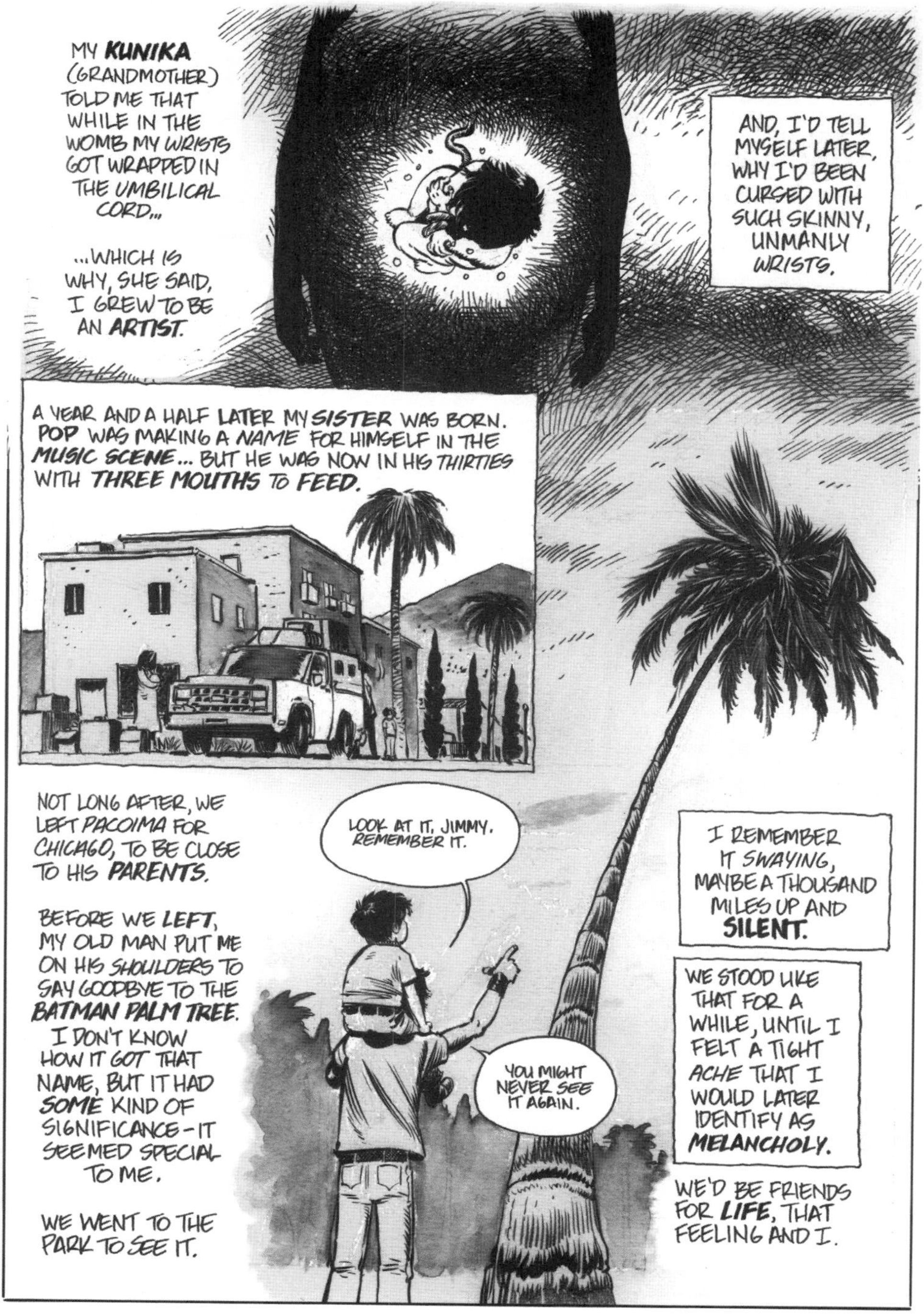
MY KUNIKA (GRANDMOTHER) TOLD ME THAT WHILE IN THE WOMB MY WRISTS GOT WRAPPED IN THE UMBILICAL CORD...
...WHICH IS WHY, SHE SAID, I GREW TO BE AN ARTIST.
AND, I'D TELL MYSELF LATER, WHY I'D BEEN CURSED WITH SUCH SKINNY, UNMANLY WRISTS.
A YEAR AND A HALF LATER MY SISTER WAS BORN. POP WAS MAKING A NAME FOR HIMSELF IN THE MUSIC SCENE... BUT HE WAS NOW IN HIS THIRTIES WITH THREE MOUTHS TO FEED.
NOT LONG AFTER, WE LEFT PACOIMA FOR CHICAGO, TO BE CLOSE TO HIS PARENTS.
BEFORE WE LEFT, MY OLD MAN PUT ME ON HIS SHOULDERS TO SAY GOODBYE TO THE BATMAN PALM TREE.
I DON'T KNOW HOW IT GOT THAT NAME, BUT IT HAD SOME KIND OF SIGNIFICANCE - IT SEEMED SPECIAL TO ME.
WE WENT TO THE PARK TO SEE IT.
LOOK AT IT, JIMMY. REMEMBER IT.
YOU MIGHT NEVER SEE IT AGAIN.
I REMEMBER IT SWAYING, MAYBE A THOUSAND MILES UP AND SILENT.
WE STOOD LIKE THAT FOR A WHILE, UNTIL I FELT A TIGHT ACHE THAT I WOULD LATER IDENTIFY AS MELANCHOLY.
WE'D BE FRIENDS FOR LIFE, THAT FEELING AND I.

POP SAID GOODBYE TO HIS FRIENDS AND HIS CAREER TRAJECTORY. HE WAS LEAVING IT ALL.

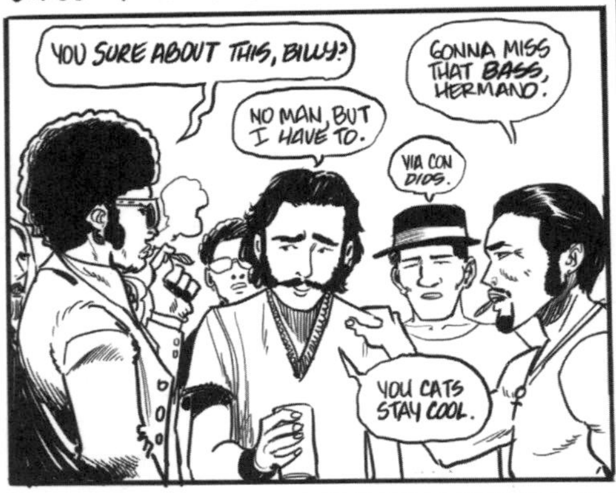
YOU SURE ABOUT THIS, BILLY?
NO MAN, BUT I HAVE TO.
GONNA MISS THAT BASS, HERMANO.
VIA CON DIOS.
YOU CATS STAY COOL.

MOM SAID GOODBYE TO THE FRIENDS SHE'D MADE. SHE WAS BEING PULLED BACK TOWARD THE WOODS.

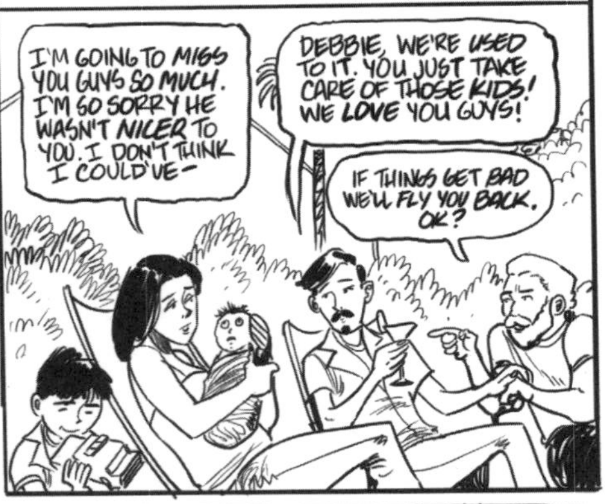
I'M GOING TO MISS YOU GUYS SO MUCH. I'M SO SORRY HE WASN'T NICER TO YOU. I DON'T THINK I COULD'VE-
DEBBIE, WE'RE USED TO IT. YOU JUST TAKE CARE OF THOSE KIDS! WE LOVE YOU GUYS!
IF THINGS GET BAD WE'LL FLY YOU BACK. OK?

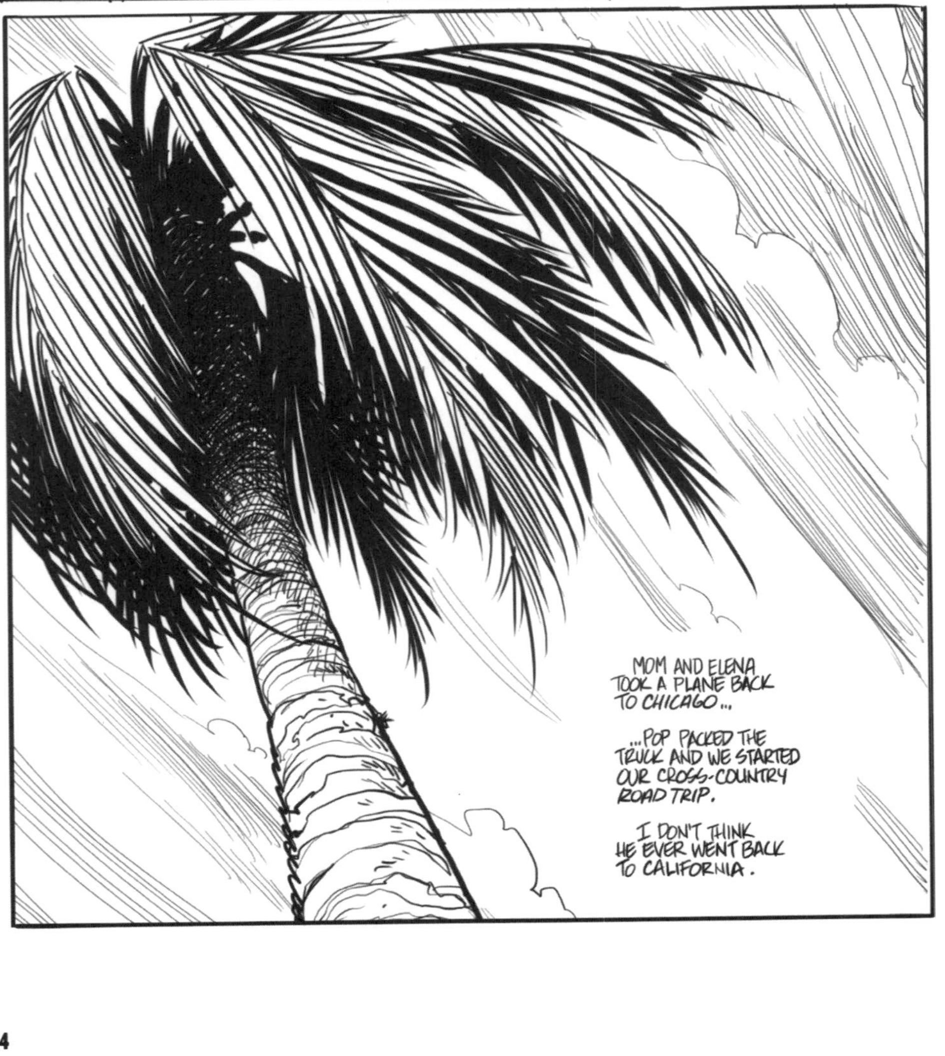
MOM AND ELENA TOOK A PLANE BACK TO CHICAGO...
...POP PACKED THE TRUCK AND WE STARTED OUR CROSS-COUNTRY ROAD TRIP.
I DON'T THINK HE EVER WENT BACK TO CALIFORNIA.

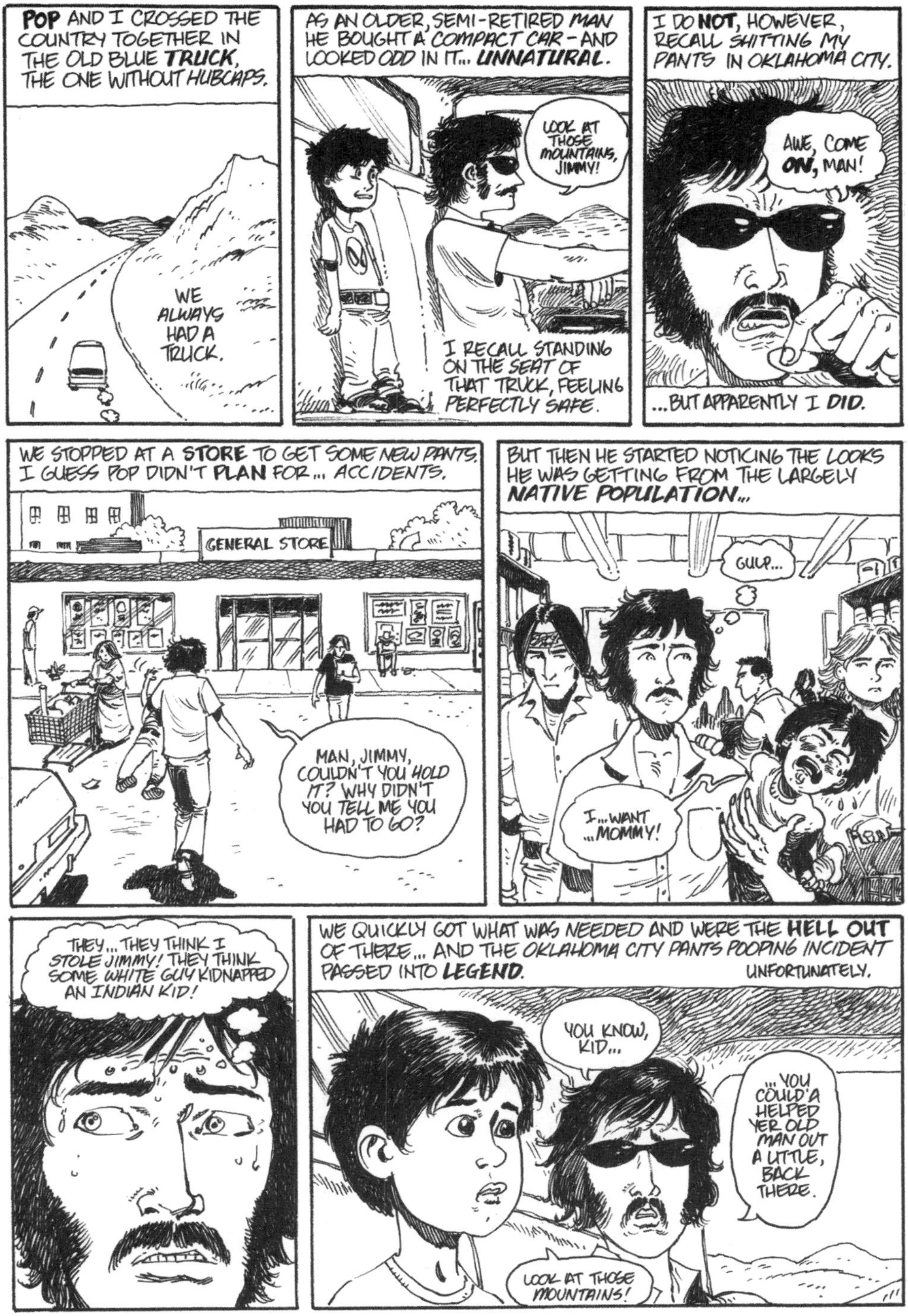
POP AND I CROSSED THE COUNTRY TOGETHER IN THE OLD BLUE TRUCK, THE ONE WITHOUT HUBCAPS.
WE ALWAYS HAD A TRUCK.
AS AN OLDER, SEMI-RETIRED MAN HE BOUGHT A COMPACT CAR - AND LOOKED ODD IN IT... UNNATURAL.
LOOK AT THOSE MOUNTAINS, JIMMY!
I RECALL STANDING ON THE SEAT OF THAT TRUCK, FEELING PERFECTLY SAFE.
I DO NOT, HOWEVER, RECALL SHITTING MY PANTS IN OKLAHOMA CITY.
AWE, COME ON, MAN!
...BUT APPARENTLY I DID.
WE STOPPED AT A STORE TO GET SOME NEW PANTS. I GUESS POP DIDN'T PLAN FOR... ACCIDENTS.
GENERAL STORE
MAN, JIMMY, COULDN'T YOU HOLD IT? WHY DIDN'T YOU TELL ME YOU HAD TO GO?
BUT THEN HE STARTED NOTICING THE LOOKS HE WAS GETTING FROM THE LARGELY NATIVE POPULATION...
GULP...
I... WANT ...MOMMY!
THEY... THEY THINK I STOLE JIMMY! THEY THINK SOME WHITE GUY KIDNAPPED AN INDIAN KID!
WE QUICKLY GOT WHAT WAS NEEDED AND WERE THE HELL OUT OF THERE... AND THE OKLAHOMA CITY PANTS POOPING INCIDENT PASSED INTO LEGEND. UNFORTUNATELY.
YOU KNOW, KID...
...YOU COULD'A HELPED YER OLD MAN OUT A LITTLE, BACK THERE.
LOOK AT THOSE MOUNTAINS!

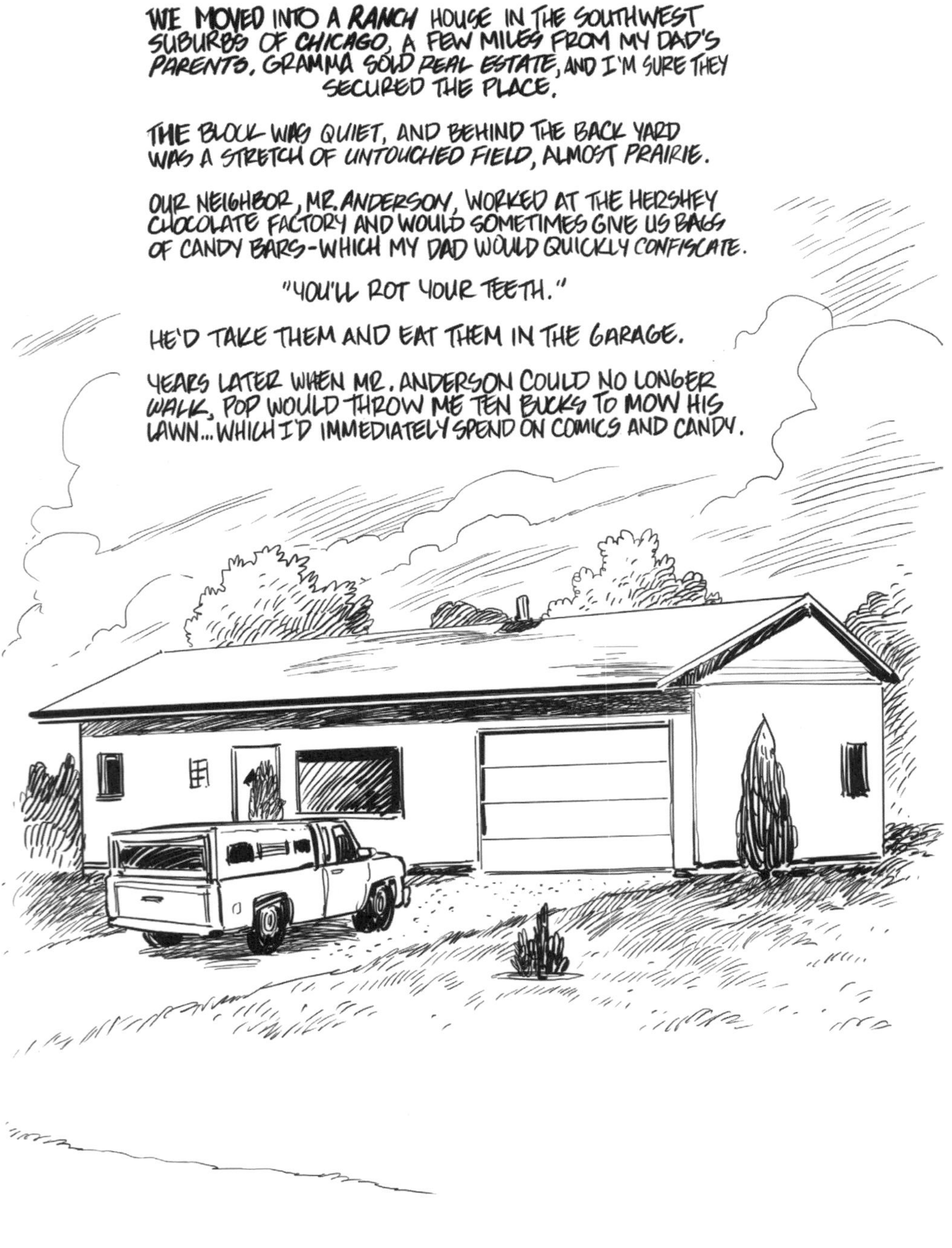
WE MOVED INTO A RANCH HOUSE IN THE SOUTHWEST SUBURBS OF CHICAGO, A FEW MILES FROM MY DAD'S PARENTS. GRAMMA SOLD REAL ESTATE, AND I'M SURE THEY SECURED THE PLACE.
THE BLOCK WAS QUIET, AND BEHIND THE BACK YARD WAS A STRETCH OF UNTOUCHED FIELD, ALMOST PRAIRIE.
OUR NEIGHBOR, MR. ANDERSON, WORKED AT THE HERSHEY CHOCOLATE FACTORY AND WOULD SOMETIMES GIVE US BAGS OF CANDY BARS-WHICH MY DAD WOULD QUICKLY CONFISCATE.
"YOU'LL ROT YOUR TEETH."
HE'D TAKE THEM AND EAT THEM IN THE GARAGE.
YEARS LATER WHEN MR. ANDERSON COULD NO LONGER WALK, POP WOULD THROW ME TEN BUCKS TO MOW HIS LAWN... WHICH I'D IMMEDIATELY SPEND ON COMICS AND CANDY.

POP GOT A JOB WITH *AL PIERSON*, PLAYING UPRIGHT **BASS** IN HIS *BIG BAND*. HE'D BE GONE FOR SEVERAL WEEKS AT A TIME.

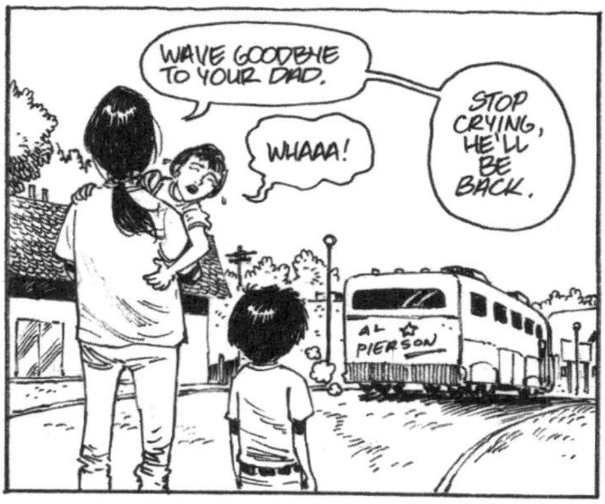
WAVE GOODBYE TO YOUR DAD.
WHAAA!
STOP CRYING, HE'LL BE BACK.
AL PIERSON

I DON'T THINK I WAS EVER **TOO** SAD WHEN HE'D LEAVE. WE WERE FREE TO DO OTHER THINGS, ALL THE STUFF HE DIDN'T GET *INTO*.

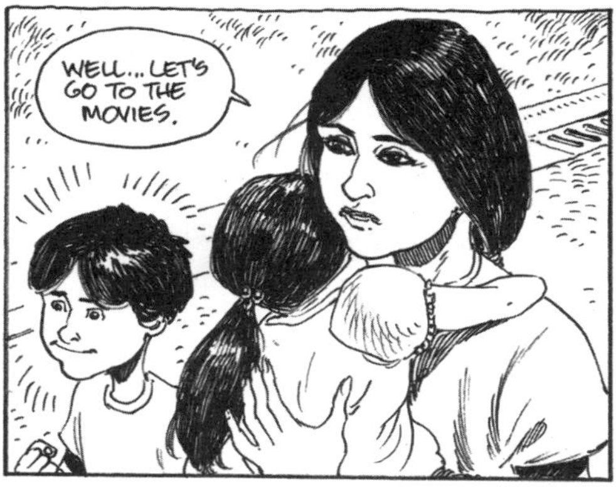
WELL... LET'S GO TO THE MOVIES.

IT WAS **MOM** WHO INTRODUCED ME TO THE **ARTS**. THE THEATER WAS A ***HOME*** TO ME.

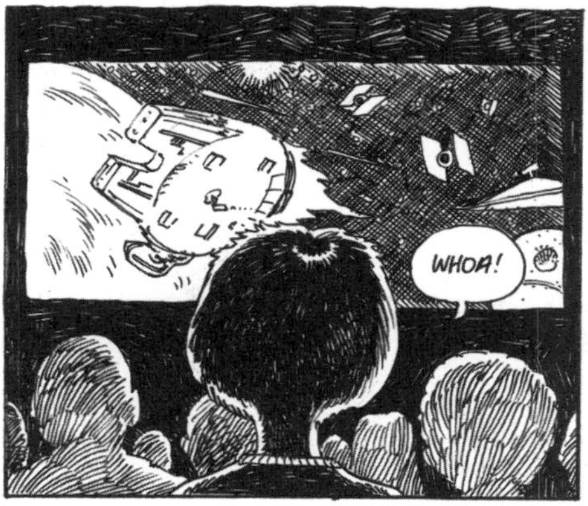
WHOA!

SHE WAS *ALWAYS READING* AND KEPT ME IN COMICS AND BOOKS. MY CHILDHOOD WITH HER WAS THE QUIET SOUND OF *PAGES* TURNING.

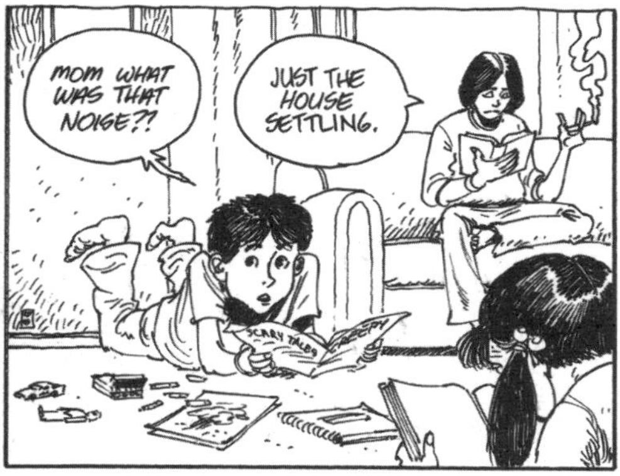
MOM WHAT WAS THAT NOISE?!
JUST THE HOUSE SETTLING.

WE WERE BROKE, BUT SOMEHOW SHE ALWAYS FOUND THE **DOUGH** FOR WHAT WOULD *FEED* MY ***BRAIN***.

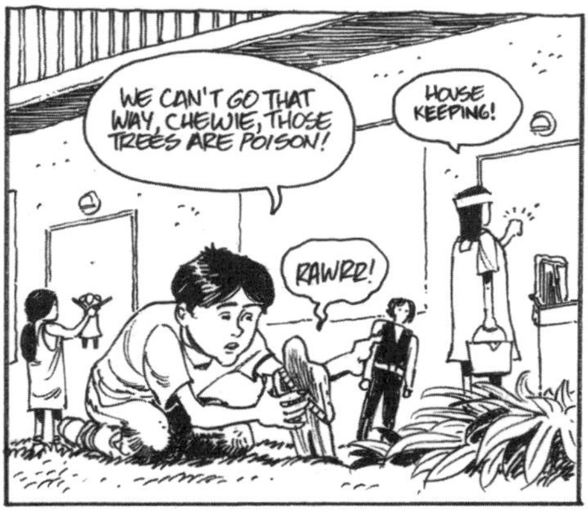
WE CAN'T GO THAT WAY, CHEWIE, THOSE TREES ARE POISON!
HOUSE KEEPING!
RAWRR!

ONCE WE SAT THROUGH "**RAIDERS OF THE LOST ARK**" TWO TIMES IN A *ROW*. I WAS WORRIED WE WERE DOING SOMETHING *WRONG* WHEN THE PLACE *EMPTIED* BETWEEN SCREENINGS...

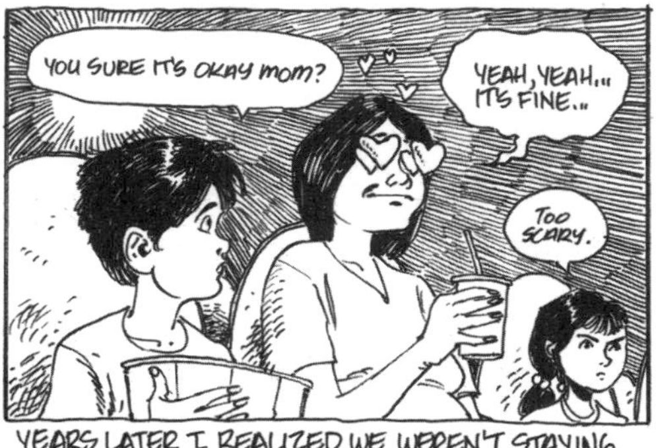
YOU SURE IT'S OKAY MOM?
YEAH, YEAH... IT'S FINE...
TOO SCARY.

YEARS LATER I REALIZED WE WEREN'T STAYING FOR *ME*, BUT FOR *HARRISON FORD*. AH WELL.

THE *BEST* WAS GOING UP TO THE **DELLS**. IT WAS THE LAND OF **TREES** AND *GO-CARTS* AND ***SWIMMING*** AND ***RUNNING AROUND*** AND THE FEEL OF THE SUN TIGHTENING YOUR SKIN AND GRASS UNDER BARE FEET. AND MOST OF ALL...

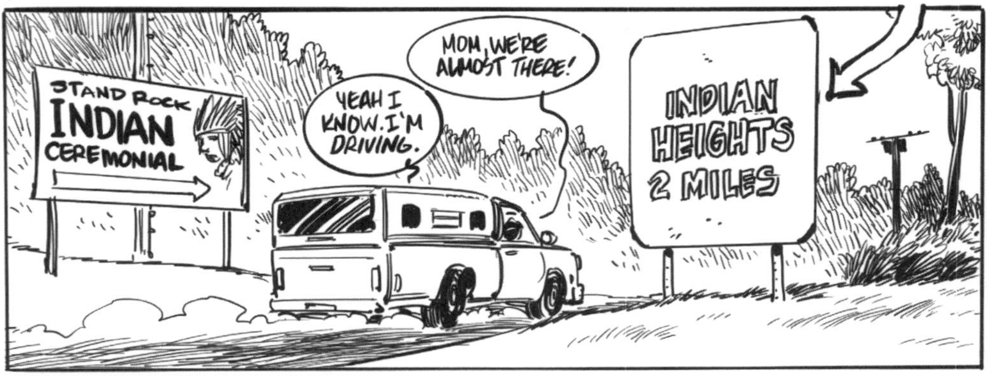
STAND ROCK
INDIAN
CEREMONIAL
YEAH I KNOW. I'M DRIVING.
MOM, WE'RE ALMOST THERE!
INDIAN HEIGHTS 2 MILES

IT WAS AN AGONIZING *FOUR HOUR DRIVE* FROM OUR HOUSE TO THE *INDIAN HEIGHTS*.

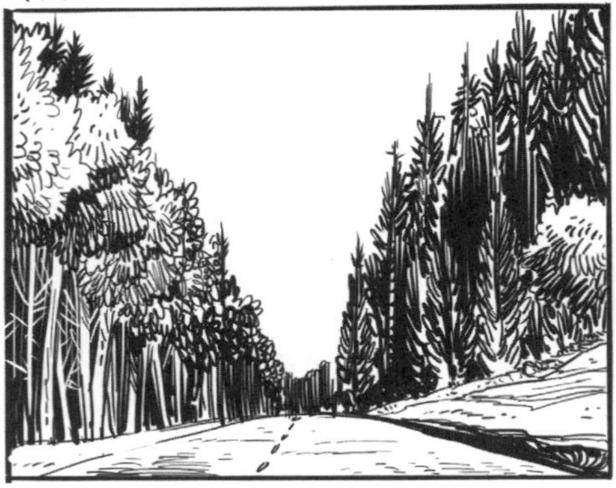

I USED TO HAVE A ***DREAM*** THAT WE HAD DISCOVERED A ***MAGIC PATH*** THROUGH A CORNFIELD THAT GOT US THERE IN *MINUTES*.

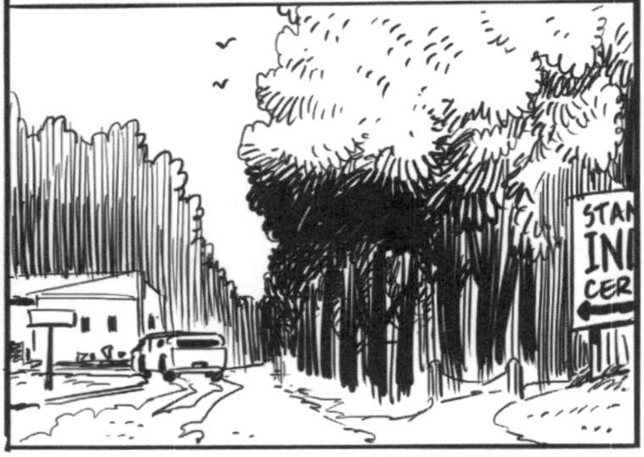
STAN
IN
CER

I COULDN'T WAIT TO SEE MY TEGAS (UNCLES), MOMS (AUNTS), ALL MY BROTHERS AND SISTERS... THERE IS NO SUCH THING AS A ***COUSIN*** IN "INDIAN WAY."

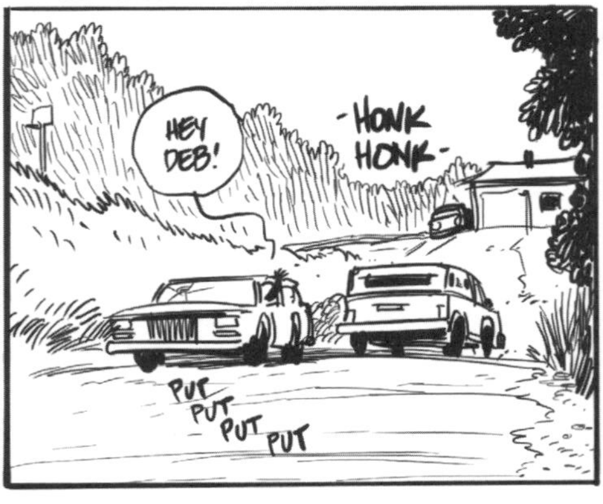
HEY DEB!
-HONK HONK-
PUT PUT PUT PUT

AND **TONY** WAS THERE.

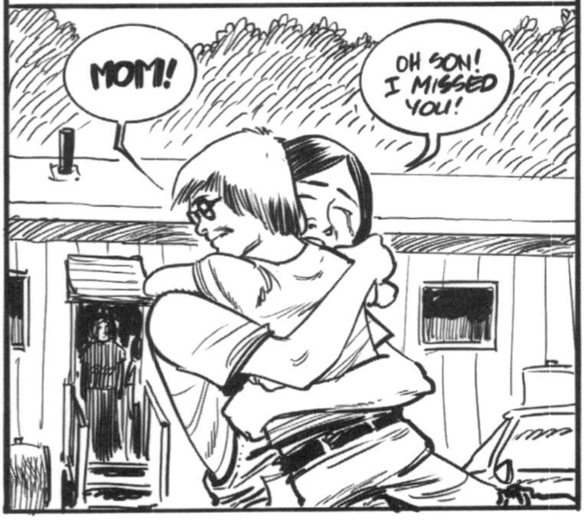
MOM!
OH SON! I MISSED YOU!

KUNIKA'S HOUSE SEEMED LIKE THE CENTER OF ACTION IN THE HEIGHTS, AND THAT IS WHERE TONY STAYED. ACCORDING TO MY MOM, DAD COULD NEVER GET PAST THE FACT THAT TONY WAS ANOTHER MAN'S SON.

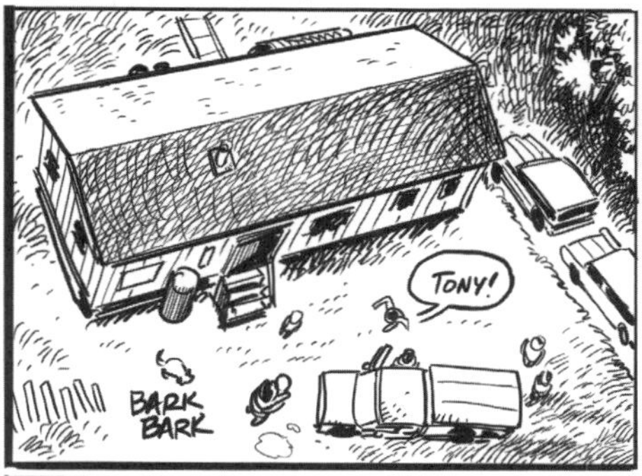
TONY!
BARK BARK

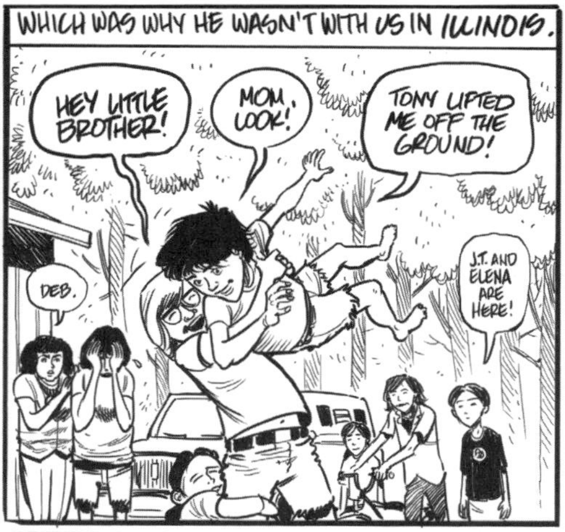
WHICH WAS WHY HE WASN'T WITH US IN ILLINOIS.
HEY LITTLE BROTHER!
MOM, LOOK!
TONY LIFTED ME OFF THE GROUND!
DEB.
J.T. AND ELENA ARE HERE!

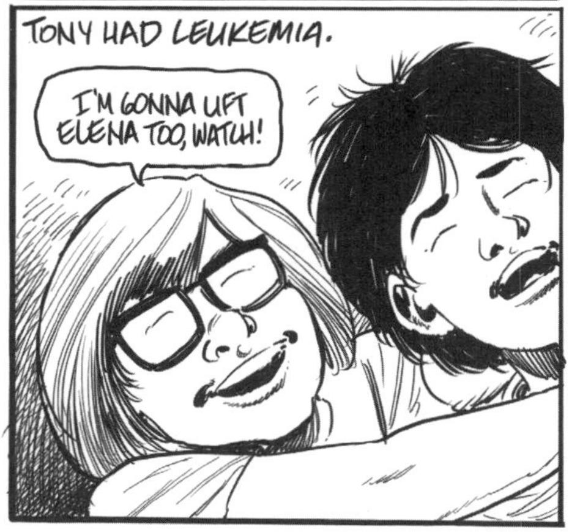
TONY HAD LEUKEMIA.
I'M GONNA LIFT ELENA TOO, WATCH!

EVERYONE KNEW HE WOULD SOON BE GONE.

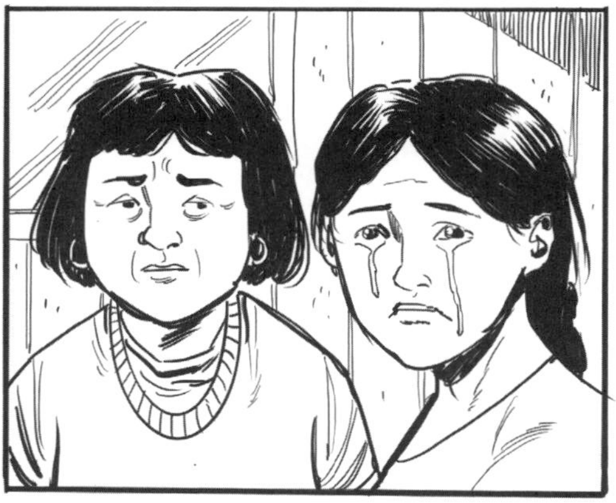

IT WAS ONLY A MATTER OF TIME.
UNTIL THEN, WE PLAYED.

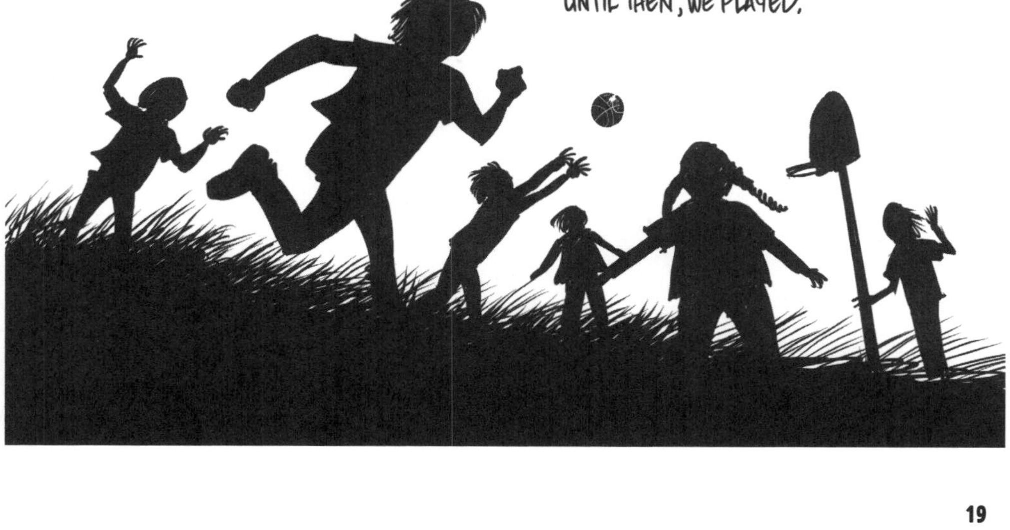

ONE DAY WHEN I WAS SIX POP CAME OUT OF THE HOUSE AND THREW ME IN THE TRUCK. WE HEADED NORTH IN *SILENCE* - MOM AND ELENA WERE ALREADY UP THERE - I'M NOT SURE WE EVEN *PACKED* A *TOOTHBRUSH*.

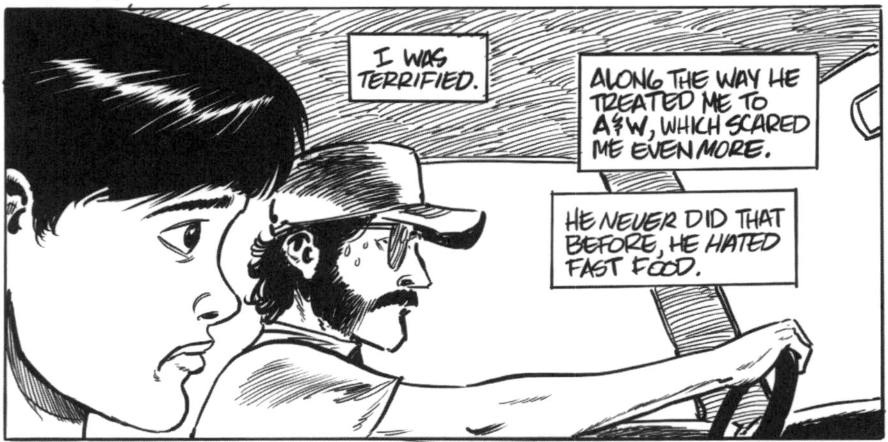
I WAS TERRIFIED.
ALONG THE WAY HE TREATED ME TO A&W, WHICH SCARED ME EVEN MORE.
HE NEVER DID THAT BEFORE, HE HATED FAST FOOD.

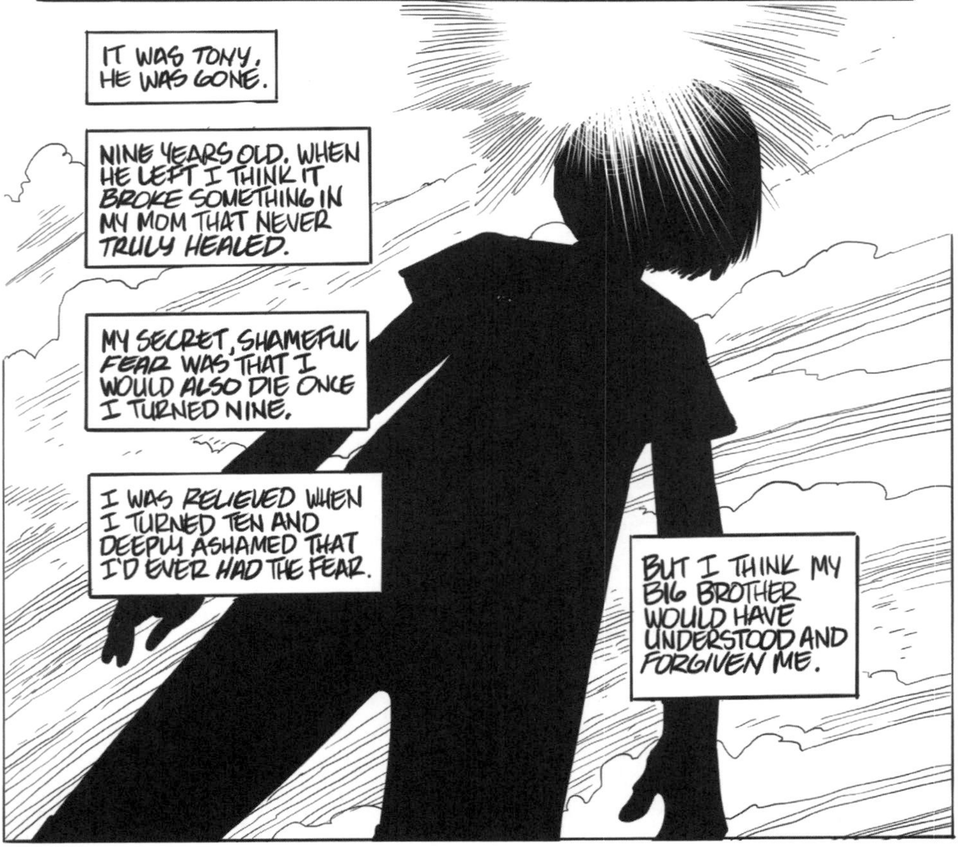
IT WAS TONY. HE WAS GONE.
NINE YEARS OLD. WHEN HE LEFT I THINK IT BROKE SOMETHING IN MY MOM THAT NEVER TRULY HEALED.
MY SECRET, SHAMEFUL FEAR WAS THAT I WOULD ALSO DIE ONCE I TURNED NINE.
I WAS RELIEVED WHEN I TURNED TEN AND DEEPLY ASHAMED THAT I'D EVER HAD THE FEAR.
BUT I THINK MY BIG BROTHER WOULD HAVE UNDERSTOOD AND FORGIVEN ME.

LIKE A SUDDEN STORM THERE WAS MISERY IN THE AIR AND POWERFUL, COMPLICATED EMOTIONS I DIDN'T UNDERSTAND. GRIEF, PAIN, AND LOSS WERE NEW AND CONFLICT WAS BECOMING FAMILIAR – SHROUDED IN A FUME OF BOOZE AND ANGER. TENSION AND UNCERTAINTY BECAME NORMAL.

A KNOT COILED IN MY GUT AND DIDN'T GO AWAY.

ELENA WAS THE ONLY CONSTANT AND WE LEANED ON EACH OTHER WITHOUT KNOWING IT. LAUGHTER THROUGH THE TEARS.

EVENTUALLY IT WAS BACK TO ILLINOIS WITH A MALIGNANT CLOUD HANGING OVER THE FAMILY.

GUILT, BLAME, SHAME, AND ANGER.

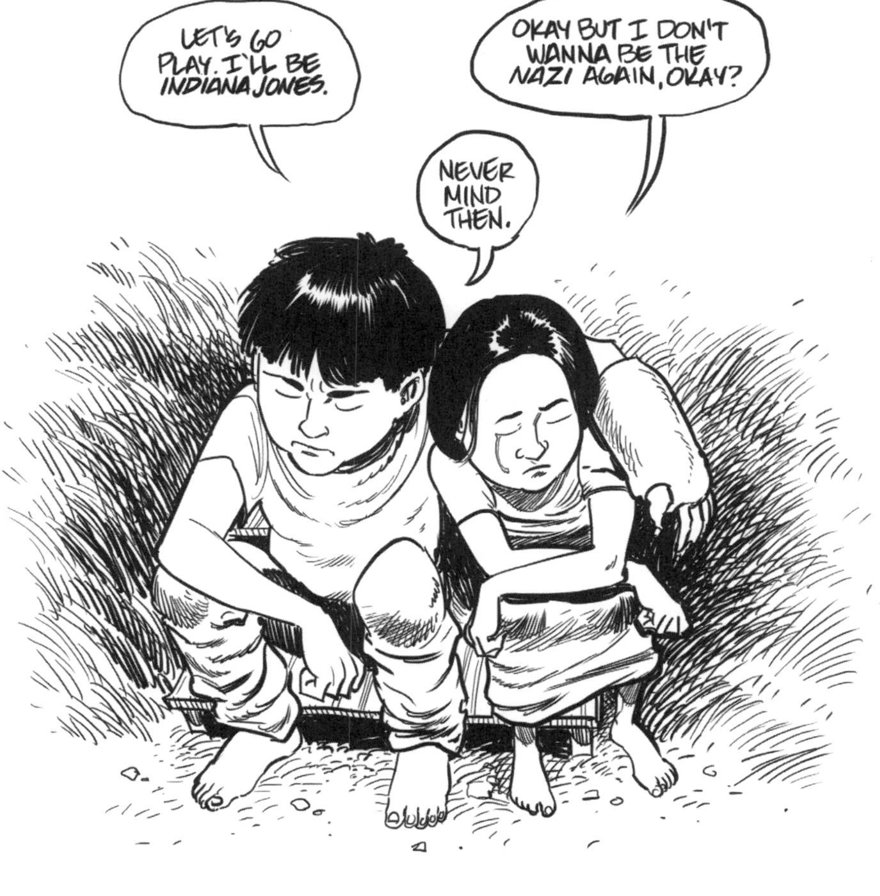
LET'S GO PLAY. I'LL BE INDIANA JONES.
OKAY BUT I DON'T WANNA BE THE NAZI AGAIN, OKAY?
NEVER MIND THEN.

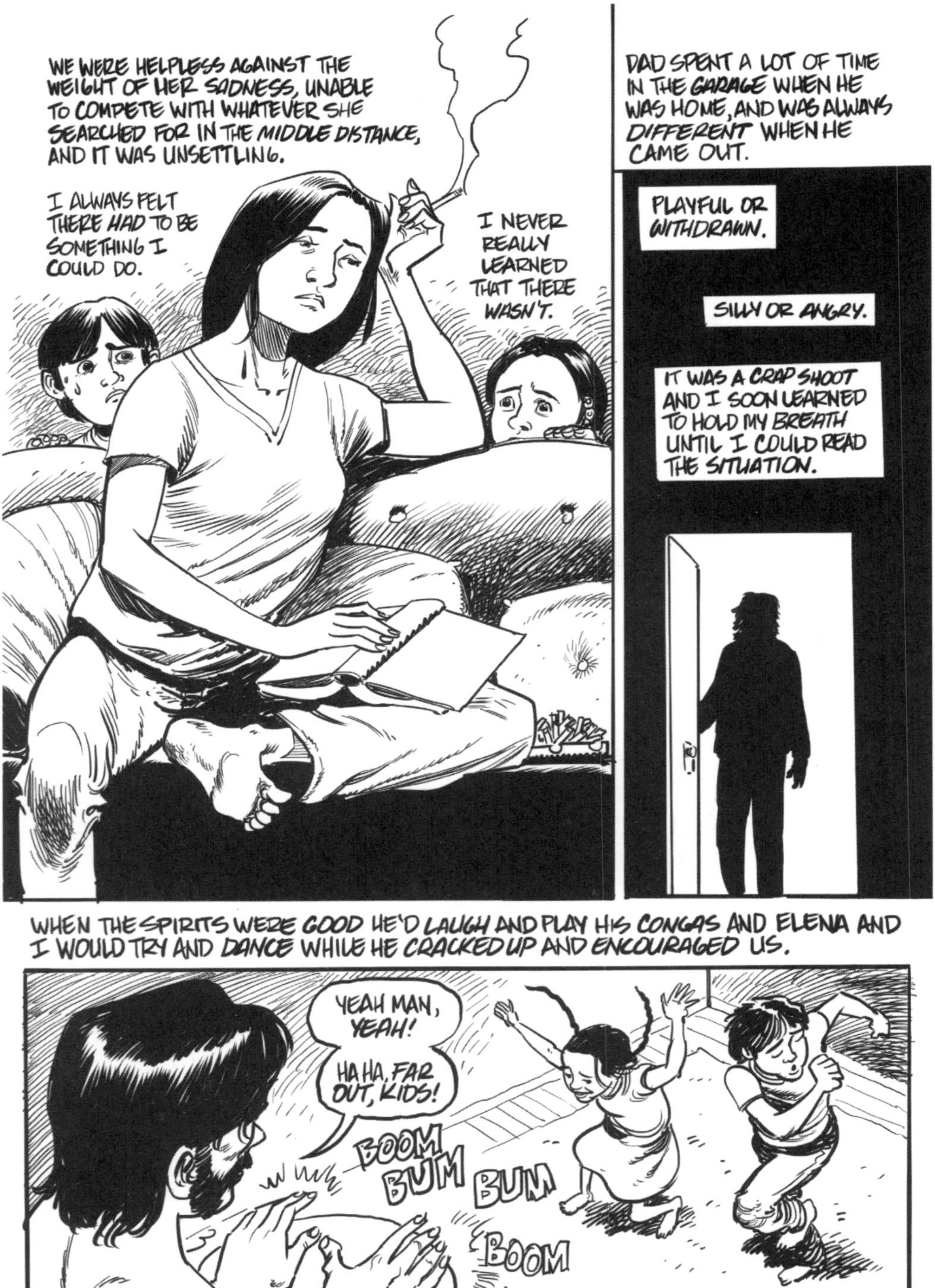
WE WERE HELPLESS AGAINST THE WEIGHT OF HER SADNESS, UNABLE TO COMPETE WITH WHATEVER SHE SEARCHED FOR IN THE MIDDLE DISTANCE, AND IT WAS UNSETTLING.
I ALWAYS FELT THERE HAD TO BE SOMETHING I COULD DO.
I NEVER REALLY LEARNED THAT THERE WASN'T.
DAD SPENT A LOT OF TIME IN THE GARAGE WHEN HE WAS HOME, AND WAS ALWAYS DIFFERENT WHEN HE CAME OUT.
PLAYFUL OR WITHDRAWN.
SILLY OR ANGRY.
IT WAS A CRAP SHOOT AND I SOON LEARNED TO HOLD MY BREATH UNTIL I COULD READ THE SITUATION.
WHEN THE SPIRITS WERE GOOD HE'D LAUGH AND PLAY HIS CONGAS AND ELENA AND I WOULD TRY AND DANCE WHILE HE CRACKED UP AND ENCOURAGED US.
YEAH MAN, YEAH!
HA HA, FAR OUT, KIDS!
BOOM
BUM
BUM
BOOM

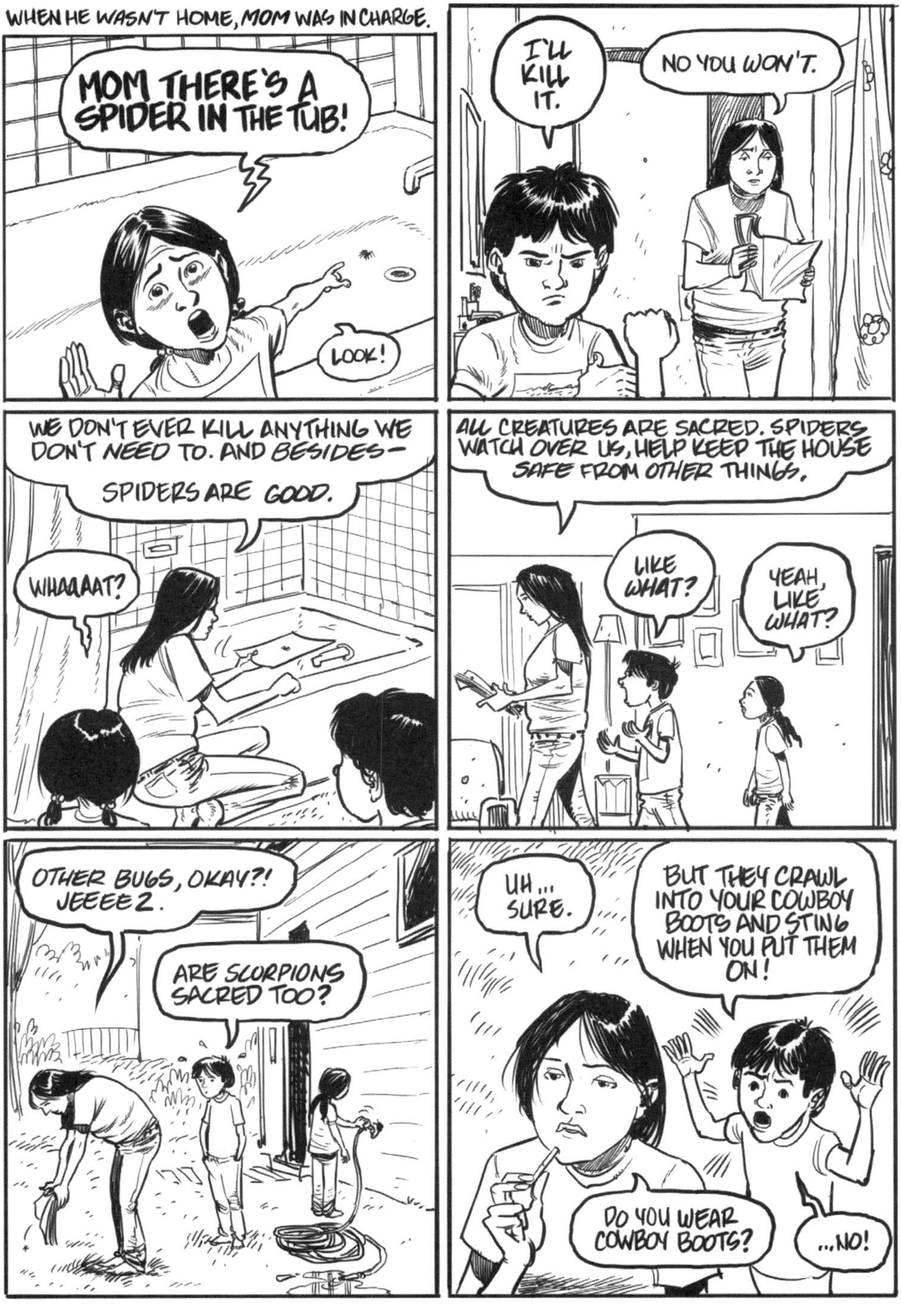
WHEN HE WASN'T HOME, MOM WAS IN CHARGE.
MOM THERE'S A SPIDER IN THE TUB!
LOOK!
I'LL KILL IT.
NO YOU WON'T.
WE DON'T EVER KILL ANYTHING WE DON'T NEED TO. AND BESIDES—
SPIDERS ARE GOOD.
WHAAAAT?
ALL CREATURES ARE SACRED. SPIDERS WATCH OVER US, HELP KEEP THE HOUSE SAFE FROM OTHER THINGS.
LIKE WHAT?
YEAH, LIKE WHAT?
OTHER BUGS, OKAY?! JEEEEZ.
ARE SCORPIONS SACRED TOO?
UH... SURE.
BUT THEY CRAWL INTO YOUR COWBOY BOOTS AND STING WHEN YOU PUT THEM ON!
DO YOU WEAR COWBOY BOOTS?
...NO!

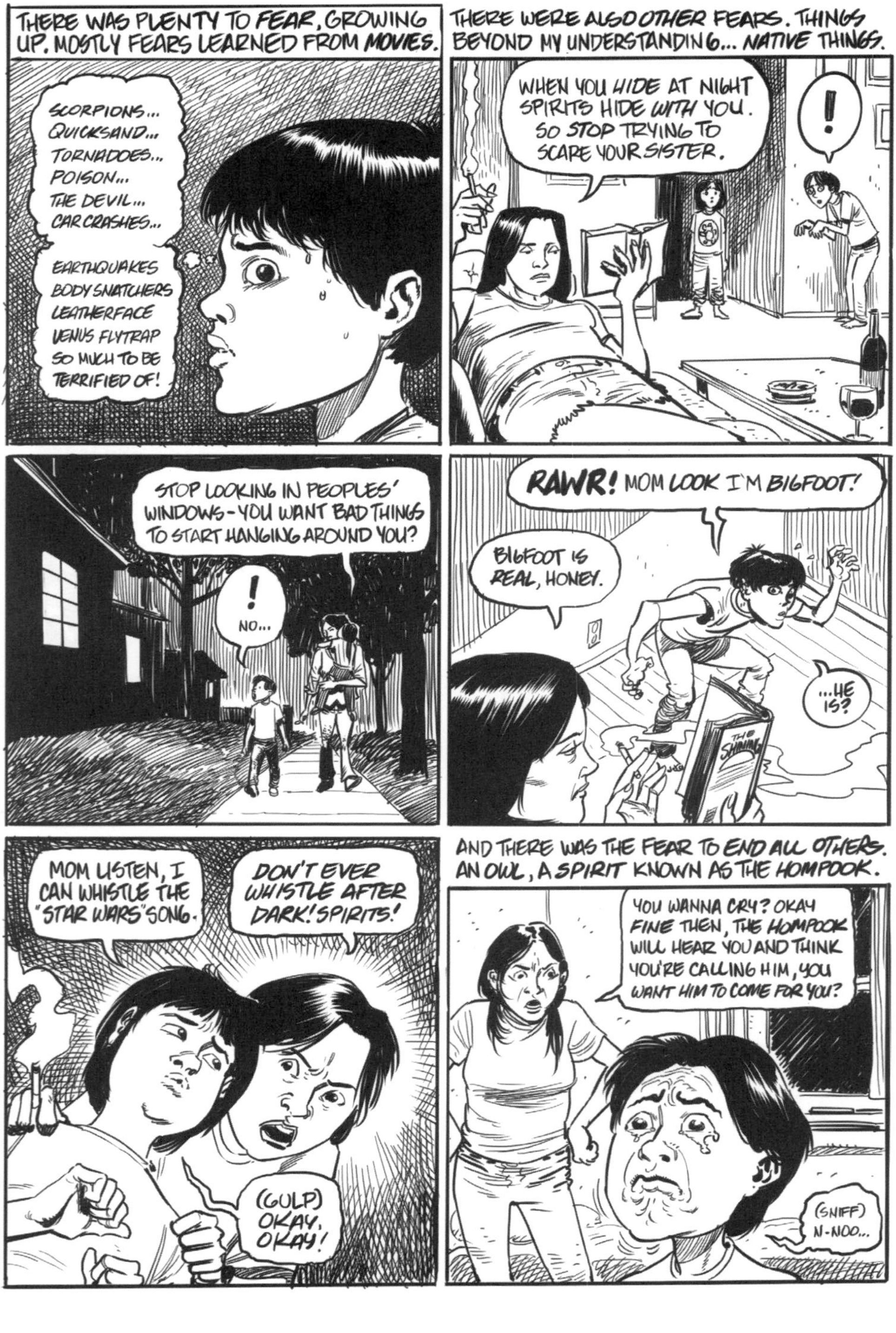
THERE WAS PLENTY TO FEAR, GROWING UP. MOSTLY FEARS LEARNED FROM MOVIES.
SCORPIONS... QUICKSAND... TORNADOES... POISON... THE DEVIL... CAR CRASHES... EARTHQUAKES BODY SNATCHERS LEATHERFACE VENUS FLYTRAP SO MUCH TO BE TERRIFIED OF!
THERE WERE ALSO OTHER FEARS. THINGS BEYOND MY UNDERSTANDING... NATIVE THINGS.
WHEN YOU HIDE AT NIGHT SPIRITS HIDE WITH YOU. SO STOP TRYING TO SCARE YOUR SISTER.
!
STOP LOOKING IN PEOPLES' WINDOWS - YOU WANT BAD THINGS TO START HANGING AROUND YOU?
! NO...
RAWR! MOM LOOK I'M BIGFOOT!
BIGFOOT IS REAL, HONEY.
...HE IS?
THE SHINING
MOM LISTEN, I CAN WHISTLE THE "STAR WARS" SONG.
DON'T EVER WHISTLE AFTER DARK! SPIRITS!
(GULP) OKAY, OKAY!
AND THERE WAS THE FEAR TO END ALL OTHERS. AN OWL, A SPIRIT KNOWN AS THE HOMPOOK.
YOU WANNA CRY? OKAY FINE THEN, THE HOMPOOK WILL HEAR YOU AND THINK YOU'RE CALLING HIM, YOU WANT HIM TO COME FOR YOU?
(SNIFF) N-NOO...

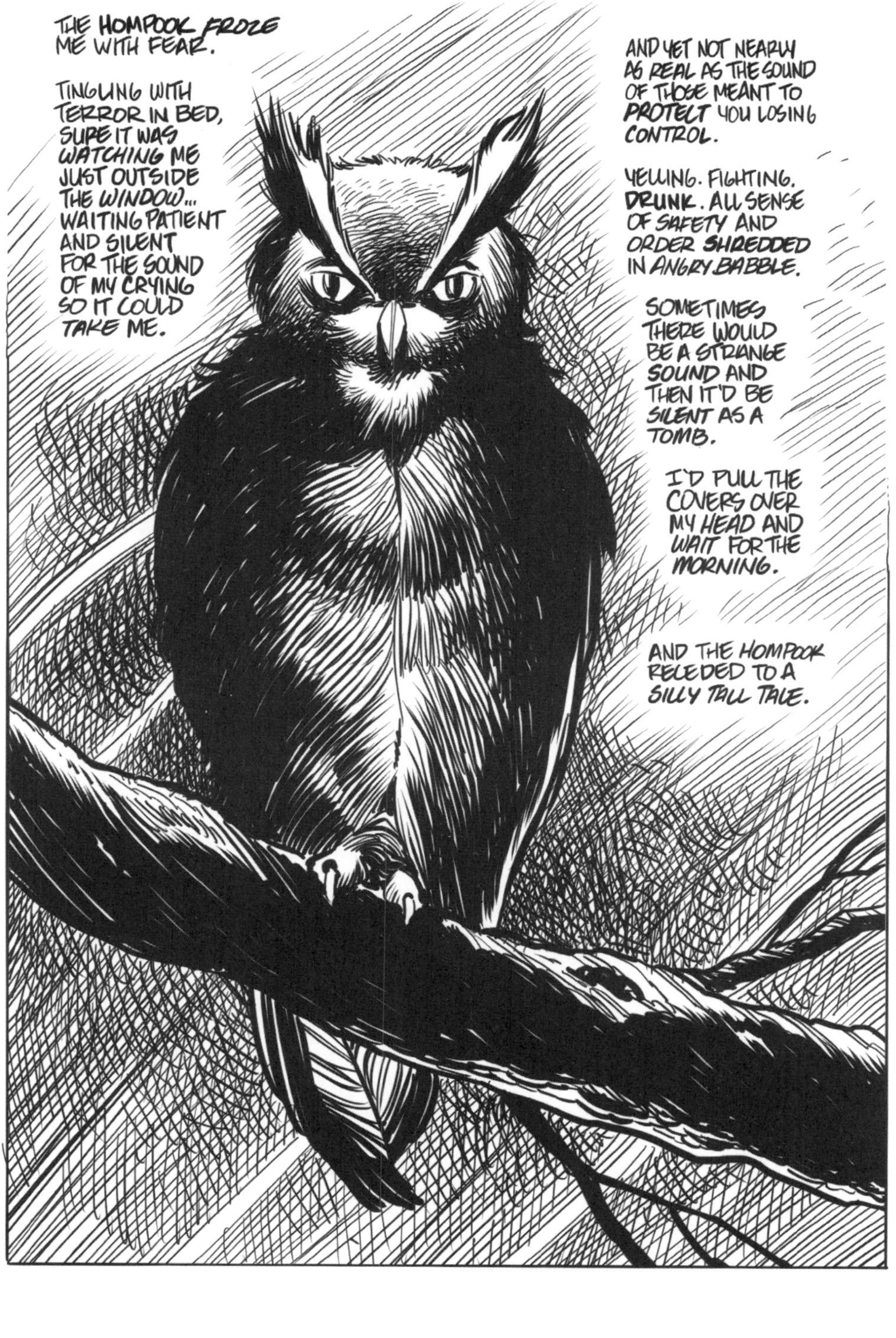
THE HOMPOOK FROZE ME WITH FEAR.
TINGLING WITH TERROR IN BED, SURE IT WAS WATCHING ME JUST OUTSIDE THE WINDOW... WAITING PATIENT AND SILENT FOR THE SOUND OF MY CRYING SO IT COULD TAKE ME.
AND YET NOT NEARLY AS REAL AS THE SOUND OF THOSE MEANT TO PROTECT YOU LOSING CONTROL.
YELLING. FIGHTING. DRUNK. ALL SENSE OF SAFETY AND ORDER SHREDDED IN ANGRY BABBLE.
SOMETIMES THERE WOULD BE A STRANGE SOUND AND THEN IT'D BE SILENT AS A TOMB.
I'D PULL THE COVERS OVER MY HEAD AND WAIT FOR THE MORNING.
AND THE HOMPOOK RECEDED TO A SILLY TALL TALE.

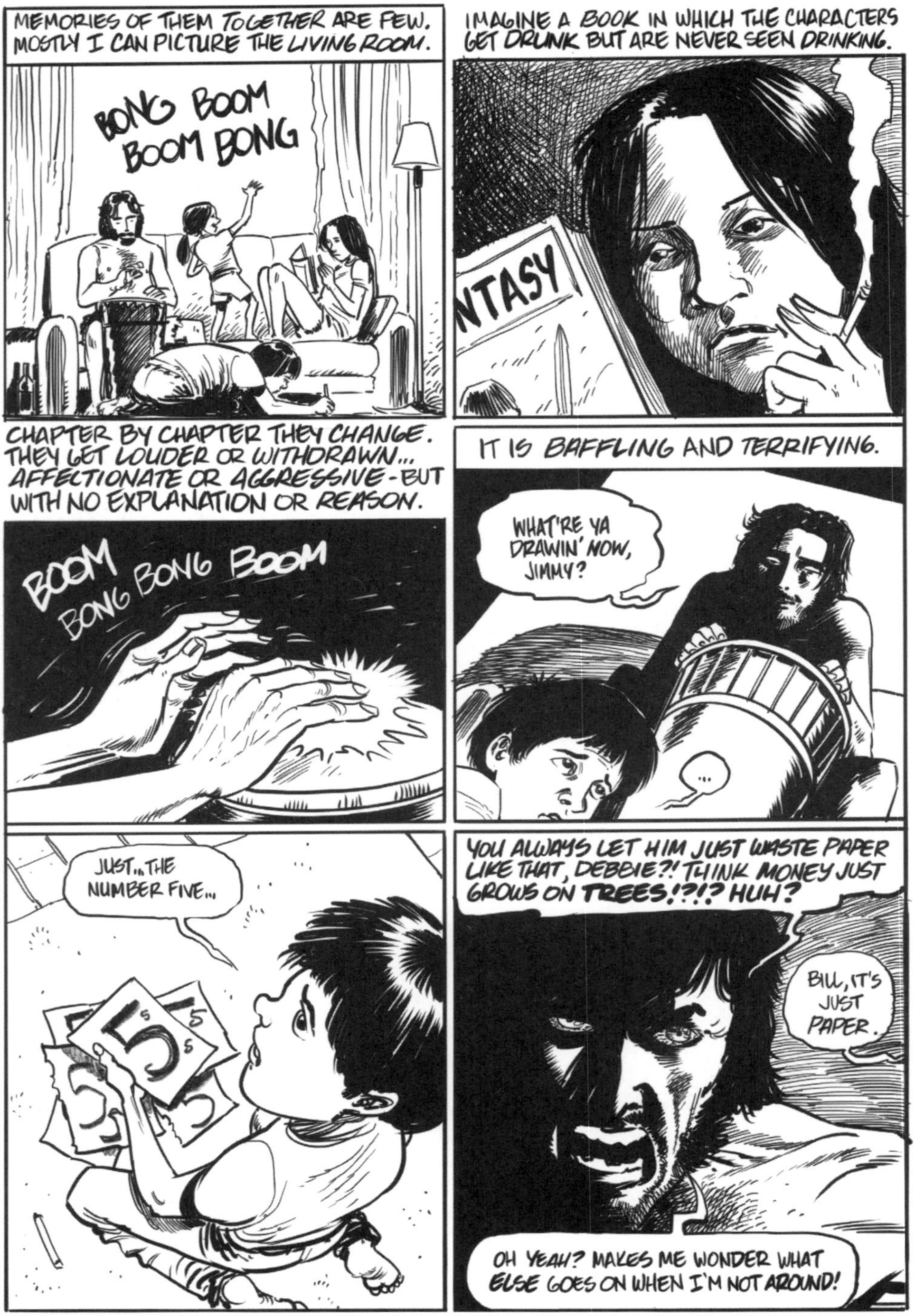
MEMORIES OF THEM TOGETHER ARE FEW. MOSTLY I CAN PICTURE THE LIVING ROOM.
BONG BOOM BOOM BONG
IMAGINE A BOOK IN WHICH THE CHARACTERS GET DRUNK BUT ARE NEVER SEEN DRINKING.
NTASY
CHAPTER BY CHAPTER THEY CHANGE. THEY GET LOUDER OR WITHDRAWN... AFFECTIONATE OR AGGRESSIVE - BUT WITH NO EXPLANATION OR REASON.
BOOM BONG BONG BOOM
IT IS BAFFLING AND TERRIFYING.
WHAT'RE YA DRAWIN' NOW, JIMMY?
...
JUST... THE NUMBER FIVE...
YOU ALWAYS LET HIM JUST WASTE PAPER LIKE THAT, DEBBIE?! THINK MONEY JUST GROWS ON TREES!?!? HUH?
BILL, IT'S JUST PAPER.
OH YEAH? MAKES ME WONDER WHAT ELSE GOES ON WHEN I'M NOT AROUND!

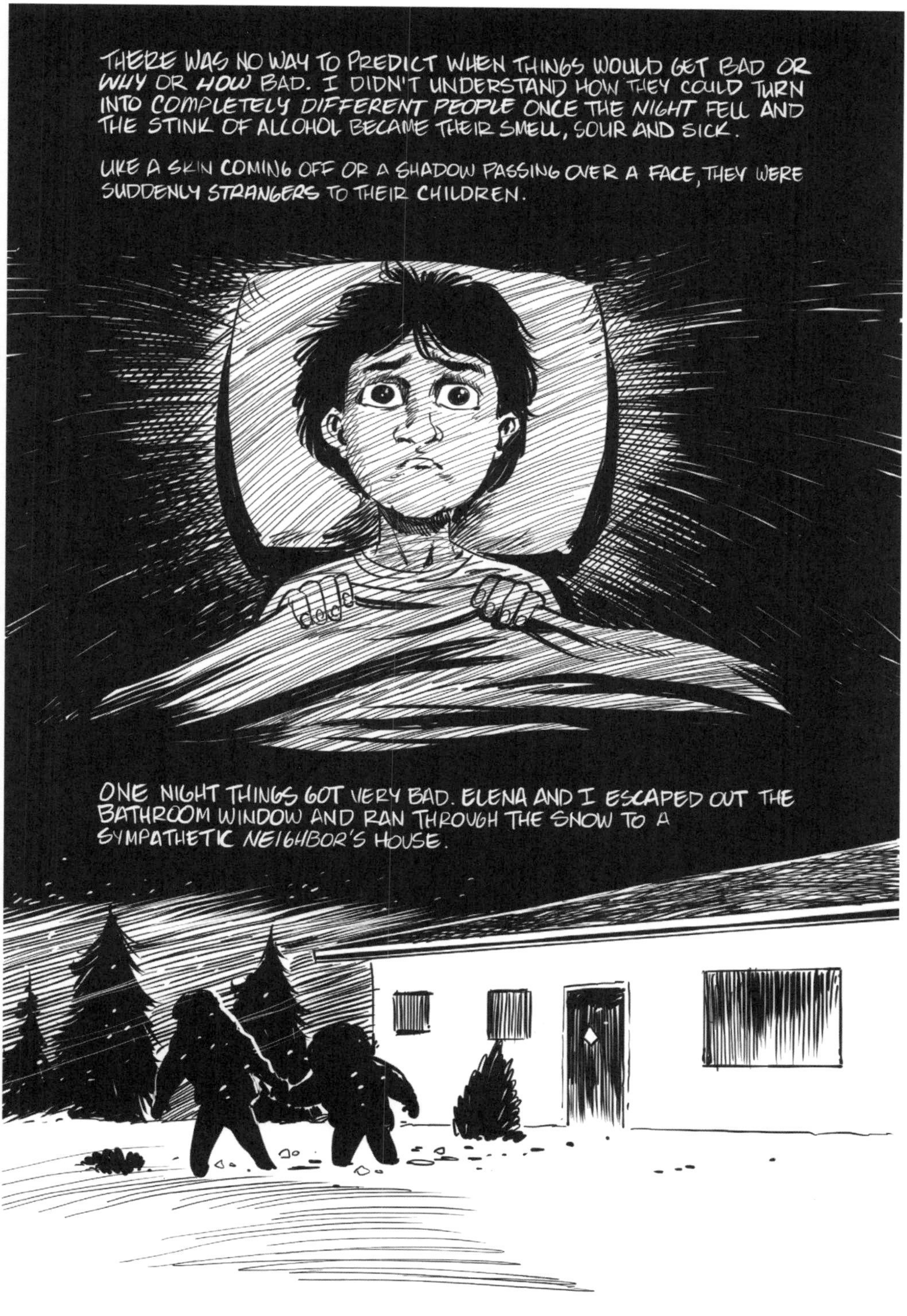
THERE WAS NO WAY TO PREDICT WHEN THINGS WOULD GET BAD OR WHY OR HOW BAD. I DIDN'T UNDERSTAND HOW THEY COULD TURN INTO COMPLETELY DIFFERENT PEOPLE ONCE THE NIGHT FELL AND THE STINK OF ALCOHOL BECAME THEIR SMELL, SOUR AND SICK.
LIKE A SKIN COMING OFF OR A SHADOW PASSING OVER A FACE, THEY WERE SUDDENLY STRANGERS TO THEIR CHILDREN.
ONE NIGHT THINGS GOT VERY BAD. ELENA AND I ESCAPED OUT THE BATHROOM WINDOW AND RAN THROUGH THE SNOW TO A SYMPATHETIC NEIGHBOR'S HOUSE.

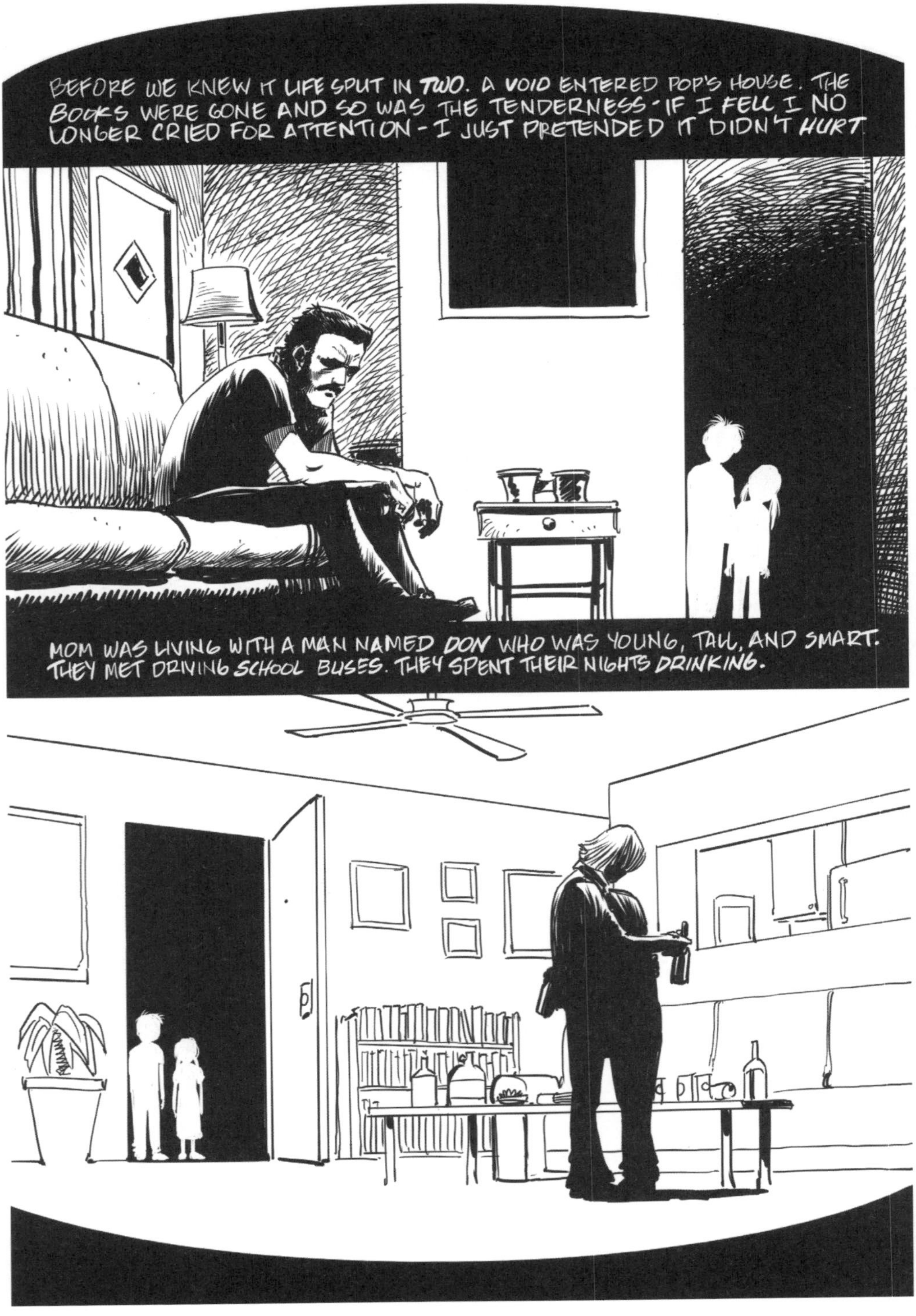
BEFORE WE KNEW IT LIFE SPLIT IN TWO. A VOID ENTERED POP'S HOUSE. THE BOOKS WERE GONE AND SO WAS THE TENDERNESS - IF I FELL I NO LONGER CRIED FOR ATTENTION - I JUST PRETENDED IT DIDN'T HURT.
MOM WAS LIVING WITH A MAN NAMED DON WHO WAS YOUNG, TALL, AND SMART. THEY MET DRIVING SCHOOL BUSES. THEY SPENT THEIR NIGHTS DRINKING.

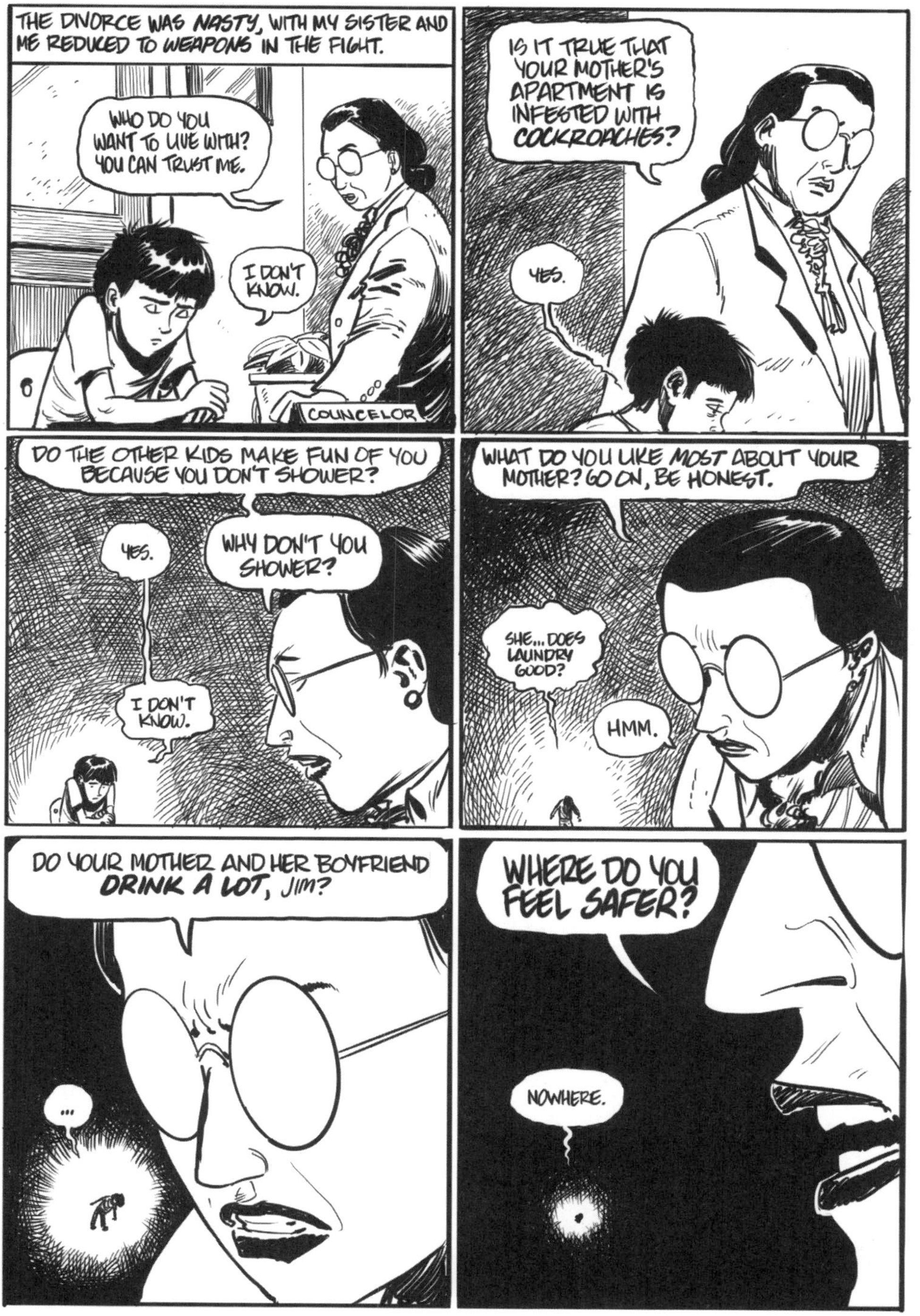
THE DIVORCE WAS NASTY, WITH MY SISTER AND ME REDUCED TO WEAPONS IN THE FIGHT.
WHO DO YOU WANT TO LIVE WITH? YOU CAN TRUST ME.
I DON'T KNOW.
COUNCELOR
IS IT TRUE THAT YOUR MOTHER'S APARTMENT IS INFESTED WITH COCKROACHES?
YES.
DO THE OTHER KIDS MAKE FUN OF YOU BECAUSE YOU DON'T SHOWER?
YES.
WHY DON'T YOU SHOWER?
I DON'T KNOW.
WHAT DO YOU LIKE MOST ABOUT YOUR MOTHER? GO ON, BE HONEST.
SHE... DOES LAUNDRY GOOD?
HMM.
DO YOUR MOTHER AND HER BOYFRIEND DRINK A LOT, JIM?
...
WHERE DO YOU FEEL SAFER?
NOWHERE.

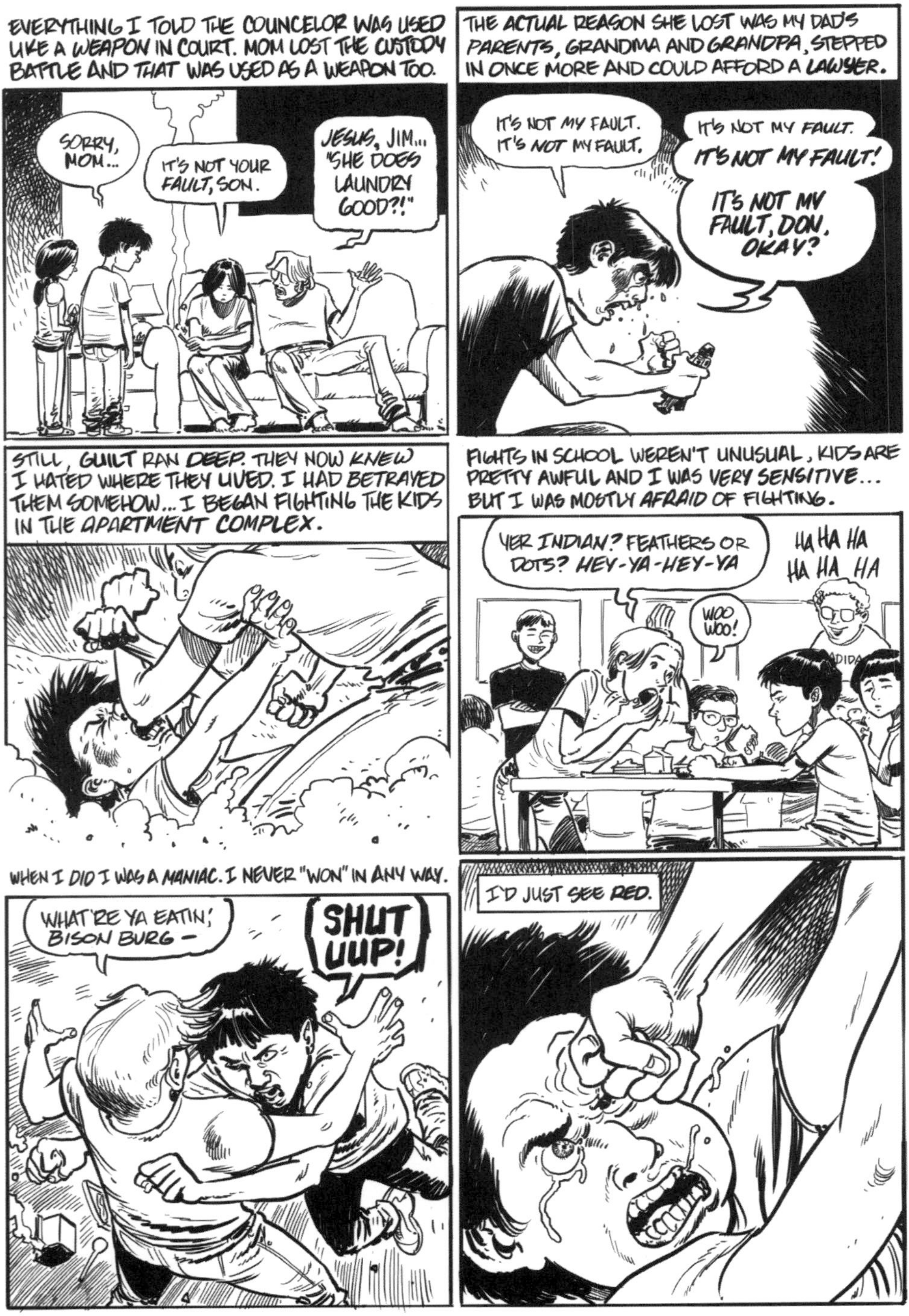
EVERYTHING I TOLD THE COUNCELOR WAS USED LIKE A WEAPON IN COURT. MOM LOST THE CUSTODY BATTLE AND THAT WAS USED AS A WEAPON TOO.
SORRY, MOM...
IT'S NOT YOUR FAULT, SON.
JESUS, JIM... "SHE DOES LAUNDRY GOOD?!"
THE ACTUAL REASON SHE LOST WAS MY DAD'S PARENTS, GRANDMA AND GRANDPA, STEPPED IN ONCE MORE AND COULD AFFORD A LAWYER.
IT'S NOT MY FAULT. IT'S NOT MY FAULT.
IT'S NOT MY FAULT. IT'S NOT MY FAULT!
IT'S NOT MY FAULT, DON, OKAY?
STILL, GUILT RAN DEEP. THEY NOW KNEW I HATED WHERE THEY LIVED. I HAD BETRAYED THEM SOMEHOW... I BEGAN FIGHTING THE KIDS IN THE APARTMENT COMPLEX.
FIGHTS IN SCHOOL WEREN'T UNUSUAL, KIDS ARE PRETTY AWFUL AND I WAS VERY SENSITIVE... BUT I WAS MOSTLY AFRAID OF FIGHTING.
YER INDIAN? FEATHERS OR DOTS? HEY-YA-HEY-YA
HA HA HA HA HA HA
WOO WOO!
WHEN I DID I WAS A MANIAC. I NEVER "WON" IN ANY WAY.
WHAT'RE YA EATIN', BISON BURG —
SHUT UUP!
I'D JUST SEE RED.

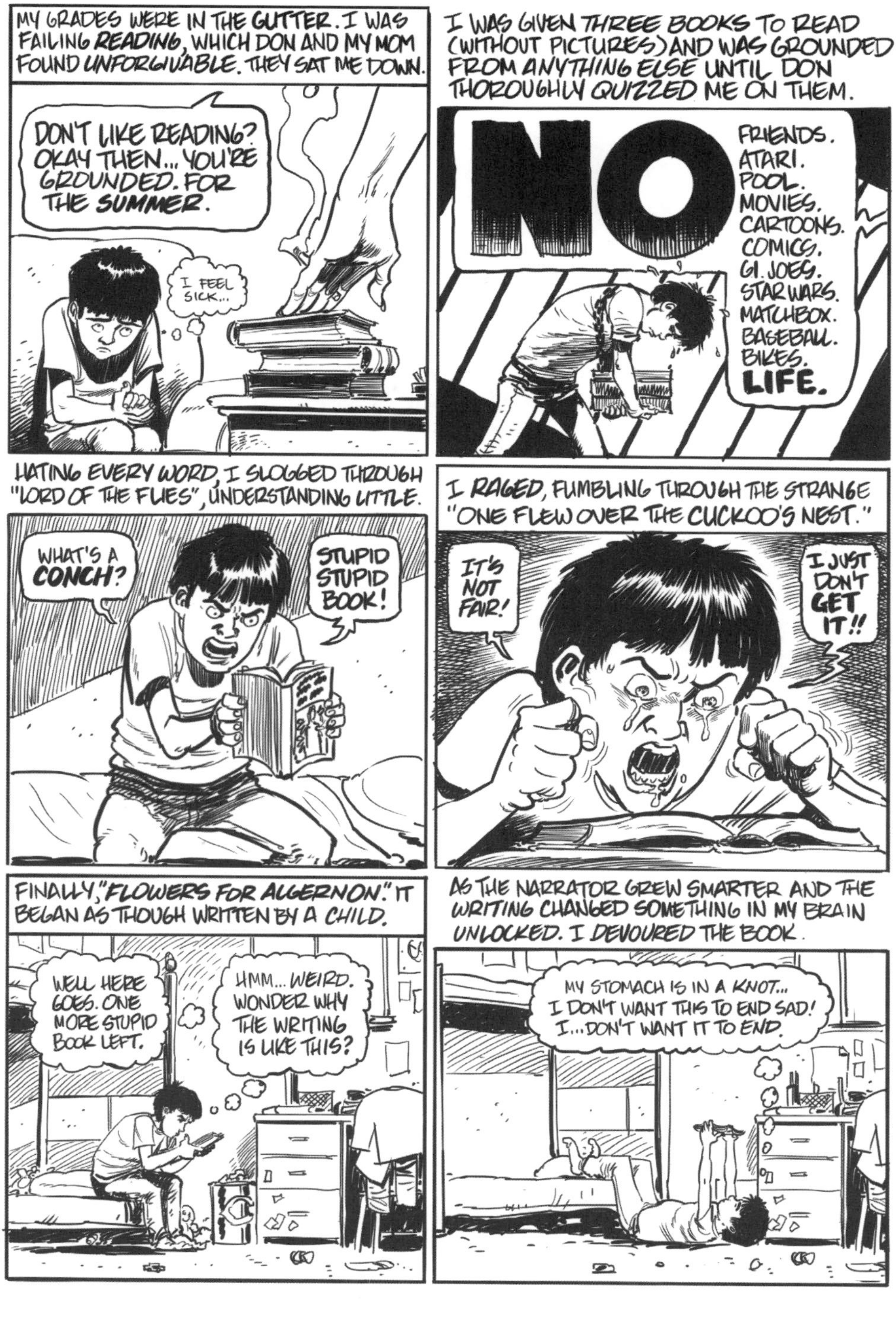

MY GRADES WERE IN THE GUTTER. I WAS FAILING READING, WHICH DON AND MY MOM FOUND UNFORGIVABLE. THEY SAT ME DOWN.
DON'T LIKE READING? OKAY THEN... YOU'RE GROUNDED. FOR THE SUMMER.
I FEEL SICK...
I WAS GIVEN THREE BOOKS TO READ (WITHOUT PICTURES) AND WAS GROUNDED FROM ANYTHING ELSE UNTIL DON THOROUGHLY QUIZZED ME ON THEM.
NO
FRIENDS. ATARI. POOL. MOVIES. CARTOONS. COMICS. GI. JOES. STAR WARS. MATCHBOX. BASEBALL. BIKES. LIFE.
HATING EVERY WORD, I SLOGGED THROUGH "LORD OF THE FLIES", UNDERSTANDING LITTLE.
WHAT'S A CONCH?
STUPID STUPID BOOK!
I RAGED, FUMBLING THROUGH THE STRANGE "ONE FLEW OVER THE CUCKOO'S NEST."
IT'S NOT FAIR!
I JUST DON'T GET IT!!
FINALLY, "FLOWERS FOR ALGERNON." IT BEGAN AS THOUGH WRITTEN BY A CHILD.
WELL HERE GOES. ONE MORE STUPID BOOK LEFT.
HMM... WEIRD. WONDER WHY THE WRITING IS LIKE THIS?
AS THE NARRATOR GREW SMARTER AND THE WRITING CHANGED SOMETHING IN MY BRAIN UNLOCKED. I DEVOURED THE BOOK.
MY STOMACH IS IN A KNOT... I DON'T WANT THIS TO END SAD! I... DON'T WANT IT TO END.

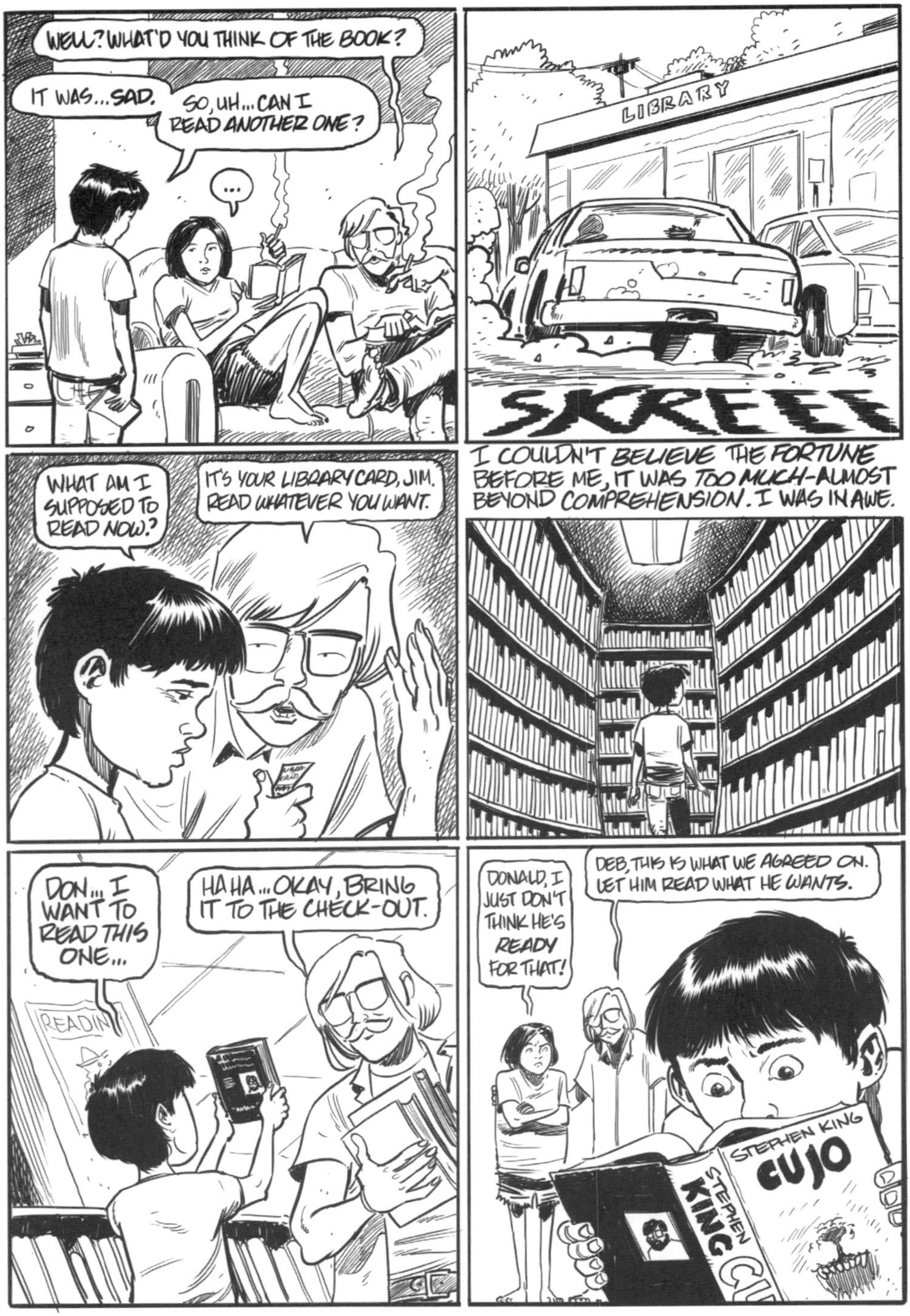
WELL? WHAT'D YOU THINK OF THE BOOK?
IT WAS... SAD.
SO, UH... CAN I READ ANOTHER ONE?
...
LIBRARY
SKREEE
WHAT AM I SUPPOSED TO READ NOW?
IT'S YOUR LIBRARY CARD, JIM. READ WHATEVER YOU WANT.
I COULDN'T BELIEVE THE FORTUNE BEFORE ME, IT WAS TOO MUCH–ALMOST BEYOND COMPREHENSION. I WAS IN AWE.
DON... I WANT TO READ THIS ONE...
HA HA... OKAY, BRING IT TO THE CHECK-OUT.
READIN
DONALD, I JUST DON'T THINK HE'S READY FOR THAT!
DEB, THIS IS WHAT WE AGREED ON. LET HIM READ WHAT HE WANTS.
STEPHEN KING
CUJO
STEPHEN KING

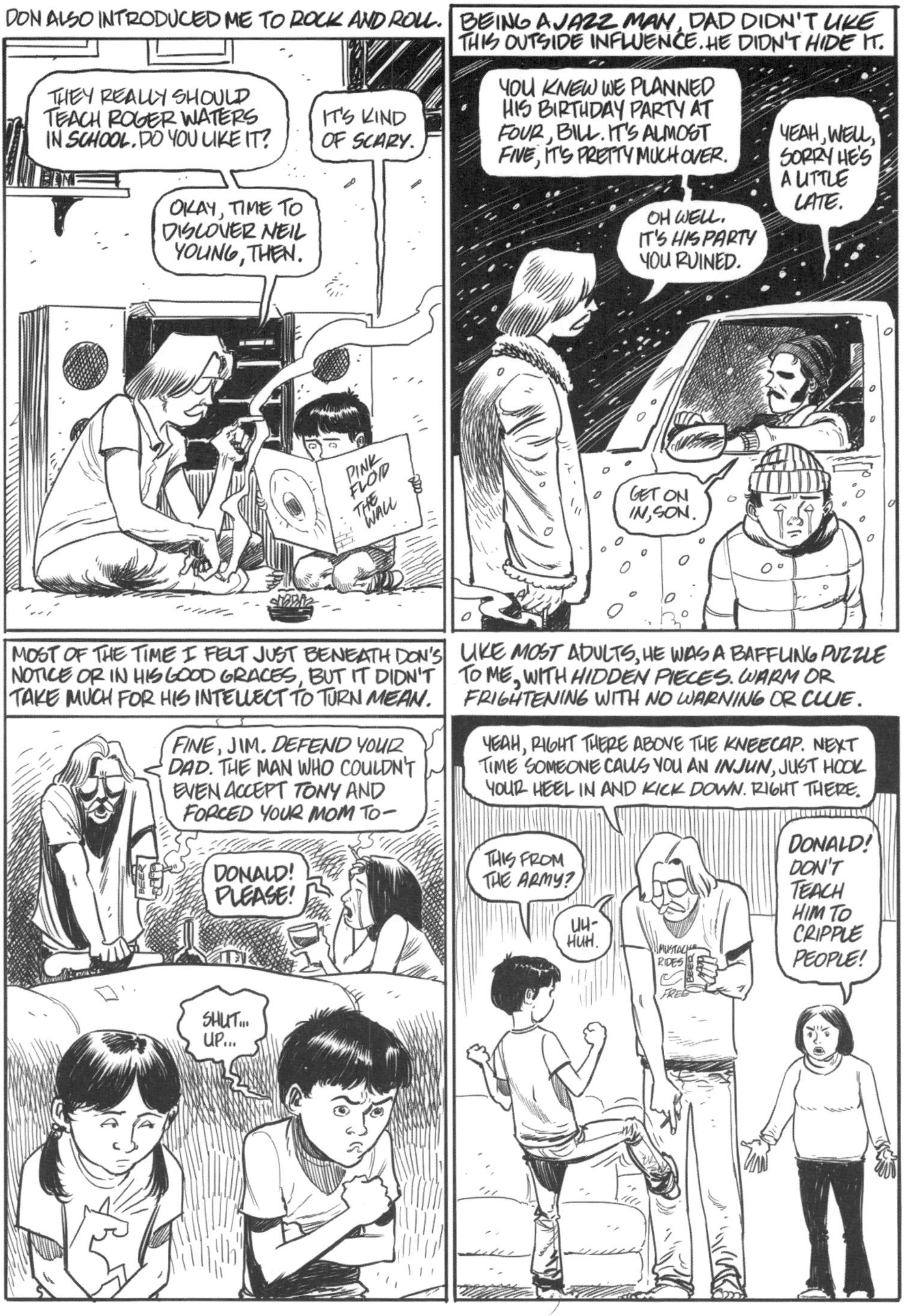
DON ALSO INTRODUCED ME TO ROCK AND ROLL.
THEY REALLY SHOULD TEACH ROGER WATERS IN SCHOOL. DO YOU LIKE IT?
IT'S KIND OF SCARY.
OKAY, TIME TO DISCOVER NEIL YOUNG, THEN.
PINK FLOID THE WALL
BEING A JAZZ MAN, DAD DIDN'T LIKE THIS OUTSIDE INFLUENCE. HE DIDN'T HIDE IT.
YOU KNEW WE PLANNED HIS BIRTHDAY PARTY AT FOUR, BILL. IT'S ALMOST FIVE, IT'S PRETTY MUCH OVER.
YEAH, WELL, SORRY HE'S A LITTLE LATE.
OH WELL. IT'S HIS PARTY YOU RUINED.
GET ON IN, SON.
MOST OF THE TIME I FELT JUST BENEATH DON'S NOTICE OR IN HIS GOOD GRACES, BUT IT DIDN'T TAKE MUCH FOR HIS INTELLECT TO TURN MEAN.
FINE, JIM. DEFEND YOUR DAD. THE MAN WHO COULDN'T EVEN ACCEPT TONY AND FORCED YOUR MOM TO—
DONALD! PLEASE!
SHUT... UP...
LIKE MOST ADULTS, HE WAS A BAFFLING PUZZLE TO ME, WITH HIDDEN PIECES. WARM OR FRIGHTENING WITH NO WARNING OR CLUE.
YEAH, RIGHT THERE ABOVE THE KNEECAP. NEXT TIME SOMEONE CALLS YOU AN INJUN, JUST HOOK YOUR HEEL IN AND KICK DOWN. RIGHT THERE.
THIS FROM THE ARMY?
UH-HUH.
DONALD! DON'T TEACH HIM TO CRIPPLE PEOPLE!
MUSTACHE RIDES FREE
BEER

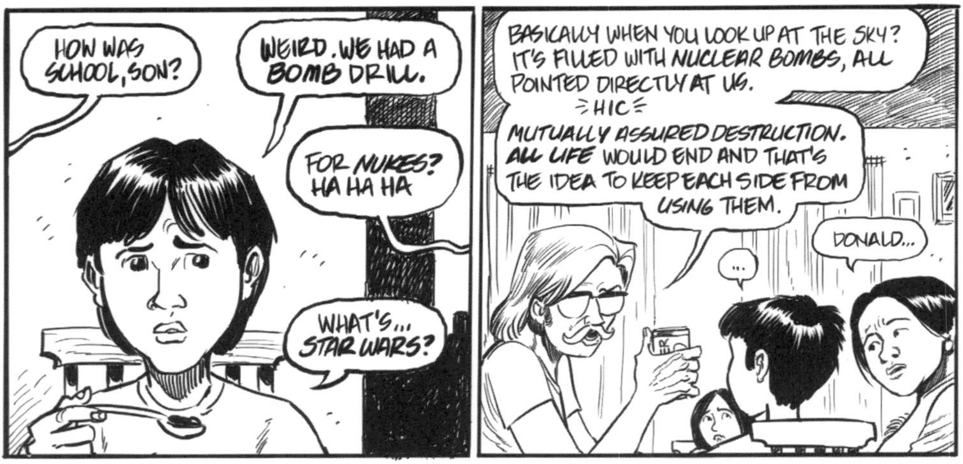
HOW WAS SCHOOL, SON?
WEIRD. WE HAD A BOMB DRILL.
FOR NUKES? HA HA HA
WHAT'S... STAR WARS?
BASICALLY WHEN YOU LOOK UP AT THE SKY? IT'S FILLED WITH NUCLEAR BOMBS, ALL POINTED DIRECTLY AT US.
HIC
MUTUALLY ASSURED DESTRUCTION. ALL LIFE WOULD END AND THAT'S THE IDEA TO KEEP EACH SIDE FROM USING THEM.
...
DONALD...

I WOULD LIE IN BED, PICTURING THE WORLD DISINTEGRATING. I COULDN'T UNDERSTAND HOW PEOPLE - JUST PEOPLE! - COULD HOLD THAT OVER US ALL.

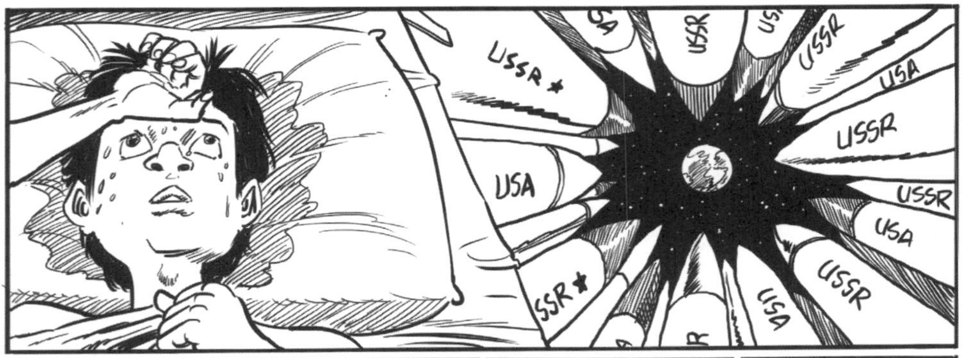
USSR
USSR
USSR
USA
USSR
USA
USSR
USA
USSR
USA
USSR

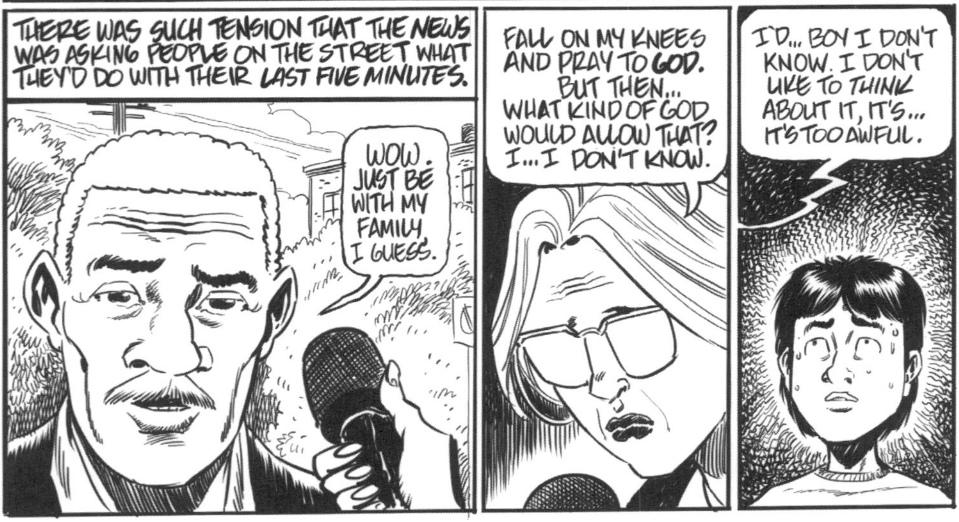
THERE WAS SUCH TENSION THAT THE NEWS WAS ASKING PEOPLE ON THE STREET WHAT THEY'D DO WITH THEIR LAST FIVE MINUTES.
WOW. JUST BE WITH MY FAMILY I GUESS.
FALL ON MY KNEES AND PRAY TO GOD. BUT THEN... WHAT KIND OF GOD WOULD ALLOW THAT? I... I DON'T KNOW.
I'D... BOY I DON'T KNOW. I DON'T LIKE TO THINK ABOUT IT, IT'S... IT'S TOO AWFUL.

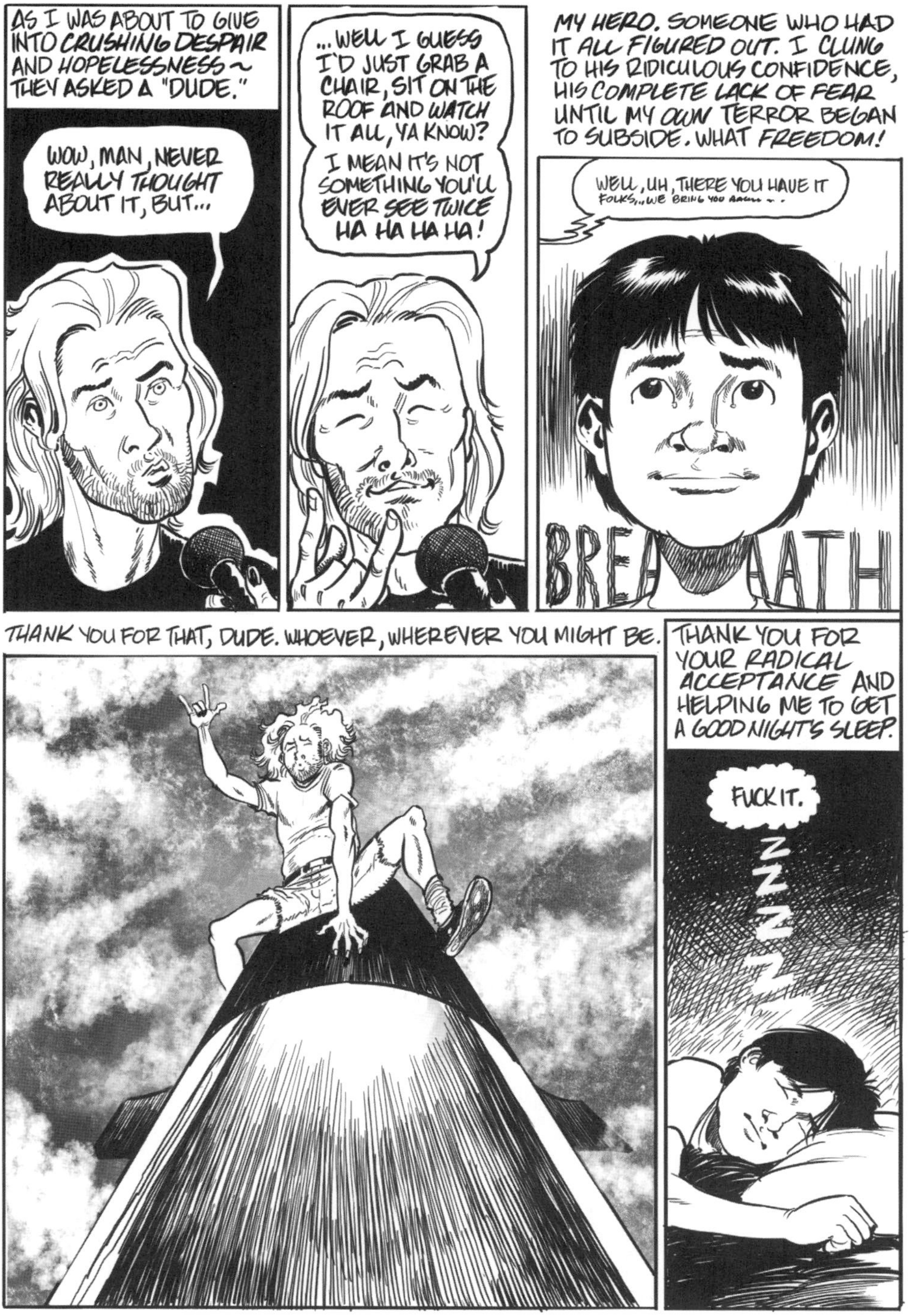
AS I WAS ABOUT TO GIVE INTO CRUSHING DESPAIR AND HOPELESSNESS ~ THEY ASKED A "DUDE."
WOW, MAN, NEVER REALLY THOUGHT ABOUT IT, BUT...
...WELL I GUESS I'D JUST GRAB A CHAIR, SIT ON THE ROOF AND WATCH IT ALL, YA KNOW?
I MEAN IT'S NOT SOMETHING YOU'LL EVER SEE TWICE HA HA HA HA!
MY HERO. SOMEONE WHO HAD IT ALL FIGURED OUT. I CLUNG TO HIS RIDICULOUS CONFIDENCE, HIS COMPLETE LACK OF FEAR UNTIL MY OWN TERROR BEGAN TO SUBSIDE. WHAT FREEDOM!
WELL, UH, THERE YOU HAVE IT
FOLKS,.. WE BRING YOU
BREAATH
THANK YOU FOR THAT, DUDE. WHOEVER, WHEREVER YOU MIGHT BE.
THANK YOU FOR YOUR RADICAL ACCEPTANCE AND HELPING ME TO GET A GOOD NIGHT'S SLEEP.
FUCK IT.
ZZZZ

DON'S TOENAILS WERE CURVED, LIKE SNAIL SHELLS. WHILE READING HE WOULD *PICK* AT THEM, ABSENTLY.

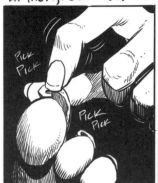

PICK PICK

PICK PICK

ELENA AND I HAD A *MORBID FASCINATION* WITH THEM.

YESSS?

HUH? NOTHIN'.

1957 STALIN YEAR

I TERRORIZED HER ABOUT THOSE THINGS.

DON'S TOENAILS...COMIN' TO *GETCHA!* HA HAA!

STOP!

SUDDENLY THE SOUND OF MOM AND DON'S LATE NIGHT *PARTYING* WOULD STOP AND WE'D FREEZE AS HE CHECKED ON US.

MELLOW...

SNORE...

ONCE THE DOOR CLOSED I'D GO RIGHT BACK TO IT WITH FRESH MATERIAL...

MELLOW YELLOW COMIN' TO GETCHA!

STOP IT!

...I

UH...

MELLOW.

SNORE...

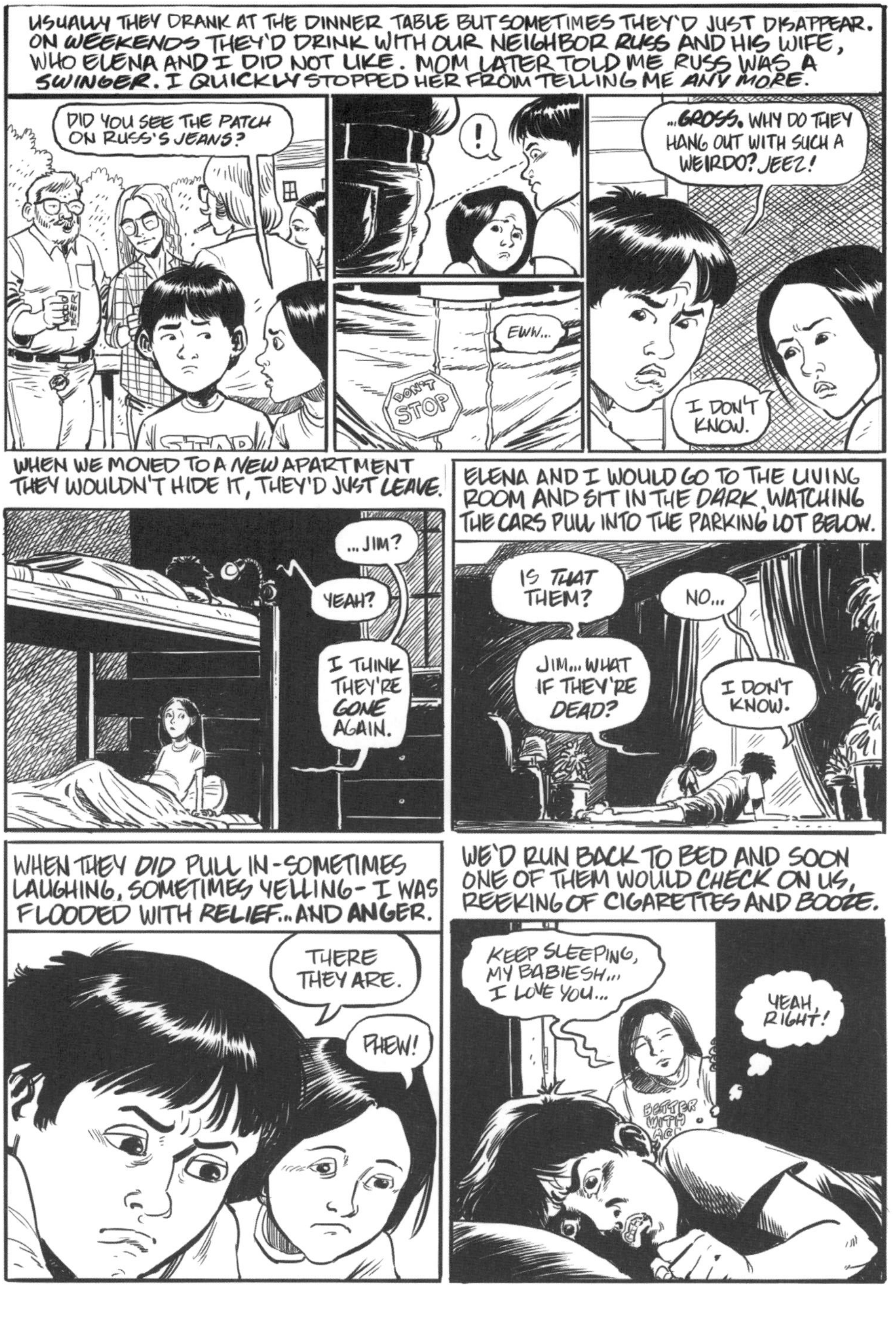
USUALLY THEY DRANK AT THE DINNER TABLE BUT SOMETIMES THEY'D JUST DISAPPEAR. ON WEEKENDS THEY'D DRINK WITH OUR NEIGHBOR RUSS AND HIS WIFE, WHO ELENA AND I DID NOT LIKE. MOM LATER TOLD ME RUSS WAS A SWINGER. I QUICKLY STOPPED HER FROM TELLING ME ANY MORE.
DID YOU SEE THE PATCH ON RUSS'S JEANS?
!
EWW...
DON'T STOP
...GROSS. WHY DO THEY HANG OUT WITH SUCH A WEIRDO? JEEZ!
I DON'T KNOW.
WHEN WE MOVED TO A NEW APARTMENT THEY WOULDN'T HIDE IT, THEY'D JUST LEAVE.
...JIM?
YEAH?
I THINK THEY'RE GONE AGAIN.
ELENA AND I WOULD GO TO THE LIVING ROOM AND SIT IN THE DARK, WATCHING THE CARS PULL INTO THE PARKING LOT BELOW.
IS THAT THEM?
NO...
JIM... WHAT IF THEY'RE DEAD?
I DON'T KNOW.
WHEN THEY DID PULL IN-SOMETIMES LAUGHING, SOMETIMES YELLING- I WAS FLOODED WITH RELIEF...AND ANGER.
THERE THEY ARE.
PHEW!
WE'D RUN BACK TO BED AND SOON ONE OF THEM WOULD CHECK ON US, REEKING OF CIGARETTES AND BOOZE.
KEEP SLEEPING, MY BABIESH... I LOVE YOU...
YEAH, RIGHT!

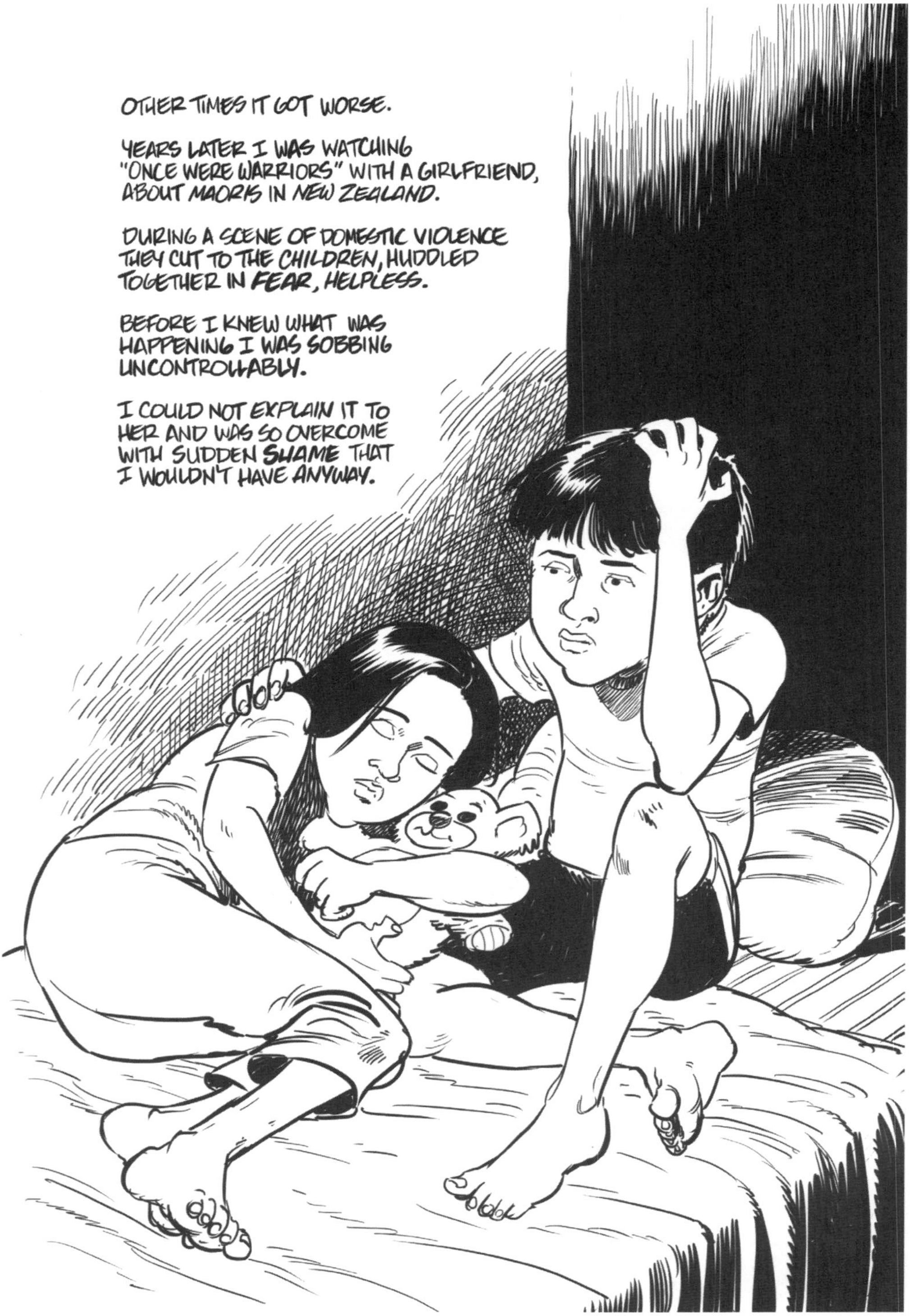
OTHER TIMES IT GOT WORSE.
YEARS LATER I WAS WATCHING "ONCE WERE WARRIORS" WITH A GIRLFRIEND, ABOUT MAORIS IN NEW ZEALAND.
DURING A SCENE OF DOMESTIC VIOLENCE THEY CUT TO THE CHILDREN, HUDDLED TOGETHER IN FEAR, HELPLESS.
BEFORE I KNEW WHAT WAS HAPPENING I WAS SOBBING UNCONTROLLABLY.
I COULD NOT EXPLAIN IT TO HER AND WAS SO OVERCOME WITH SUDDEN SHAME THAT I WOULDN'T HAVE ANYWAY.

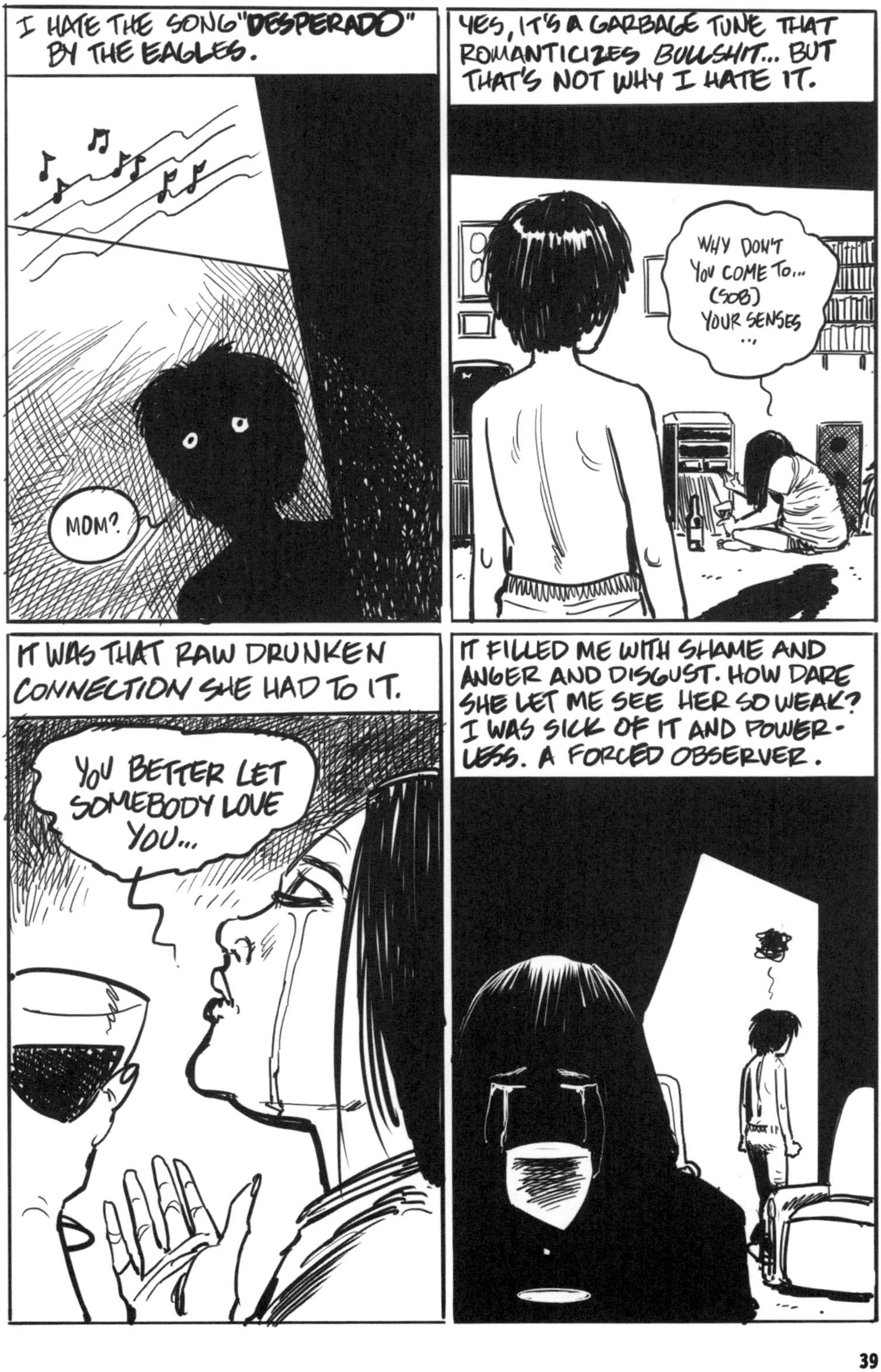
I HATE THE SONG "DESPERADO" BY THE EAGLES.
MOM?
YES, IT'S A GARBAGE TUNE THAT ROMANTICIZES BULLSHIT... BUT THAT'S NOT WHY I HATE IT.
WHY DON'T YOU COME TO... (SOB) YOUR SENSES ...
IT WAS THAT RAW DRUNKEN CONNECTION SHE HAD TO IT.
YOU BETTER LET SOMEBODY LOVE YOU...
IT FILLED ME WITH SHAME AND ANGER AND DISGUST. HOW DARE SHE LET ME SEE HER SO WEAK? I WAS SICK OF IT AND POWER-LESS. A FORCED OBSERVER.

IN THE LIGHT OF DAY EVERYTHING FELT JUST FINE. THE HOT SUN BURNED AWAY RESIDUAL *ANGER* AND *SHAME* LIKE MORNING *FOG*, AND I BECAME *ACCUSTOMED* TO THE FLICKERING SENSE OF *TENSION* AND *UNEASE* IN MY STOMACH.

THERE WAS ALSO A WHISPER IN MY MIND, A GROWING IDEA THAT SOMEWHERE I'D DONE SOMETHING *WRONG* AND IT'D CHANGED HOW MOM *FELT* ABOUT ME.

WHY ELSE WOULD SHE ALWAYS SEEM SO *UNHAPPY*?

IT ***HAD*** TO BE SOMETHING I'D DONE.

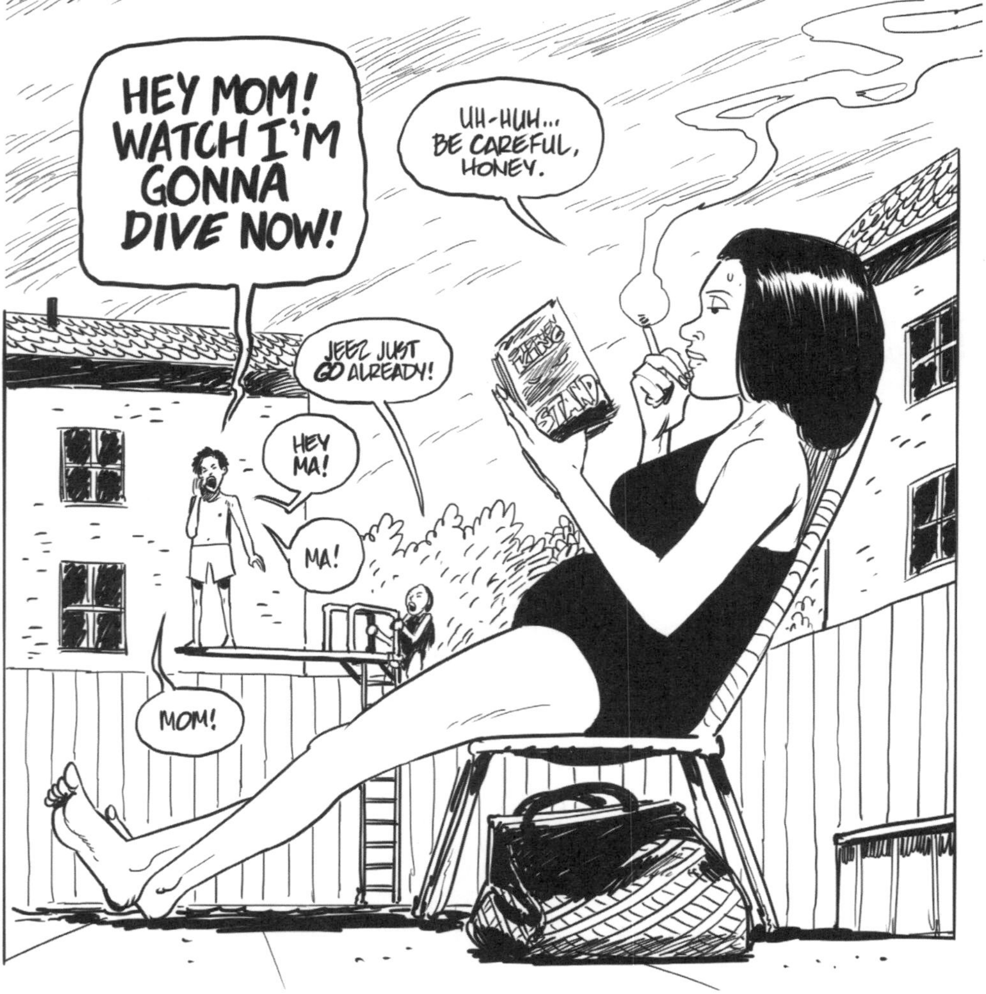
HEY MOM! WATCH I'M GONNA *DIVE* NOW!
UH-HUH... BE CAREFUL, HONEY.
JEEZ JUST *GO* ALREADY!
HEY MA!
MA!
MOM!
STAND

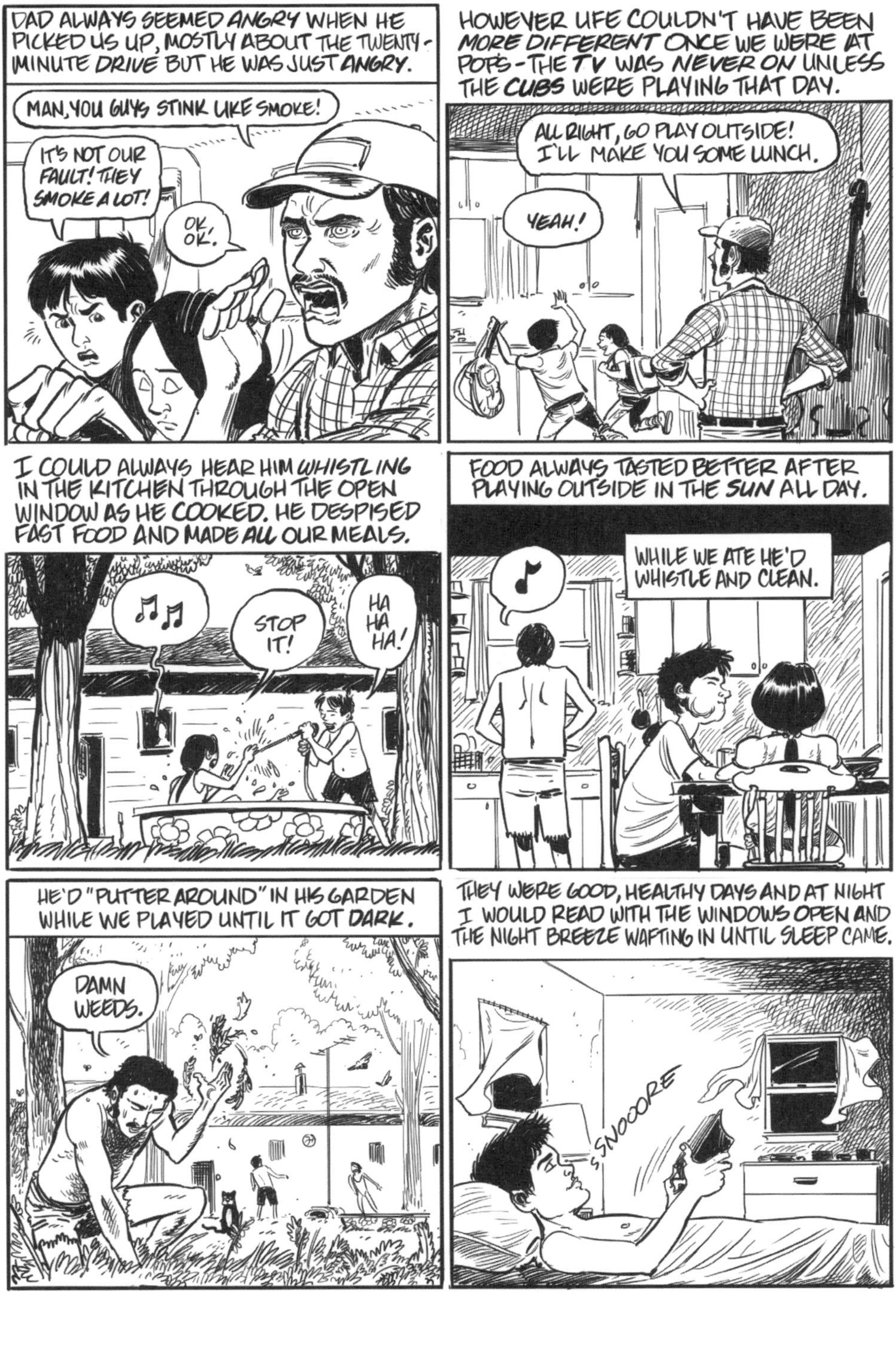
DAD ALWAYS SEEMED ANGRY WHEN HE PICKED US UP, MOSTLY ABOUT THE TWENTY-MINUTE DRIVE BUT HE WAS JUST ANGRY.
MAN, YOU GUYS STINK LIKE SMOKE!
IT'S NOT OUR FAULT! THEY SMOKE A LOT!
OK! OK.
HOWEVER LIFE COULDN'T HAVE BEEN MORE DIFFERENT ONCE WE WERE AT POP'S - THE TV WAS NEVER ON UNLESS THE CUBS WERE PLAYING THAT DAY.
ALL RIGHT, GO PLAY OUTSIDE! I'LL MAKE YOU SOME LUNCH.
YEAH!
I COULD ALWAYS HEAR HIM WHISTLING IN THE KITCHEN THROUGH THE OPEN WINDOW AS HE COOKED. HE DESPISED FAST FOOD AND MADE ALL OUR MEALS.
STOP IT!
HA HA HA!
FOOD ALWAYS TASTED BETTER AFTER PLAYING OUTSIDE IN THE SUN ALL DAY.
WHILE WE ATE HE'D WHISTLE AND CLEAN.
HE'D "PUTTER AROUND" IN HIS GARDEN WHILE WE PLAYED UNTIL IT GOT DARK.
DAMN WEEDS.
THEY WERE GOOD, HEALTHY DAYS AND AT NIGHT I WOULD READ WITH THE WINDOWS OPEN AND THE NIGHT BREEZE WAFTING IN UNTIL SLEEP CAME.
SNOOORE

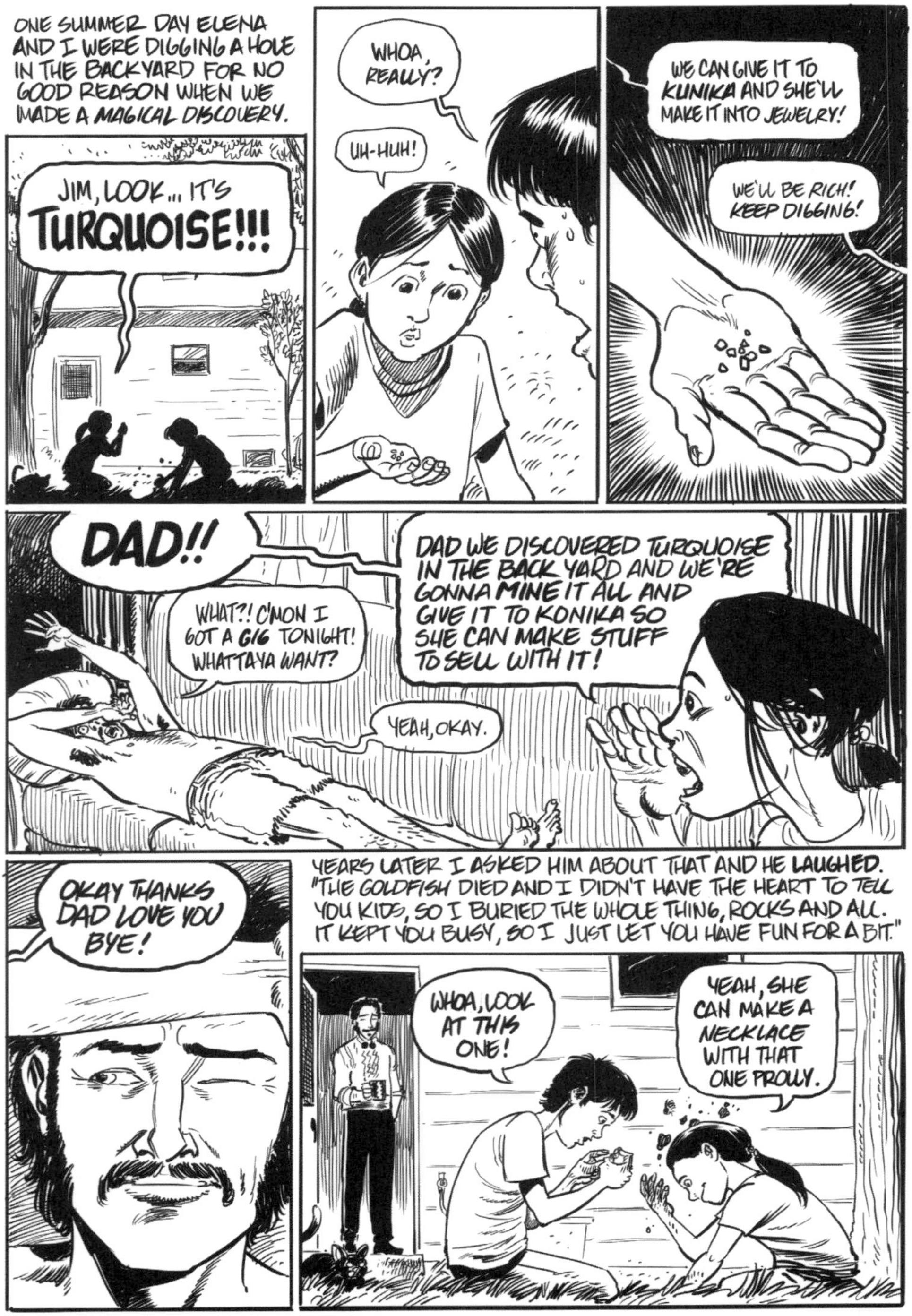
ONE SUMMER DAY ELENA AND I WERE DIGGING A HOLE IN THE BACKYARD FOR NO GOOD REASON WHEN WE MADE A MAGICAL DISCOVERY.
JIM, LOOK... IT'S TURQUOISE!!!
WHOA, REALLY?
UH-HUH!
WE CAN GIVE IT TO KUNIKA AND SHE'LL MAKE IT INTO JEWELRY!
WE'LL BE RICH! KEEP DIGGING!
DAD!!
WHAT?! C'MON I GOT A GIG TONIGHT! WHATTAYA WANT?
DAD WE DISCOVERED TURQUOISE IN THE BACK YARD AND WE'RE GONNA MINE IT ALL AND GIVE IT TO KONIKA SO SHE CAN MAKE STUFF TO SELL WITH IT!
YEAH, OKAY.
OKAY THANKS DAD LOVE YOU BYE!
YEARS LATER I ASKED HIM ABOUT THAT AND HE LAUGHED. "THE GOLDFISH DIED AND I DIDN'T HAVE THE HEART TO TELL YOU KIDS, SO I BURIED THE WHOLE THING, ROCKS AND ALL. IT KEPT YOU BUSY, SO I JUST LET YOU HAVE FUN FOR A BIT."
WHOA, LOOK AT THIS ONE!
YEAH, SHE CAN MAKE A NECKLACE WITH THAT ONE PROLLY.

POP DID HIS **BEST** TO MAKE SURE WE DIDN'T GROW UP KNOWING NOTHING BUT THE **SUBURBS** SO WE SPENT A LOT OF TIME IN THE ***CITY***.

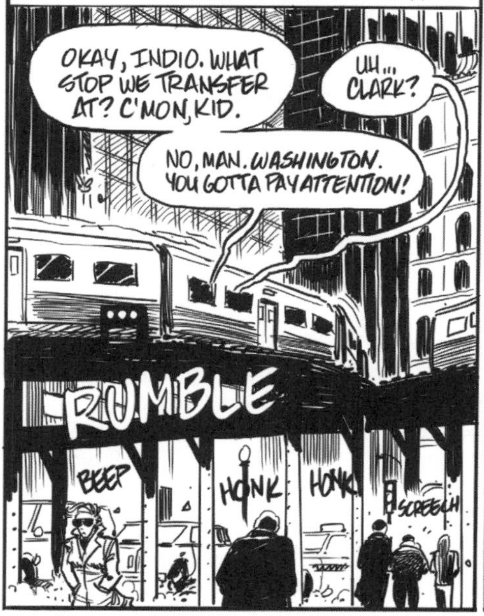
OKAY, INDIO. WHAT STOP WE TRANSFER AT? C'MON, KID.
UH... CLARK?
NO, MAN. *WASHINGTON*. YOU GOTTA PAY ATTENTION!
RUMBLE
BEEP
HONK
HONK
SCREECH

HE HAD PLENTY OF **LADY FRIENDS** THAT WE'D GO VISIT. I LOVED THE FOOD THEY'D COOK AND THEY USUALLY HAD **KIDS** OUR AGE TO PLAY WITH.

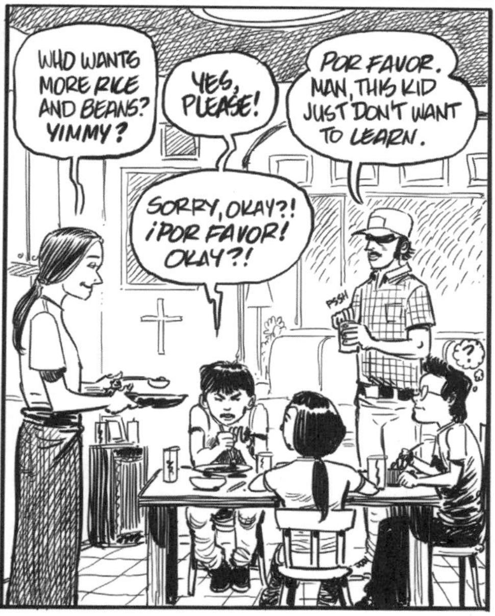
WHO WANTS MORE *RICE* AND BEANS? **YIMMY?**
YES, PLEASE!
POR FAVOR. MAN, THIS KID JUST DON'T WANT TO *LEARN*.
SORRY, OKAY?! *¡POR FAVOR!* OKAY?!
PSSH

THE CITY WAS ***DANGEROUS*** AND HE WANTED US TO ***UNDERSTAND*** THAT. WE'D BEEN ROBBED IN THE STREET, THE BUS WE WERE RIDING GOT CAUGHT IN THE MIDDLE OF A SHOOT-OUT... I SAW A KID GET KILLED BY A CAR COMING OUT OF AN ***ALLEY***.

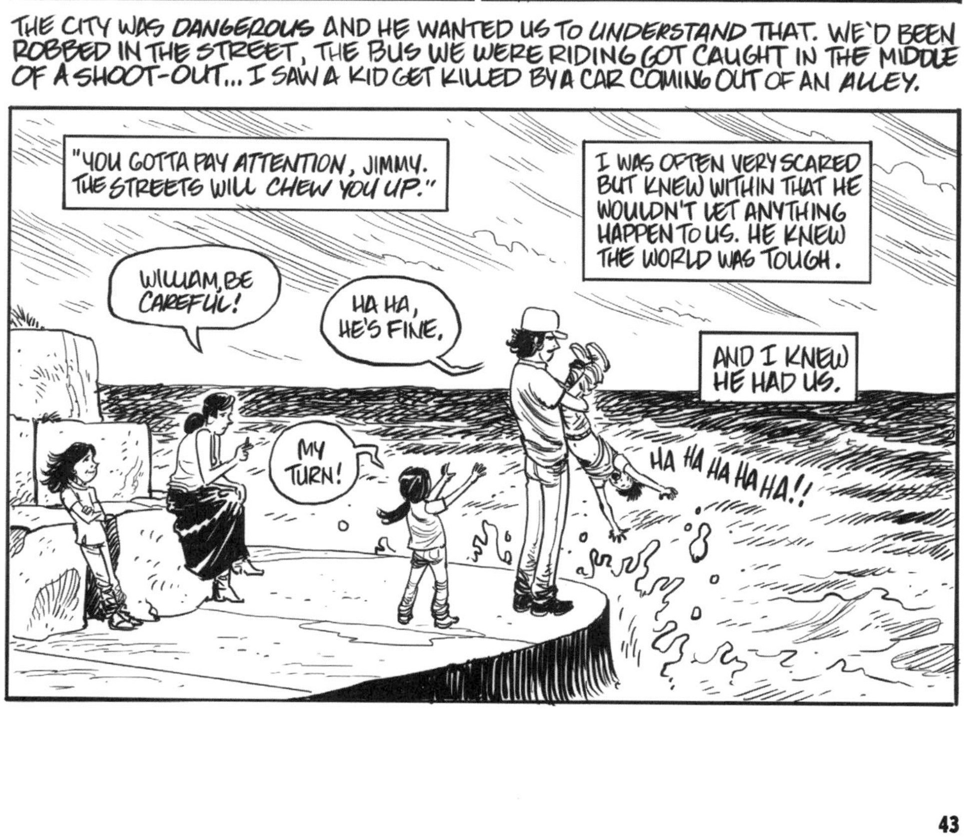
"YOU GOTTA PAY *ATTENTION*, JIMMY. THE STREETS WILL *CHEW YOU UP*."
I WAS OFTEN VERY SCARED BUT KNEW WITHIN THAT HE WOULDN'T LET ANYTHING HAPPEN TO US. HE KNEW THE WORLD WAS TOUGH.
WILLIAM, BE CAREFUL!
HA HA, HE'S FINE.
AND I KNEW HE HAD US.
MY TURN!
HA HA HA HA HA!!

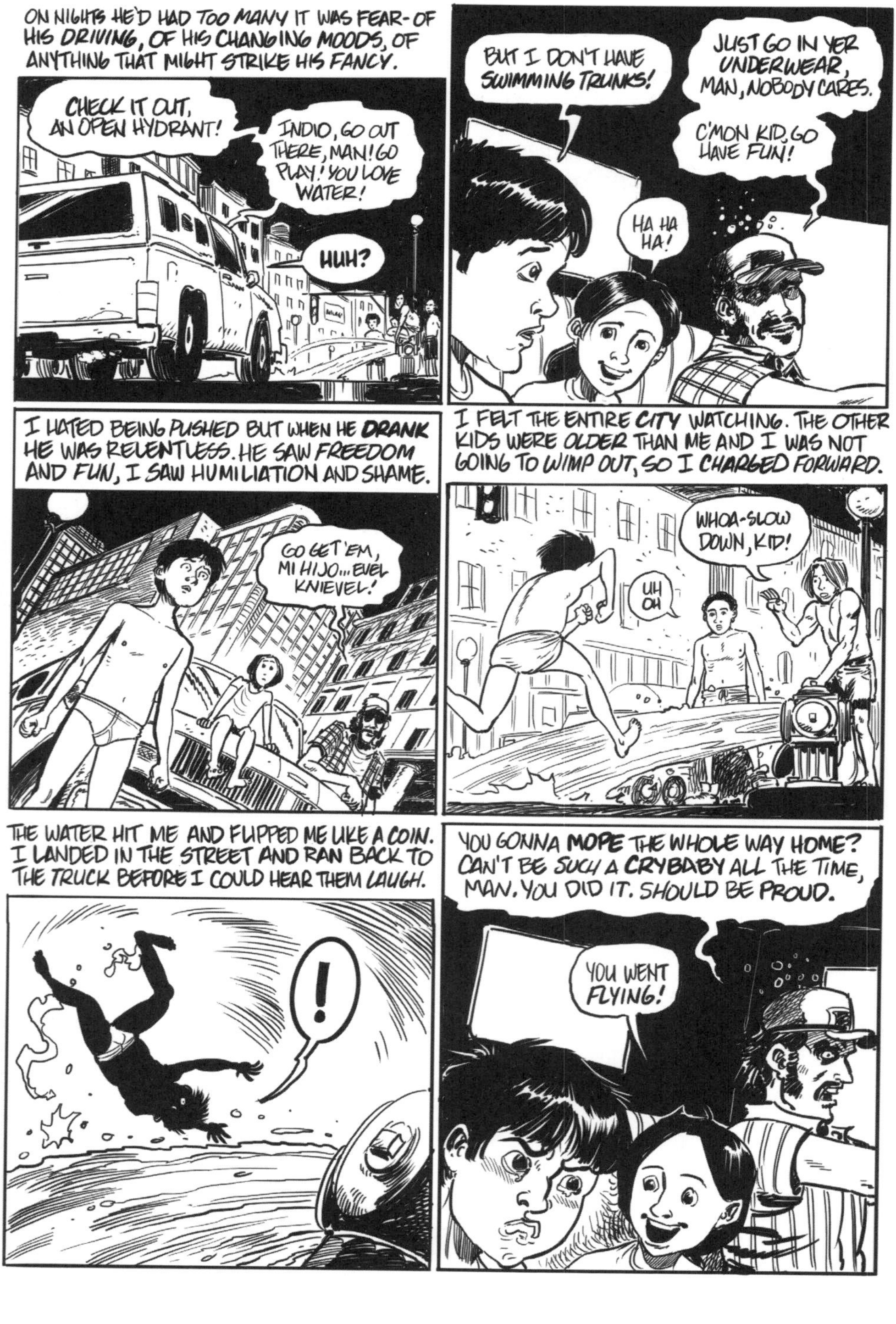

ON NIGHTS HE'D HAD TOO MANY IT WAS FEAR- OF HIS DRIVING, OF HIS CHANGING MOODS, OF ANYTHING THAT MIGHT STRIKE HIS FANCY.
CHECK IT OUT, AN OPEN HYDRANT!
INDIO, GO OUT THERE, MAN! GO PLAY! YOU LOVE WATER!
HUH?
BUT I DON'T HAVE SWIMMING TRUNKS!
JUST GO IN YER UNDERWEAR, MAN, NOBODY CARES.
C'MON KID, GO HAVE FUN!
HA HA HA!
I HATED BEING PUSHED BUT WHEN HE DRANK HE WAS RELENTLESS. HE SAW FREEDOM AND FUN, I SAW HUMILIATION AND SHAME.
GO GET 'EM, MI HIJO... EVEL KNIEVEL!
I FELT THE ENTIRE CITY WATCHING. THE OTHER KIDS WERE OLDER THAN ME AND I WAS NOT GOING TO WIMP OUT, SO I CHARGED FORWARD.
WHOA-SLOW DOWN, KID!
UH OH
THE WATER HIT ME AND FLIPPED ME LIKE A COIN. I LANDED IN THE STREET AND RAN BACK TO THE TRUCK BEFORE I COULD HEAR THEM LAUGH.
!
YOU GONNA MOPE THE WHOLE WAY HOME? CAN'T BE SUCH A CRYBABY ALL THE TIME, MAN. YOU DID IT. SHOULD BE PROUD.
YOU WENT FLYING!

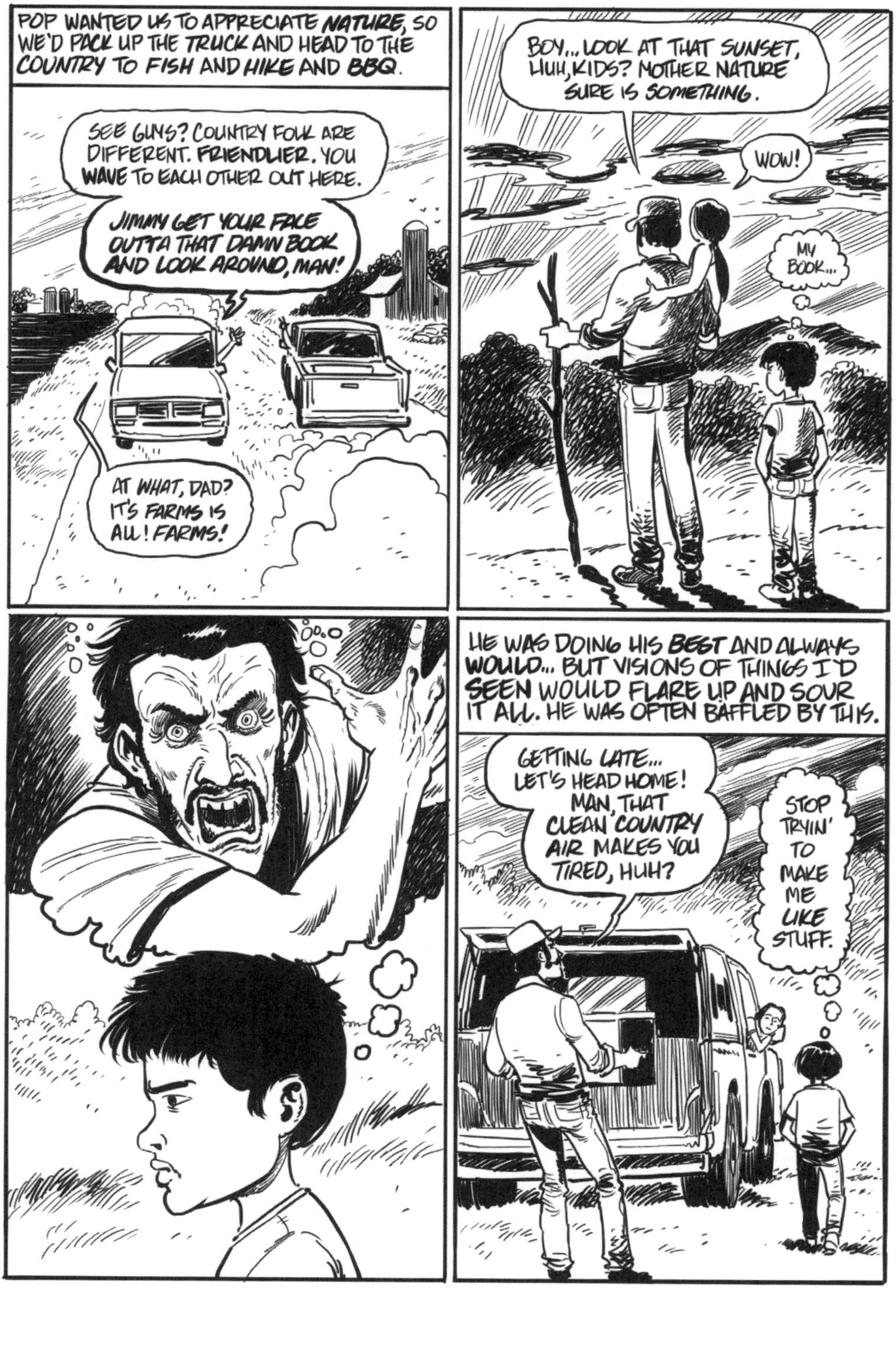
POP WANTED US TO APPRECIATE NATURE, SO WE'D PACK UP THE TRUCK AND HEAD TO THE COUNTRY TO FISH AND HIKE AND BBQ.
SEE GUYS? COUNTRY FOLK ARE DIFFERENT. FRIENDLIER. YOU WAVE TO EACH OTHER OUT HERE.
JIMMY GET YOUR FACE OUTTA THAT DAMN BOOK AND LOOK AROUND, MAN!
AT WHAT, DAD? IT'S FARMS IS ALL! FARMS!
BOY... LOOK AT THAT SUNSET, HUH, KIDS? MOTHER NATURE SURE IS SOMETHING.
WOW!
MY BOOK...
HE WAS DOING HIS BEST AND ALWAYS WOULD... BUT VISIONS OF THINGS I'D SEEN WOULD FLARE UP AND SOUR IT ALL. HE WAS OFTEN BAFFLED BY THIS.
GETTING LATE... LET'S HEAD HOME! MAN, THAT CLEAN COUNTRY AIR MAKES YOU TIRED, HUH?
STOP TRYIN' TO MAKE ME LIKE STUFF.

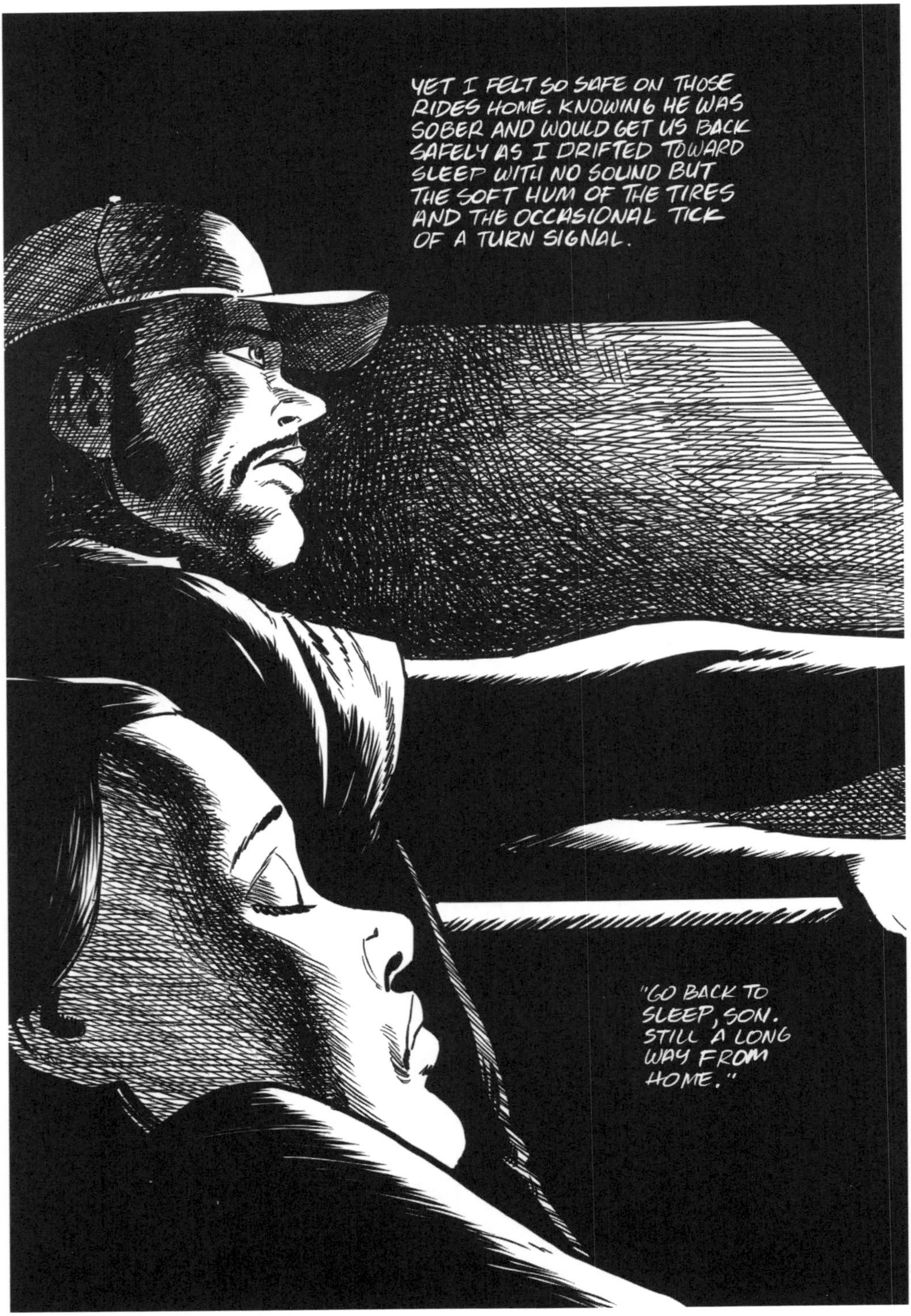
YET I FELT SO SAFE ON THOSE RIDES HOME. KNOWING HE WAS SOBER AND WOULD GET US BACK SAFELY AS I DRIFTED TOWARD SLEEP WITH NO SOUND BUT THE SOFT HUM OF THE TIRES AND THE OCCASIONAL TICK OF A TURN SIGNAL.
"GO BACK TO SLEEP, SON. STILL A LONG WAY FROM HOME."

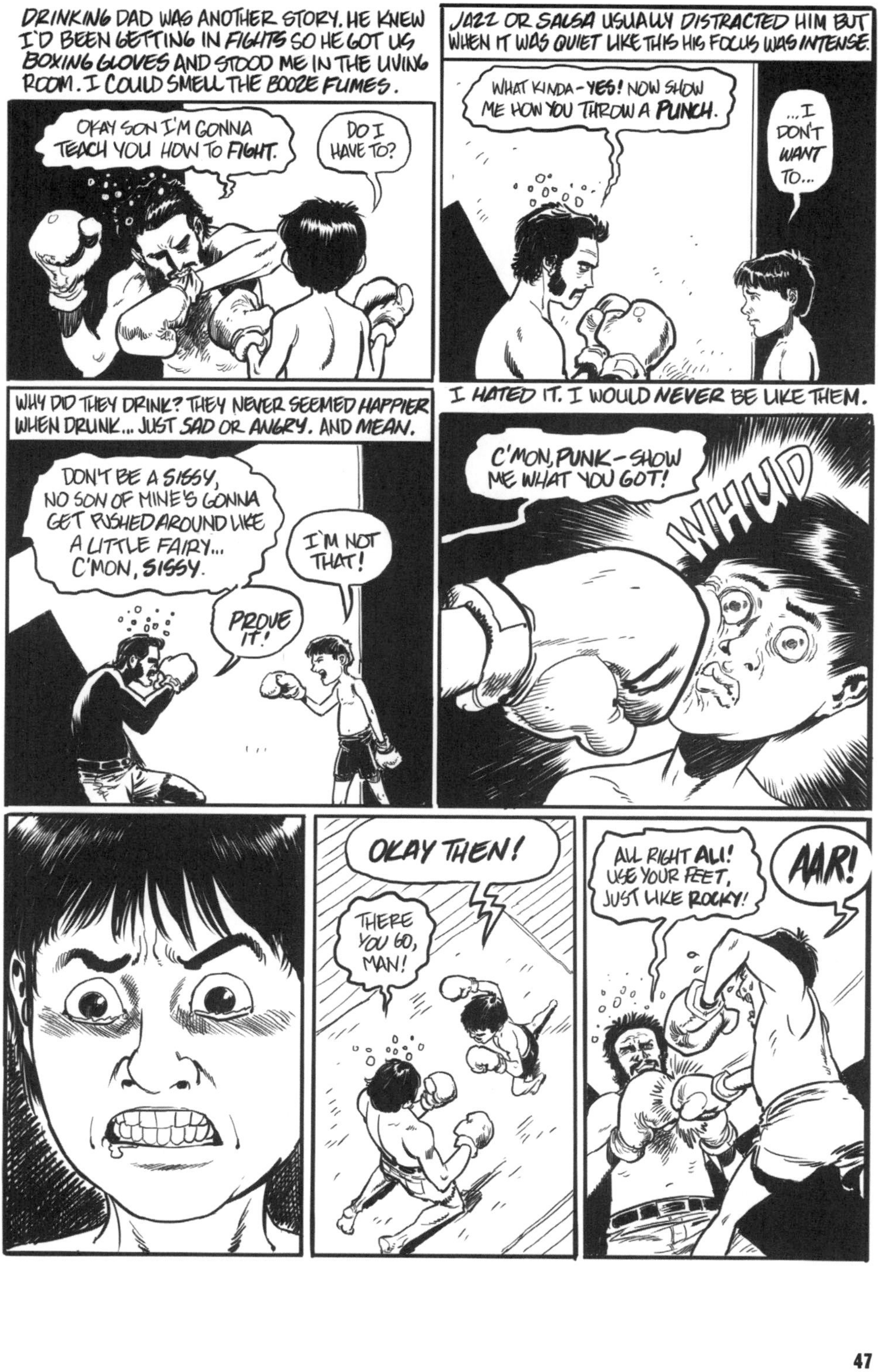
DRINKING DAD WAS ANOTHER STORY. HE KNEW I'D BEEN GETTING IN FIGHTS SO HE GOT US BOXING GLOVES AND STOOD ME IN THE LIVING ROOM. I COULD SMELL THE BOOZE FUMES.
OKAY SON I'M GONNA TEACH YOU HOW TO FIGHT.
DO I HAVE TO?
JAZZ OR SALSA USUALLY DISTRACTED HIM BUT WHEN IT WAS QUIET LIKE THIS HIS FOCUS WAS INTENSE.
WHAT KINDA - YES! NOW SHOW ME HOW YOU THROW A PUNCH.
...I DON'T WANT TO...
WHY DID THEY DRINK? THEY NEVER SEEMED HAPPIER WHEN DRUNK... JUST SAD OR ANGRY. AND MEAN.
DON'T BE A SISSY, NO SON OF MINE'S GONNA GET PUSHED AROUND LIKE A LITTLE FAIRY... C'MON, SISSY.
I'M NOT THAT!
PROVE IT!
I HATED IT. I WOULD NEVER BE LIKE THEM.
C'MON, PUNK - SHOW ME WHAT YOU GOT!
WHUD
OKAY THEN!
THERE YOU GO, MAN!
ALL RIGHT ALI! USE YOUR FEET, JUST LIKE ROCKY!
AAR!

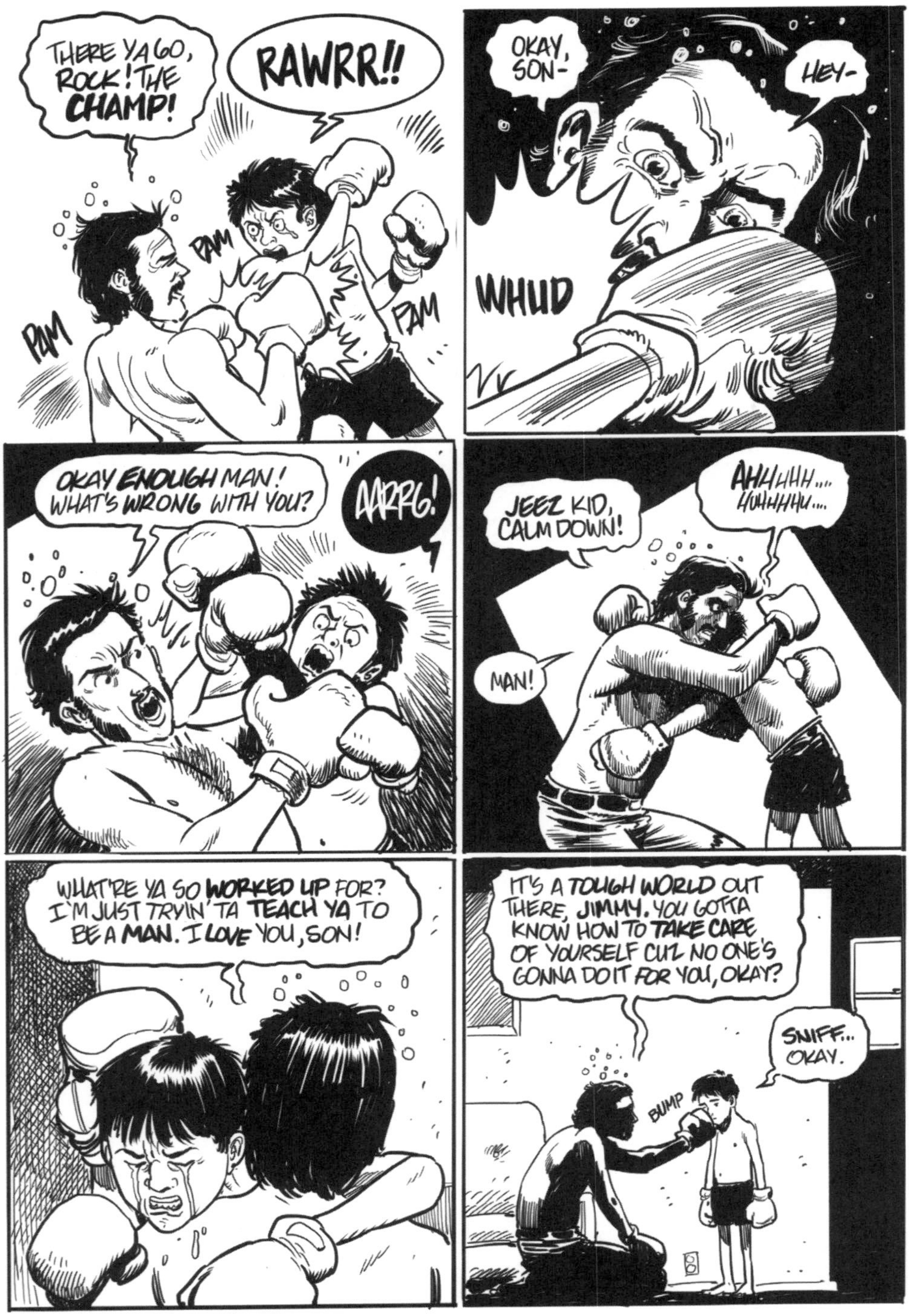
THERE YA GO, ROCK! THE CHAMP!
RAWRR!!
PAM
PAM
PAM
PAM
OKAY, SON-
HEY-
WHUD
OKAY ENOUGH MAN! WHAT'S WRONG WITH YOU?
AARRG!
JEEZ KID, CALM DOWN!
AHHHHH.... HUHHHHU....
MAN!
WHAT'RE YA SO WORKED UP FOR? I'M JUST TRYIN' TA TEACH YA TO BE A MAN. I LOVE YOU, SON!
IT'S A TOUGH WORLD OUT THERE, JIMMY. YOU GOTTA KNOW HOW TO TAKE CARE OF YOURSELF CUZ NO ONE'S GONNA DO IT FOR YOU, OKAY?
SNIFF... OKAY.
BUMP

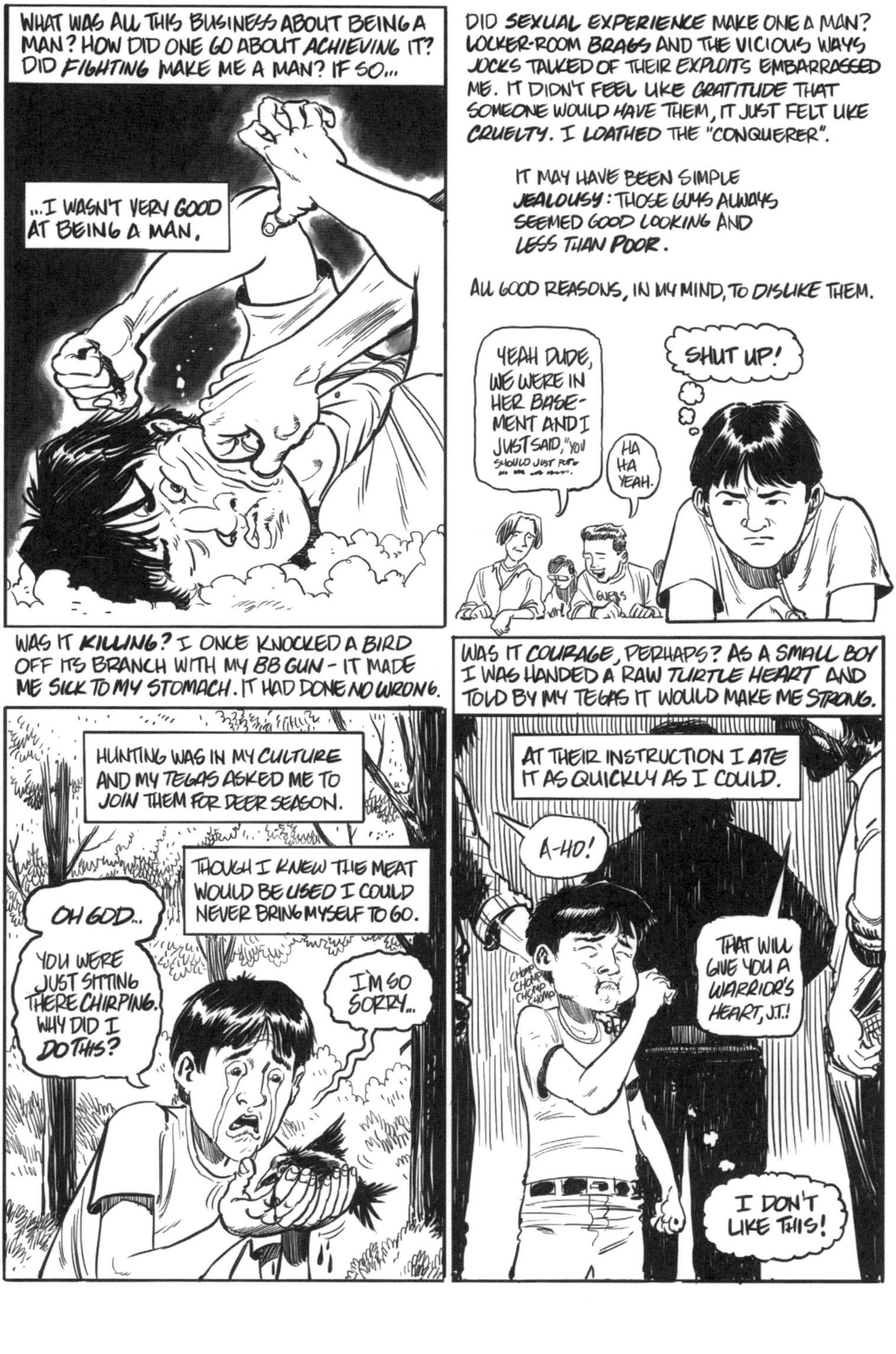
WHAT WAS ALL THIS BUSINESS ABOUT BEING A MAN? HOW DID ONE GO ABOUT ACHIEVING IT? DID FIGHTING MAKE ME A MAN? IF SO...
...I WASN'T VERY GOOD AT BEING A MAN.
DID SEXUAL EXPERIENCE MAKE ONE A MAN? LOCKER-ROOM BRAGS AND THE VICIOUS WAYS JOCKS TALKED OF THEIR EXPLOITS EMBARRASSED ME. IT DIDN'T FEEL LIKE GRATITUDE THAT SOMEONE WOULD HAVE THEM, IT JUST FELT LIKE CRUELTY. I LOATHED THE "CONQUERER".
IT MAY HAVE BEEN SIMPLE JEALOUSY: THOSE GUYS ALWAYS SEEMED GOOD LOOKING AND LESS THAN POOR.
ALL GOOD REASONS, IN MY MIND, TO DISLIKE THEM.
YEAH DUDE, WE WERE IN HER BASEMENT AND I JUST SAID, "YOU SHOULD JUST PUT
HA HA YEAH.
SHUT UP!
GUESS
WAS IT KILLING? I ONCE KNOCKED A BIRD OFF ITS BRANCH WITH MY BB GUN - IT MADE ME SICK TO MY STOMACH. IT HAD DONE NO WRONG.
HUNTING WAS IN MY CULTURE AND MY TEGAS ASKED ME TO JOIN THEM FOR DEER SEASON.
THOUGH I KNEW THE MEAT WOULD BE USED I COULD NEVER BRING MYSELF TO GO.
OH GOD.. YOU WERE JUST SITTING THERE CHIRPING. WHY DID I DO THIS?
I'M SO SORRY...
WAS IT COURAGE, PERHAPS? AS A SMALL BOY I WAS HANDED A RAW TURTLE HEART AND TOLD BY MY TEGAS IT WOULD MAKE ME STRONG.
AT THEIR INSTRUCTION I ATE IT AS QUICKLY AS I COULD.
A-HO!
THAT WILL GIVE YOU A WARRIOR'S HEART, J.T.!
CHOMP CHOMP CHOMP CHOMP
I DON'T LIKE THIS!

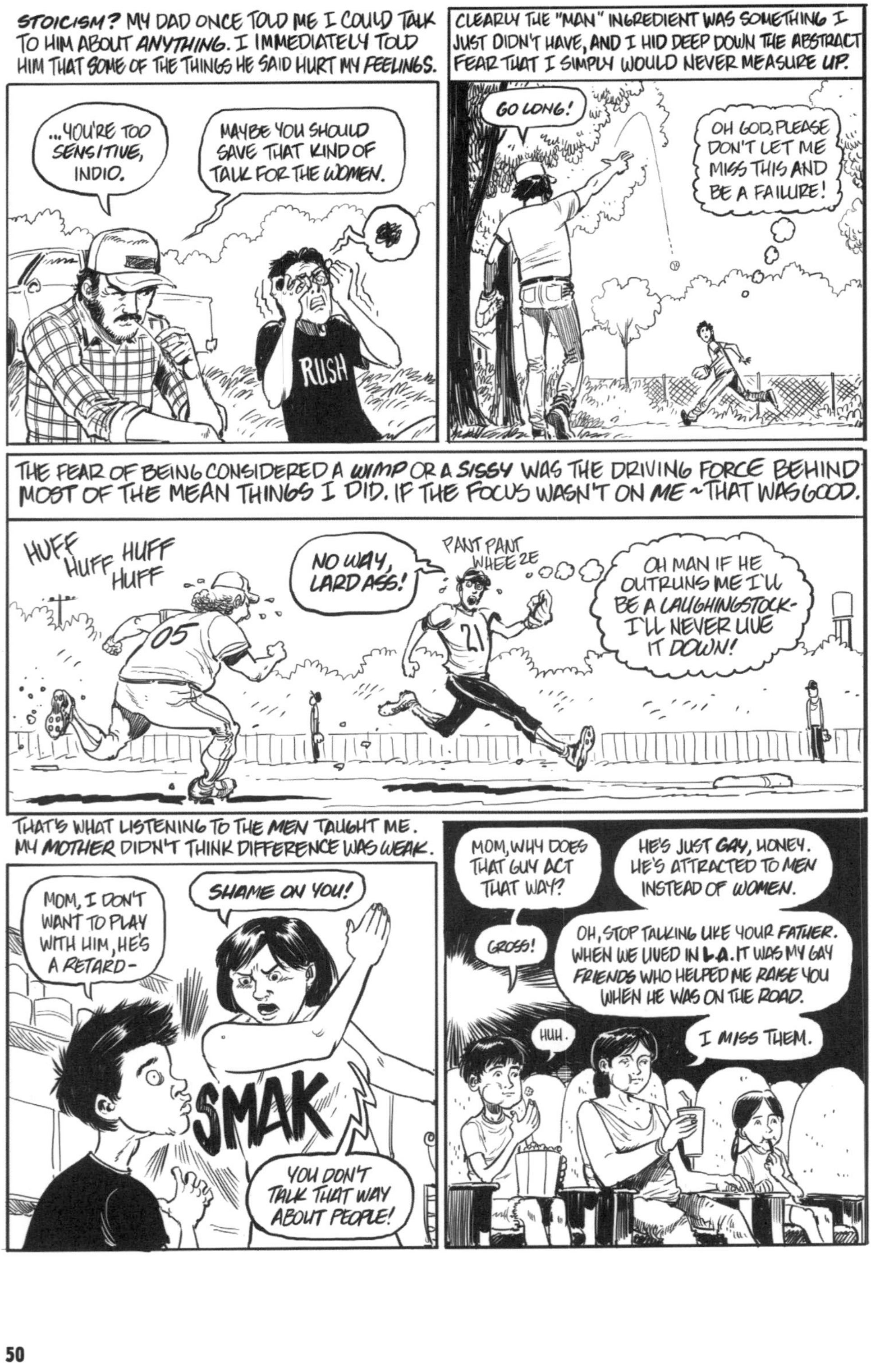
STOICISM? MY DAD ONCE TOLD ME I COULD TALK TO HIM ABOUT ANYTHING. I IMMEDIATELY TOLD HIM THAT SOME OF THE THINGS HE SAID HURT MY FEELINGS.
...YOU'RE TOO SENSITIVE, INDIO.
MAYBE YOU SHOULD SAVE THAT KIND OF TALK FOR THE WOMEN.
RUSH
CLEARLY THE "MAN" INGREDIENT WAS SOMETHING I JUST DIDN'T HAVE, AND I HID DEEP DOWN THE ABSTRACT FEAR THAT I SIMPLY WOULD NEVER MEASURE UP.
GO LONG!
OH GOD, PLEASE DON'T LET ME MISS THIS AND BE A FAILURE!
THE FEAR OF BEING CONSIDERED A WIMP OR A SISSY WAS THE DRIVING FORCE BEHIND MOST OF THE MEAN THINGS I DID. IF THE FOCUS WASN'T ON ME ~ THAT WAS GOOD.
HUFF HUFF HUFF HUFF
05
NO WAY, LARD ASS!
PANT PANT WHEEZE
21
OH MAN IF HE OUTRUNS ME I'LL BE A LAUGHINGSTOCK- I'LL NEVER LIVE IT DOWN!
THAT'S WHAT LISTENING TO THE MEN TAUGHT ME. MY MOTHER DIDN'T THINK DIFFERENCE WAS WEAK.
MOM, I DON'T WANT TO PLAY WITH HIM, HE'S A RETARD-
SHAME ON YOU!
SMAK
YOU DON'T TALK THAT WAY ABOUT PEOPLE!
MOM, WHY DOES THAT GUY ACT THAT WAY?
HE'S JUST GAY, HONEY. HE'S ATTRACTED TO MEN INSTEAD OF WOMEN.
GROSS!
OH, STOP TALKING LIKE YOUR FATHER. WHEN WE LIVED IN L.A. IT WAS MY GAY FRIENDS WHO HELPED ME RAISE YOU WHEN HE WAS ON THE ROAD.
HUH.
I MISS THEM.

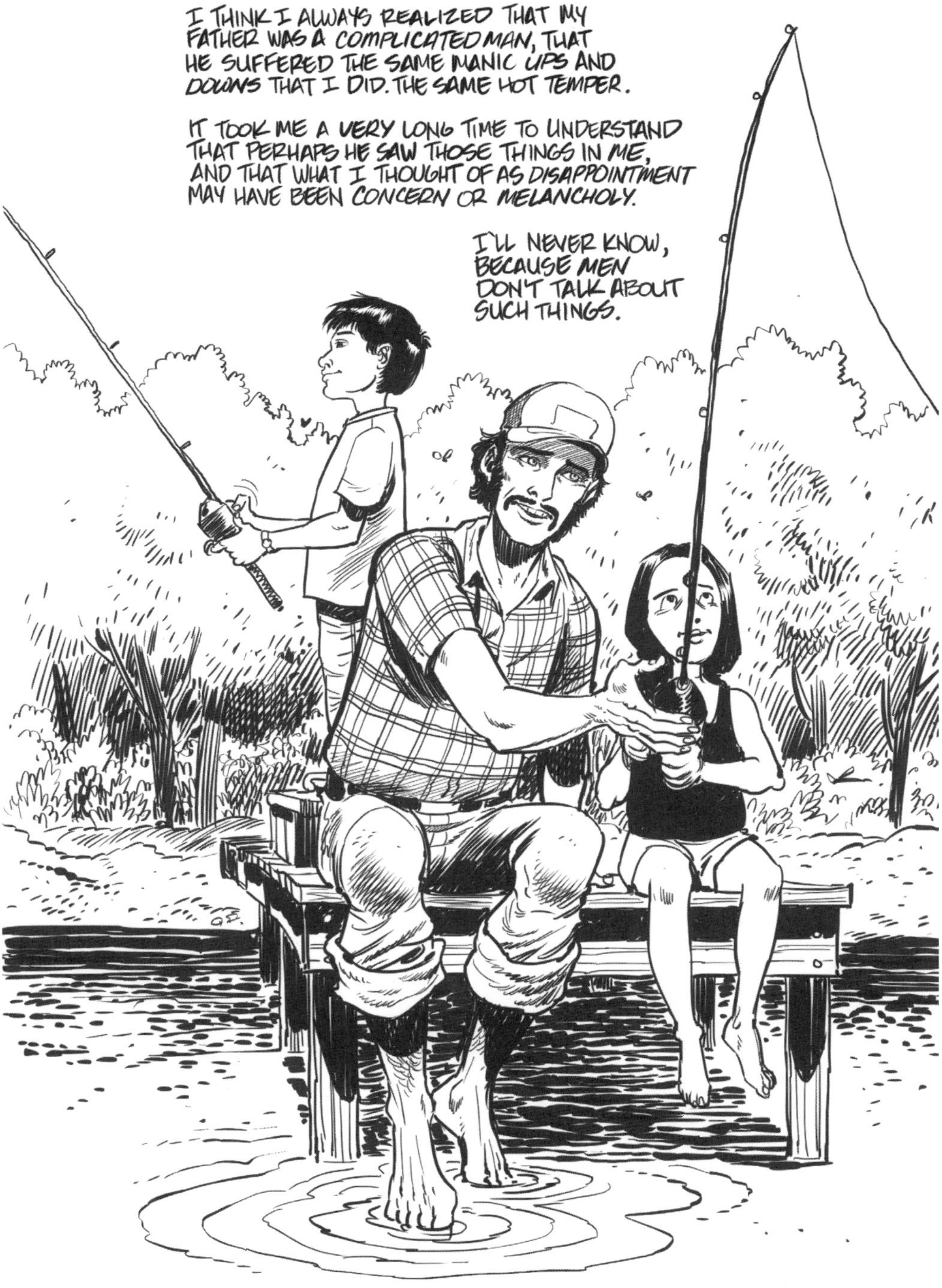
I THINK I ALWAYS REALIZED THAT MY FATHER WAS A COMPLICATED MAN, THAT HE SUFFERED THE SAME MANIC UPS AND DOWNS THAT I DID. THE SAME HOT TEMPER.
IT TOOK ME A VERY LONG TIME TO UNDERSTAND THAT PERHAPS HE SAW THOSE THINGS IN ME, AND THAT WHAT I THOUGHT OF AS DISAPPOINTMENT MAY HAVE BEEN CONCERN OR MELANCHOLY.
I'LL NEVER KNOW, BECAUSE MEN DON'T TALK ABOUT SUCH THINGS.

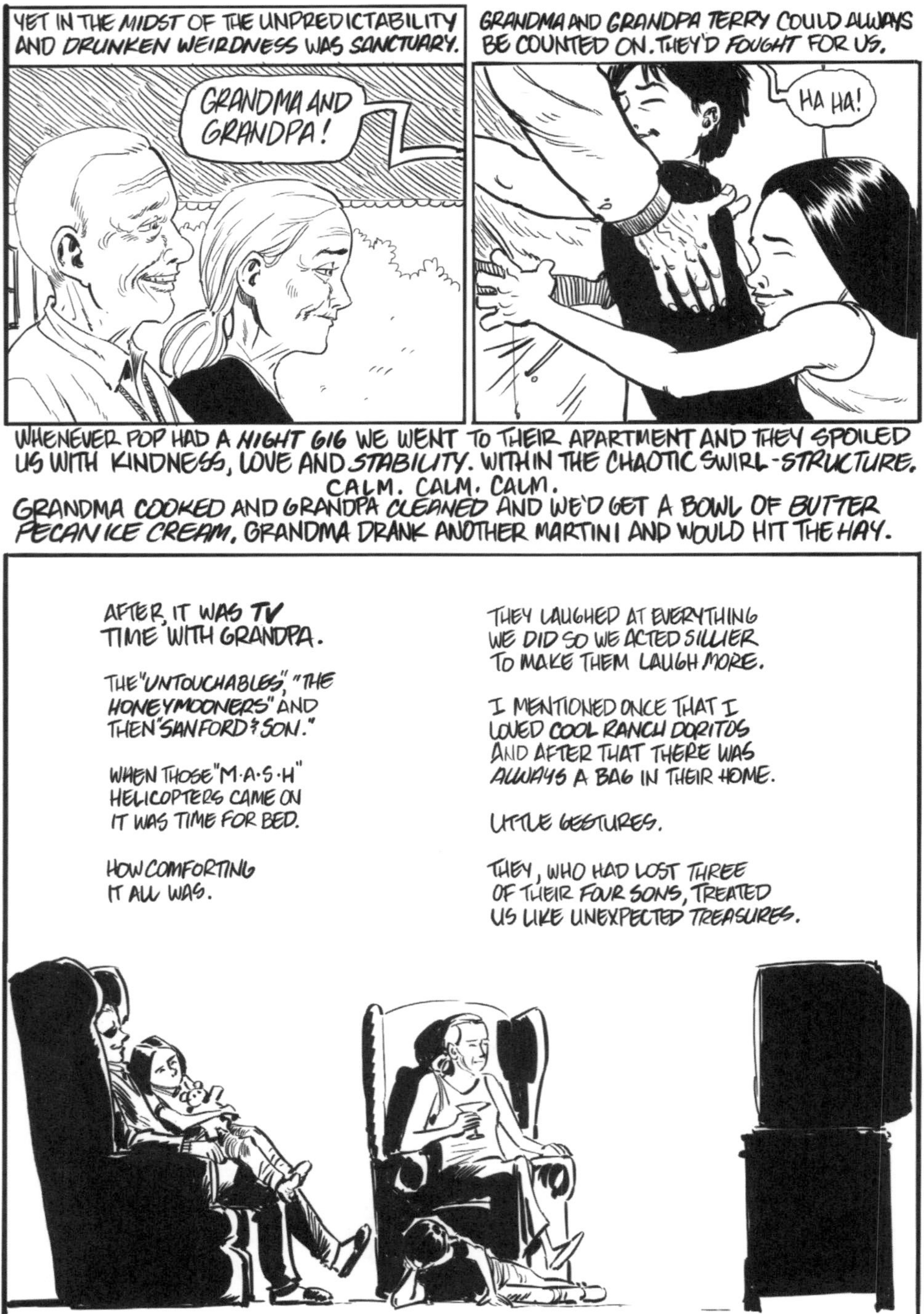
YET IN THE MIDST OF THE UNPREDICTABILITY AND DRUNKEN WEIRDNESS WAS SANCTUARY.
GRANDMA AND GRANDPA!
GRANDMA AND GRANDPA TERRY COULD ALWAYS BE COUNTED ON. THEY'D FOUGHT FOR US.
HA HA!
WHENEVER POP HAD A NIGHT GIG WE WENT TO THEIR APARTMENT AND THEY SPOILED US WITH KINDNESS, LOVE AND STABILITY. WITHIN THE CHAOTIC SWIRL-STRUCTURE.
CALM. CALM. CALM.
GRANDMA COOKED AND GRANDPA CLEANED AND WE'D GET A BOWL OF BUTTER PECAN ICE CREAM. GRANDMA DRANK ANOTHER MARTINI AND WOULD HIT THE HAY.
AFTER, IT WAS TV TIME WITH GRANDPA.
THE "UNTOUCHABLES," "THE HONEYMOONERS" AND THEN "SANFORD & SON."
WHEN THOSE "M·A·S·H" HELICOPTERS CAME ON IT WAS TIME FOR BED.
HOW COMFORTING IT ALL WAS.
THEY LAUGHED AT EVERYTHING WE DID SO WE ACTED SILLIER TO MAKE THEM LAUGH MORE.
I MENTIONED ONCE THAT I LOVED COOL RANCH DORITOS AND AFTER THAT THERE WAS ALWAYS A BAG IN THEIR HOME.
LITTLE GESTURES.
THEY, WHO HAD LOST THREE OF THEIR FOUR SONS, TREATED US LIKE UNEXPECTED TREASURES.

MOST SUNDAYS POP WORKED THE WILLOWBROOK BALLROOM - WHICH HE WASN'T CRAZY ABOUT. "BORING WALTZES FOR A BUNCH OF OLD FOLKS." HE'D DROP US OFF AT GRANDMA AND GRANDPA'S AND WE'D PLAY OUTSIDE UNTIL WE HEARD GRANDPA'S WHISTLE.

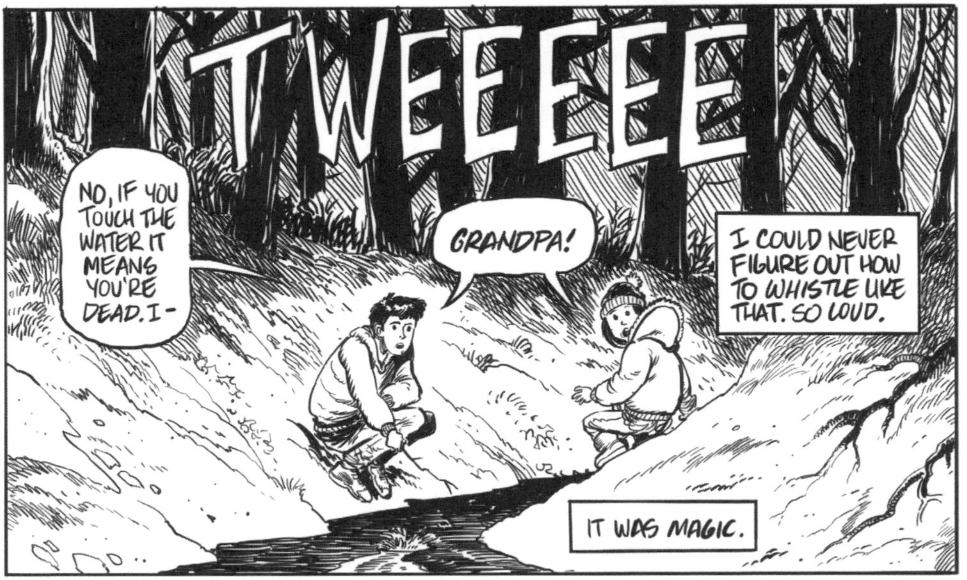
TWEEEEE
NO, IF YOU TOUCH THE WATER IT MEANS YOU'RE DEAD. I-
GRANDPA!
I COULD NEVER FIGURE OUT HOW TO WHISTLE LIKE THAT. SO LOUD.
IT WAS MAGIC.

SOMETIMES GRANDMA WOULD HAVE TOO MANY MARTINIS AND GET A BIT NASTY BUT GRANDPA WOULD JUST LAUGH IT OFF. HE SAW HOW SENSITIVE I WAS AND WOULD SAY-

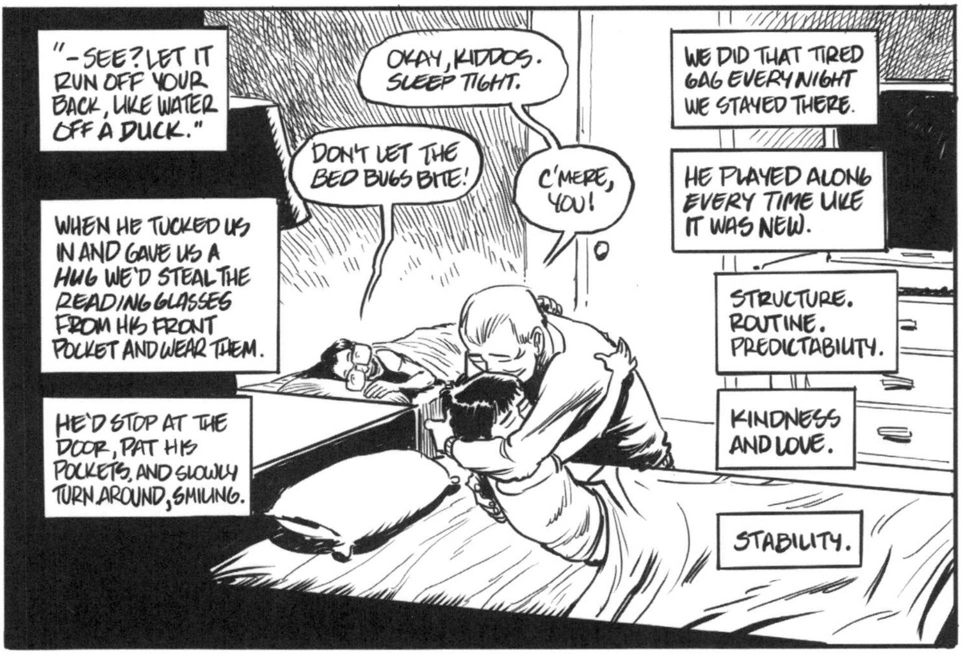
"-SEE? LET IT RUN OFF YOUR BACK, LIKE WATER OFF A DUCK."
WHEN HE TUCKED US IN AND GAVE US A HUG WE'D STEAL THE READING GLASSES FROM HIS FRONT POCKET AND WEAR THEM.
HE'D STOP AT THE DOOR, PAT HIS POCKETS, AND SLOWLY TURN AROUND, SMILING.
OKAY, KIDDOS. SLEEP TIGHT.
DON'T LET THE BED BUGS BITE!
C'MERE, YOU!
WE DID THAT TIRED GAG EVERY NIGHT WE STAYED THERE.
HE PLAYED ALONG EVERY TIME LIKE IT WAS NEW.
STRUCTURE. ROUTINE. PREDICTABILITY.
KINDNESS AND LOVE.
STABILITY.

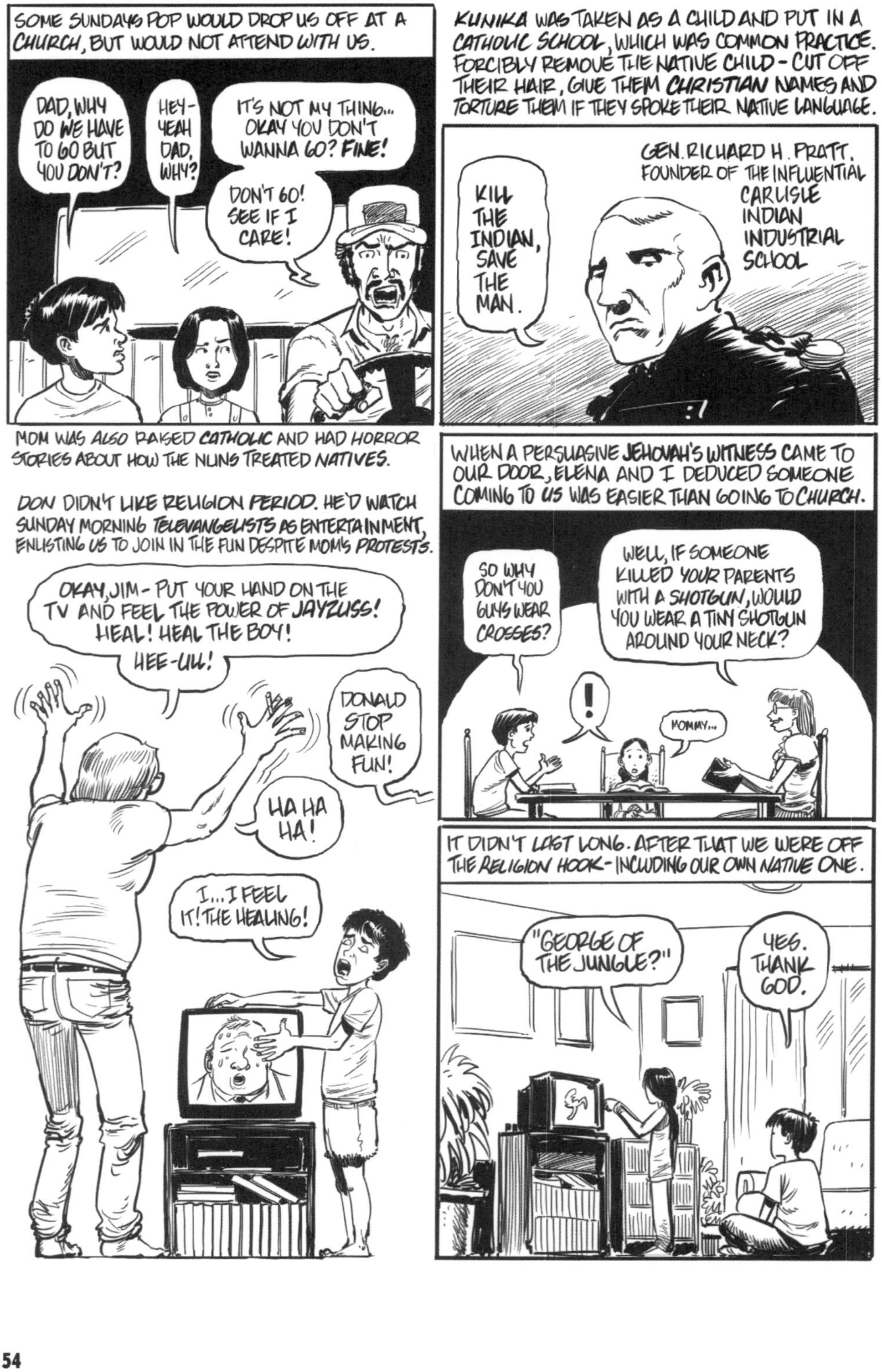
SOME SUNDAYS POP WOULD DROP US OFF AT A CHURCH, BUT WOULD NOT ATTEND WITH US.
DAD, WHY DO WE HAVE TO GO BUT YOU DON'T?
HEY-YEAH DAD, WHY?
IT'S NOT MY THING... OKAY YOU DON'T WANNA GO? FINE!
DON'T GO! SEE IF I CARE!
KUNIKA WAS TAKEN AS A CHILD AND PUT IN A CATHOLIC SCHOOL, WHICH WAS COMMON PRACTICE. FORCIBLY REMOVE THE NATIVE CHILD - CUT OFF THEIR HAIR, GIVE THEM CHRISTIAN NAMES AND TORTURE THEM IF THEY SPOKE THEIR NATIVE LANGUAGE.
GEN. RICHARD H. PRATT. FOUNDER OF THE INFLUENTIAL CARLISLE INDIAN INDUSTRIAL SCHOOL
KILL THE INDIAN, SAVE THE MAN.
MOM WAS ALSO RAISED CATHOLIC AND HAD HORROR STORIES ABOUT HOW THE NUNS TREATED NATIVES.
DON DIDN'T LIKE RELIGION PERIOD. HE'D WATCH SUNDAY MORNING TELEVANGELISTS AS ENTERTAINMENT, ENLISTING US TO JOIN IN THE FUN DESPITE MOM'S PROTESTS.
OKAY, JIM - PUT YOUR HAND ON THE TV AND FEEL THE POWER OF JAYZUSS! HEAL! HEAL THE BOY!
HEE-ULL!
DONALD STOP MAKING FUN!
HA HA HA!
I... I FEEL IT! THE HEALING!
WHEN A PERSUASIVE JEHOVAH'S WITNESS CAME TO OUR DOOR, ELENA AND I DEDUCED SOMEONE COMING TO US WAS EASIER THAN GOING TO CHURCH.
SO WHY DON'T YOU GUYS WEAR CROSSES?
WELL, IF SOMEONE KILLED YOUR PARENTS WITH A SHOTGUN, WOULD YOU WEAR A TINY SHOTGUN AROUND YOUR NECK?
!
MOMMY...
IT DIDN'T LAST LONG. AFTER THAT WE WERE OFF THE RELIGION HOOK - INCLUDING OUR OWN NATIVE ONE.
"GEORGE OF THE JUNGLE?"
YES. THANK GOD.

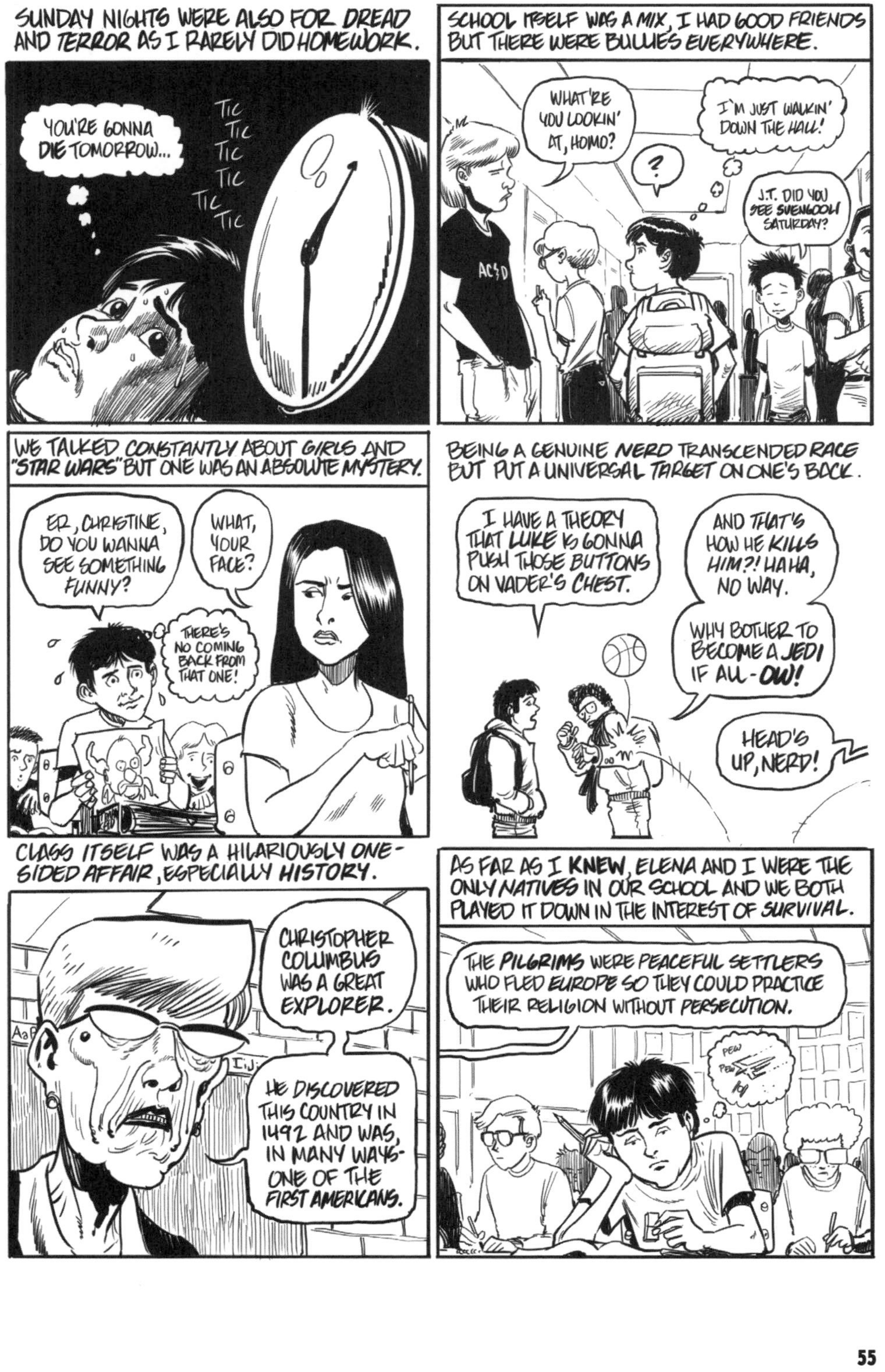
SUNDAY NIGHTS WERE ALSO FOR DREAD AND TERROR AS I RARELY DID HOMEWORK.
YOU'RE GONNA DIE TOMORROW...
TIC TIC TIC TIC TIC TIC
SCHOOL ITSELF WAS A MIX, I HAD GOOD FRIENDS BUT THERE WERE BULLIES EVERYWHERE.
WHAT'RE YOU LOOKIN' AT, HOMO?
?
I'M JUST WALKIN' DOWN THE HALL!
J.T. DID YOU SEE SVENGOOLI SATURDAY?
AC/DC
WE TALKED CONSTANTLY ABOUT GIRLS AND "STAR WARS" BUT ONE WAS AN ABSOLUTE MYSTERY.
ER, CHRISTINE, DO YOU WANNA SEE SOMETHING FUNNY?
WHAT, YOUR FACE?
THERE'S NO COMING BACK FROM THAT ONE!
BEING A GENUINE NERD TRANSCENDED RACE BUT PUT A UNIVERSAL TARGET ON ONE'S BACK.
I HAVE A THEORY THAT LUKE IS GONNA PUSH THOSE BUTTONS ON VADER'S CHEST.
AND THAT'S HOW HE KILLS HIM?! HA HA, NO WAY.
WHY BOTHER TO BECOME A JEDI IF ALL-OW!
HEAD'S UP, NERD!
CLASS ITSELF WAS A HILARIOUSLY ONE-SIDED AFFAIR, ESPECIALLY HISTORY.
CHRISTOPHER COLUMBUS WAS A GREAT EXPLORER.
HE DISCOVERED THIS COUNTRY IN 1492 AND WAS, IN MANY WAYS, ONE OF THE FIRST AMERICANS.
AS FAR AS I KNEW, ELENA AND I WERE THE ONLY NATIVES IN OUR SCHOOL AND WE BOTH PLAYED IT DOWN IN THE INTEREST OF SURVIVAL.
THE PILGRIMS WERE PEACEFUL SETTLERS WHO FLED EUROPE SO THEY COULD PRACTICE THEIR RELIGION WITHOUT PERSECUTION.
PEW PEW

I TOOK IT IN, I MEMORIZED THE DATES AND DREW PICTURES OF THE *MAYFLOWER*.

THANKSGIVING IS A HOLIDAY OF *PEACE* AND *SHARING*. IT IS THE DAY THE *PILGRIMS* INVITED THE *INDIANS* TO SHARE IN THEIR *BOUNTY*.

THE *TRAGEDY* IS I BELIEVED IT ALL. WHY WOULD THEY *LIE*? I WASN'T TAUGHT ANYTHING DIFFERENT AT *HOME*, ON *TV* OR AT THE *MOVIES*.

ANDREW JACKSON WAS THE *COMMON PEOPLE'S* PRESIDENT.

IN FACT HE ONCE OPENED THE *WHITE HOUSE* AND INVITED ANYONE TO JUST DROP ON IN! IT WAS... QUITE A PARTY!

HA HA HA REALLY? AWESOME! DUDE! WHAT A COOL GUY!

ANDREW "INDIAN KILLER" JACKSON WAS ON *MONEY* NEXT TO GOD'S NAME. HIS *INDIAN RELOCATION ACT* WAS NEVER MENTIONED IN OUR TEXT AND THE *TRAIL OF TEARS* WAS A *PARAGRAPH.* A *FOOTNOTE*.

NOR A MENTION THAT THE PILGRIMS WERE CONSIDERED *FANATICS* BACK HOME AND WERE EATING *BELTS, SHOES,* AND POSSIBLY *EACH OTHER* BEFORE THE NATIVES STEPPED IN.

OR THAT COLUMBUS CHOPPED THE HANDS OFF NATIVES WHEN THEY COULD NOT SUPPLY HIM WITH THE GOLD HE WAS CONVINCED THEY HAD ~

~ HE DID NOT REALIZE THAT ALMOST ALL THE GOLD HE SAW WAS GOLD THE NATIVES FOUND ON THE SHORES, WASHED UP FROM SUNKEN SPANISH SHIPS. *

* I'D READ THIS ALL LATER, AFTER I WAS ALLOWED TO DEVELOP A MIND OF MY OWN.

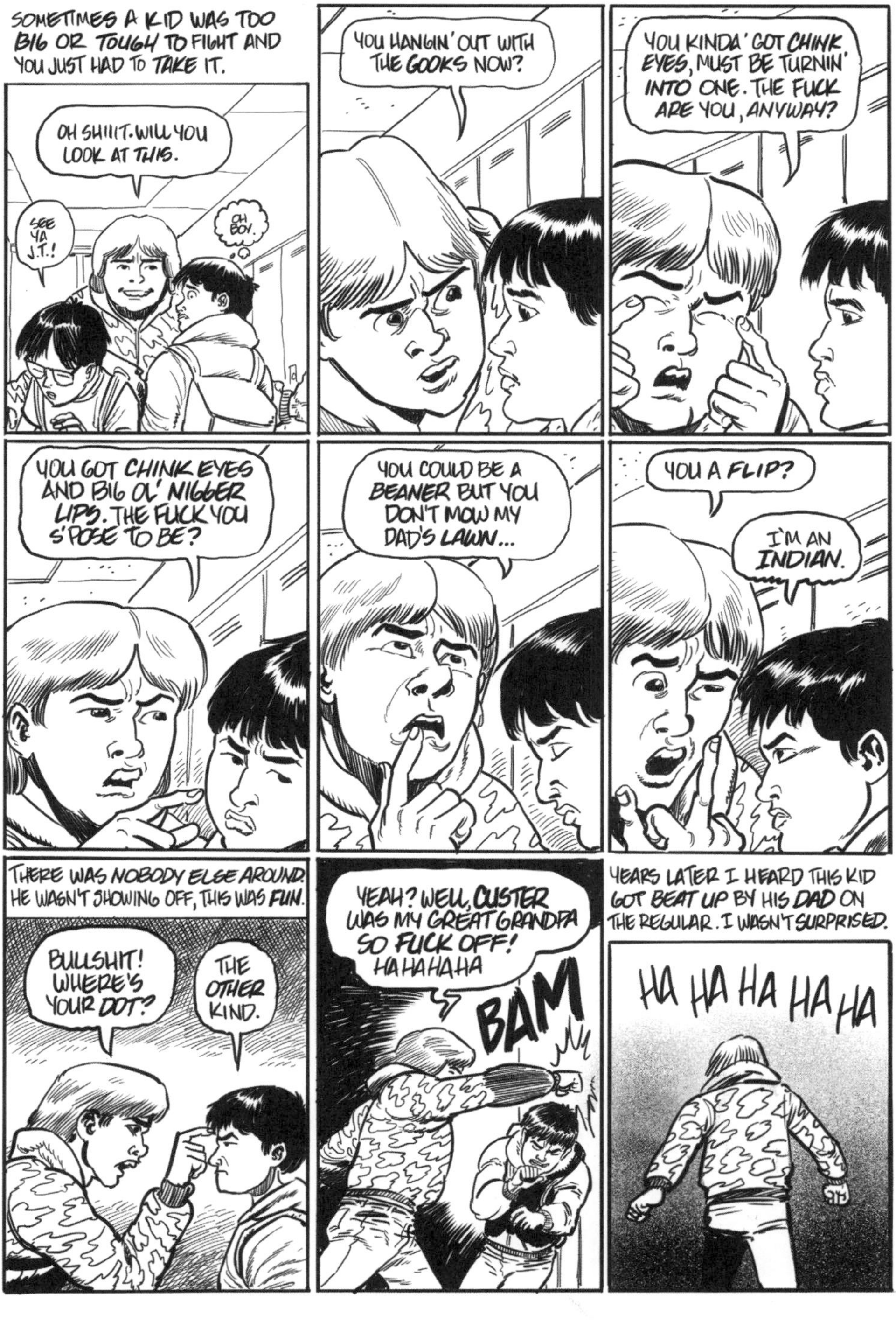
SOMETIMES A KID WAS TOO BIG OR TOUGH TO FIGHT AND YOU JUST HAD TO TAKE IT.
OH SHIIIT. WILL YOU LOOK AT THIS.
SEE YA J.T.!
OH BOY.
YOU HANGIN' OUT WITH THE GOOKS NOW?
YOU KINDA' GOT CHINK EYES, MUST BE TURNIN' INTO ONE. THE FUCK ARE YOU, ANYWAY?
YOU GOT CHINK EYES AND BIG OL' NIGGER LIPS. THE FUCK YOU S'POSE TO BE?
YOU COULD BE A BEANER BUT YOU DON'T MOW MY DAD'S LAWN...
YOU A FLIP?
I'M AN INDIAN.
THERE WAS NOBODY ELSE AROUND. HE WASN'T SHOWING OFF, THIS WAS FUN.
BULLSHIT! WHERE'S YOUR DOT?
THE OTHER KIND.
YEAH? WELL, CUSTER WAS MY GREAT GRANDPA SO FUCK OFF! HA HA HA HA
BAM
YEARS LATER I HEARD THIS KID GOT BEAT UP BY HIS DAD ON THE REGULAR. I WASN'T SURPRISED.
HA HA HA HA HA

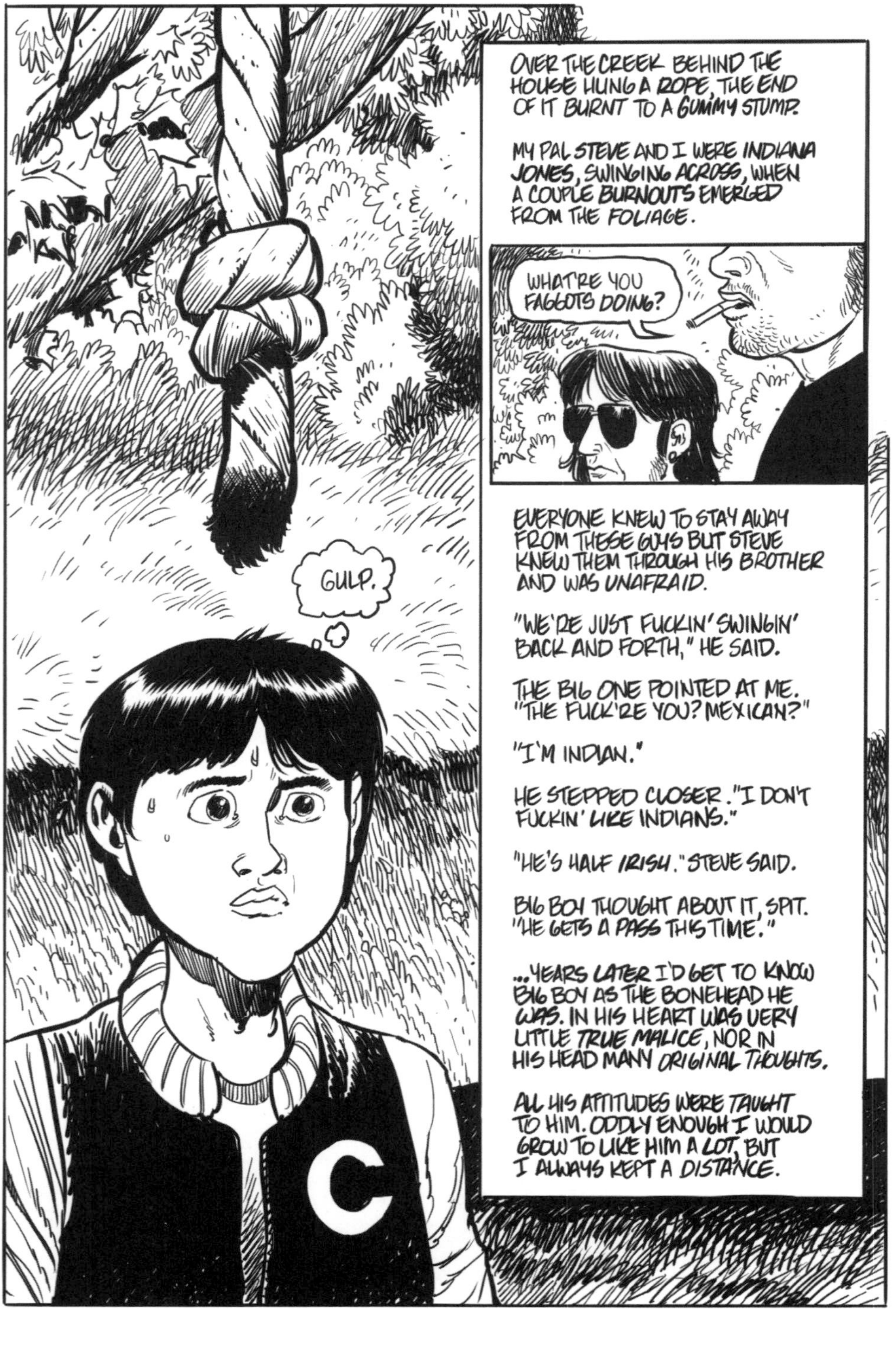
OVER THE CREEK BEHIND THE HOUSE HUNG A ROPE, THE END OF IT BURNT TO A GUMMY STUMP.
MY PAL STEVE AND I WERE INDIANA JONES, SWINGING ACROSS, WHEN A COUPLE BURNOUTS EMERGED FROM THE FOLIAGE.
WHAT'RE YOU FAGGOTS DOING?
GULP.
EVERYONE KNEW TO STAY AWAY FROM THESE GUYS BUT STEVE KNEW THEM THROUGH HIS BROTHER AND WAS UNAFRAID.
"WE'RE JUST FUCKIN' SWINGIN' BACK AND FORTH," HE SAID.
THE BIG ONE POINTED AT ME. "THE FUCK'RE YOU? MEXICAN?"
"I'M INDIAN."
HE STEPPED CLOSER. "I DON'T FUCKIN' LIKE INDIANS."
"HE'S HALF IRISH." STEVE SAID.
BIG BOY THOUGHT ABOUT IT, SPIT. "HE GETS A PASS THIS TIME."
...YEARS LATER I'D GET TO KNOW BIG BOY AS THE BONEHEAD HE WAS. IN HIS HEART WAS VERY LITTLE TRUE MALICE, NOR IN HIS HEAD MANY ORIGINAL THOUGHTS.
ALL HIS ATTITUDES WERE TAUGHT TO HIM. ODDLY ENOUGH I WOULD GROW TO LIKE HIM A LOT, BUT I ALWAYS KEPT A DISTANCE.

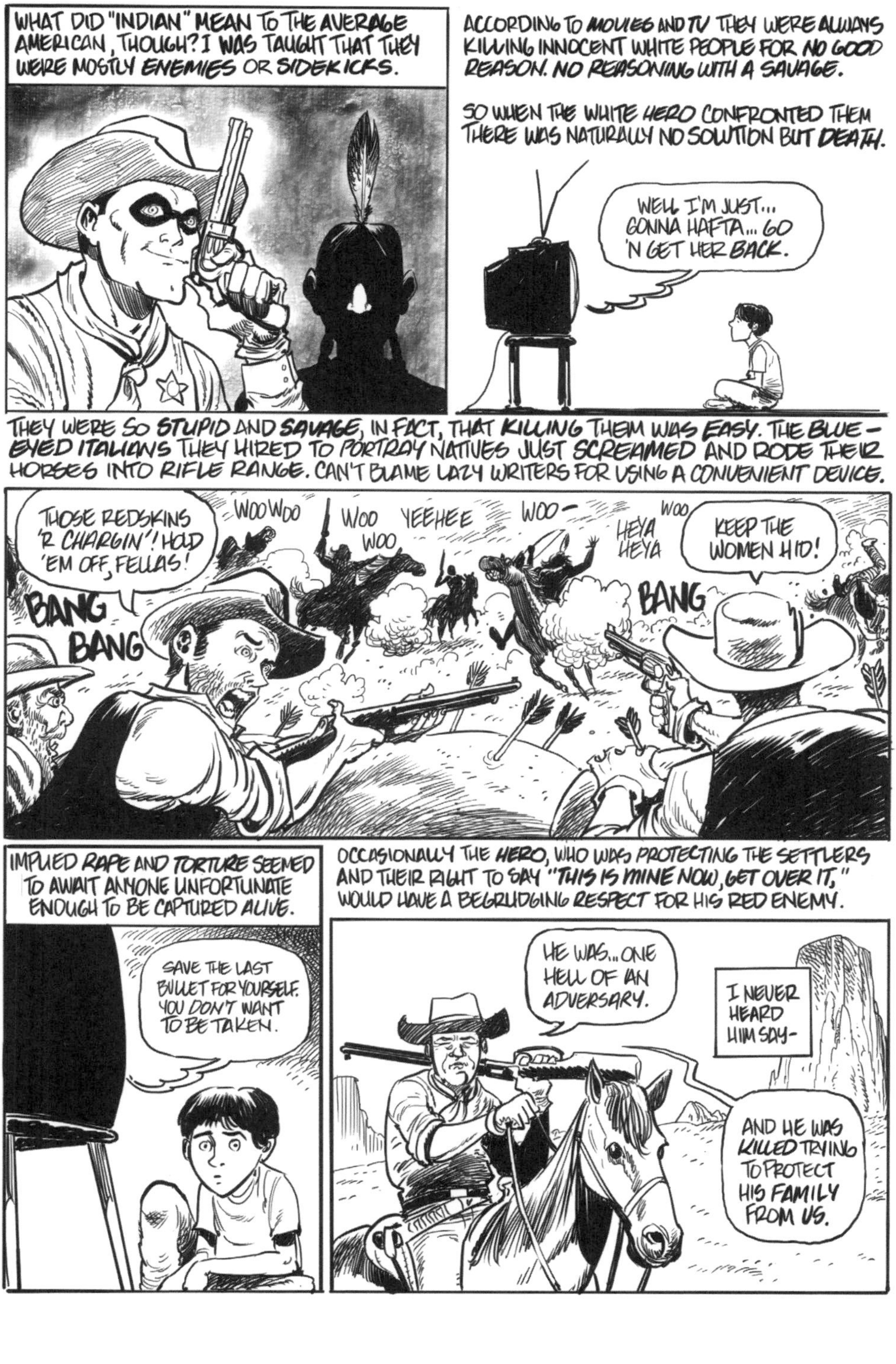

WHAT DID "INDIAN" MEAN TO THE AVERAGE AMERICAN, THOUGH? I WAS TAUGHT THAT THEY WERE MOSTLY ENEMIES OR SIDEKICKS.
ACCORDING TO MOVIES AND TV THEY WERE ALWAYS KILLING INNOCENT WHITE PEOPLE FOR NO GOOD REASON. NO REASONING WITH A SAVAGE.
SO WHEN THE WHITE HERO CONFRONTED THEM THERE WAS NATURALLY NO SOLUTION BUT DEATH.
WELL I'M JUST... GONNA HAFTA... GO 'N GET HER BACK.
THEY WERE SO STUPID AND SAVAGE, IN FACT, THAT KILLING THEM WAS EASY. THE BLUE-EYED ITALIANS THEY HIRED TO PORTRAY NATIVES JUST SCREAMED AND RODE THEIR HORSES INTO RIFLE RANGE. CAN'T BLAME LAZY WRITERS FOR USING A CONVENIENT DEVICE.
THOSE REDSKINS 'R CHARGIN'! HOLD 'EM OFF, FELLAS!
WOO WOO
WOO WOO
YEEHEE
WOO-
HEYA HEYA
WOO
KEEP THE WOMEN HID!
BANG
BANG
BANG
IMPLIED RAPE AND TORTURE SEEMED TO AWAIT ANYONE UNFORTUNATE ENOUGH TO BE CAPTURED ALIVE.
SAVE THE LAST BULLET FOR YOURSELF. YOU DON'T WANT TO BE TAKEN.
OCCASIONALLY THE HERO, WHO WAS PROTECTING THE SETTLERS AND THEIR RIGHT TO SAY "THIS IS MINE NOW, GET OVER IT," WOULD HAVE A BEGRUDGING RESPECT FOR HIS RED ENEMY.
HE WAS... ONE HELL OF AN ADVERSARY.
I NEVER HEARD HIM SAY-
AND HE WAS KILLED TRYING TO PROTECT HIS FAMILY FROM US.

I BURIED MYSELF IN *COMICS, MOVIES,* AND *BOOKS.*

I DIDN'T DREAM OF BEING *GERONIMO* – I DIDN'T KNOW HIM AS THE *UNCOMPROMISING TACTICAL GENIUS* WHO EVADED THE U.S. ARMY FOR *YEARS* – I KNEW HIM AS WHAT WHITE GUYS JOKINGLY YELLED WHEN THEY HAD TO JUMP *OUT* OF SOMETHING.

MY DAD THOUGHT INDIANS OF OLD WERE ABOUT THE *WISEST* AND *TOUGHEST* PEOPLE THAT EVER LIVED. WHEN I TOLD MY MOM THAT HE USED TO DREAM HE WAS INDIAN (WHICH HE INDEED SAID TO ME) SHE CHUCKLED AND ROLLED HER EYES.

"OF COURSE HE DID, HE WAS A BOY."

MOM – ESPECIALLY *DRUNK* – WOULD ACT AS THOUGH BEING NATIVE WAS THE *HARDEST* THING THAT COULD *HAPPEN* TO SOMEONE. THAT *SORROW* AND *TRAUMA* RAN IN OUR VEINS, GENERATIONAL WOUNDS SO DEEP THAT ONE DIDN'T *DETECT* IT UNTIL LIFE *CRUSHED* THEM.

YET SHE *LAUGHED* MORE THAN ANYONE I'VE EVER KNOWN AND ALWAYS HAMMERED HOME THAT THE *INDIAN WAY* WAS DIFFERENT. BE GOOD TO EVERYONE. HELP. BE GOOD. I DON'T KNOW IF THAT'S THE "INDIAN WAY" OR *NOT* BUT I THINK IT WAS *HER* WAY.

SHE DIDN'T TEACH ME ABOUT *GERONIMO,* CHEWIE, AND I DIDN'T GROW UP WITH OTHER *NATIVES.*

I GREW UP WITH *MOVIES.*

KINDA *HID* THAT I WAS NATIVE.

UNLESS I WAS IN THE *DELLS,* OF COURSE. THEN I COULD *RELAX.*

SORT OF.

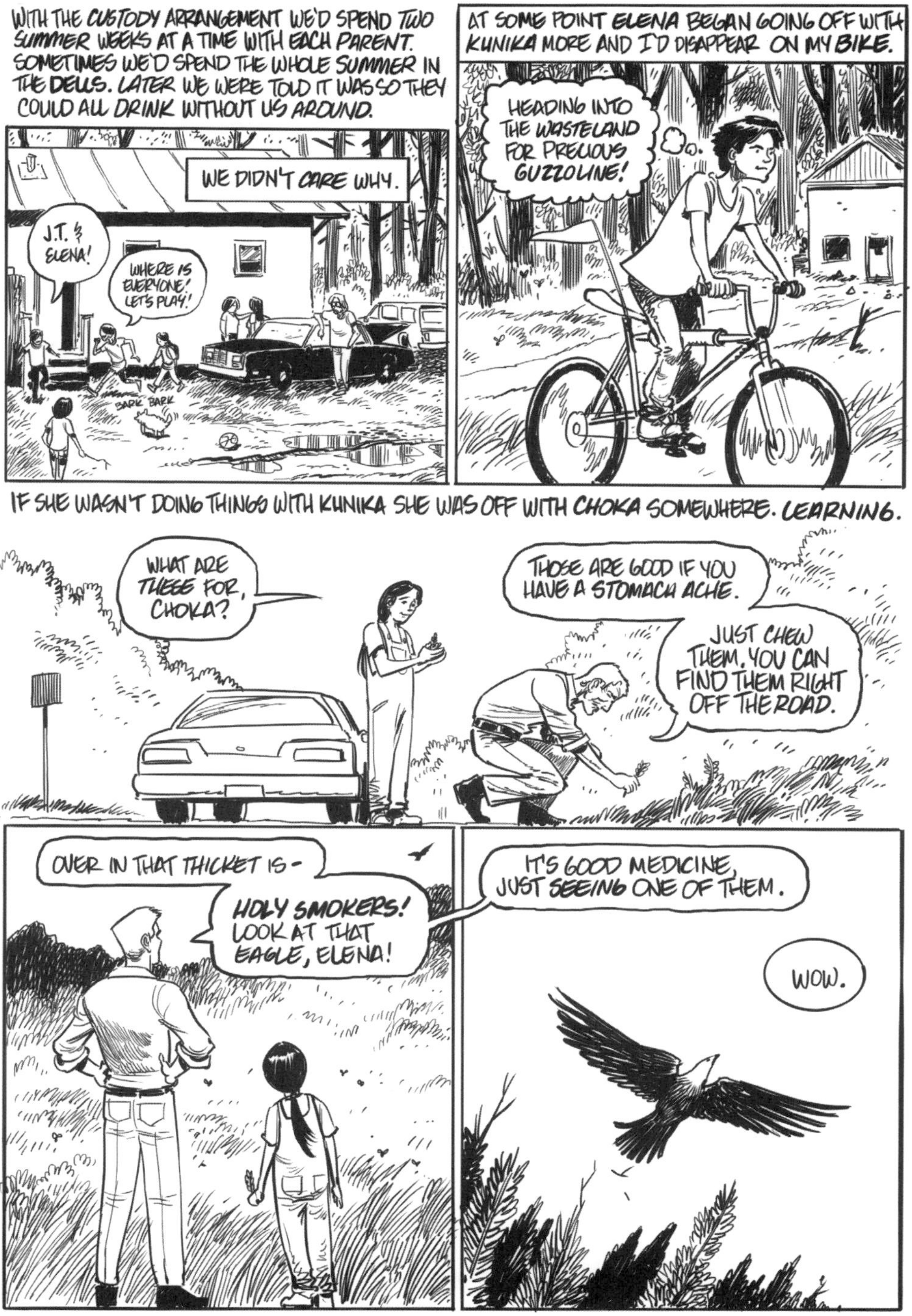
WITH THE CUSTODY ARRANGEMENT WE'D SPEND TWO SUMMER WEEKS AT A TIME WITH EACH PARENT. SOMETIMES WE'D SPEND THE WHOLE SUMMER IN THE DELLS. LATER WE WERE TOLD IT WAS SO THEY COULD ALL DRINK WITHOUT US AROUND.
WE DIDN'T CARE WHY.
J.T. & ELENA!
WHERE IS EVERYONE! LET'S PLAY!
BARK BARK
AT SOME POINT ELENA BEGAN GOING OFF WITH KUNIKA MORE AND I'D DISAPPEAR ON MY BIKE.
HEADING INTO THE WASTELAND FOR PRECIOUS GUZZOLINE!
IF SHE WASN'T DOING THINGS WITH KUNIKA SHE WAS OFF WITH CHOKA SOMEWHERE. LEARNING.
WHAT ARE THESE FOR, CHOKA?
THOSE ARE GOOD IF YOU HAVE A STOMACH ACHE.
JUST CHEW THEM. YOU CAN FIND THEM RIGHT OFF THE ROAD.
OVER IN THAT THICKET IS-
HOLY SMOKERS! LOOK AT THAT EAGLE, ELENA!
IT'S GOOD MEDICINE, JUST SEEING ONE OF THEM.
WOW.

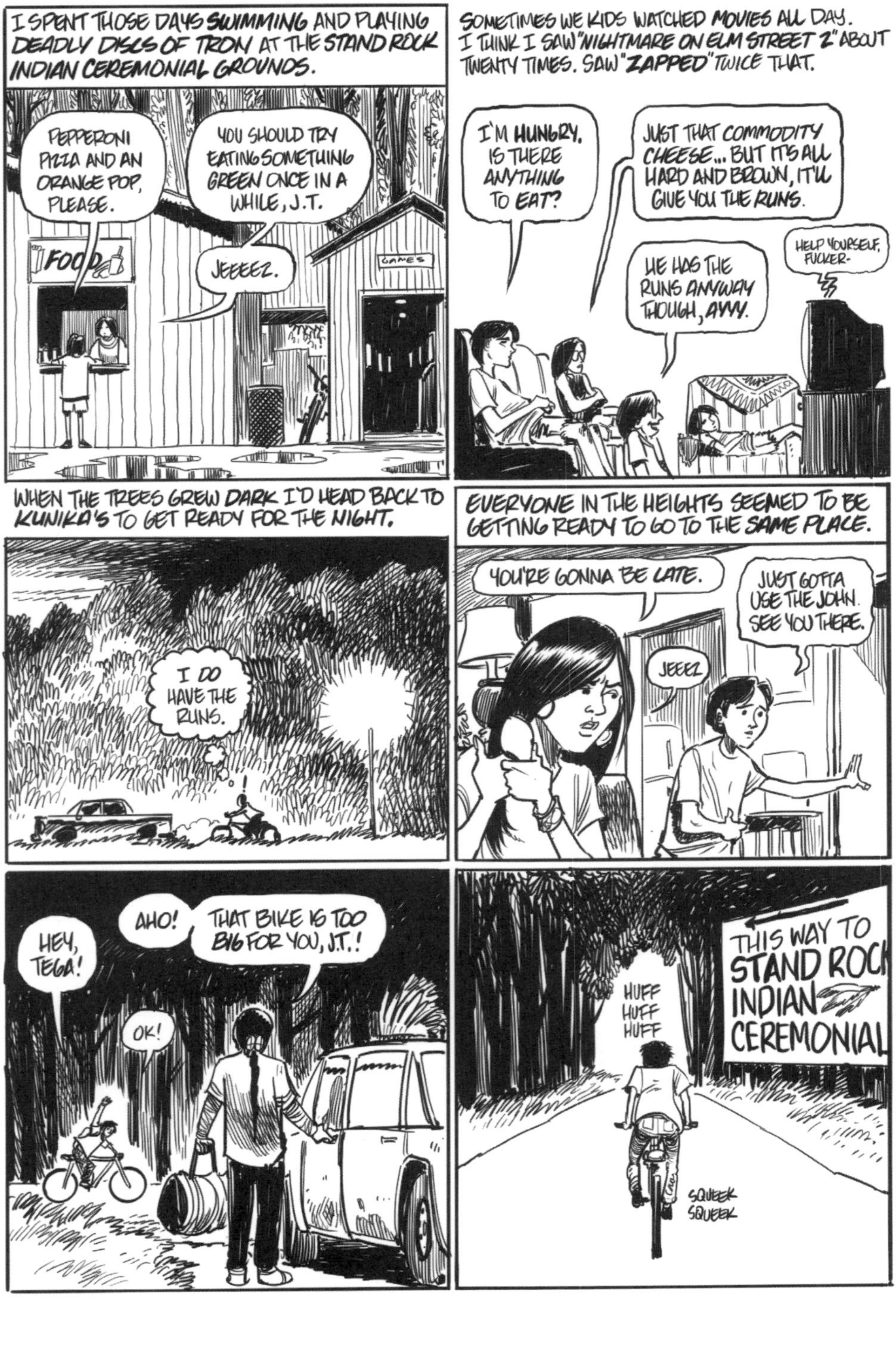
I SPENT THOSE DAYS SWIMMING AND PLAYING DEADLY DISCS OF TRON AT THE STAND ROCK INDIAN CEREMONIAL GROUNDS.
PEPPERONI PIZZA AND AN ORANGE POP, PLEASE.
YOU SHOULD TRY EATING SOMETHING GREEN ONCE IN A WHILE, J.T.
JEEEEZ.
FOOD
GAMES
SOMETIMES WE KIDS WATCHED MOVIES ALL DAY. I THINK I SAW "NIGHTMARE ON ELM STREET 2" ABOUT TWENTY TIMES. SAW "ZAPPED" TWICE THAT.
I'M HUNGRY. IS THERE ANYTHING TO EAT?
JUST THAT COMMODITY CHEESE... BUT IT'S ALL HARD AND BROWN, IT'LL GIVE YOU THE RUNS.
HE HAS THE RUNS ANYWAY THOUGH, AYYY.
HELP YOURSELF, FUCKER-
WHEN THE TREES GREW DARK I'D HEAD BACK TO KUNIKA'S TO GET READY FOR THE NIGHT.
I DO HAVE THE RUNS.
EVERYONE IN THE HEIGHTS SEEMED TO BE GETTING READY TO GO TO THE SAME PLACE.
YOU'RE GONNA BE LATE.
JUST GOTTA USE THE JOHN. SEE YOU THERE.
JEEEZ
HEY, TEGA!
AHO!
THAT BIKE IS TOO BIG FOR YOU, J.T.!
OK!
THIS WAY TO STAND ROCK INDIAN CEREMONIAL
HUFF HUFF HUFF
SQUEEK SQUEEK

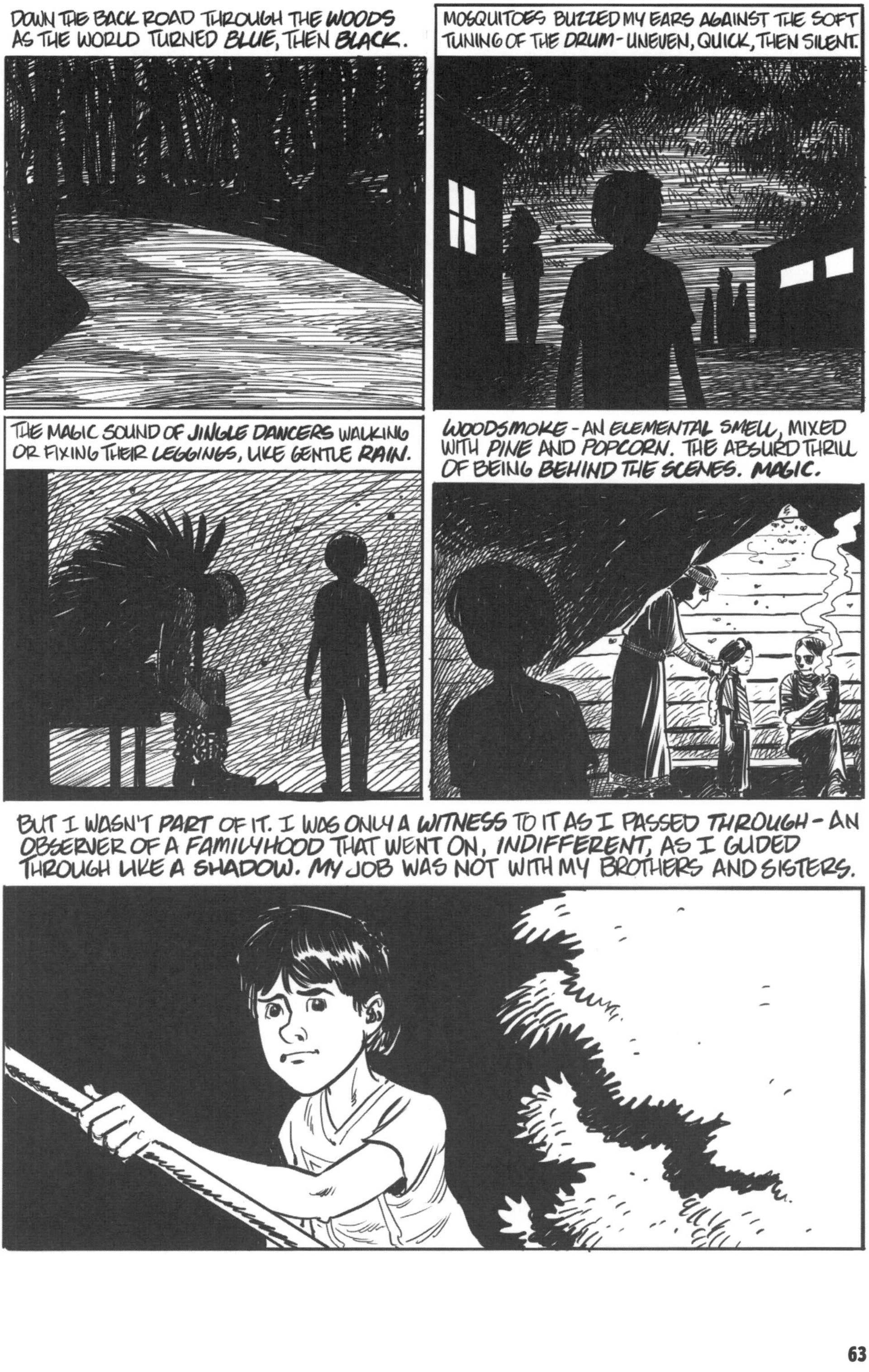
DOWN THE BACK ROAD THROUGH THE WOODS AS THE WORLD TURNED BLUE, THEN BLACK.
MOSQUITOES BUZZED MY EARS AGAINST THE SOFT TUNING OF THE DRUM - UNEVEN, QUICK, THEN SILENT.
THE MAGIC SOUND OF JINGLE DANCERS WALKING OR FIXING THEIR LEGGINGS, LIKE GENTLE RAIN.
WOODSMOKE - AN ELEMENTAL SMELL, MIXED WITH PINE AND POPCORN. THE ABSURD THRILL OF BEING BEHIND THE SCENES. MAGIC.
BUT I WASN'T PART OF IT. I WAS ONLY A WITNESS TO IT AS I PASSED THROUGH - AN OBSERVER OF A FAMILYHOOD THAT WENT ON, INDIFFERENT, AS I GLIDED THROUGH LIKE A SHADOW. MY JOB WAS NOT WITH MY BROTHERS AND SISTERS.

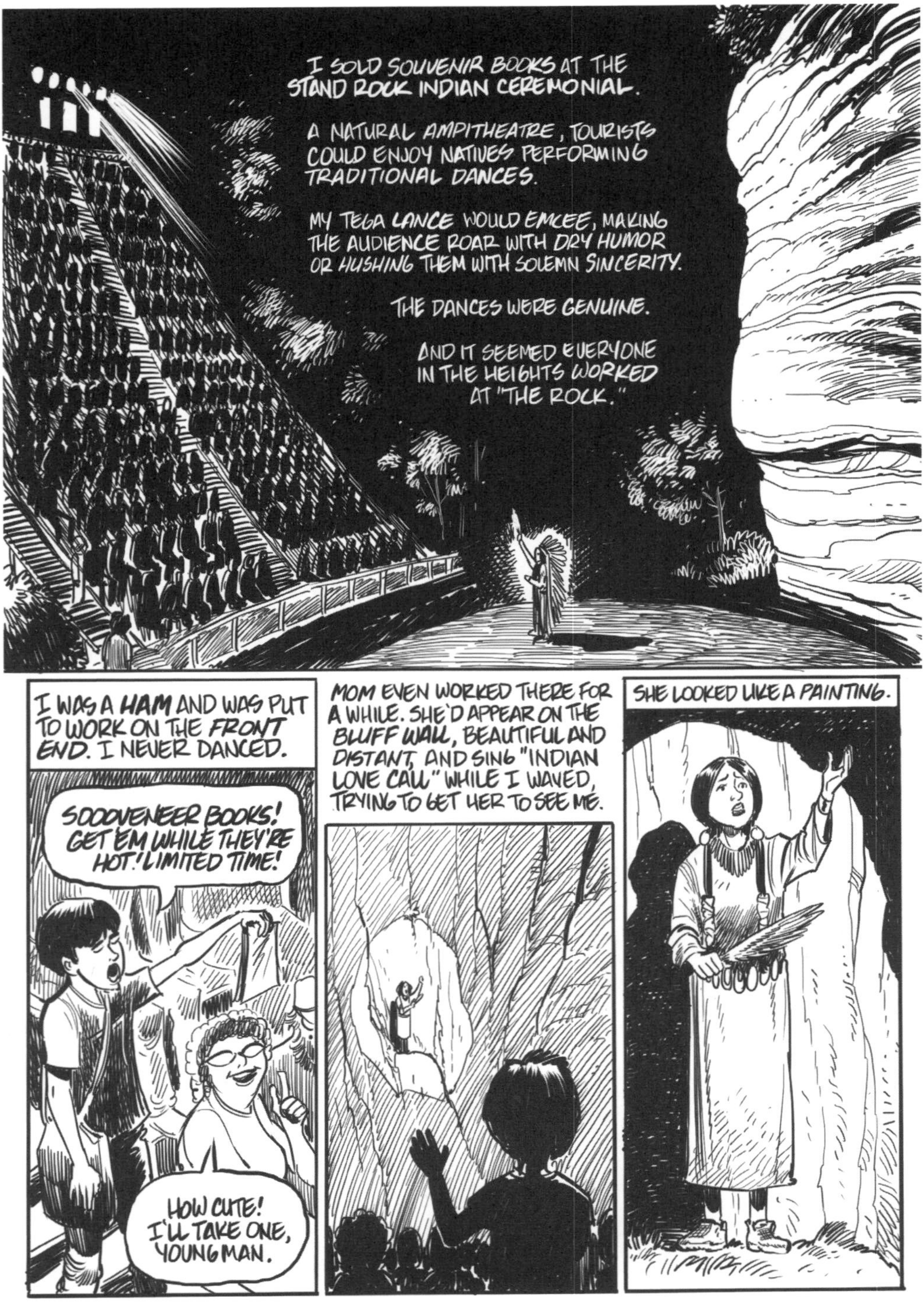
I SOLD SOUVENIR BOOKS AT THE STAND ROCK INDIAN CEREMONIAL.
A NATURAL AMPITHEATRE, TOURISTS COULD ENJOY NATIVES PERFORMING TRADITIONAL DANCES.
MY TEGA LANCE WOULD EMCEE, MAKING THE AUDIENCE ROAR WITH DRY HUMOR OR HUSHING THEM WITH SOLEMN SINCERITY.
THE DANCES WERE GENUINE.
AND IT SEEMED EVERYONE IN THE HEIGHTS WORKED AT "THE ROCK."
I WAS A HAM AND WAS PUT TO WORK ON THE FRONT END. I NEVER DANCED.
SOOOVENEER BOOKS! GET 'EM WHILE THEY'RE HOT! LIMITED TIME!
HOW CUTE! I'LL TAKE ONE, YOUNG MAN.
MOM EVEN WORKED THERE FOR A WHILE. SHE'D APPEAR ON THE BLUFF WALL, BEAUTIFUL AND DISTANT, AND SING "INDIAN LOVE CALL" WHILE I WAVED, TRYING TO GET HER TO SEE ME.
SHE LOOKED LIKE A PAINTING.

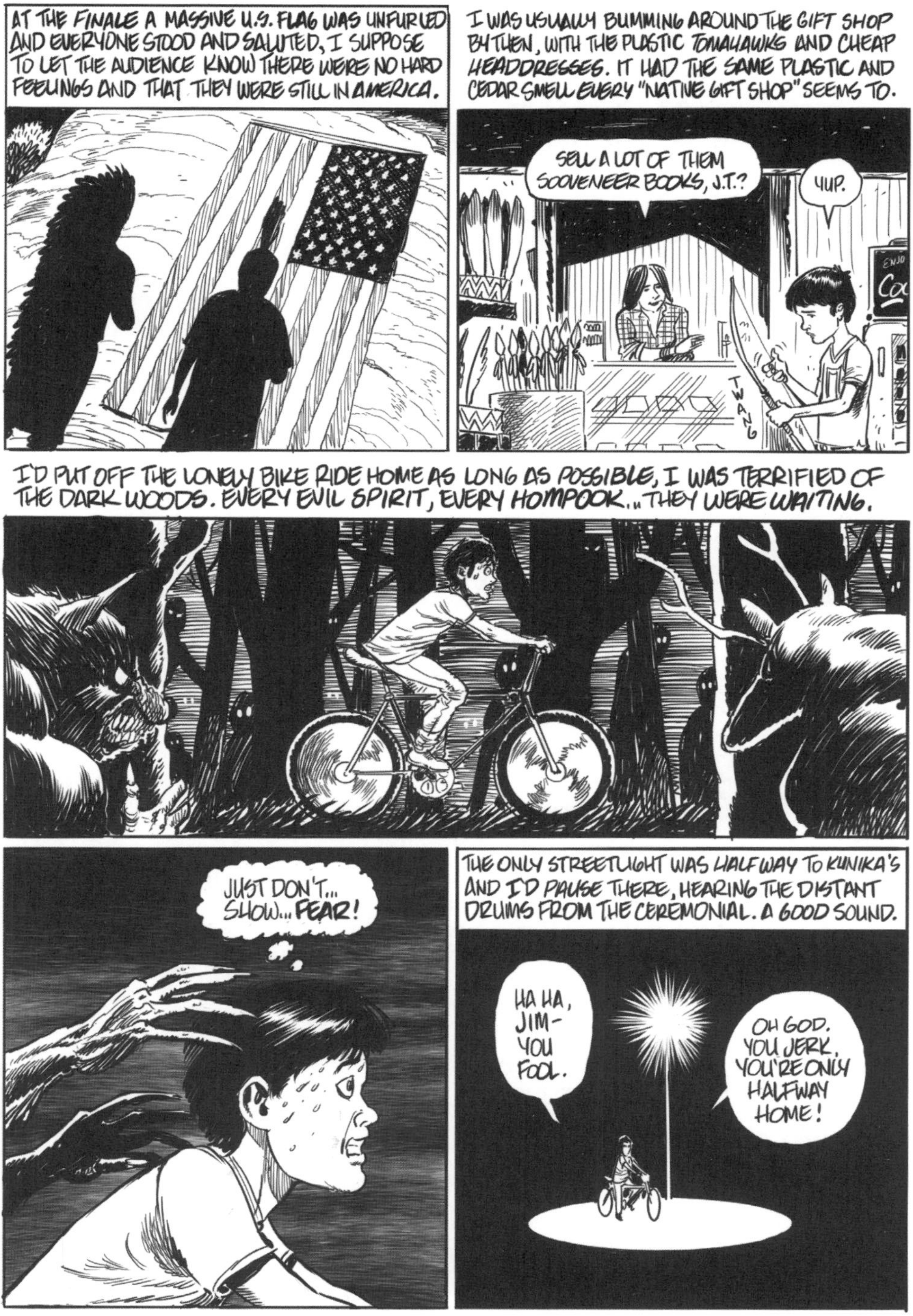
AT THE FINALE A MASSIVE U.S. FLAG WAS UNFURLED AND EVERYONE STOOD AND SALUTED, I SUPPOSE TO LET THE AUDIENCE KNOW THERE WERE NO HARD FEELINGS AND THAT THEY WERE STILL IN AMERICA.
I WAS USUALLY BUMMING AROUND THE GIFT SHOP BY THEN, WITH THE PLASTIC TOMAHAWKS AND CHEAP HEADDRESSES. IT HAD THE SAME PLASTIC AND CEDAR SMELL EVERY "NATIVE GIFT SHOP" SEEMS TO.
SELL A LOT OF THEM SOOVENEER BOOKS, J.T.?
YUP.
TWANG
I'D PUT OFF THE LONELY BIKE RIDE HOME AS LONG AS POSSIBLE, I WAS TERRIFIED OF THE DARK WOODS. EVERY EVIL SPIRIT, EVERY HOMPOOK... THEY WERE WAITING.
JUST DON'T... SHOW... FEAR!
THE ONLY STREETLIGHT WAS HALFWAY TO KUNIKA'S AND I'D PAUSE THERE, HEARING THE DISTANT DRUMS FROM THE CEREMONIAL. A GOOD SOUND.
HA HA, JIM- YOU FOOL.
OH GOD. YOU JERK, YOU'RE ONLY HALFWAY HOME!

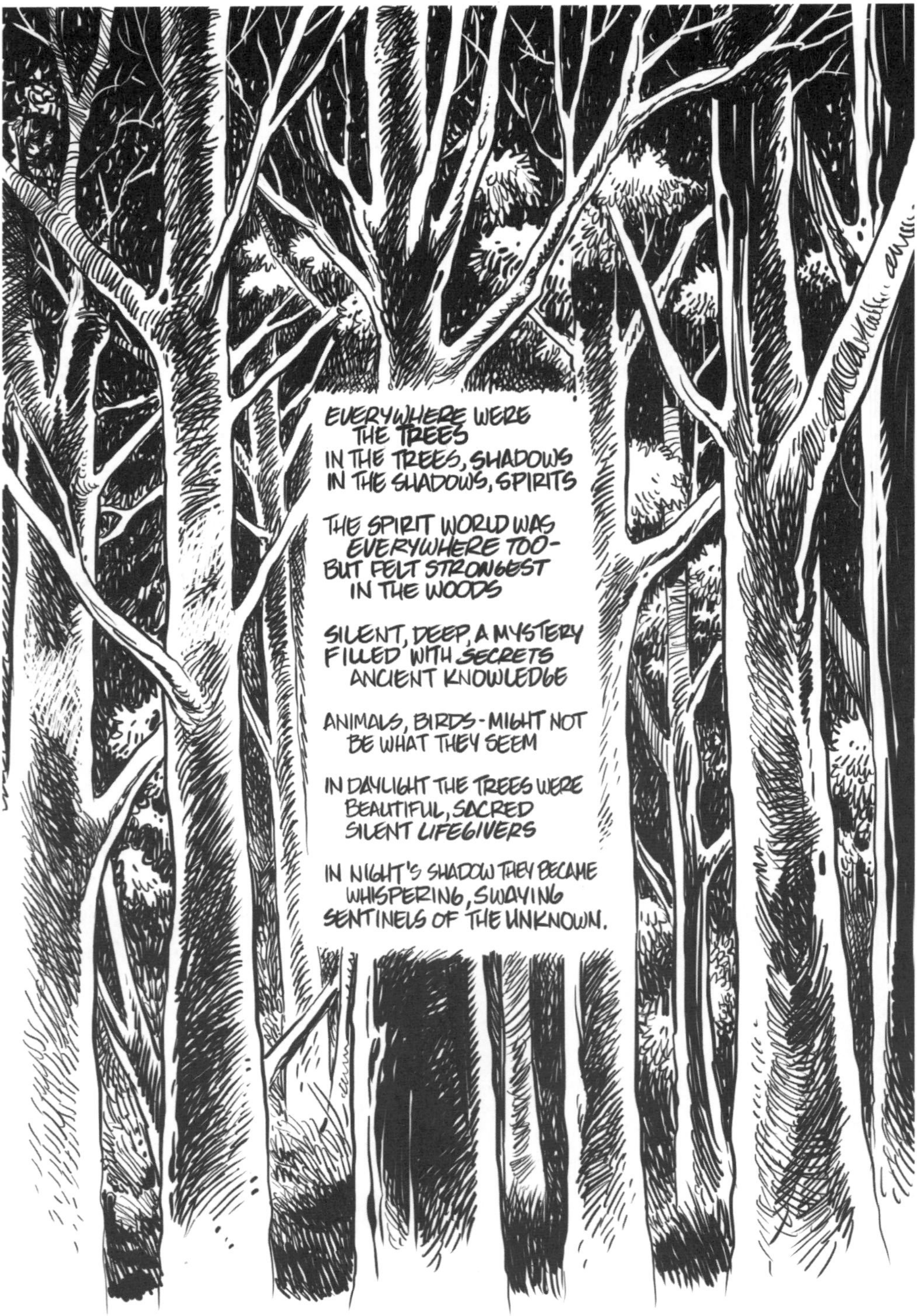
EVERYWHERE WERE THE TREES
IN THE TREES, SHADOWS
IN THE SHADOWS, SPIRITS
THE SPIRIT WORLD WAS EVERYWHERE TOO- BUT FELT STRONGEST IN THE WOODS
SILENT, DEEP, A MYSTERY FILLED WITH SECRETS ANCIENT KNOWLEDGE
ANIMALS, BIRDS - MIGHT NOT BE WHAT THEY SEEM
IN DAYLIGHT THE TREES WERE BEAUTIFUL, SACRED SILENT LIFEGIVERS
IN NIGHT'S SHADOW THEY BECAME WHISPERING, SWAYING SENTINELS OF THE UNKNOWN.

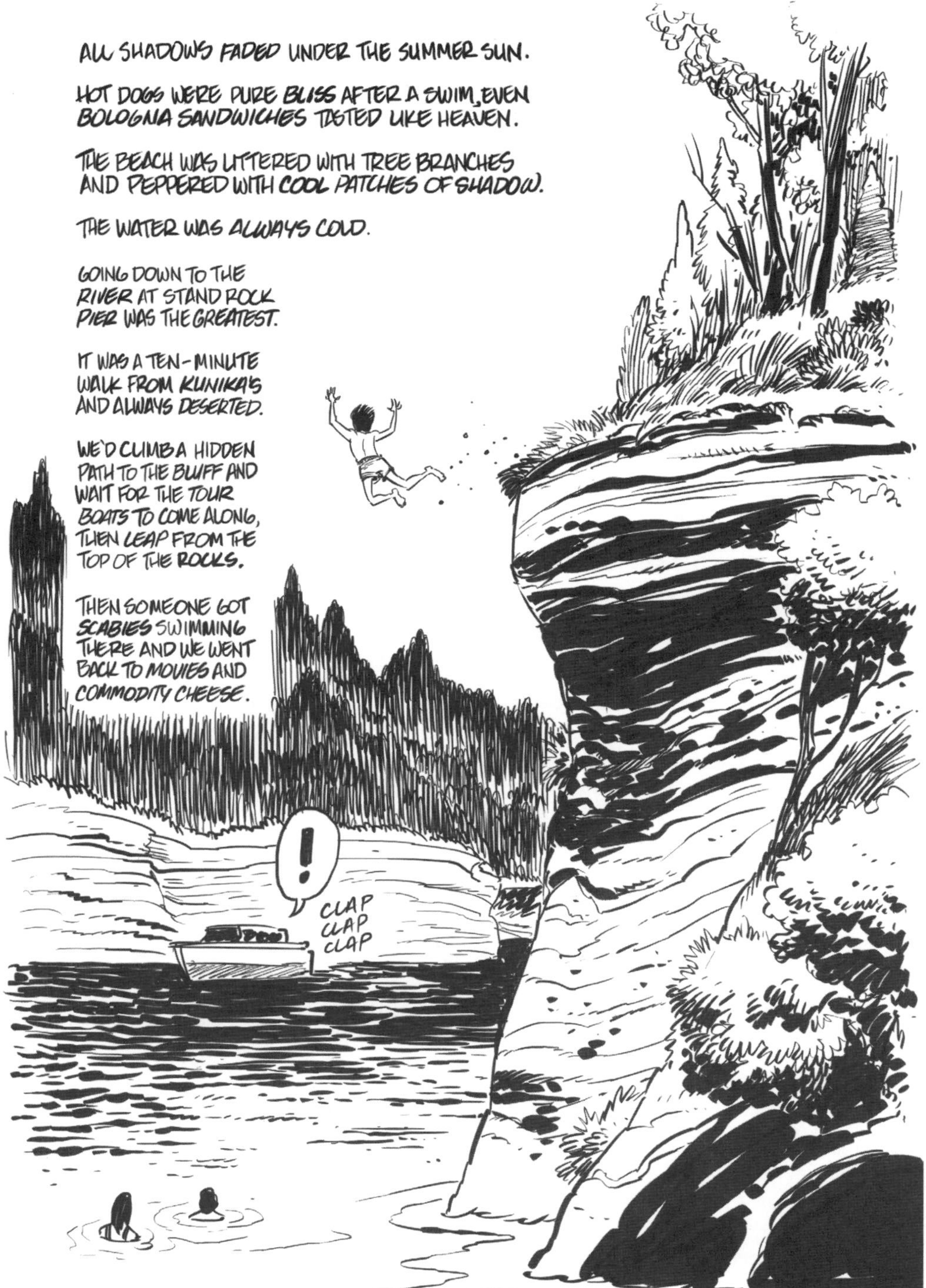
ALL SHADOWS FADED UNDER THE SUMMER SUN.
HOT DOGS WERE PURE BLISS AFTER A SWIM, EVEN BOLOGNA SANDWICHES TASTED LIKE HEAVEN.
THE BEACH WAS LITTERED WITH TREE BRANCHES AND PEPPERED WITH COOL PATCHES OF SHADOW.
THE WATER WAS ALWAYS COLD.
GOING DOWN TO THE RIVER AT STAND ROCK PIER WAS THE GREATEST.
IT WAS A TEN-MINUTE WALK FROM KUNIKA'S AND ALWAYS DESERTED.
WE'D CLIMB A HIDDEN PATH TO THE BLUFF AND WAIT FOR THE TOUR BOATS TO COME ALONG, THEN LEAP FROM THE TOP OF THE ROCKS.
THEN SOMEONE GOT SCABIES SWIMMING THERE AND WE WENT BACK TO MOVIES AND COMMODITY CHEESE.
!
CLAP CLAP CLAP

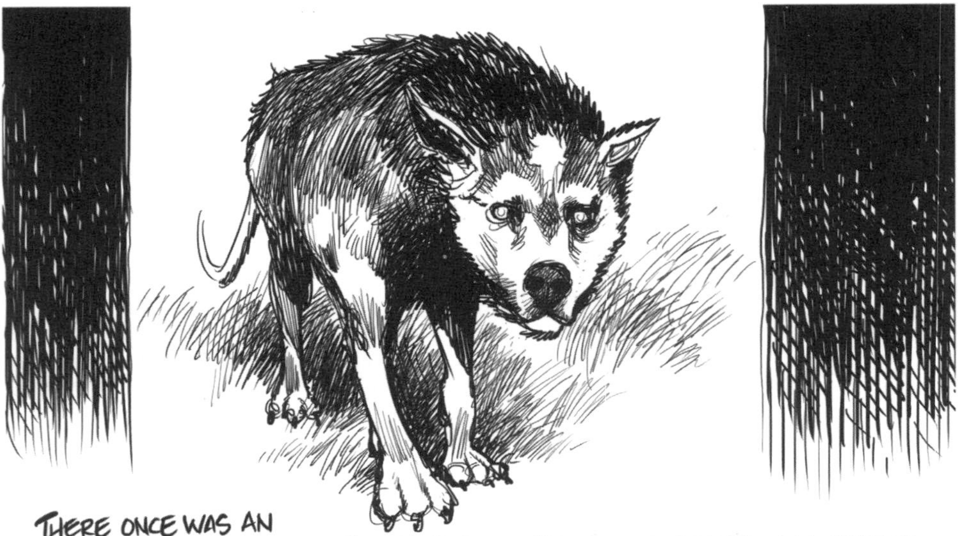

THERE ONCE WAS AN OLD GRAY DOG THAT WANDERED THE NEIGHBORHOOD, GENTLE AND KNOWING. THE ELDERS SPOKE TO HIM AS ONE OF THEIR OWN AND HIS SAD, INTELLIGENT EYES UNDERSTOOD.

THE CHILDREN JUMPED ON HIS ANCIENT BACK AND HE CRUMPLED BENEATH THEM UNTIL THEY RAN OFF, THEN ROSE AND QUIETLY PADDED AWAY.

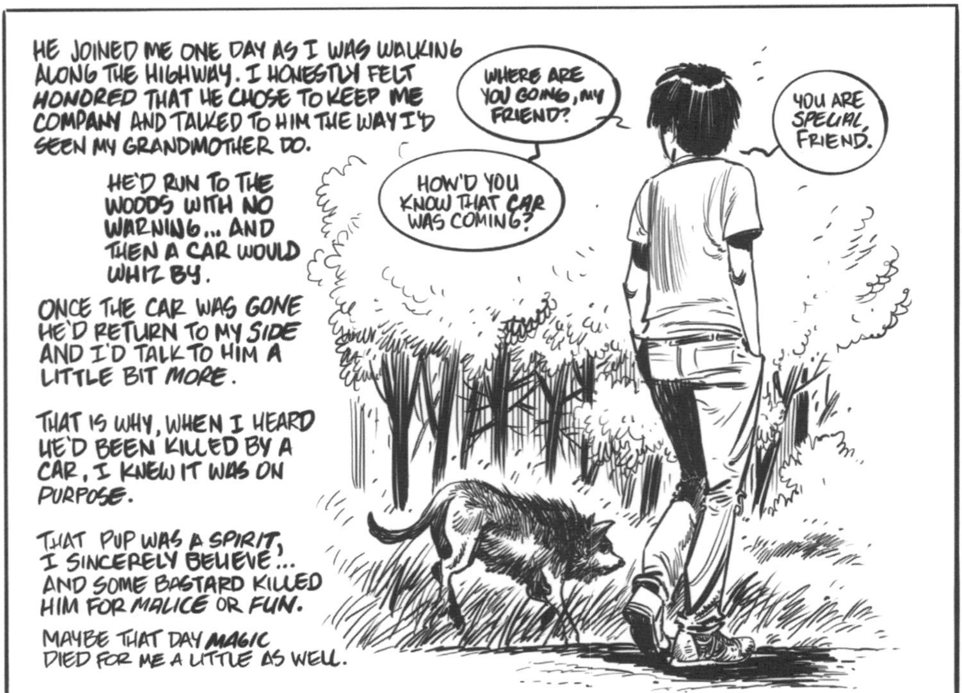
HE JOINED ME ONE DAY AS I WAS WALKING ALONG THE HIGHWAY. I HONESTLY FELT HONORED THAT HE CHOSE TO KEEP ME COMPANY AND TALKED TO HIM THE WAY I'D SEEN MY GRANDMOTHER DO.
WHERE ARE YOU GOING, MY FRIEND?
YOU ARE SPECIAL, FRIEND.
HE'D RUN TO THE WOODS WITH NO WARNING... AND THEN A CAR WOULD WHIZ BY.
HOW'D YOU KNOW THAT CAR WAS COMING?
ONCE THE CAR WAS GONE HE'D RETURN TO MY SIDE AND I'D TALK TO HIM A LITTLE BIT MORE.
THAT IS WHY, WHEN I HEARD HE'D BEEN KILLED BY A CAR, I KNEW IT WAS ON PURPOSE.
THAT PUP WAS A SPIRIT, I SINCERELY BELIEVE... AND SOME BASTARD KILLED HIM FOR MALICE OR FUN.
MAYBE THAT DAY MAGIC DIED FOR ME A LITTLE AS WELL.

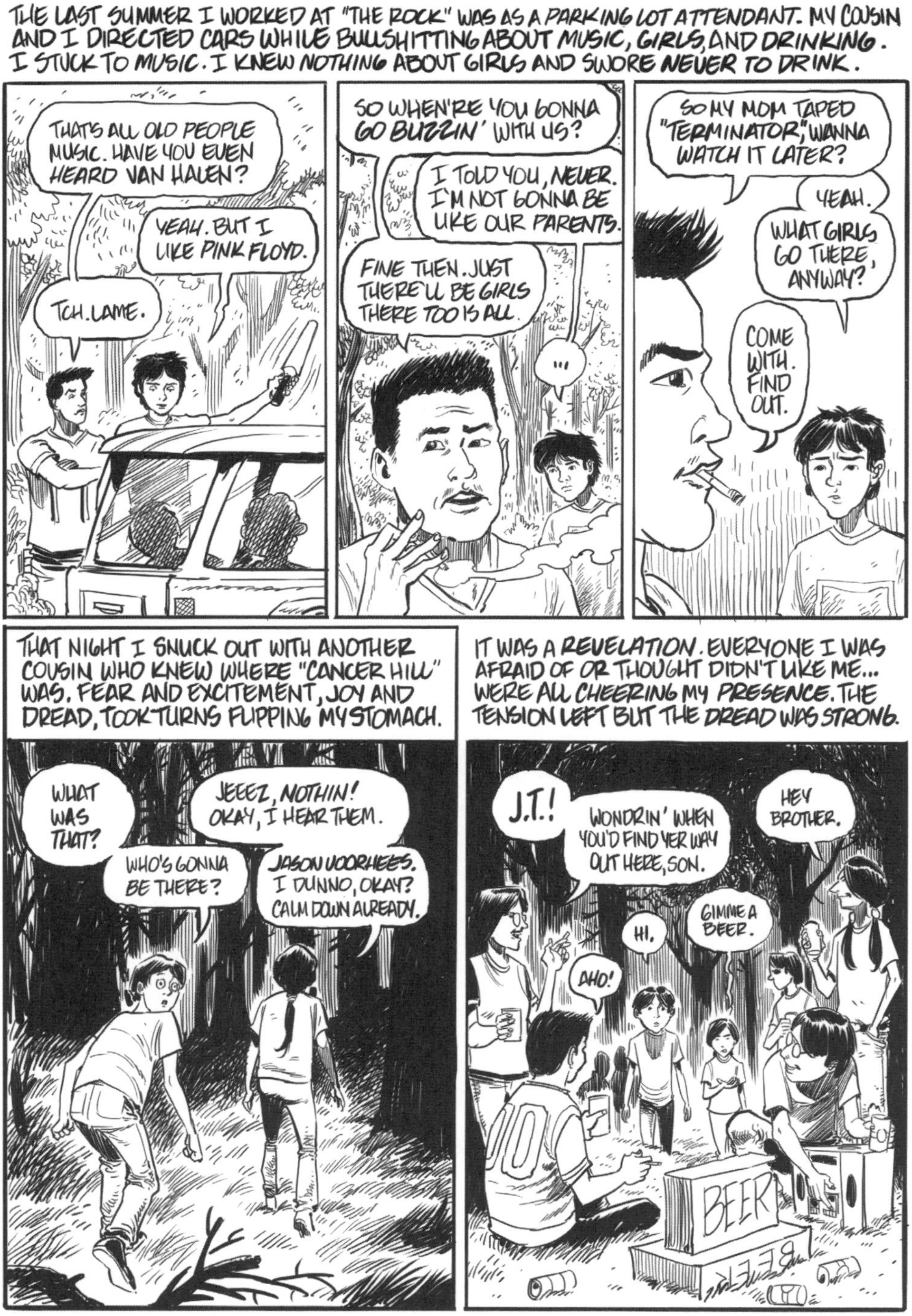
THE LAST SUMMER I WORKED AT "THE ROCK" WAS AS A PARKING LOT ATTENDANT. MY COUSIN AND I DIRECTED CARS WHILE BULLSHITTING ABOUT MUSIC, GIRLS, AND DRINKING. I STUCK TO MUSIC. I KNEW NOTHING ABOUT GIRLS AND SWORE NEVER TO DRINK.
THAT'S ALL OLD PEOPLE MUSIC. HAVE YOU EVEN HEARD VAN HALEN?
YEAH. BUT I LIKE PINK FLOYD.
TCH. LAME.
SO WHEN'RE YOU GONNA GO BUZZIN' WITH US?
I TOLD YOU, NEVER. I'M NOT GONNA BE LIKE OUR PARENTS.
FINE THEN. JUST THERE'LL BE GIRLS THERE TOO IS ALL.
...
SO MY MOM TAPED "TERMINATOR," WANNA WATCH IT LATER?
YEAH.
WHAT GIRLS GO THERE, ANYWAY?
COME WITH. FIND OUT.
THAT NIGHT I SNUCK OUT WITH ANOTHER COUSIN WHO KNEW WHERE "CANCER HILL" WAS. FEAR AND EXCITEMENT, JOY AND DREAD, TOOK TURNS FLIPPING MY STOMACH.
WHAT WAS THAT?
JEEEZ, NOTHIN! OKAY, I HEAR THEM.
WHO'S GONNA BE THERE?
JASON VOORHEES. I DUNNO, OKAY? CALM DOWN ALREADY.
IT WAS A REVELATION. EVERYONE I WAS AFRAID OF OR THOUGHT DIDN'T LIKE ME... WERE ALL CHEERING MY PRESENCE. THE TENSION LEFT BUT THE DREAD WAS STRONG.
J.T.!
WONDRIN' WHEN YOU'D FIND YER WAY OUT HERE, SON.
HEY BROTHER.
HI.
GIMME A BEER.
AHO!
00
BEER
BEER

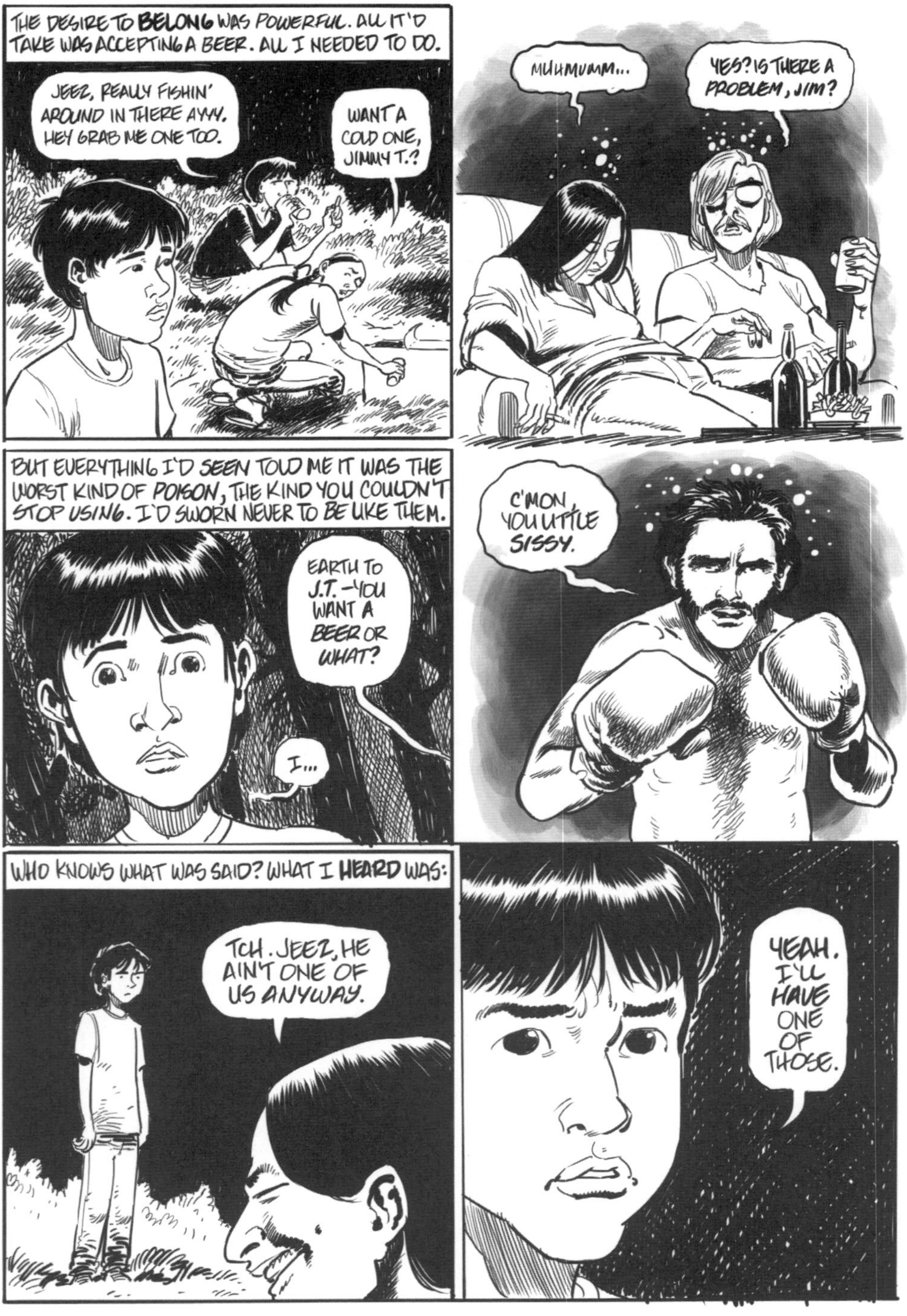

THE DESIRE TO BELONG WAS POWERFUL. ALL IT'D TAKE WAS ACCEPTING A BEER. ALL I NEEDED TO DO.
JEEZ, REALLY FISHIN' AROUND IN THERE AYYY. HEY GRAB ME ONE TOO.
WANT A COLD ONE, JIMMY T.?
MUHMUMM...
YES? IS THERE A PROBLEM, JIM?
BUT EVERYTHING I'D SEEN TOLD ME IT WAS THE WORST KIND OF POISON, THE KIND YOU COULDN'T STOP USING. I'D SWORN NEVER TO BE LIKE THEM.
EARTH TO J.T.—YOU WANT A BEER OR WHAT?
I...
C'MON, YOU LITTLE SISSY.
WHO KNOWS WHAT WAS SAID? WHAT I HEARD WAS:
TCH. JEEZ, HE AIN'T ONE OF US ANYWAY.
YEAH. I'LL HAVE ONE OF THOSE.

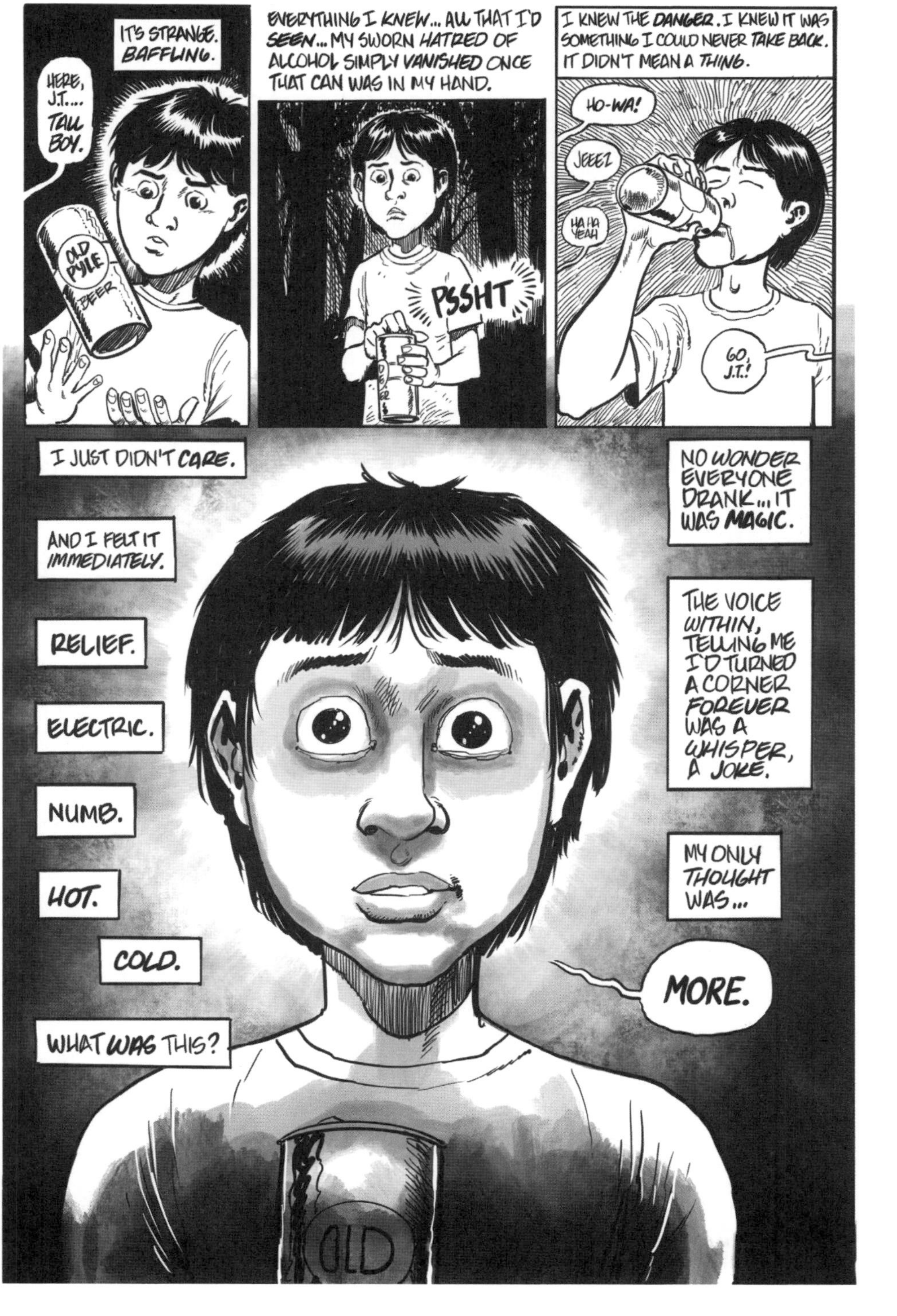
IT'S STRANGE. BAFFLING.
HERE, J.T.... TALL BOY.
OLD PYLE BEER
EVERYTHING I KNEW... ALL THAT I'D SEEN... MY SWORN HATRED OF ALCOHOL SIMPLY VANISHED ONCE THAT CAN WAS IN MY HAND.
PSSHT
I KNEW THE DANGER. I KNEW IT WAS SOMETHING I COULD NEVER TAKE BACK. IT DIDN'T MEAN A THING.
HO-WA!
JEEEZ
HA HA YEAH
GO, J.T.!
I JUST DIDN'T CARE.
AND I FELT IT IMMEDIATELY.
RELIEF.
ELECTRIC.
NUMB.
HOT.
COLD.
WHAT WAS THIS?
NO WONDER EVERYONE DRANK... IT WAS MAGIC.
THE VOICE WITHIN, TELLING ME I'D TURNED A CORNER FOREVER WAS A WHISPER, A JOKE.
MY ONLY THOUGHT WAS...
MORE.
OLD

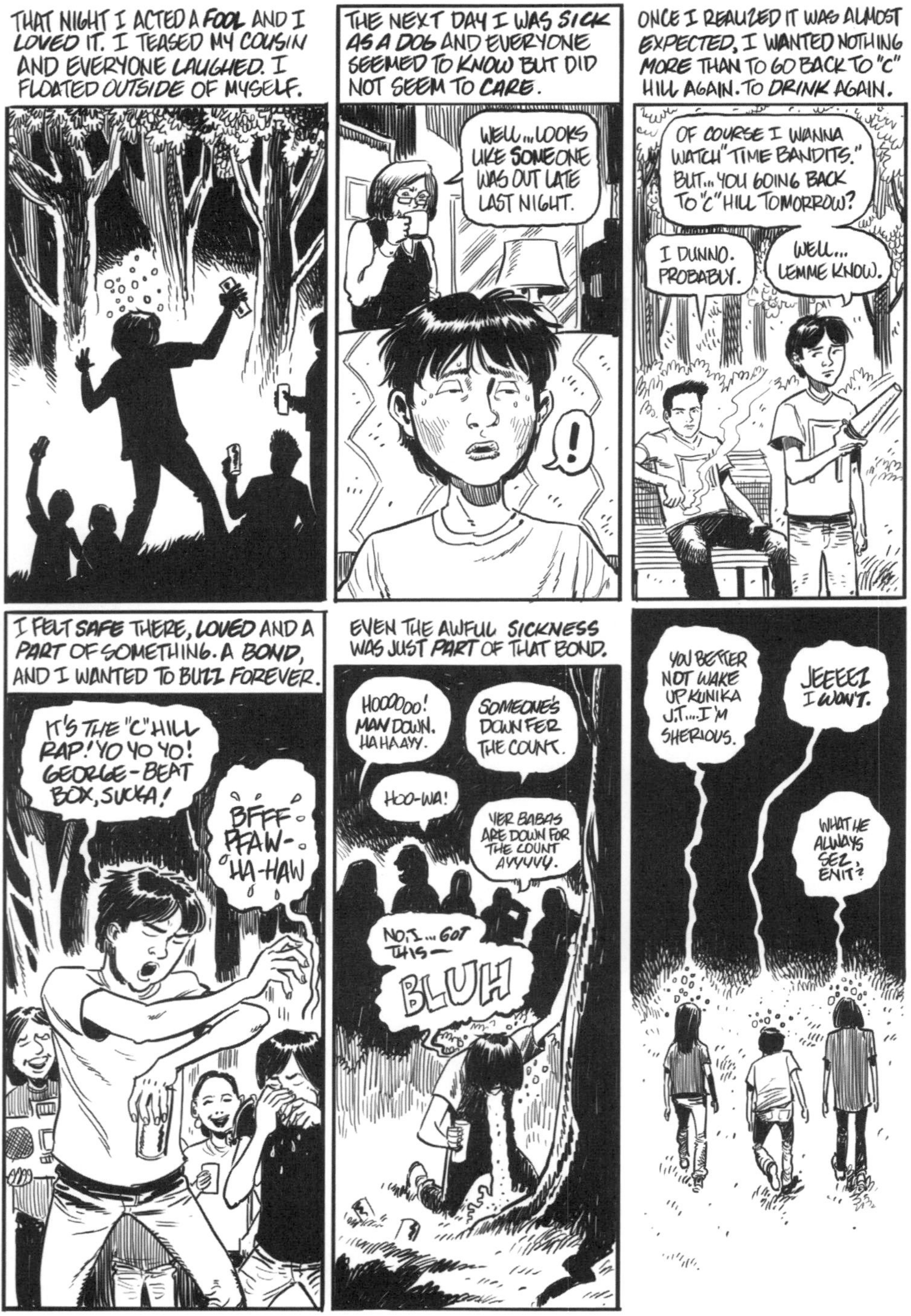
THAT NIGHT I ACTED A FOOL AND I LOVED IT. I TEASED MY COUSIN AND EVERYONE LAUGHED. I FLOATED OUTSIDE OF MYSELF.
THE NEXT DAY I WAS SICK AS A DOG AND EVERYONE SEEMED TO KNOW BUT DID NOT SEEM TO CARE.
WELL... LOOKS LIKE SOMEONE WAS OUT LATE LAST NIGHT.
!
ONCE I REALIZED IT WAS ALMOST EXPECTED, I WANTED NOTHING MORE THAN TO GO BACK TO "C" HILL AGAIN. TO DRINK AGAIN.
OF COURSE I WANNA WATCH "TIME BANDITS." BUT... YOU GOING BACK TO "C" HILL TOMORROW?
I DUNNO. PROBABLY.
WELL... LEMME KNOW.
I FELT SAFE THERE, LOVED AND A PART OF SOMETHING. A BOND, AND I WANTED TO BUZZ FOREVER.
IT'S THE "C" HILL RAP! YO YO YO! GEORGE-BEAT BOX, SUCKA!
BFFF PFAW-HA-HAW
EVEN THE AWFUL SICKNESS WAS JUST PART OF THAT BOND.
HOOOOOO! MAN DOWN. HAHAAYY.
SOMEONE'S DOWN FER THE COUNT.
HOO-WA!
YER BABAS ARE DOWN FOR THE COUNT AYYYYY.
NO, I... GOT THIS—
BLUH
YOU BETTER NOT WAKE UP KUNIKA J.T.... I'M SHERIOUS.
JEEEEZ I WON'T.
WHAT HE ALWAYS SEZ, ENIT?

BEFORE LONG IT WAS ALL I REALLY *THOUGHT* ABOUT, AND I BECAME A COLOSSAL PEST.

YEAH, SO THEN SHE COMES ALONG AND—*WHAT, J.T.*?

NOTHIN'... JUST ARE YOU GOIN' "*BUZZIN*" LATER?

MAYBE, OKAY? JEEZ!

ANYWAYS—

WELL—LEMME KNOW.

THE NIGHT NO LONGER MEANT *FEAR OF SPIRITS* OR THE *THRILL* OF THE *SHOW*... IT NOW MEANT THE CHANCE TO *SNEAK OUT* AND *DRINK*. I TRIED TO HIDE IT FROM *ELENA* BUT SHE SAW WHAT WAS HAPPENING.

YOU THREE SHOULD TRY STAYING *IN* FOR A NIGHT.

YEAH OKAY MA... WE WERE JUST GONNA WATCH "*ZAPPED*" AGAIN ANYWAY TONIGHT, ENIT.

YUP.

I KNEW, EVERY STEP OF THE WAY, THAT BOOZING WAS A *BAD PATH* — I JUST DIDN'T *CARE* ANYMORE. THAT DIDN'T MEAN I WANTED ELENA TO SEE ME DRINKING. THE *THOUGHT* OF THAT FILLED ME WITH *GUILT* AND *SHAME*.

THE COMMUNITY WAS *ALREADY* SMALL ENOUGH.

WELL LOOK AT THIS. *JIMMY T.* SAY IT FOR YOUR *TEGA*. SAY "*D'LIN D'LIN HEIGHTS*" FOR ME.

OH GOD HE'S HERE? TIME TO GO!

SOME OF THOSE GUYS *SCARED* ME AND THEY ALL THOUGHT THEY WERE MY *TEGA*. MEN WITH AN AURA OF *DANGER*, AND NOT THE "*COOL*" KIND. *HAUNTED* MEN, *BROKEN* MEN, *ANGRY* MEN WITH WARRIOR SPIRITS GONE TWISTED WITH *IMPOTENT RAGE* AND SOURED BY BOOZE.

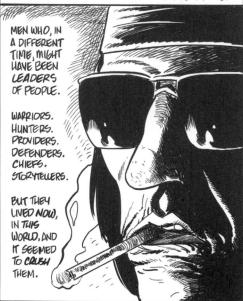

MEN WHO, IN A DIFFERENT TIME, MIGHT HAVE BEEN *LEADERS* OF PEOPLE.

WARRIORS. HUNTERS. PROVIDERS. DEFENDERS. CHIEFS. STORYTELLERS.

BUT THEY LIVED *NOW*, IN THIS WORLD, AND IT SEEMED TO *CRUSH* THEM.

BOOZE MADE ME **MAUDLIN** AND EVEN **MORE** EMOTIONAL THAN I ALREADY **WAS**, WHICH LED TO MANY AWKWARD OUTBURSTS AND **CONFESSIONS** - WHICH WERE ACCEPTED WITHOUT **COMMENT**, **QUESTION**, OR **JUDGMENT**.

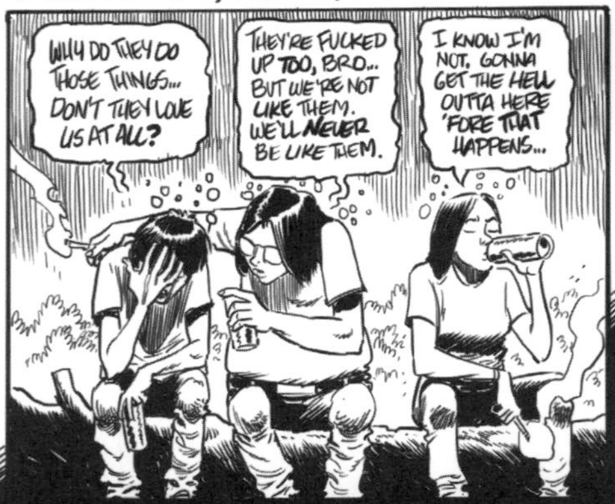
WHY DO THEY DO THOSE THINGS... DON'T THEY LOVE US AT ALL?
THEY'RE FUCKED UP TOO, BRO... BUT WE'RE NOT LIKE THEM. WE'LL NEVER BE LIKE THEM.
I KNOW I'M NOT. GONNA GET THE HELL OUTTA HERE 'FORE THAT HAPPENS...

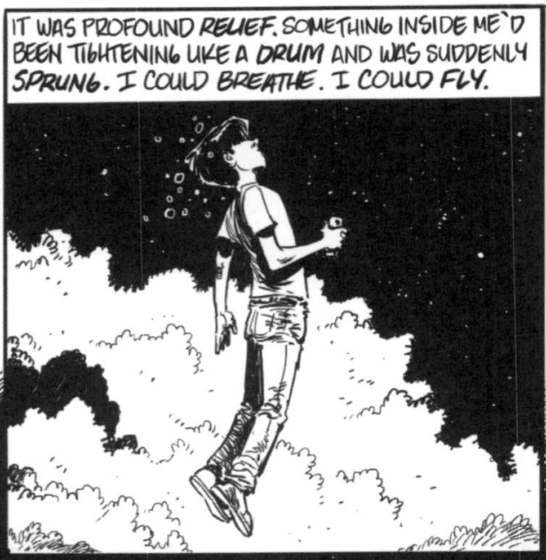
IT WAS PROFOUND RELIEF. SOMETHING INSIDE ME'D BEEN TIGHTENING LIKE A DRUM AND WAS SUDDENLY SPRUNG. I COULD BREATHE. I COULD FLY.

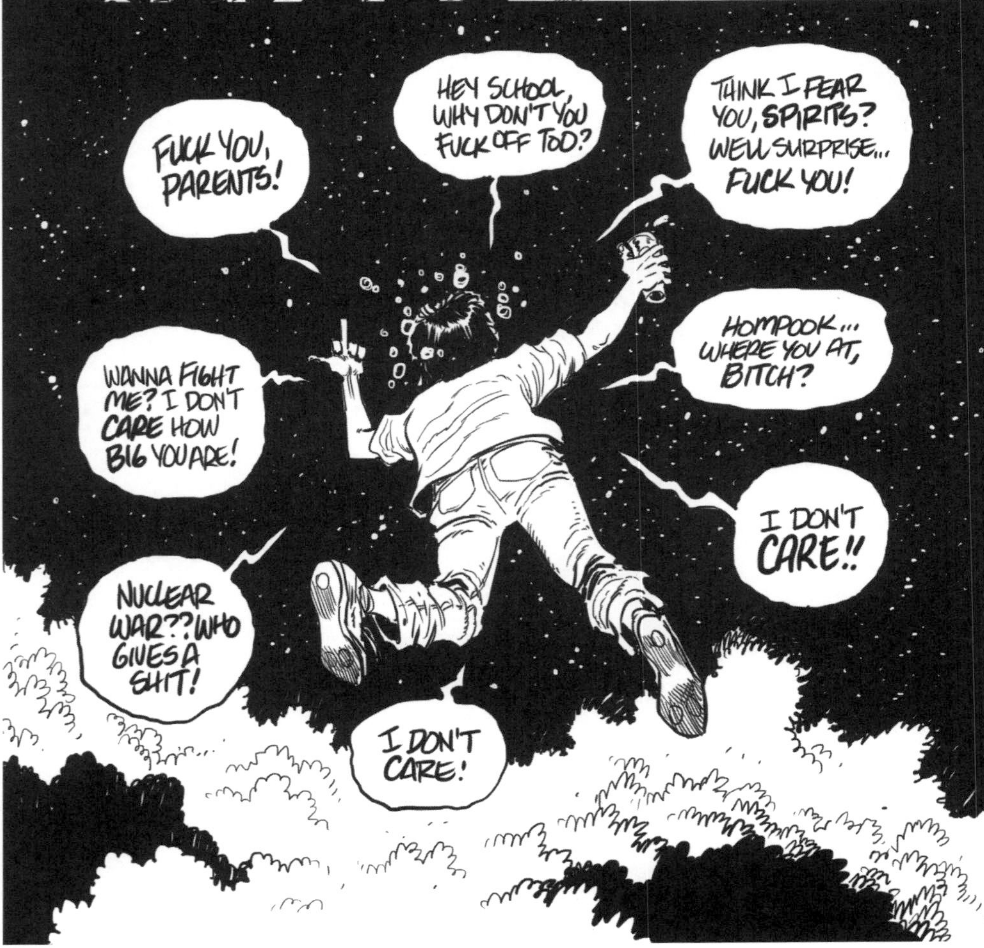
FUCK YOU, PARENTS!
HEY SCHOOL, WHY DON'T YOU FUCK OFF TOO?
THINK I FEAR YOU, SPIRITS? WELL SURPRISE... FUCK YOU!
WANNA FIGHT ME? I DON'T CARE HOW BIG YOU ARE!
HOMPOOK... WHERE YOU AT, BITCH?
I DON'T CARE!!
NUCLEAR WAR?? WHO GIVES A SHIT!
I DON'T CARE!

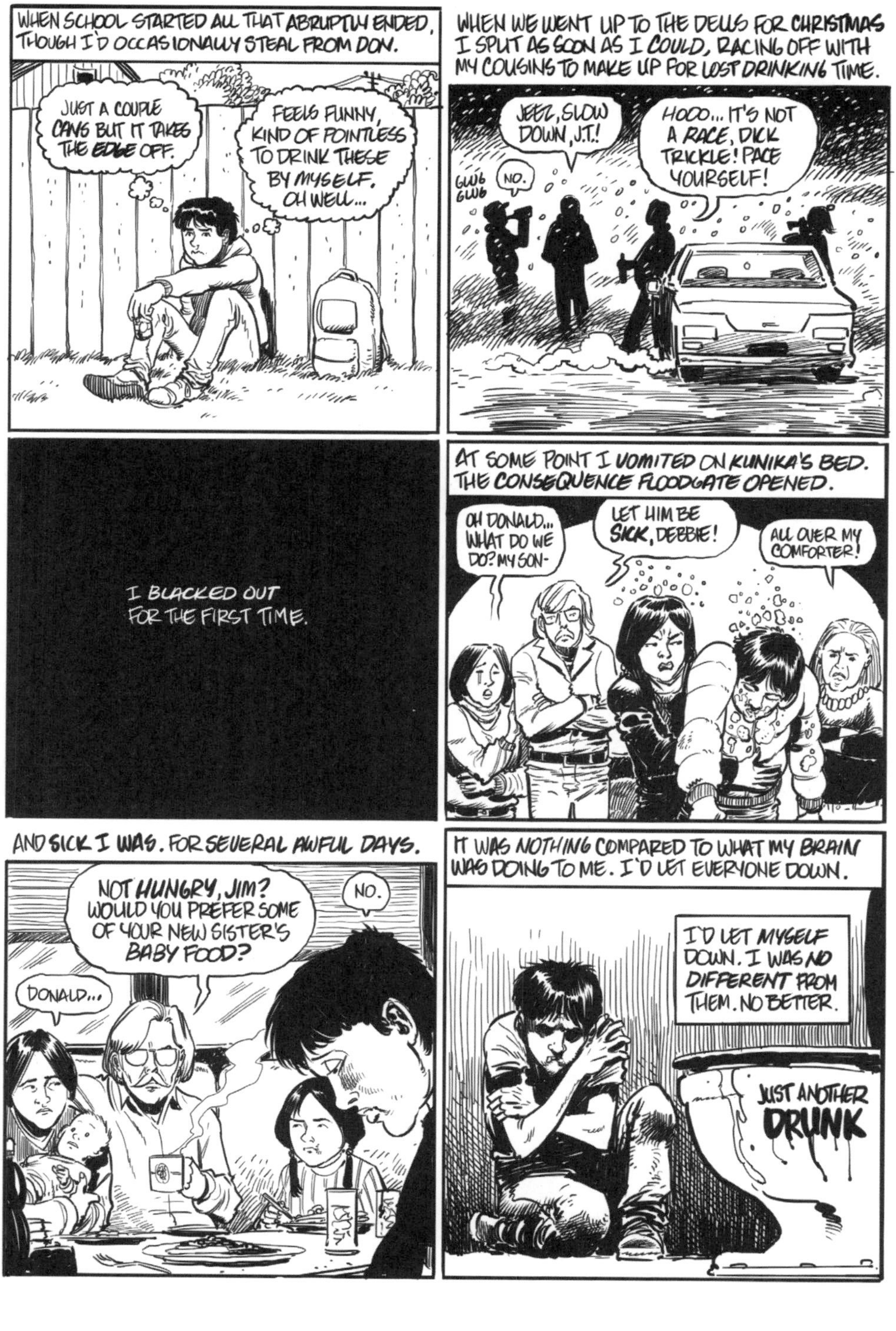
WHEN SCHOOL STARTED ALL THAT ABRUPTLY ENDED, THOUGH I'D OCCASIONALLY STEAL FROM DON.
JUST A COUPLE CANS BUT IT TAKES THE EDGE OFF.
FEELS FUNNY, KIND OF POINTLESS TO DRINK THESE BY MYSELF. OH WELL...
WHEN WE WENT UP TO THE DELLS FOR CHRISTMAS I SPLIT AS SOON AS I COULD, RACING OFF WITH MY COUSINS TO MAKE UP FOR LOST DRINKING TIME.
JEEZ, SLOW DOWN, J.T.!
HOOO... IT'S NOT A RACE, DICK TRICKLE! PACE YOURSELF!
GLUG GLUG
NO.
I BLACKED OUT FOR THE FIRST TIME.
AT SOME POINT I VOMITED ON KUNIKA'S BED. THE CONSEQUENCE FLOODGATE OPENED.
OH DONALD... WHAT DO WE DO? MY SON-
LET HIM BE SICK, DEBBIE!
ALL OVER MY COMFORTER!
AND SICK I WAS. FOR SEVERAL AWFUL DAYS.
NOT HUNGRY, JIM? WOULD YOU PREFER SOME OF YOUR NEW SISTER'S BABY FOOD?
NO.
DONALD...
IT WAS NOTHING COMPARED TO WHAT MY BRAIN WAS DOING TO ME. I'D LET EVERYONE DOWN.
I'D LET MYSELF DOWN. I WAS NO DIFFERENT FROM THEM. NO BETTER.
JUST ANOTHER DRUNK

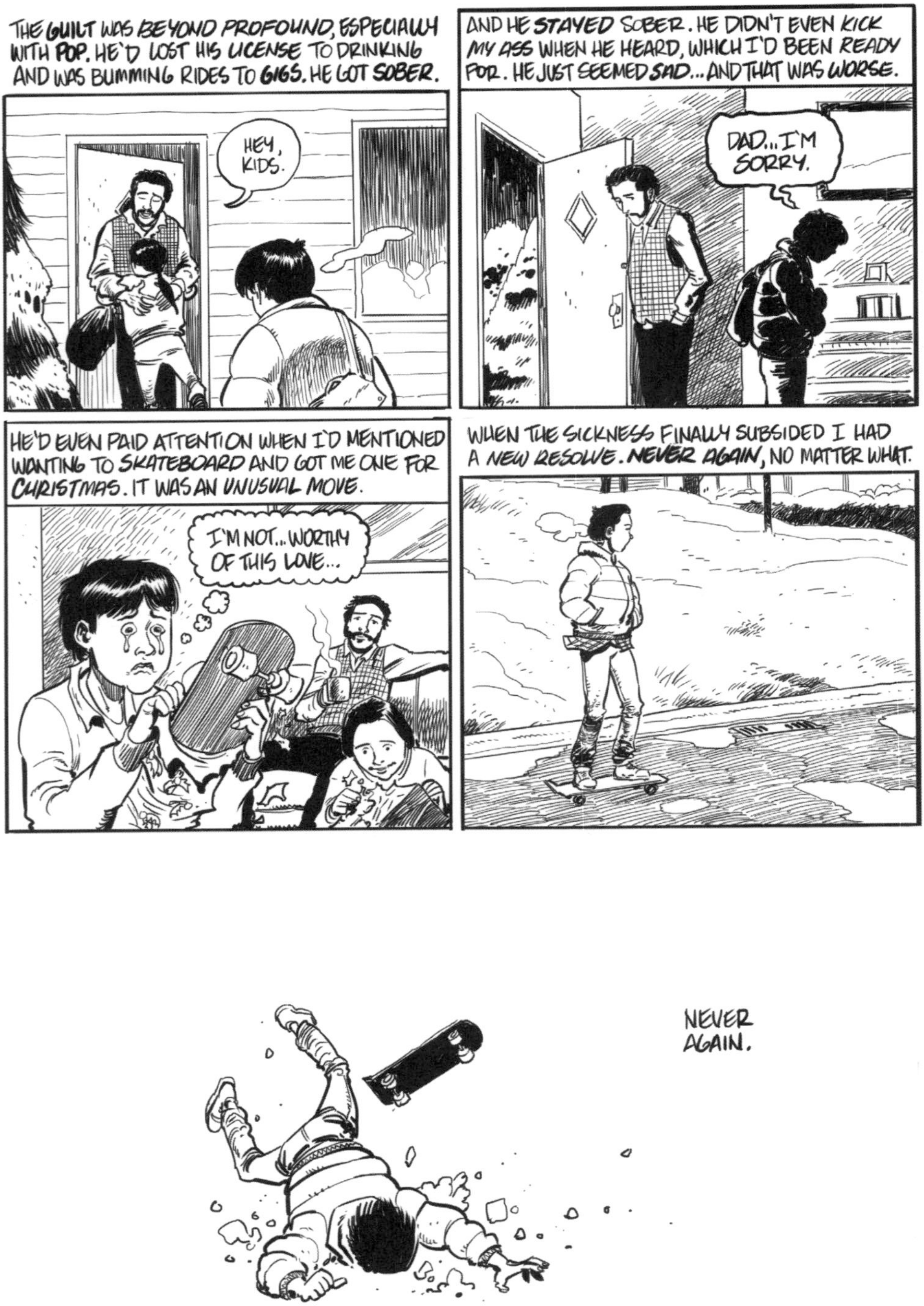
THE GUILT WAS BEYOND PROFOUND, ESPECIALLY WITH POP. HE'D LOST HIS LICENSE TO DRINKING AND WAS BUMMING RIDES TO GIGS. HE GOT SOBER.
HEY, KIDS.
AND HE STAYED SOBER. HE DIDN'T EVEN KICK MY ASS WHEN HE HEARD, WHICH I'D BEEN READY FOR. HE JUST SEEMED SAD... AND THAT WAS WORSE.
DAD... I'M SORRY.
HE'D EVEN PAID ATTENTION WHEN I'D MENTIONED WANTING TO SKATEBOARD AND GOT ME ONE FOR CHRISTMAS. IT WAS AN UNUSUAL MOVE.
I'M NOT... WORTHY OF THIS LOVE...
WHEN THE SICKNESS FINALLY SUBSIDED I HAD A NEW RESOLVE. NEVER AGAIN, NO MATTER WHAT.
NEVER AGAIN.

PART 2

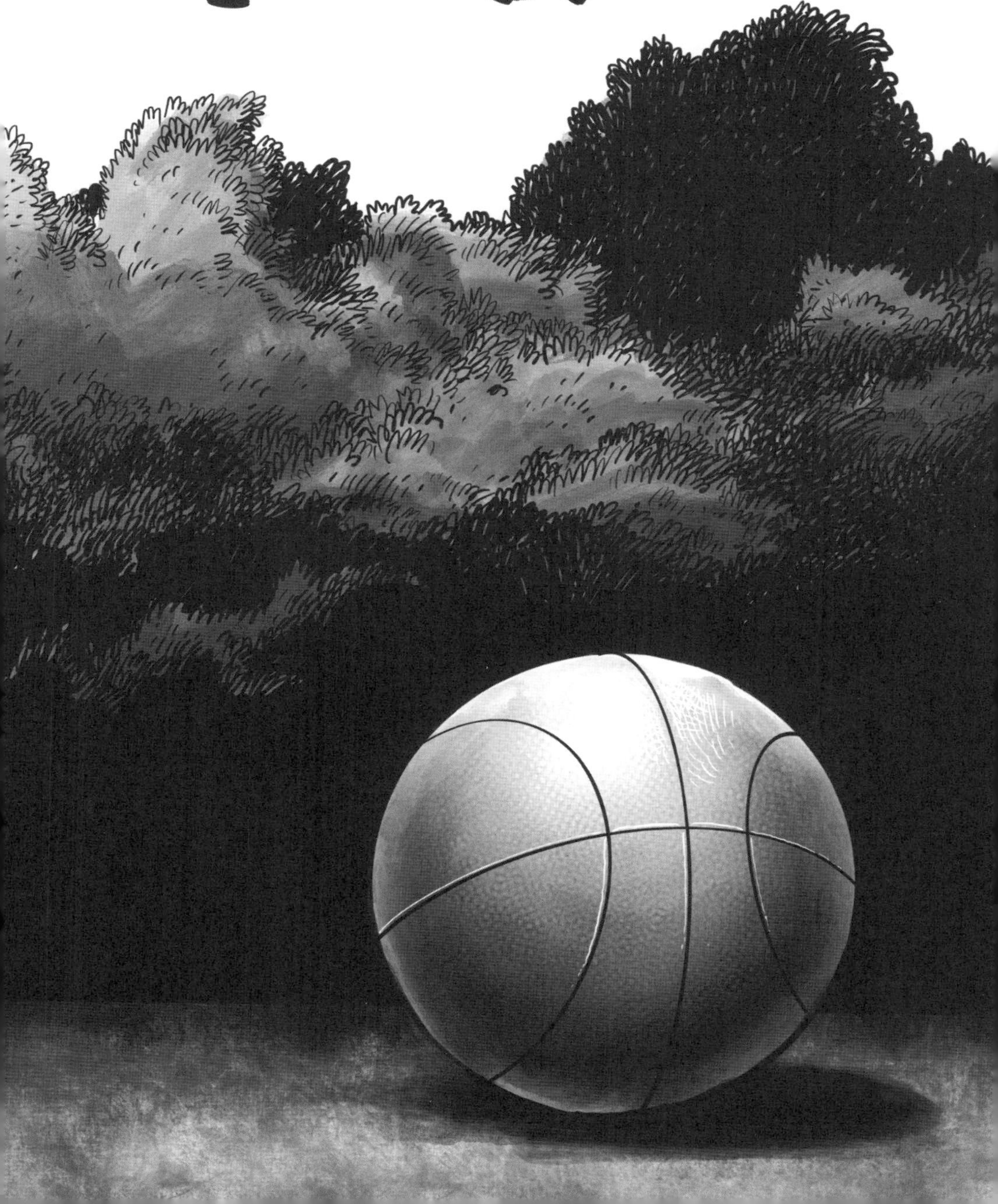

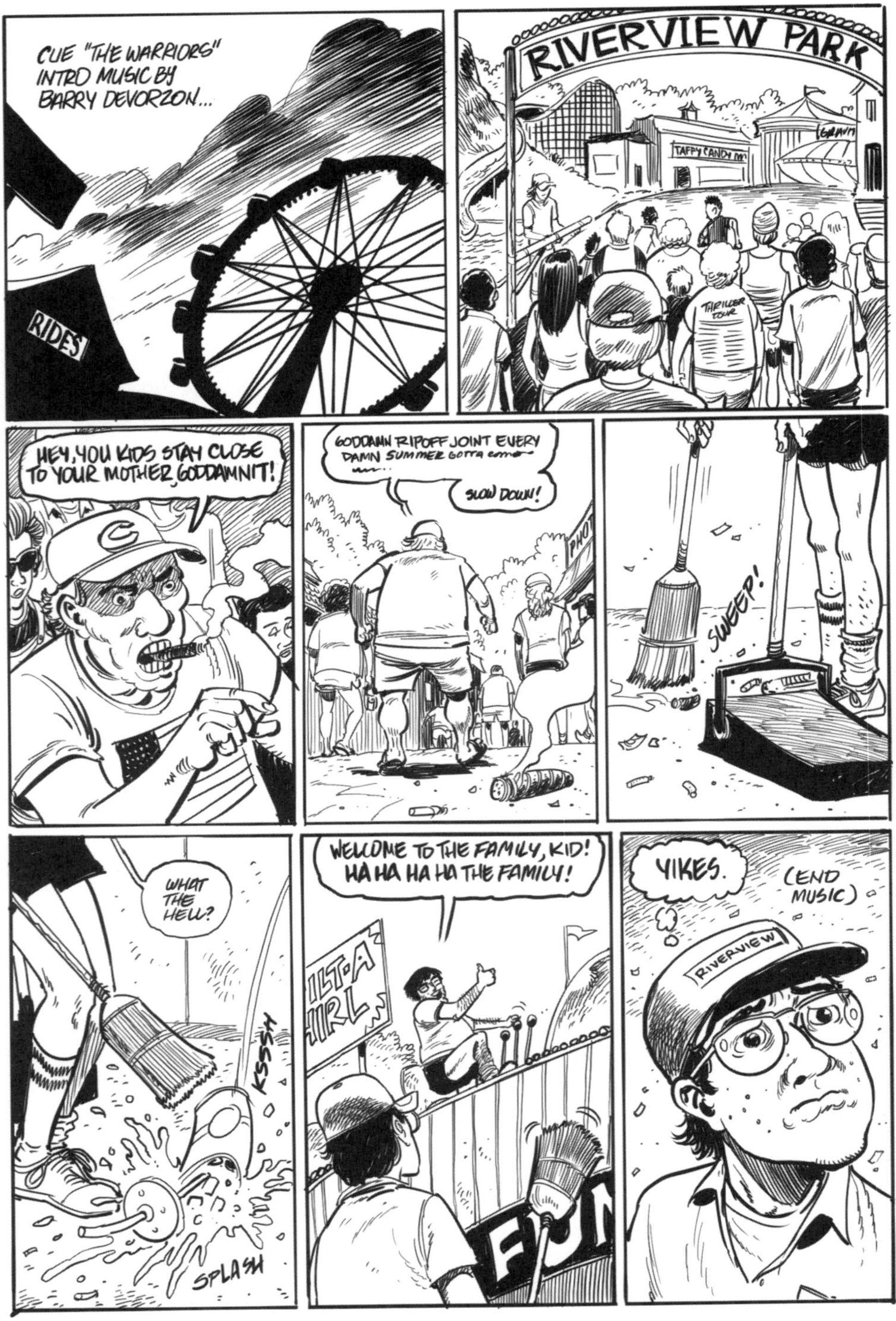
CUE "THE WARRIORS" INTRO MUSIC BY BARRY DEVORZON...
RIDES
RIVERVIEW PARK
THRILLER TOUR
HEY, YOU KIDS STAY CLOSE TO YOUR MOTHER, GODDAMNIT!
GODDAMN RIPOFF JOINT EVERY DAMN SUMMER GOTTA
SLOW DOWN!
SWEEP!
WHAT THE HELL?
KSSSH
SPLASH
WELCOME TO THE FAMILY, KID! HA HA HA HA THE FAMILY!
YIKES.
(END MUSIC)
RIVERVIEW

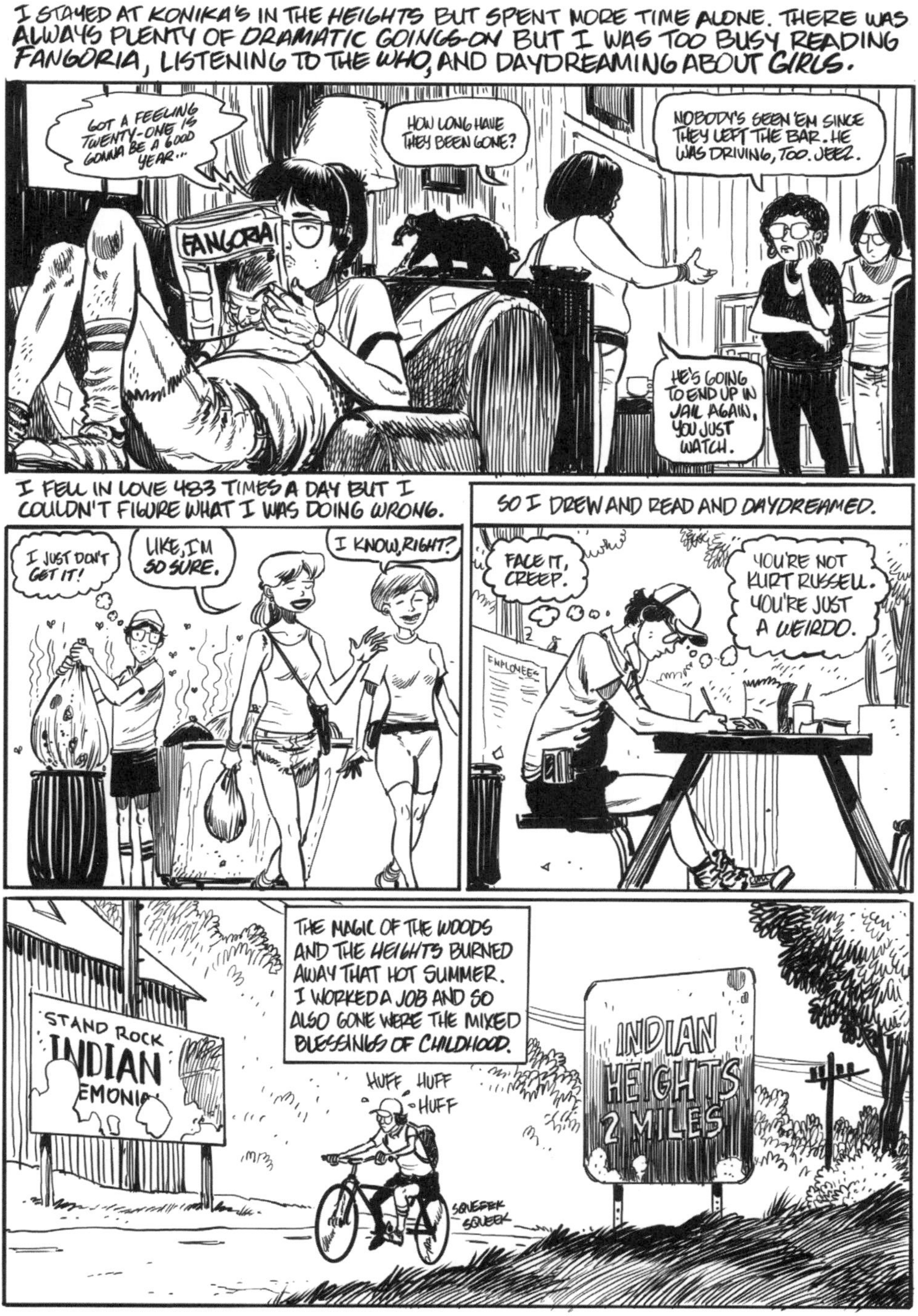
I STAYED AT KONIKA'S IN THE HEIGHTS BUT SPENT MORE TIME ALONE. THERE WAS ALWAYS PLENTY OF DRAMATIC GOINGS-ON BUT I WAS TOO BUSY READING FANGORIA, LISTENING TO THE WHO, AND DAYDREAMING ABOUT GIRLS.
GOT A FEELING TWENTY-ONE IS GONNA BE A GOOD YEAR...
FANGORIA
HOW LONG HAVE THEY BEEN GONE?
NOBODY'S SEEN 'EM SINCE THEY LEFT THE BAR. HE WAS DRIVING, TOO. JEEZ.
HE'S GOING TO END UP IN JAIL AGAIN, YOU JUST WATCH.
I FELL IN LOVE 483 TIMES A DAY BUT I COULDN'T FIGURE WHAT I WAS DOING WRONG.
I JUST DON'T GET IT!
LIKE, I'M SO SURE.
I KNOW, RIGHT?
SO I DREW AND READ AND DAYDREAMED.
FACE IT, CREEP.
YOU'RE NOT KURT RUSSELL. YOU'RE JUST A WEIRDO.
EMPLOYEES
THE MAGIC OF THE WOODS AND THE HEIGHTS BURNED AWAY THAT HOT SUMMER. I WORKED A JOB AND SO ALSO GONE WERE THE MIXED BLESSINGS OF CHILDHOOD.
STAND ROCK INDIAN EMONIA
HUFF HUFF HUFF
INDIAN HEIGHTS 2 MILES
SQUEEEK SQUEEK

HORMONES, MY LOVE OF THE *WEIRD* AND *MACABRE*, AND MY VERY BEING IN *GENERAL* MADE ME *FEEL DIFFERENT.*

AS I GOT OLDER I BEGAN TO SEE *FAMILY POLITICS*. MY *MOTHER* WAS A *HOTBUTTON*. SHE *LEFT*. SHE WENT TO LIVE IN THE *WHITE WORLD*. SHE WAS ALWAYS *READING* AND THOUGHT SHE WAS *BETTER* **THAN.**

THE FACT THAT MY FATHER WAS *WHITE* AND THAT I WASN'T FROM THE *HEIGHTS* FELT MORE THAN EVER LIKE *DEFINING CHARACTERISTICS.*

I WAS NOT A "TOUGH GUY" AND WAS ABOUT AS *STOIC* AS *WET CARDBOARD*. EVERYONE WAS PLAYING *BASKETBALL* WHILE I READ *"DAREDEVIL"* AND RAY *BRADBURY*... I COULD NOT DO THE *"HARD INDIAN FACE"* WITHOUT BUSTING INTO A GIGGLE.

AND I WAS NO LONGER *DRINKING*, SO I WAS SIMPLY *LEFT OUT.*

WITHOUT COMPLAINT, I DRIFTED FROM IT ALL. IF THEY HAD A PROBLEM WITH ME OR DIDN'T THINK I *BELONGED*... WELL, GOODBYE.

SADLY IT WAS THE LAST SUMMER I SPENT UP THERE.

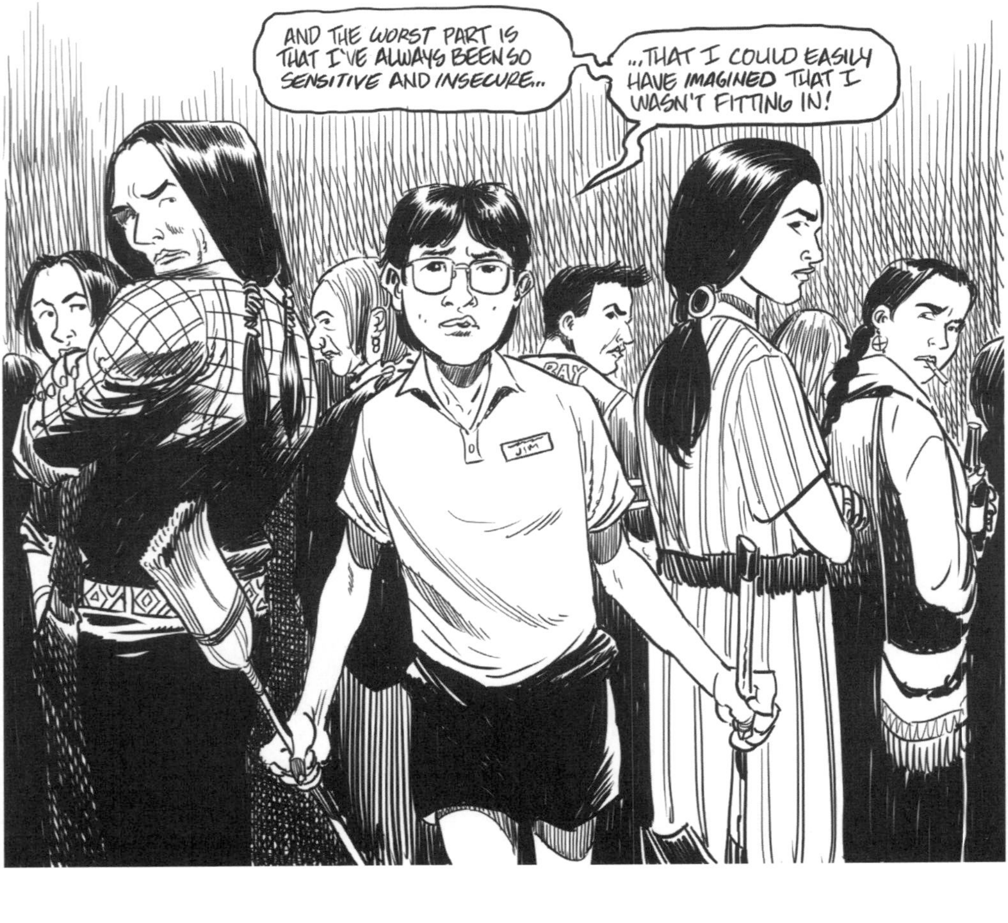
AND THE WORST PART IS THAT I'VE ALWAYS BEEN SO SENSITIVE AND INSECURE...
...THAT I COULD EASILY HAVE IMAGINED THAT I WASN'T FITTING IN!
RAY
JIM

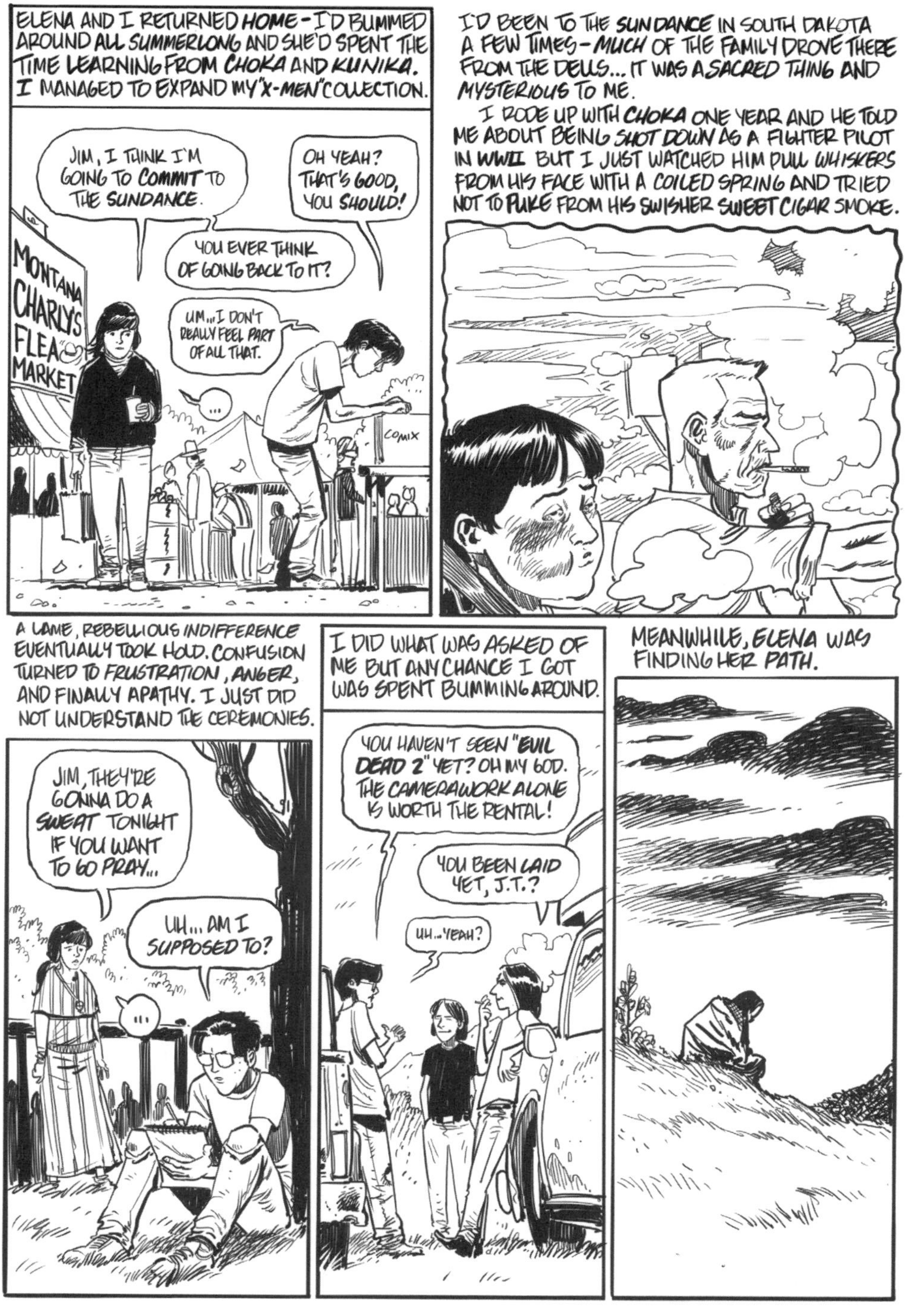
ELENA AND I RETURNED HOME - I'D BUMMED AROUND ALL SUMMERLONG AND SHE'D SPENT THE TIME LEARNING FROM CHOKA AND KUNIKA. I MANAGED TO EXPAND MY "X-MEN" COLLECTION.
JIM, I THINK I'M GOING TO COMMIT TO THE SUNDANCE.
OH YEAH? THAT'S GOOD, YOU SHOULD!
YOU EVER THINK OF GOING BACK TO IT?
UM...I DON'T REALLY FEEL PART OF ALL THAT.
...
MONTANA CHARLY'S FLEA MARKET
COMIX
I'D BEEN TO THE SUNDANCE IN SOUTH DAKOTA A FEW TIMES - MUCH OF THE FAMILY DROVE THERE FROM THE DELLS... IT WAS A SACRED THING AND MYSTERIOUS TO ME.
I RODE UP WITH CHOKA ONE YEAR AND HE TOLD ME ABOUT BEING SHOT DOWN AS A FIGHTER PILOT IN WWII BUT I JUST WATCHED HIM PULL WHISKERS FROM HIS FACE WITH A COILED SPRING AND TRIED NOT TO PUKE FROM HIS SWISHER SWEET CIGAR SMOKE.
A LAME, REBELLIOUS INDIFFERENCE EVENTUALLY TOOK HOLD. CONFUSION TURNED TO FRUSTRATION, ANGER, AND FINALLY APATHY. I JUST DID NOT UNDERSTAND THE CEREMONIES.
JIM, THEY'RE GONNA DO A SWEAT TONIGHT IF YOU WANT TO GO PRAY...
UH... AM I SUPPOSED TO?
...
I DID WHAT WAS ASKED OF ME BUT ANY CHANCE I GOT WAS SPENT BUMMING AROUND.
YOU HAVEN'T SEEN "EVIL DEAD 2" YET? OH MY GOD. THE CAMERAWORK ALONE IS WORTH THE RENTAL!
YOU BEEN LAID YET, J.T.?
UH...YEAH?
MEANWHILE, ELENA WAS FINDING HER PATH.

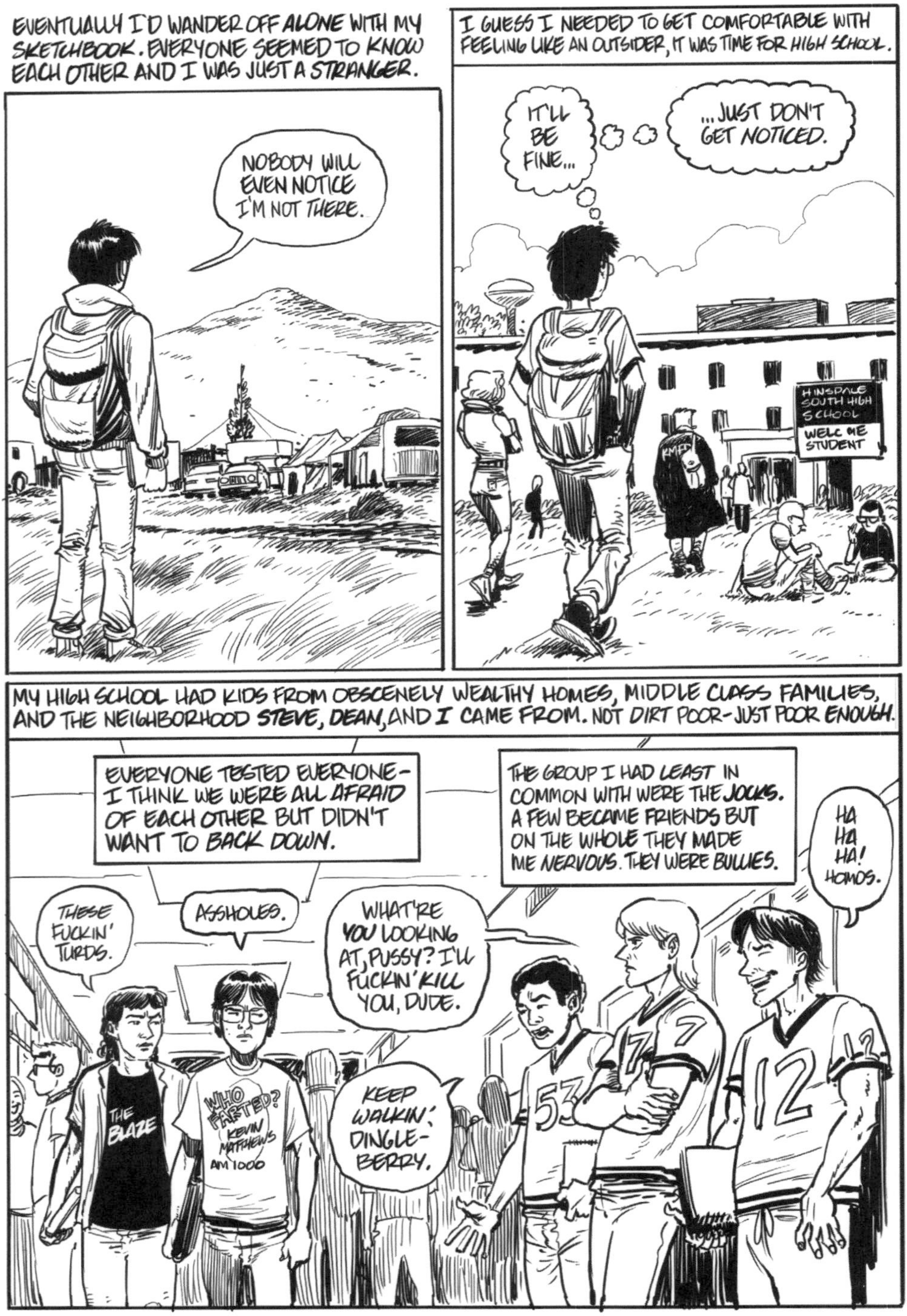
EVENTUALLY I'D WANDER OFF ALONE WITH MY SKETCHBOOK. EVERYONE SEEMED TO KNOW EACH OTHER AND I WAS JUST A STRANGER.
NOBODY WILL EVEN NOTICE I'M NOT THERE.
I GUESS I NEEDED TO GET COMFORTABLE WITH FEELING LIKE AN OUTSIDER, IT WAS TIME FOR HIGH SCHOOL.
IT'LL BE FINE...
...JUST DON'T GET NOTICED.
HINSDALE SOUTH HIGH SCHOOL
WELC ME STUDENT
MY HIGH SCHOOL HAD KIDS FROM OBSCENELY WEALTHY HOMES, MIDDLE CLASS FAMILIES, AND THE NEIGHBORHOOD STEVE, DEAN, AND I CAME FROM. NOT DIRT POOR- JUST POOR ENOUGH.
EVERYONE TESTED EVERYONE- I THINK WE WERE ALL AFRAID OF EACH OTHER BUT DIDN'T WANT TO BACK DOWN.
THE GROUP I HAD LEAST IN COMMON WITH WERE THE JOCKS. A FEW BECAME FRIENDS BUT ON THE WHOLE THEY MADE ME NERVOUS. THEY WERE BULLIES.
HA HA HA! HOMOS.
WHAT'RE YOU LOOKING AT, PUSSY? I'LL FUCKIN' KILL YOU, DUDE.
ASSHOLES.
THESE FUCKIN' TURDS.
KEEP WALKIN', DINGLE-BERRY.
THE BLAZE
WHO FARTED? KEVIN MATTHEWS AM 1000

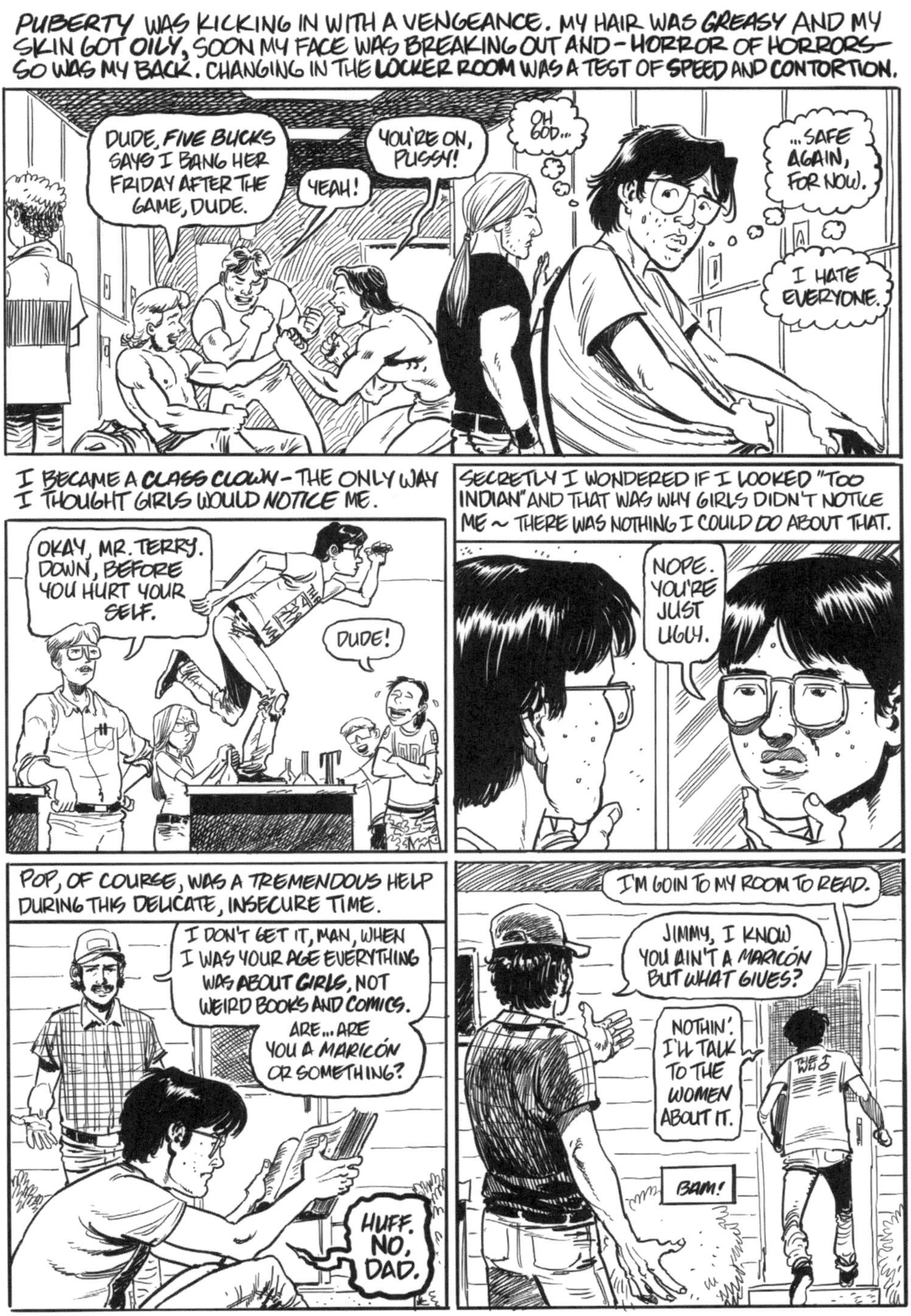
PUBERTY WAS KICKING IN WITH A VENGEANCE. MY HAIR WAS GREASY AND MY SKIN GOT OILY, SOON MY FACE WAS BREAKING OUT AND - HORROR OF HORRORS - SO WAS MY BACK. CHANGING IN THE LOCKER ROOM WAS A TEST OF SPEED AND CONTORTION.
DUDE, FIVE BUCKS SAYS I BANG HER FRIDAY AFTER THE GAME, DUDE.
YEAH!
YOU'RE ON, PUSSY!
OH GOD...
...SAFE AGAIN, FOR NOW.
I HATE EVERYONE.
I BECAME A CLASS CLOWN - THE ONLY WAY I THOUGHT GIRLS WOULD NOTICE ME.
OKAY, MR. TERRY. DOWN, BEFORE YOU HURT YOUR SELF.
DUDE!
SECRETLY I WONDERED IF I LOOKED "TOO INDIAN" AND THAT WAS WHY GIRLS DIDN'T NOTICE ME ~ THERE WAS NOTHING I COULD DO ABOUT THAT.
NOPE. YOU'RE JUST UGLY.
POP, OF COURSE, WAS A TREMENDOUS HELP DURING THIS DELICATE, INSECURE TIME.
I DON'T GET IT, MAN, WHEN I WAS YOUR AGE EVERYTHING WAS ABOUT GIRLS, NOT WEIRD BOOKS AND COMICS.
ARE... ARE YOU A MARICÓN OR SOMETHING?
HUFF. NO, DAD.
I'M GOIN TO MY ROOM TO READ.
JIMMY, I KNOW YOU AIN'T A MARICÓN BUT WHAT GIVES?
NOTHIN'. I'LL TALK TO THE WOMEN ABOUT IT.
BAM!

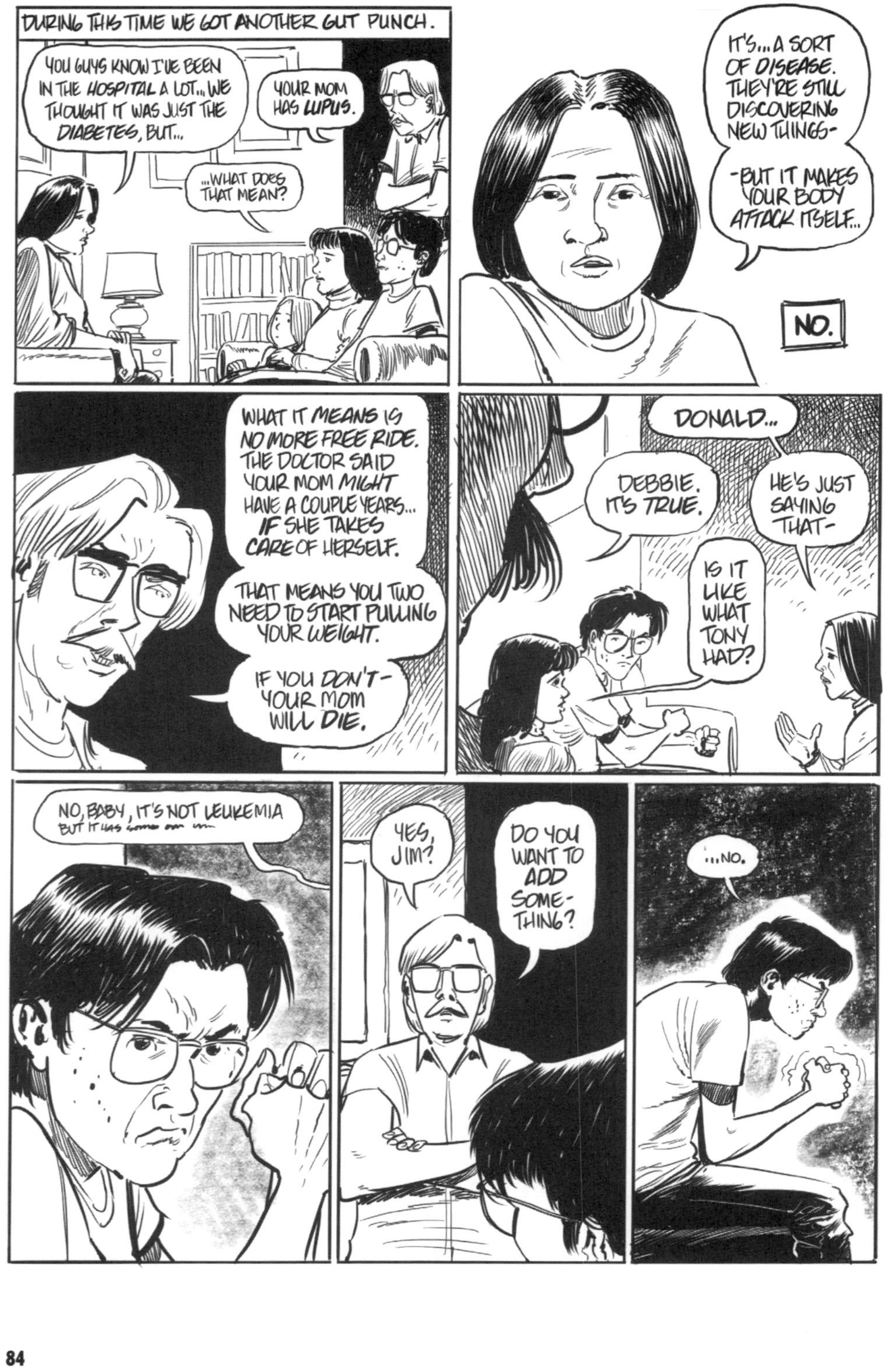
DURING THIS TIME WE GOT ANOTHER GUT PUNCH.
YOU GUYS KNOW I'VE BEEN IN THE HOSPITAL A LOT... WE THOUGHT IT WAS JUST THE DIABETES, BUT...
YOUR MOM HAS LUPUS.
...WHAT DOES THAT MEAN?
IT'S... A SORT OF DISEASE. THEY'RE STILL DISCOVERING NEW THINGS-
-BUT IT MAKES YOUR BODY ATTACK ITSELF...
NO.
WHAT IT MEANS IS NO MORE FREE RIDE. THE DOCTOR SAID YOUR MOM MIGHT HAVE A COUPLE YEARS... IF SHE TAKES CARE OF HERSELF.
THAT MEANS YOU TWO NEED TO START PULLING YOUR WEIGHT.
IF YOU DON'T- YOUR MOM WILL DIE.
DONALD...
DEBBIE. IT'S TRUE.
HE'S JUST SAYING THAT-
IS IT LIKE WHAT TONY HAD?
NO, BABY, IT'S NOT LEUKEMIA
BUT IT HAS
YES, JIM?
DO YOU WANT TO ADD SOME-THING?
...NO.

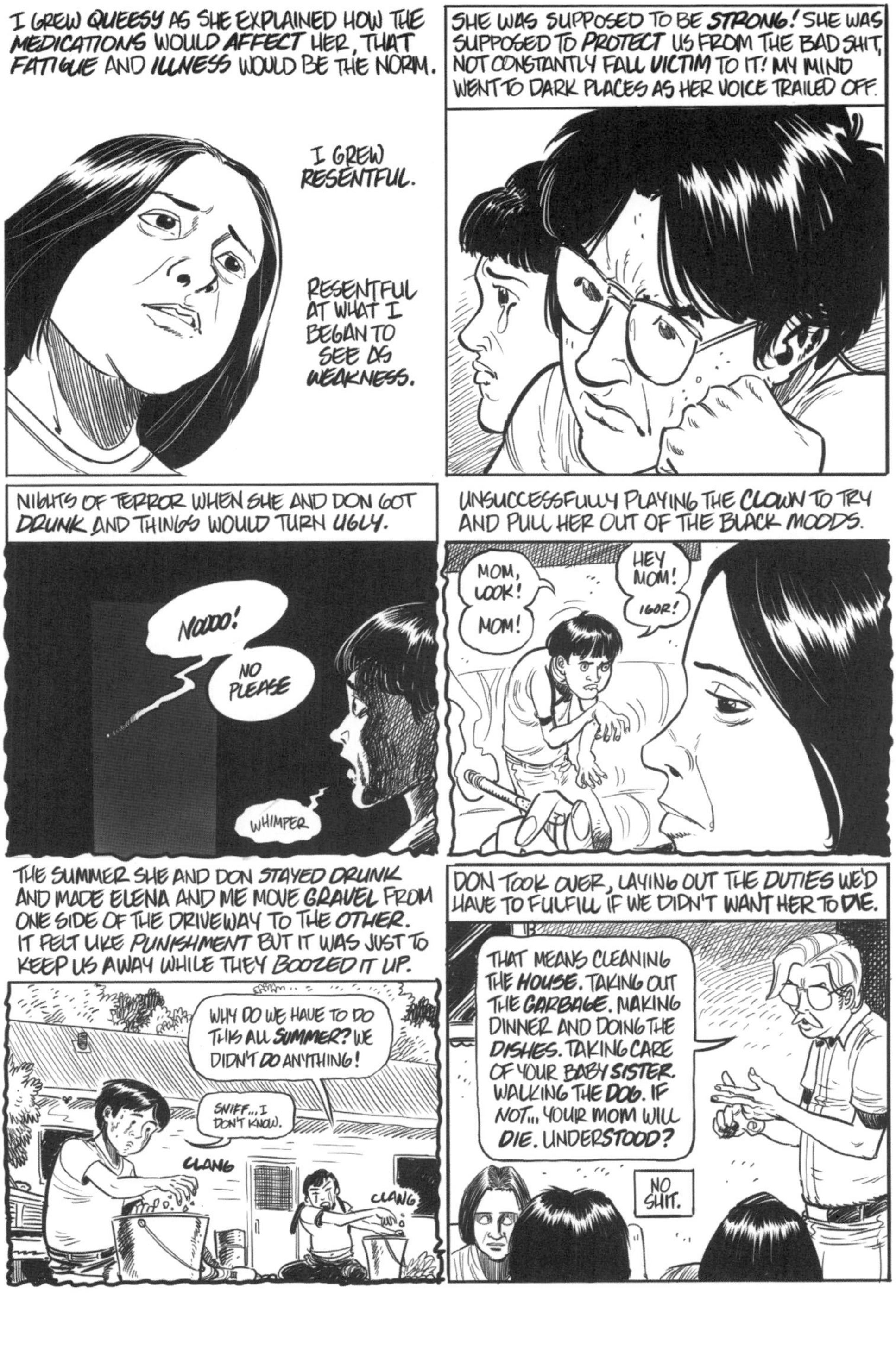
I GREW QUEESY AS SHE EXPLAINED HOW THE MEDICATIONS WOULD AFFECT HER, THAT FATIGUE AND ILLNESS WOULD BE THE NORM.
I GREW RESENTFUL.
RESENTFUL AT WHAT I BEGAN TO SEE AS WEAKNESS.
SHE WAS SUPPOSED TO BE STRONG! SHE WAS SUPPOSED TO PROTECT US FROM THE BAD SHIT, NOT CONSTANTLY FALL VICTIM TO IT! MY MIND WENT TO DARK PLACES AS HER VOICE TRAILED OFF.
NIGHTS OF TERROR WHEN SHE AND DON GOT DRUNK AND THINGS WOULD TURN UGLY.
NOOOO!
NO PLEASE
WHIMPER
UNSUCCESSFULLY PLAYING THE CLOWN TO TRY AND PULL HER OUT OF THE BLACK MOODS.
MOM, LOOK!
MOM!
HEY MOM!
IGOR!
THE SUMMER SHE AND DON STAYED DRUNK AND MADE ELENA AND ME MOVE GRAVEL FROM ONE SIDE OF THE DRIVEWAY TO THE OTHER. IT FELT LIKE PUNISHMENT BUT IT WAS JUST TO KEEP US AWAY WHILE THEY BOOZED IT UP.
WHY DO WE HAVE TO DO THIS ALL SUMMER? WE DIDN'T DO ANYTHING!
SNIFF... I DON'T KNOW.
CLANG
CLANG
DON TOOK OVER, LAYING OUT THE DUTIES WE'D HAVE TO FULFILL IF WE DIDN'T WANT HER TO DIE.
THAT MEANS CLEANING THE HOUSE. TAKING OUT THE GARBAGE. MAKING DINNER AND DOING THE DISHES. TAKING CARE OF YOUR BABY SISTER. WALKING THE DOG. IF NOT... YOUR MOM WILL DIE. UNDERSTOOD?
NO SHIT.

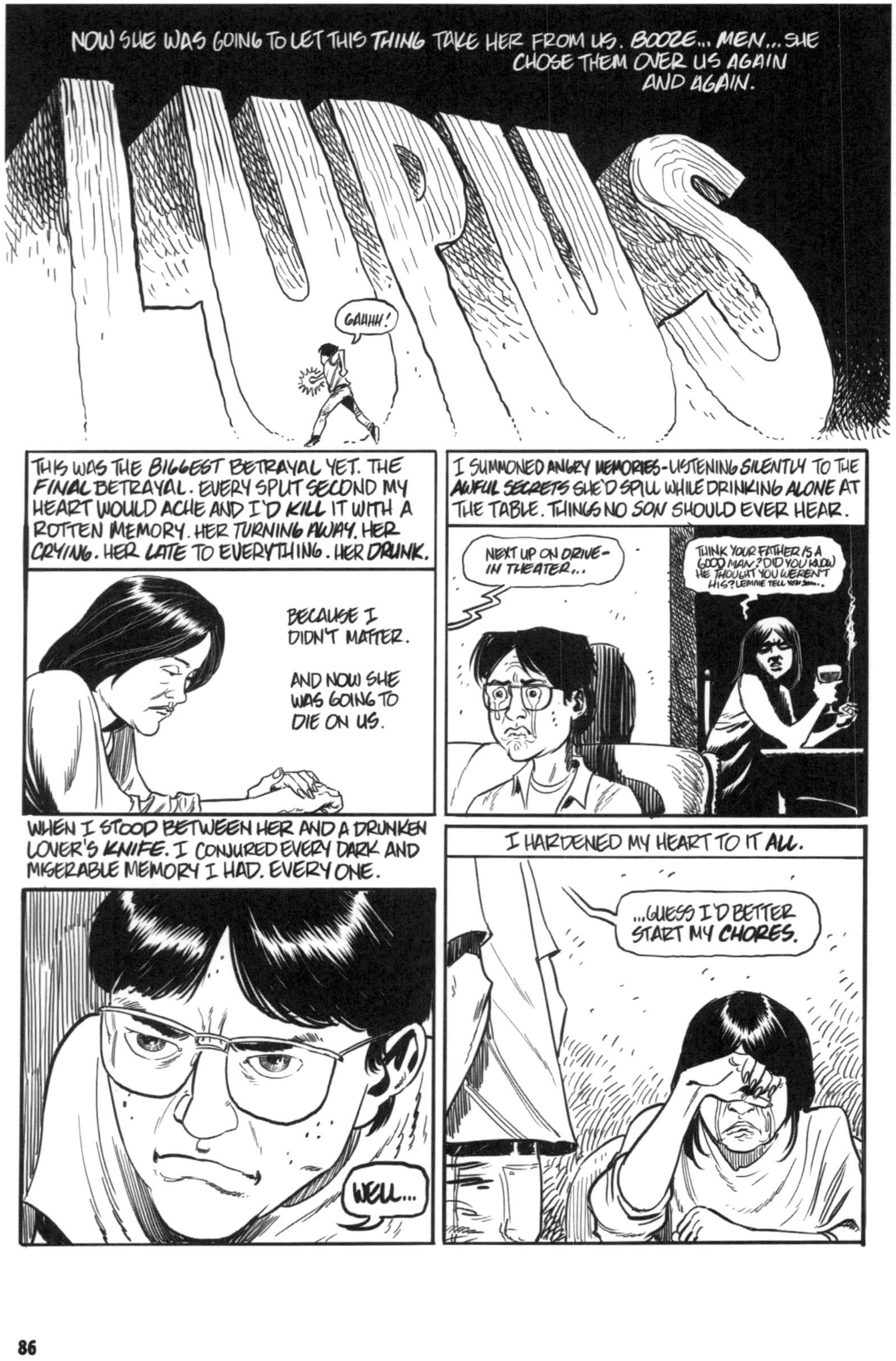
NOW SHE WAS GOING TO LET THIS THING TAKE HER FROM US. BOOZE... MEN... SHE CHOSE THEM OVER US AGAIN AND AGAIN.
LUPUS
GAHHH!
THIS WAS THE BIGGEST BETRAYAL YET. THE FINAL BETRAYAL. EVERY SPLIT SECOND MY HEART WOULD ACHE AND I'D KILL IT WITH A ROTTEN MEMORY. HER TURNING AWAY. HER CRYING. HER LATE TO EVERYTHING. HER DRUNK.
BECAUSE I DIDN'T MATTER.
AND NOW SHE WAS GOING TO DIE ON US.
I SUMMONED ANGRY MEMORIES-LISTENING SILENTLY TO THE AWFUL SECRETS SHE'D SPILL WHILE DRINKING ALONE AT THE TABLE. THINGS NO SON SHOULD EVER HEAR.
NEXT UP ON DRIVE-IN THEATER...
THINK YOUR FATHER IS A GOOD MAN? DID YOU KNOW HE THOUGHT YOU WEREN'T HIS? LEMME TELL
WHEN I STOOD BETWEEN HER AND A DRUNKEN LOVER'S KNIFE. I CONJURED EVERY DARK AND MISERABLE MEMORY I HAD. EVERY ONE.
WELL...
I HARDENED MY HEART TO IT ALL.
...GUESS I'D BETTER START MY CHORES.

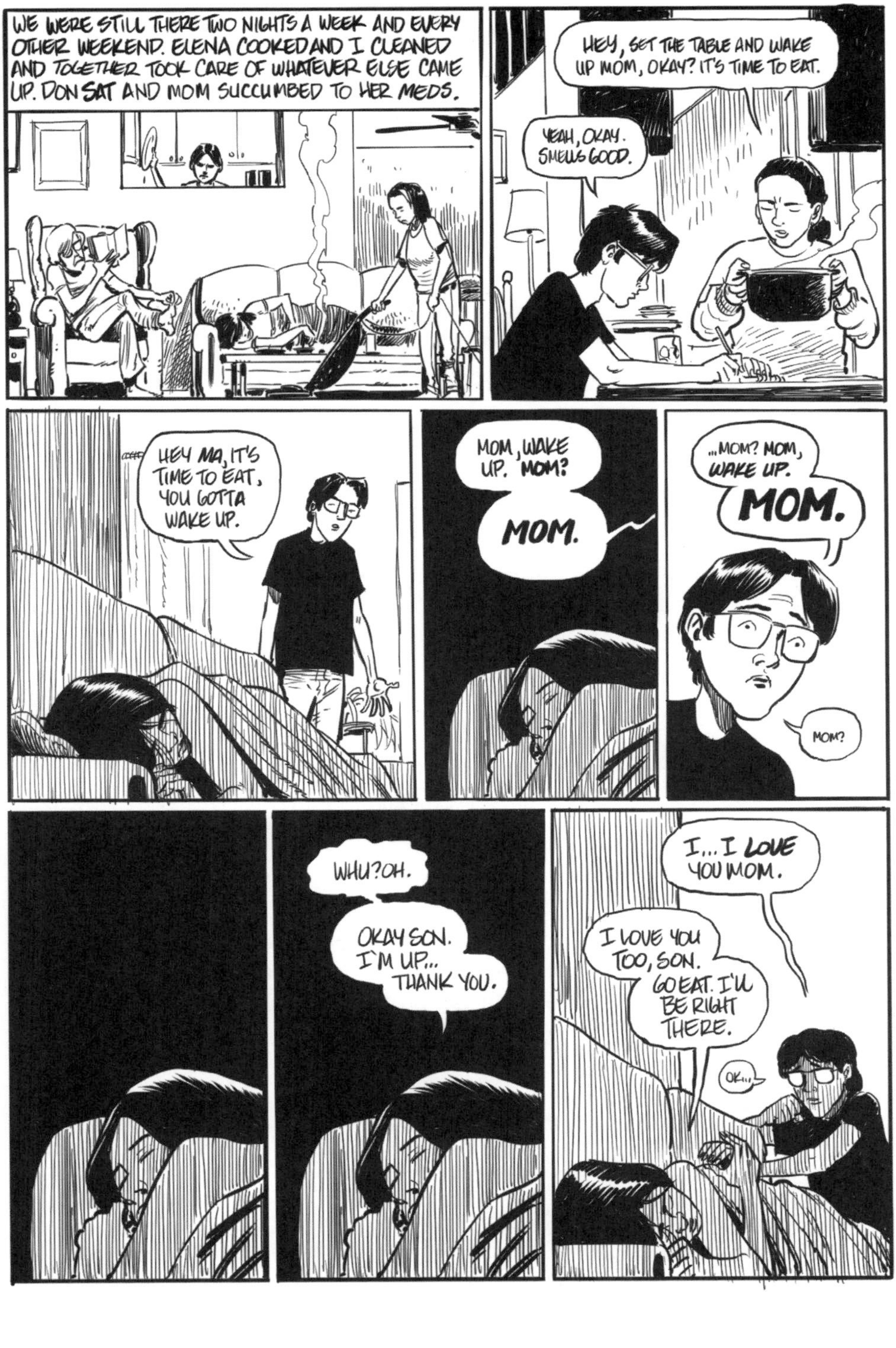
WE WERE STILL THERE TWO NIGHTS A WEEK AND EVERY OTHER WEEKEND. ELENA COOKED AND I CLEANED AND TOGETHER TOOK CARE OF WHATEVER ELSE CAME UP. DON SAT AND MOM SUCCUMBED TO HER MEDS.
HEY, SET THE TABLE AND WAKE UP MOM, OKAY? IT'S TIME TO EAT.
YEAH, OKAY. SMELLS GOOD.
HEY MA, IT'S TIME TO EAT, YOU GOTTA WAKE UP.
MOM, WAKE UP. MOM?
MOM.
...MOM? MOM, WAKE UP.
MOM.
MOM?
WHU? OH.
OKAY SON. I'M UP... THANK YOU.
I... I LOVE YOU MOM.
I LOVE YOU TOO, SON. GO EAT. I'LL BE RIGHT THERE.
OK...

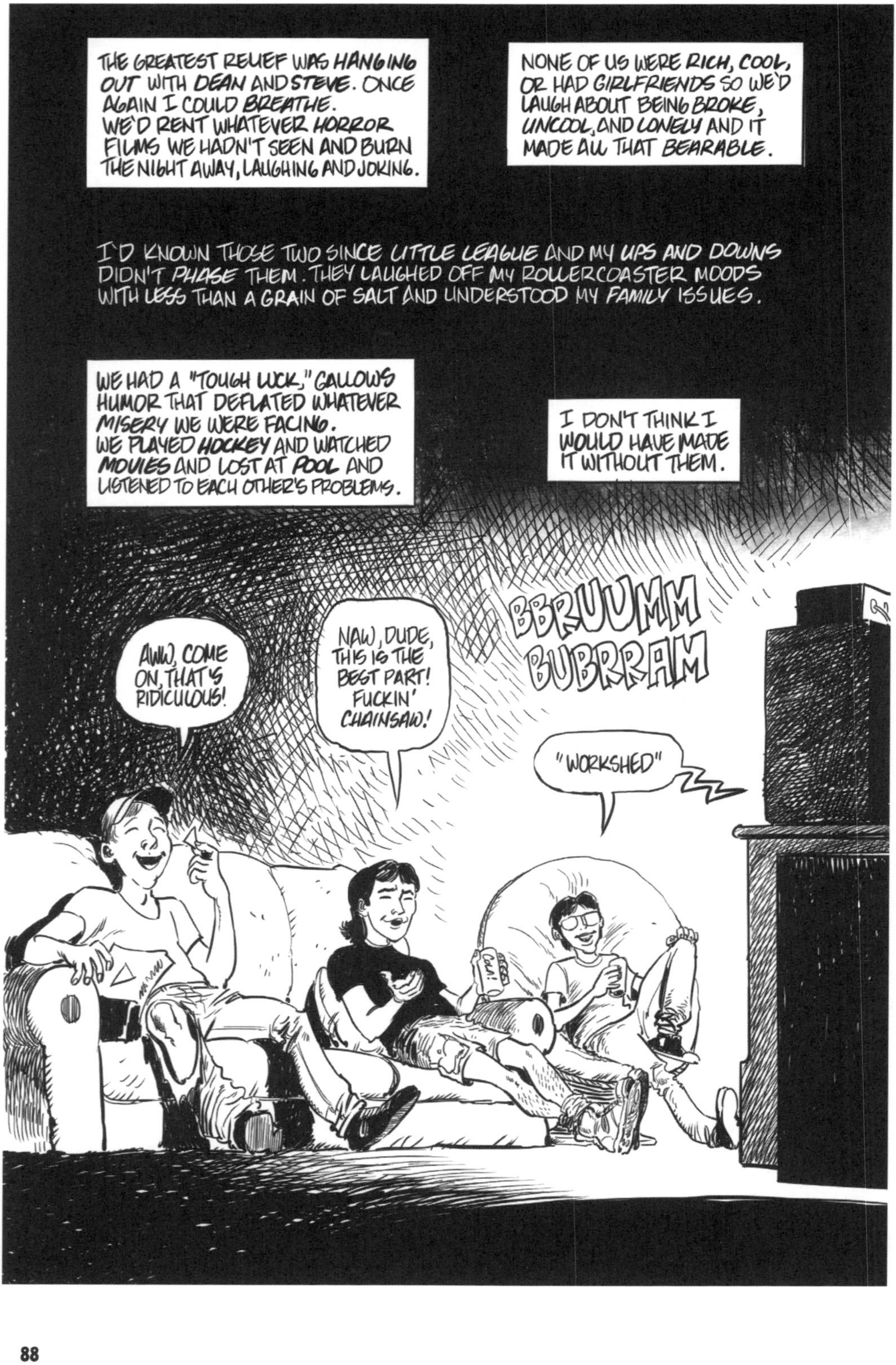
THE GREATEST RELIEF WAS HANGING OUT WITH DEAN AND STEVE. ONCE AGAIN I COULD BREATHE. WE'D RENT WHATEVER HORROR FILMS WE HADN'T SEEN AND BURN THE NIGHT AWAY, LAUGHING AND JOKING.
NONE OF US WERE RICH, COOL, OR HAD GIRLFRIENDS SO WE'D LAUGH ABOUT BEING BROKE, UNCOOL, AND LONELY AND IT MADE ALL THAT BEARABLE.
I'D KNOWN THOSE TWO SINCE LITTLE LEAGUE AND MY UPS AND DOWNS DIDN'T PHASE THEM. THEY LAUGHED OFF MY ROLLERCOASTER MOODS WITH LESS THAN A GRAIN OF SALT AND UNDERSTOOD MY FAMILY ISSUES.
WE HAD A "TOUGH LUCK," GALLOWS HUMOR THAT DEFLATED WHATEVER MISERY WE WERE FACING. WE PLAYED HOCKEY AND WATCHED MOVIES AND LOST AT POOL AND LISTENED TO EACH OTHER'S PROBLEMS.
I DON'T THINK I WOULD HAVE MADE IT WITHOUT THEM.
BBRUUMM BUBRRAM
AWW, COME ON, THAT'S RIDICULOUS!
NAW, DUDE, THIS IS THE BEST PART! FUCKIN' CHAINSAW!
"WORKSHED"
COLA!

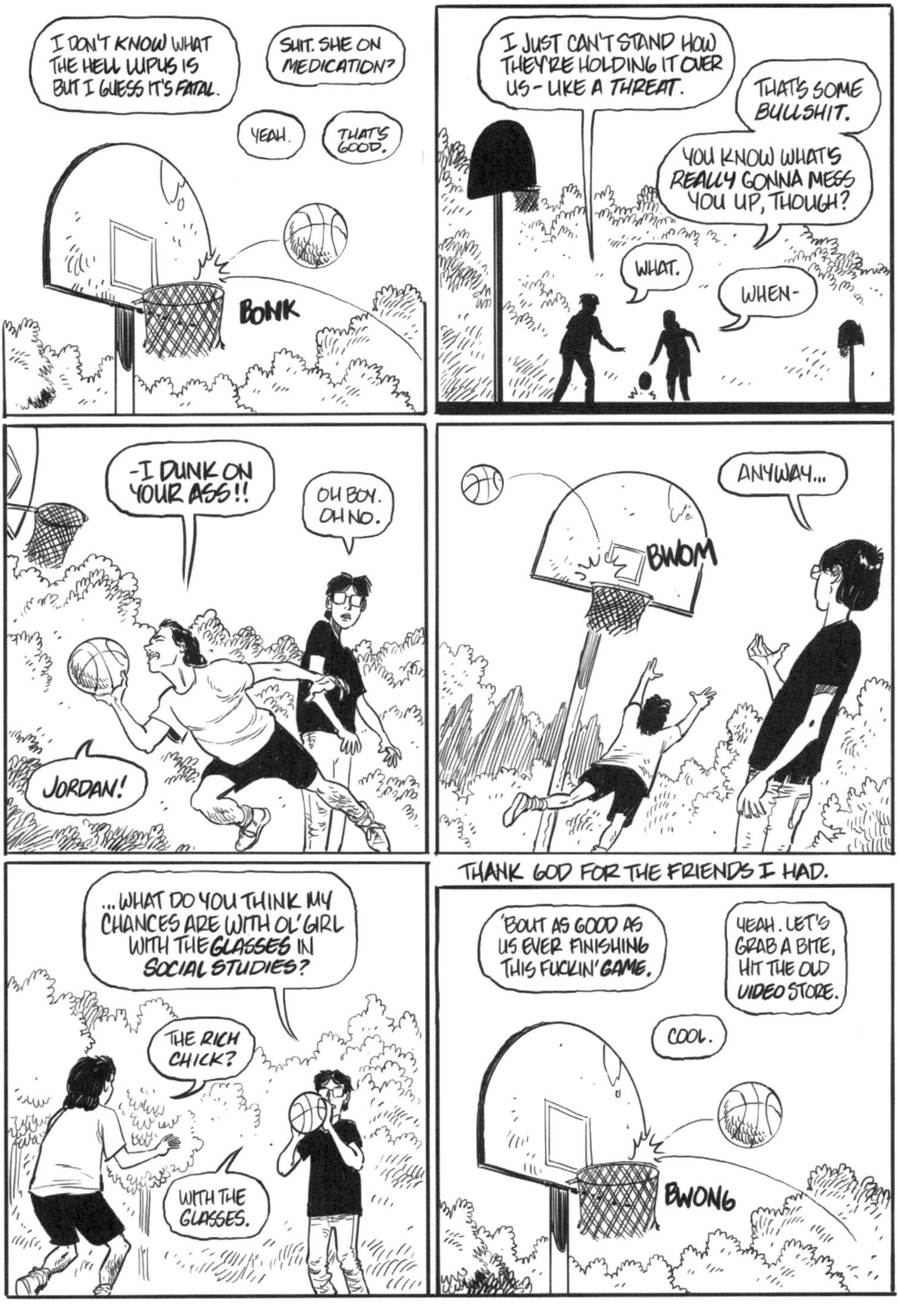
I DON'T KNOW WHAT THE HELL LUPUS IS BUT I GUESS IT'S FATAL.
SHIT. SHE ON MEDICATION?
YEAH.
THAT'S GOOD.
BONK
I JUST CAN'T STAND HOW THEY'RE HOLDING IT OVER US - LIKE A THREAT.
THAT'S SOME BULLSHIT.
YOU KNOW WHAT'S REALLY GONNA MESS YOU UP, THOUGH?
WHAT.
WHEN-
-I DUNK ON YOUR ASS!!
OH BOY. OH NO.
JORDAN!
ANYWAY...
BWOM
...WHAT DO YOU THINK MY CHANCES ARE WITH OL' GIRL WITH THE GLASSES IN SOCIAL STUDIES?
THE RICH CHICK?
WITH THE GLASSES.
THANK GOD FOR THE FRIENDS I HAD.
'BOUT AS GOOD AS US EVER FINISHING THIS FUCKIN' GAME.
YEAH. LET'S GRAB A BITE, HIT THE OLD VIDEO STORE.
COOL.
BWONG

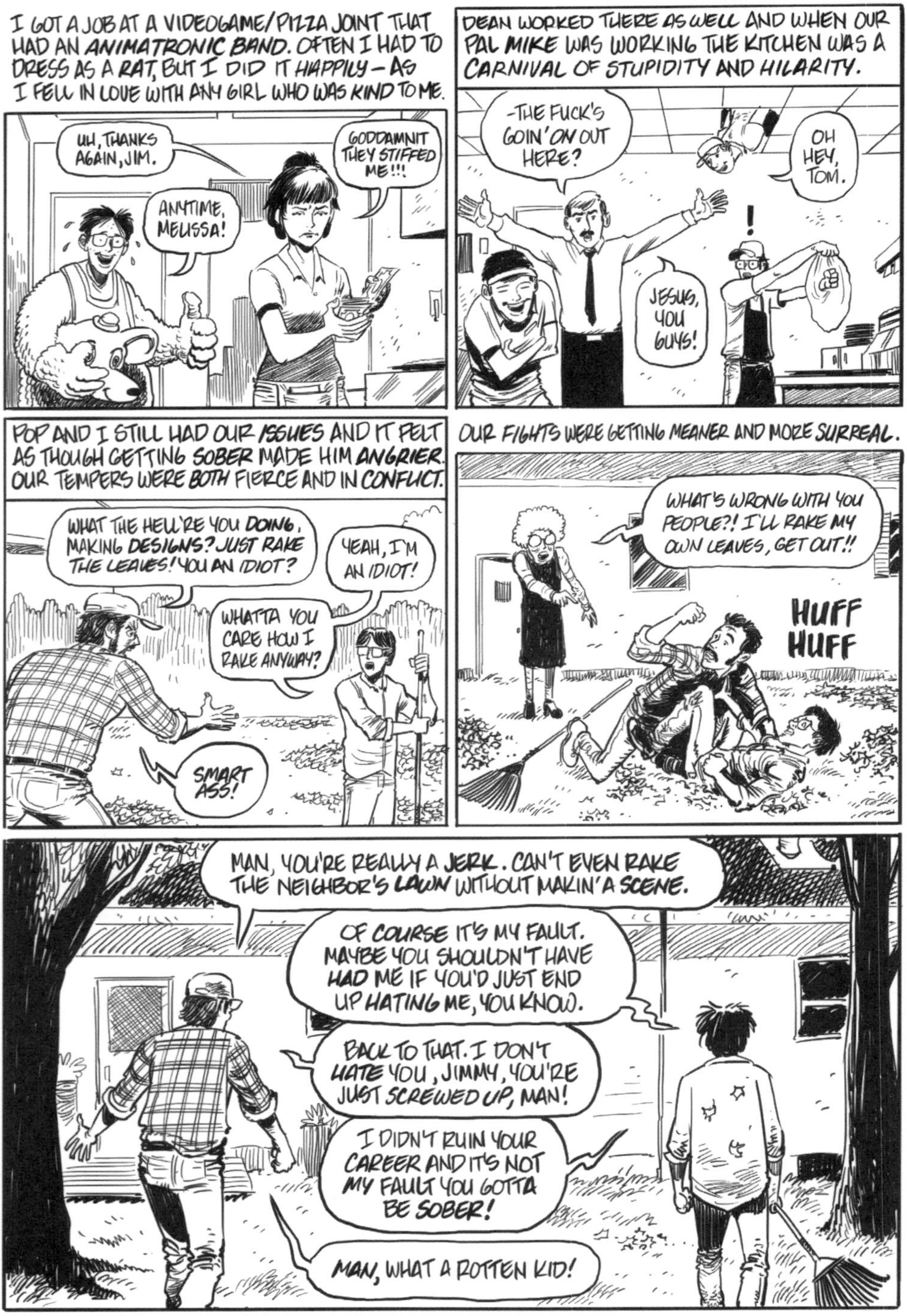
I GOT A JOB AT A VIDEOGAME/PIZZA JOINT THAT HAD AN ANIMATRONIC BAND. OFTEN I HAD TO DRESS AS A RAT, BUT I DID IT HAPPILY — AS I FELL IN LOVE WITH ANY GIRL WHO WAS KIND TO ME.
UH, THANKS AGAIN, JIM.
GODDAMNIT THEY STIFFED ME!!!
ANYTIME, MELISSA!
DEAN WORKED THERE AS WELL AND WHEN OUR PAL MIKE WAS WORKING THE KITCHEN WAS A CARNIVAL OF STUPIDITY AND HILARITY.
-THE FUCK'S GOIN' ON OUT HERE?
OH HEY, TOM.
!
JESUS, YOU GUYS!
POP AND I STILL HAD OUR ISSUES AND IT FELT AS THOUGH GETTING SOBER MADE HIM ANGRIER. OUR TEMPERS WERE BOTH FIERCE AND IN CONFLICT.
WHAT THE HELL'RE YOU DOING, MAKING DESIGNS? JUST RAKE THE LEAVES! YOU AN IDIOT?
YEAH, I'M AN IDIOT!
WHATTA YOU CARE HOW I RAKE ANYWAY?
SMART ASS!
OUR FIGHTS WERE GETTING MEANER AND MORE SURREAL.
WHAT'S WRONG WITH YOU PEOPLE?! I'LL RAKE MY OWN LEAVES, GET OUT!!
HUFF HUFF
MAN, YOU'RE REALLY A JERK. CAN'T EVEN RAKE THE NEIGHBOR'S LAWN WITHOUT MAKIN' A SCENE.
OF COURSE IT'S MY FAULT. MAYBE YOU SHOULDN'T HAVE HAD ME IF YOU'D JUST END UP HATING ME, YOU KNOW.
BACK TO THAT. I DON'T HATE YOU, JIMMY, YOU'RE JUST SCREWED UP, MAN!
I DIDN'T RUIN YOUR CAREER AND IT'S NOT MY FAULT YOU GOTTA BE SOBER!
MAN, WHAT A ROTTEN KID!

WE HAD A BIG **ART** SHOW AT SCHOOL AND POP ACTUALLY SHOWED UP FOR IT. HE WAS TAKEN ASIDE BY MY ART TEACHER "ON THE Q.T."

MR. TERRY... THE THINGS JIM *DRAWS*... I'M... CONCERNED.

YEAH HE'S A *WEIRD* KID, I KNOW.

I GOT AN EARFUL *LATER* BUT IT WASN'T *NEW*.

MAN I HAD TO LISTEN TO THAT **CREEPY** CHICK ASK IF YOU'RE SOME KINDA' *SUICIDE RISK*?

JIMMY... ARE YOU THAT *MESSED UP*?

NO I'M *NOT*, OKAY? *JEEZ* I CAN'T BELIEVE HER - IT WAS JUST A DRAWING OF THE GRIM REAPER!

WHEN POP TALKED TO *MOM* ABOUT IT SHE HAD AN ENTIRELY DIFFERENT *REACTION*.

WAIT, **WHAT?**

WHAT'S THIS **ASSHOLE'S** NAME? *YES* I'M GONNA CALL HER, BILL!

DID YOU *BOTHER* *TALKING* TO MY SON OR DID YOU SIMPLY JUMP TO A *POORLY INFORMED CONCLUSION*? HE HAS A *HEALTHY IMAGINATION* AND LIKES "SCARY THINGS", SO WHAT? TALK TO *HIM* AND HE'LL GO ON *ALL DAY* ABOUT WHO HIS "INFLUENCES" ARE I COULD TELL RIGHT NOW YOU'VE NEVER READ "CONAN", "TALES FROM THE *CRYPT*" OR "EERIE"... ZINE- YES I HAVE... SU...... ON AND OF COL..... U...... READ IT, WHY...... I? FRANKLY I'M... LITTLE DISTU... THAT YOU DID... TALK TO HIM...

I *KNOW* THAT *MENTAL WELL BEING* IS AN IMPORTANT ISSUE AND THAT MY TEACHER'S INTENTIONS WERE *GOOD*... BUT I WASN'T *SUICIDAL*. I *WAS* LONELY. I *KNEW* I WAS A *WEIRDO*. I *KNEW* THAT I WAS STRANGE.

WHAT KIND OF DUMBASS ART TEACHER DOESN'T KNOW WHO *FRANK FRAZETTA* IS?

WHAT MY MOM *DID* THAT DAY WAS TO TELL ME THAT IT WAS *OKAY* TO BE THOSE THINGS.

THANKS, MOM.

LOVE YOU, SON.

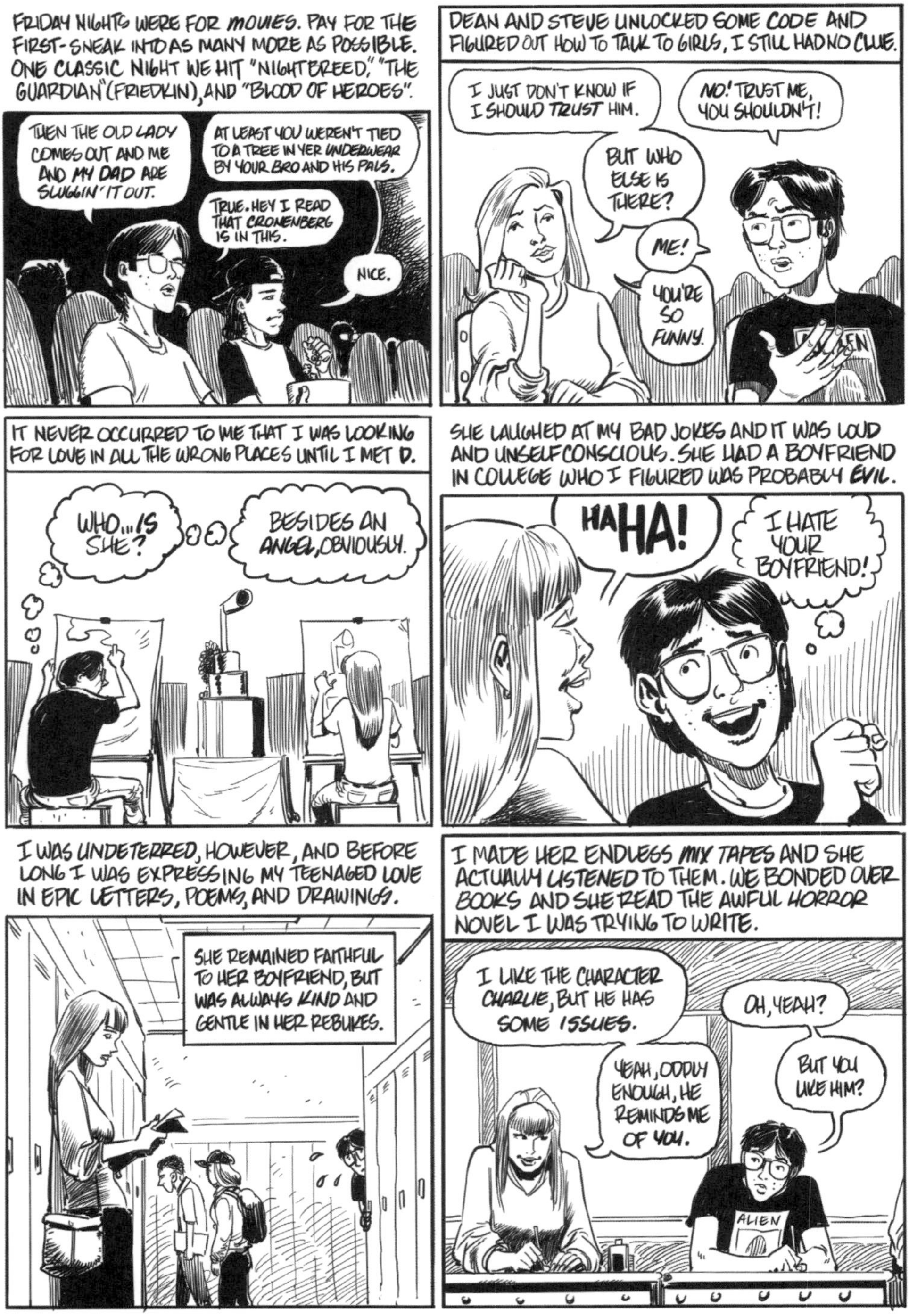
FRIDAY NIGHTS WERE FOR MOVIES. PAY FOR THE FIRST-SNEAK INTO AS MANY MORE AS POSSIBLE. ONE CLASSIC NIGHT WE HIT "NIGHTBREED," "THE GUARDIAN"(FRIEDKIN), AND "BLOOD OF HEROES".
THEN THE OLD LADY COMES OUT AND ME AND MY DAD ARE SLUGGIN' IT OUT.
AT LEAST YOU WEREN'T TIED TO A TREE IN YER UNDERWEAR BY YOUR BRO AND HIS PALS.
TRUE. HEY I READ THAT CRONENBERG IS IN THIS.
NICE.
DEAN AND STEVE UNLOCKED SOME CODE AND FIGURED OUT HOW TO TALK TO GIRLS, I STILL HAD NO CLUE.
I JUST DON'T KNOW IF I SHOULD TRUST HIM.
NO! TRUST ME, YOU SHOULDN'T!
BUT WHO ELSE IS THERE?
ME!
YOU'RE SO FUNNY.
IT NEVER OCCURRED TO ME THAT I WAS LOOKING FOR LOVE IN ALL THE WRONG PLACES UNTIL I MET D.
WHO...IS SHE?
BESIDES AN ANGEL, OBVIOUSLY.
SHE LAUGHED AT MY BAD JOKES AND IT WAS LOUD AND UNSELFCONSCIOUS. SHE HAD A BOYFRIEND IN COLLEGE WHO I FIGURED WAS PROBABLY EVIL.
HA HA!
I HATE YOUR BOYFRIEND!
I WAS UNDETERRED, HOWEVER, AND BEFORE LONG I WAS EXPRESSING MY TEENAGED LOVE IN EPIC LETTERS, POEMS, AND DRAWINGS.
SHE REMAINED FAITHFUL TO HER BOYFRIEND, BUT WAS ALWAYS KIND AND GENTLE IN HER REBUKES.
I MADE HER ENDLESS MIX TAPES AND SHE ACTUALLY LISTENED TO THEM. WE BONDED OVER BOOKS AND SHE READ THE AWFUL HORROR NOVEL I WAS TRYING TO WRITE.
I LIKE THE CHARACTER CHARLIE, BUT HE HAS SOME ISSUES.
OH, YEAH?
YEAH, ODDLY ENOUGH, HE REMINDS ME OF YOU.
BUT YOU LIKE HIM?
ALIEN

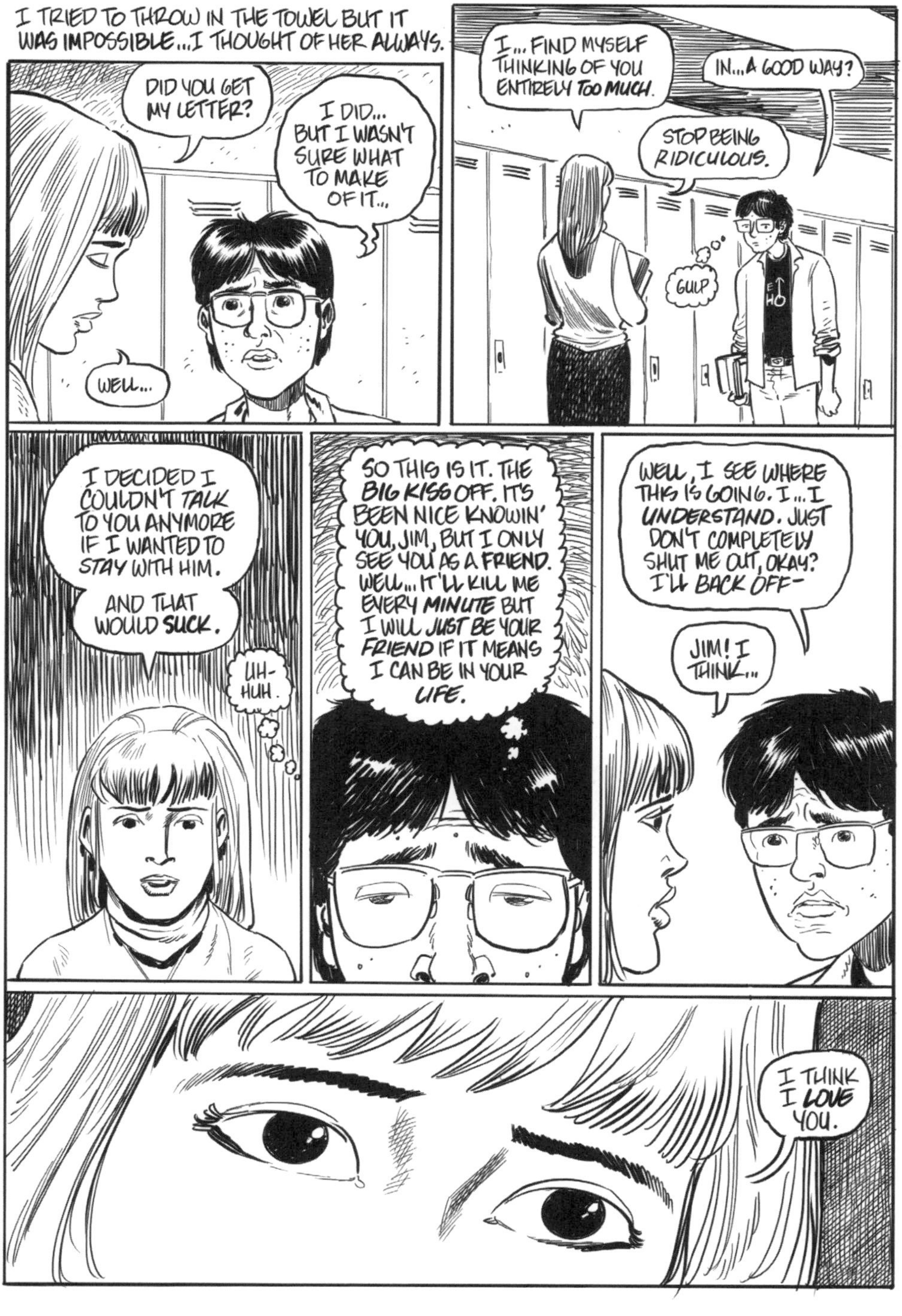
I TRIED TO THROW IN THE TOWEL BUT IT WAS IMPOSSIBLE...I THOUGHT OF HER ALWAYS.
DID YOU GET MY LETTER?
I DID... BUT I WASN'T SURE WHAT TO MAKE OF IT...
WELL...
I... FIND MYSELF THINKING OF YOU ENTIRELY TOO MUCH.
IN... A GOOD WAY?
STOP BEING RIDICULOUS.
GULP
I DECIDED I COULDN'T TALK TO YOU ANYMORE IF I WANTED TO STAY WITH HIM.
AND THAT WOULD SUCK.
UH-HUH.
SO THIS IS IT. THE BIG KISS OFF. IT'S BEEN NICE KNOWIN' YOU, JIM, BUT I ONLY SEE YOU AS A FRIEND. WELL... IT'LL KILL ME EVERY MINUTE BUT I WILL JUST BE YOUR FRIEND IF IT MEANS I CAN BE IN YOUR LIFE.
WELL, I SEE WHERE THIS IS GOING. I... I UNDERSTAND. JUST DON'T COMPLETELY SHUT ME OUT, OKAY? I'LL BACK OFF-
JIM! I THINK...
I THINK I LOVE YOU.

LOVE.

SHE SAID SHE **LOVED** ME. SHE ACTUALLY EXHALED AND WHILE DOING SO MOVED HER LIPS AND TONGUE SO THEY WOULD FORM THOSE *IMPOSSIBLE*, *MAGIC* WORDS.

I HAD BEEN SO IN LOVE WITH EVERYTHING ABOUT HER FOR SO ***LONG*** IT ***COULDN'T*** HAVE BEEN REAL. SHE WAS ***SMART***. ***FUNNY***. BEAUTIFUL. SHE WAS A ***GOOD PERSON***.

AND SHE **LOVED** ME.

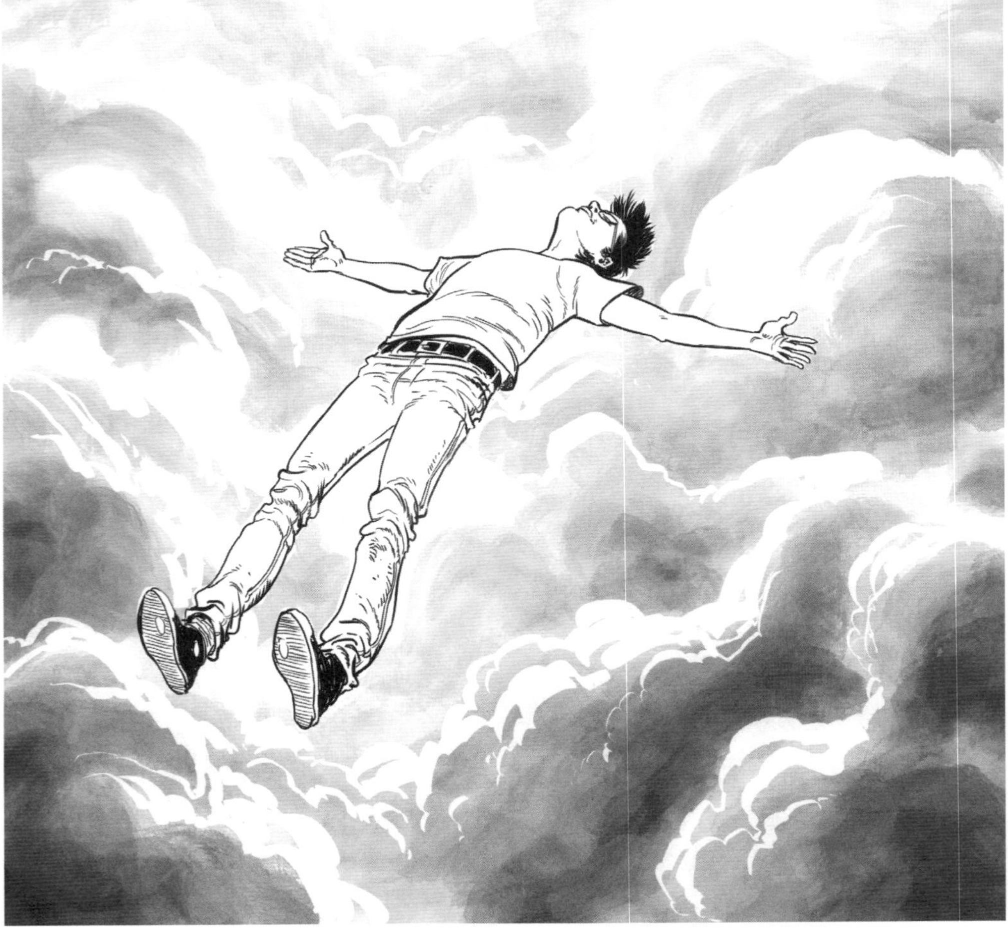

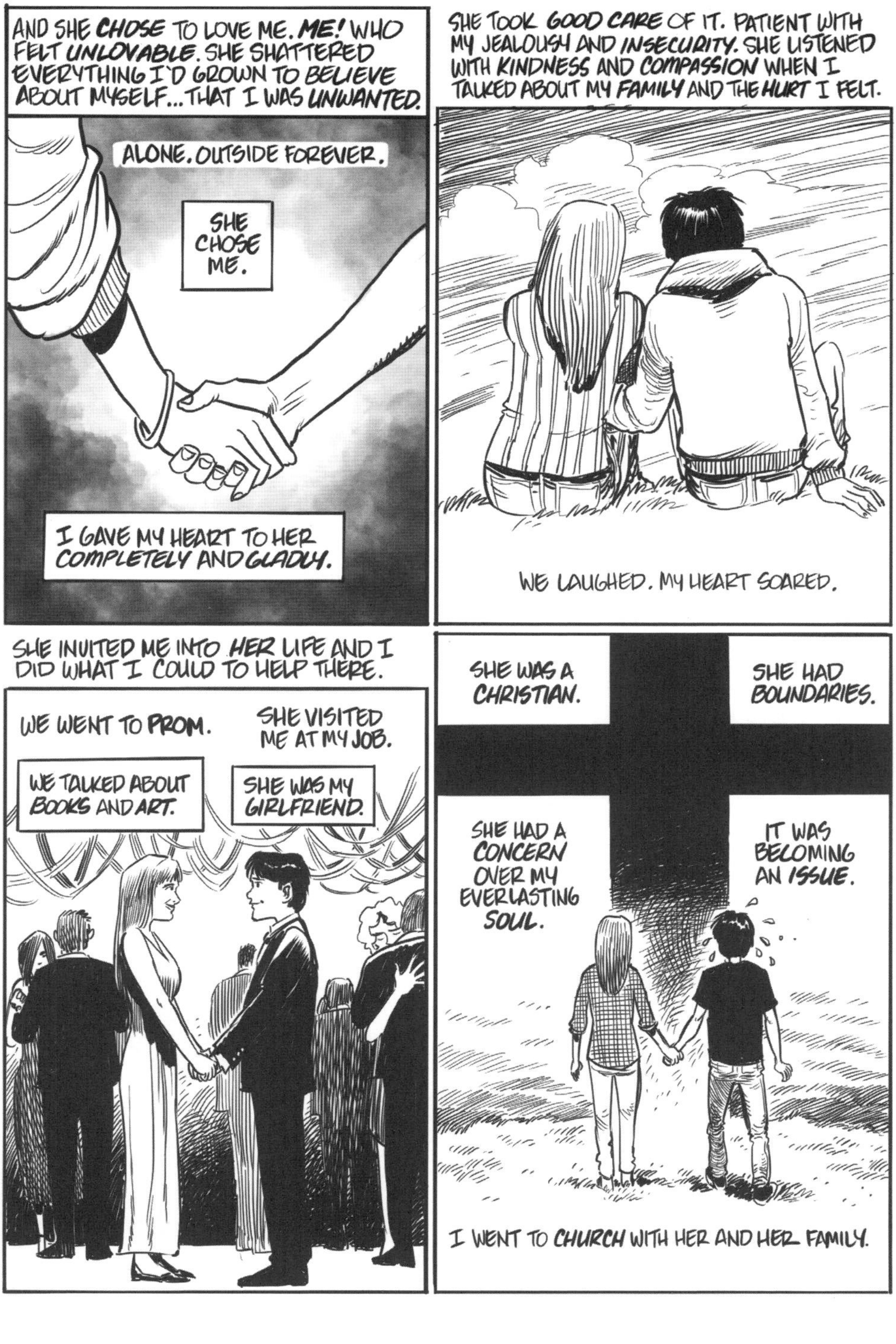
AND SHE CHOSE TO LOVE ME. ME! WHO FELT UNLOVABLE. SHE SHATTERED EVERYTHING I'D GROWN TO BELIEVE ABOUT MYSELF... THAT I WAS UNWANTED.
ALONE. OUTSIDE FOREVER.
SHE CHOSE ME.
I GAVE MY HEART TO HER COMPLETELY AND GLADLY.
SHE TOOK GOOD CARE OF IT. PATIENT WITH MY JEALOUSY AND INSECURITY. SHE LISTENED WITH KINDNESS AND COMPASSION WHEN I TALKED ABOUT MY FAMILY AND THE HURT I FELT.
WE LAUGHED. MY HEART SOARED.
SHE INVITED ME INTO HER LIFE AND I DID WHAT I COULD TO HELP THERE.
WE WENT TO PROM.
SHE VISITED ME AT MY JOB.
WE TALKED ABOUT BOOKS AND ART.
SHE WAS MY GIRLFRIEND.
SHE WAS A CHRISTIAN.
SHE HAD BOUNDARIES.
SHE HAD A CONCERN OVER MY EVERLASTING SOUL.
IT WAS BECOMING AN ISSUE.
I WENT TO CHURCH WITH HER AND HER FAMILY.

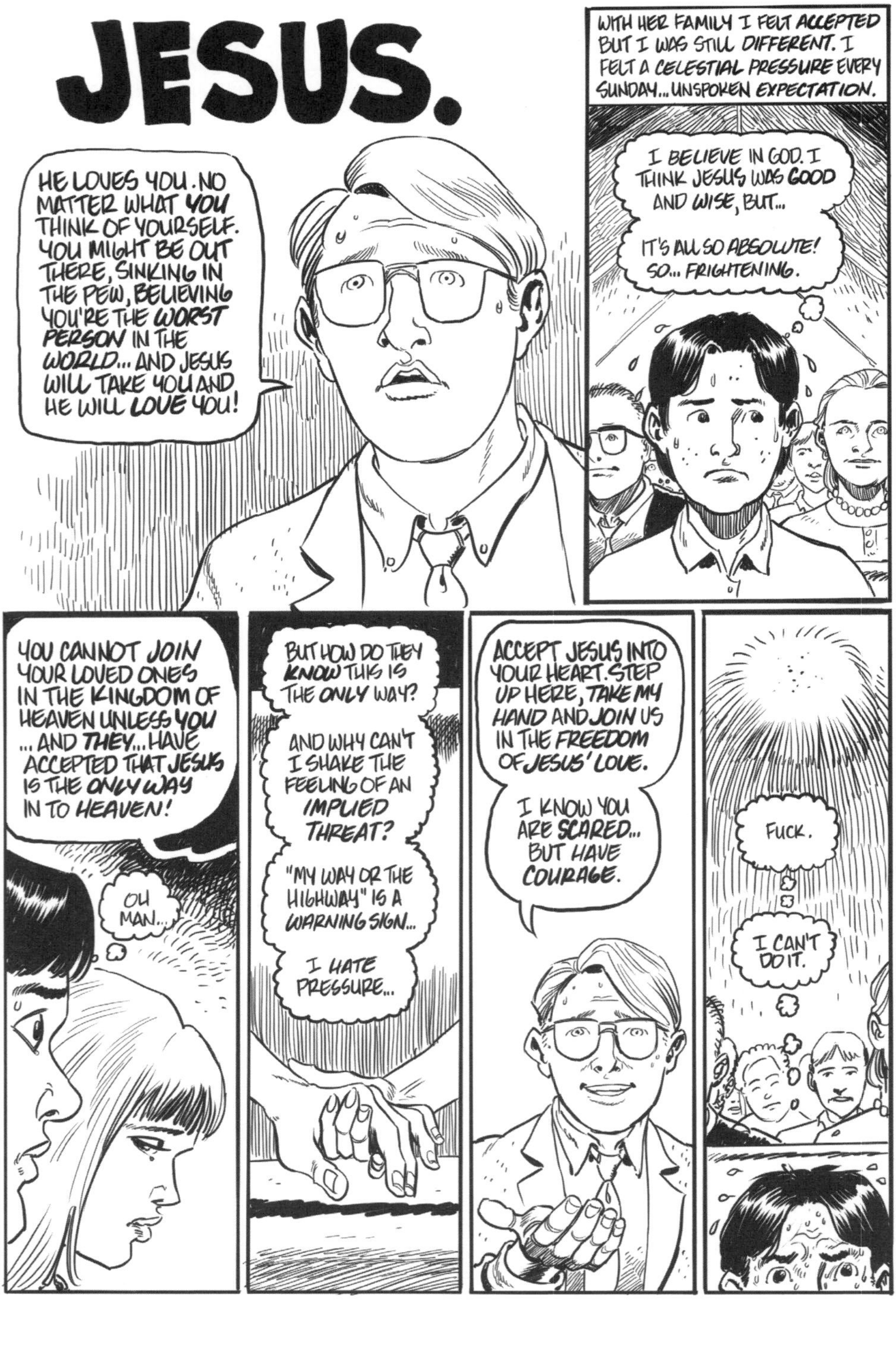
JESUS.
HE LOVES YOU. NO MATTER WHAT YOU THINK OF YOURSELF. YOU MIGHT BE OUT THERE, SINKING IN THE PEW, BELIEVING YOU'RE THE WORST PERSON IN THE WORLD... AND JESUS WILL TAKE YOU AND HE WILL LOVE YOU!
WITH HER FAMILY I FELT ACCEPTED BUT I WAS STILL DIFFERENT. I FELT A CELESTIAL PRESSURE EVERY SUNDAY... UNSPOKEN EXPECTATION.
I BELIEVE IN GOD. I THINK JESUS WAS GOOD AND WISE, BUT...
IT'S ALL SO ABSOLUTE! SO... FRIGHTENING.
YOU CANNOT JOIN YOUR LOVED ONES IN THE KINGDOM OF HEAVEN UNLESS YOU ... AND THEY... HAVE ACCEPTED THAT JESUS IS THE ONLY WAY IN TO HEAVEN!
OH MAN...
BUT HOW DO THEY KNOW THIS IS THE ONLY WAY?
AND WHY CAN'T I SHAKE THE FEELING OF AN IMPLIED THREAT?
"MY WAY OR THE HIGHWAY" IS A WARNING SIGN...
I HATE PRESSURE...
ACCEPT JESUS INTO YOUR HEART. STEP UP HERE, TAKE MY HAND AND JOIN US IN THE FREEDOM OF JESUS' LOVE.
I KNOW YOU ARE SCARED... BUT HAVE COURAGE.
FUCK.
I CAN'T DO IT.

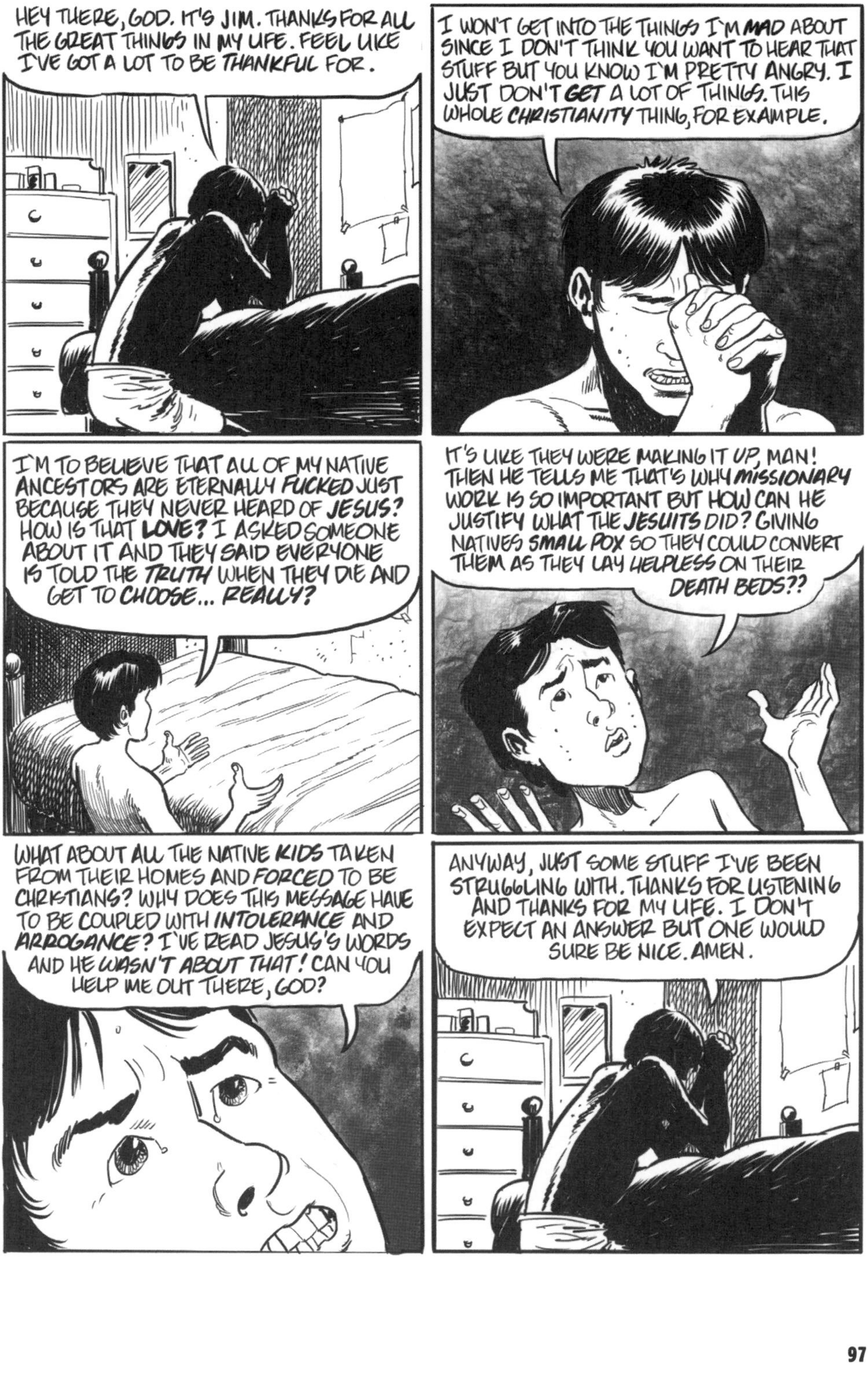
HEY THERE, GOD. IT'S JIM. THANKS FOR ALL THE GREAT THINGS IN MY LIFE. FEEL LIKE I'VE GOT A LOT TO BE THANKFUL FOR.
I WON'T GET INTO THE THINGS I'M MAD ABOUT SINCE I DON'T THINK YOU WANT TO HEAR THAT STUFF BUT YOU KNOW I'M PRETTY ANGRY. I JUST DON'T GET A LOT OF THINGS. THIS WHOLE CHRISTIANITY THING, FOR EXAMPLE.
I'M TO BELIEVE THAT ALL OF MY NATIVE ANCESTORS ARE ETERNALLY FUCKED JUST BECAUSE THEY NEVER HEARD OF JESUS? HOW IS THAT LOVE? I ASKED SOMEONE ABOUT IT AND THEY SAID EVERYONE IS TOLD THE TRUTH WHEN THEY DIE AND GET TO CHOOSE... REALLY?
IT'S LIKE THEY WERE MAKING IT UP, MAN! THEN HE TELLS ME THAT'S WHY MISSIONARY WORK IS SO IMPORTANT BUT HOW CAN HE JUSTIFY WHAT THE JESUITS DID? GIVING NATIVES SMALL POX SO THEY COULD CONVERT THEM AS THEY LAY HELPLESS ON THEIR DEATH BEDS??
WHAT ABOUT ALL THE NATIVE KIDS TAKEN FROM THEIR HOMES AND FORCED TO BE CHRISTIANS? WHY DOES THIS MESSAGE HAVE TO BE COUPLED WITH INTOLERANCE AND ARROGANCE? I'VE READ JESUS'S WORDS AND HE WASN'T ABOUT THAT! CAN YOU HELP ME OUT THERE, GOD?
ANYWAY, JUST SOME STUFF I'VE BEEN STRUGGLING WITH. THANKS FOR LISTENING AND THANKS FOR MY LIFE. I DON'T EXPECT AN ANSWER BUT ONE WOULD SURE BE NICE. AMEN.

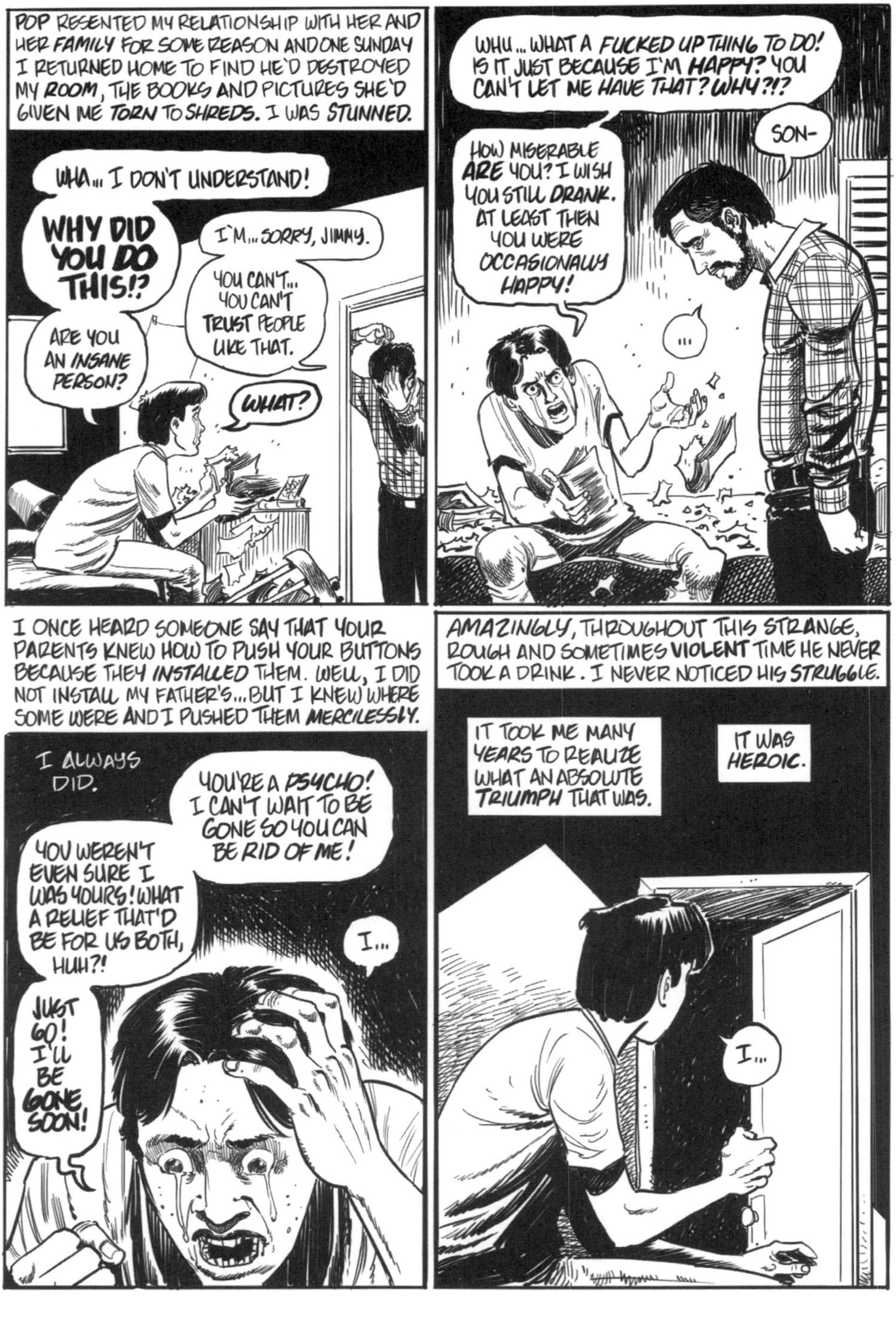
POP RESENTED MY RELATIONSHIP WITH HER AND HER FAMILY FOR SOME REASON AND ONE SUNDAY I RETURNED HOME TO FIND HE'D DESTROYED MY ROOM, THE BOOKS AND PICTURES SHE'D GIVEN ME TORN TO SHREDS. I WAS STUNNED.
WHA... I DON'T UNDERSTAND!
WHY DID YOU DO THIS!?
I'M... SORRY, JIMMY.
YOU CAN'T... YOU CAN'T TRUST PEOPLE LIKE THAT.
ARE YOU AN INSANE PERSON?
WHAT?
WHU... WHAT A FUCKED UP THING TO DO! IS IT JUST BECAUSE I'M HAPPY? YOU CAN'T LET ME HAVE THAT? WHY?!?
SON-
HOW MISERABLE ARE YOU? I WISH YOU STILL DRANK. AT LEAST THEN YOU WERE OCCASIONALLY HAPPY!
...
I ONCE HEARD SOMEONE SAY THAT YOUR PARENTS KNEW HOW TO PUSH YOUR BUTTONS BECAUSE THEY INSTALLED THEM. WELL, I DID NOT INSTALL MY FATHER'S... BUT I KNEW WHERE SOME WERE AND I PUSHED THEM MERCILESSLY.
I ALWAYS DID.
YOU'RE A PSYCHO! I CAN'T WAIT TO BE GONE SO YOU CAN BE RID OF ME!
YOU WEREN'T EVEN SURE I WAS YOURS! WHAT A RELIEF THAT'D BE FOR US BOTH, HUH?!
I...
JUST GO! I'LL BE GONE SOON!
AMAZINGLY, THROUGHOUT THIS STRANGE, ROUGH AND SOMETIMES VIOLENT TIME HE NEVER TOOK A DRINK. I NEVER NOTICED HIS STRUGGLE.
IT TOOK ME MANY YEARS TO REALIZE WHAT AN ABSOLUTE TRIUMPH THAT WAS.
IT WAS HEROIC.
I...

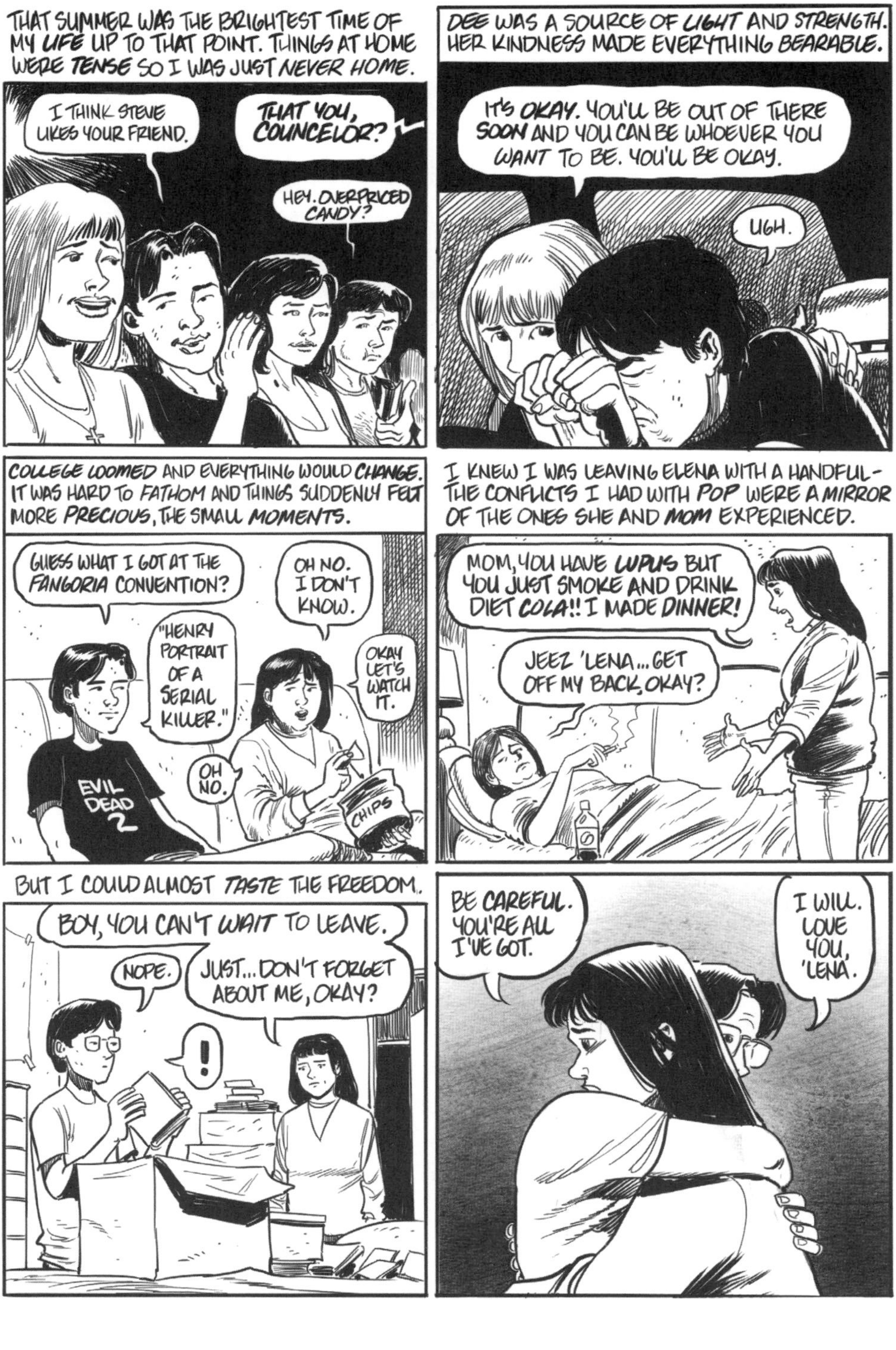
THAT SUMMER WAS THE BRIGHTEST TIME OF MY LIFE UP TO THAT POINT. THINGS AT HOME WERE TENSE SO I WAS JUST NEVER HOME.
I THINK STEVE LIKES YOUR FRIEND.
THAT YOU, COUNCELOR?
HEY. OVERPRICED CANDY?
DEE WAS A SOURCE OF LIGHT AND STRENGTH. HER KINDNESS MADE EVERYTHING BEARABLE.
IT'S OKAY. YOU'LL BE OUT OF THERE SOON AND YOU CAN BE WHOEVER YOU WANT TO BE. YOU'LL BE OKAY.
UGH.
COLLEGE LOOMED AND EVERYTHING WOULD CHANGE. IT WAS HARD TO FATHOM AND THINGS SUDDENLY FELT MORE PRECIOUS, THE SMALL MOMENTS.
GUESS WHAT I GOT AT THE FANGORIA CONVENTION?
OH NO. I DON'T KNOW.
"HENRY PORTRAIT OF A SERIAL KILLER."
OKAY LET'S WATCH IT.
OH NO.
EVIL DEAD 2
CHIPS
I KNEW I WAS LEAVING ELENA WITH A HANDFUL- THE CONFLICTS I HAD WITH POP WERE A MIRROR OF THE ONES SHE AND MOM EXPERIENCED.
MOM, YOU HAVE LUPUS BUT YOU JUST SMOKE AND DRINK DIET COLA!! I MADE DINNER!
JEEZ 'LENA... GET OFF MY BACK, OKAY?
BUT I COULD ALMOST TASTE THE FREEDOM.
BOY, YOU CAN'T WAIT TO LEAVE.
NOPE.
JUST... DON'T FORGET ABOUT ME, OKAY?
!
BE CAREFUL. YOU'RE ALL I'VE GOT.
I WILL. LOVE YOU, 'LENA.

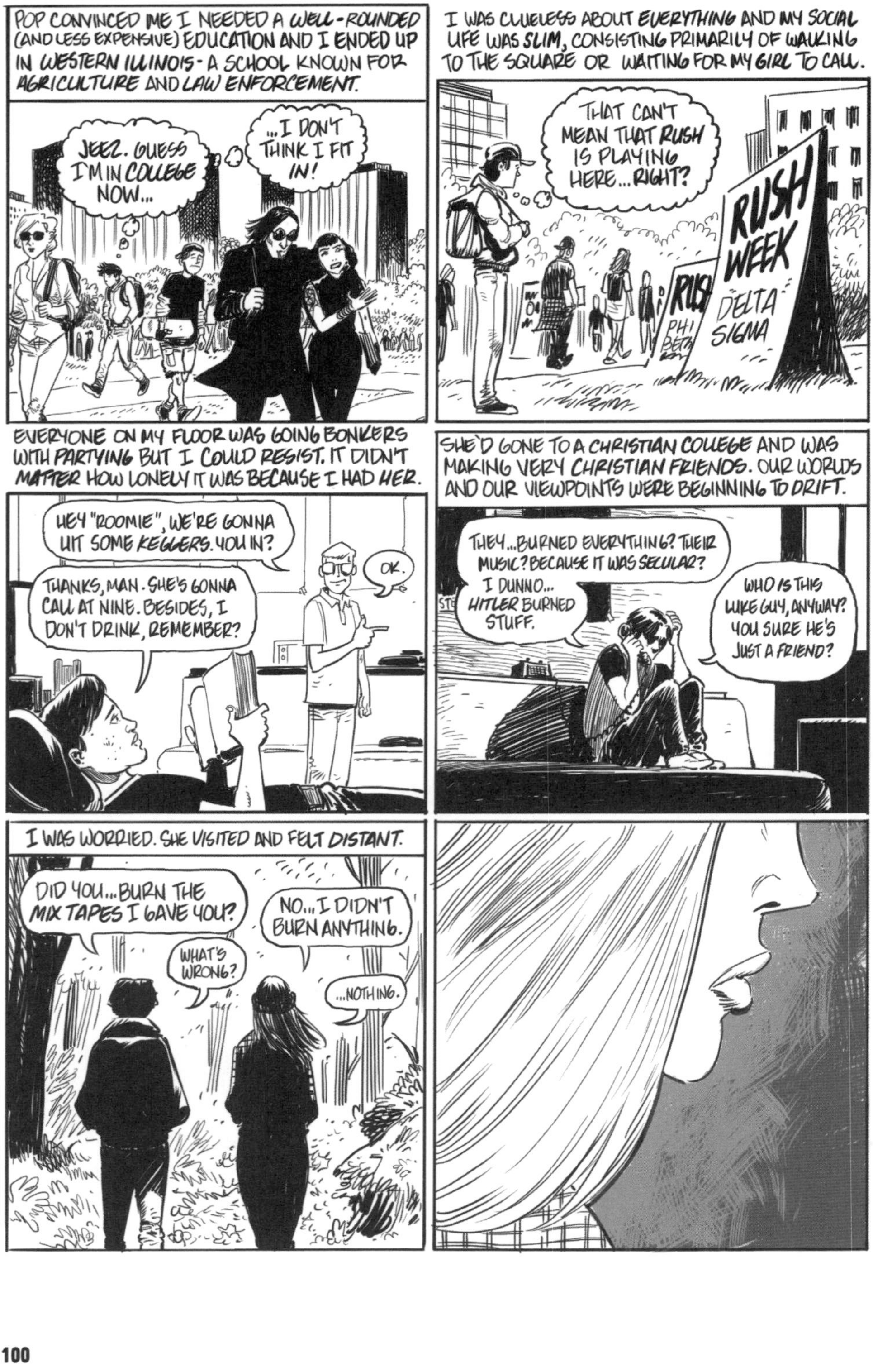
POP CONVINCED ME I NEEDED A WELL-ROUNDED (AND LESS EXPENSIVE) EDUCATION AND I ENDED UP IN WESTERN ILLINOIS - A SCHOOL KNOWN FOR AGRICULTURE AND LAW ENFORCEMENT.
JEEZ. GUESS I'M IN COLLEGE NOW...
...I DON'T THINK I FIT IN!
I WAS CLUELESS ABOUT EVERYTHING AND MY SOCIAL LIFE WAS SLIM, CONSISTING PRIMARILY OF WALKING TO THE SQUARE OR WAITING FOR MY GIRL TO CALL.
THAT CAN'T MEAN THAT RUSH IS PLAYING HERE... RIGHT?
RUSH WEEK
DELTA SIGMA
RUSH
PHI BETA
EVERYONE ON MY FLOOR WAS GOING BONKERS WITH PARTYING BUT I COULD RESIST. IT DIDN'T MATTER HOW LONELY IT WAS BECAUSE I HAD HER.
HEY "ROOMIE", WE'RE GONNA HIT SOME KEGGERS. YOU IN?
THANKS, MAN. SHE'S GONNA CALL AT NINE. BESIDES, I DON'T DRINK, REMEMBER?
OK.
SHE'D GONE TO A CHRISTIAN COLLEGE AND WAS MAKING VERY CHRISTIAN FRIENDS. OUR WORLDS AND OUR VIEWPOINTS WERE BEGINNING TO DRIFT.
THEY... BURNED EVERYTHING? THEIR MUSIC? BECAUSE IT WAS SECULAR?
I DUNNO... HITLER BURNED STUFF.
WHO IS THIS MIKE GUY, ANYWAY? YOU SURE HE'S JUST A FRIEND?
I WAS WORRIED. SHE VISITED AND FELT DISTANT.
DID YOU... BURN THE MIX TAPES I GAVE YOU?
NO... I DIDN'T BURN ANYTHING.
WHAT'S WRONG?
...NOTHING.

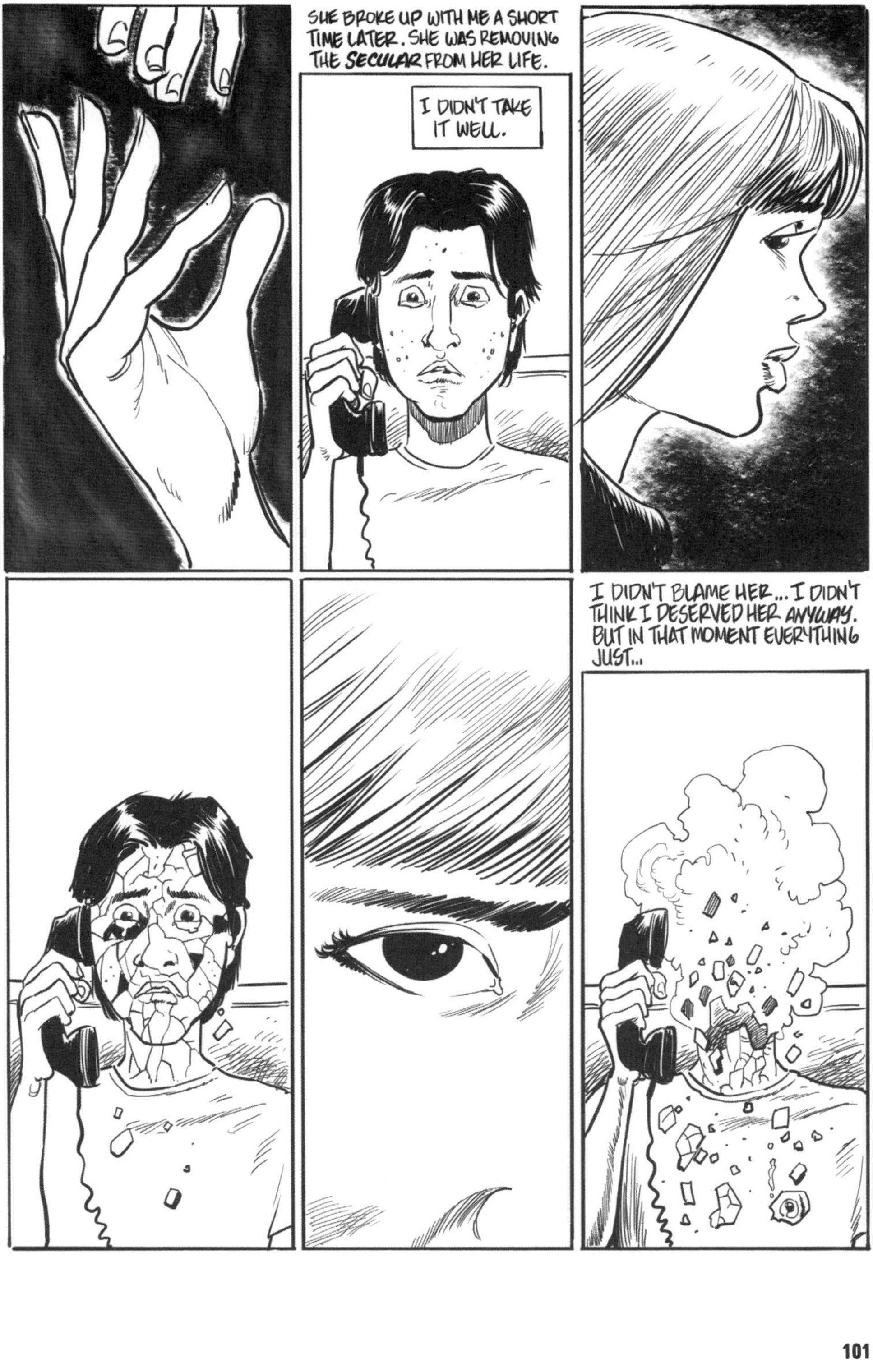
SHE BROKE UP WITH ME A SHORT TIME LATER. SHE WAS REMOVING THE SECULAR FROM HER LIFE.
I DIDN'T TAKE IT WELL.
I DIDN'T BLAME HER... I DIDN'T THINK I DESERVED HER ANYWAY. BUT IN THAT MOMENT EVERYTHING JUST...

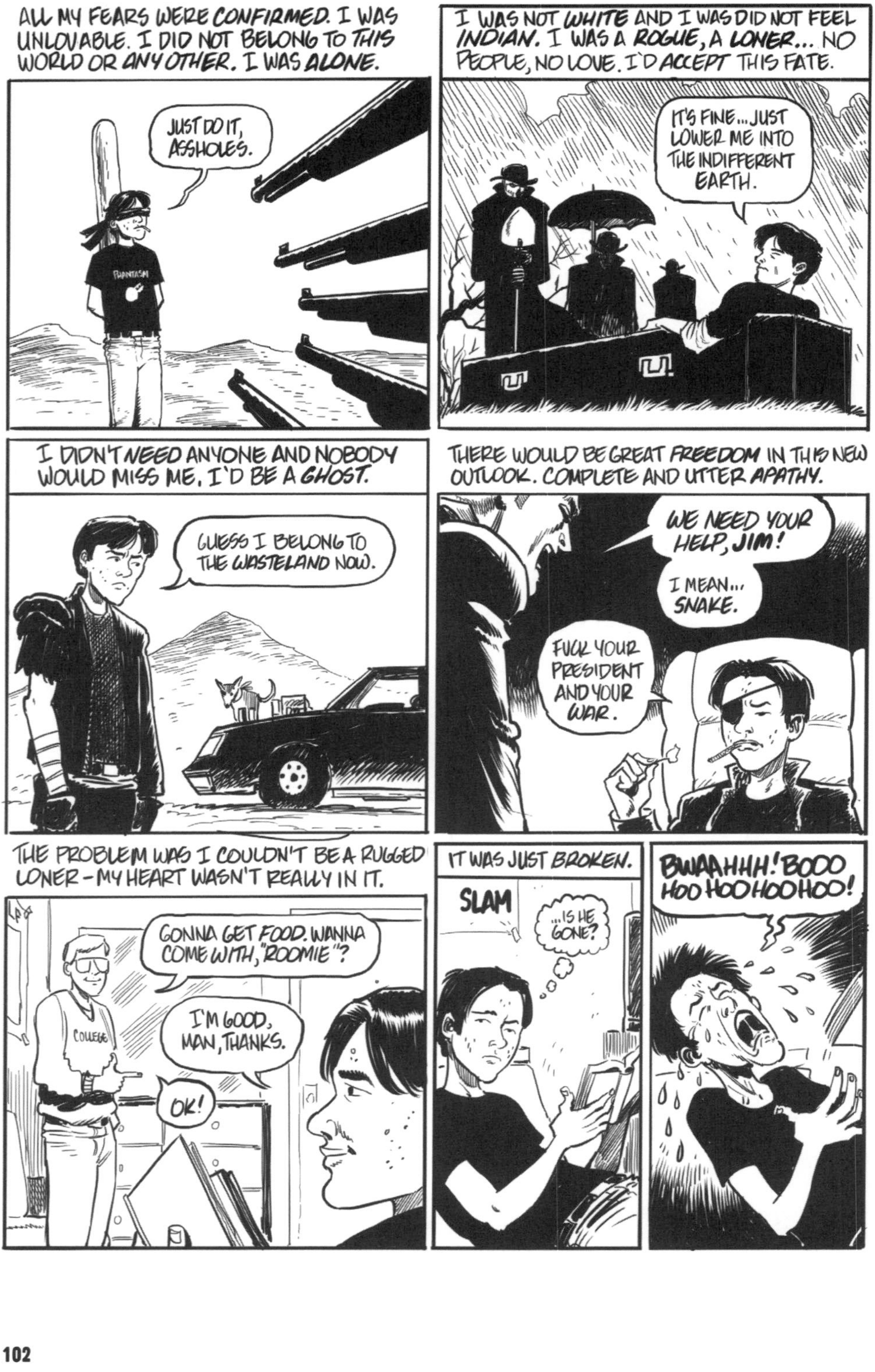
ALL MY FEARS WERE CONFIRMED. I WAS UNLOVABLE. I DID NOT BELONG TO THIS WORLD OR ANY OTHER. I WAS ALONE.
JUST DO IT, ASSHOLES.
PHANTASM
I WAS NOT WHITE AND I WAS DID NOT FEEL INDIAN. I WAS A ROGUE, A LONER... NO PEOPLE, NO LOVE. I'D ACCEPT THIS FATE.
IT'S FINE... JUST LOWER ME INTO THE INDIFFERENT EARTH.
I DIDN'T NEED ANYONE AND NOBODY WOULD MISS ME. I'D BE A GHOST.
GUESS I BELONG TO THE WASTELAND NOW.
THERE WOULD BE GREAT FREEDOM IN THIS NEW OUTLOOK. COMPLETE AND UTTER APATHY.
WE NEED YOUR HELP, JIM!
I MEAN... SNAKE.
FUCK YOUR PRESIDENT AND YOUR WAR.
THE PROBLEM WAS I COULDN'T BE A RUGGED LONER - MY HEART WASN'T REALLY IN IT.
GONNA GET FOOD. WANNA COME WITH, "ROOMIE"?
COLLEGE
I'M GOOD, MAN, THANKS.
OK!
IT WAS JUST BROKEN.
SLAM
...IS HE GONE?
BWAAHHH! BOOO HOO HOO HOO HOO!

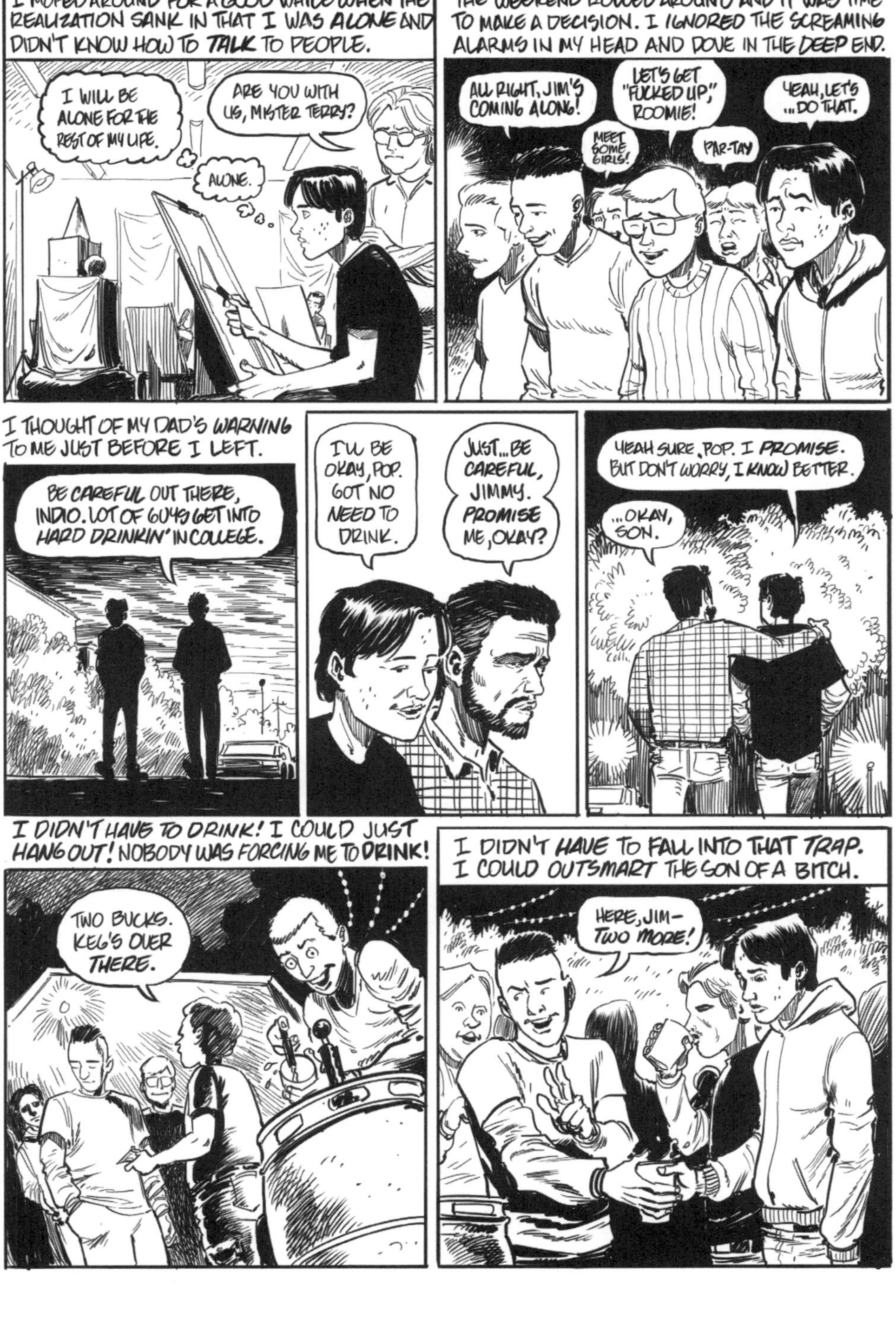
I MOPED AROUND FOR A GOOD WHILE WHEN THE REALIZATION SANK IN THAT I WAS ALONE AND DIDN'T KNOW HOW TO TALK TO PEOPLE.
I WILL BE ALONE FOR THE REST OF MY LIFE.
ARE YOU WITH US, MISTER TERRY?
ALONE.
THE WEEKEND ROLLED AROUND AND IT WAS TIME TO MAKE A DECISION. I IGNORED THE SCREAMING ALARMS IN MY HEAD AND DOVE IN THE DEEP END.
ALL RIGHT, JIM'S COMING ALONG!
MEET SOME GIRLS!
LET'S GET "FUCKED UP," ROOMIE!
PAR-TAY
YEAH, LET'S ...DO THAT.
I THOUGHT OF MY DAD'S WARNING TO ME JUST BEFORE I LEFT.
BE CAREFUL OUT THERE, INDIO. LOT OF GUYS GET INTO HARD DRINKIN' IN COLLEGE.
I'LL BE OKAY, POP. GOT NO NEED TO DRINK.
JUST... BE CAREFUL, JIMMY. PROMISE ME, OKAY?
YEAH SURE, POP. I PROMISE. BUT DON'T WORRY, I KNOW BETTER.
...OKAY, SON.
I DIDN'T HAVE TO DRINK! I COULD JUST HANG OUT! NOBODY WAS FORCING ME TO DRINK!
TWO BUCKS. KEG'S OVER THERE.
I DIDN'T HAVE TO FALL INTO THAT TRAP. I COULD OUTSMART THE SON OF A BITCH.
HERE, JIM- TWO MORE!

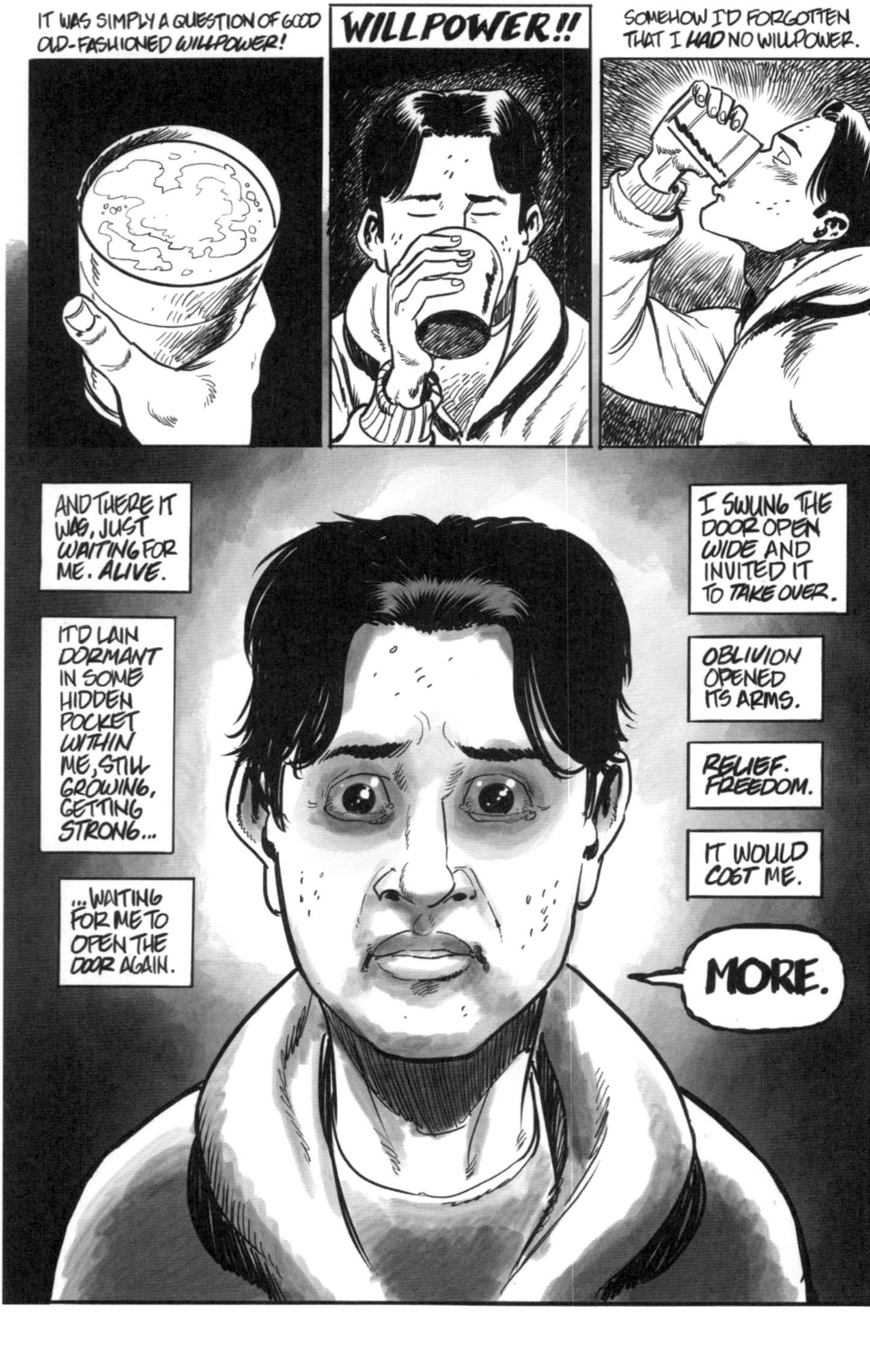
IT WAS SIMPLY A QUESTION OF GOOD OLD-FASHIONED *WILLPOWER*!
WILLPOWER!!
SOMEHOW I'D FORGOTTEN THAT I *HAD* NO WILLPOWER.
AND THERE IT WAS, JUST *WAITING* FOR ME. *ALIVE*.
IT'D LAIN *DORMANT* IN SOME HIDDEN POCKET *WITHIN* ME, STILL *GROWING*, GETTING STRONG...
...WAITING FOR ME TO OPEN THE *DOOR* AGAIN.
I SWUNG THE DOOR OPEN *WIDE* AND INVITED IT TO *TAKE OVER*.
OBLIVION OPENED ITS ARMS.
RELIEF. FREEDOM.
IT WOULD *COST* ME.
MORE.

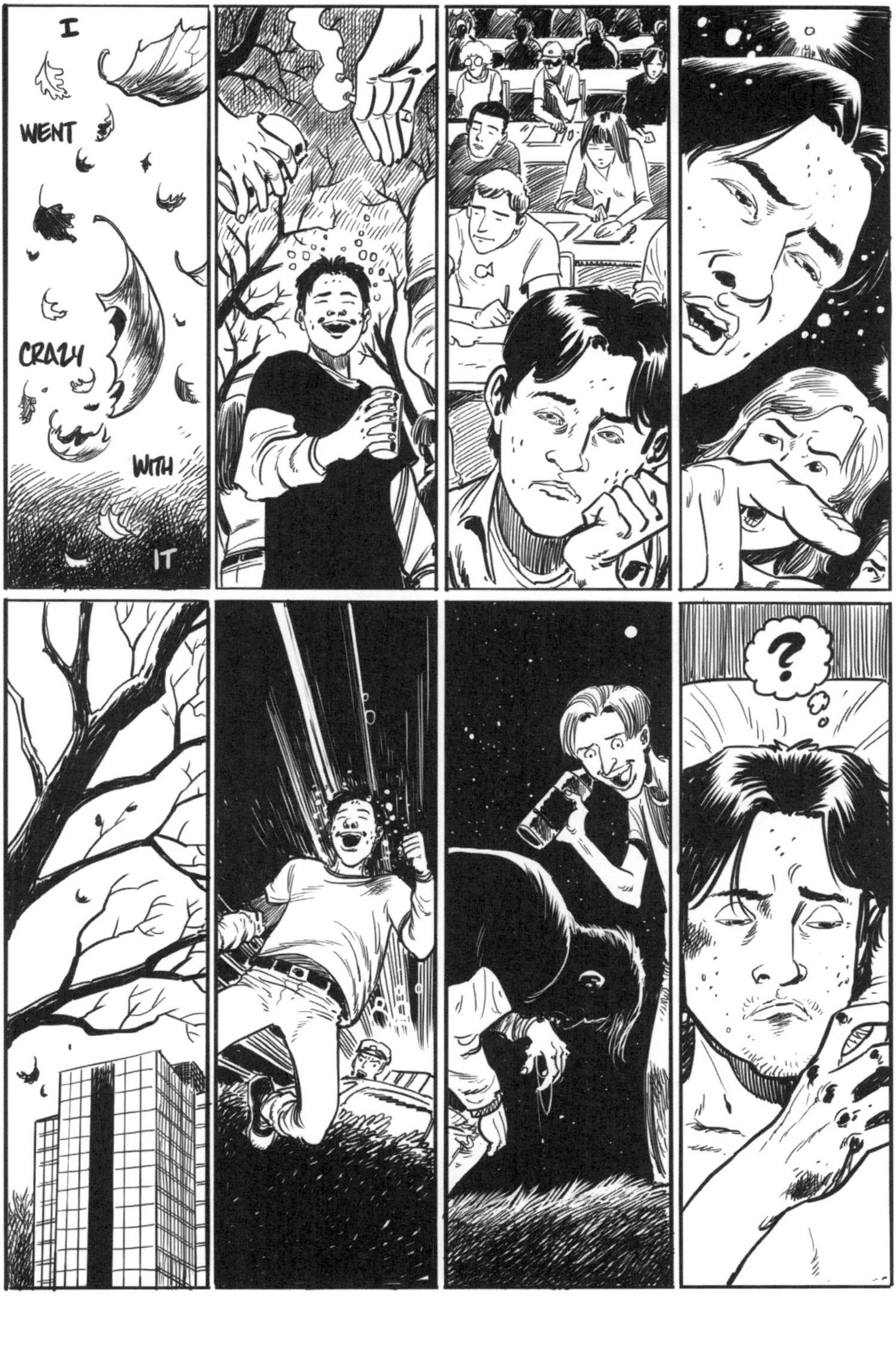
I
WENT
CRAZY
WITH
IT
?

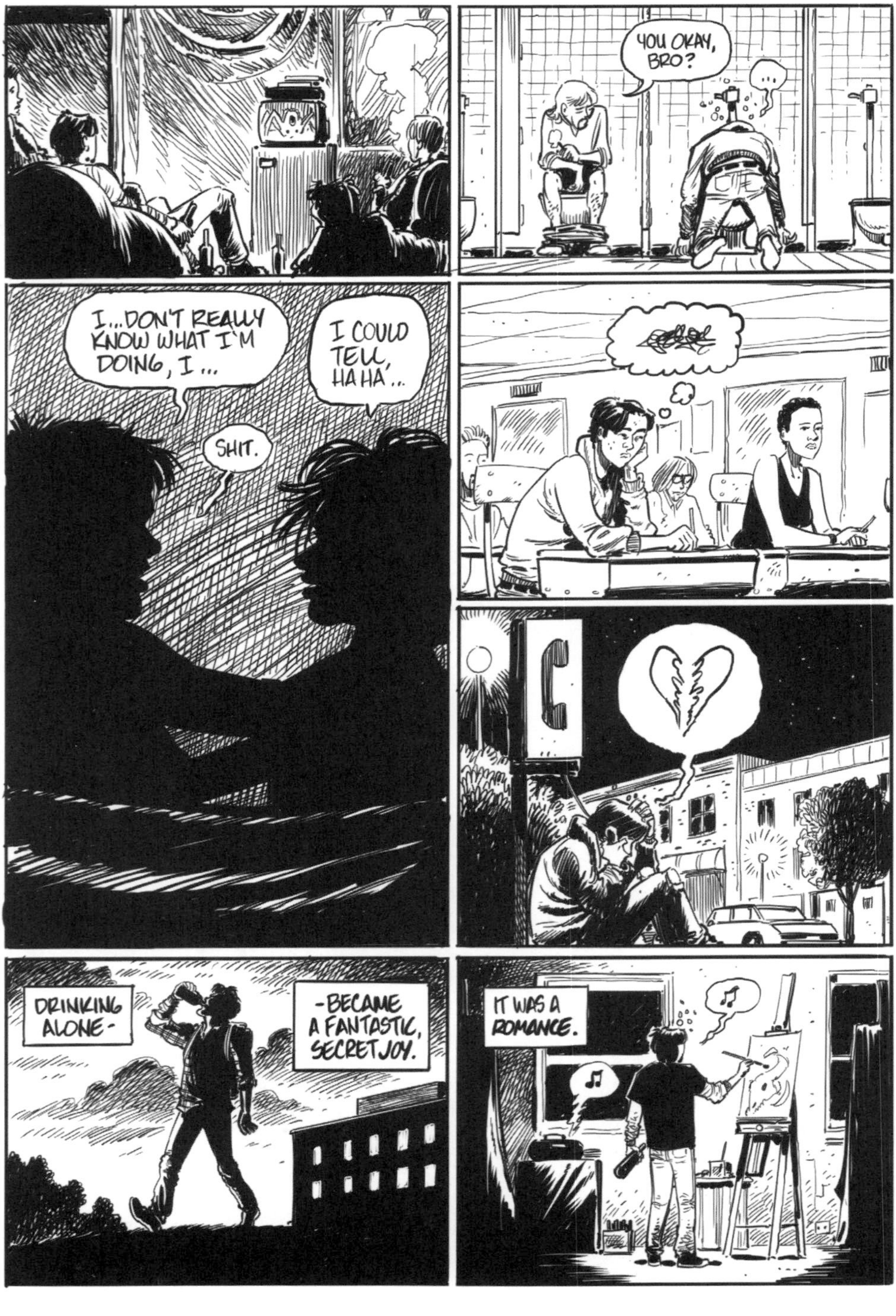
YOU OKAY, BRO?
...
I...DON'T REALLY KNOW WHAT I'M DOING, I...
SHIT.
I COULD TELL, HA HA...
DRINKING ALONE-
-BECAME A FANTASTIC, SECRET JOY.
IT WAS A ROMANCE.

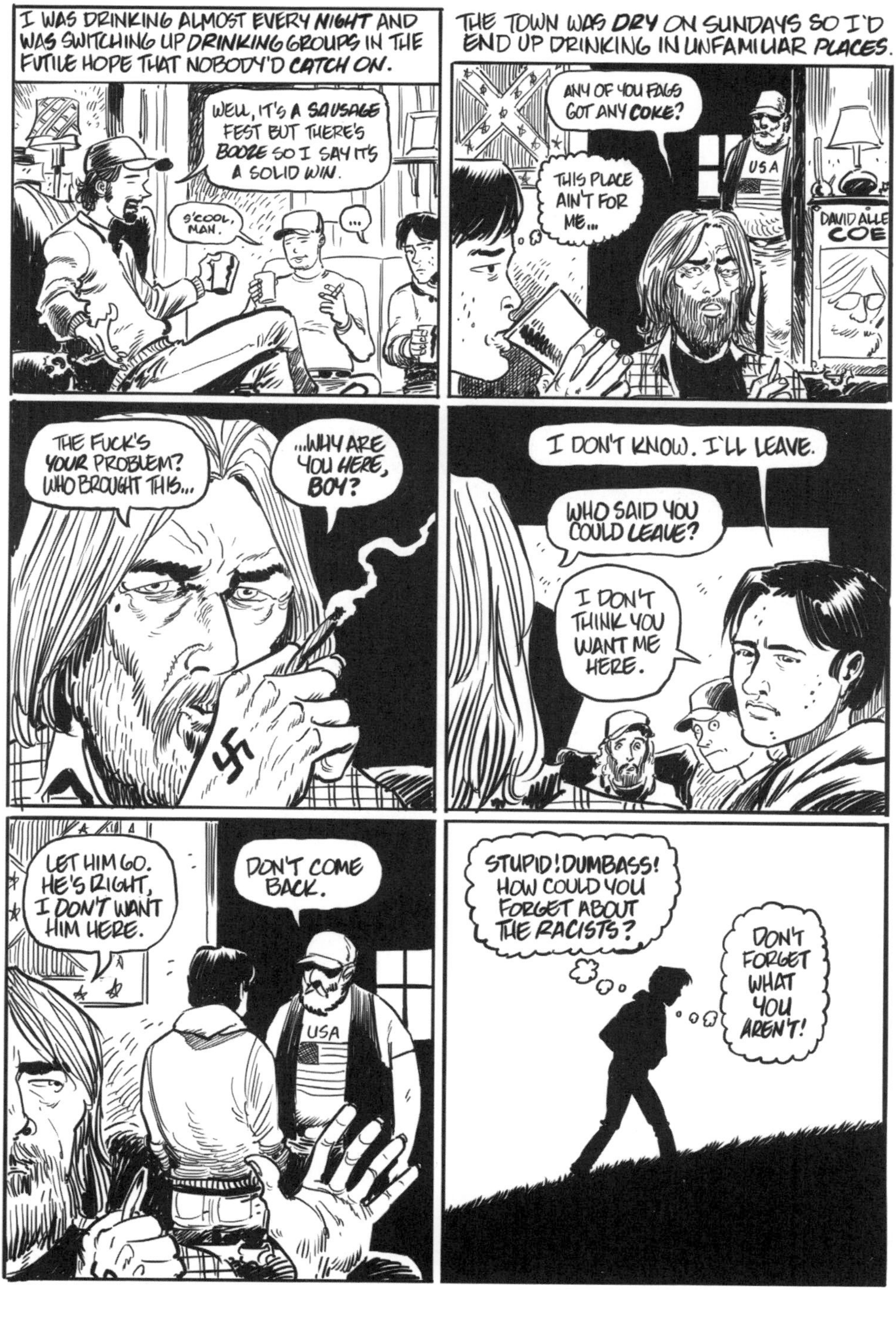
I WAS DRINKING ALMOST EVERY NIGHT AND WAS SWITCHING UP DRINKING GROUPS IN THE FUTILE HOPE THAT NOBODY'D CATCH ON.
WELL, IT'S A SAUSAGE FEST BUT THERE'S BOOZE SO I SAY IT'S A SOLID WIN.
S'COOL, MAN.
...
THE TOWN WAS DRY ON SUNDAYS SO I'D END UP DRINKING IN UNFAMILIAR PLACES.
ANY OF YOU FAGS GOT ANY COKE?
THIS PLACE AIN'T FOR ME...
USA
DAVID ALLE
COE
THE FUCK'S YOUR PROBLEM? WHO BROUGHT THIS...
...WHY ARE YOU HERE, BOY?
I DON'T KNOW. I'LL LEAVE.
WHO SAID YOU COULD LEAVE?
I DON'T THINK YOU WANT ME HERE.
LET HIM GO. HE'S RIGHT, I DON'T WANT HIM HERE.
DON'T COME BACK.
USA
STUPID! DUMBASS! HOW COULD YOU FORGET ABOUT THE RACISTS?
DON'T FORGET WHAT YOU AREN'T!

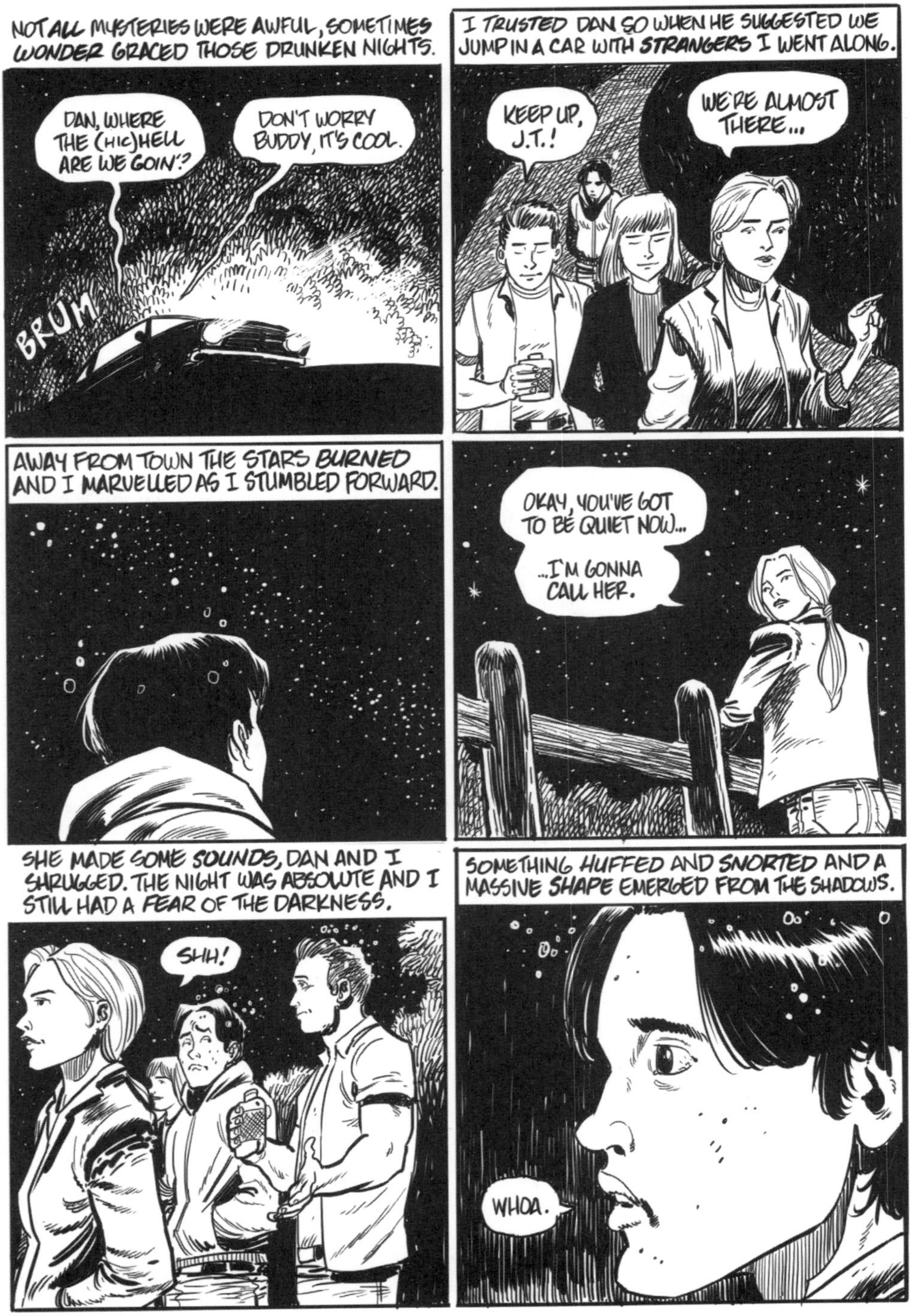
NOT ALL MYSTERIES WERE AWFUL, SOMETIMES WONDER GRACED THOSE DRUNKEN NIGHTS.
DAN, WHERE THE (HIC) HELL ARE WE GOIN'?
DON'T WORRY BUDDY, IT'S COOL.
BRUM
I TRUSTED DAN SO WHEN HE SUGGESTED WE JUMP IN A CAR WITH STRANGERS I WENT ALONG.
KEEP UP, J.T.!
WE'RE ALMOST THERE...
AWAY FROM TOWN THE STARS BURNED AND I MARVELLED AS I STUMBLED FORWARD.
OKAY, YOU'VE GOT TO BE QUIET NOW...
...I'M GONNA CALL HER.
SHE MADE SOME SOUNDS, DAN AND I SHRUGGED. THE NIGHT WAS ABSOLUTE AND I STILL HAD A FEAR OF THE DARKNESS.
SHH!
SOMETHING HUFFED AND SNORTED AND A MASSIVE SHAPE EMERGED FROM THE SHADOWS.
WHOA.

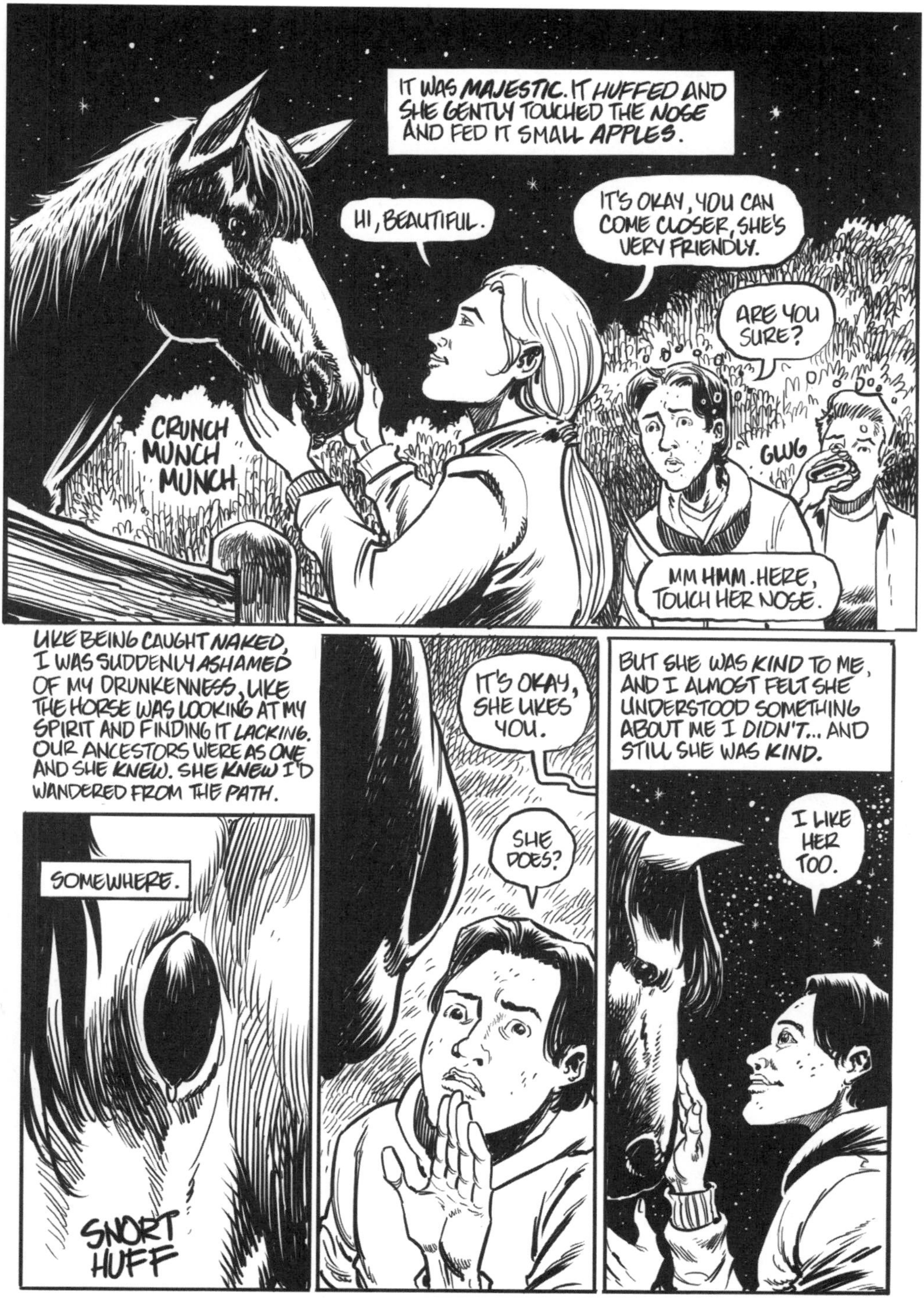
IT WAS MAJESTIC. IT HUFFED AND SHE GENTLY TOUCHED THE NOSE AND FED IT SMALL APPLES.
HI, BEAUTIFUL.
IT'S OKAY, YOU CAN COME CLOSER, SHE'S VERY FRIENDLY.
ARE YOU SURE?
CRUNCH MUNCH MUNCH
GLUG
MM HMM. HERE, TOUCH HER NOSE.
LIKE BEING CAUGHT NAKED, I WAS SUDDENLY ASHAMED OF MY DRUNKENNESS, LIKE THE HORSE WAS LOOKING AT MY SPIRIT AND FINDING IT LACKING. OUR ANCESTORS WERE AS ONE AND SHE KNEW. SHE KNEW I'D WANDERED FROM THE PATH.
SOMEWHERE.
SNORT HUFF
IT'S OKAY, SHE LIKES YOU.
SHE DOES?
BUT SHE WAS KIND TO ME, AND I ALMOST FELT SHE UNDERSTOOD SOMETHING ABOUT ME I DIDN'T... AND STILL SHE WAS KIND.
I LIKE HER TOO.

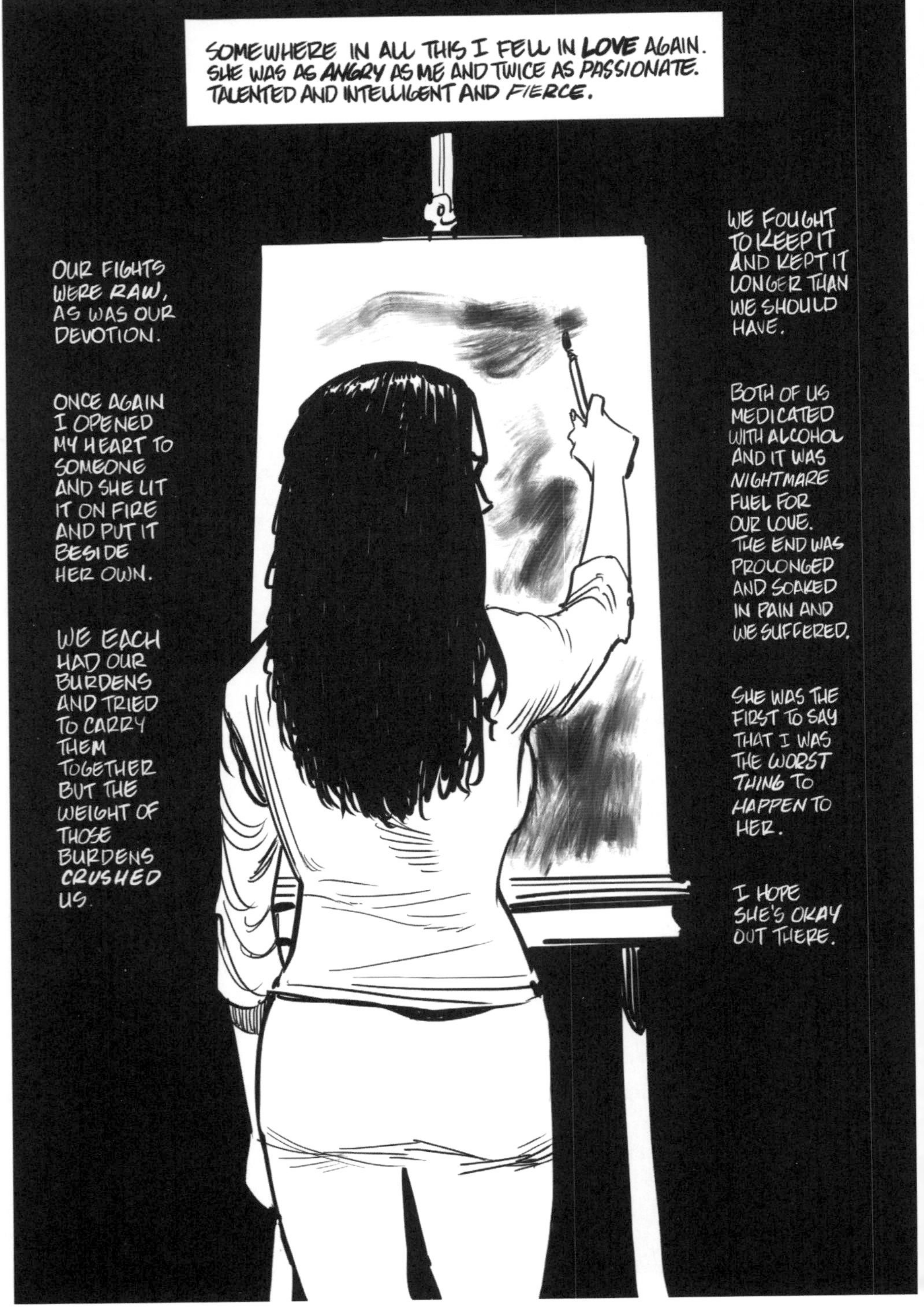
SOMEWHERE IN ALL THIS I FELL IN LOVE AGAIN. SHE WAS AS ANGRY AS ME AND TWICE AS PASSIONATE. TALENTED AND INTELLIGENT AND FIERCE.
OUR FIGHTS WERE RAW, AS WAS OUR DEVOTION.
ONCE AGAIN I OPENED MY HEART TO SOMEONE AND SHE LIT IT ON FIRE AND PUT IT BESIDE HER OWN.
WE EACH HAD OUR BURDENS AND TRIED TO CARRY THEM TOGETHER BUT THE WEIGHT OF THOSE BURDENS CRUSHED US.
WE FOUGHT TO KEEP IT AND KEPT IT LONGER THAN WE SHOULD HAVE.
BOTH OF US MEDICATED WITH ALCOHOL AND IT WAS NIGHTMARE FUEL FOR OUR LOVE. THE END WAS PROLONGED AND SOAKED IN PAIN AND WE SUFFERED.
SHE WAS THE FIRST TO SAY THAT I WAS THE WORST THING TO HAPPEN TO HER.
I HOPE SHE'S OKAY OUT THERE.

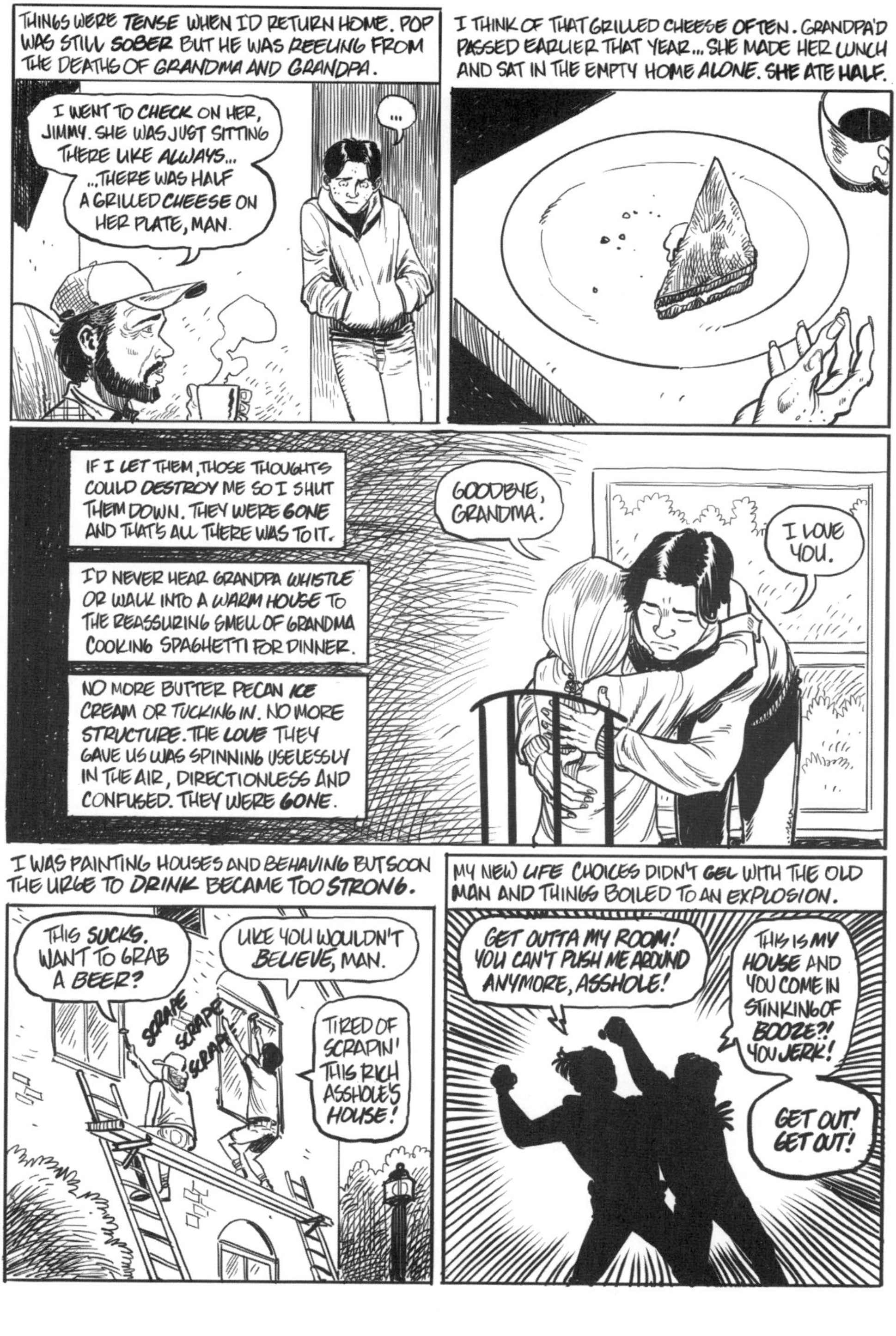
THINGS WERE TENSE WHEN I'D RETURN HOME. POP WAS STILL SOBER BUT HE WAS REELING FROM THE DEATHS OF GRANDMA AND GRANDPA.
I WENT TO CHECK ON HER, JIMMY. SHE WAS JUST SITTING THERE LIKE ALWAYS... ...THERE WAS HALF A GRILLED CHEESE ON HER PLATE, MAN.
...
I THINK OF THAT GRILLED CHEESE OFTEN. GRANDPA'D PASSED EARLIER THAT YEAR... SHE MADE HER LUNCH AND SAT IN THE EMPTY HOME ALONE. SHE ATE HALF.
IF I LET THEM, THOSE THOUGHTS COULD DESTROY ME SO I SHUT THEM DOWN. THEY WERE GONE AND THAT'S ALL THERE WAS TO IT.
I'D NEVER HEAR GRANDPA WHISTLE OR WALK INTO A WARM HOUSE TO THE REASSURING SMELL OF GRANDMA COOKING SPAGHETTI FOR DINNER.
NO MORE BUTTER PECAN ICE CREAM OR TUCKING IN. NO MORE STRUCTURE. THE LOVE THEY GAVE US WAS SPINNING USELESSLY IN THE AIR, DIRECTIONLESS AND CONFUSED. THEY WERE GONE.
GOODBYE, GRANDMA.
I LOVE YOU.
I WAS PAINTING HOUSES AND BEHAVING BUT SOON THE URGE TO DRINK BECAME TOO STRONG.
THIS SUCKS. WANT TO GRAB A BEER?
LIKE YOU WOULDN'T BELIEVE, MAN.
SCRAPE SCRAPE SCRAPE
TIRED OF SCRAPIN' THIS RICH ASSHOLE'S HOUSE!
MY NEW LIFE CHOICES DIDN'T GEL WITH THE OLD MAN AND THINGS BOILED TO AN EXPLOSION.
GET OUTTA MY ROOM! YOU CAN'T PUSH ME AROUND ANYMORE, ASSHOLE!
THIS IS MY HOUSE AND YOU COME IN STINKING OF BOOZE?! YOU JERK!
GET OUT! GET OUT!

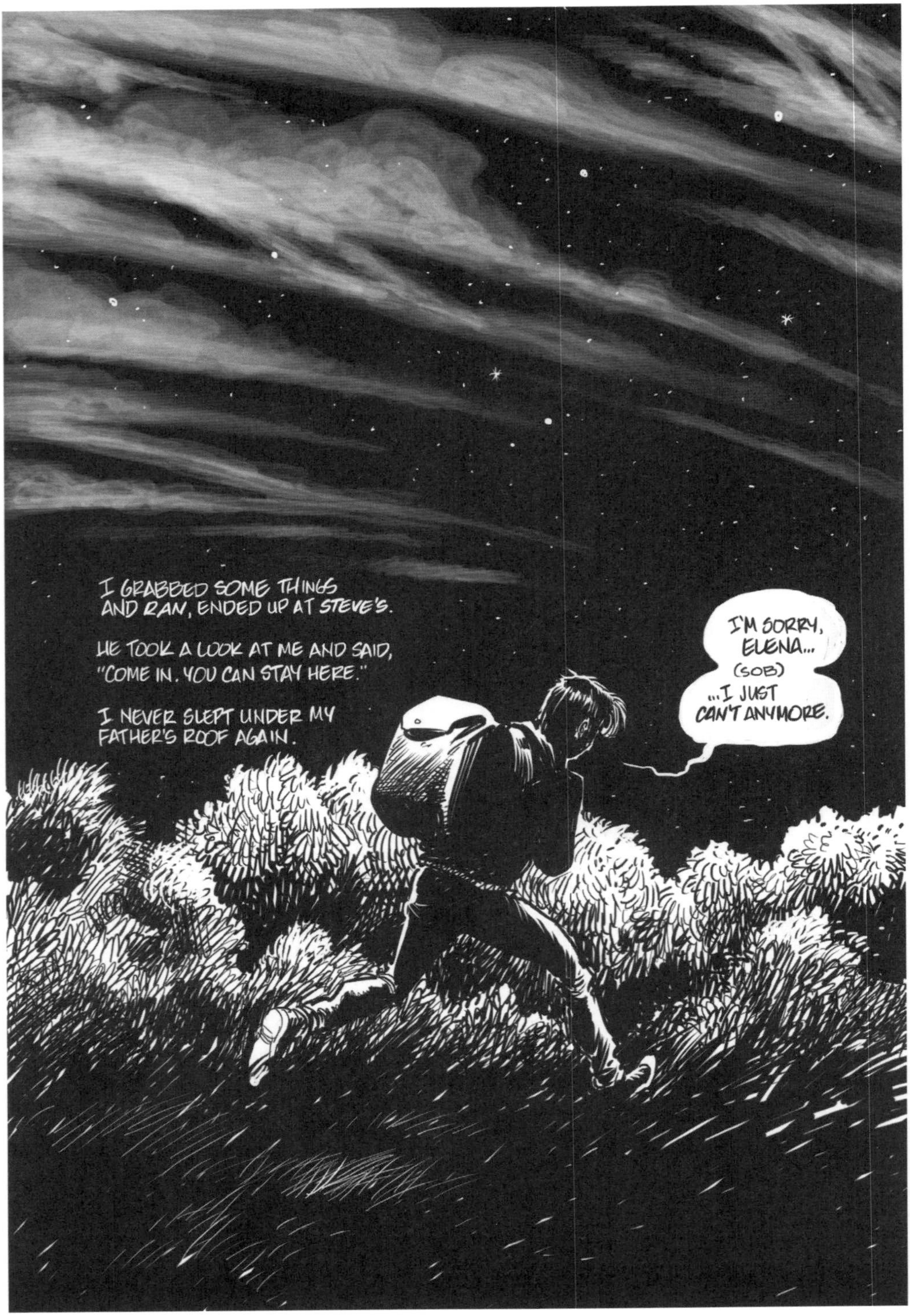
I GRABBED SOME THINGS AND RAN, ENDED UP AT STEVE'S.
HE TOOK A LOOK AT ME AND SAID, "COME IN. YOU CAN STAY HERE."
I NEVER SLEPT UNDER MY FATHER'S ROOF AGAIN.
I'M SORRY, ELENA... (SOB) ...I JUST CAN'T ANYMORE.

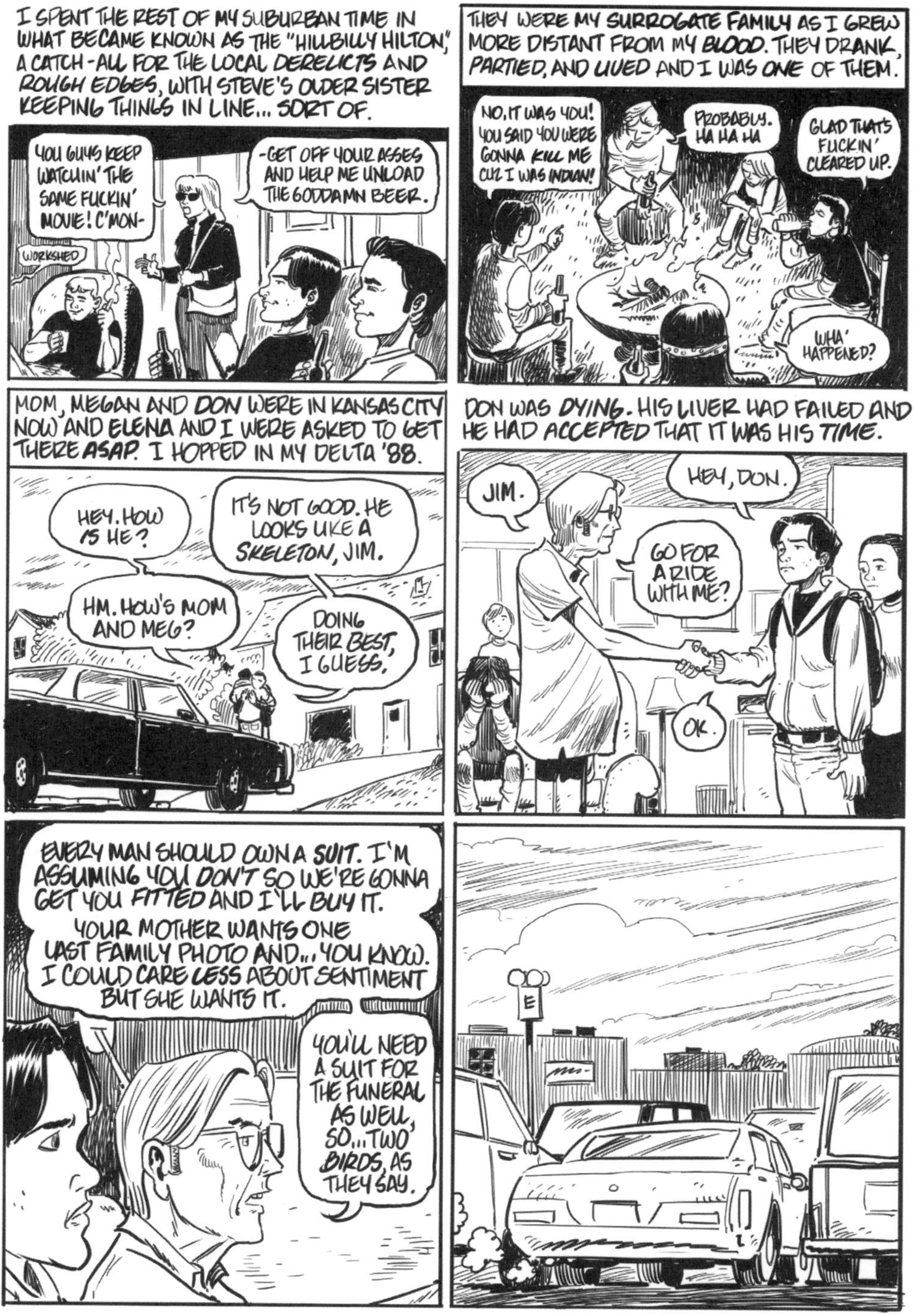
I SPENT THE REST OF MY SUBURBAN TIME IN WHAT BECAME KNOWN AS THE "HILLBILLY HILTON," A CATCH-ALL FOR THE LOCAL DERELICTS AND ROUGH EDGES, WITH STEVE'S OLDER SISTER KEEPING THINGS IN LINE... SORT OF.
YOU GUYS KEEP WATCHIN' THE SAME FUCKIN' MOVIE! C'MON-
-GET OFF YOUR ASSES AND HELP ME UNLOAD THE GODDAMN BEER.
WORKSHED
THEY WERE MY SURROGATE FAMILY AS I GREW MORE DISTANT FROM MY BLOOD. THEY DRANK, PARTIED, AND LIVED AND I WAS ONE OF THEM.
NO, IT WAS YOU! YOU SAID YOU WERE GONNA KILL ME CUZ I WAS INDIAN!
PROBABLY. HA HA HA
GLAD THAT'S FUCKIN' CLEARED UP.
WHA' HAPPENED?
MOM, MEGAN AND DON WERE IN KANSAS CITY NOW AND ELENA AND I WERE ASKED TO GET THERE ASAP. I HOPPED IN MY DELTA '88.
HEY. HOW IS HE?
IT'S NOT GOOD. HE LOOKS LIKE A SKELETON, JIM.
HM. HOW'S MOM AND MEG?
DOING THEIR BEST, I GUESS.
DON WAS DYING. HIS LIVER HAD FAILED AND HE HAD ACCEPTED THAT IT WAS HIS TIME.
JIM.
HEY, DON.
GO FOR A RIDE WITH ME?
OK.
EVERY MAN SHOULD OWN A SUIT. I'M ASSUMING YOU DON'T SO WE'RE GONNA GET YOU FITTED AND I'LL BUY IT.
YOUR MOTHER WANTS ONE LAST FAMILY PHOTO AND... YOU KNOW. I COULD CARE LESS ABOUT SENTIMENT BUT SHE WANTS IT.
YOU'LL NEED A SUIT FOR THE FUNERAL AS WELL, SO... TWO BIRDS, AS THEY SAY.
E

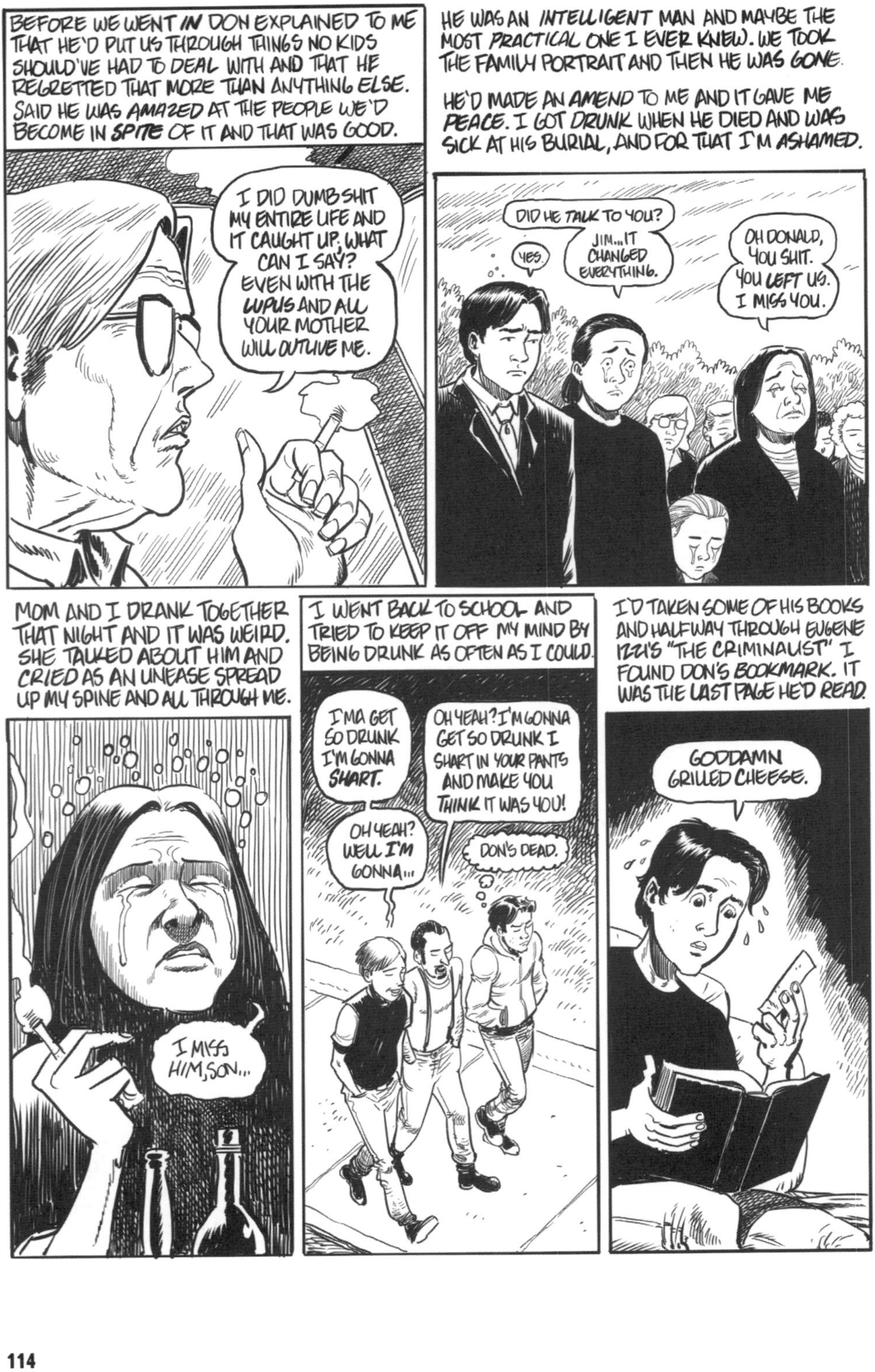
BEFORE WE WENT IN DON EXPLAINED TO ME THAT HE'D PUT US THROUGH THINGS NO KIDS SHOULD'VE HAD TO DEAL WITH AND THAT HE REGRETTED THAT MORE THAN ANYTHING ELSE. SAID HE WAS AMAZED AT THE PEOPLE WE'D BECOME IN SPITE OF IT AND THAT WAS GOOD.
I DID DUMB SHIT MY ENTIRE LIFE AND IT CAUGHT UP. WHAT CAN I SAY? EVEN WITH THE LUPUS AND ALL YOUR MOTHER WILL OUTLIVE ME.
HE WAS AN INTELLIGENT MAN AND MAYBE THE MOST PRACTICAL ONE I EVER KNEW. WE TOOK THE FAMILY PORTRAIT AND THEN HE WAS GONE.
HE'D MADE AN AMEND TO ME AND IT GAVE ME PEACE. I GOT DRUNK WHEN HE DIED AND WAS SICK AT HIS BURIAL, AND FOR THAT I'M ASHAMED.
DID HE TALK TO YOU?
YES.
JIM... IT CHANGED EVERYTHING.
OH DONALD, YOU SHIT. YOU LEFT US. I MISS YOU.
MOM AND I DRANK TOGETHER THAT NIGHT AND IT WAS WEIRD. SHE TALKED ABOUT HIM AND CRIED AS AN UNEASE SPREAD UP MY SPINE AND ALL THROUGH ME.
I MISS HIM, SON...
I WENT BACK TO SCHOOL AND TRIED TO KEEP IT OFF MY MIND BY BEING DRUNK AS OFTEN AS I COULD.
I'MA GET SO DRUNK I'M GONNA SHART.
OH YEAH? I'M GONNA GET SO DRUNK I SHART IN YOUR PANTS AND MAKE YOU THINK IT WAS YOU!
OH YEAH? WELL I'M GONNA...
DON'S DEAD.
I'D TAKEN SOME OF HIS BOOKS AND HALFWAY THROUGH EUGENE IZZI'S "THE CRIMINALIST" I FOUND DON'S BOOKMARK. IT WAS THE LAST PAGE HE'D READ.
GODDAMN GRILLED CHEESE.

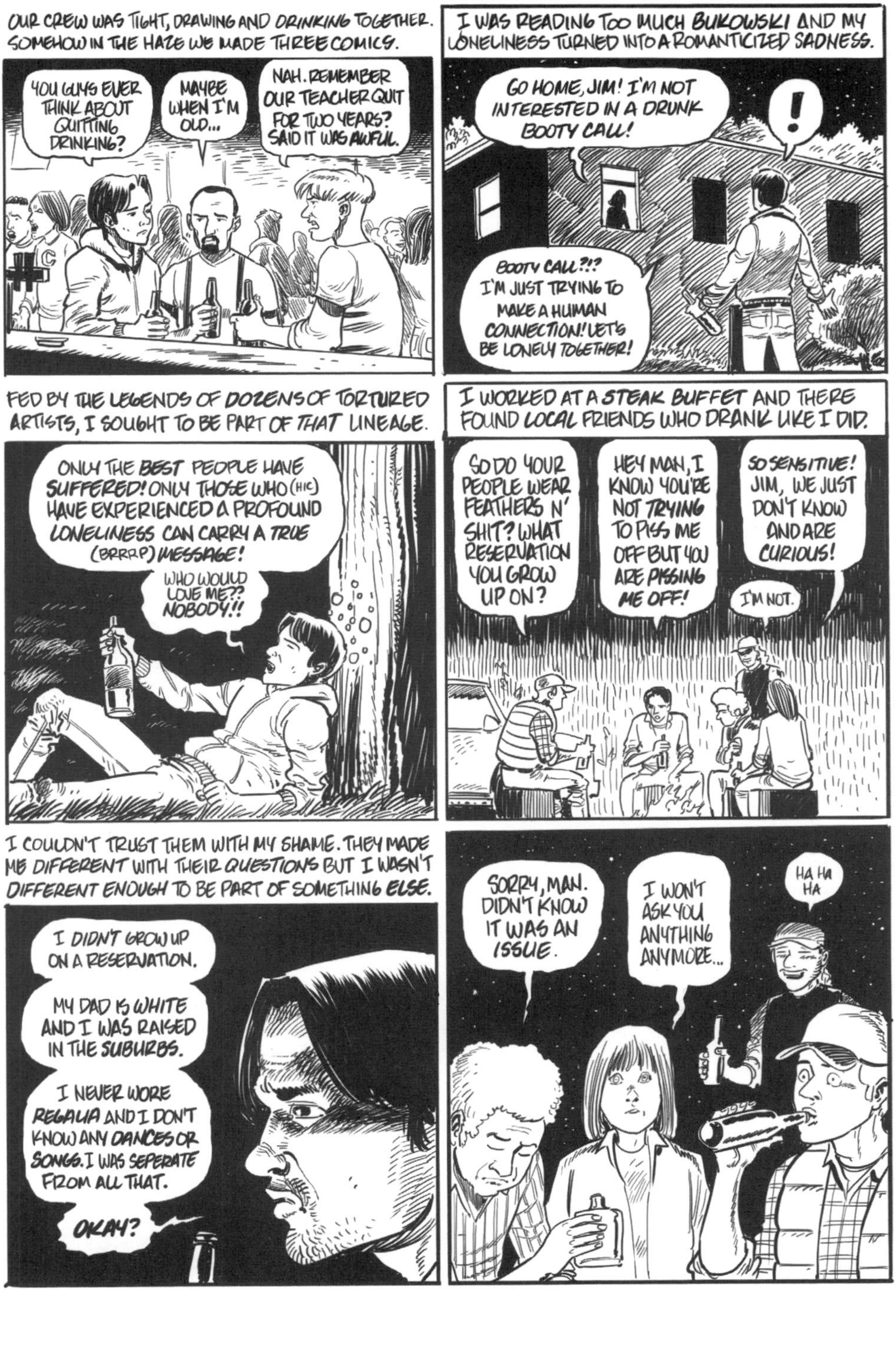
OUR CREW WAS TIGHT, DRAWING AND DRINKING TOGETHER. SOMEHOW IN THE HAZE WE MADE THREE COMICS.
YOU GUYS EVER THINK ABOUT QUITTING DRINKING?
MAYBE WHEN I'M OLD...
NAH. REMEMBER OUR TEACHER QUIT FOR TWO YEARS? SAID IT WAS AWFUL.
I WAS READING TOO MUCH BUKOWSKI AND MY LONELINESS TURNED INTO A ROMANTICIZED SADNESS.
GO HOME, JIM! I'M NOT INTERESTED IN A DRUNK BOOTY CALL!
!
BOOTY CALL?!? I'M JUST TRYING TO MAKE A HUMAN CONNECTION! LET'S BE LONELY TOGETHER!
FED BY THE LEGENDS OF DOZENS OF TORTURED ARTISTS, I SOUGHT TO BE PART OF THAT LINEAGE.
ONLY THE BEST PEOPLE HAVE SUFFERED! ONLY THOSE WHO (HIC) HAVE EXPERIENCED A PROFOUND LONELINESS CAN CARRY A TRUE (BRRRP) MESSAGE!
WHO WOULD LOVE ME?? NOBODY!!
I WORKED AT A STEAK BUFFET AND THERE FOUND LOCAL FRIENDS WHO DRANK LIKE I DID.
SO DO YOUR PEOPLE WEAR FEATHERS N' SHIT? WHAT RESERVATION YOU GROW UP ON?
HEY MAN, I KNOW YOU'RE NOT TRYING TO PISS ME OFF BUT YOU ARE PISSING ME OFF!
SO SENSITIVE! JIM, WE JUST DON'T KNOW AND ARE CURIOUS!
I'M NOT.
I COULDN'T TRUST THEM WITH MY SHAME. THEY MADE ME DIFFERENT WITH THEIR QUESTIONS BUT I WASN'T DIFFERENT ENOUGH TO BE PART OF SOMETHING ELSE.
I DIDN'T GROW UP ON A RESERVATION.
MY DAD IS WHITE AND I WAS RAISED IN THE SUBURBS.
I NEVER WORE REGALIA AND I DON'T KNOW ANY DANCES OR SONGS. I WAS SEPERATE FROM ALL THAT.
OKAY?
SORRY, MAN. DIDN'T KNOW IT WAS AN ISSUE.
I WON'T ASK YOU ANYTHING ANYMORE...
HA HA HA

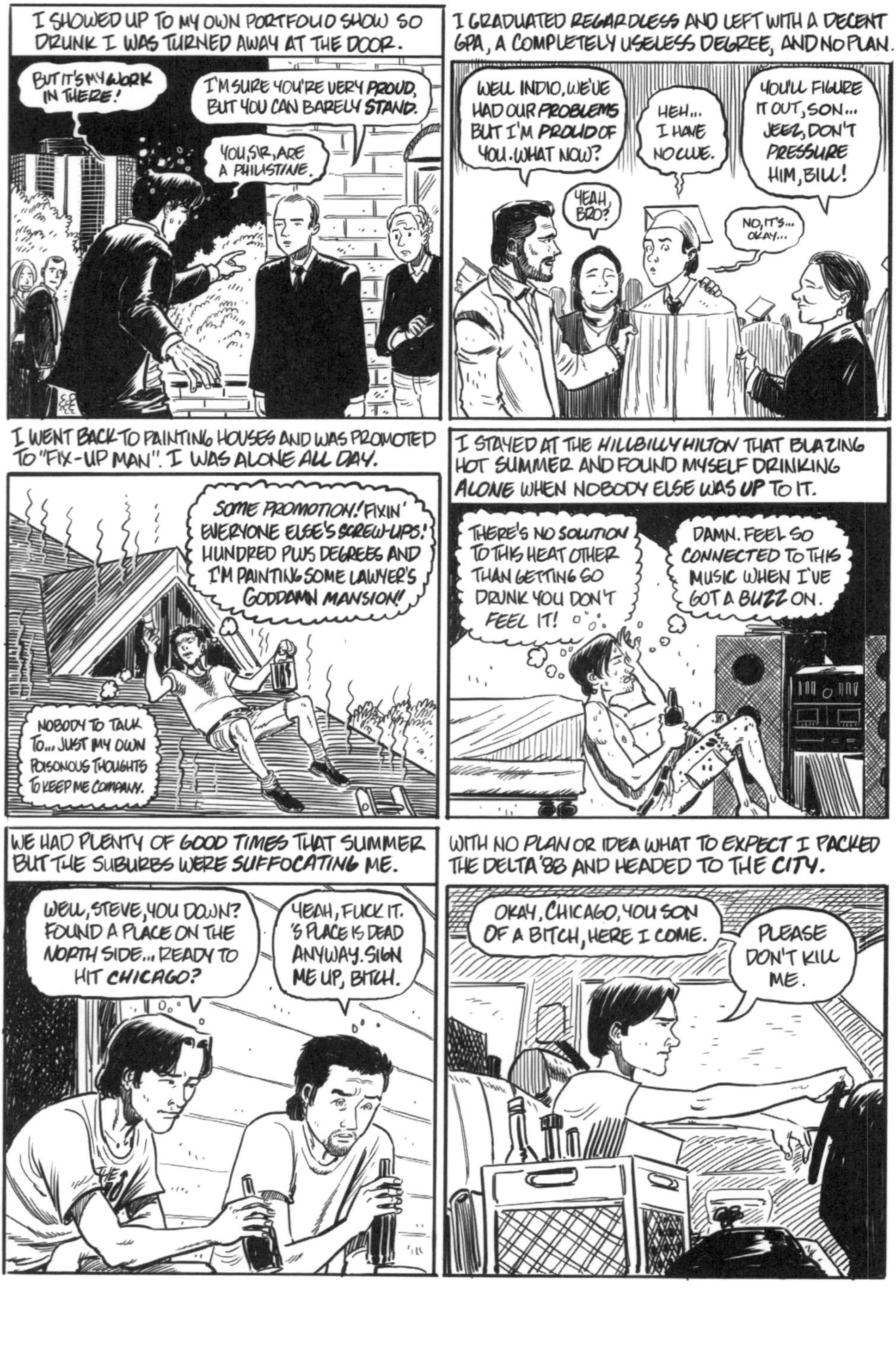
I SHOWED UP TO MY OWN PORTFOLIO SHOW SO DRUNK I WAS TURNED AWAY AT THE DOOR.
BUT IT'S MY WORK IN THERE!
I'M SURE YOU'RE VERY PROUD, BUT YOU CAN BARELY STAND.
YOU, SIR, ARE A PHILISTINE.
I GRADUATED REGARDLESS AND LEFT WITH A DECENT GPA, A COMPLETELY USELESS DEGREE, AND NO PLAN.
WELL INDIO, WE'VE HAD OUR PROBLEMS BUT I'M PROUD OF YOU. WHAT NOW?
HEH... I HAVE NO CLUE.
YOU'LL FIGURE IT OUT, SON... JEEZ, DON'T PRESSURE HIM, BILL!
YEAH, BRO?
NO, IT'S... OKAY...
I WENT BACK TO PAINTING HOUSES AND WAS PROMOTED TO "FIX-UP MAN". I WAS ALONE ALL DAY.
SOME PROMOTION! FIXIN' EVERYONE ELSE'S SCREW-UPS! HUNDRED PLUS DEGREES AND I'M PAINTING SOME LAWYER'S GODDAMN MANSION!
NOBODY TO TALK TO... JUST MY OWN POISONOUS THOUGHTS TO KEEP ME COMPANY.
I STAYED AT THE HILLBILLY HILTON THAT BLAZING HOT SUMMER AND FOUND MYSELF DRINKING ALONE WHEN NOBODY ELSE WAS UP TO IT.
THERE'S NO SOLUTION TO THIS HEAT OTHER THAN GETTING SO DRUNK YOU DON'T FEEL IT!
DAMN. FEEL SO CONNECTED TO THIS MUSIC WHEN I'VE GOT A BUZZ ON.
WE HAD PLENTY OF GOOD TIMES THAT SUMMER BUT THE SUBURBS WERE SUFFOCATING ME.
WELL, STEVE, YOU DOWN? FOUND A PLACE ON THE NORTH SIDE... READY TO HIT CHICAGO?
YEAH, FUCK IT. 'S PLACE IS DEAD ANYWAY. SIGN ME UP, BITCH.
WITH NO PLAN OR IDEA WHAT TO EXPECT I PACKED THE DELTA '88 AND HEADED TO THE CITY.
OKAY, CHICAGO, YOU SON OF A BITCH, HERE I COME.
PLEASE DON'T KILL ME.

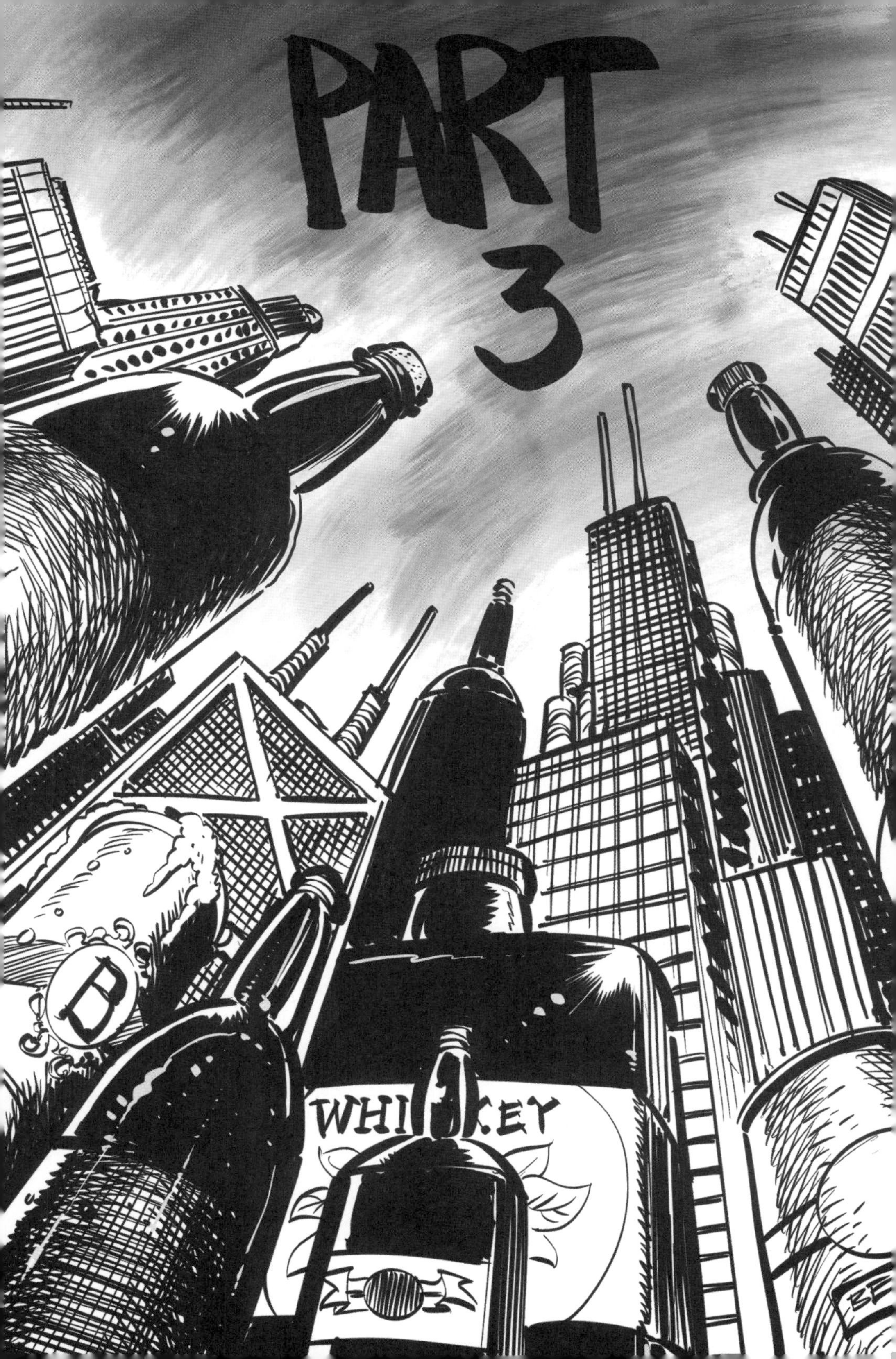
PART
3
WHI
KEY

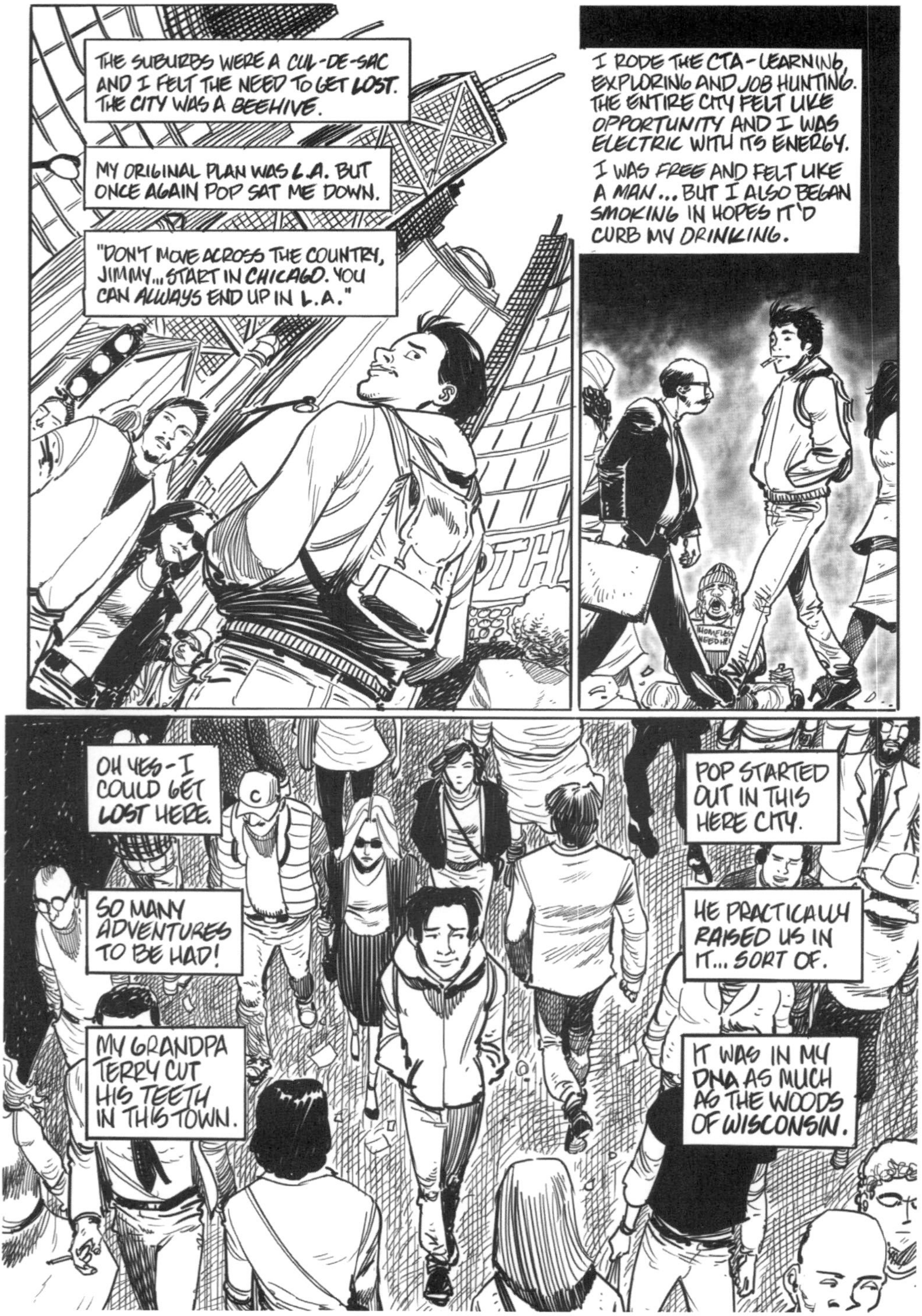

THE SUBURBS WERE A CUL-DE-SAC AND I FELT THE NEED TO GET LOST. THE CITY WAS A BEEHIVE.
MY ORIGINAL PLAN WAS L.A. BUT ONCE AGAIN POP SAT ME DOWN.
"DON'T MOVE ACROSS THE COUNTRY, JIMMY... START IN CHICAGO. YOU CAN ALWAYS END UP IN L.A."
I RODE THE CTA - LEARNING, EXPLORING AND JOB HUNTING. THE ENTIRE CITY FELT LIKE OPPORTUNITY AND I WAS ELECTRIC WITH ITS ENERGY.
I WAS FREE AND FELT LIKE A MAN... BUT I ALSO BEGAN SMOKING IN HOPES IT'D CURB MY DRINKING.
OH YES - I COULD GET LOST HERE.
SO MANY ADVENTURES TO BE HAD!
MY GRANDPA TERRY CUT HIS TEETH IN THIS TOWN.
POP STARTED OUT IN THIS HERE CITY.
HE PRACTICALLY RAISED US IN IT... SORT OF.
IT WAS IN MY DNA AS MUCH AS THE WOODS OF WISCONSIN.

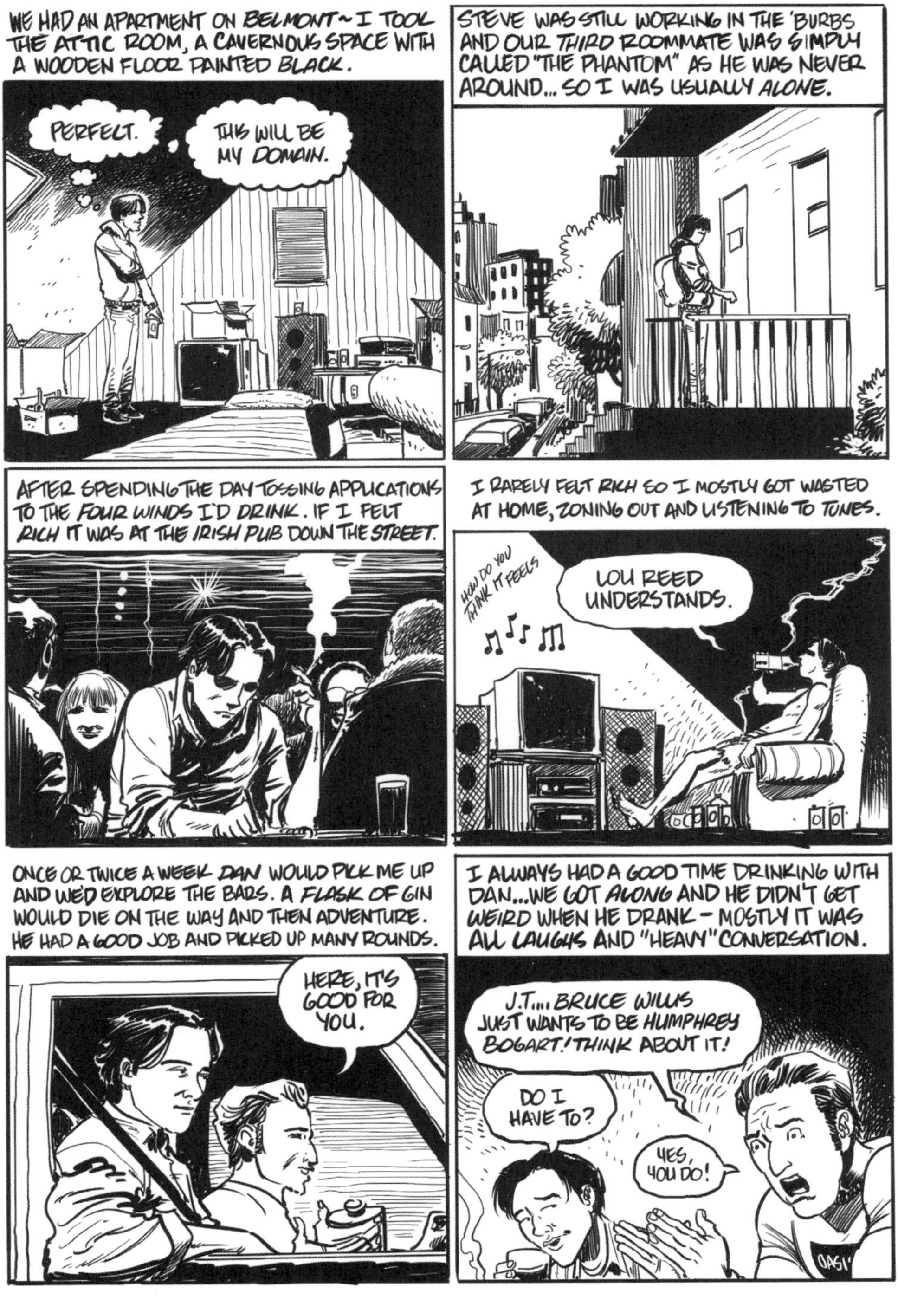
WE HAD AN APARTMENT ON BELMONT ~ I TOOK THE ATTIC ROOM, A CAVERNOUS SPACE WITH A WOODEN FLOOR PAINTED BLACK.
PERFECT.
THIS WILL BE MY DOMAIN.
STEVE WAS STILL WORKING IN THE 'BURBS AND OUR THIRD ROOMMATE WAS SIMPLY CALLED "THE PHANTOM" AS HE WAS NEVER AROUND... SO I WAS USUALLY ALONE.
AFTER SPENDING THE DAY TOSSING APPLICATIONS TO THE FOUR WINDS I'D DRINK. IF I FELT RICH IT WAS AT THE IRISH PUB DOWN THE STREET.
I RARELY FELT RICH SO I MOSTLY GOT WASTED AT HOME, ZONING OUT AND LISTENING TO TUNES.
HOW DO YOU THINK IT FEELS
LOU REED UNDERSTANDS.
ONCE OR TWICE A WEEK DAN WOULD PICK ME UP AND WE'D EXPLORE THE BARS. A FLASK OF GIN WOULD DIE ON THE WAY AND THEN ADVENTURE. HE HAD A GOOD JOB AND PICKED UP MANY ROUNDS.
HERE, IT'S GOOD FOR YOU.
I ALWAYS HAD A GOOD TIME DRINKING WITH DAN... WE GOT ALONG AND HE DIDN'T GET WEIRD WHEN HE DRANK – MOSTLY IT WAS ALL LAUGHS AND "HEAVY" CONVERSATION.
J.T.... BRUCE WILLIS JUST WANTS TO BE HUMPHREY BOGART! THINK ABOUT IT!
DO I HAVE TO?
YES, YOU DO!

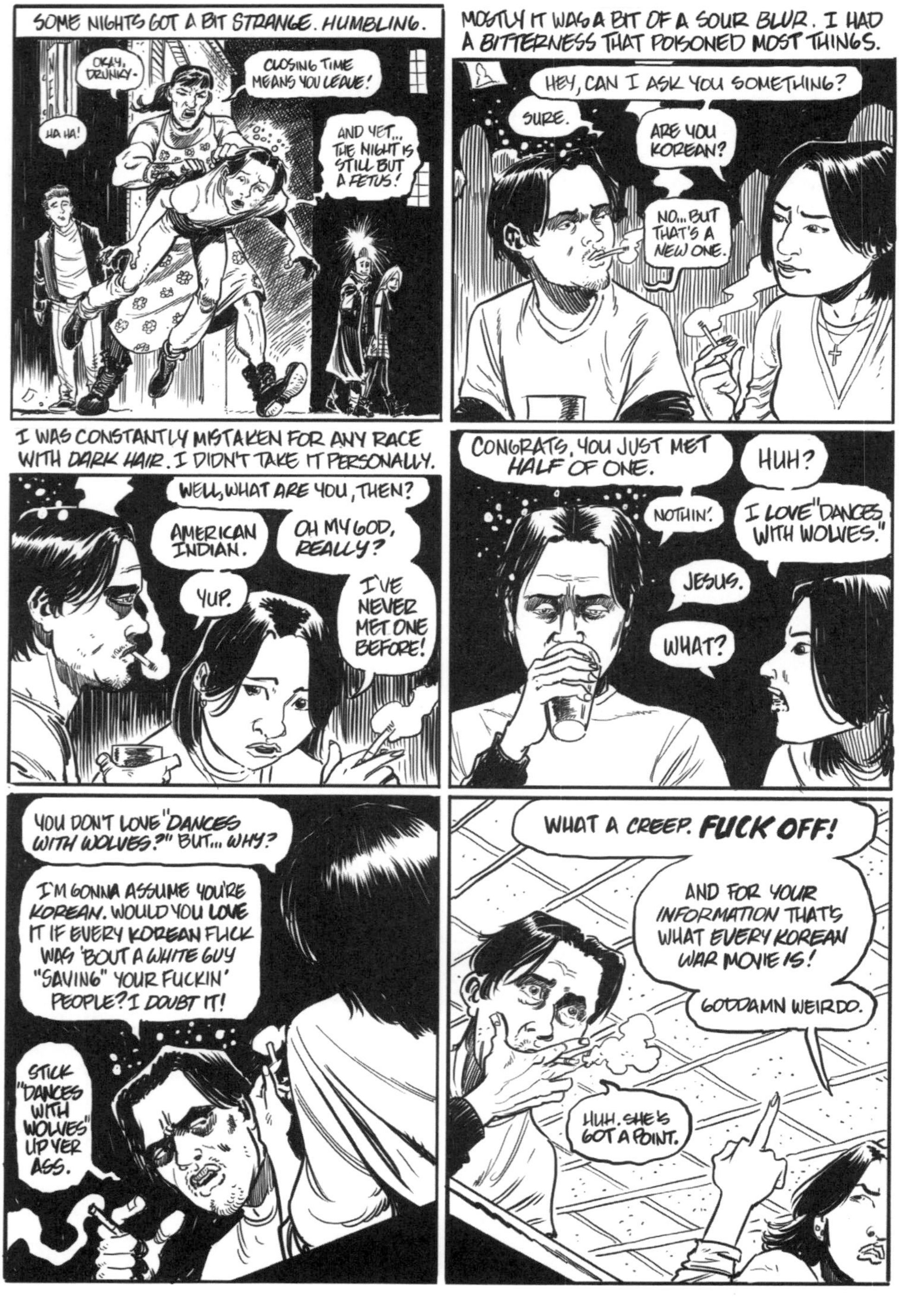
SOME NIGHTS GOT A BIT STRANGE. HUMBLING.
OKAY, DRUNKY.
CLOSING TIME MEANS YOU LEAVE!
HA HA!
AND YET... THE NIGHT IS STILL BUT A FETUS!
MOSTLY IT WAS A BIT OF A SOUR BLUR. I HAD A BITTERNESS THAT POISONED MOST THINGS.
HEY, CAN I ASK YOU SOMETHING?
SURE.
ARE YOU KOREAN?
NO... BUT THAT'S A NEW ONE.
I WAS CONSTANTLY MISTAKEN FOR ANY RACE WITH DARK HAIR. I DIDN'T TAKE IT PERSONALLY.
WELL, WHAT ARE YOU, THEN?
AMERICAN INDIAN.
OH MY GOD, REALLY?
YUP.
I'VE NEVER MET ONE BEFORE!
CONGRATS, YOU JUST MET HALF OF ONE.
HUH?
NOTHIN'.
I LOVE "DANCES WITH WOLVES."
JESUS.
WHAT?
YOU DON'T LOVE "DANCES WITH WOLVES?" BUT... WHY?
I'M GONNA ASSUME YOU'RE KOREAN. WOULD YOU LOVE IT IF EVERY KOREAN FLICK WAS 'BOUT A WHITE GUY "SAVING" YOUR FUCKIN' PEOPLE? I DOUBT IT!
STICK "DANCES WITH WOLVES" UP YER ASS.
WHAT A CREEP. FUCK OFF!
AND FOR YOUR INFORMATION THAT'S WHAT EVERY KOREAN WAR MOVIE IS!
GODDAMN WEIRDO.
HUH. SHE'S GOT A POINT.

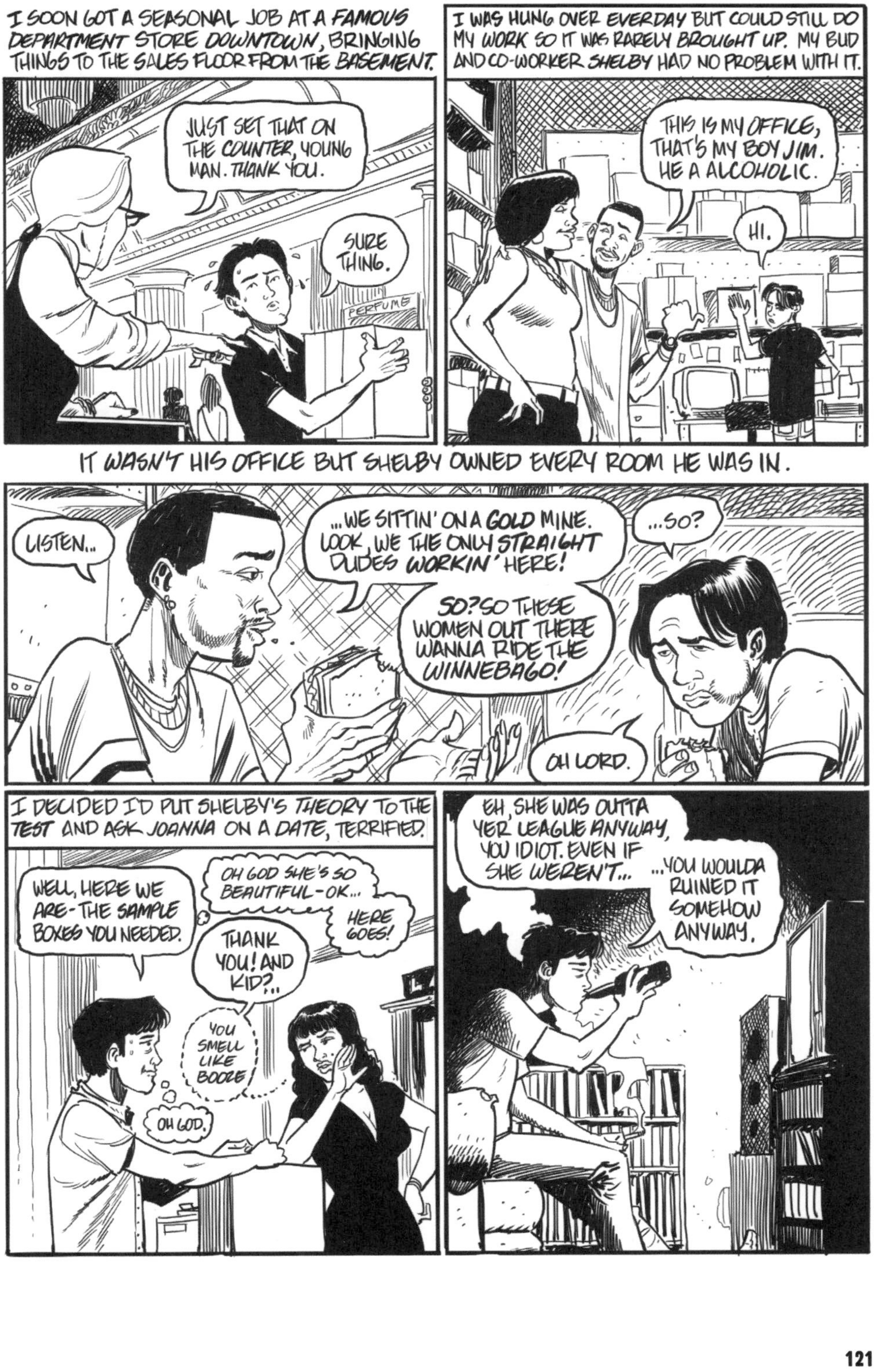
I SOON GOT A SEASONAL JOB AT A FAMOUS DEPARTMENT STORE DOWNTOWN, BRINGING THINGS TO THE SALES FLOOR FROM THE BASEMENT.
JUST SET THAT ON THE COUNTER, YOUNG MAN. THANK YOU.
SURE THING.
PERFUME
I WAS HUNG OVER EVERDAY BUT COULD STILL DO MY WORK SO IT WAS RARELY BROUGHT UP. MY BUD AND CO-WORKER SHELBY HAD NO PROBLEM WITH IT.
THIS IS MY OFFICE, THAT'S MY BOY JIM. HE A ALCOHOLIC.
HI.
IT WASN'T HIS OFFICE BUT SHELBY OWNED EVERY ROOM HE WAS IN.
LISTEN...
...WE SITTIN' ON A GOLD MINE. LOOK, WE THE ONLY STRAIGHT DUDES WORKIN' HERE!
...SO?
SO? SO THESE WOMEN OUT THERE WANNA RIDE THE WINNEBAGO!
OH LORD.
I DECIDED I'D PUT SHELBY'S THEORY TO THE TEST AND ASK JOANNA ON A DATE, TERRIFIED.
WELL, HERE WE ARE- THE SAMPLE BOXES YOU NEEDED.
OH GOD SHE'S SO BEAUTIFUL- OK...
HERE GOES!
THANK YOU! AND KID?...
YOU SMELL LIKE BOOZE
OH GOD.
EH, SHE WAS OUTTA YER LEAGUE ANYWAY, YOU IDIOT. EVEN IF SHE WEREN'T...
...YOU WOULDA RUINED IT SOMEHOW ANYWAY.

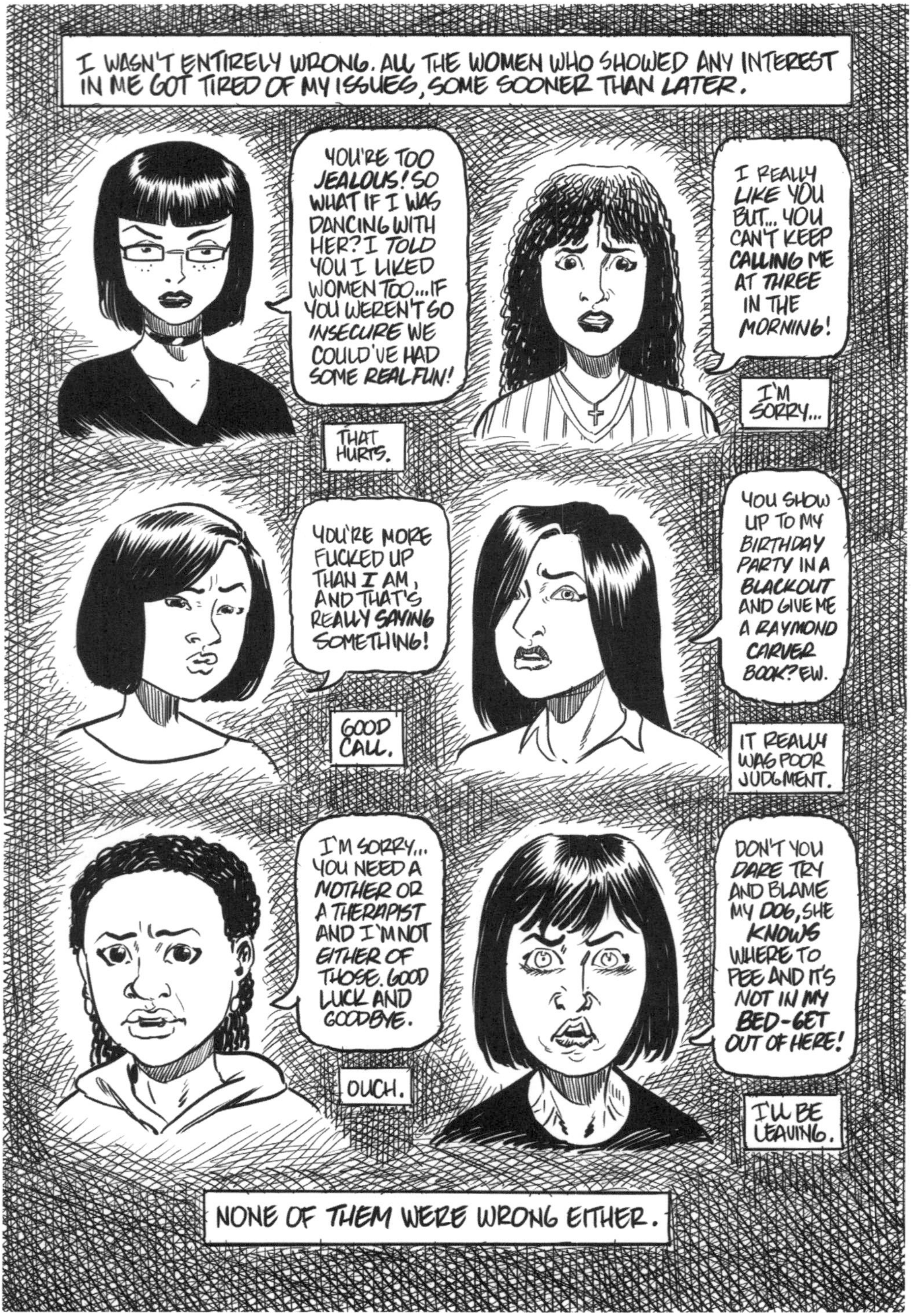
I WASN'T ENTIRELY WRONG. ALL THE WOMEN WHO SHOWED ANY INTEREST IN ME GOT TIRED OF MY ISSUES, SOME SOONER THAN LATER.
YOU'RE TOO JEALOUS! SO WHAT IF I WAS DANCING WITH HER? I TOLD YOU I LIKED WOMEN TOO... IF YOU WEREN'T SO INSECURE WE COULD'VE HAD SOME REAL FUN!
THAT HURTS.
I REALLY LIKE YOU BUT... YOU CAN'T KEEP CALLING ME AT THREE IN THE MORNING!
I'M SORRY...
YOU'RE MORE FUCKED UP THAN I AM, AND THAT'S REALLY SAYING SOMETHING!
GOOD CALL.
YOU SHOW UP TO MY BIRTHDAY PARTY IN A BLACKOUT AND GIVE ME A RAYMOND CARVER BOOK? EW.
IT REALLY WAS POOR JUDGMENT.
I'M SORRY... YOU NEED A MOTHER OR A THERAPIST AND I'M NOT EITHER OF THOSE. GOOD LUCK AND GOODBYE.
OUCH.
DON'T YOU DARE TRY AND BLAME MY DOG, SHE KNOWS WHERE TO PEE AND IT'S NOT IN MY BED-GET OUT OF HERE!
I'LL BE LEAVING.
NONE OF THEM WERE WRONG EITHER.

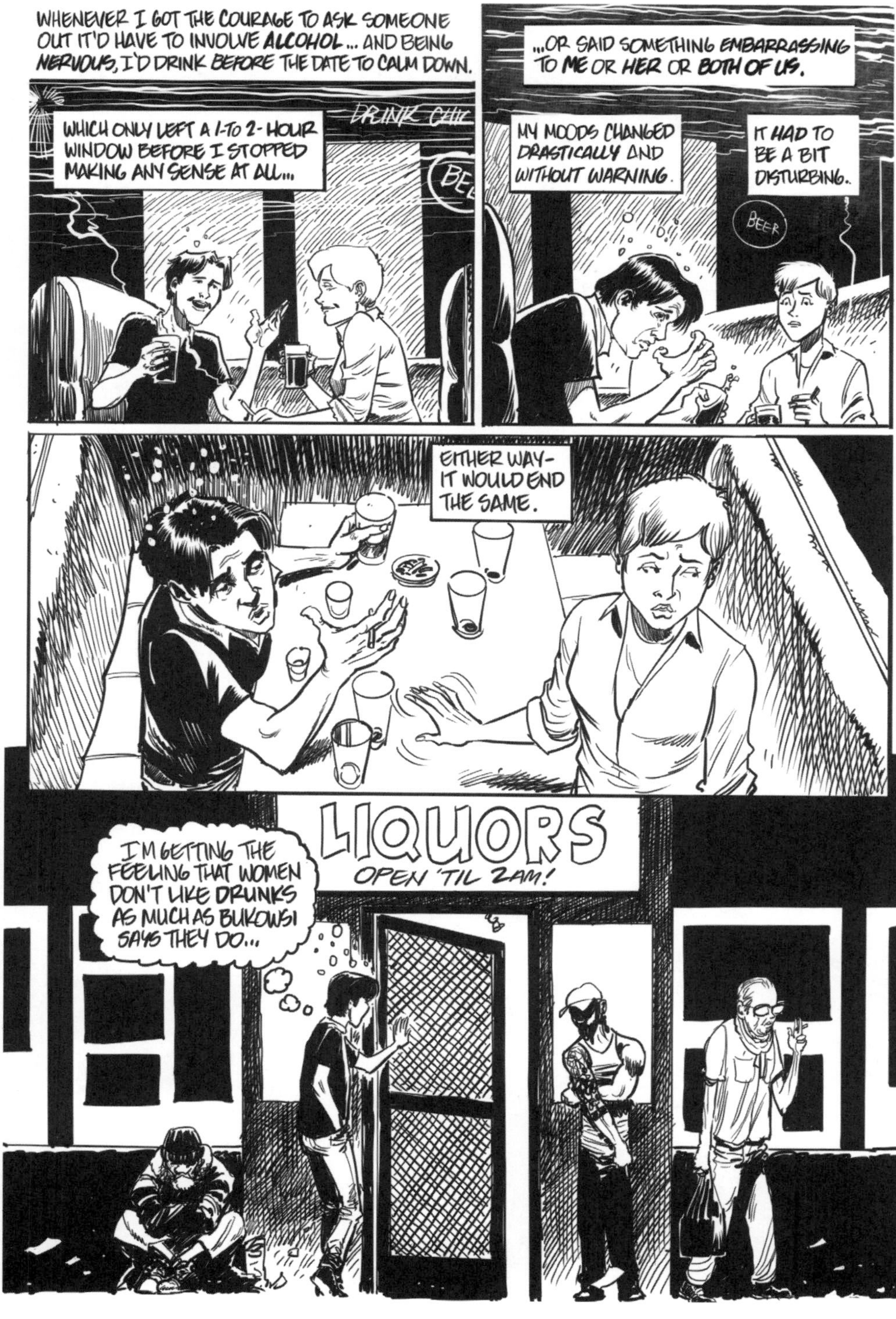
WHENEVER I GOT THE COURAGE TO ASK SOMEONE OUT IT'D HAVE TO INVOLVE **ALCOHOL**... AND BEING **NERVOUS**, I'D DRINK **BEFORE** THE DATE TO CALM DOWN.
WHICH ONLY LEFT A 1-TO 2-HOUR WINDOW BEFORE I STOPPED MAKING ANY SENSE AT ALL...
...OR SAID SOMETHING EMBARRASSING TO **ME** OR **HER** OR **BOTH OF US**.
MY MOODS CHANGED **DRASTICALLY** AND WITHOUT WARNING.
IT **HAD** TO BE A BIT DISTURBING.
BEER
EITHER WAY- IT WOULD END THE SAME.
LIQUORS
OPEN 'TIL 2AM!
I'M GETTING THE FEELING THAT WOMEN DON'T LIKE **DRUNKS** AS MUCH AS BUKOWSI SAYS THEY DO...

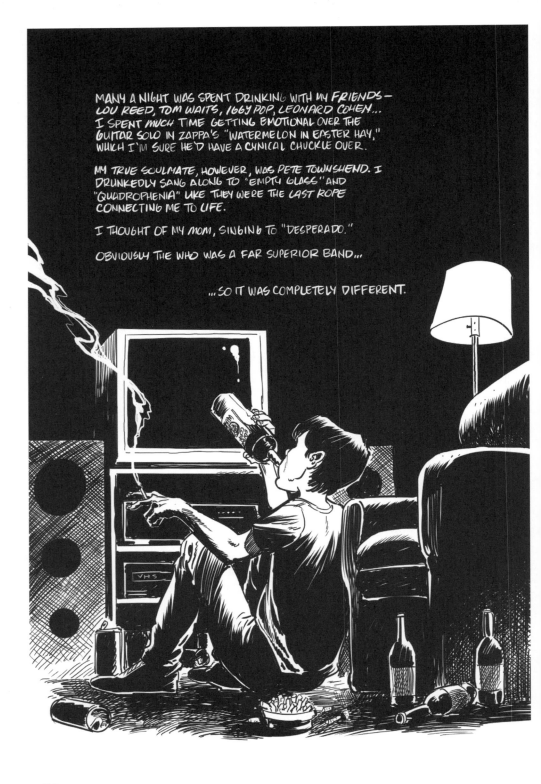

MANY A NIGHT WAS SPENT DRINKING WITH MY *FRIENDS* — LOU REED, TOM WAITS, IGGY POP, LEONARD COHEN... I SPENT *MUCH* TIME GETTING EMOTIONAL OVER THE GUITAR SOLO IN ZAPPA'S "WATERMELON IN EASTER HAY," WHICH I'M SURE HE'D HAVE A CYNICAL CHUCKLE OVER.

MY *TRUE* SOULMATE, HOWEVER, WAS PETE TOWNSHEND. I DRUNKEDLY SANG ALONG TO "EMPTY GLASS" AND "QUADROPHENIA" LIKE THEY WERE THE LAST ROPE CONNECTING ME TO LIFE.

I THOUGHT OF MY MOM, SINGING TO "DESPERADO."

OBVIOUSLY THE WHO WAS A FAR SUPERIOR BAND...

...SO IT WAS COMPLETELY DIFFERENT.

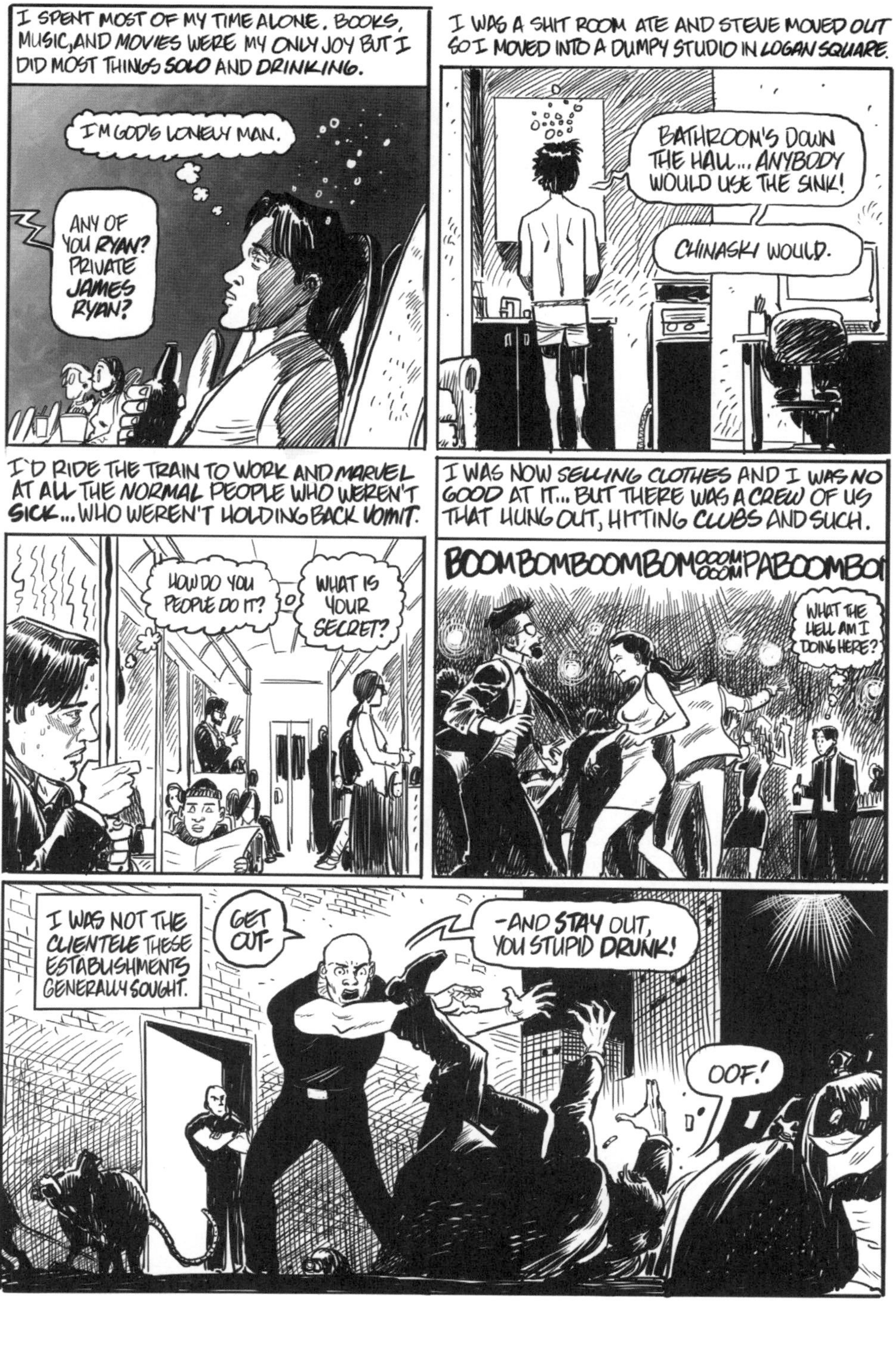
I SPENT MOST OF MY TIME ALONE. BOOKS, MUSIC, AND MOVIES WERE MY ONLY JOY BUT I DID MOST THINGS SOLO AND DRINKING.
I'M GOD'S LONELY MAN.
ANY OF YOU RYAN? PRIVATE JAMES RYAN?
I WAS A SHIT ROOM ATE AND STEVE MOVED OUT SO I MOVED INTO A DUMPY STUDIO IN LOGAN SQUARE.
BATHROOM'S DOWN THE HALL... ANYBODY WOULD USE THE SINK!
CHINASKI WOULD.
I'D RIDE THE TRAIN TO WORK AND MARVEL AT ALL THE NORMAL PEOPLE WHO WEREN'T SICK... WHO WEREN'T HOLDING BACK VOMIT.
HOW DO YOU PEOPLE DO IT?
WHAT IS YOUR SECRET?
I WAS NOW SELLING CLOTHES AND I WAS NO GOOD AT IT... BUT THERE WAS A CREW OF US THAT HUNG OUT, HITTING CLUBS AND SUCH.
BOOMBOMBOOMBOMOOMOOMPABOOMBO
WHAT THE HELL AM I DOING HERE?
I WAS NOT THE CLIENTELE THESE ESTABLISHMENTS GENERALLY SOUGHT.
GET OUT-
-AND STAY OUT, YOU STUPID DRUNK!
OOF!

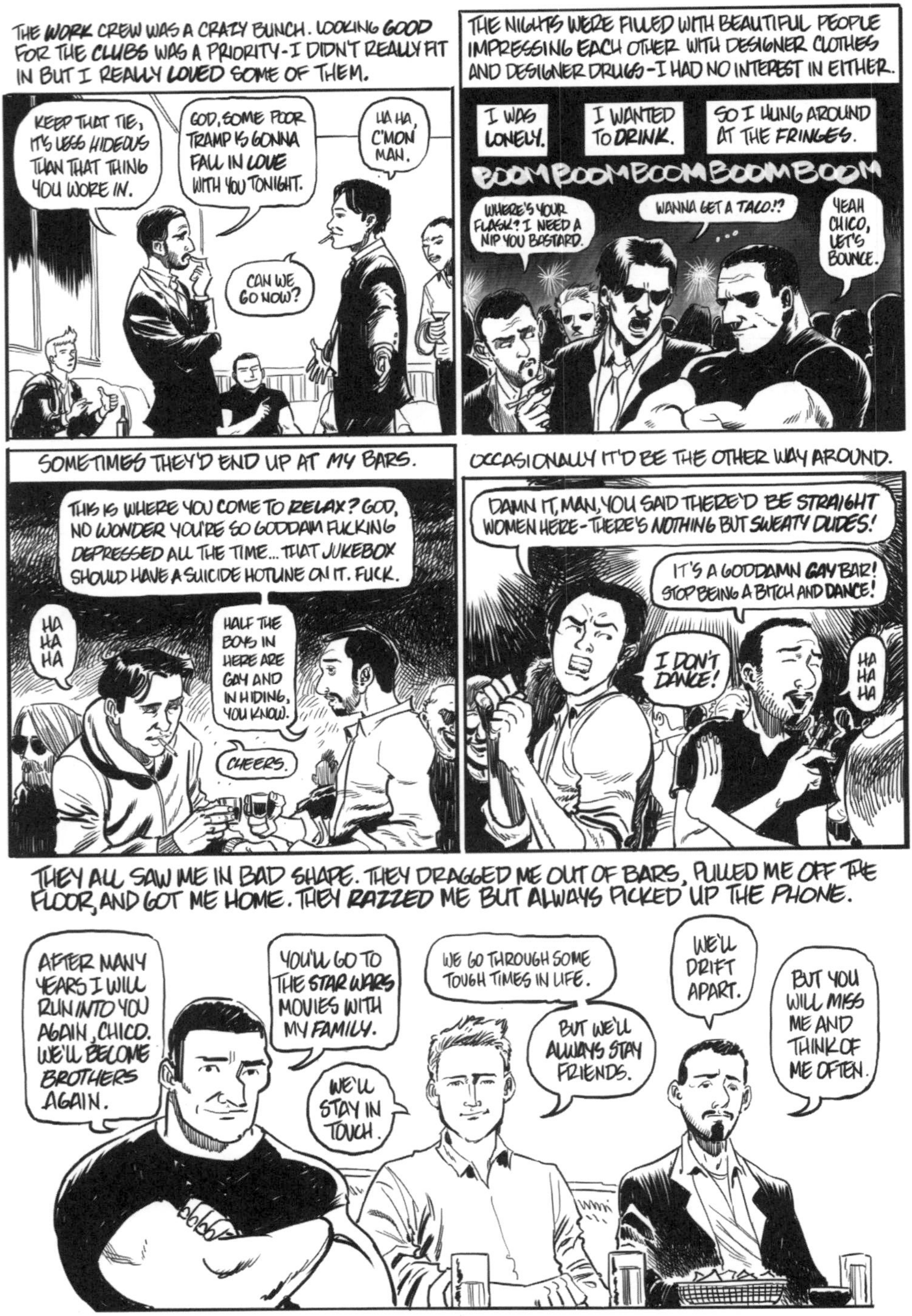
THE WORK CREW WAS A CRAZY BUNCH. LOOKING GOOD FOR THE CLUBS WAS A PRIORITY-I DIDN'T REALLY FIT IN BUT I REALLY LOVED SOME OF THEM.
KEEP THAT TIE, IT'S LESS HIDEOUS THAN THAT THING YOU WORE IN.
GOD, SOME POOR TRAMP IS GONNA FALL IN LOVE WITH YOU TONIGHT.
HA HA, C'MON MAN.
CAN WE GO NOW?
THE NIGHTS WERE FILLED WITH BEAUTIFUL PEOPLE IMPRESSING EACH OTHER WITH DESIGNER CLOTHES AND DESIGNER DRUGS-I HAD NO INTEREST IN EITHER.
I WAS LONELY.
I WANTED TO DRINK.
SO I HUNG AROUND AT THE FRINGES.
BOOM BOOM BOOM BOOM BOOM
WHERE'S YOUR FLASK? I NEED A NIP YOU BASTARD.
WANNA GET A TACO!?
...
YEAH CHICO, LET'S BOUNCE.
SOMETIMES THEY'D END UP AT MY BARS.
THIS IS WHERE YOU COME TO RELAX? GOD, NO WONDER YOU'RE SO GODDAM FUCKING DEPRESSED ALL THE TIME... THAT JUKEBOX SHOULD HAVE A SUICIDE HOTLINE ON IT. FUCK.
HA HA HA
HALF THE BOYS IN HERE ARE GAY AND IN HIDING, YOU KNOW.
CHEERS.
OCCASIONALLY IT'D BE THE OTHER WAY AROUND.
DAMN IT, MAN, YOU SAID THERE'D BE STRAIGHT WOMEN HERE-THERE'S NOTHING BUT SWEATY DUDES!
IT'S A GODDAMN GAY BAR! STOP BEING A BITCH AND DANCE!
I DON'T DANCE!
HA HA HA
THEY ALL SAW ME IN BAD SHAPE. THEY DRAGGED ME OUT OF BARS, PULLED ME OFF THE FLOOR, AND GOT ME HOME. THEY RAZZED ME BUT ALWAYS PICKED UP THE PHONE.
AFTER MANY YEARS I WILL RUN INTO YOU AGAIN, CHICO. WE'LL BECOME BROTHERS AGAIN.
YOU'LL GO TO THE STAR WARS MOVIES WITH MY FAMILY.
WE'LL STAY IN TOUCH.
WE GO THROUGH SOME TOUGH TIMES IN LIFE.
BUT WE'LL ALWAYS STAY FRIENDS.
WE'LL DRIFT APART.
BUT YOU WILL MISS ME AND THINK OF ME OFTEN.

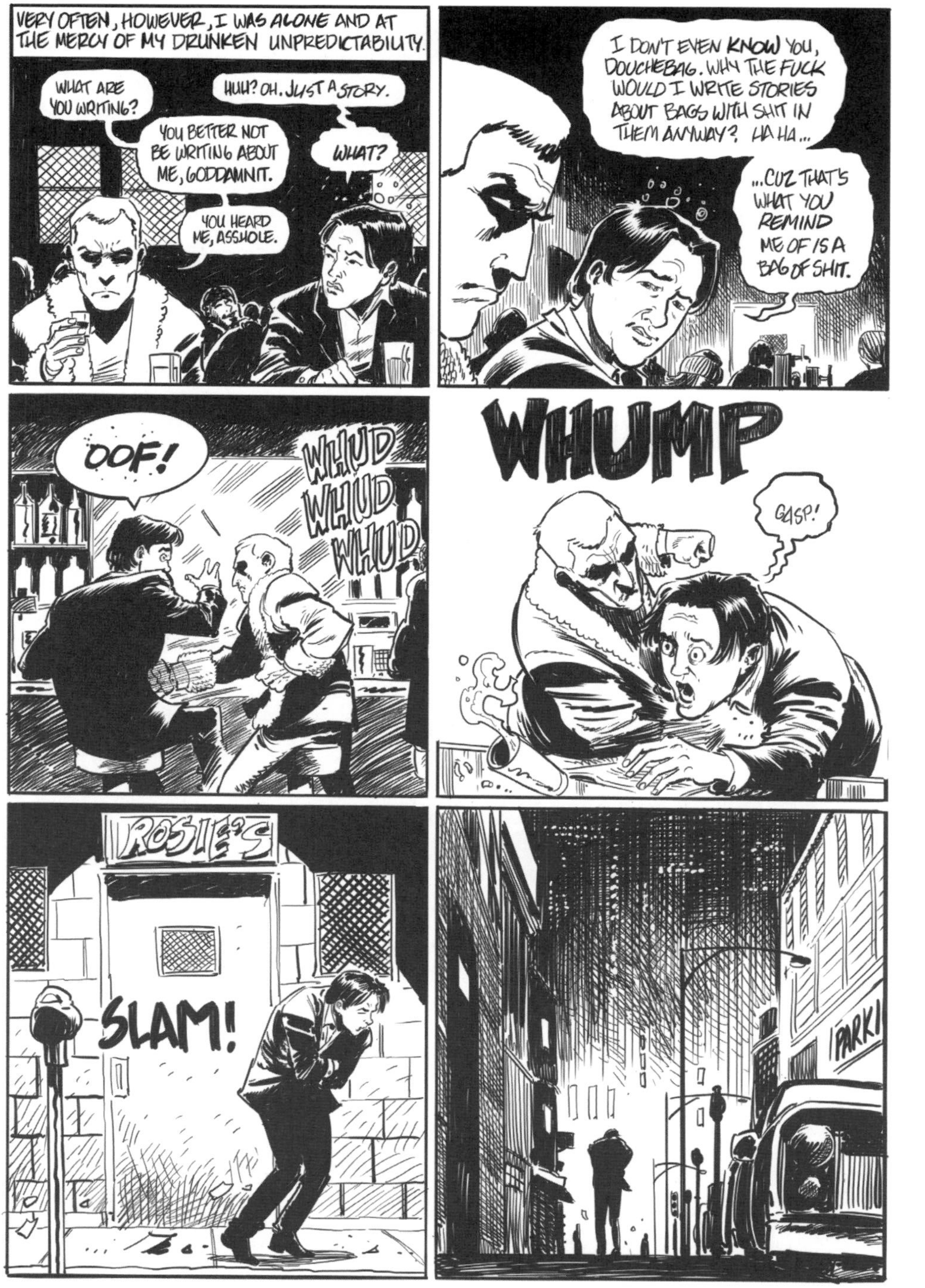
VERY OFTEN, HOWEVER, I WAS ALONE AND AT THE MERCY OF MY DRUNKEN UNPREDICTABILITY.
WHAT ARE YOU WRITING?
HUH? OH. JUST A STORY.
YOU BETTER NOT BE WRITING ABOUT ME, GODDAMNIT.
WHAT?
YOU HEARD ME, ASSHOLE.
I DON'T EVEN KNOW YOU, DOUCHEBAG. WHY THE FUCK WOULD I WRITE STORIES ABOUT BAGS WITH SHIT IN THEM ANYWAY? HA HA...
...CUZ THAT'S WHAT YOU REMIND ME OF IS A BAG OF SHIT.
OOF!
WHUD WHUD WHUD
WHUMP
GASP!
ROSIE'S
SLAM!
PARK

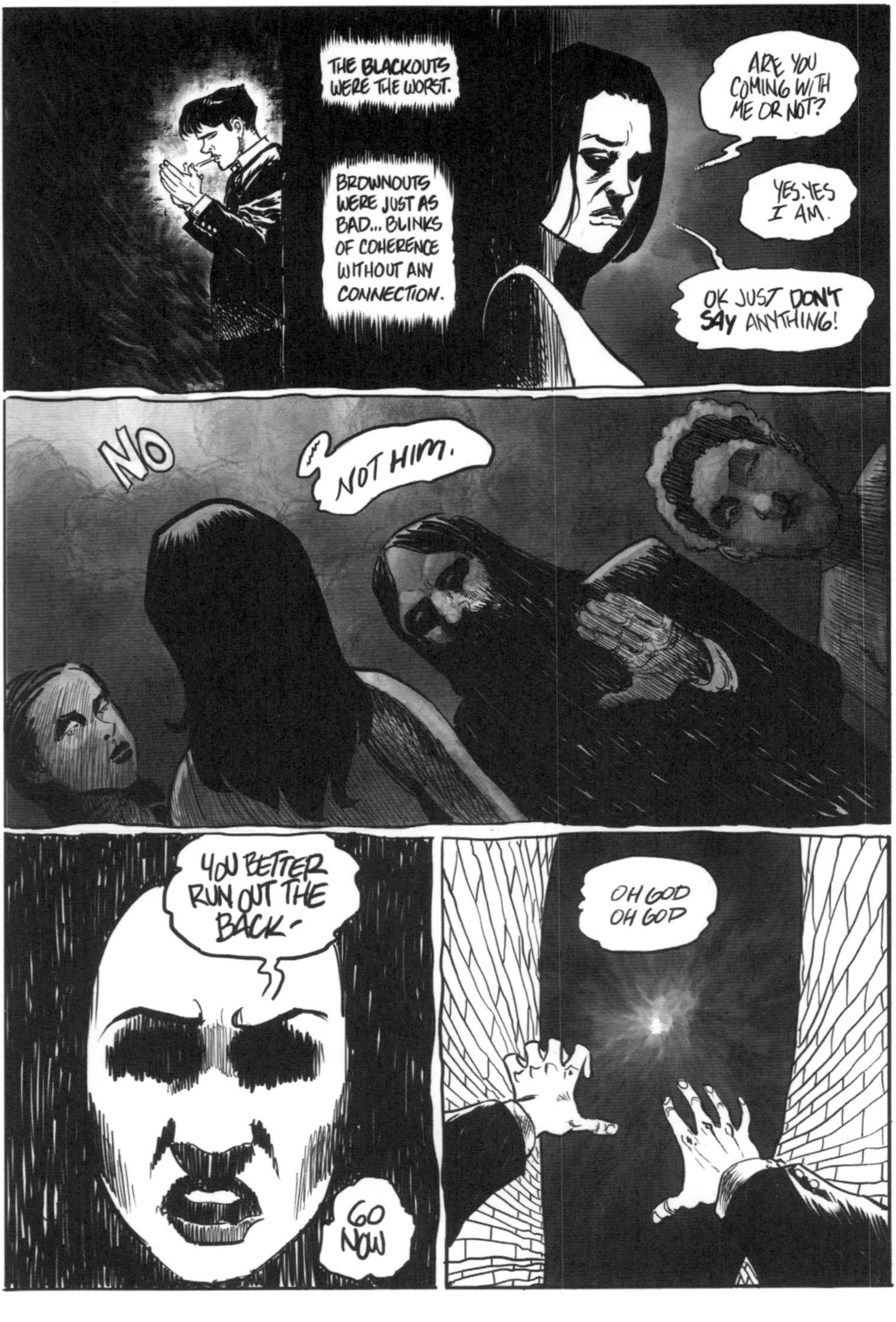
THE BLACKOUTS WERE THE WORST.
BROWNOUTS WERE JUST AS BAD... BLINKS OF COHERENCE WITHOUT ANY CONNECTION.
ARE YOU COMING WITH ME OR NOT?
YES. YES I AM.
OK JUST DON'T SAY ANYTHING!
NO
NOT HIM.
YOU BETTER RUN OUT THE BACK-
GO NOW
OH GOD OH GOD

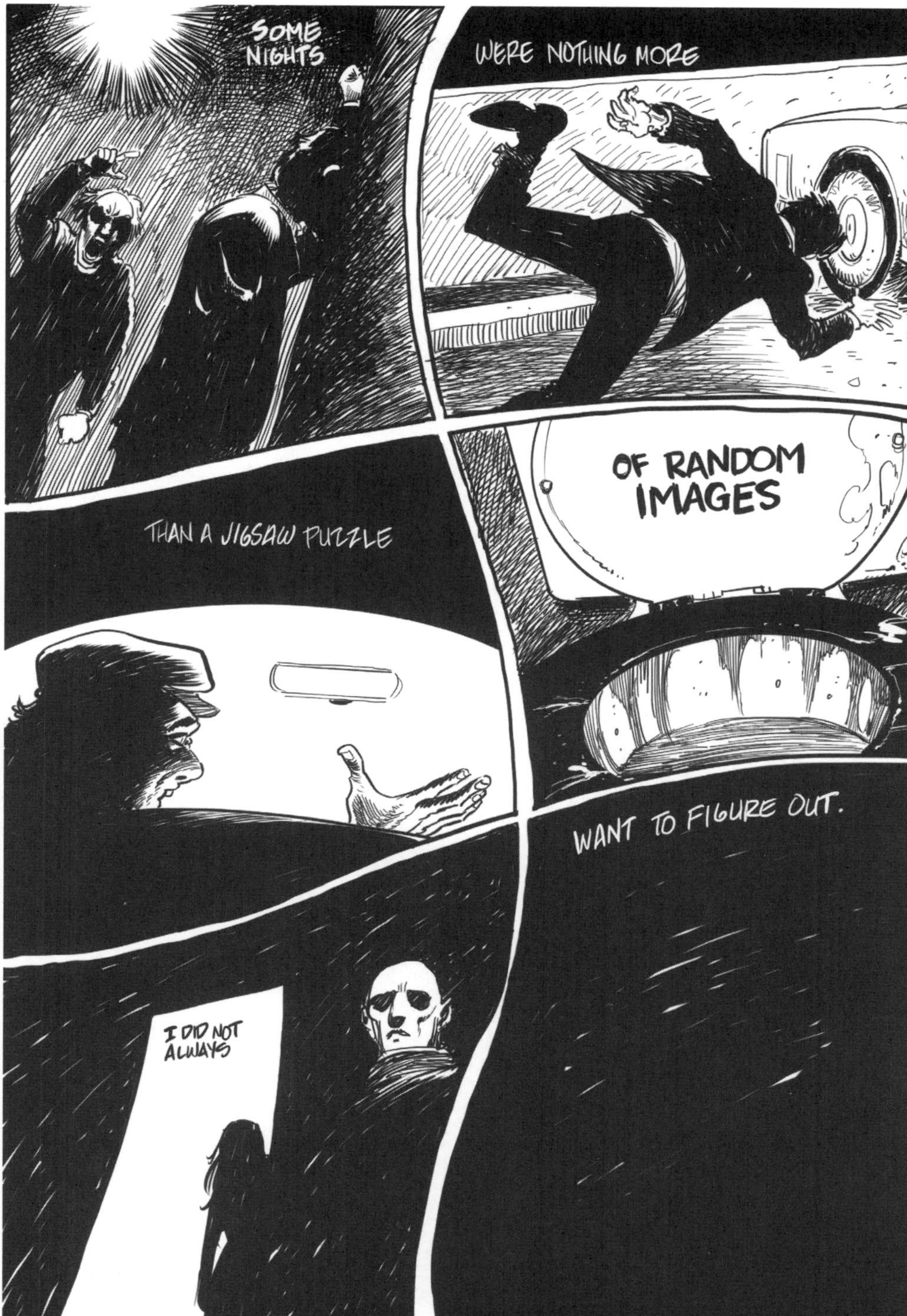
SOME NIGHTS
WERE NOTHING MORE
THAN A JIGSAW PUZZLE
OF RANDOM IMAGES
I DID NOT ALWAYS
WANT TO FIGURE OUT.

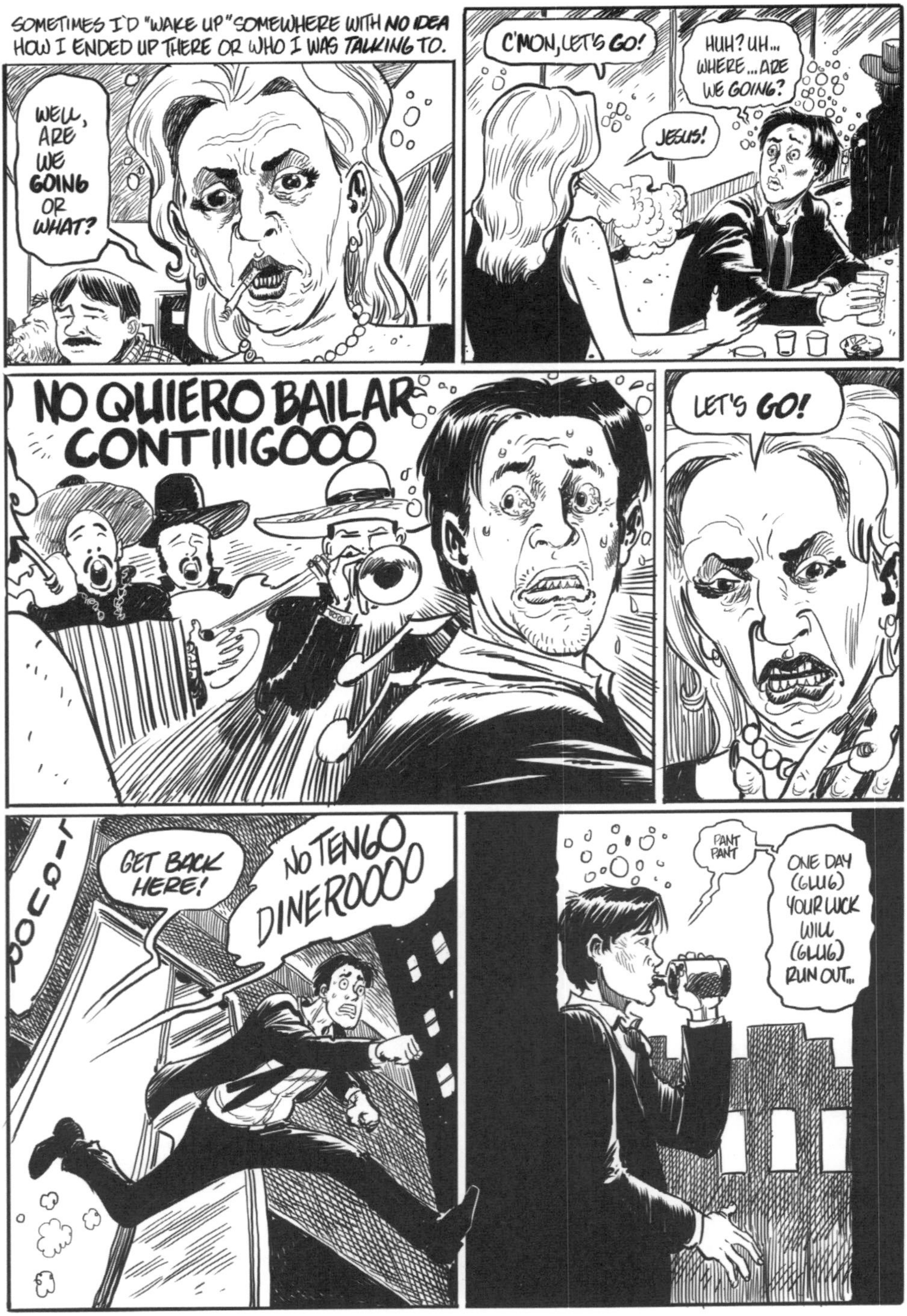
SOMETIMES I'D "WAKE UP" SOMEWHERE WITH NO IDEA HOW I ENDED UP THERE OR WHO I WAS TALKING TO.
WELL, ARE WE GOING OR WHAT?
C'MON, LET'S GO!
HUH? UH... WHERE... ARE WE GOING?
JESUS!
NO QUIERO BAILAR CONTIIIGOOO
LET'S GO!
GET BACK HERE!
NO TENGO DINEROOOO
PANT PANT
ONE DAY (GLUG) YOUR LUCK WILL (GLUG) RUN OUT...

THE CRUSHING **FEAR** AND **PARANOIA** POST-**BLACKOUT** WERE PROFOUND.

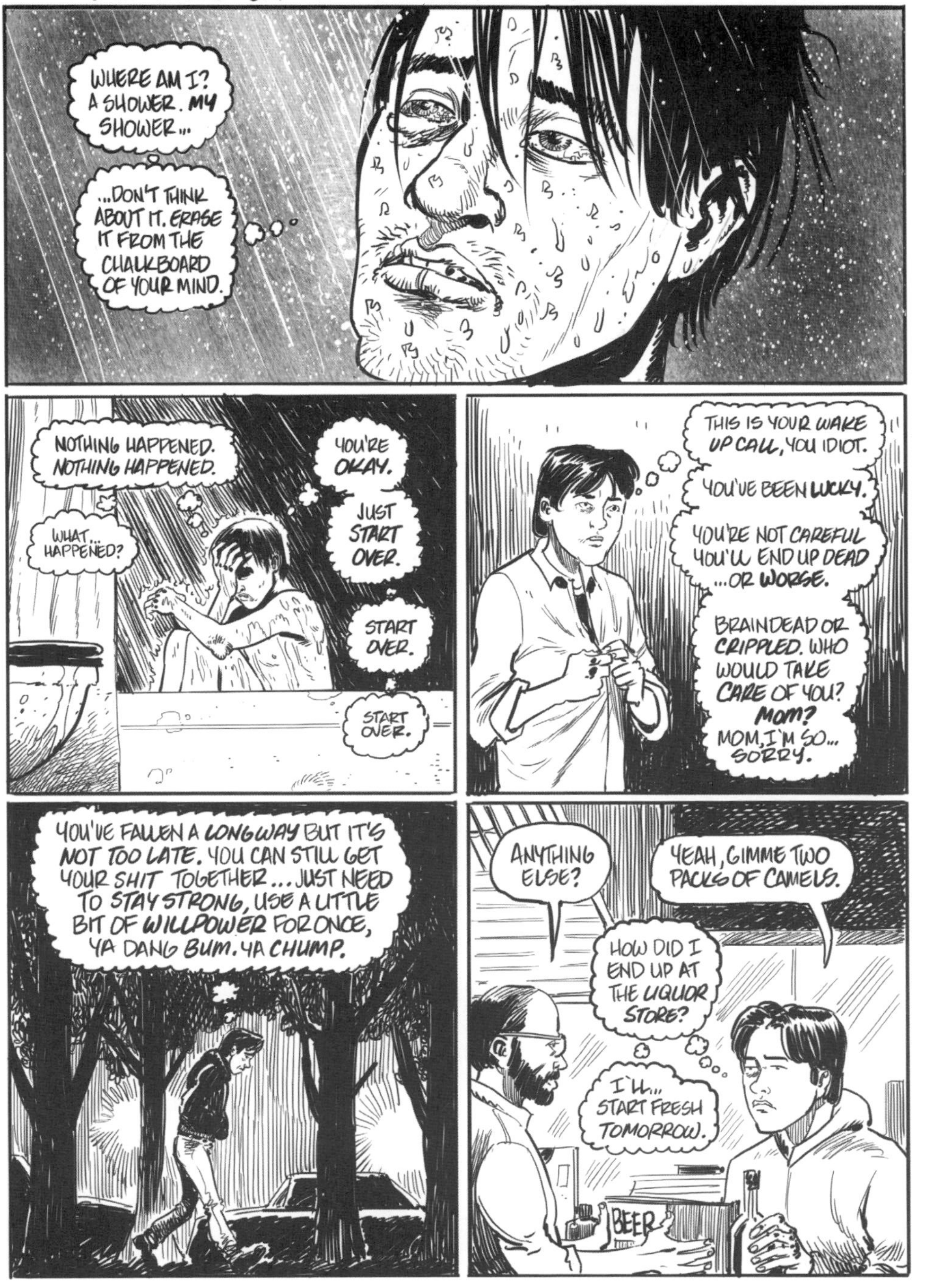
WHERE AM I? A SHOWER. **MY** SHOWER...
...DON'T THINK ABOUT IT. ERASE IT FROM THE CHALKBOARD OF YOUR MIND.
NOTHING HAPPENED. NOTHING HAPPENED.
WHAT... HAPPENED?
YOU'RE **OKAY.**
JUST **START OVER.**
START OVER.
START OVER.
THIS IS YOUR **WAKE UP CALL,** YOU IDIOT.
YOU'VE BEEN **LUCKY.**
YOU'RE NOT **CAREFUL** YOU'LL END UP **DEAD** ...OR **WORSE.**
BRAINDEAD OR **CRIPPLED.** WHO WOULD TAKE **CARE** OF YOU? **MOM?** MOM, I'M SO... SORRY.
YOU'VE FALLEN A **LONG WAY** BUT IT'S **NOT TOO LATE.** YOU CAN STILL GET YOUR SHIT TOGETHER... JUST NEED TO **STAY STRONG,** USE A LITTLE BIT OF **WILLPOWER** FOR ONCE, YA DANG **BUM.** YA **CHUMP.**
ANYTHING ELSE?
YEAH, GIMME TWO PACKS OF CAMELS.
HOW DID I END UP AT THE **LIQUOR STORE?**
I'LL... START FRESH TOMORROW.
BEER

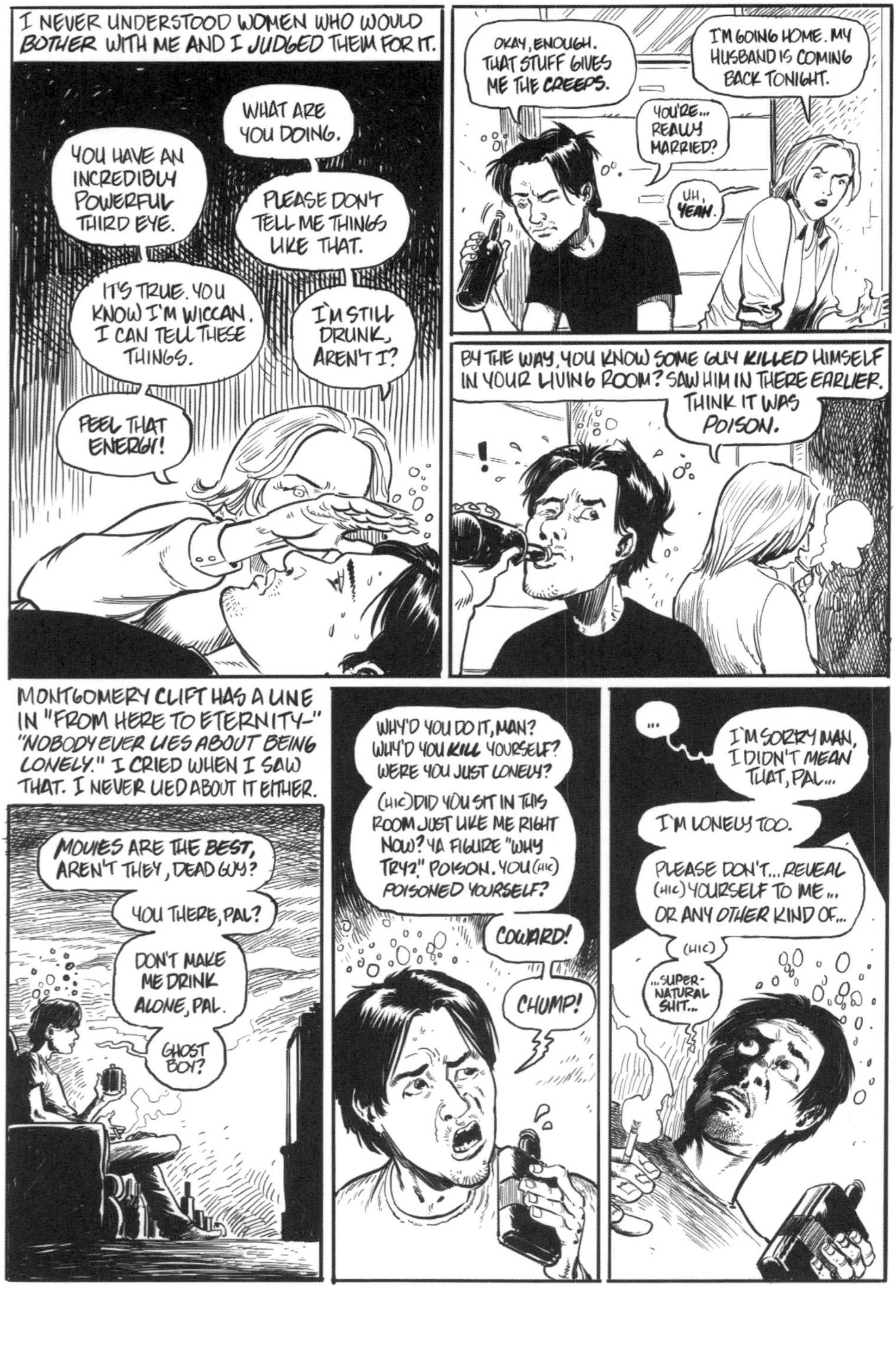
I NEVER UNDERSTOOD WOMEN WHO WOULD BOTHER WITH ME AND I JUDGED THEM FOR IT.
WHAT ARE YOU DOING.
YOU HAVE AN INCREDIBLY POWERFUL THIRD EYE.
PLEASE DON'T TELL ME THINGS LIKE THAT.
IT'S TRUE. YOU KNOW I'M WICCAN. I CAN TELL THESE THINGS.
I'M STILL DRUNK, AREN'T I?
FEEL THAT ENERGY!
OKAY, ENOUGH. THAT STUFF GIVES ME THE CREEPS.
I'M GOING HOME. MY HUSBAND IS COMING BACK TONIGHT.
YOU'RE... REALLY MARRIED?
UH, YEAH.
BY THE WAY, YOU KNOW SOME GUY KILLED HIMSELF IN YOUR LIVING ROOM? SAW HIM IN THERE EARLIER.
THINK IT WAS POISON.
!
MONTGOMERY CLIFT HAS A LINE IN "FROM HERE TO ETERNITY-" "NOBODY EVER LIES ABOUT BEING LONELY." I CRIED WHEN I SAW THAT. I NEVER LIED ABOUT IT EITHER.
MOVIES ARE THE BEST, AREN'T THEY, DEAD GUY?
YOU THERE, PAL?
DON'T MAKE ME DRINK ALONE, PAL.
GHOST BOY?
WHY'D YOU DO IT, MAN? WHY'D YOU KILL YOURSELF? WERE YOU JUST LONELY?
(HIC) DID YOU SIT IN THIS ROOM JUST LIKE ME RIGHT NOW? YA FIGURE "WHY TRY?" POISON. YOU (HIC) POISONED YOURSELF?
COWARD!
CHUMP!
...
I'M SORRY MAN, I DIDN'T MEAN THAT, PAL...
I'M LONELY TOO.
PLEASE DON'T... REVEAL (HIC) YOURSELF TO ME... OR ANY OTHER KIND OF...
(HIC)
...SUPER-NATURAL SHIT...

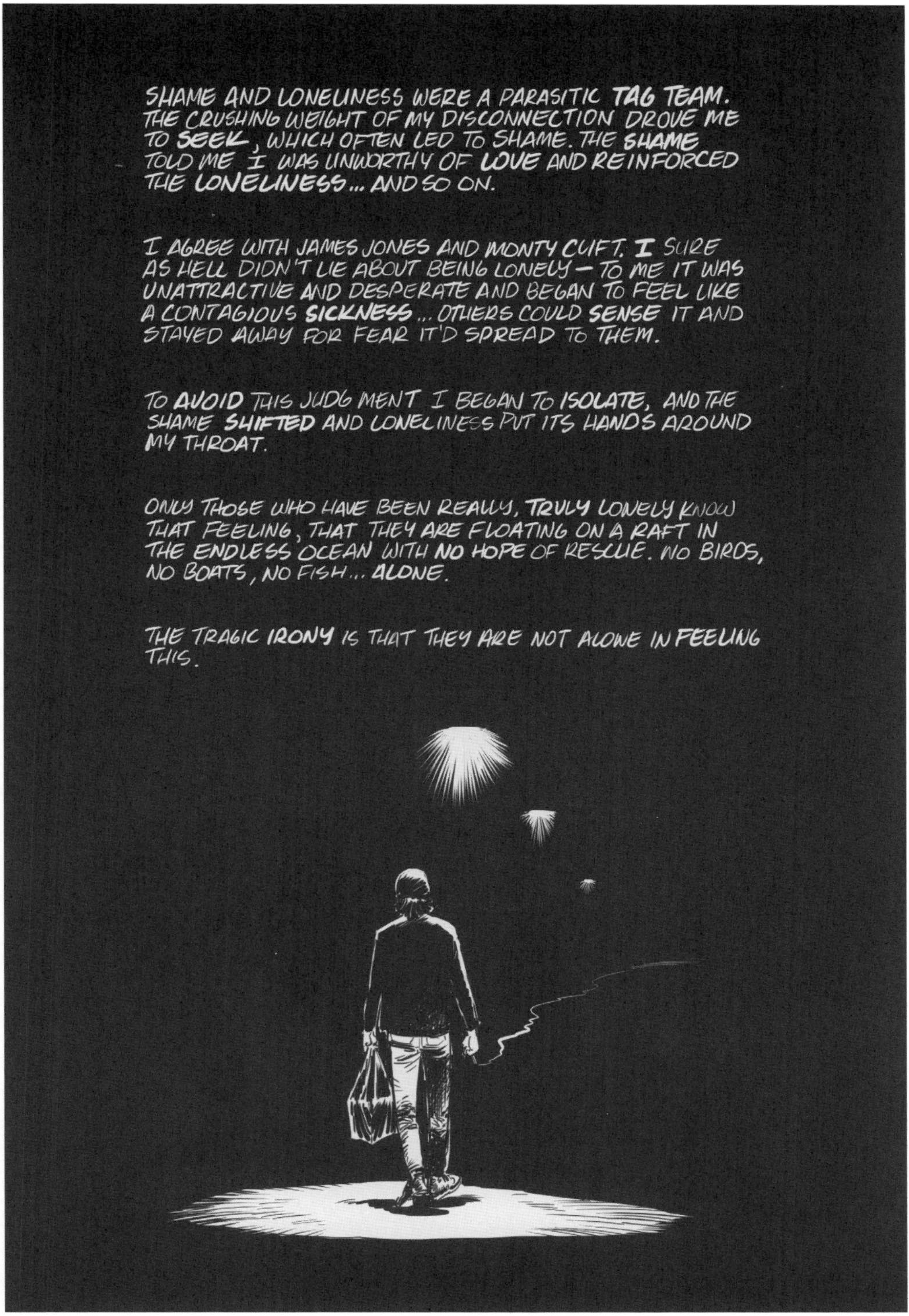
SHAME AND LONELINESS WERE A PARASITIC **TAG TEAM.** THE CRUSHING WEIGHT OF MY DISCONNECTION DROVE ME TO **SEEK**, WHICH OFTEN LED TO SHAME. THE **SHAME** TOLD ME I WAS UNWORTHY OF **LOVE** AND REINFORCED THE **LONELINESS**... AND SO ON.
I AGREE WITH JAMES JONES AND MONTY CLIFT. **I** SURE AS HELL DIDN'T LIE ABOUT BEING LONELY — TO ME IT WAS UNATTRACTIVE AND DESPERATE AND BEGAN TO FEEL LIKE A CONTAGIOUS **SICKNESS**... OTHERS COULD **SENSE** IT AND STAYED AWAY FOR FEAR IT'D SPREAD TO THEM.
TO **AVOID** THIS JUDGMENT I BEGAN TO **ISOLATE,** AND THE SHAME **SHIFTED** AND LONELINESS PUT ITS HANDS AROUND MY THROAT.
ONLY THOSE WHO HAVE BEEN REALLY, **TRULY** LONELY KNOW THAT FEELING, THAT THEY **ARE** FLOATING ON A RAFT IN THE **ENDLESS** OCEAN WITH **NO HOPE** OF RESCUE. NO BIRDS, NO BOATS, NO FISH... **ALONE**.
THE TRAGIC **IRONY** IS THAT THEY ARE NOT ALONE IN **FEELING** THIS.

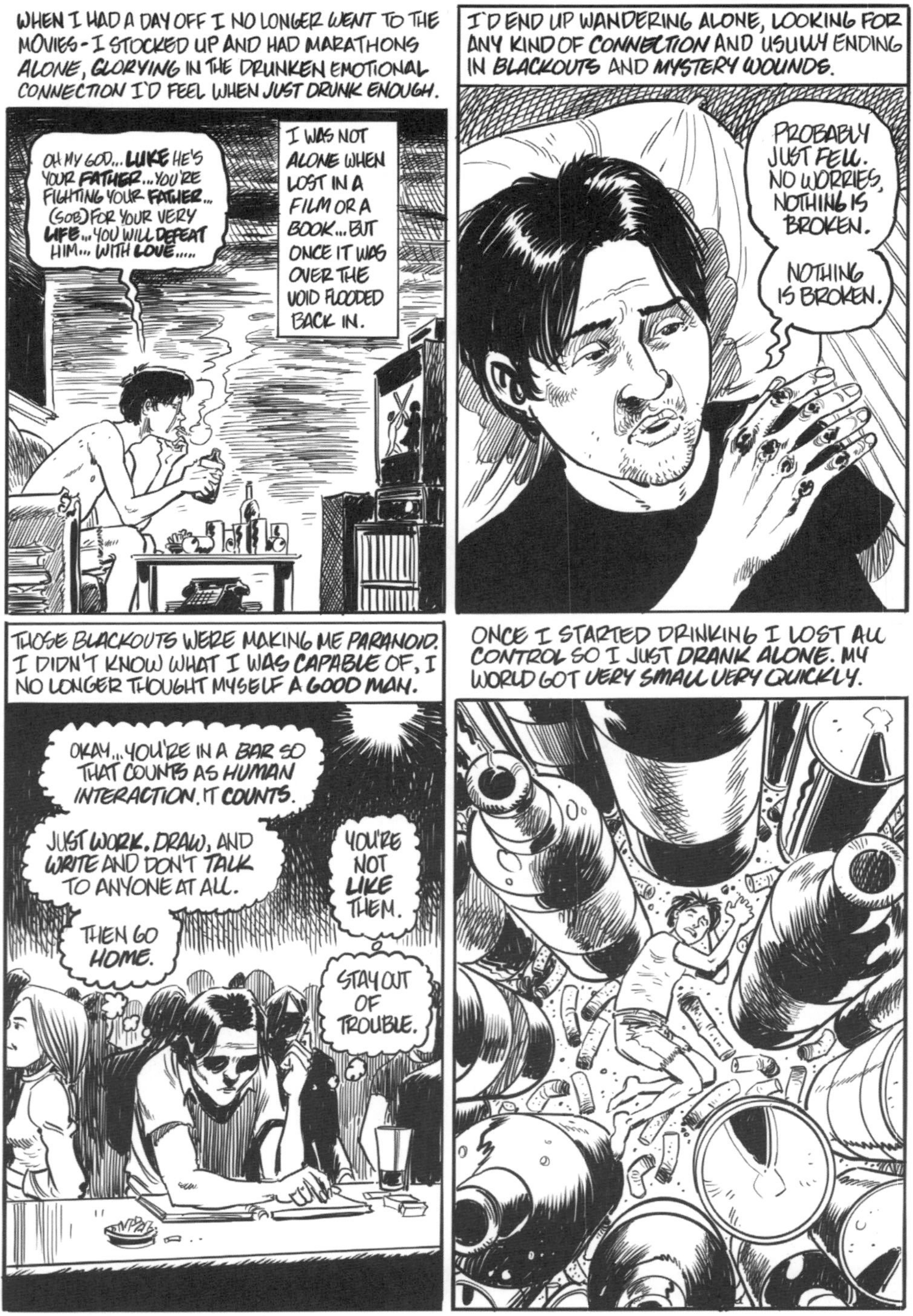
WHEN I HAD A DAY OFF I NO LONGER WENT TO THE MOVIES - I STOCKED UP AND HAD MARATHONS ALONE, GLORYING IN THE DRUNKEN EMOTIONAL CONNECTION I'D FEEL WHEN JUST DRUNK ENOUGH.
OH MY GOD... LUKE HE'S YOUR FATHER... YOU'RE FIGHTING YOUR FATHER... (SOB) FOR YOUR VERY LIFE... YOU WILL DEFEAT HIM... WITH LOVE.....
I WAS NOT ALONE WHEN LOST IN A FILM OR A BOOK... BUT ONCE IT WAS OVER THE VOID FLOODED BACK IN.
I'D END UP WANDERING ALONE, LOOKING FOR ANY KIND OF CONNECTION AND USUALLY ENDING IN BLACKOUTS AND MYSTERY WOUNDS.
PROBABLY JUST FELL. NO WORRIES, NOTHING IS BROKEN.
NOTHING IS BROKEN.
THOSE BLACKOUTS WERE MAKING ME PARANOID. I DIDN'T KNOW WHAT I WAS CAPABLE OF, I NO LONGER THOUGHT MYSELF A GOOD MAN.
OKAY... YOU'RE IN A BAR SO THAT COUNTS AS HUMAN INTERACTION. IT COUNTS.
JUST WORK. DRAW, AND WRITE AND DON'T TALK TO ANYONE AT ALL.
THEN GO HOME.
YOU'RE NOT LIKE THEM.
STAY OUT OF TROUBLE.
ONCE I STARTED DRINKING I LOST ALL CONTROL SO I JUST DRANK ALONE. MY WORLD GOT VERY SMALL VERY QUICKLY.

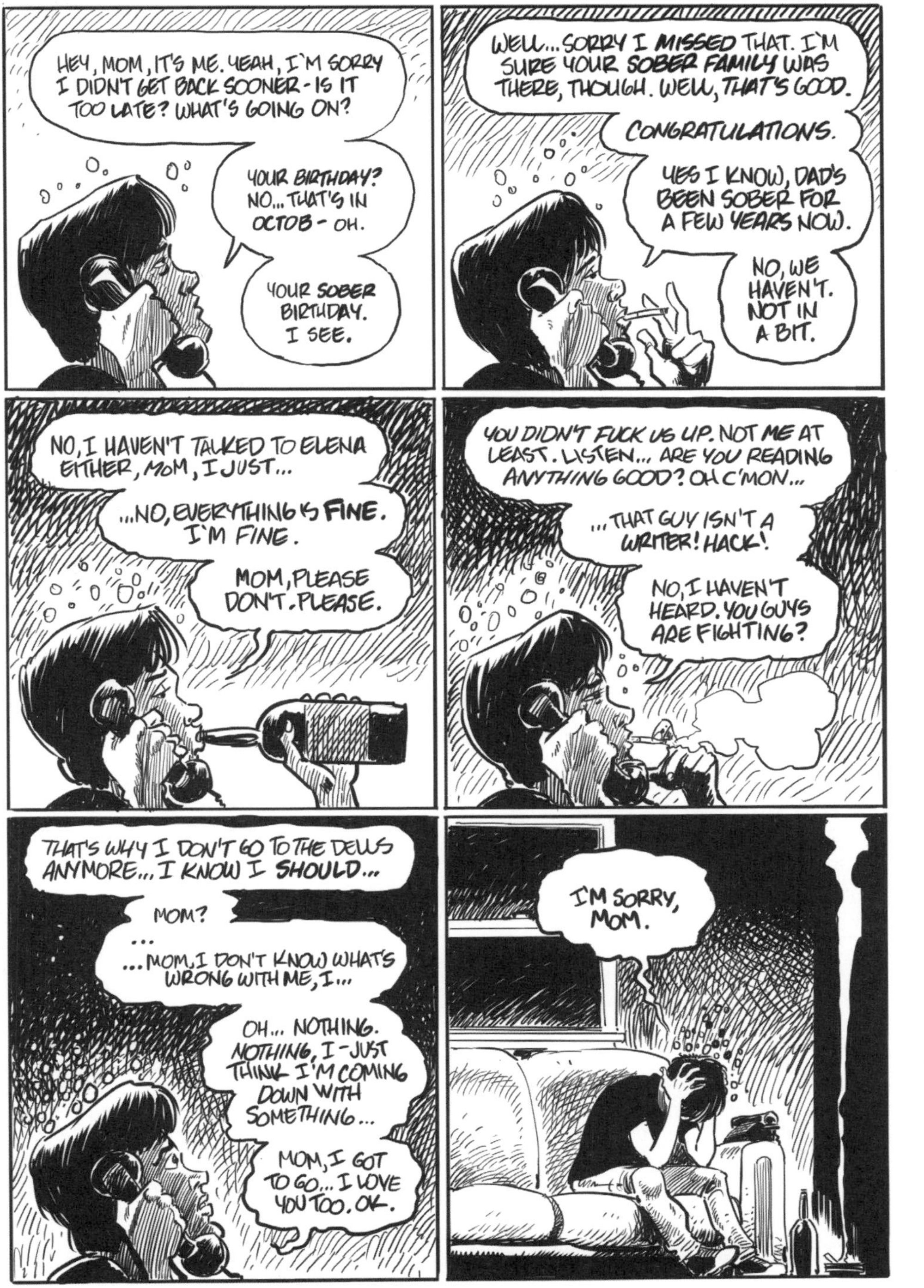

HEY, MOM, IT'S ME. YEAH, I'M SORRY I DIDN'T GET BACK SOONER - IS IT TOO LATE? WHAT'S GOING ON?
YOUR BIRTHDAY? NO... THAT'S IN OCTOB - OH.
YOUR SOBER BIRTHDAY. I SEE.
WELL... SORRY I MISSED THAT. I'M SURE YOUR SOBER FAMILY WAS THERE, THOUGH. WELL, THAT'S GOOD.
CONGRATULATIONS.
YES I KNOW, DAD'S BEEN SOBER FOR A FEW YEARS NOW.
NO, WE HAVEN'T. NOT IN A BIT.
NO, I HAVEN'T TALKED TO ELENA EITHER, MOM, I JUST...
...NO, EVERYTHING'S FINE. I'M FINE.
MOM, PLEASE DON'T. PLEASE.
YOU DIDN'T FUCK US UP. NOT ME AT LEAST. LISTEN... ARE YOU READING ANYTHING GOOD? OH C'MON...
...THAT GUY ISN'T A WRITER! HACK!
NO, I HAVEN'T HEARD. YOU GUYS ARE FIGHTING?
THAT'S WHY I DON'T GO TO THE DELLS ANYMORE... I KNOW I SHOULD...
MOM?
...
...MOM, I DON'T KNOW WHAT'S WRONG WITH ME, I...
OH... NOTHING. NOTHING, I - JUST THINK I'M COMING DOWN WITH SOMETHING...
MOM, I GOT TO GO... I LOVE YOU TOO. OK.
I'M SORRY, MOM.

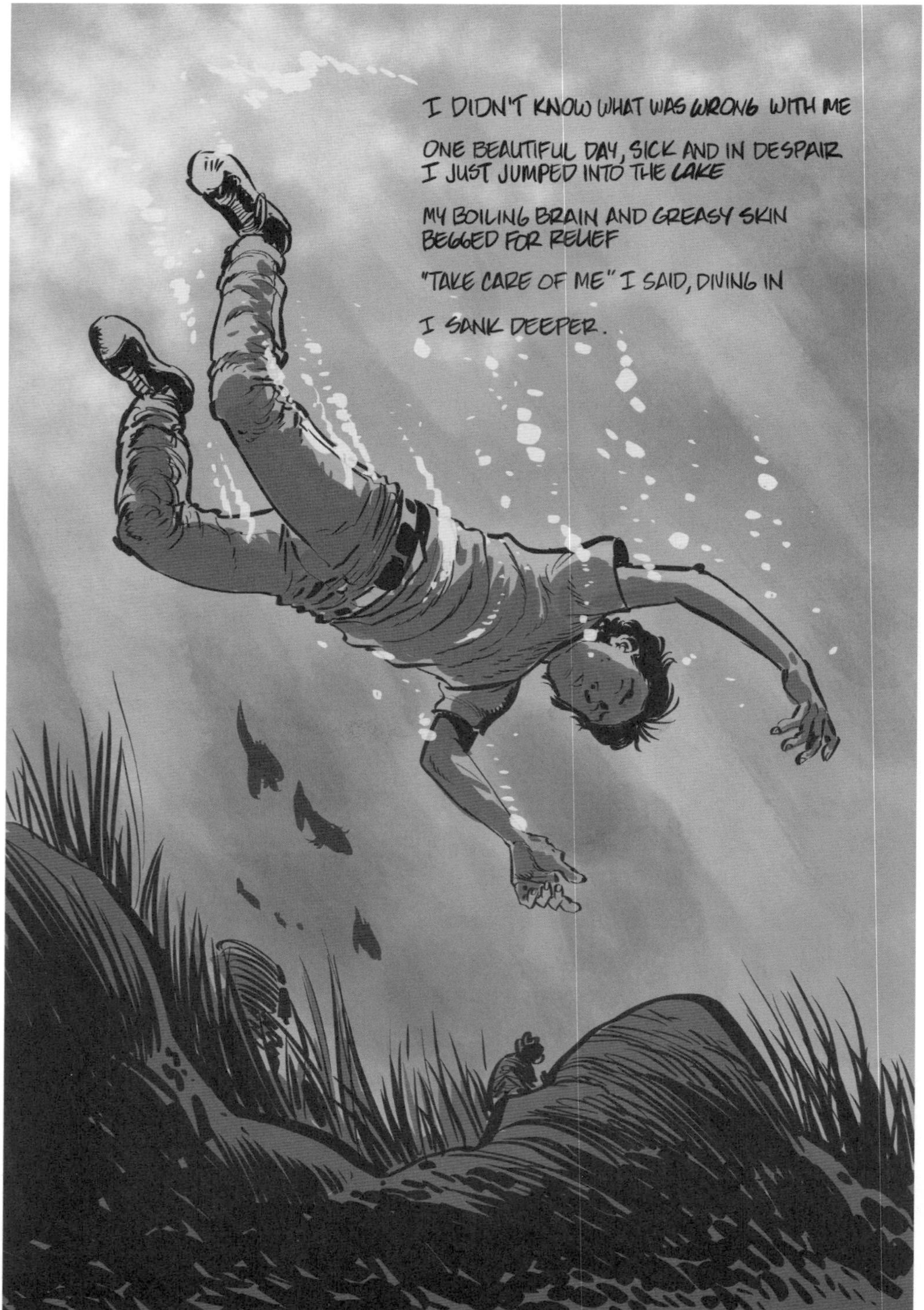
I DIDN'T KNOW WHAT WAS WRONG WITH ME
ONE BEAUTIFUL DAY, SICK AND IN DESPAIR I JUST JUMPED INTO THE LAKE
MY BOILING BRAIN AND GREASY SKIN BEGGED FOR RELIEF
"TAKE CARE OF ME" I SAID, DIVING IN
I SANK DEEPER.

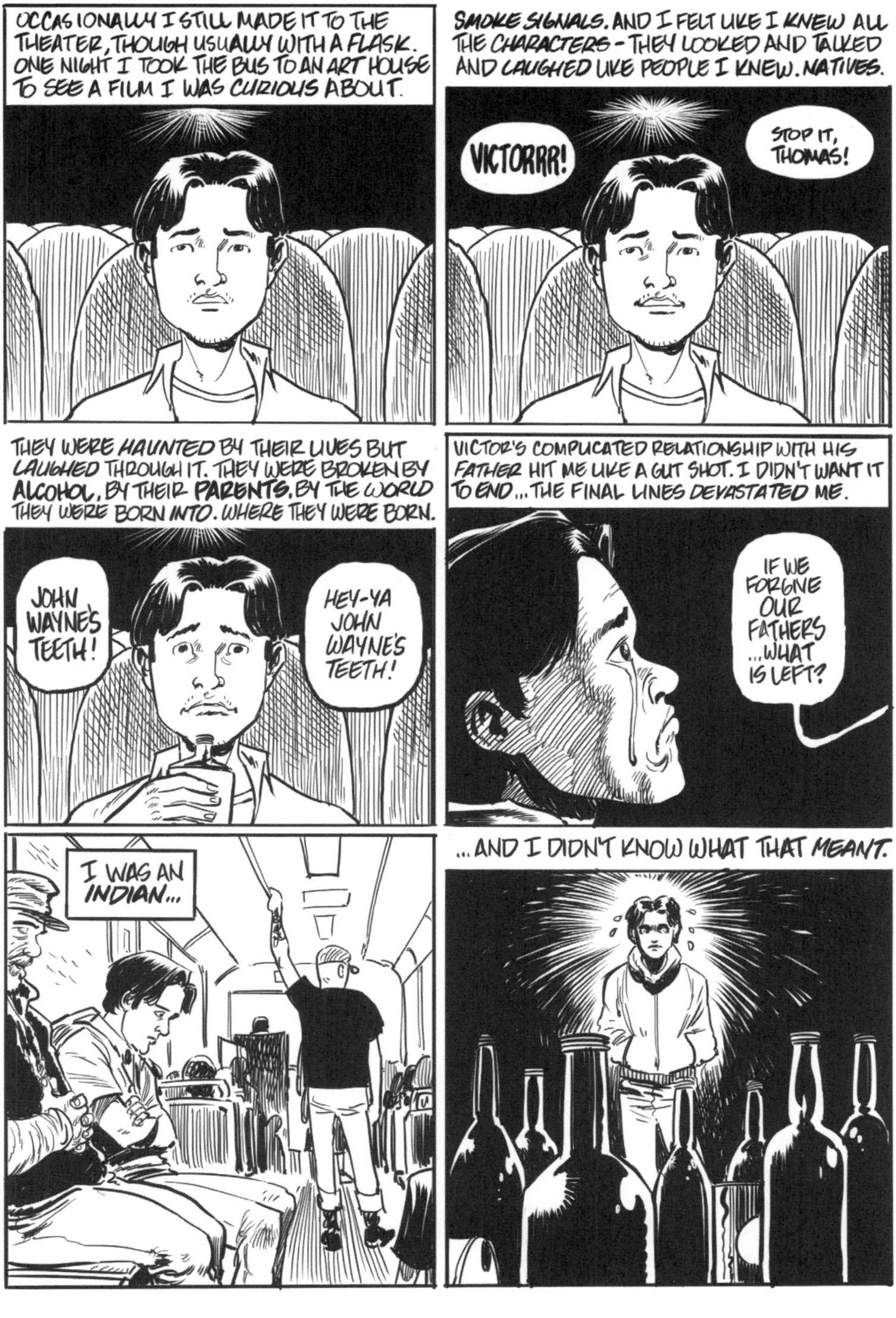
OCCASIONALLY I STILL MADE IT TO THE THEATER, THOUGH USUALLY WITH A FLASK. ONE NIGHT I TOOK THE BUS TO AN ART HOUSE TO SEE A FILM I WAS CURIOUS ABOUT.
SMOKE SIGNALS. AND I FELT LIKE I KNEW ALL THE CHARACTERS - THEY LOOKED AND TALKED AND LAUGHED LIKE PEOPLE I KNEW. NATIVES.
VICTORRR!
STOP IT, THOMAS!
THEY WERE HAUNTED BY THEIR LIVES BUT LAUGHED THROUGH IT. THEY WERE BROKEN BY ALCOHOL, BY THEIR PARENTS, BY THE WORLD THEY WERE BORN INTO. WHERE THEY WERE BORN.
JOHN WAYNE'S TEETH!
HEY-YA JOHN WAYNE'S TEETH!
VICTOR'S COMPLICATED RELATIONSHIP WITH HIS FATHER HIT ME LIKE A GUT SHOT. I DIDN'T WANT IT TO END... THE FINAL LINES DEVASTATED ME.
IF WE FORGIVE OUR FATHERS ...WHAT IS LEFT?
I WAS AN INDIAN...
...AND I DIDN'T KNOW WHAT THAT MEANT.

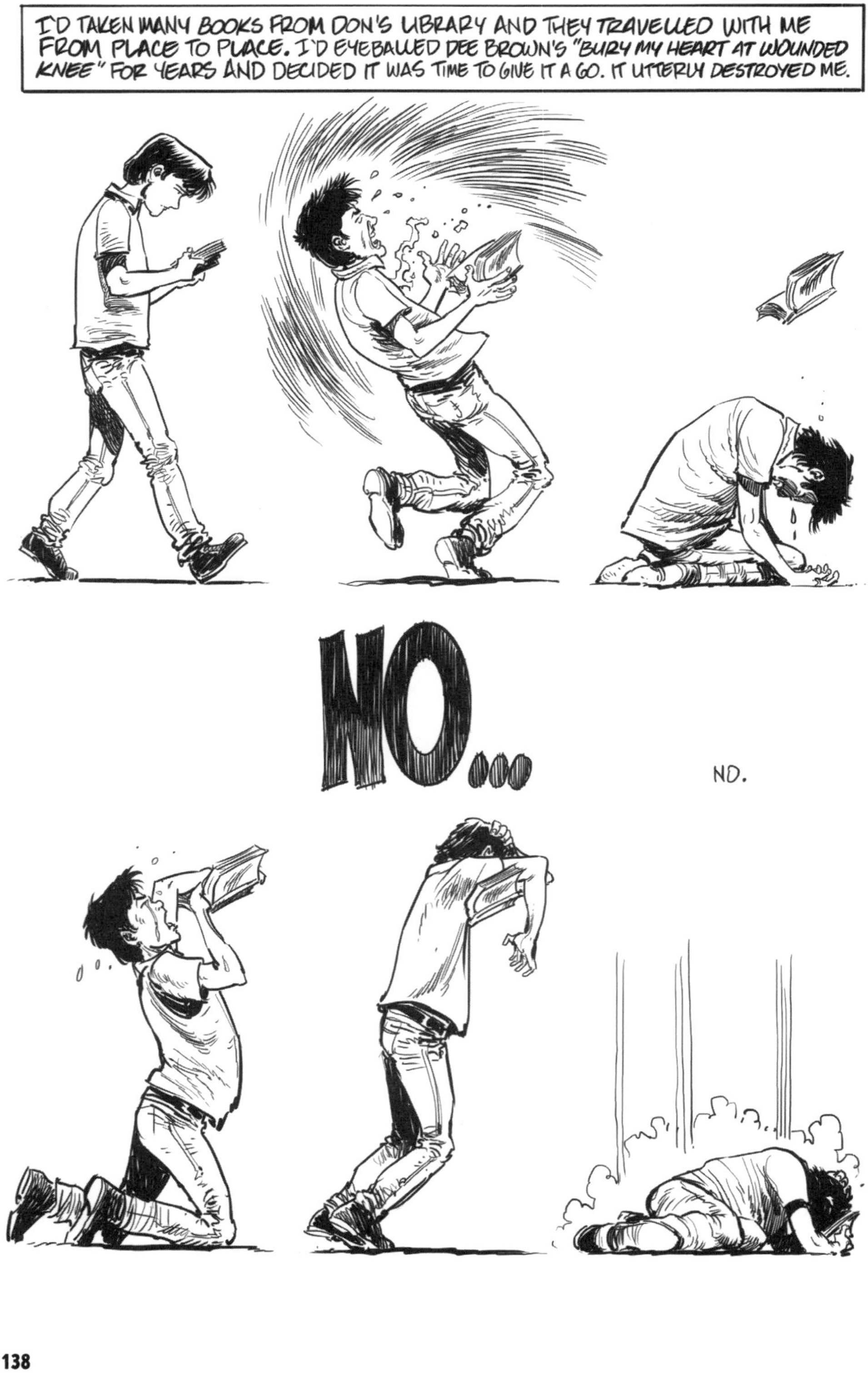
I'D TAKEN MANY BOOKS FROM DON'S LIBRARY AND THEY TRAVELLED WITH ME FROM PLACE TO PLACE. I'D EYEBALLED DEE BROWN'S "BURY MY HEART AT WOUNDED KNEE" FOR YEARS AND DECIDED IT WAS TIME TO GIVE IT A GO. IT UTTERLY DESTROYED ME.
NO...
NO.

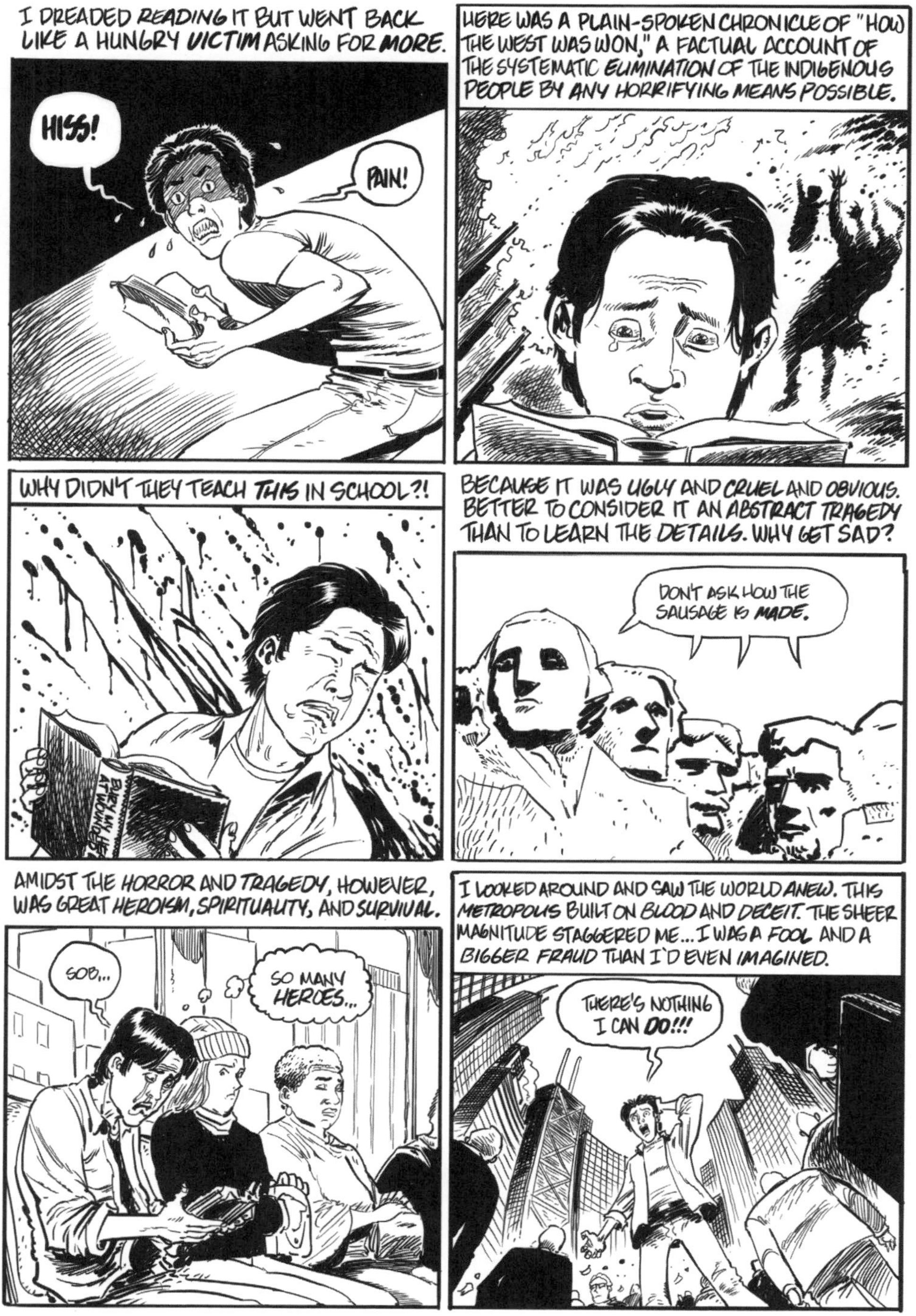
I DREADED READING IT BUT WENT BACK LIKE A HUNGRY VICTIM ASKING FOR MORE.
HISS!
PAIN!
HERE WAS A PLAIN-SPOKEN CHRONICLE OF "HOW THE WEST WAS WON," A FACTUAL ACCOUNT OF THE SYSTEMATIC ELIMINATION OF THE INDIGENOUS PEOPLE BY ANY HORRIFYING MEANS POSSIBLE.
WHY DIDN'T THEY TEACH THIS IN SCHOOL?!
BECAUSE IT WAS UGLY AND CRUEL AND OBVIOUS. BETTER TO CONSIDER IT AN ABSTRACT TRAGEDY THAN TO LEARN THE DETAILS. WHY GET SAD?
DON'T ASK HOW THE SAUSAGE IS MADE.
AMIDST THE HORROR AND TRAGEDY, HOWEVER, WAS GREAT HEROISM, SPIRITUALITY, AND SURVIVAL.
SOB...
SO MANY HEROES...
I LOOKED AROUND AND SAW THE WORLD ANEW. THIS METROPOLIS BUILT ON BLOOD AND DECEIT. THE SHEER MAGNITUDE STAGGERED ME... I WAS A FOOL AND A BIGGER FRAUD THAN I'D EVEN IMAGINED.
THERE'S NOTHING I CAN DO!!!

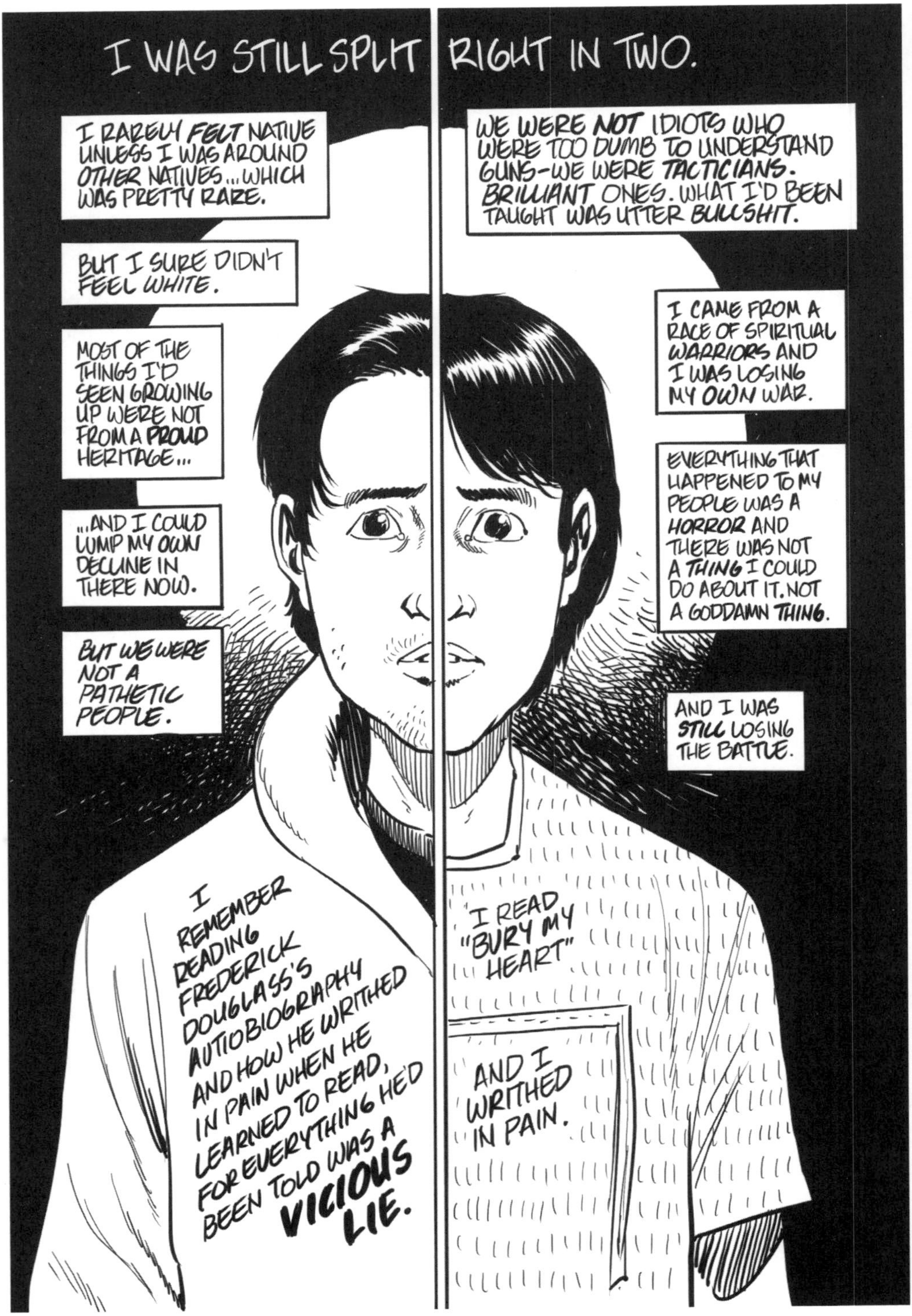
I WAS STILL SPLIT RIGHT IN TWO.
I RARELY FELT NATIVE UNLESS I WAS AROUND OTHER NATIVES... WHICH WAS PRETTY RARE.
BUT I SURE DIDN'T FEEL WHITE.
MOST OF THE THINGS I'D SEEN GROWING UP WERE NOT FROM A PROUD HERITAGE...
...AND I COULD LUMP MY OWN DECLINE IN THERE NOW.
BUT WE WERE NOT A PATHETIC PEOPLE.
WE WERE NOT IDIOTS WHO WERE TOO DUMB TO UNDERSTAND GUNS-WE WERE TACTICIANS. BRILLIANT ONES. WHAT I'D BEEN TAUGHT WAS UTTER BULLSHIT.
I CAME FROM A RACE OF SPIRITUAL WARRIORS AND I WAS LOSING MY OWN WAR.
EVERYTHING THAT HAPPENED TO MY PEOPLE WAS A HORROR AND THERE WAS NOT A THING I COULD DO ABOUT IT. NOT A GODDAMN THING.
AND I WAS STILL LOSING THE BATTLE.
I REMEMBER READING FREDERICK DOUGLASS'S AUTOBIOGRAPHY AND HOW HE WRITHED IN PAIN WHEN HE LEARNED TO READ, FOR EVERYTHING HE'D BEEN TOLD WAS A VICIOUS LIE.
I READ "BURY MY HEART"
AND I WRITHED IN PAIN.

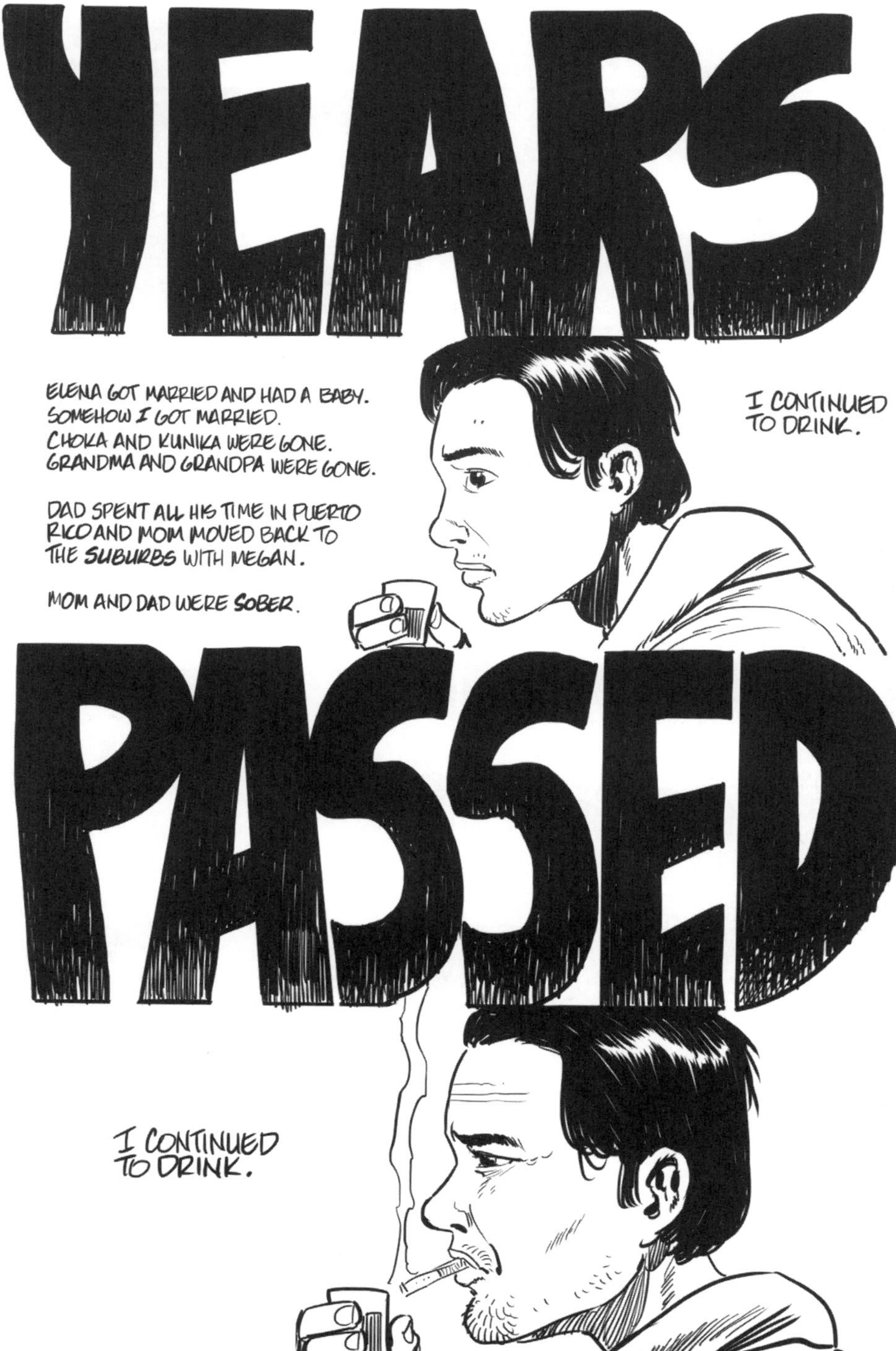
YEARS
ELENA GOT MARRIED AND HAD A BABY.
SOMEHOW I GOT MARRIED.
CHOKA AND KUNIKA WERE GONE.
GRANDMA AND GRANDPA WERE GONE.
DAD SPENT ALL HIS TIME IN PUERTO RICO AND MOM MOVED BACK TO THE SUBURBS WITH MEGAN.
MOM AND DAD WERE SOBER.
I CONTINUED TO DRINK.
PASSED
I CONTINUED TO DRINK.

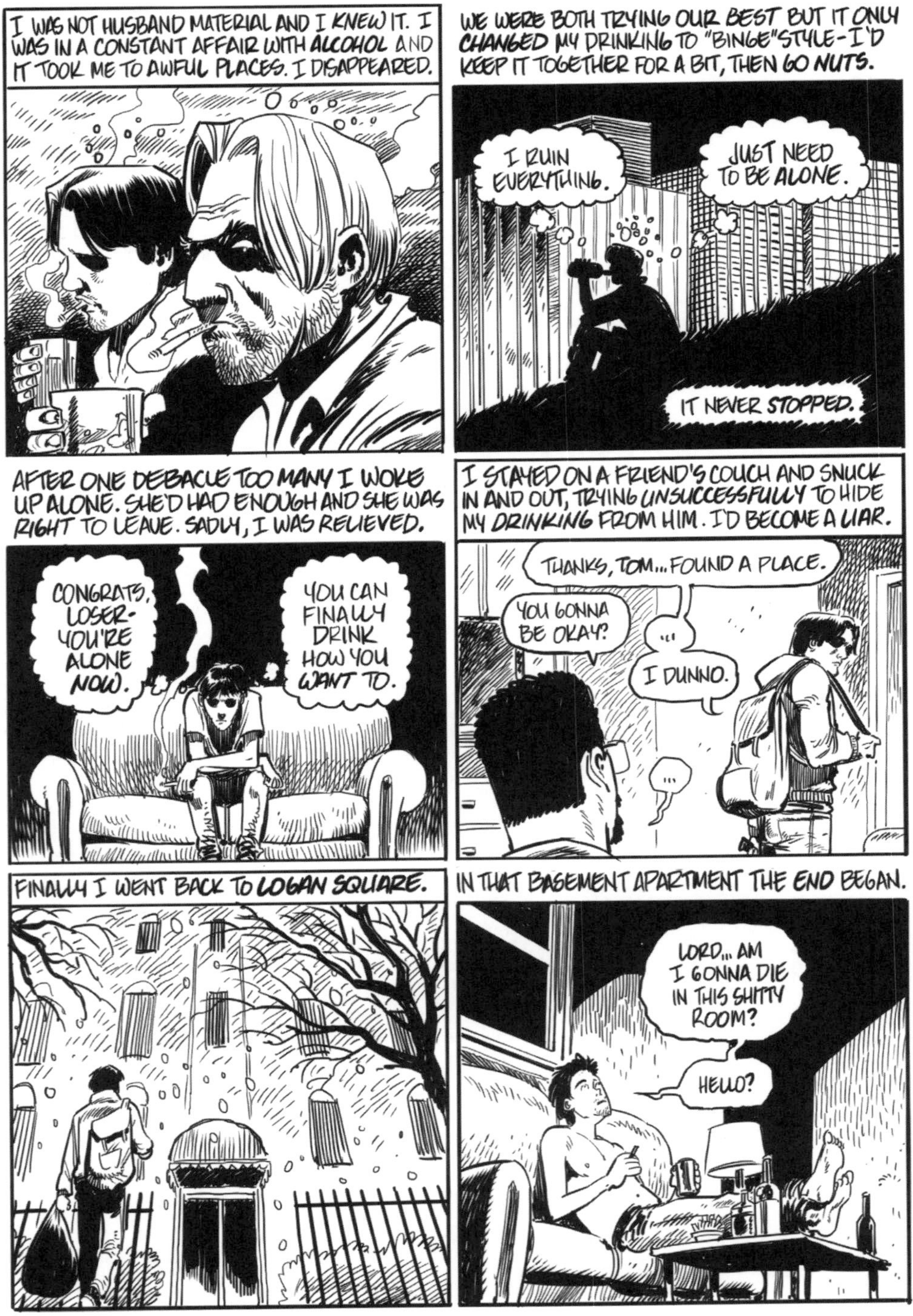
I WAS NOT HUSBAND MATERIAL AND I KNEW IT. I WAS IN A CONSTANT AFFAIR WITH ALCOHOL AND IT TOOK ME TO AWFUL PLACES. I DISAPPEARED.
WE WERE BOTH TRYING OUR BEST BUT IT ONLY CHANGED MY DRINKING TO "BINGE" STYLE - I'D KEEP IT TOGETHER FOR A BIT, THEN GO NUTS.
I RUIN EVERYTHING.
JUST NEED TO BE ALONE.
IT NEVER STOPPED.
AFTER ONE DEBACLE TOO MANY I WOKE UP ALONE. SHE'D HAD ENOUGH AND SHE WAS RIGHT TO LEAVE. SADLY, I WAS RELIEVED.
CONGRATS, LOSER- YOU'RE ALONE NOW.
YOU CAN FINALLY DRINK HOW YOU WANT TO.
I STAYED ON A FRIEND'S COUCH AND SNUCK IN AND OUT, TRYING UNSUCCESSFULLY TO HIDE MY DRINKING FROM HIM. I'D BECOME A LIAR.
THANKS, TOM... FOUND A PLACE.
YOU GONNA BE OKAY?
...
I DUNNO.
...
FINALLY I WENT BACK TO LOGAN SQUARE.
IN THAT BASEMENT APARTMENT THE END BEGAN.
LORD... AM I GONNA DIE IN THIS SHITTY ROOM?
HELLO?

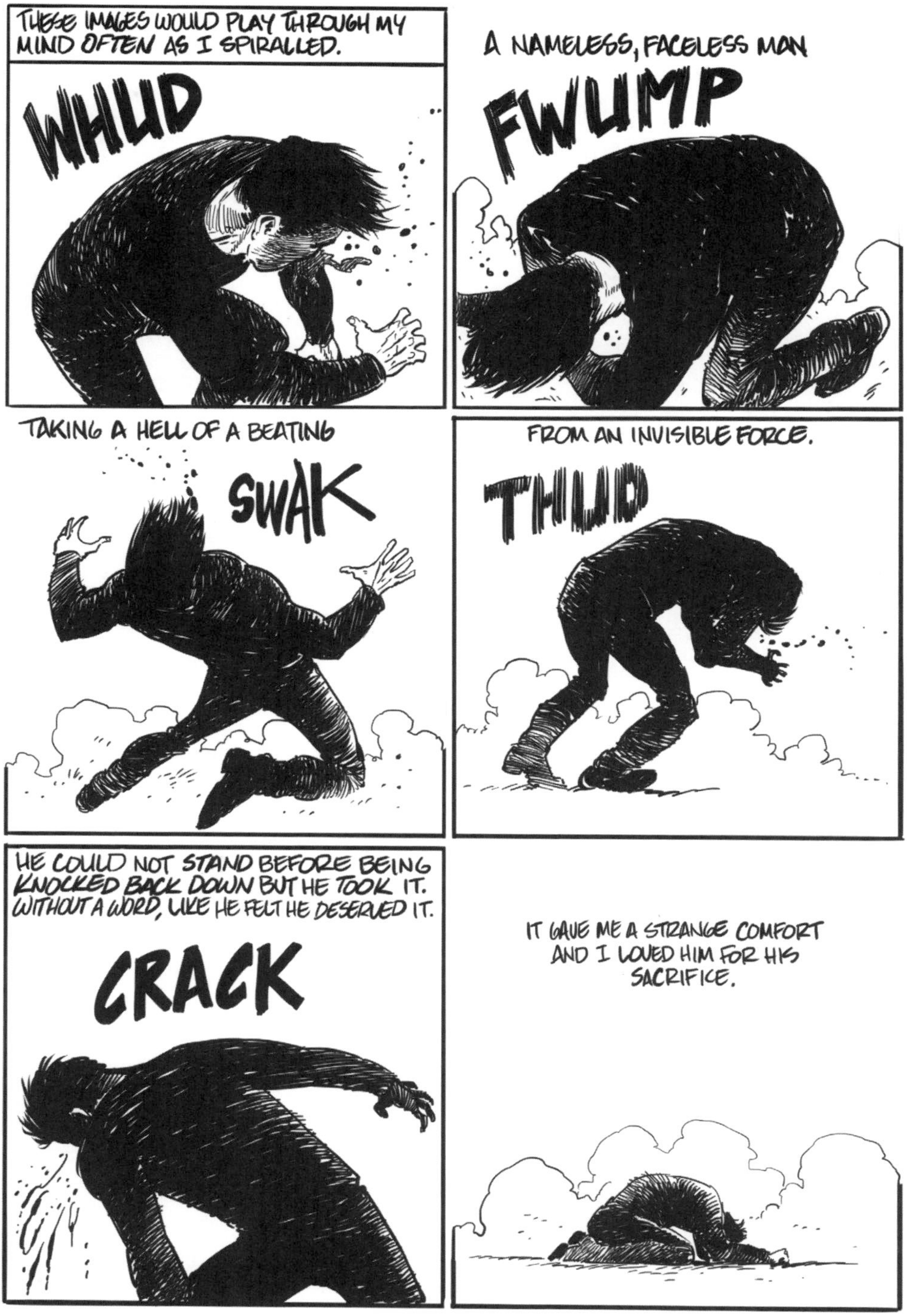
THESE IMAGES WOULD PLAY THROUGH MY MIND OFTEN AS I SPIRALLED.
WHUD
A NAMELESS, FACELESS MAN
FWUMP
TAKING A HELL OF A BEATING
SWAK
FROM AN INVISIBLE FORCE.
THUD
HE COULD NOT STAND BEFORE BEING KNOCKED BACK DOWN BUT HE TOOK IT. WITHOUT A WORD, LIKE HE FELT HE DESERVED IT.
CRACK
IT GAVE ME A STRANGE COMFORT AND I LOVED HIM FOR HIS SACRIFICE.

I RESIGNED MYSELF TO MY FATE—I WORKED AND I **DRANK** AND ALL ELSE FELL AWAY.

ALMOST TO MY STOP... MIGHT HAVE TO GET OFF EARLY AND PUKE ON THE PLATFORM...

ONCE I HAD MY *BOOZE* AND *SMOKES* I WAS *KING OF THE WORLD* AGAIN. THE FIRST DRINK WAS TOUGH.

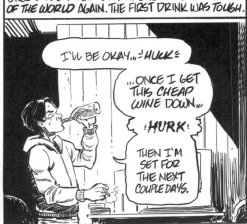

I'LL BE OKAY... ≥HUKK≥

...ONCE I GET THIS *CHEAP WINE* DOWN...

≥HURK≥

THEN I'M SET FOR THE NEXT COUPLE DAYS.

THERE WAS NO GREATER FEELING THAN KNOWING I'D BE IN *OBLIVION* FOR A WHILE. EVERYTHING FELL FROM MY SHOULDERS AND I WAS SORT OF FREE.

THERE IT IS.

AND HERE WE ARE.

MY OLD FRIEND.

I'D DRINK, SMOKE, AND WATCH MOVIES UNTIL I PASSED OUT, WAKE UP AND CARRY THE DRUNK OVER.

LOOKS LIKE A NICE SUNNY DAY OUT THERE.

IT HURTS MY SOUL.

THE APARTMENT WAS A *CAVE*, THE RADIATOR WAS ATTACHED TO THE CEILING AND IT MADE SUDDEN, TERRIFYING *NOISES* OUT OF THE BLUE.

CLANK CLUNK

THE HELL... TRYNA *WATCH* "THE THIN RED LINE" HERE...

BOOM CRACK CRACK PING AARGH FWOOM

MY FRIENDS STILL *CALLED* BUT I DIDN'T ANSWER. IT WAS JUST *EASIER* THIS WAY... I LOVED THEM BUT COULD *NEVER* EXPLAIN THE HOLLOW SHADOW THAT FILLED MY INSIDES. I THOUGHT IT'D *SCARE* THEM.

THE LOST, BUSTED WAY YOU FEEL RIGHT NOW IS THE WAY YOU WILL FEEL *FOREVER*.

THE ONLY ANSWER IS TO STAY *NUMB*.

OBLIVION.

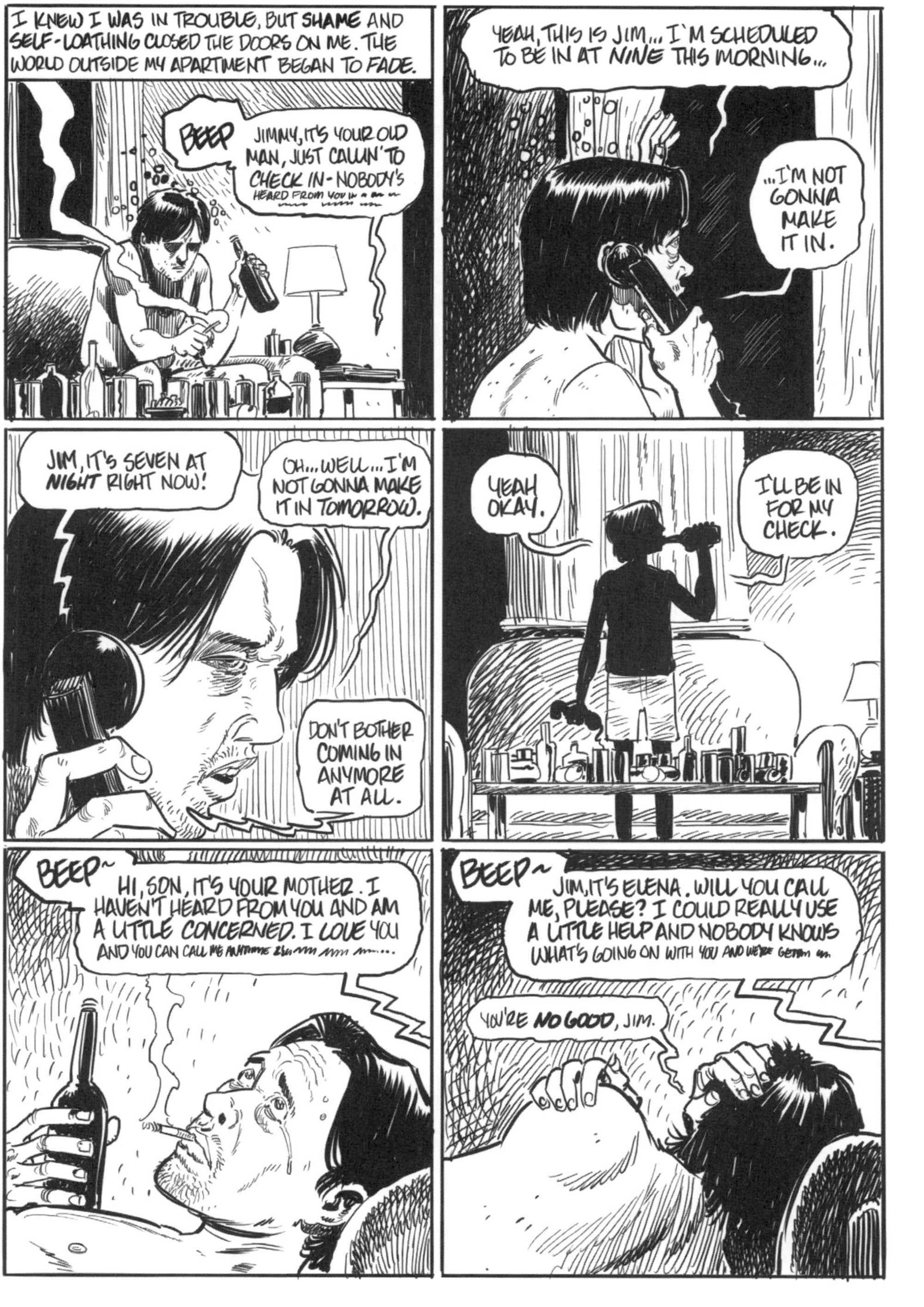
I KNEW I WAS IN TROUBLE, BUT **SHAME** AND **SELF-LOATHING** CLOSED THE DOORS ON ME. THE WORLD OUTSIDE MY APARTMENT BEGAN TO *FADE*.
BEEP
JIMMY, IT'S YOUR OLD MAN, JUST CALLIN' TO CHECK IN - NOBODY'S HEARD FROM YOU IN A
YEAH, THIS IS JIM... I'M SCHEDULED TO BE IN AT *NINE* THIS MORNING...
...I'M NOT GONNA MAKE IT IN.
JIM, IT'S SEVEN AT ***NIGHT*** RIGHT NOW!
OH... WELL... I'M NOT GONNA MAKE IT IN *TOMORROW*.
DON'T BOTHER COMING IN ANYMORE AT ALL.
YEAH OKAY.
I'LL BE IN FOR MY CHECK.
BEEP~
HI, SON, IT'S YOUR MOTHER. I HAVEN'T HEARD FROM YOU AND AM A LITTLE *CONCERNED*. I *LOVE* YOU AND YOU CAN CALL ME ANYTIME
BEEP~
JIM, IT'S ELENA. WILL YOU CALL ME, PLEASE? I COULD REALLY USE A LITTLE HELP AND NOBODY KNOWS WHAT'S GOING ON WITH YOU
YOU'RE ***NO GOOD***, JIM.

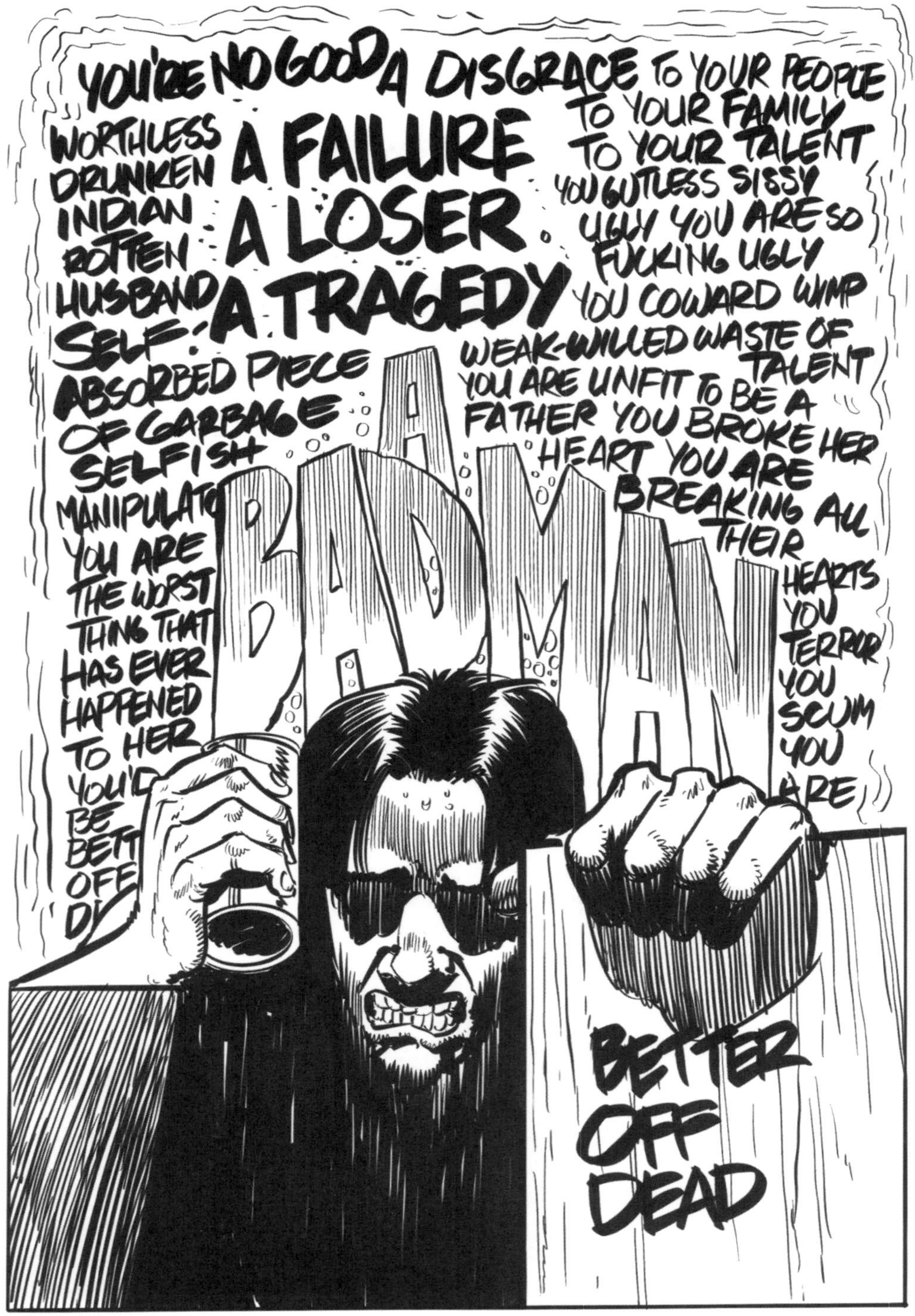
YOU'RE NO GOOD A DISGRACE TO YOUR PEOPLE
TO YOUR FAMILY
TO YOUR TALENT
WORTHLESS
DRUNKEN
INDIAN
ROTTEN
HUSBAND
SELF-
ABSORBED PIECE
OF GARBAGE
SELFISH
MANIPULATO
YOU ARE
THE WORST
THING THAT
HAS EVER
HAPPENED
TO HER
YOU'D
BE
BETT
OFF
D
A FAILURE
A LOSER
A TRAGEDY
YOU GUTLESS SISSY
UGLY YOU ARE SO
FUCKING UGLY
YOU COWARD WIMP
WEAK-WILLED WASTE OF
TALENT
YOU ARE UNFIT TO BE A
FATHER YOU BROKE HER
HEART YOU ARE
BREAKING ALL
THEIR
HEARTS
YOU
TERROR
YOU
SCUM
YOU
ARE
BAD MAN
BETTER
OFF
DEAD

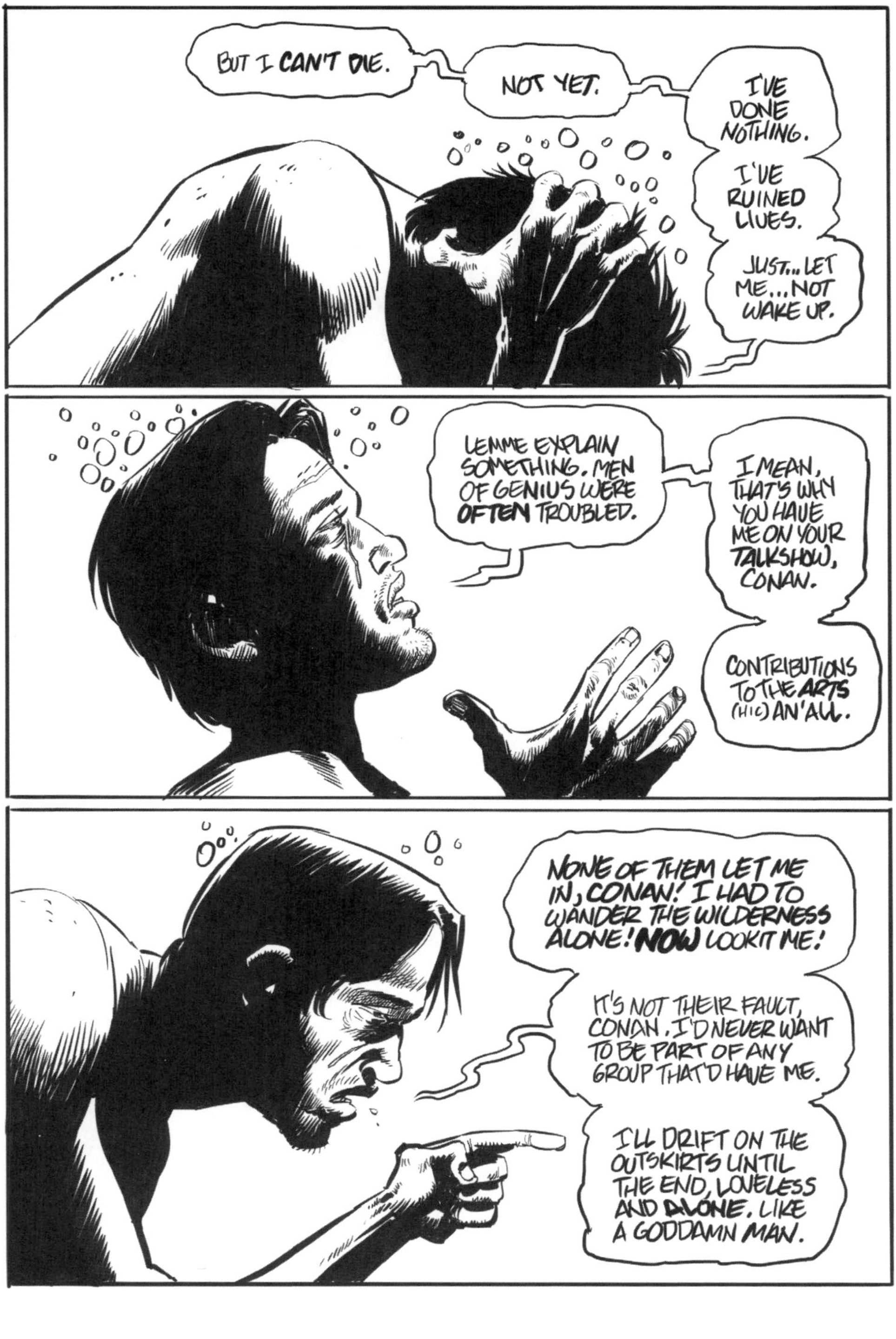

BUT I CAN'T DIE.
NOT YET.
I'VE DONE NOTHING.
I'VE RUINED LIVES.
JUST... LET ME... NOT WAKE UP.
LEMME EXPLAIN SOMETHING. MEN OF GENIUS WERE OFTEN TROUBLED.
I MEAN, THAT'S WHY YOU HAVE ME ON YOUR TALKSHOW, CONAN.
CONTRIBUTIONS TO THE ARTS (HIC) AN'ALL.
NONE OF THEM LET ME IN, CONAN! I HAD TO WANDER THE WILDERNESS ALONE! NOW LOOKIT ME!
IT'S NOT THEIR FAULT, CONAN. I'D NEVER WANT TO BE PART OF ANY GROUP THAT'D HAVE ME.
I'LL DRIFT ON THE OUTSKIRTS UNTIL THE END, LOVELESS AND ALONE. LIKE A GODDAMN MAN.

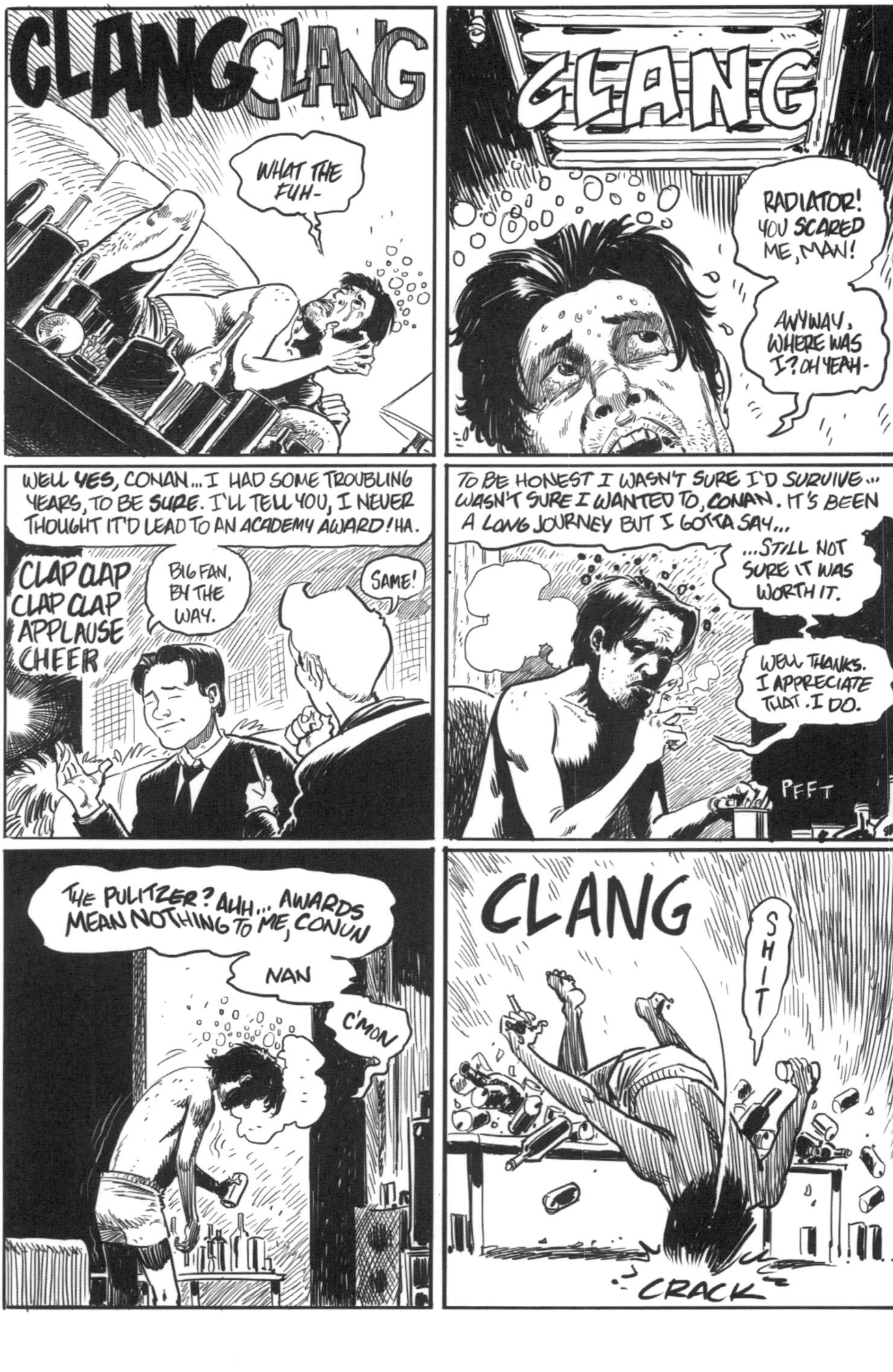
CLANG CLANG
WHAT THE FUH-
CLANG
RADIATOR! YOU SCARED ME, MAN!
ANYWAY, WHERE WAS I? OH YEAH-
WELL YES, CONAN... I HAD SOME TROUBLING YEARS, TO BE SURE. I'LL TELL YOU, I NEVER THOUGHT IT'D LEAD TO AN ACADEMY AWARD! HA.
CLAP CLAP CLAP CLAP APPLAUSE CHEER
BIG FAN, BY THE WAY.
SAME!
TO BE HONEST I WASN'T SURE I'D SURVIVE... WASN'T SURE I WANTED TO, CONAN. IT'S BEEN A LONG JOURNEY BUT I GOTTA SAY...
...STILL NOT SURE IT WAS WORTH IT.
WELL THANKS. I APPRECIATE THAT. I DO.
PFFT
THE PULITZER? AHH... AWARDS MEAN NOTHING TO ME, CONUN
NAN
C'MON
CLANG
SHIT
CRACK

Ssssssssss...

KLANG

I CAN'T **KILL** MYSELF... IT WOULD DESTROY THE FAMILY... SO JUST... TAKE ME IN MY SLEEP, LORD.

DON'T LET ME WAKE UP. HAVE MERCY ON ME.

KANG
CLUNK HISSSSSSSS...

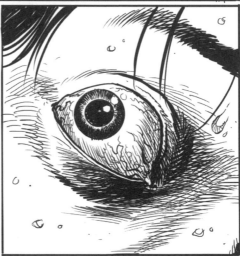

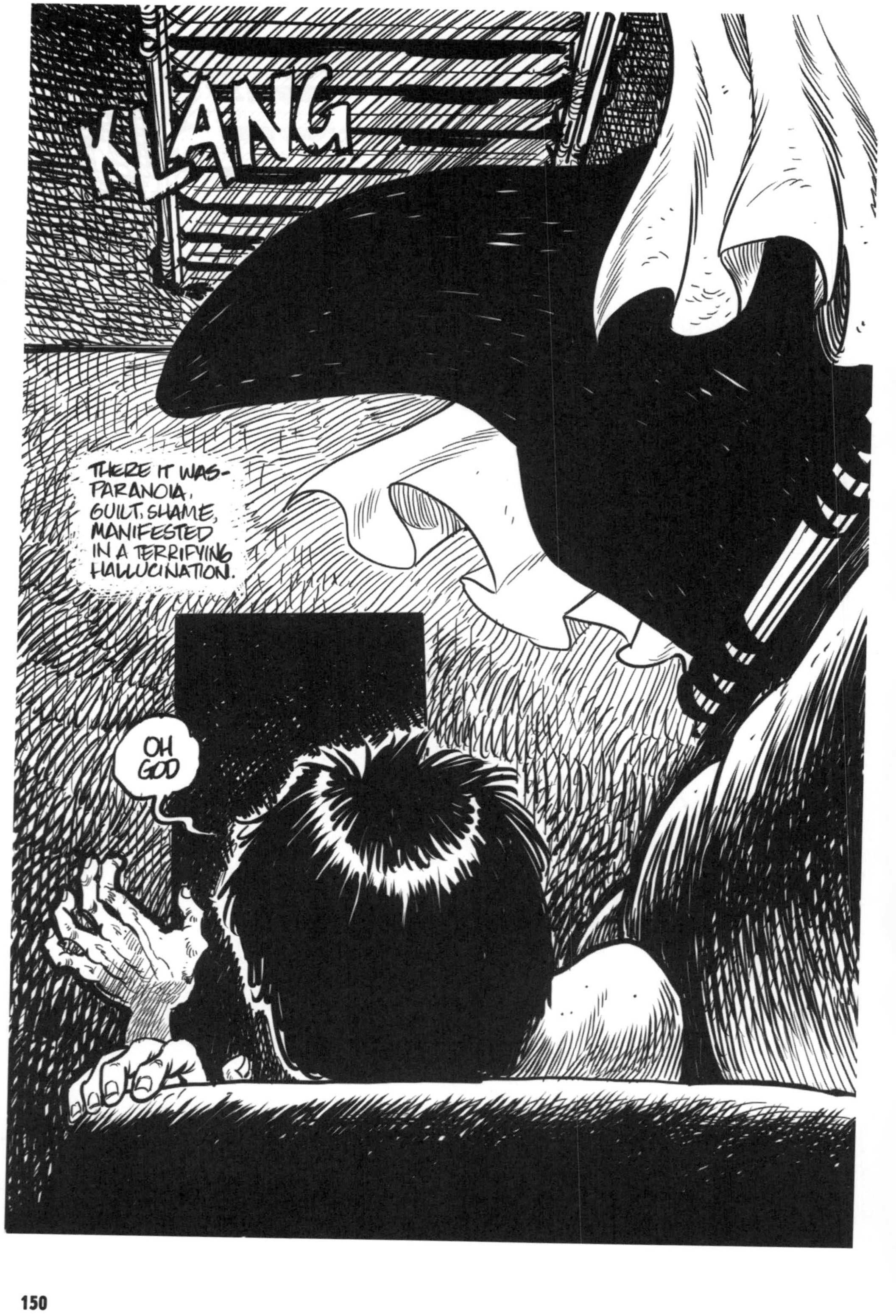
KLANG
THERE IT WAS- PARANOIA, GUILT, SHAME, MANIFESTED IN A TERRIFYING HALLUCINATION.
OH GOD

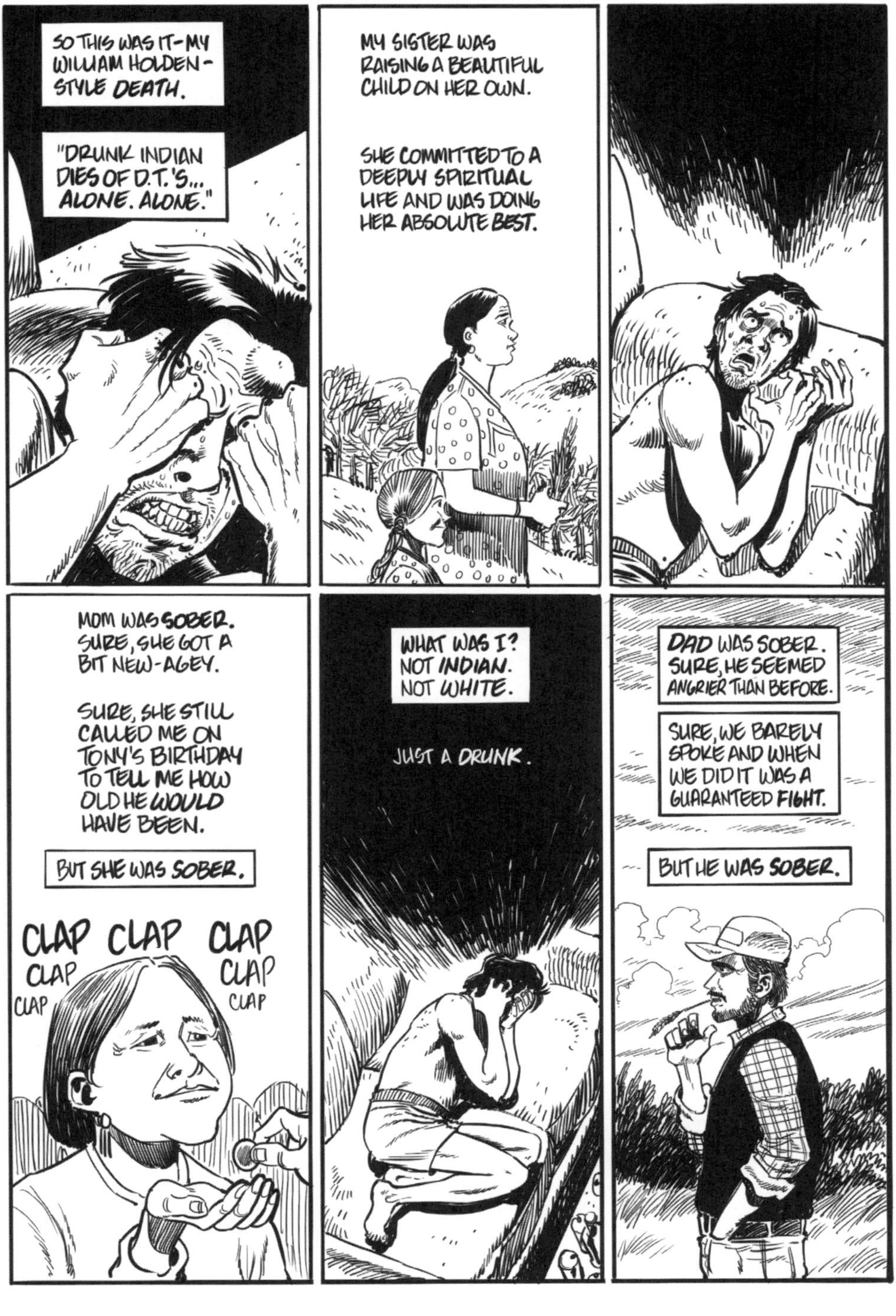

SO THIS WAS IT-MY WILLIAM HOLDEN-STYLE DEATH.
"DRUNK INDIAN DIES OF D.T.'S... ALONE. ALONE."
MY SISTER WAS RAISING A BEAUTIFUL CHILD ON HER OWN.
SHE COMMITTED TO A DEEPLY SPIRITUAL LIFE AND WAS DOING HER ABSOLUTE BEST.
MOM WAS SOBER. SURE, SHE GOT A BIT NEW-AGEY.
SURE, SHE STILL CALLED ME ON TONY'S BIRTHDAY TO TELL ME HOW OLD HE WOULD HAVE BEEN.
BUT SHE WAS SOBER.
CLAP CLAP CLAP
CLAP CLAP
CLAP CLAP
WHAT WAS I? NOT INDIAN. NOT WHITE.
JUST A DRUNK.
DAD WAS SOBER. SURE, HE SEEMED ANGRIER THAN BEFORE.
SURE, WE BARELY SPOKE AND WHEN WE DID IT WAS A GUARANTEED FIGHT.
BUT HE WAS SOBER.

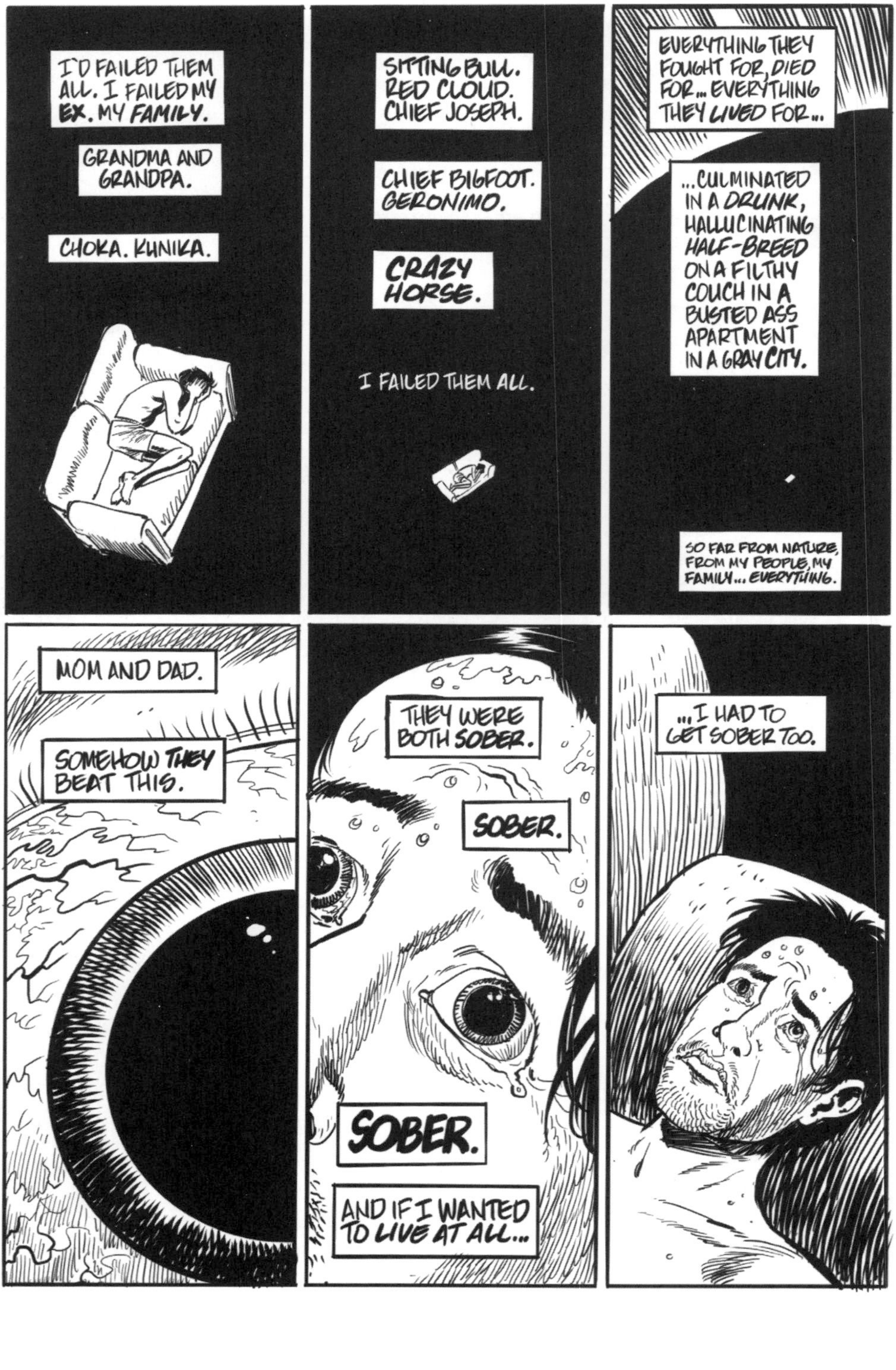
I'D FAILED THEM ALL. I FAILED MY EX. MY FAMILY.
GRANDMA AND GRANDPA.
CHOKA. KUNIKA.
SITTING BULL. RED CLOUD. CHIEF JOSEPH.
CHIEF BIGFOOT. GERONIMO.
CRAZY HORSE.
I FAILED THEM ALL.
EVERYTHING THEY FOUGHT FOR, DIED FOR... EVERYTHING THEY LIVED FOR...
...CULMINATED IN A DRUNK, HALLUCINATING HALF-BREED ON A FILTHY COUCH IN A BUSTED ASS APARTMENT IN A GRAY CITY.
SO FAR FROM NATURE, FROM MY PEOPLE, MY FAMILY... EVERYTHING.
MOM AND DAD.
SOMEHOW THEY BEAT THIS.
THEY WERE BOTH SOBER.
SOBER.
SOBER.
AND IF I WANTED TO LIVE AT ALL...
...I HAD TO GET SOBER TOO.

I COULD NOT GO A DAY WITHOUT BOOZE.

I DIDN'T KNOW HOW TO *LIVE* WITHOUT IT ANYMORE.

THEY WENT TO MEETINGS, THAT MUCH I KNEW.

THERE WAS REALLY NOTHING TO LOSE.

SO I GAVE IT A TRY.

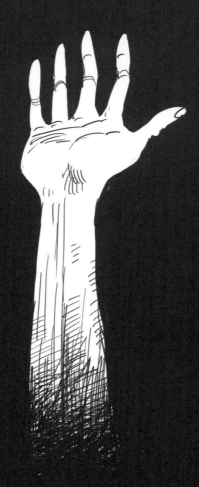

PART 4

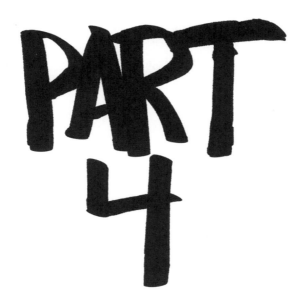

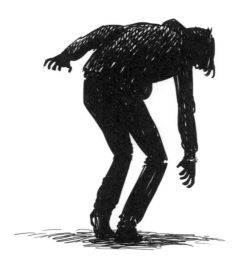

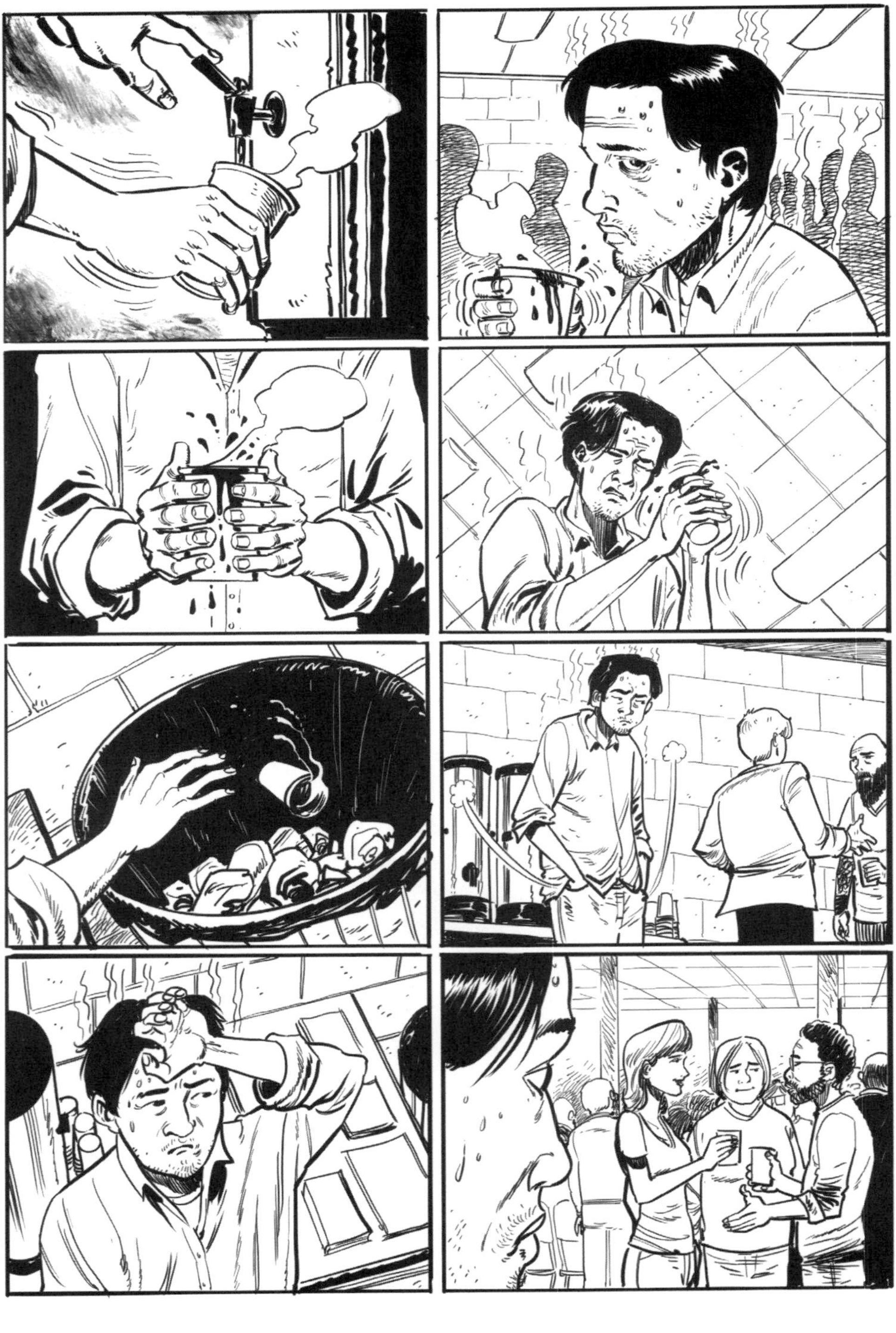

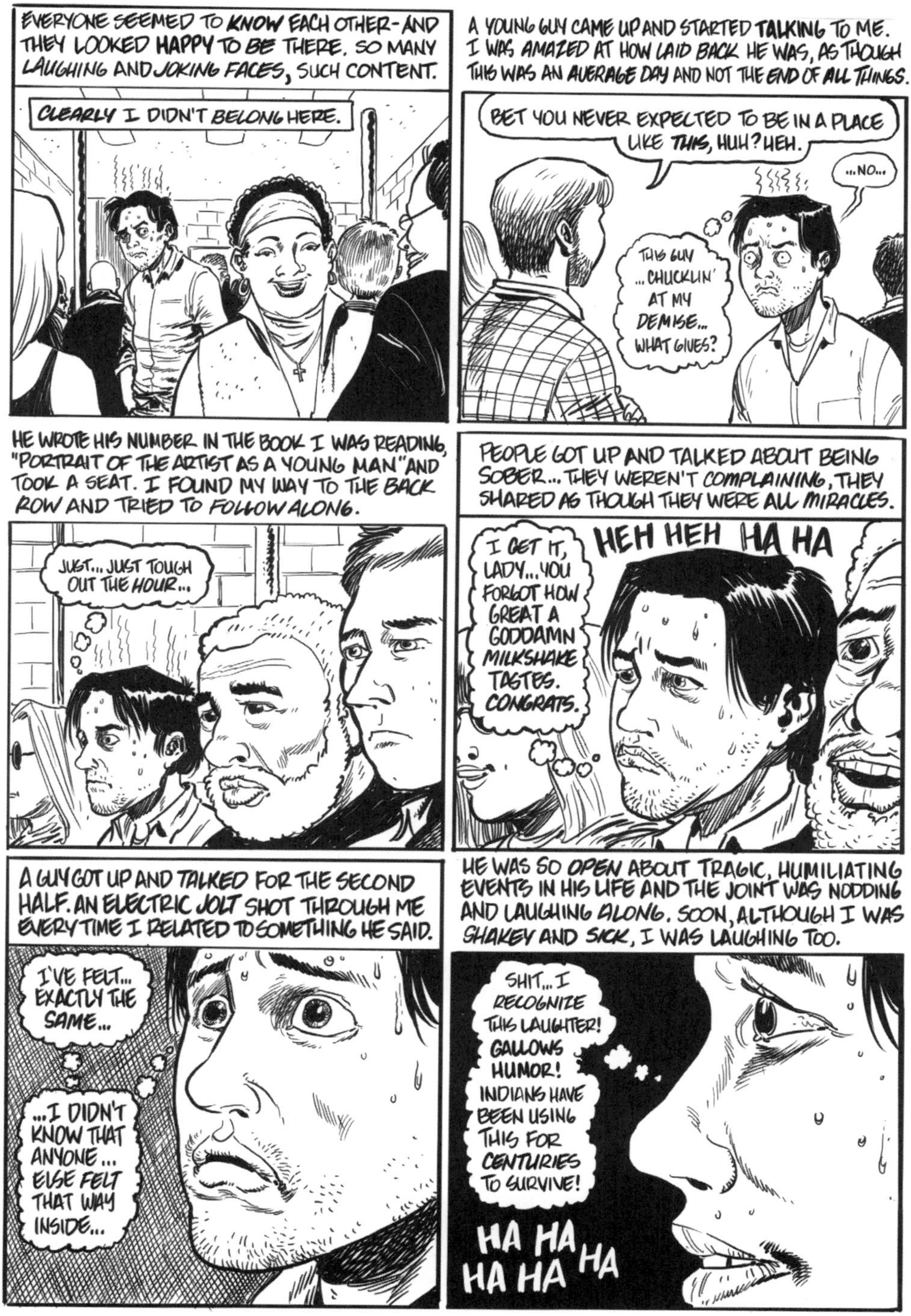
EVERYONE SEEMED TO KNOW EACH OTHER- AND THEY LOOKED HAPPY TO BE THERE. SO MANY LAUGHING AND JOKING FACES, SUCH CONTENT.
CLEARLY I DIDN'T BELONG HERE.
A YOUNG GUY CAME UP AND STARTED TALKING TO ME. I WAS AMAZED AT HOW LAID BACK HE WAS, AS THOUGH THIS WAS AN AVERAGE DAY AND NOT THE END OF ALL THINGS.
BET YOU NEVER EXPECTED TO BE IN A PLACE LIKE THIS, HUH? HEH.
...NO...
THIS GUY ...CHUCKLIN' AT MY DEMISE... WHAT GIVES?
HE WROTE HIS NUMBER IN THE BOOK I WAS READING, "PORTRAIT OF THE ARTIST AS A YOUNG MAN" AND TOOK A SEAT. I FOUND MY WAY TO THE BACK ROW AND TRIED TO FOLLOW ALONG.
JUST... JUST TOUGH OUT THE HOUR...
PEOPLE GOT UP AND TALKED ABOUT BEING SOBER... THEY WEREN'T COMPLAINING, THEY SHARED AS THOUGH THEY WERE ALL MIRACLES.
HEH HEH HA HA
I GET IT, LADY... YOU FORGOT HOW GREAT A GODDAMN MILKSHAKE TASTES. CONGRATS.
A GUY GOT UP AND TALKED FOR THE SECOND HALF. AN ELECTRIC JOLT SHOT THROUGH ME EVERY TIME I RELATED TO SOMETHING HE SAID.
I'VE FELT... EXACTLY THE SAME...
...I DIDN'T KNOW THAT ANYONE... ELSE FELT THAT WAY INSIDE...
HE WAS SO OPEN ABOUT TRAGIC, HUMILIATING EVENTS IN HIS LIFE AND THE JOINT WAS NODDING AND LAUGHING ALONG. SOON, ALTHOUGH I WAS SHAKEY AND SICK, I WAS LAUGHING TOO.
SHIT... I RECOGNIZE THIS LAUGHTER! GALLOWS HUMOR! INDIANS HAVE BEEN USING THIS FOR CENTURIES TO SURVIVE!
HA HA HA HA HA HA

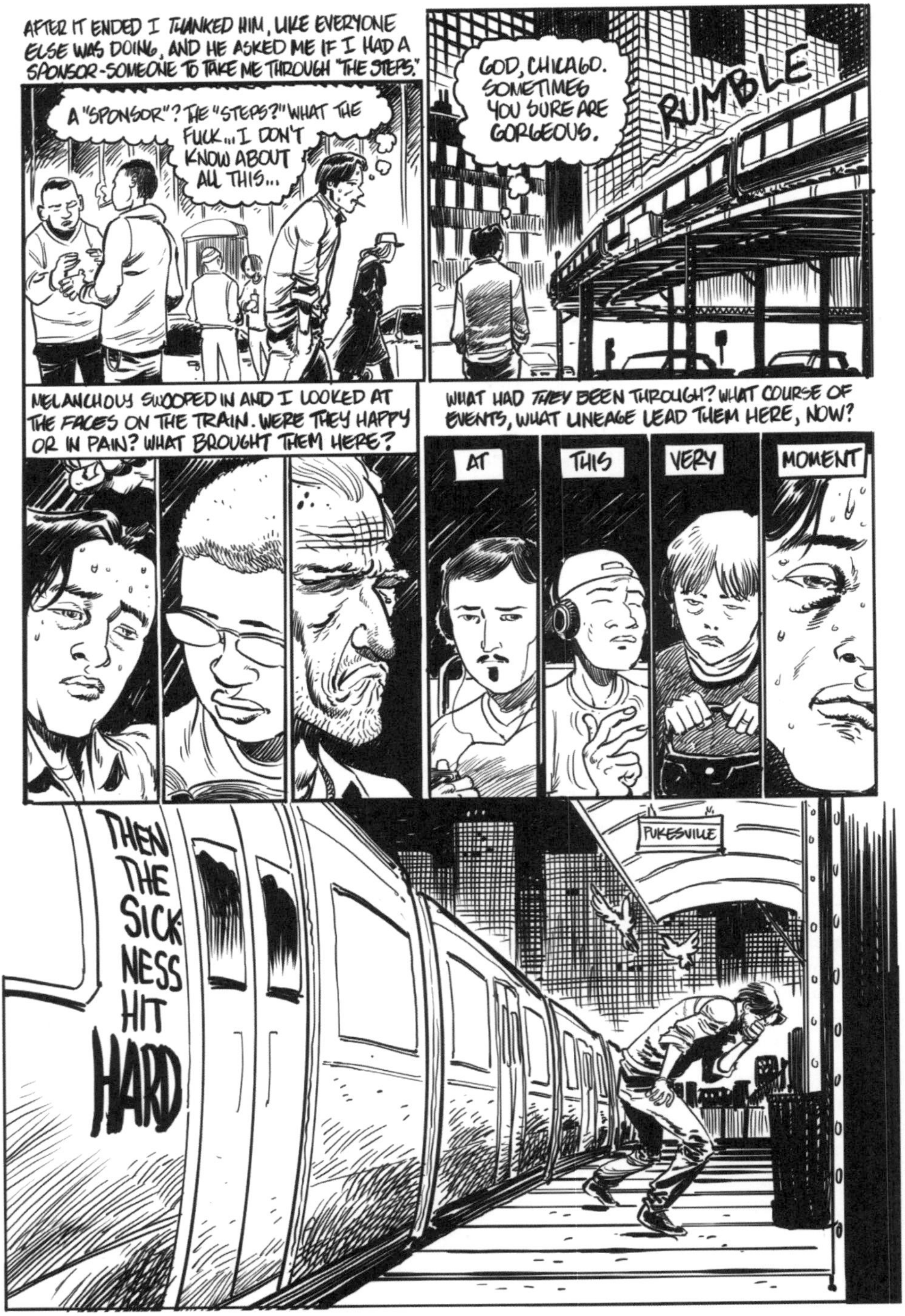
AFTER IT ENDED I THANKED HIM, LIKE EVERYONE ELSE WAS DOING, AND HE ASKED ME IF I HAD A SPONSOR-SOMEONE TO TAKE ME THROUGH "THE STEPS."
A "SPONSOR"? THE "STEPS?" WHAT THE FUCK... I DON'T KNOW ABOUT ALL THIS...
GOD, CHICAGO. SOMETIMES YOU SURE ARE GORGEOUS.
RUMBLE
MELANCHOLY SWOOPED IN AND I LOOKED AT THE FACES ON THE TRAIN. WERE THEY HAPPY OR IN PAIN? WHAT BROUGHT THEM HERE?
WHAT HAD THEY BEEN THROUGH? WHAT COURSE OF EVENTS, WHAT LINEAGE LEAD THEM HERE, NOW?
AT
THIS
VERY
MOMENT
PUKESVILLE
THEN THE SICKNESS HIT HARD

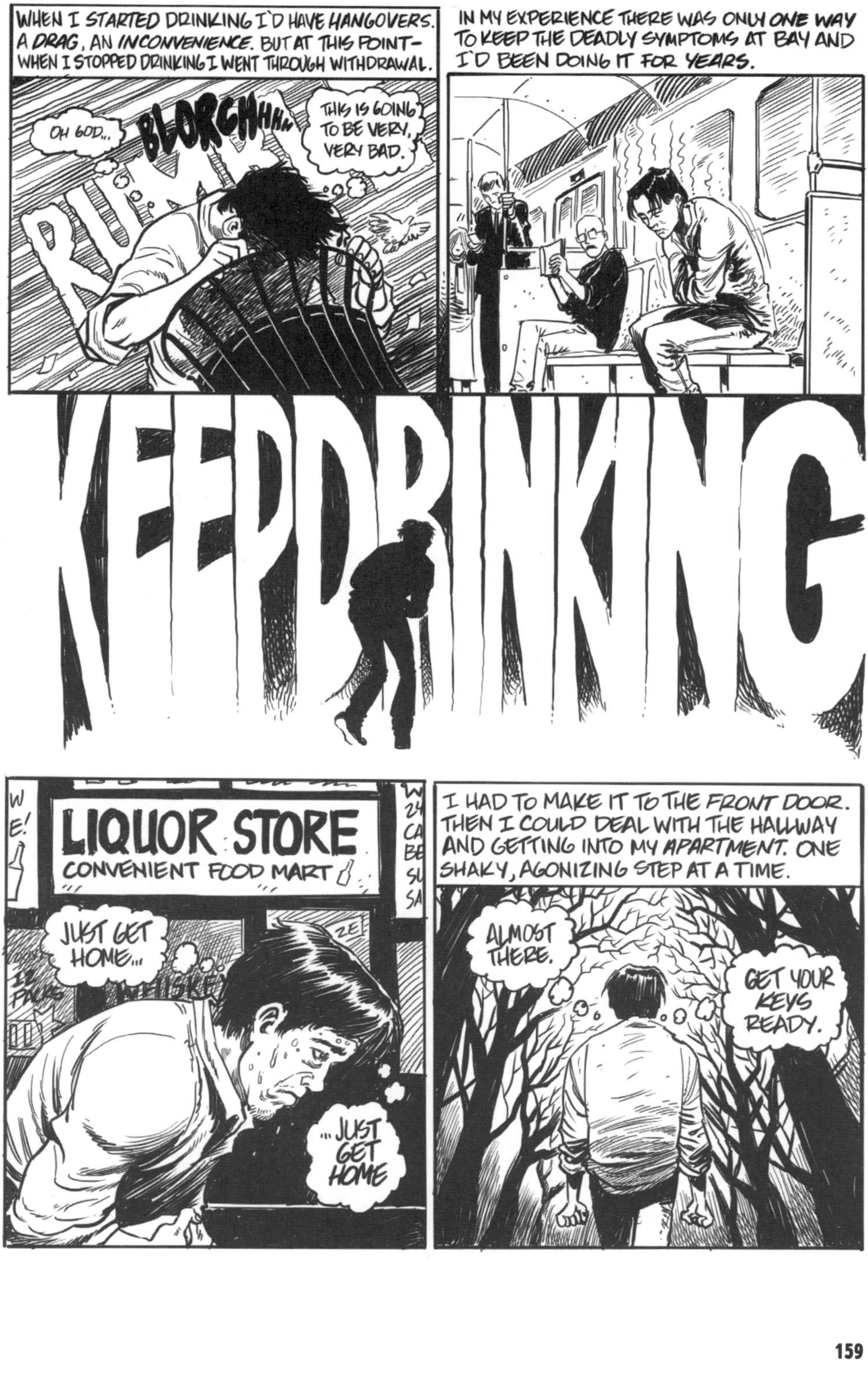

WHEN I STARTED DRINKING I'D HAVE HANGOVERS. A DRAG, AN INCONVENIENCE. BUT AT THIS POINT- WHEN I STOPPED DRINKING I WENT THROUGH WITHDRAWAL.
OH GOD...
BLORCHHHH
THIS IS GOING TO BE VERY, VERY BAD.
IN MY EXPERIENCE THERE WAS ONLY ONE WAY TO KEEP THE DEADLY SYMPTOMS AT BAY AND I'D BEEN DOING IT FOR YEARS.
KEEP DRINKING
LIQUOR STORE
CONVENIENT FOOD MART
JUST GET HOME...
...JUST GET HOME
I HAD TO MAKE IT TO THE FRONT DOOR. THEN I COULD DEAL WITH THE HALLWAY AND GETTING INTO MY APARTMENT. ONE SHAKY, AGONIZING STEP AT A TIME.
ALMOST THERE.
GET YOUR KEYS READY.

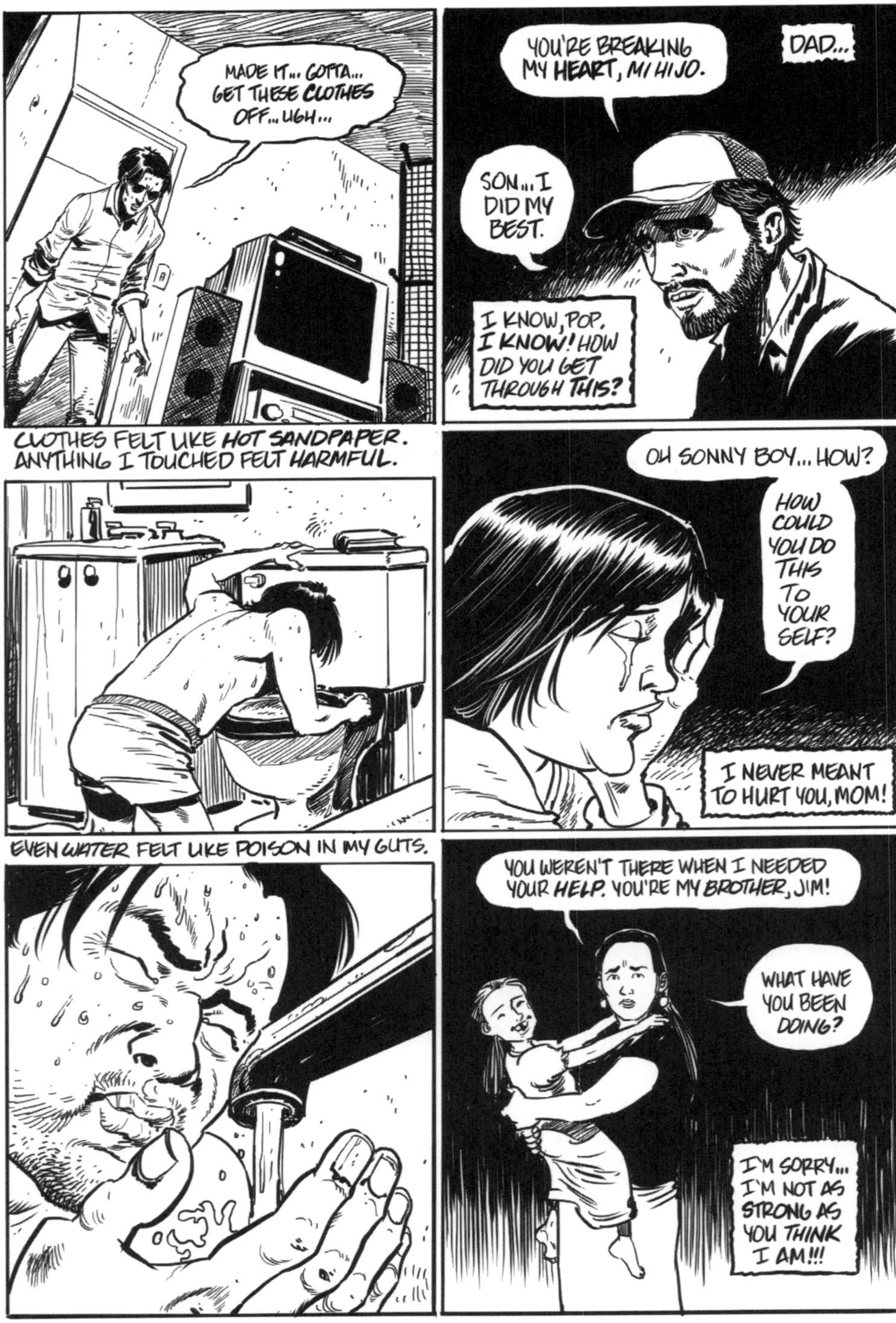
MADE IT... GOTTA... GET THESE CLOTHES OFF... UGH...
YOU'RE BREAKING MY HEART, MI HIJO.
DAD...
SON... I DID MY BEST.
I KNOW, POP, I KNOW! HOW DID YOU GET THROUGH THIS?
CLOTHES FELT LIKE HOT SANDPAPER. ANYTHING I TOUCHED FELT HARMFUL.
OH SONNY BOY... HOW?
HOW COULD YOU DO THIS TO YOUR SELF?
I NEVER MEANT TO HURT YOU, MOM!
EVEN WATER FELT LIKE POISON IN MY GUTS.
YOU WEREN'T THERE WHEN I NEEDED YOUR HELP. YOU'RE MY BROTHER, JIM!
WHAT HAVE YOU BEEN DOING?
I'M SORRY... I'M NOT AS STRONG AS YOU THINK I AM!!!

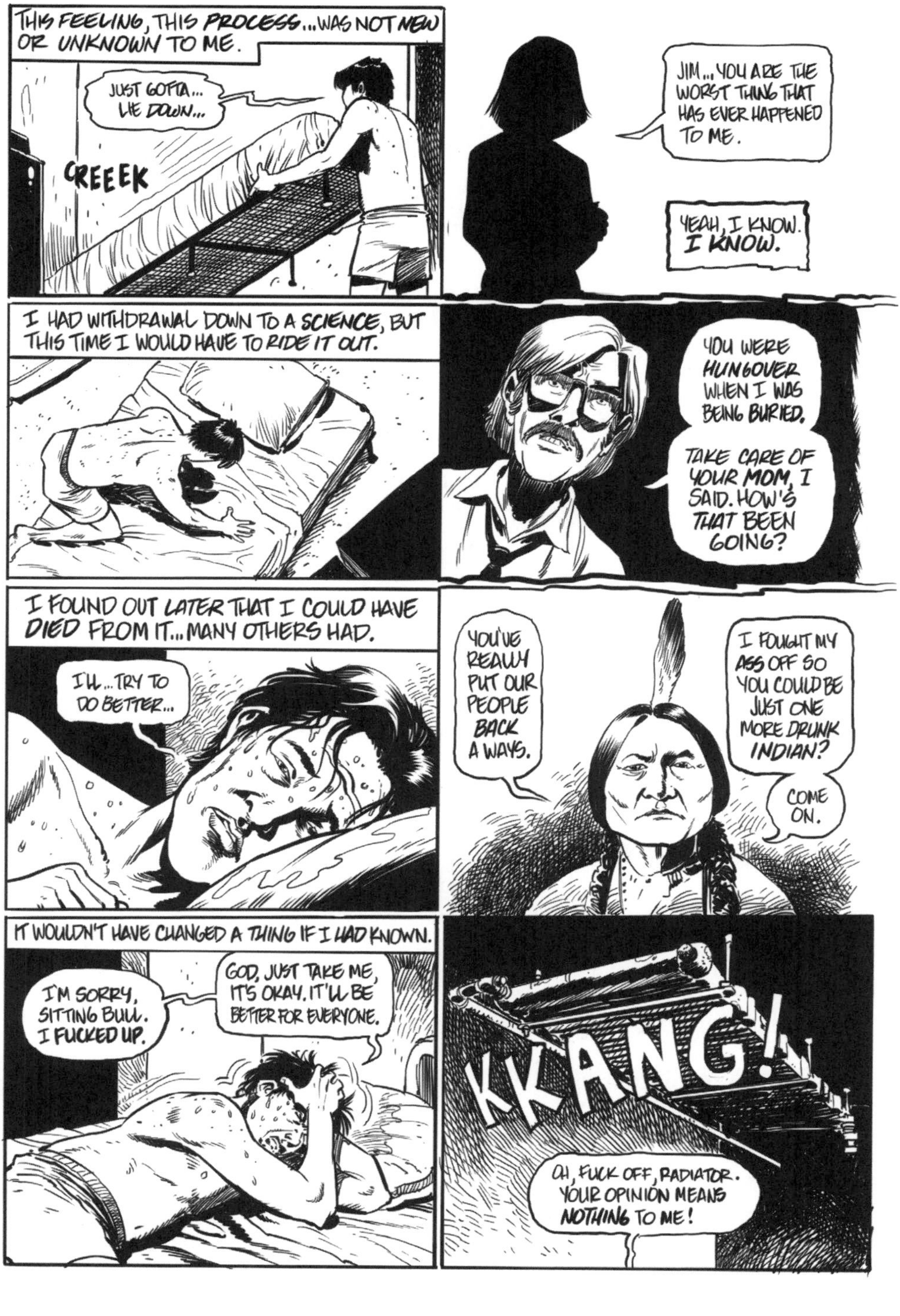
THIS FEELING, THIS PROCESS... WAS NOT NEW OR UNKNOWN TO ME.
JUST GOTTA... LIE DOWN...
CREEEK
JIM... YOU ARE THE WORST THING THAT HAS EVER HAPPENED TO ME.
YEAH, I KNOW. I KNOW.
I HAD WITHDRAWAL DOWN TO A SCIENCE, BUT THIS TIME I WOULD HAVE TO RIDE IT OUT.
YOU WERE HUNGOVER WHEN I WAS BEING BURIED.
TAKE CARE OF YOUR MOM, I SAID. HOW'S THAT BEEN GOING?
I FOUND OUT LATER THAT I COULD HAVE DIED FROM IT... MANY OTHERS HAD.
I'LL... TRY TO DO BETTER...
YOU'VE REALLY PUT OUR PEOPLE BACK A WAYS.
I FOUGHT MY ASS OFF SO YOU COULD BE JUST ONE MORE DRUNK INDIAN?
COME ON.
IT WOULDN'T HAVE CHANGED A THING IF I HAD KNOWN.
I'M SORRY, SITTING BULL. I FUCKED UP.
GOD, JUST TAKE ME, IT'S OKAY. IT'LL BE BETTER FOR EVERYONE.
KKANG!
OH, FUCK OFF, RADIATOR. YOUR OPINION MEANS NOTHING TO ME!

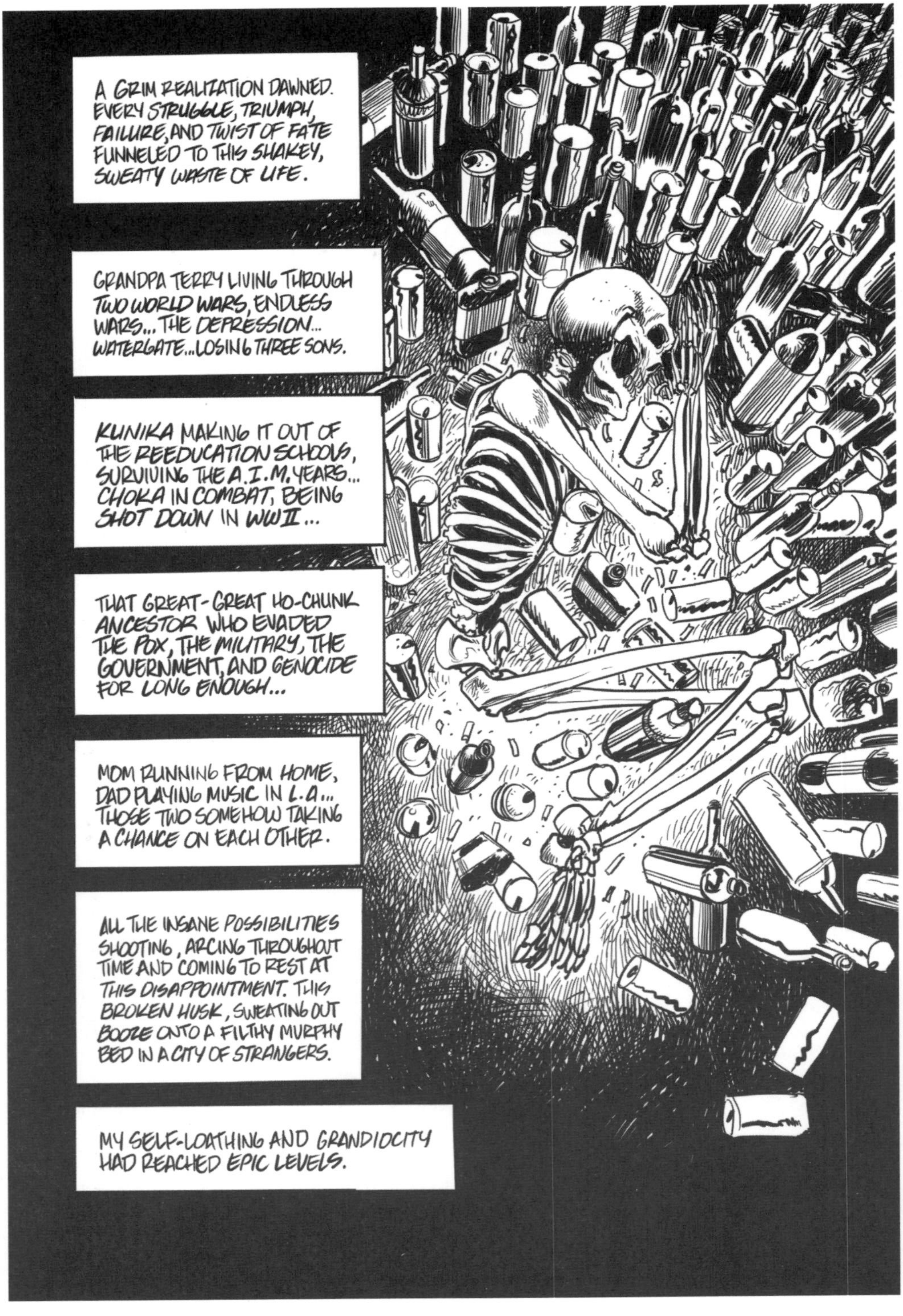
A GRIM REALIZATION DAWNED. EVERY STRUGGLE, TRIUMPH, FAILURE, AND TWIST OF FATE FUNNELED TO THIS SHAKEY, SWEATY WASTE OF LIFE.
GRANDPA TERRY LIVING THROUGH TWO WORLD WARS, ENDLESS WARS... THE DEPRESSION... WATERGATE...LOSING THREE SONS.
KUNIKA MAKING IT OUT OF THE REEDUCATION SCHOOLS, SURVIVING THE A.I.M. YEARS... CHOKA IN COMBAT, BEING SHOT DOWN IN WW II...
THAT GREAT-GREAT HO-CHUNK ANCESTOR WHO EVADED THE POX, THE MILITARY, THE GOVERNMENT, AND GENOCIDE FOR LONG ENOUGH...
MOM RUNNING FROM HOME, DAD PLAYING MUSIC IN L.A... THOSE TWO SOMEHOW TAKING A CHANCE ON EACH OTHER.
ALL THE INSANE POSSIBILITIES SHOOTING, ARCING THROUGHOUT TIME AND COMING TO REST AT THIS DISAPPOINTMENT. THIS BROKEN HUSK, SWEATING OUT BOOZE ONTO A FILTHY MURPHY BED IN A CITY OF STRANGERS.
MY SELF-LOATHING AND GRANDIOCITY HAD REACHED EPIC LEVELS.

I TOSSED AND TURNED AND THE SHEETS WERE FIBERGLASS – CLINGING TO THE COLD SWEAT, PULLING AND SCRAPING WITH EVERY MOVE I MADE.

MY LIMBS ACHED. MY STOMACH WAS AN EMPTY CRAMP. ANY ATTEMPT TO PURGE IT WAS ACIDIC NOTHING.

THIS THING....

IT'S IN YOUR BLOOD, MAN. ON BOTH SIDES. YOU'RE IN REAL TROUBLE, INDIO.

JUST...

SON.... THE NIGHT WE CAME BACK FROM BURYING DON WE DRANK TOGETHER. IT WAS THE WORST I EVER FELT AND THE REASON I QUIT. SEEING YOU DRINK BROKE ME, SON.

...GOTTA...

MY BRAIN FELT LIKE A FILTHY, TOXIC COTTON BALL. INVISIBLE MAGGOTS WRITHED JUST BENEATH THE SKIN ON MY BACK, RIPPLES OF REVULSION.

YOU'RE BROKEN, JIM. I'M GLAD WE DIDN'T HAVE CHILDREN. YOU'RE JUST... TOO SELFISH.

...SURVIVE...

I TRIED TO ENVISION GERONIMO RUNNING THROUGH CANYONS, SILENT. CRAZY HORSE IN DEFIANCE ON THE PLAIN. TECUMSEH IN QUIET CONTEMPLATION. CHOKA AND HIS DAMNED SWISHER SWEETS. I NEEDED STRENGTH.

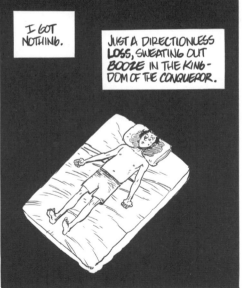

I GOT NOTHING.

JUST A DIRECTIONLESS LOSS, SWEATING OUT BOOZE IN THE KINGDOM OF THE CONQUEROR.

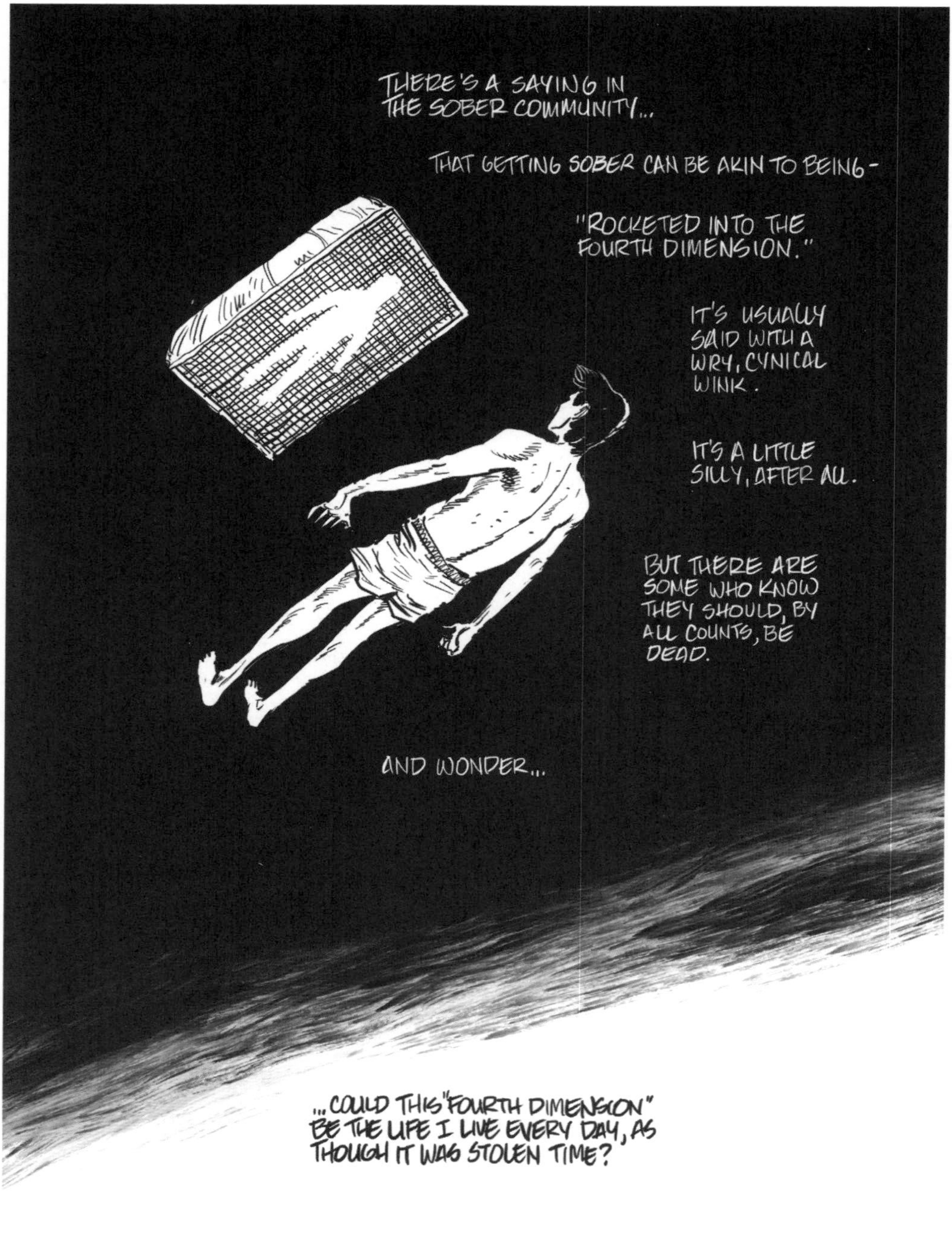
THERE'S A SAYING IN THE SOBER COMMUNITY...
THAT GETTING SOBER CAN BE AKIN TO BEING -
"ROCKETED INTO THE FOURTH DIMENSION."
IT'S USUALLY SAID WITH A WRY, CYNICAL WINK.
IT'S A LITTLE SILLY, AFTER ALL.
BUT THERE ARE SOME WHO KNOW THEY SHOULD, BY ALL COUNTS, BE DEAD.
AND WONDER...
...COULD THIS "FOURTH DIMENSION" BE THE LIFE I LIVE EVERY DAY, AS THOUGH IT WAS STOLEN TIME?

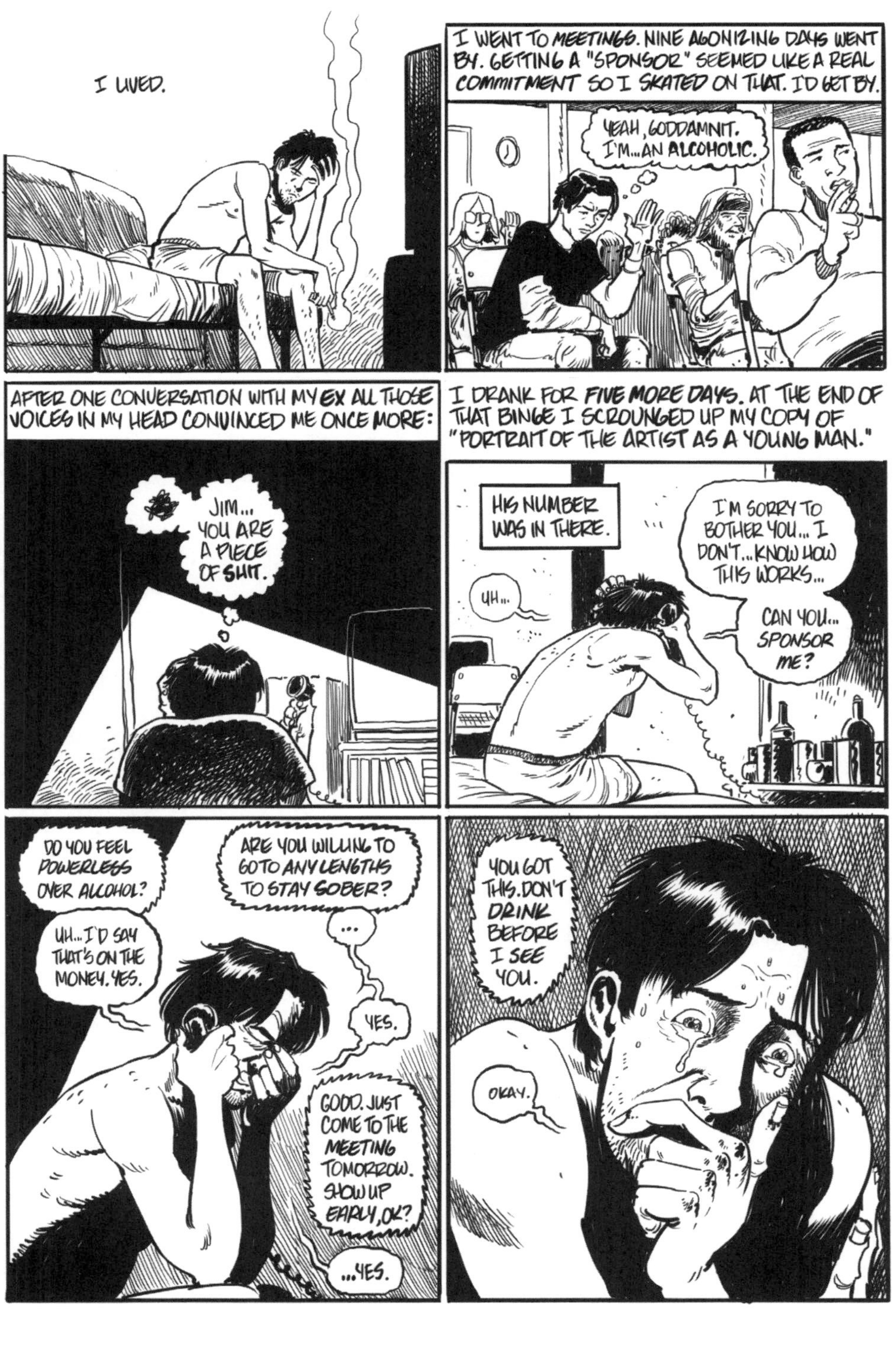
I LIVED.
I WENT TO MEETINGS. NINE AGONIZING DAYS WENT BY. GETTING A "SPONSOR" SEEMED LIKE A REAL COMMITMENT SO I SKATED ON THAT. I'D GET BY.
YEAH, GODDAMNIT. I'M...AN ALCOHOLIC.
AFTER ONE CONVERSATION WITH MY EX ALL THOSE VOICES IN MY HEAD CONVINCED ME ONCE MORE:
JIM... YOU ARE A PIECE OF SHIT.
I DRANK FOR FIVE MORE DAYS. AT THE END OF THAT BINGE I SCROUNGED UP MY COPY OF "PORTRAIT OF THE ARTIST AS A YOUNG MAN."
HIS NUMBER WAS IN THERE.
I'M SORRY TO BOTHER YOU... I DON'T...KNOW HOW THIS WORKS...
UH...
CAN YOU... SPONSOR ME?
DO YOU FEEL POWERLESS OVER ALCOHOL?
ARE YOU WILLING TO GO TO ANY LENGTHS TO STAY SOBER?
UH...I'D SAY THAT'S ON THE MONEY. YES.
...
YES.
GOOD. JUST COME TO THE MEETING TOMORROW. SHOW UP EARLY, OK?
...YES.
YOU GOT THIS. DON'T DRINK BEFORE I SEE YOU.
OKAY.

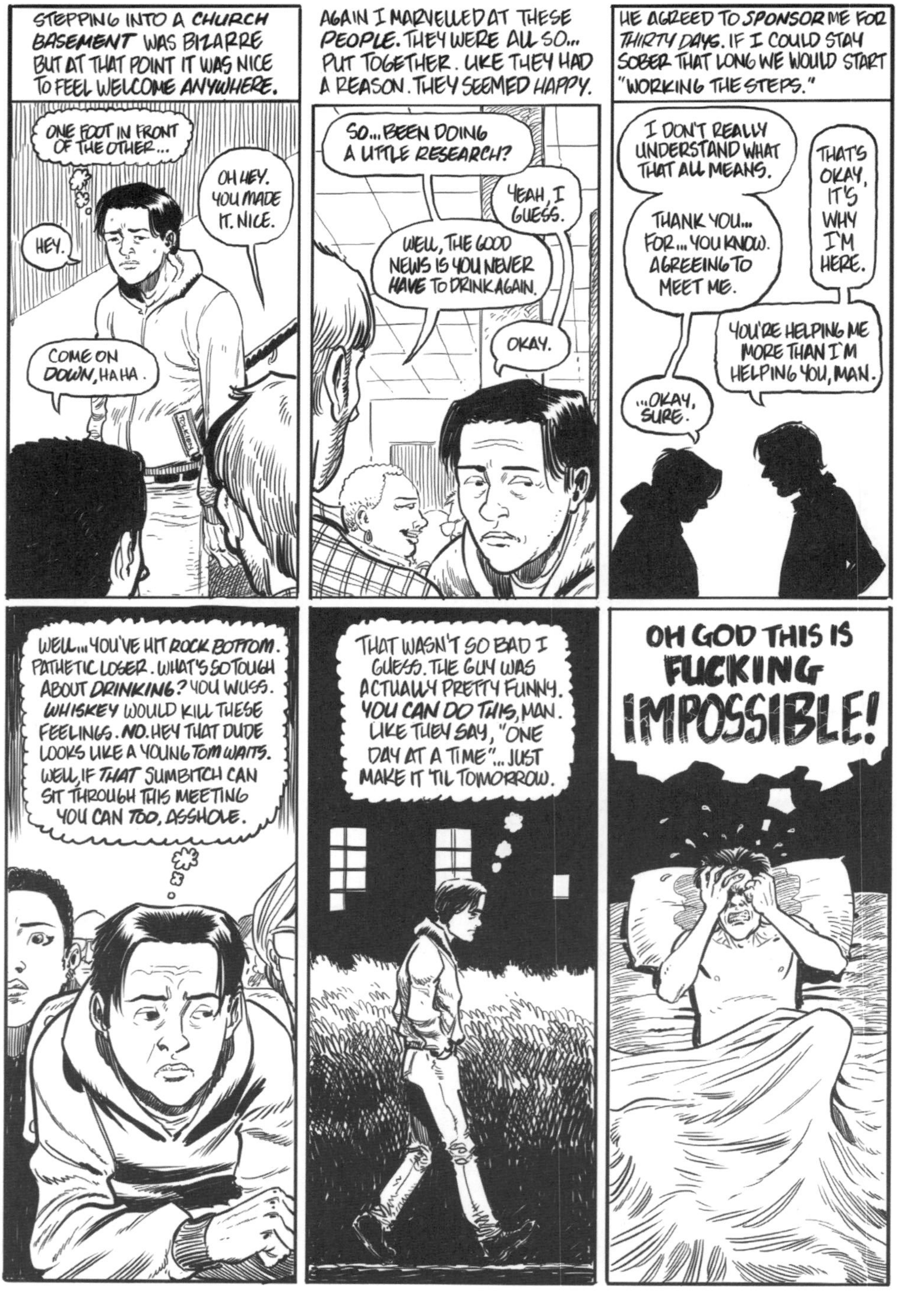
STEPPING INTO A CHURCH BASEMENT WAS BIZARRE BUT AT THAT POINT IT WAS NICE TO FEEL WELCOME ANYWHERE.
ONE FOOT IN FRONT OF THE OTHER...
OH HEY. YOU MADE IT. NICE.
HEY.
COME ON DOWN, HAHA.
AGAIN I MARVELLED AT THESE PEOPLE. THEY WERE ALL SO... PUT TOGETHER. LIKE THEY HAD A REASON. THEY SEEMED HAPPY.
SO... BEEN DOING A LITTLE RESEARCH?
YEAH, I GUESS.
WELL, THE GOOD NEWS IS YOU NEVER HAVE TO DRINK AGAIN.
OKAY.
HE AGREED TO SPONSOR ME FOR THIRTY DAYS. IF I COULD STAY SOBER THAT LONG WE WOULD START "WORKING THE STEPS."
I DON'T REALLY UNDERSTAND WHAT THAT ALL MEANS.
THAT'S OKAY, IT'S WHY I'M HERE.
THANK YOU... FOR... YOU KNOW. AGREEING TO MEET ME.
YOU'RE HELPING ME MORE THAN I'M HELPING YOU, MAN.
...OKAY, SURE.
WELL... YOU'VE HIT ROCK BOTTOM. PATHETIC LOSER. WHAT'S SO TOUGH ABOUT DRINKING? YOU WUSS. WHISKEY WOULD KILL THESE FEELINGS. NO. HEY THAT DUDE LOOKS LIKE A YOUNG TOM WAITS. WELL, IF THAT SUMBITCH CAN SIT THROUGH THIS MEETING YOU CAN TOO, ASSHOLE.
THAT WASN'T SO BAD I GUESS. THE GUY WAS ACTUALLY PRETTY FUNNY. YOU CAN DO THIS, MAN. LIKE THEY SAY, "ONE DAY AT A TIME"... JUST MAKE IT 'TIL TOMORROW.
OH GOD THIS IS FUCKING IMPOSSIBLE!

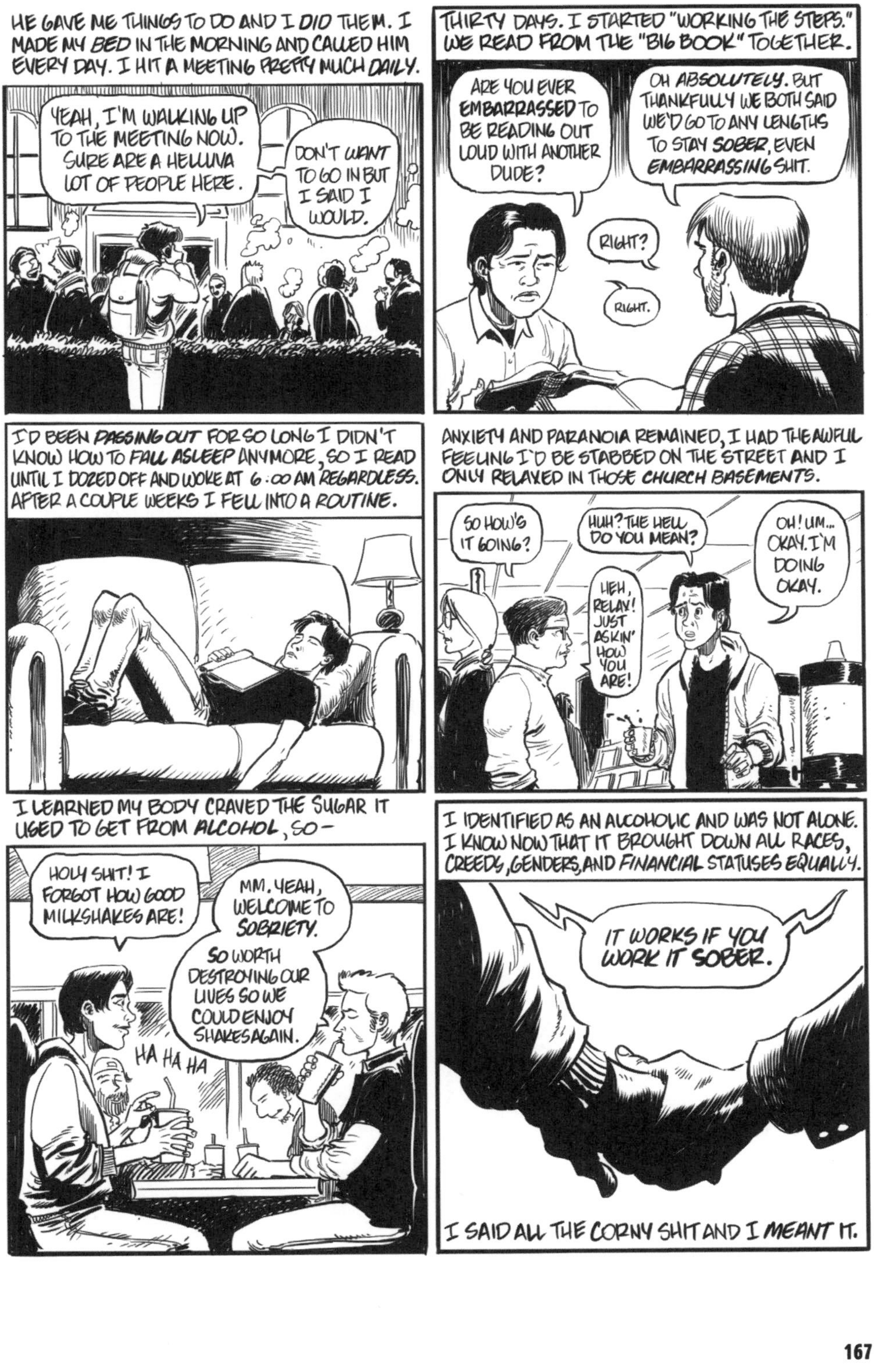
HE GAVE ME THINGS TO DO AND I DID THEM. I MADE MY BED IN THE MORNING AND CALLED HIM EVERY DAY. I HIT A MEETING PRETTY MUCH DAILY.
YEAH, I'M WALKING UP TO THE MEETING NOW. SURE ARE A HELLUVA LOT OF PEOPLE HERE.
DON'T WANT TO GO IN BUT I SAID I WOULD.
THIRTY DAYS. I STARTED "WORKING THE STEPS." WE READ FROM THE "BIG BOOK" TOGETHER.
ARE YOU EVER EMBARRASSED TO BE READING OUT LOUD WITH ANOTHER DUDE?
OH ABSOLUTELY. BUT THANKFULLY WE BOTH SAID WE'D GO TO ANY LENGTHS TO STAY SOBER, EVEN EMBARRASSING SHIT.
RIGHT?
RIGHT.
I'D BEEN PASSING OUT FOR SO LONG I DIDN'T KNOW HOW TO FALL ASLEEP ANYMORE, SO I READ UNTIL I DOZED OFF AND WOKE AT 6:00 AM REGARDLESS. AFTER A COUPLE WEEKS I FELL INTO A ROUTINE.
ANXIETY AND PARANOIA REMAINED, I HAD THE AWFUL FEELING I'D BE STABBED ON THE STREET AND I ONLY RELAXED IN THOSE CHURCH BASEMENTS.
SO HOW'S IT GOING?
HUH? THE HELL DO YOU MEAN?
HEH, RELAX! JUST ASKIN' HOW YOU ARE!
OH! UM... OKAY. I'M DOING OKAY.
I LEARNED MY BODY CRAVED THE SUGAR IT USED TO GET FROM ALCOHOL, SO—
HOLY SHIT! I FORGOT HOW GOOD MILKSHAKES ARE!
MM. YEAH, WELCOME TO SOBRIETY.
SO WORTH DESTROYING OUR LIVES SO WE COULD ENJOY SHAKES AGAIN.
HA HA HA
I IDENTIFIED AS AN ALCOHOLIC AND WAS NOT ALONE. I KNOW NOW THAT IT BROUGHT DOWN ALL RACES, CREEDS, GENDERS, AND FINANCIAL STATUSES EQUALLY.
IT WORKS IF YOU WORK IT SOBER.
I SAID ALL THE CORNY SHIT AND I MEANT IT.

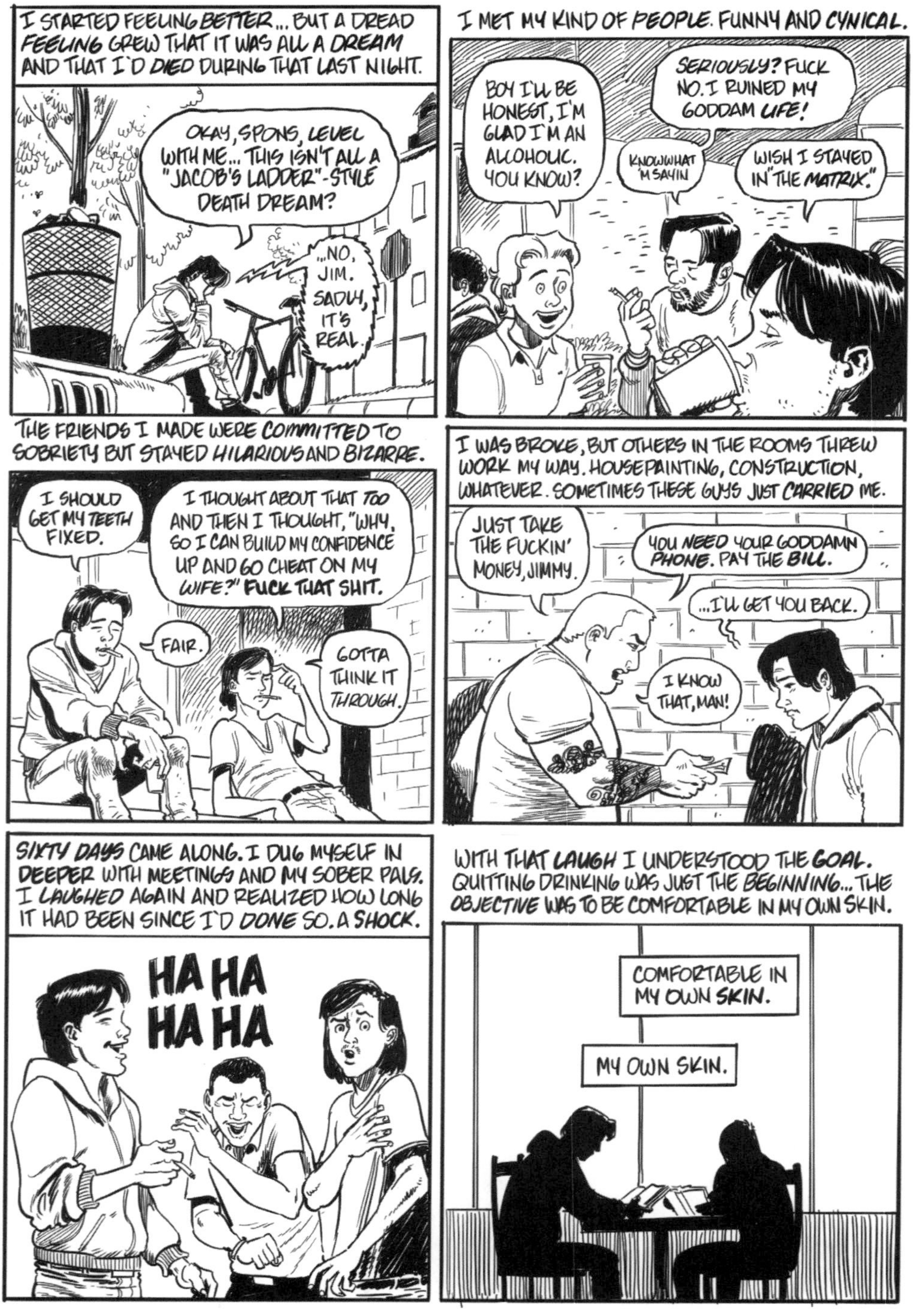
I STARTED FEELING BETTER... BUT A DREAD FEELING GREW THAT IT WAS ALL A DREAM AND THAT I'D DIED DURING THAT LAST NIGHT.
OKAY, SPONS, LEVEL WITH ME... THIS ISN'T ALL A "JACOB'S LADDER"-STYLE DEATH DREAM?
...NO, JIM. SADLY, IT'S REAL.
I MET MY KIND OF PEOPLE. FUNNY AND CYNICAL.
BOY I'LL BE HONEST, I'M GLAD I'M AN ALCOHOLIC. YOU KNOW?
SERIOUSLY? FUCK NO. I RUINED MY GODDAM LIFE!
KNOWWHAT 'M SAYIN
WISH I STAYED IN "THE MATRIX."
THE FRIENDS I MADE WERE COMMITTED TO SOBRIETY BUT STAYED HILARIOUS AND BIZARRE.
I SHOULD GET MY TEETH FIXED.
I THOUGHT ABOUT THAT TOO AND THEN I THOUGHT, "WHY, SO I CAN BUILD MY CONFIDENCE UP AND GO CHEAT ON MY WIFE?" FUCK THAT SHIT.
FAIR.
GOTTA THINK IT THROUGH.
I WAS BROKE, BUT OTHERS IN THE ROOMS THREW WORK MY WAY. HOUSEPAINTING, CONSTRUCTION, WHATEVER. SOMETIMES THESE GUYS JUST CARRIED ME.
JUST TAKE THE FUCKIN' MONEY, JIMMY.
YOU NEED YOUR GODDAMN PHONE. PAY THE BILL.
...I'LL GET YOU BACK.
I KNOW THAT, MAN!
SIXTY DAYS CAME ALONG. I DUG MYSELF IN DEEPER WITH MEETINGS AND MY SOBER PALS. I LAUGHED AGAIN AND REALIZED HOW LONG IT HAD BEEN SINCE I'D DONE SO. A SHOCK.
HA HA HA HA
WITH THAT LAUGH I UNDERSTOOD THE GOAL. QUITTING DRINKING WAS JUST THE BEGINNING... THE OBJECTIVE WAS TO BE COMFORTABLE IN MY OWN SKIN.
COMFORTABLE IN MY OWN SKIN.
MY OWN SKIN.

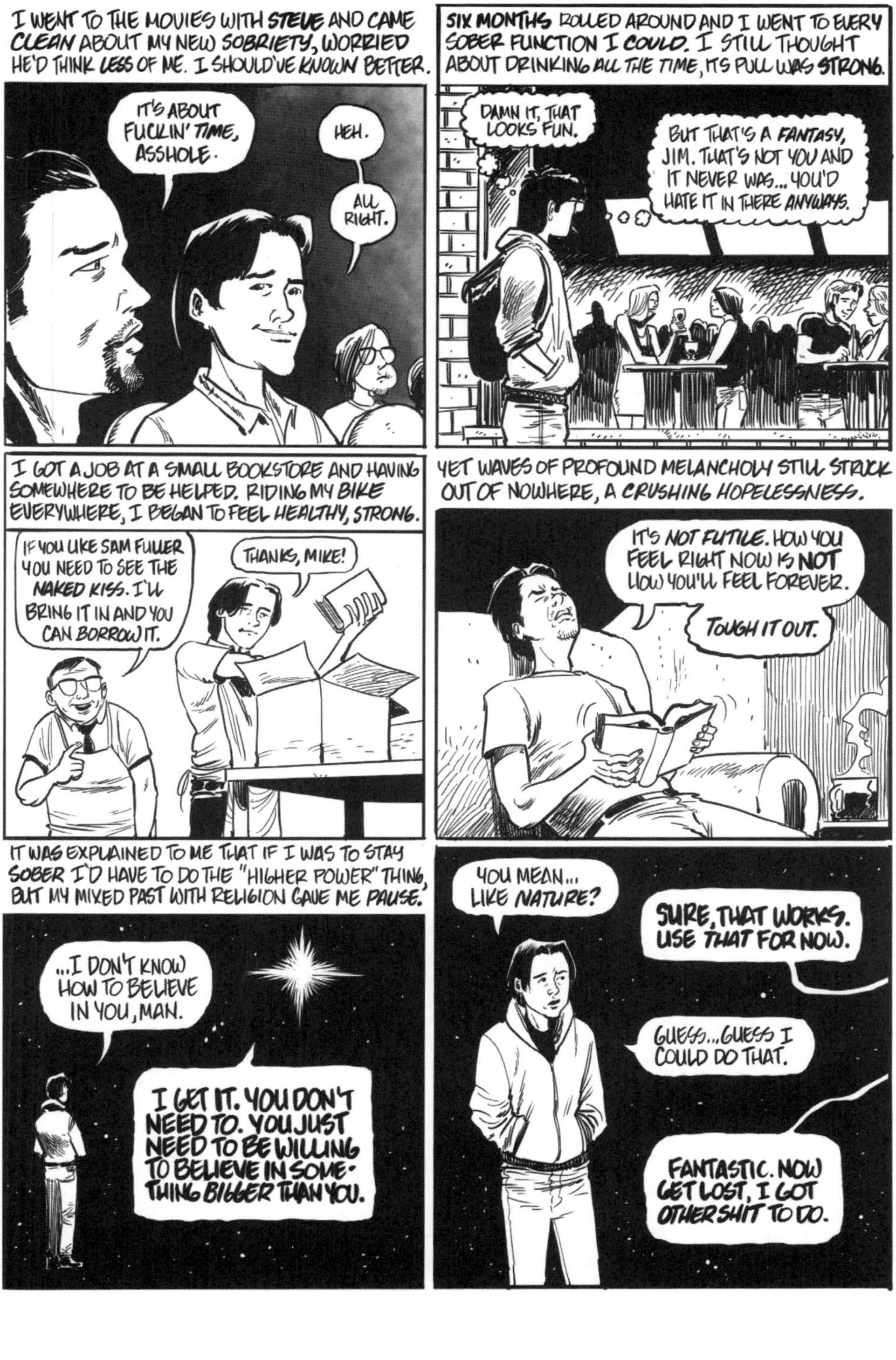
I WENT TO THE MOVIES WITH STEVE AND CAME CLEAN ABOUT MY NEW SOBRIETY, WORRIED HE'D THINK LESS OF ME. I SHOULD'VE KNOWN BETTER.
IT'S ABOUT FUCKIN' TIME, ASSHOLE.
HEH.
ALL RIGHT.
SIX MONTHS ROLLED AROUND AND I WENT TO EVERY SOBER FUNCTION I COULD. I STILL THOUGHT ABOUT DRINKING ALL THE TIME, ITS PULL WAS STRONG.
DAMN IT, THAT LOOKS FUN.
BUT THAT'S A FANTASY, JIM. THAT'S NOT YOU AND IT NEVER WAS... YOU'D HATE IT IN THERE ANYWAYS.
I GOT A JOB AT A SMALL BOOKSTORE AND HAVING SOMEWHERE TO BE HELPED. RIDING MY BIKE EVERYWHERE, I BEGAN TO FEEL HEALTHY, STRONG.
IF YOU LIKE SAM FULLER YOU NEED TO SEE THE NAKED KISS. I'LL BRING IT IN AND YOU CAN BORROW IT.
THANKS, MIKE!
YET WAVES OF PROFOUND MELANCHOLY STILL STRUCK OUT OF NOWHERE, A CRUSHING HOPELESSNESS.
IT'S NOT FUTILE. HOW YOU FEEL RIGHT NOW IS NOT HOW YOU'LL FEEL FOREVER.
TOUGH IT OUT.
IT WAS EXPLAINED TO ME THAT IF I WAS TO STAY SOBER I'D HAVE TO DO THE "HIGHER POWER" THING, BUT MY MIXED PAST WITH RELIGION GAVE ME PAUSE.
...I DON'T KNOW HOW TO BELIEVE IN YOU, MAN.
I GET IT. YOU DON'T NEED TO. YOU JUST NEED TO BE WILLING TO BELIEVE IN SOME-THING BIGGER THAN YOU.
YOU MEAN... LIKE NATURE?
SURE, THAT WORKS. USE THAT FOR NOW.
GUESS...GUESS I COULD DO THAT.
FANTASTIC. NOW GET LOST, I GOT OTHER SHIT TO DO.

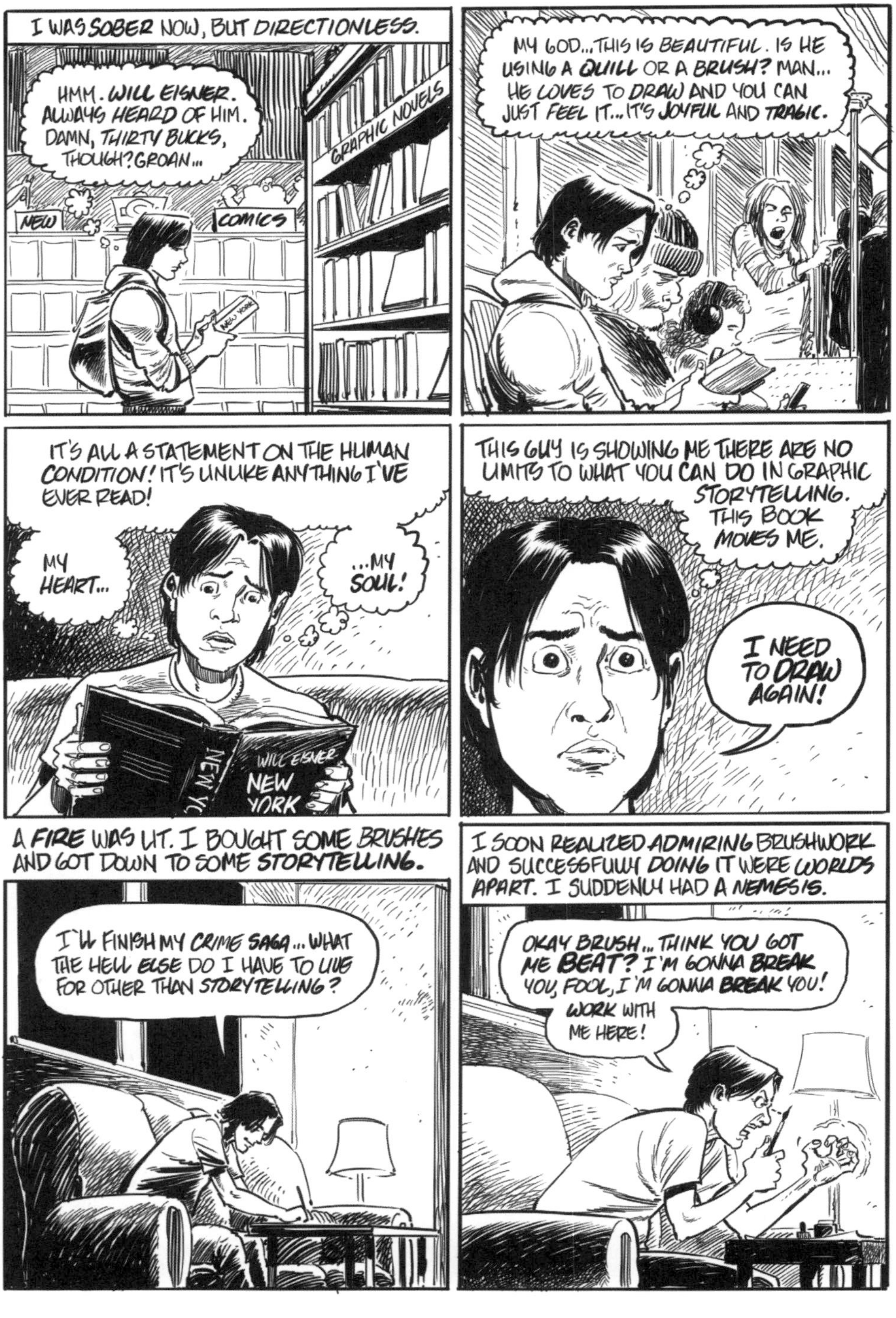

I WAS SOBER NOW, BUT DIRECTIONLESS.
HMM. WILL EISNER. ALWAYS HEARD OF HIM. DAMN, THIRTY BUCKS, THOUGH? GROAN...
GRAPHIC NOVELS
NEW
COMICS
NEW YORK
MY GOD... THIS IS BEAUTIFUL. IS HE USING A QUILL OR A BRUSH? MAN... HE LOVES TO DRAW AND YOU CAN JUST FEEL IT... IT'S JOYFUL AND TRAGIC.
IT'S ALL A STATEMENT ON THE HUMAN CONDITION! IT'S UNLIKE ANYTHING I'VE EVER READ!
MY HEART...
...MY SOUL!
WILL EISNER
NEW YORK
THIS GUY IS SHOWING ME THERE ARE NO LIMITS TO WHAT YOU CAN DO IN GRAPHIC STORYTELLING. THIS BOOK MOVES ME.
I NEED TO DRAW AGAIN!
A FIRE WAS LIT. I BOUGHT SOME BRUSHES AND GOT DOWN TO SOME STORYTELLING.
I'LL FINISH MY CRIME SAGA... WHAT THE HELL ELSE DO I HAVE TO LIVE FOR OTHER THAN STORYTELLING?
I SOON REALIZED ADMIRING BRUSHWORK AND SUCCESSFULLY DOING IT WERE WORLDS APART. I SUDDENLY HAD A NEMESIS.
OKAY BRUSH... THINK YOU GOT ME BEAT? I'M GONNA BREAK YOU, FOOL, I'M GONNA BREAK YOU!
WORK WITH ME HERE!

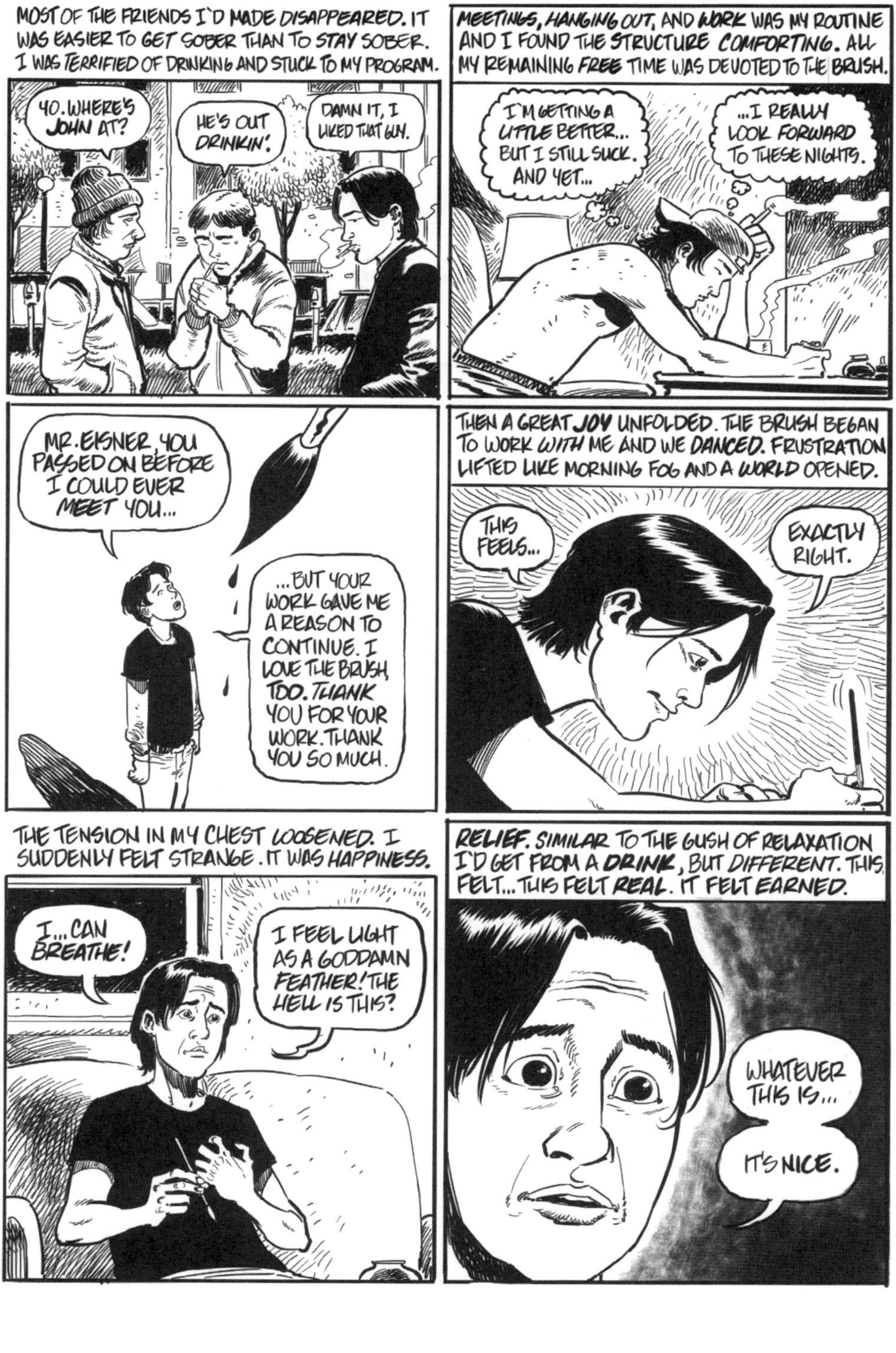
MOST OF THE FRIENDS I'D MADE DISAPPEARED. IT WAS EASIER TO GET SOBER THAN TO STAY SOBER. I WAS TERRIFIED OF DRINKING AND STUCK TO MY PROGRAM.
YO. WHERE'S JOHN AT?
HE'S OUT DRINKIN'.
DAMN IT, I LIKED THAT GUY.
MEETINGS, HANGING OUT, AND WORK WAS MY ROUTINE AND I FOUND THE STRUCTURE COMFORTING. ALL MY REMAINING FREE TIME WAS DEVOTED TO THE BRUSH.
I'M GETTING A LITTLE BETTER... BUT I STILL SUCK. AND YET...
...I REALLY LOOK FORWARD TO THESE NIGHTS.
MR. EISNER, YOU PASSED ON BEFORE I COULD EVER MEET YOU...
...BUT YOUR WORK GAVE ME A REASON TO CONTINUE. I LOVE THE BRUSH, TOO. THANK YOU FOR YOUR WORK. THANK YOU SO MUCH.
THEN A GREAT JOY UNFOLDED. THE BRUSH BEGAN TO WORK WITH ME AND WE DANCED. FRUSTRATION LIFTED LIKE MORNING FOG AND A WORLD OPENED.
THIS FEELS...
EXACTLY RIGHT.
THE TENSION IN MY CHEST LOOSENED. I SUDDENLY FELT STRANGE. IT WAS HAPPINESS.
I... CAN BREATHE!
I FEEL LIGHT AS A GODDAMN FEATHER! THE HELL IS THIS?
RELIEF. SIMILAR TO THE GUSH OF RELAXATION I'D GET FROM A DRINK, BUT DIFFERENT. THIS FELT... THIS FELT REAL. IT FELT EARNED.
WHATEVER THIS IS...
IT'S NICE.

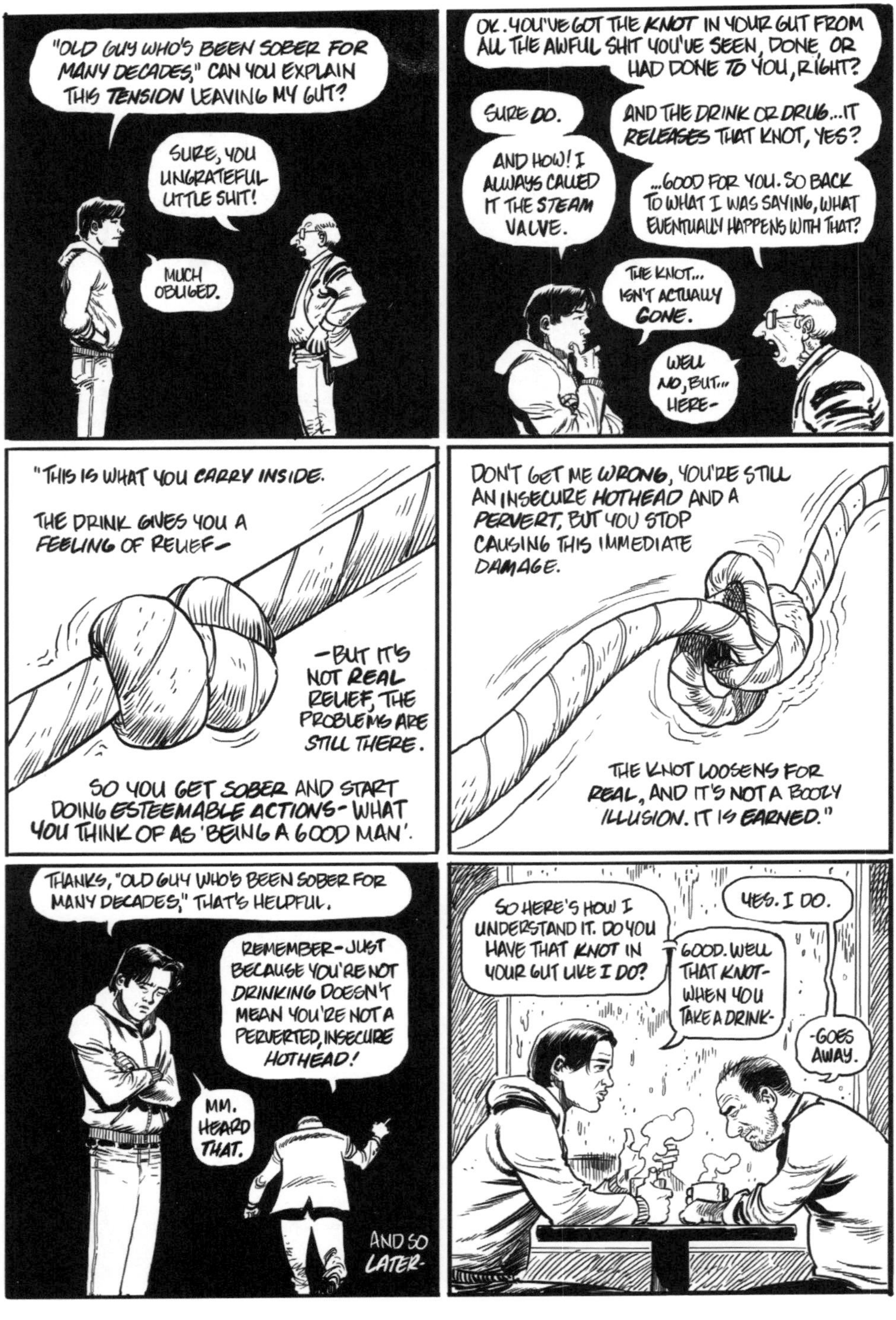
"OLD GUY WHO'S BEEN SOBER FOR MANY DECADES," CAN YOU EXPLAIN THIS TENSION LEAVING MY GUT?
SURE, YOU UNGRATEFUL LITTLE SHIT!
MUCH OBLIGED.
OK. YOU'VE GOT THE KNOT IN YOUR GUT FROM ALL THE AWFUL SHIT YOU'VE SEEN, DONE, OR HAD DONE TO YOU, RIGHT?
SURE DO.
AND THE DRINK OR DRUG... IT RELEASES THAT KNOT, YES?
AND HOW! I ALWAYS CALLED IT THE STEAM VALVE.
...GOOD FOR YOU. SO BACK TO WHAT I WAS SAYING, WHAT EVENTUALLY HAPPENS WITH THAT?
THE KNOT... ISN'T ACTUALLY GONE.
WELL NO, BUT... HERE-
"THIS IS WHAT YOU CARRY INSIDE.
THE DRINK GIVES YOU A FEELING OF RELIEF-
-BUT IT'S NOT REAL RELIEF, THE PROBLEMS ARE STILL THERE.
SO YOU GET SOBER AND START DOING ESTEEMABLE ACTIONS- WHAT YOU THINK OF AS 'BEING A GOOD MAN'.
DON'T GET ME WRONG, YOU'RE STILL AN INSECURE HOTHEAD AND A PERVERT, BUT YOU STOP CAUSING THIS IMMEDIATE DAMAGE.
THE KNOT LOOSENS FOR REAL, AND IT'S NOT A BOOZY ILLUSION. IT IS EARNED."
THANKS, "OLD GUY WHO'S BEEN SOBER FOR MANY DECADES," THAT'S HELPFUL.
REMEMBER- JUST BECAUSE YOU'RE NOT DRINKING DOESN'T MEAN YOU'RE NOT A PERVERTED, INSECURE HOTHEAD!
MM. HEARD THAT.
AND SO LATER-
SO HERE'S HOW I UNDERSTAND IT. DO YOU HAVE THAT KNOT IN YOUR GUT LIKE I DO?
YES. I DO.
GOOD. WELL THAT KNOT- WHEN YOU TAKE A DRINK-
-GOES AWAY.

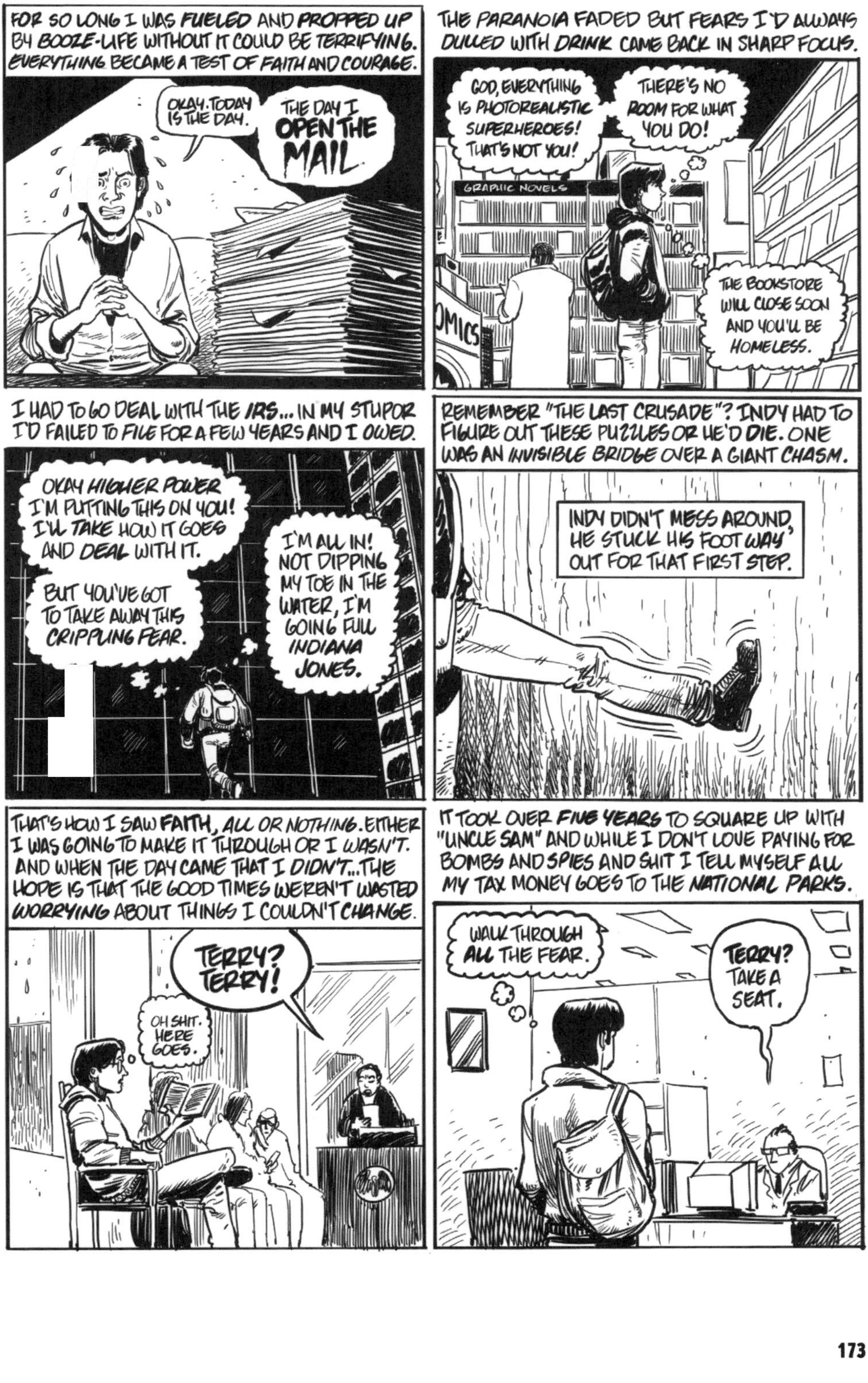
FOR SO LONG I WAS FUELED AND PROPPED UP BY BOOZE-LIFE WITHOUT IT COULD BE TERRIFYING. EVERYTHING BECAME A TEST OF FAITH AND COURAGE.
OKAY. TODAY IS THE DAY.
THE DAY I OPEN THE MAIL
THE PARANOIA FADED BUT FEARS I'D ALWAYS DULLED WITH DRINK CAME BACK IN SHARP FOCUS.
GOD, EVERYTHING IS PHOTOREALISTIC SUPERHEROES! THAT'S NOT YOU!
THERE'S NO ROOM FOR WHAT YOU DO!
GRAPHIC NOVELS
THE BOOKSTORE WILL CLOSE SOON AND YOU'LL BE HOMELESS.
I HAD TO GO DEAL WITH THE IRS... IN MY STUPOR I'D FAILED TO FILE FOR A FEW YEARS AND I OWED.
OKAY HIGHER POWER I'M PUTTING THIS ON YOU! I'LL TAKE HOW IT GOES AND DEAL WITH IT.
BUT YOU'VE GOT TO TAKE AWAY THIS CRIPPLING FEAR.
I'M ALL IN! NOT DIPPING MY TOE IN THE WATER, I'M GOING FULL INDIANA JONES.
REMEMBER "THE LAST CRUSADE"? INDY HAD TO FIGURE OUT THESE PUZZLES OR HE'D DIE. ONE WAS AN INVISIBLE BRIDGE OVER A GIANT CHASM.
INDY DIDN'T MESS AROUND, HE STUCK HIS FOOT WAY OUT FOR THAT FIRST STEP.
THAT'S HOW I SAW FAITH, ALL OR NOTHING. EITHER I WAS GOING TO MAKE IT THROUGH OR I WASN'T. AND WHEN THE DAY CAME THAT I DIDN'T... THE HOPE IS THAT THE GOOD TIMES WEREN'T WASTED WORRYING ABOUT THINGS I COULDN'T CHANGE.
TERRY? TERRY!
OH SHIT. HERE GOES.
IT TOOK OVER FIVE YEARS TO SQUARE UP WITH "UNCLE SAM" AND WHILE I DON'T LOVE PAYING FOR BOMBS AND SPIES AND SHIT I TELL MYSELF ALL MY TAX MONEY GOES TO THE NATIONAL PARKS.
WALK THROUGH ALL THE FEAR.
TERRY? TAKE A SEAT.

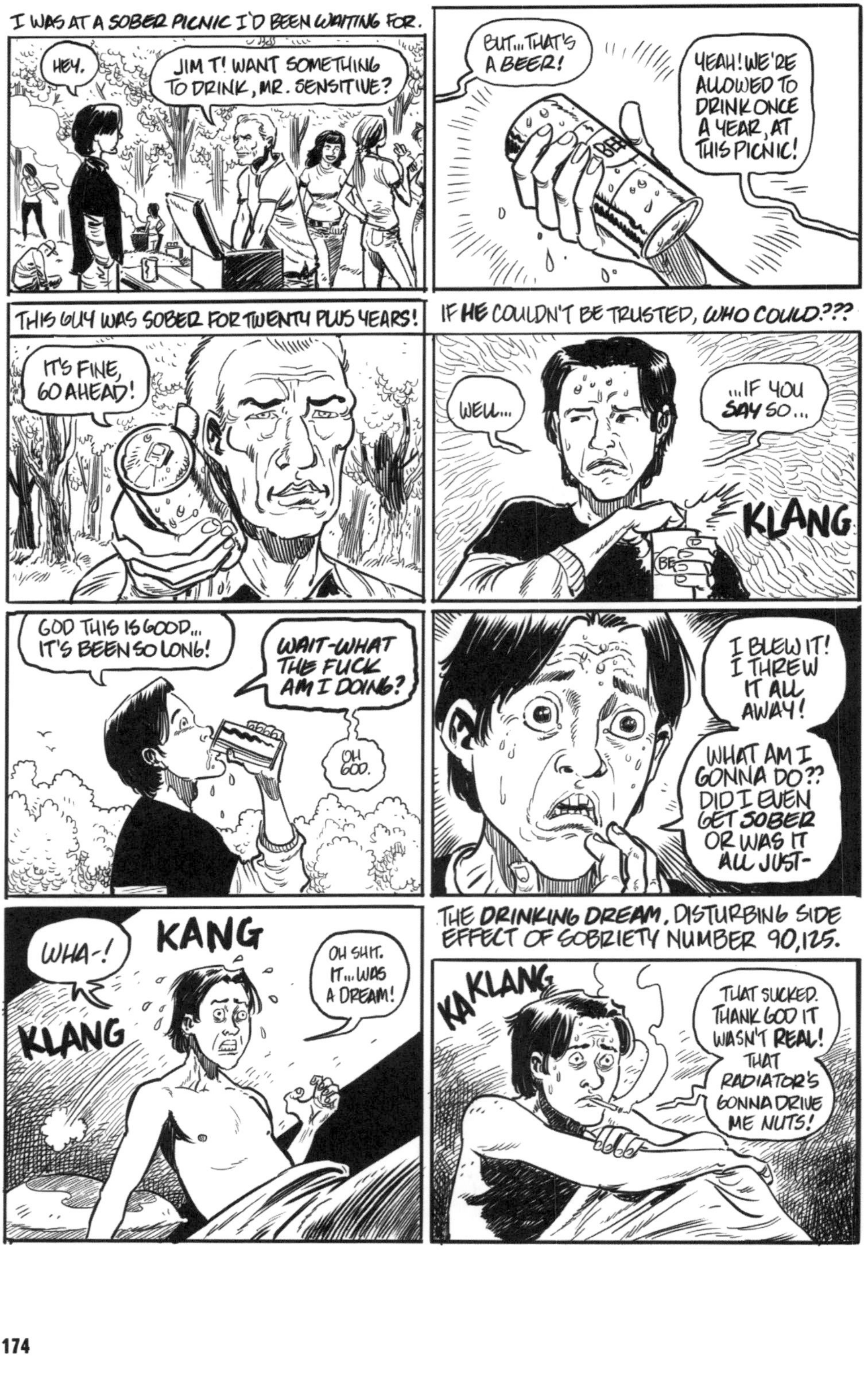

I WAS AT A SOBER PICNIC I'D BEEN WAITING FOR.
HEY.
JIM T! WANT SOMETHING TO DRINK, MR. SENSITIVE?
BUT... THAT'S A BEER!
YEAH! WE'RE ALLOWED TO DRINK ONCE A YEAR, AT THIS PICNIC!
THIS GUY WAS SOBER FOR TWENTY PLUS YEARS!
IT'S FINE, GO AHEAD!
IF HE COULDN'T BE TRUSTED, WHO COULD???
WELL...
...IF YOU SAY SO...
KLANG
GOD THIS IS GOOD... IT'S BEEN SO LONG!
WAIT-WHAT THE FUCK AM I DOING?
OH GOD.
I BLEW IT! I THREW IT ALL AWAY!
WHAT AM I GONNA DO?? DID I EVEN GET SOBER OR WAS IT ALL JUST-
WHA-!
KANG
KLANG
OH SHIT. IT... WAS A DREAM!
THE DRINKING DREAM. DISTURBING SIDE EFFECT OF SOBRIETY NUMBER 90,125.
KAKLANG
THAT SUCKED. THANK GOD IT WASN'T REAL! THAT RADIATOR'S GONNA DRIVE ME NUTS!

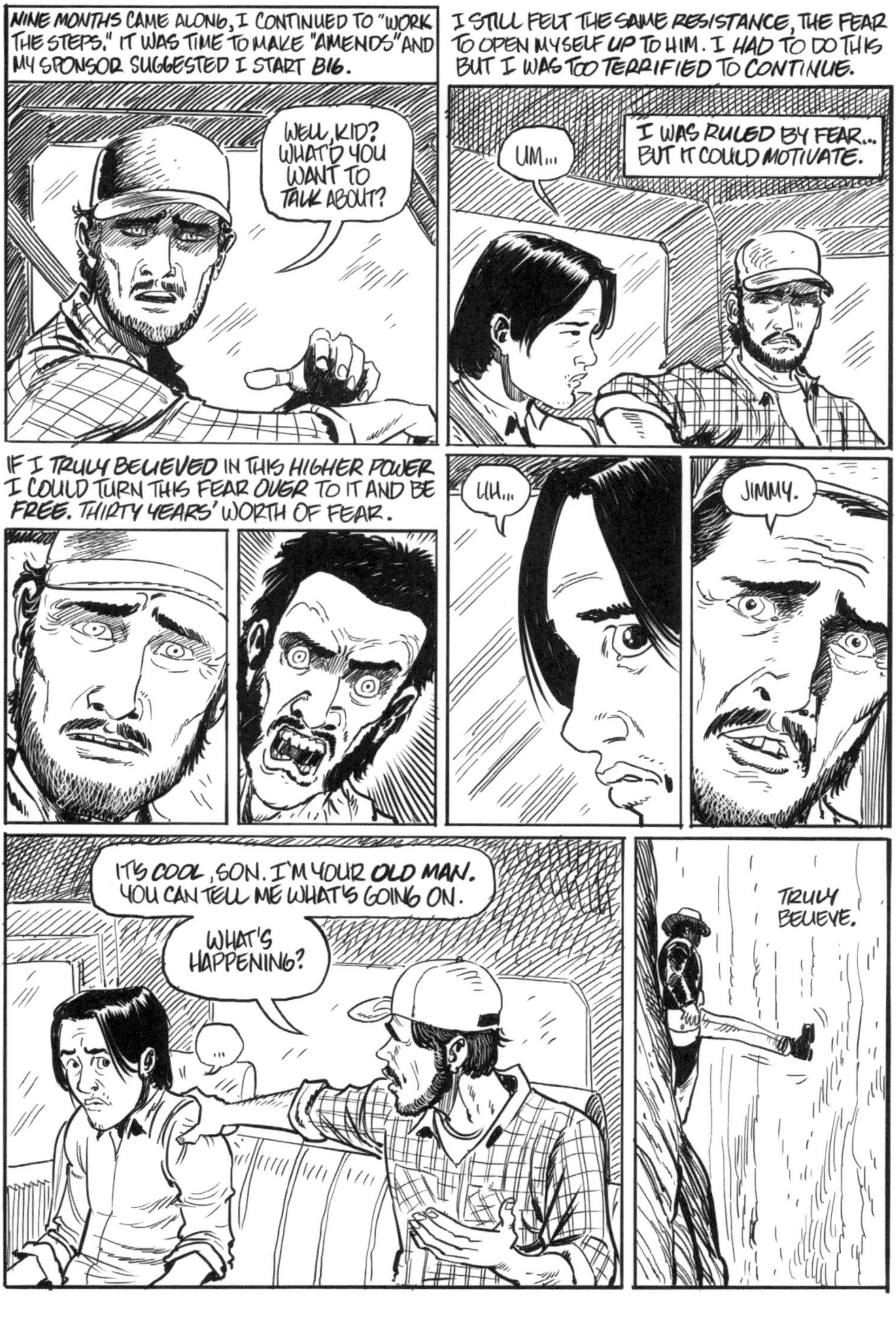
NINE MONTHS CAME ALONG, I CONTINUED TO "WORK THE STEPS." IT WAS TIME TO MAKE "AMENDS" AND MY SPONSOR SUGGESTED I START BIG.
WELL, KID? WHAT'D YOU WANT TO TALK ABOUT?
I STILL FELT THE SAME RESISTANCE, THE FEAR TO OPEN MYSELF UP TO HIM. I HAD TO DO THIS BUT I WAS TOO TERRIFIED TO CONTINUE.
UM...
I WAS RULED BY FEAR... BUT IT COULD MOTIVATE.
IF I TRULY BELIEVED IN THIS HIGHER POWER I COULD TURN THIS FEAR OVER TO IT AND BE FREE. THIRTY YEARS' WORTH OF FEAR.
UH...
JIMMY.
IT'S COOL, SON. I'M YOUR OLD MAN. YOU CAN TELL ME WHAT'S GOING ON.
WHAT'S HAPPENING?
...
TRULY BELIEVE.

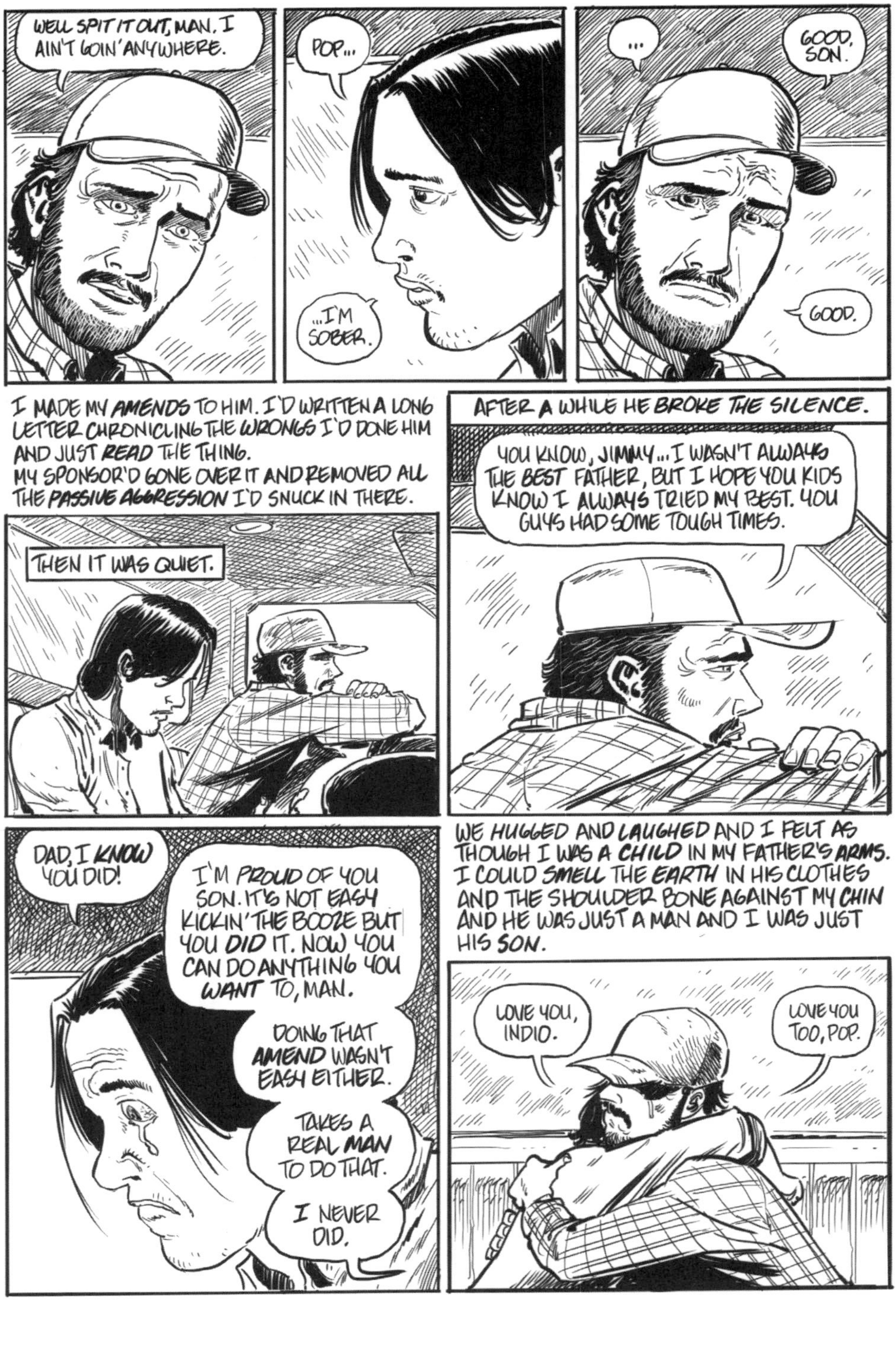
WELL SPIT IT OUT, MAN. I AIN'T GOIN' ANYWHERE.
POP...
...I'M SOBER.
...
GOOD, SON.
GOOD.
I MADE MY AMENDS TO HIM. I'D WRITTEN A LONG LETTER CHRONICLING THE WRONGS I'D DONE HIM AND JUST READ THE THING.
MY SPONSOR'D GONE OVER IT AND REMOVED ALL THE PASSIVE AGGRESSION I'D SNUCK IN THERE.
THEN IT WAS QUIET.
AFTER A WHILE HE BROKE THE SILENCE.
YOU KNOW, JIMMY... I WASN'T ALWAYS THE BEST FATHER, BUT I HOPE YOU KIDS KNOW I ALWAYS TRIED MY BEST. YOU GUYS HAD SOME TOUGH TIMES.
DAD, I KNOW YOU DID!
I'M PROUD OF YOU SON. IT'S NOT EASY KICKIN' THE BOOZE BUT YOU DID IT. NOW YOU CAN DO ANYTHING YOU WANT TO, MAN.
DOING THAT AMEND WASN'T EASY EITHER.
TAKES A REAL MAN TO DO THAT.
I NEVER DID.
WE HUGGED AND LAUGHED AND I FELT AS THOUGH I WAS A CHILD IN MY FATHER'S ARMS. I COULD SMELL THE EARTH IN HIS CLOTHES AND THE SHOULDER BONE AGAINST MY CHIN AND HE WAS JUST A MAN AND I WAS JUST HIS SON.
LOVE YOU, INDIO.
LOVE YOU TOO, POP.

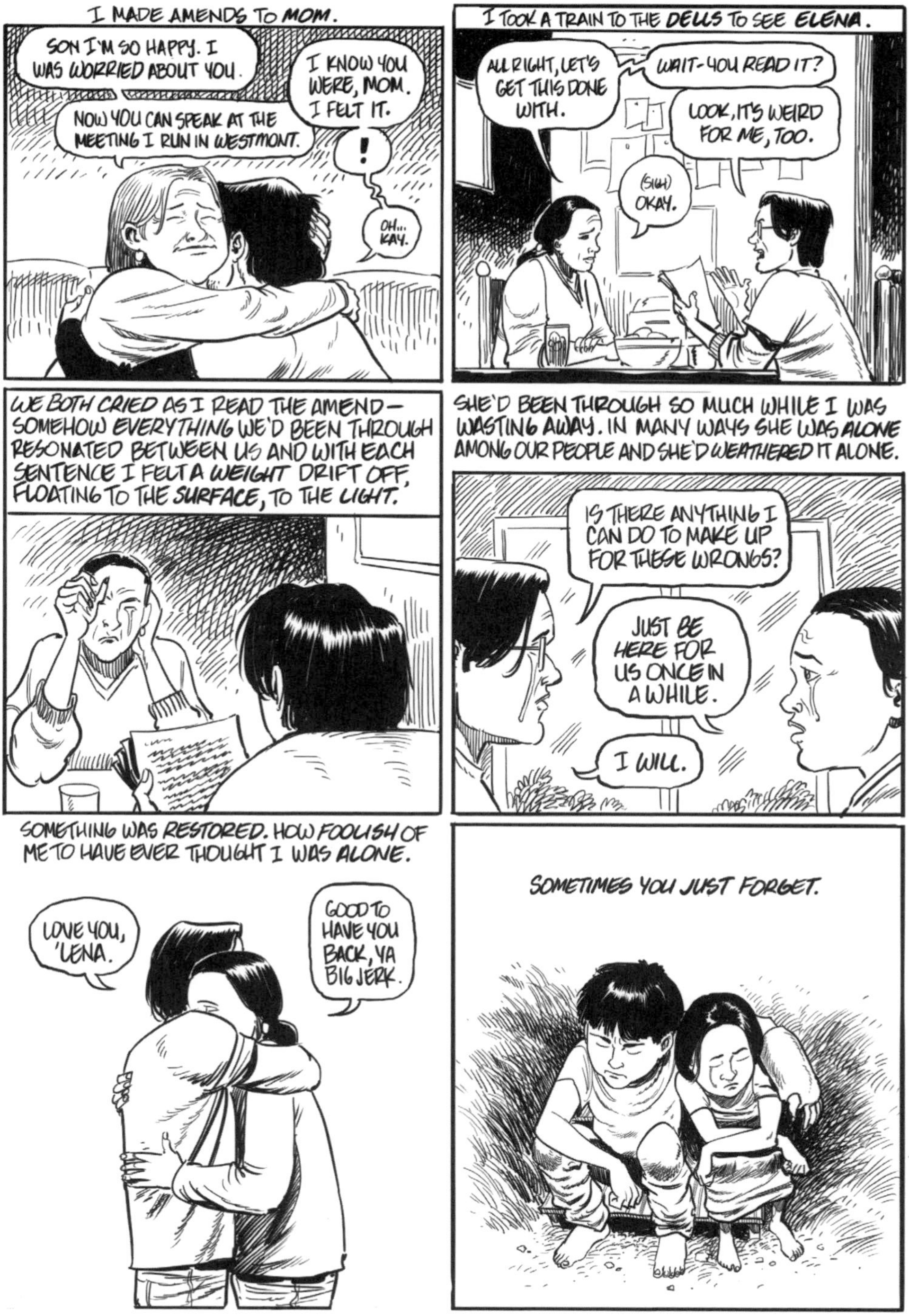
I MADE AMENDS TO MOM.
SON I'M SO HAPPY. I WAS WORRIED ABOUT YOU.
NOW YOU CAN SPEAK AT THE MEETING I RUN IN WESTMONT.
I KNOW YOU WERE, MOM. I FELT IT.
!
OH... KAY.
I TOOK A TRAIN TO THE DELLS TO SEE ELENA.
ALL RIGHT, LET'S GET THIS DONE WITH.
WAIT- YOU READ IT?
LOOK, IT'S WEIRD FOR ME, TOO.
(SIGH) OKAY.
WE BOTH CRIED AS I READ THE AMEND— SOMEHOW EVERYTHING WE'D BEEN THROUGH RESONATED BETWEEN US AND WITH EACH SENTENCE I FELT A WEIGHT DRIFT OFF, FLOATING TO THE SURFACE, TO THE LIGHT.
SHE'D BEEN THROUGH SO MUCH WHILE I WAS WASTING AWAY. IN MANY WAYS SHE WAS ALONE AMONG OUR PEOPLE AND SHE'D WEATHERED IT ALONE.
IS THERE ANYTHING I CAN DO TO MAKE UP FOR THESE WRONGS?
JUST BE HERE FOR US ONCE IN A WHILE.
I WILL.
SOMETHING WAS RESTORED. HOW FOOLISH OF ME TO HAVE EVER THOUGHT I WAS ALONE.
LOVE YOU, 'LENA.
GOOD TO HAVE YOU BACK, YA BIG JERK.
SOMETIMES YOU JUST FORGET.

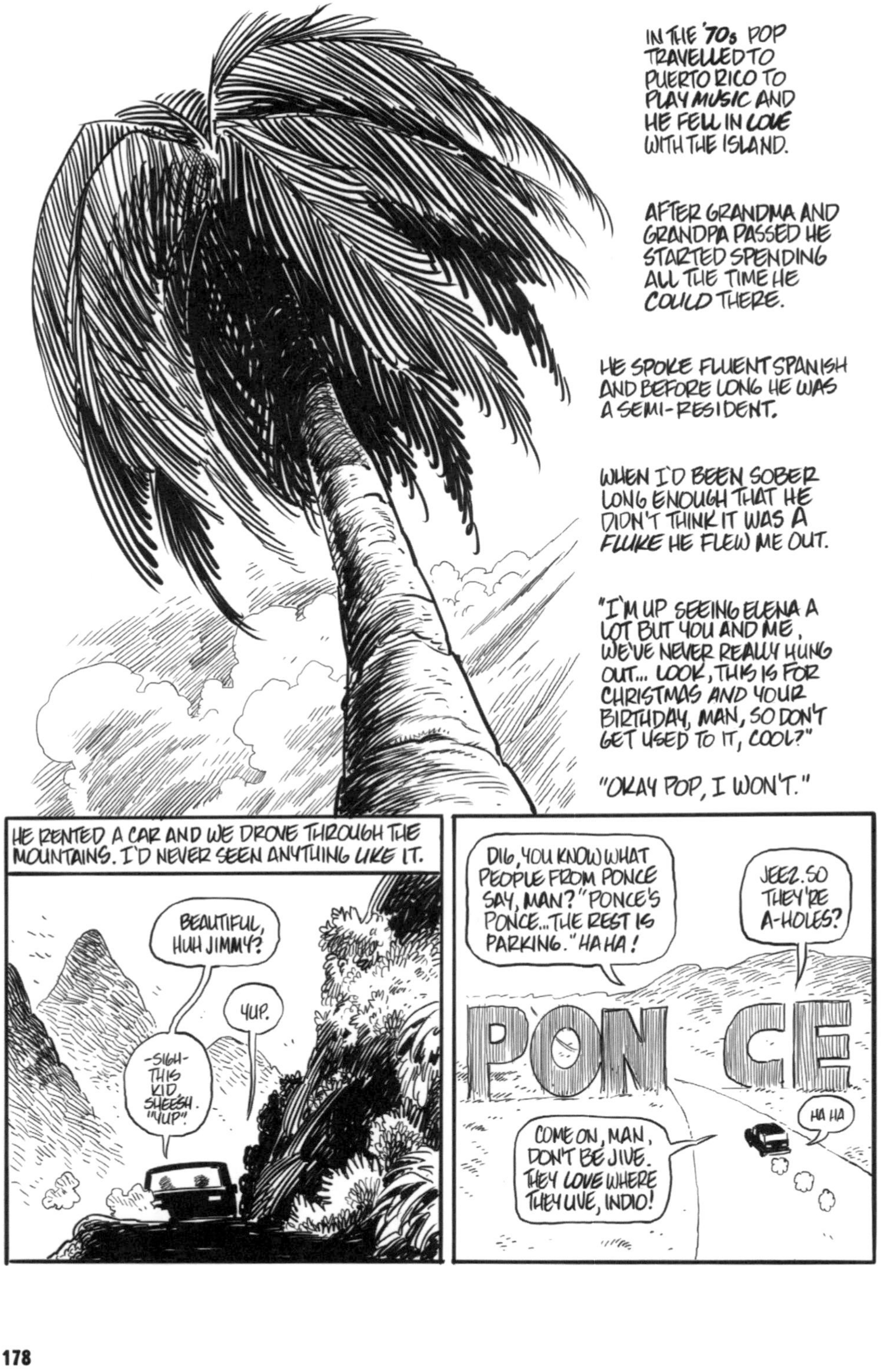
IN THE '70s POP TRAVELLED TO PUERTO RICO TO PLAY MUSIC AND HE FELL IN LOVE WITH THE ISLAND.
AFTER GRANDMA AND GRANDPA PASSED HE STARTED SPENDING ALL THE TIME HE COULD THERE.
HE SPOKE FLUENT SPANISH AND BEFORE LONG HE WAS A SEMI-RESIDENT.
WHEN I'D BEEN SOBER LONG ENOUGH THAT HE DIDN'T THINK IT WAS A FLUKE HE FLEW ME OUT.
"I'M UP SEEING ELENA A LOT BUT YOU AND ME, WE'VE NEVER REALLY HUNG OUT... LOOK, THIS IS FOR CHRISTMAS AND YOUR BIRTHDAY, MAN, SO DON'T GET USED TO IT, COOL?"
"OKAY POP, I WON'T."
HE RENTED A CAR AND WE DROVE THROUGH THE MOUNTAINS. I'D NEVER SEEN ANYTHING LIKE IT.
BEAUTIFUL, HUH JIMMY?
YUP.
-SIGH- THIS KID. SHEESH. "YUP."
DIG, YOU KNOW WHAT PEOPLE FROM PONCE SAY, MAN? "PONCE'S PONCE... THE REST IS PARKING." HA HA!
JEEZ. SO THEY'RE A-HOLES?
PONCE
COME ON, MAN, DON'T BE JIVE. THEY LOVE WHERE THEY LIVE, INDIO!
HA HA

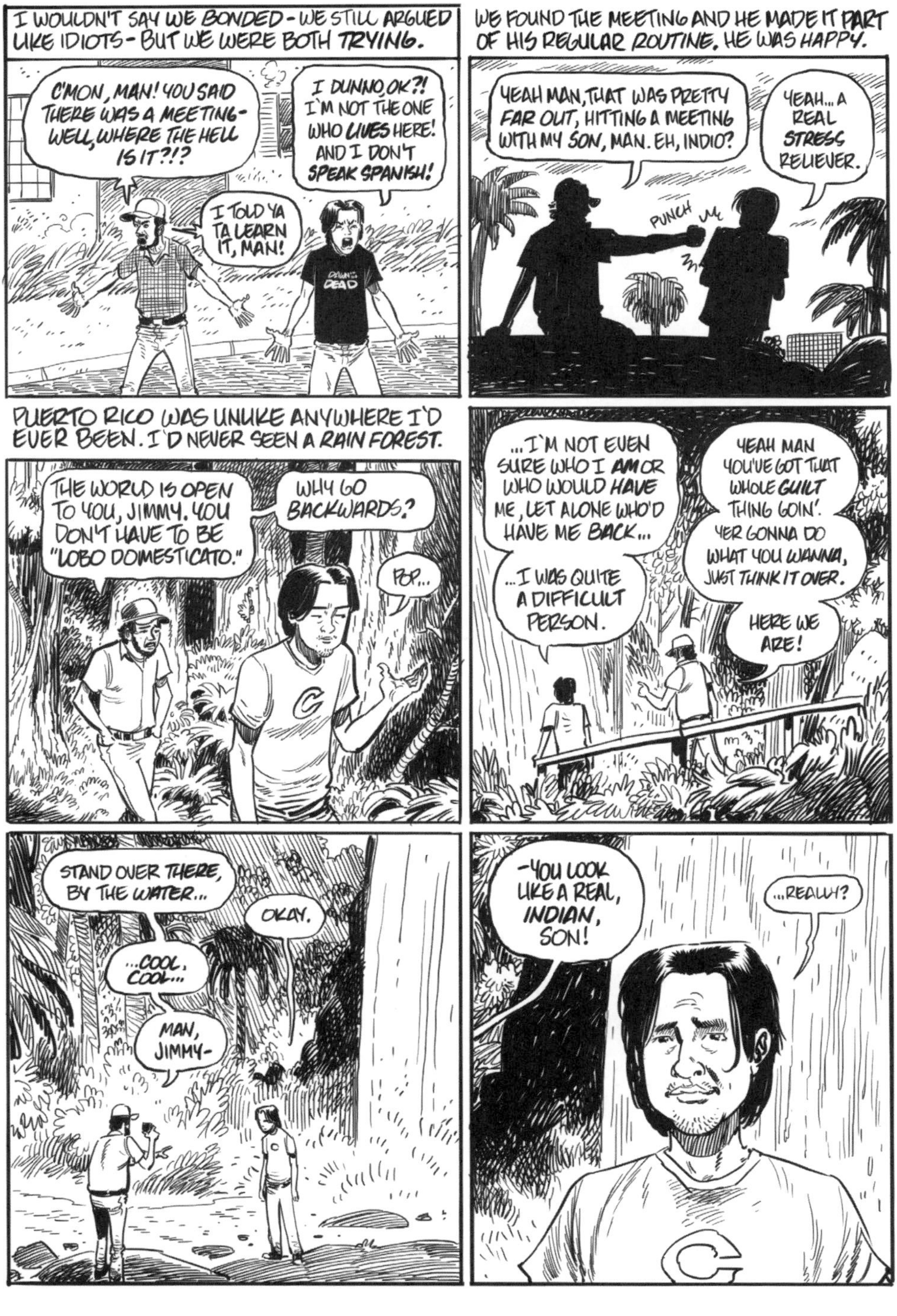
I WOULDN'T SAY WE BONDED - WE STILL ARGUED LIKE IDIOTS - BUT WE WERE BOTH TRYING.
C'MON, MAN! YOU SAID THERE WAS A MEETING - WELL, WHERE THE HELL IS IT?!?
I DUNNO, OK?! I'M NOT THE ONE WHO LIVES HERE! AND I DON'T SPEAK SPANISH!
I TOLD YA TA LEARN IT, MAN!
DAWN OF THE DEAD
WE FOUND THE MEETING AND HE MADE IT PART OF HIS REGULAR ROUTINE. HE WAS HAPPY.
YEAH MAN, THAT WAS PRETTY FAR OUT, HITTING A MEETING WITH MY SON, MAN. EH, INDIO?
PUNCH
YEAH... A REAL STRESS RELIEVER.
PUERTO RICO WAS UNLIKE ANYWHERE I'D EVER BEEN. I'D NEVER SEEN A RAIN FOREST.
THE WORLD IS OPEN TO YOU, JIMMY. YOU DON'T HAVE TO BE "LOBO DOMESTICATO."
WHY GO BACKWARDS?
POP...
...I'M NOT EVEN SURE WHO I AM OR WHO WOULD HAVE ME, LET ALONE WHO'D HAVE ME BACK...
...I WAS QUITE A DIFFICULT PERSON.
YEAH MAN YOU'VE GOT THAT WHOLE GUILT THING GOIN'.
YER GONNA DO WHAT YOU WANNA, JUST THINK IT OVER.
HERE WE ARE!
STAND OVER THERE, BY THE WATER...
OKAY.
...COOL. COOL...
MAN, JIMMY-
-YOU LOOK LIKE A REAL, INDIAN, SON!
...REALLY?

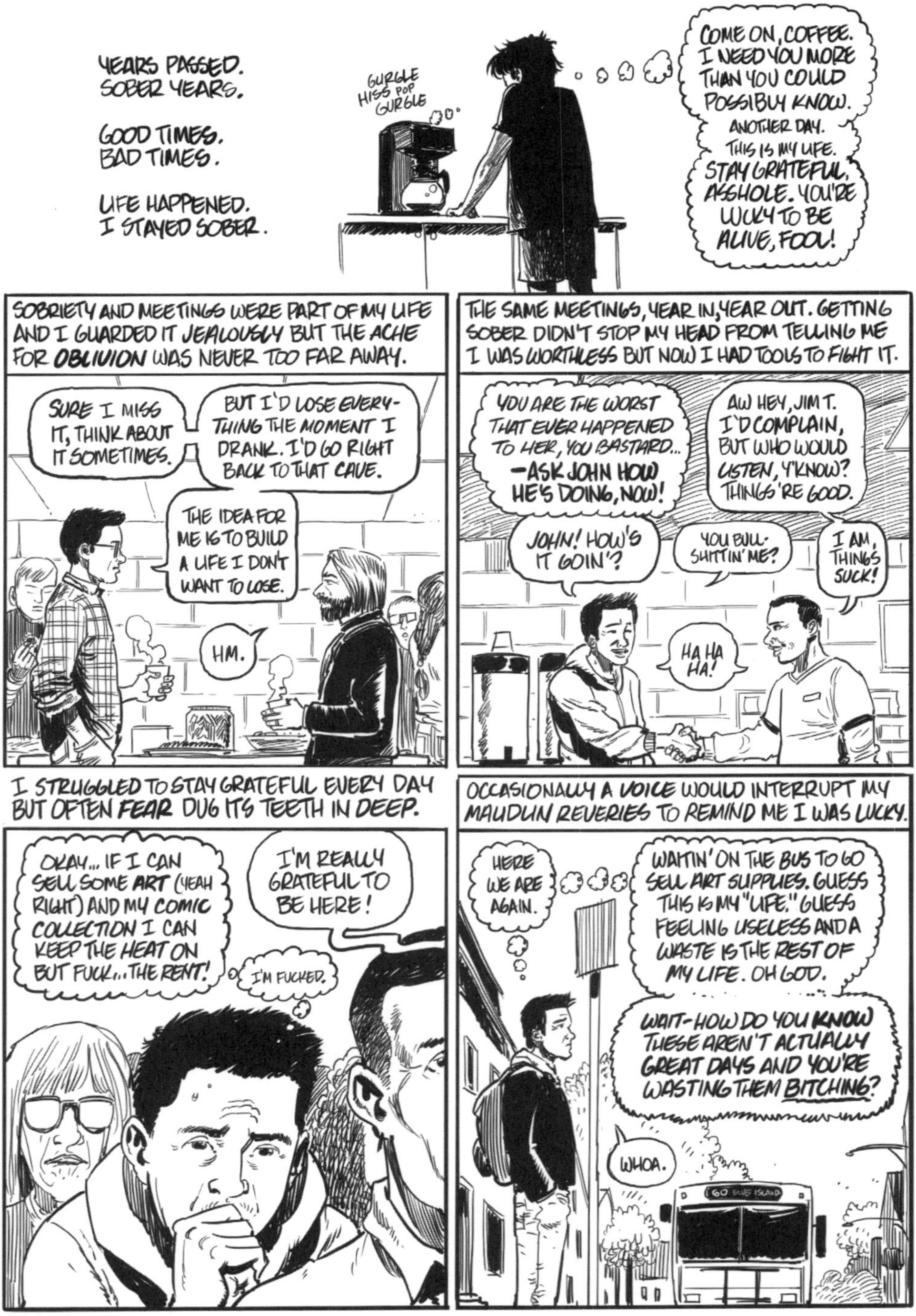
YEARS PASSED. SOBER YEARS.
GOOD TIMES. BAD TIMES.
LIFE HAPPENED. I STAYED SOBER.
GURGLE HISS POP GURGLE
COME ON, COFFEE. I NEED YOU MORE THAN YOU COULD POSSIBLY KNOW. ANOTHER DAY. THIS IS MY LIFE. STAY GRATEFUL, ASSHOLE. YOU'RE LUCKY TO BE ALIVE, FOOL!
SOBRIETY AND MEETINGS WERE PART OF MY LIFE AND I GUARDED IT JEALOUSLY BUT THE ACHE FOR OBLIVION WAS NEVER TOO FAR AWAY.
SURE I MISS IT, THINK ABOUT IT SOMETIMES.
BUT I'D LOSE EVERYTHING THE MOMENT I DRANK. I'D GO RIGHT BACK TO THAT CAVE.
THE IDEA FOR ME IS TO BUILD A LIFE I DON'T WANT TO LOSE.
HM.
THE SAME MEETINGS, YEAR IN, YEAR OUT. GETTING SOBER DIDN'T STOP MY HEAD FROM TELLING ME I WAS WORTHLESS BUT NOW I HAD TOOLS TO FIGHT IT.
YOU ARE THE WORST THAT EVER HAPPENED TO HER, YOU BASTARD... —ASK JOHN HOW HE'S DOING, NOW!
AW HEY, JIM T. I'D COMPLAIN, BUT WHO WOULD LISTEN, Y'KNOW? THINGS'RE GOOD.
JOHN! HOW'S IT GOIN'?
YOU BULLSHITTIN' ME?
I AM, THINGS SUCK!
HA HA HA!
I STRUGGLED TO STAY GRATEFUL EVERY DAY BUT OFTEN FEAR DUG ITS TEETH IN DEEP.
OKAY... IF I CAN SELL SOME ART (YEAH RIGHT) AND MY COMIC COLLECTION I CAN KEEP THE HEAT ON BUT FUCK... THE RENT!
I'M FUCKED.
I'M REALLY GRATEFUL TO BE HERE!
OCCASIONALLY A VOICE WOULD INTERRUPT MY MAUDLIN REVERIES TO REMIND ME I WAS LUCKY.
HERE WE ARE AGAIN.
WAITIN' ON THE BUS TO GO SELL ART SUPPLIES. GUESS THIS IS MY "LIFE." GUESS FEELING USELESS AND A WASTE IS THE REST OF MY LIFE. OH GOD.
WAIT- HOW DO YOU KNOW THESE AREN'T ACTUALLY GREAT DAYS AND YOU'RE WASTING THEM BITCHING?
WHOA.
60 BLUE ISLAND

AT SOME POINT DURING MY **DRINKING** I'D THROWN SOME **SAMPLE PAGES** ON THE TABLE OF THE **CROW** CREATOR **JAMES O'BARR** AT A COMICON.

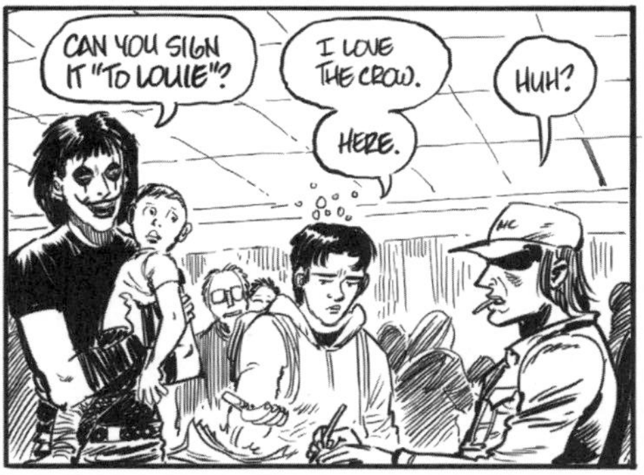
CAN YOU SIGN IT "TO LOUIE"?
I LOVE THE CROW.
HERE.
HUH?

SOME **FOUR YEARS LATER** HE SENT AN **EMAIL** TO SAY HE'D **LIKED** THEM AND WE **BECAME FRIENDS** OVER OLD **MOVIES, BOOKS**, AND **ARTISTS**. WE BOTH ALSO UNDERSTOOD **LONELINESS** AND THE **GREAT MELANCHOLY**, HAVING SPENT PLENTY OF TIME THERE.

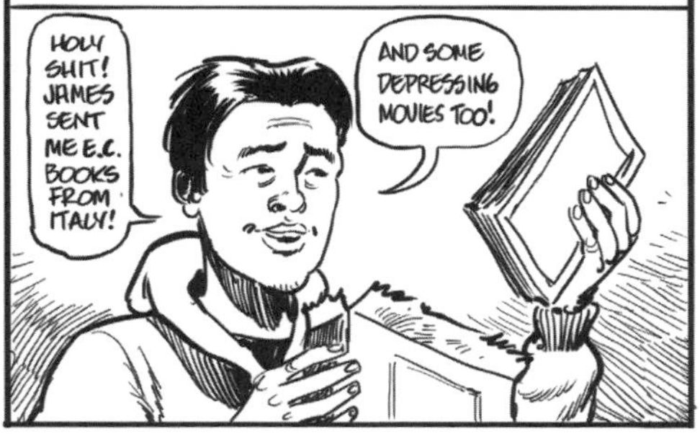
HOLY SHIT! JAMES SENT ME E.C. BOOKS FROM ITALY!
AND SOME DEPRESSING MOVIES TOO!

I FLEW TO **DALLAS** AND DID SOME **SHOWS** WITH HIM. THE DRIVE TO **AUSTIN** WAS A STORYTELLING **CONFESSIONAL** AND WE LAUGHED PLENTY.

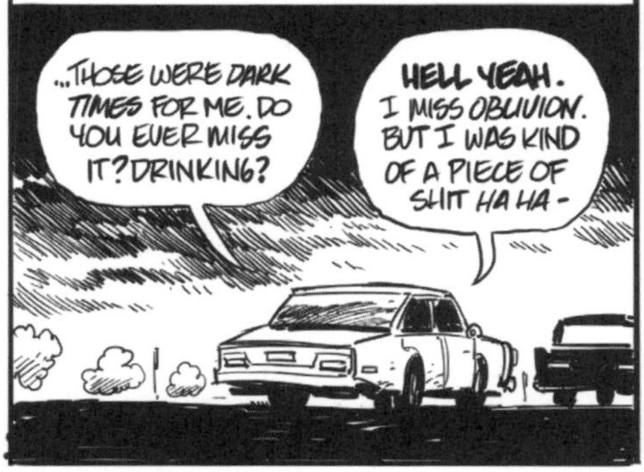
...THOSE WERE DARK TIMES FOR ME. DO YOU EVER MISS IT? DRINKING?
HELL YEAH. I MISS OBLIVION. BUT I WAS KIND OF A PIECE OF SHIT HA HA-

I WAS **AMAZED** AT THEIR **COMICS COMMUNITY**.

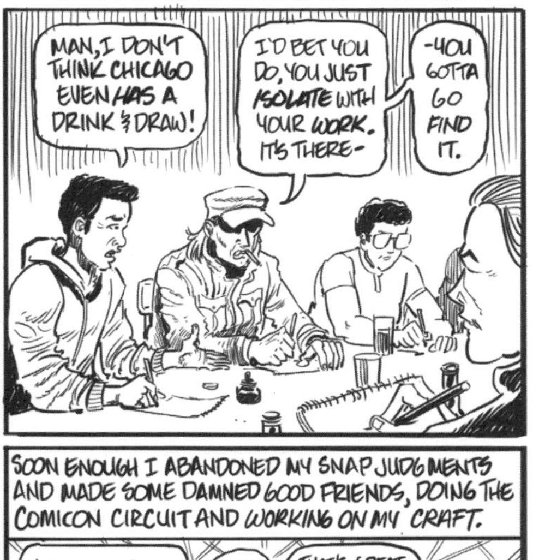
MAN, I DON'T THINK CHICAGO EVEN HAS A DRINK & DRAW!
I'D BET YOU DO, YOU JUST ISOLATE WITH YOUR WORK. IT'S THERE-
-YOU GOTTA GO FIND IT.

I FOUND IT-EVERYONE SEEMED TO **KNOW** EACH OTHER AND **HOVERED** AROUND THE **SUCCESSES**.

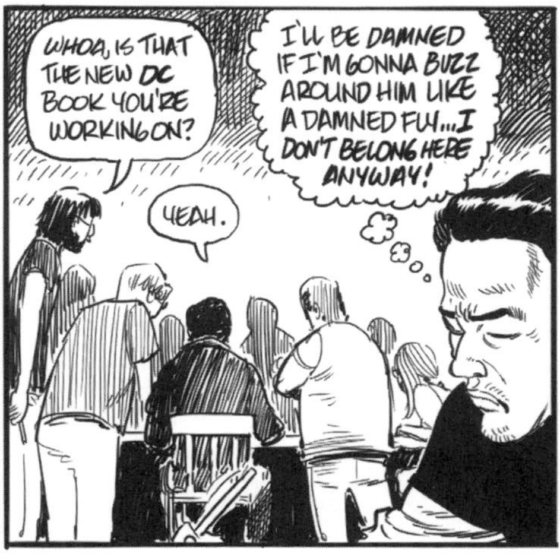
WHOA, IS THAT THE NEW DC BOOK YOU'RE WORKING ON?
YEAH.
I'LL BE DAMNED IF I'M GONNA BUZZ AROUND HIM LIKE A DAMNED FLY...I DON'T BELONG HERE ANYWAY!

SOON ENOUGH I ABANDONED MY SNAP JUDGMENTS AND MADE SOME DAMNED GOOD FRIENDS, DOING THE COMICON CIRCUIT AND **WORKING ON MY CRAFT**.

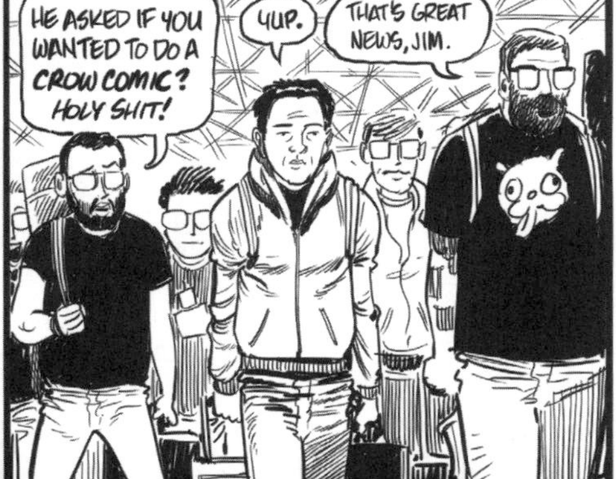
HE ASKED IF YOU WANTED TO DO A CROW COMIC? HOLY SHIT!
YUP.
THAT'S GREAT NEWS, JIM.

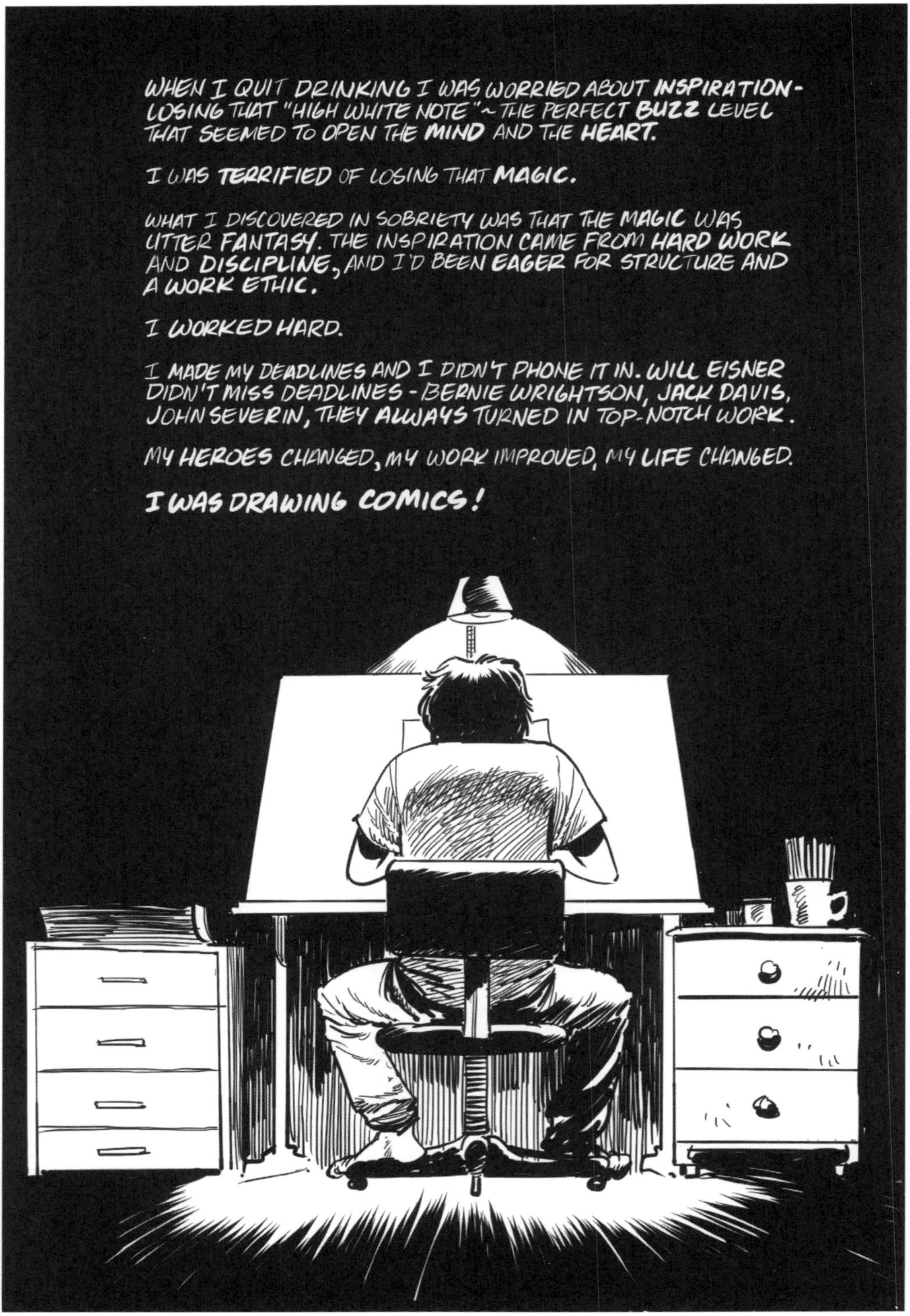
WHEN I QUIT DRINKING I WAS WORRIED ABOUT INSPIRATION- LOSING THAT "HIGH WHITE NOTE" ~ THE PERFECT BUZZ LEVEL THAT SEEMED TO OPEN THE MIND AND THE HEART.
I WAS TERRIFIED OF LOSING THAT MAGIC.
WHAT I DISCOVERED IN SOBRIETY WAS THAT THE MAGIC WAS UTTER FANTASY. THE INSPIRATION CAME FROM HARD WORK AND DISCIPLINE, AND I'D BEEN EAGER FOR STRUCTURE AND A WORK ETHIC.
I WORKED HARD.
I MADE MY DEADLINES AND I DIDN'T PHONE IT IN. WILL EISNER DIDN'T MISS DEADLINES - BERNIE WRIGHTSON, JACK DAVIS, JOHN SEVERIN, THEY ALWAYS TURNED IN TOP-NOTCH WORK.
MY HEROES CHANGED, MY WORK IMPROVED, MY LIFE CHANGED.
I WAS DRAWING COMICS!

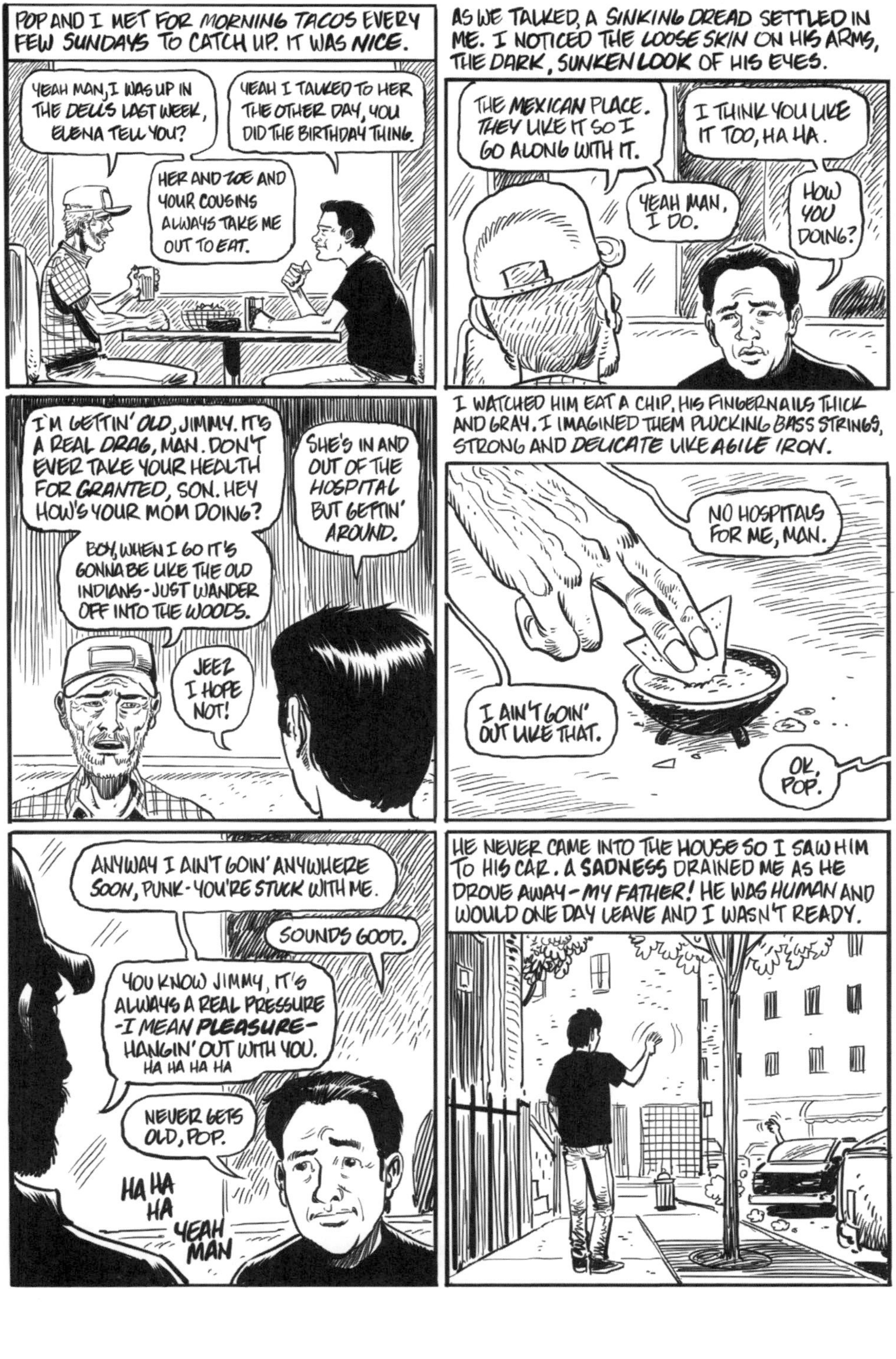
POP AND I MET FOR MORNING TACOS EVERY FEW SUNDAYS TO CATCH UP. IT WAS NICE.
YEAH MAN, I WAS UP IN THE DELLS LAST WEEK, ELENA TELL YOU?
YEAH I TALKED TO HER THE OTHER DAY, YOU DID THE BIRTHDAY THING.
HER AND ZOE AND YOUR COUSINS ALWAYS TAKE ME OUT TO EAT.
AS WE TALKED, A SINKING DREAD SETTLED IN ME. I NOTICED THE LOOSE SKIN ON HIS ARMS, THE DARK, SUNKEN LOOK OF HIS EYES.
THE MEXICAN PLACE. THEY LIKE IT SO I GO ALONG WITH IT.
I THINK YOU LIKE IT TOO, HA HA.
YEAH MAN, I DO.
HOW YOU DOING?
I'M GETTIN' OLD, JIMMY. IT'S A REAL DRAG, MAN. DON'T EVER TAKE YOUR HEALTH FOR GRANTED, SON. HEY HOW'S YOUR MOM DOING?
SHE'S IN AND OUT OF THE HOSPITAL BUT GETTIN' AROUND.
BOY, WHEN I GO IT'S GONNA BE LIKE THE OLD INDIANS - JUST WANDER OFF INTO THE WOODS.
JEEZ I HOPE NOT!
I WATCHED HIM EAT A CHIP, HIS FINGERNAILS THICK AND GRAY. I IMAGINED THEM PLUCKING BASS STRINGS, STRONG AND DELICATE LIKE AGILE IRON.
NO HOSPITALS FOR ME, MAN.
I AIN'T GOIN' OUT LIKE THAT.
OK, POP.
ANYWAY I AIN'T GOIN' ANYWHERE SOON, PUNK - YOU'RE STUCK WITH ME.
SOUNDS GOOD.
YOU KNOW JIMMY, IT'S ALWAYS A REAL PRESSURE - I MEAN PLEASURE - HANGIN' OUT WITH YOU.
HA HA HA HA
NEVER GETS OLD, POP.
HA HA HA
YEAH MAN
HE NEVER CAME INTO THE HOUSE SO I SAW HIM TO HIS CAR. A SADNESS DRAINED ME AS HE DROVE AWAY - MY FATHER! HE WAS HUMAN AND WOULD ONE DAY LEAVE AND I WASN'T READY.

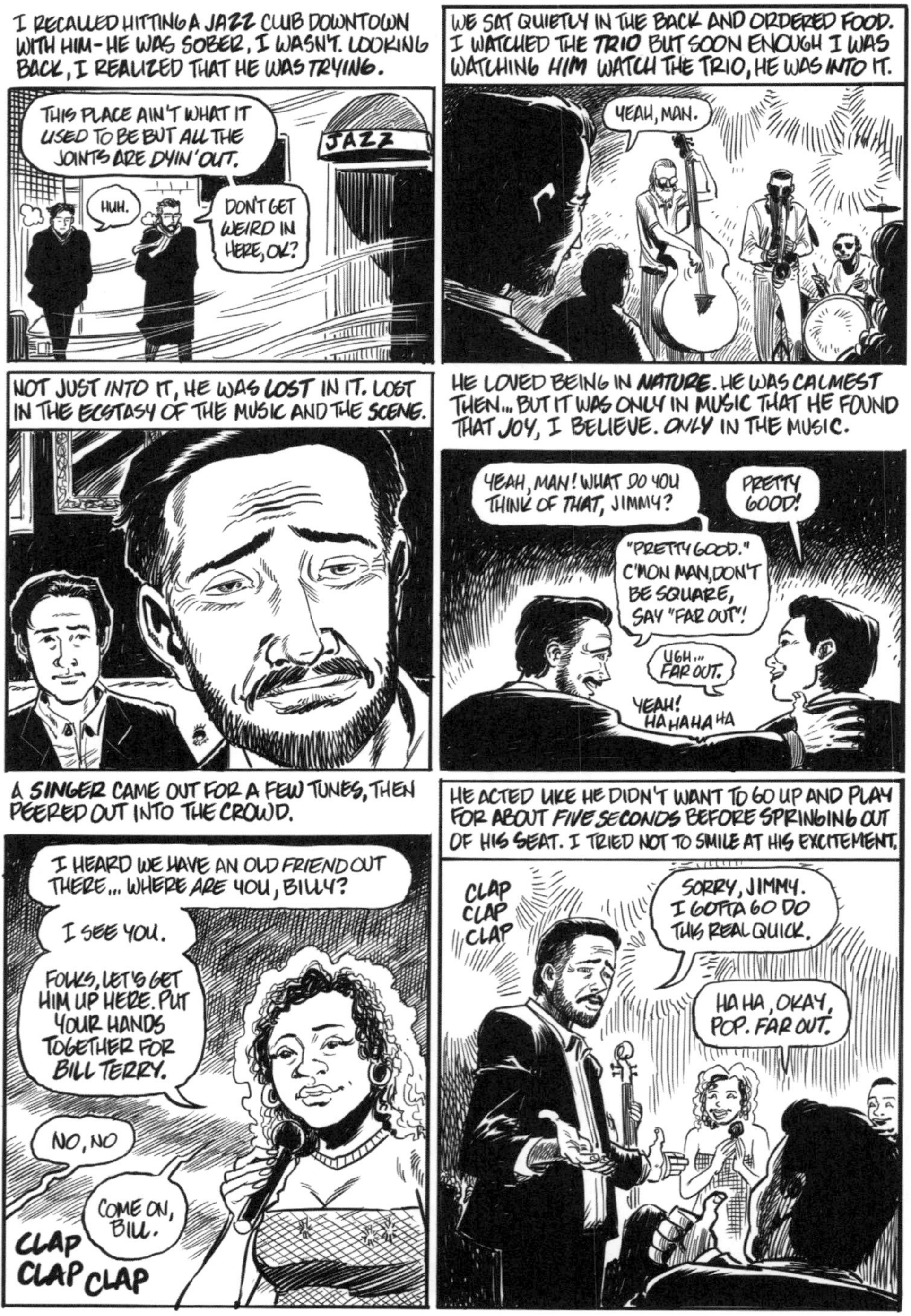

I RECALLED HITTING A JAZZ CLUB DOWNTOWN WITH HIM - HE WAS SOBER, I WASN'T. LOOKING BACK, I REALIZED THAT HE WAS TRYING.
THIS PLACE AIN'T WHAT IT USED TO BE BUT ALL THE JOINTS ARE DYIN' OUT.
JAZZ
HUH.
DON'T GET WEIRD IN HERE, OK?
WE SAT QUIETLY IN THE BACK AND ORDERED FOOD. I WATCHED THE TRIO BUT SOON ENOUGH I WAS WATCHING HIM WATCH THE TRIO, HE WAS INTO IT.
YEAH, MAN.
NOT JUST INTO IT, HE WAS LOST IN IT. LOST IN THE ECSTASY OF THE MUSIC AND THE SCENE.
HE LOVED BEING IN NATURE. HE WAS CALMEST THEN... BUT IT WAS ONLY IN MUSIC THAT HE FOUND THAT JOY, I BELIEVE. ONLY IN THE MUSIC.
YEAH, MAN! WHAT DO YOU THINK OF THAT, JIMMY?
PRETTY GOOD!
"PRETTY GOOD." C'MON MAN, DON'T BE SQUARE, SAY "FAR OUT"!
UGH... FAR OUT.
YEAH! HA HAHA HA
A SINGER CAME OUT FOR A FEW TUNES, THEN PEERED OUT INTO THE CROWD.
I HEARD WE HAVE AN OLD FRIEND OUT THERE... WHERE ARE YOU, BILLY?
I SEE YOU.
FOLKS, LET'S GET HIM UP HERE. PUT YOUR HANDS TOGETHER FOR BILL TERRY.
NO, NO
COME ON, BILL.
CLAP CLAP CLAP
HE ACTED LIKE HE DIDN'T WANT TO GO UP AND PLAY FOR ABOUT FIVE SECONDS BEFORE SPRINGING OUT OF HIS SEAT. I TRIED NOT TO SMILE AT HIS EXCITEMENT.
CLAP CLAP CLAP
SORRY, JIMMY. I GOTTA GO DO THIS REAL QUICK.
HA HA, OKAY, POP. FAR OUT.

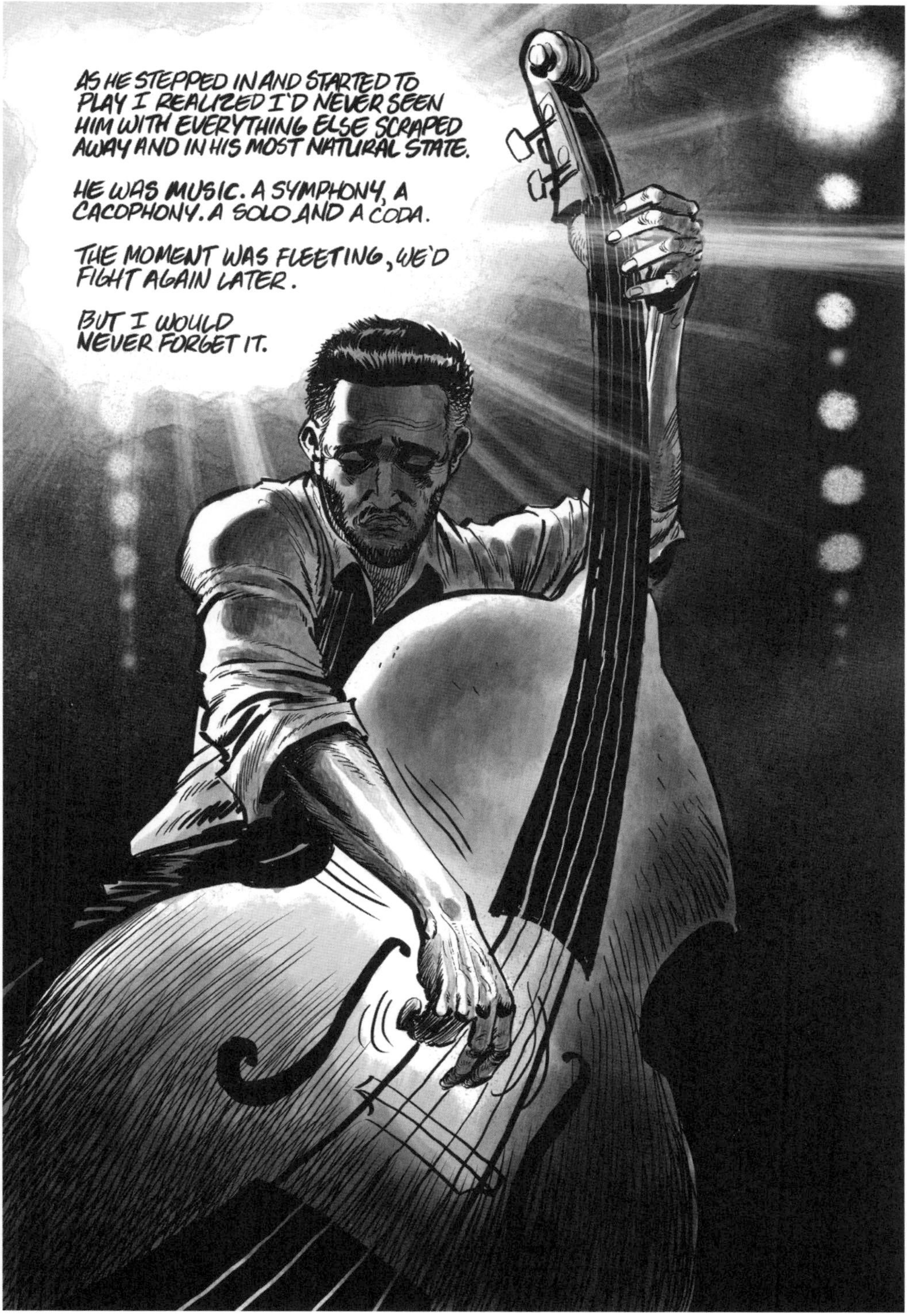
AS HE STEPPED IN AND STARTED TO PLAY I REALIZED I'D NEVER SEEN HIM WITH EVERYTHING ELSE SCRAPED AWAY AND IN HIS MOST NATURAL STATE.
HE WAS MUSIC. A SYMPHONY, A CACOPHONY. A SOLO AND A CODA.
THE MOMENT WAS FLEETING, WE'D FIGHT AGAIN LATER.
BUT I WOULD NEVER FORGET IT.

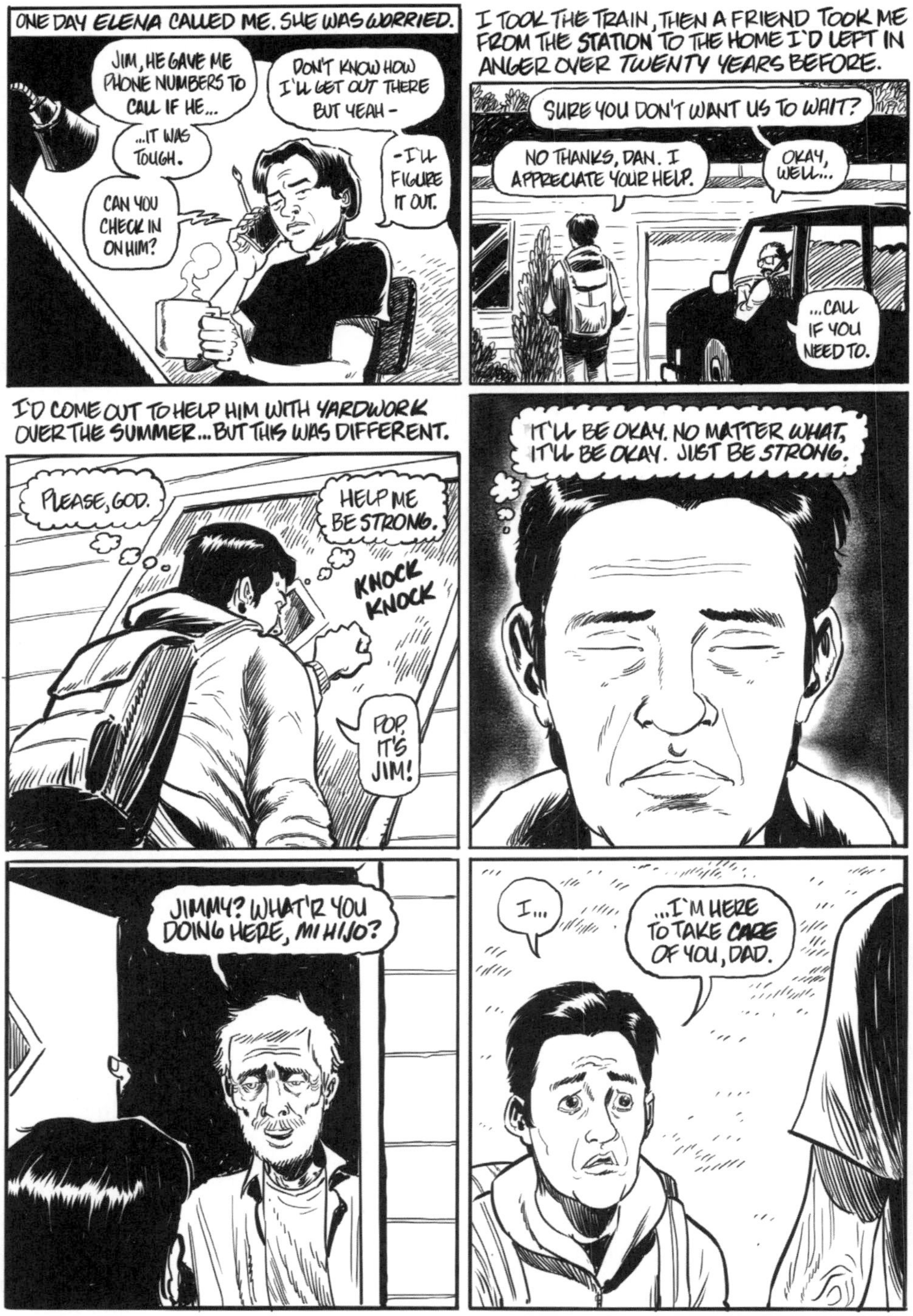
ONE DAY ELENA CALLED ME. SHE WAS WORRIED.
JIM, HE GAVE ME PHONE NUMBERS TO CALL IF HE...
...IT WAS TOUGH.
CAN YOU CHECK IN ON HIM?
DON'T KNOW HOW I'LL GET OUT THERE BUT YEAH -
-I'LL FIGURE IT OUT.
I TOOK THE TRAIN, THEN A FRIEND TOOK ME FROM THE STATION TO THE HOME I'D LEFT IN ANGER OVER TWENTY YEARS BEFORE.
SURE YOU DON'T WANT US TO WAIT?
NO THANKS, DAN. I APPRECIATE YOUR HELP.
OKAY, WELL...
...CALL IF YOU NEED TO.
I'D COME OUT TO HELP HIM WITH YARDWORK OVER THE SUMMER... BUT THIS WAS DIFFERENT.
PLEASE, GOD.
HELP ME BE STRONG.
KNOCK KNOCK
POP, IT'S JIM!
IT'LL BE OKAY. NO MATTER WHAT, IT'LL BE OKAY. JUST BE STRONG.
JIMMY? WHAT'R YOU DOING HERE, MI HIJO?
I...
...I'M HERE TO TAKE CARE OF YOU, DAD.

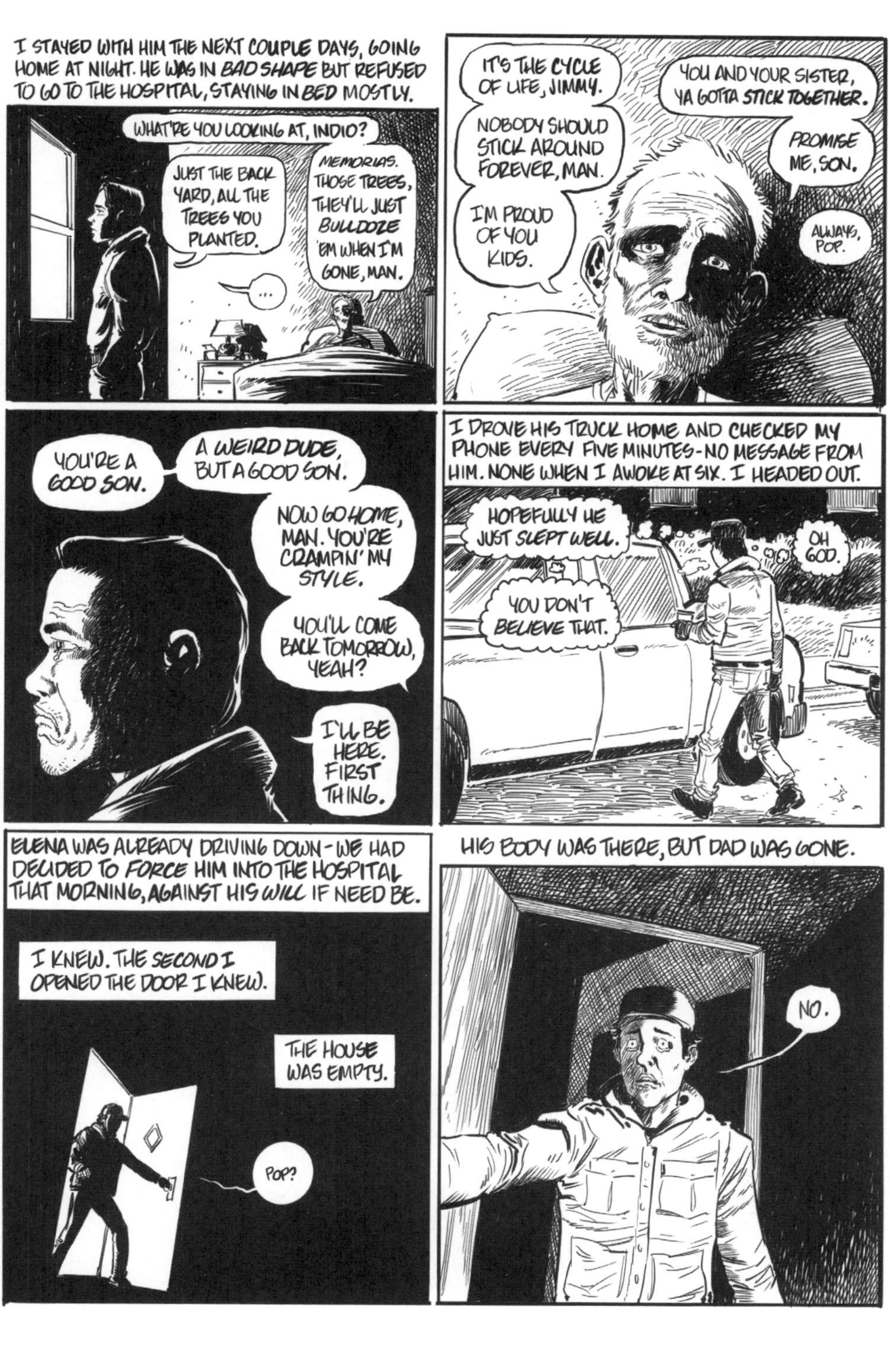
I STAYED WITH HIM THE NEXT COUPLE DAYS, GOING HOME AT NIGHT. HE WAS IN BAD SHAPE BUT REFUSED TO GO TO THE HOSPITAL, STAYING IN BED MOSTLY.
WHAT'RE YOU LOOKING AT, INDIO?
JUST THE BACK YARD, ALL THE TREES YOU PLANTED.
MEMORIAS. THOSE TREES, THEY'LL JUST BULLDOZE 'EM WHEN I'M GONE, MAN.
...
IT'S THE CYCLE OF LIFE, JIMMY.
NOBODY SHOULD STICK AROUND FOREVER, MAN.
I'M PROUD OF YOU KIDS.
YOU AND YOUR SISTER, YA GOTTA STICK TOGETHER.
PROMISE ME, SON.
ALWAYS, POP.
YOU'RE A GOOD SON.
A WEIRD DUDE, BUT A GOOD SON.
NOW GO HOME, MAN. YOU'RE CRAMPIN' MY STYLE.
YOU'LL COME BACK TOMORROW, YEAH?
I'LL BE HERE. FIRST THING.
I DROVE HIS TRUCK HOME AND CHECKED MY PHONE EVERY FIVE MINUTES - NO MESSAGE FROM HIM. NONE WHEN I AWOKE AT SIX. I HEADED OUT.
HOPEFULLY HE JUST SLEPT WELL.
YOU DON'T BELIEVE THAT.
OH GOD.
ELENA WAS ALREADY DRIVING DOWN - WE HAD DECIDED TO FORCE HIM INTO THE HOSPITAL THAT MORNING, AGAINST HIS WILL IF NEED BE.
I KNEW. THE SECOND I OPENED THE DOOR I KNEW.
THE HOUSE WAS EMPTY.
POP?
HIS BODY WAS THERE, BUT DAD WAS GONE.
NO.

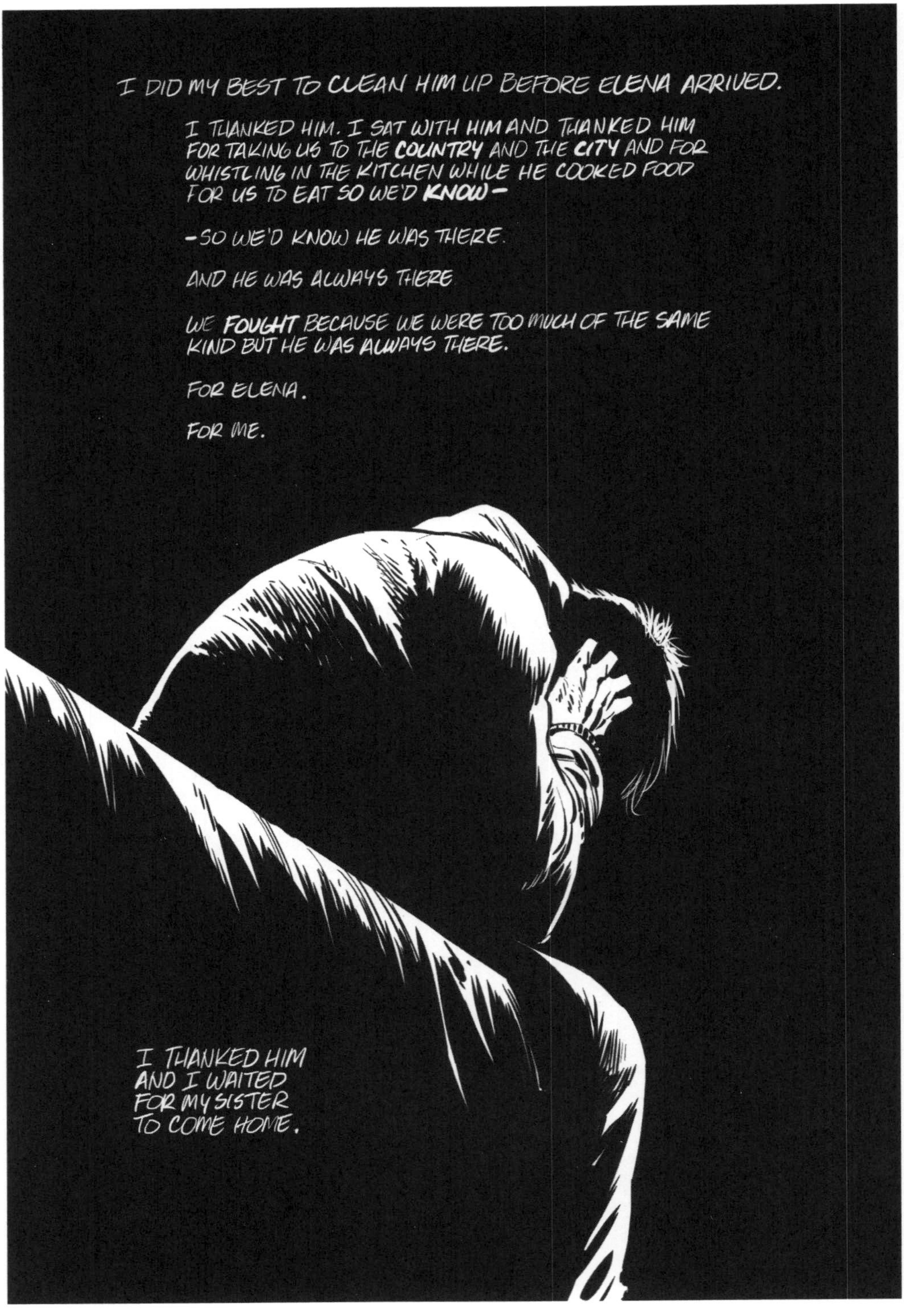
I DID MY BEST TO CLEAN HIM UP BEFORE ELENA ARRIVED.
I THANKED HIM. I SAT WITH HIM AND THANKED HIM FOR TAKING US TO THE COUNTRY AND THE CITY AND FOR WHISTLING IN THE KITCHEN WHILE HE COOKED FOOD FOR US TO EAT SO WE'D KNOW—
—SO WE'D KNOW HE WAS THERE.
AND HE WAS ALWAYS THERE
WE FOUGHT BECAUSE WE WERE TOO MUCH OF THE SAME KIND BUT HE WAS ALWAYS THERE.
FOR ELENA.
FOR ME.
I THANKED HIM AND I WAITED FOR MY SISTER TO COME HOME.

THERE IS NO RIGHT WAY TO GRIEVE. WE ALL CARRY THE BURDEN OUR OWN WAY AND I CRAMMED MY GRIEF DOWN LOW.

HE WENT OUT THE WAY HE WANTED. HE SAID HIS PIECE AND SET HIS THINGS IN ORDER AND STAYED THE HELL OUT OF THE HOSPITAL WITH THEIR "TUBES AND MACHINES", AS HE PUT IT.

MOM SHOWED UP WITH HER BROTHERS AND SISTERS AND THEIR SORROW WAS GENUINE. BILL STAYED PART OF THE FAMILY. HE DROVE UP TO THE DELLS WITH THE LAWNMOWER IN THE TRUCK SO HE COULD MOW KUNIKA'S LAWN. HE TOOK ALL THOSE KIDS ON AS HIS OWN. HE WAS BELOVED BY THEM AND THIS DISCOVERY MADE MY HEART SWELL.

I LEANED ON ELENA, MY FRIENDS, AND THE THINGS I'D LEARED IN THE PROGRAM.

DEAN CAME OUT OF THE WOODWORK FOR THE FUNERAL, AS DID MANY FRIENDS. WE BURIED HIM ON A FROZEN DECEMBER DAY.

I WAS NOT ANGRY AT GOD. WASN'T ANGRY AT POP. I WAS GRATEFUL WE'D PARTED AS FATHER AND SON. ON GOOD TERMS. WITH LOVE.

HE WAS AT REST NOW WITH HIS MOTHER AND FATHER. AND HIS BROTHERS. JAMES, BOBBY, AND TOMMY.

ELENA AND I WERE THE LAST.

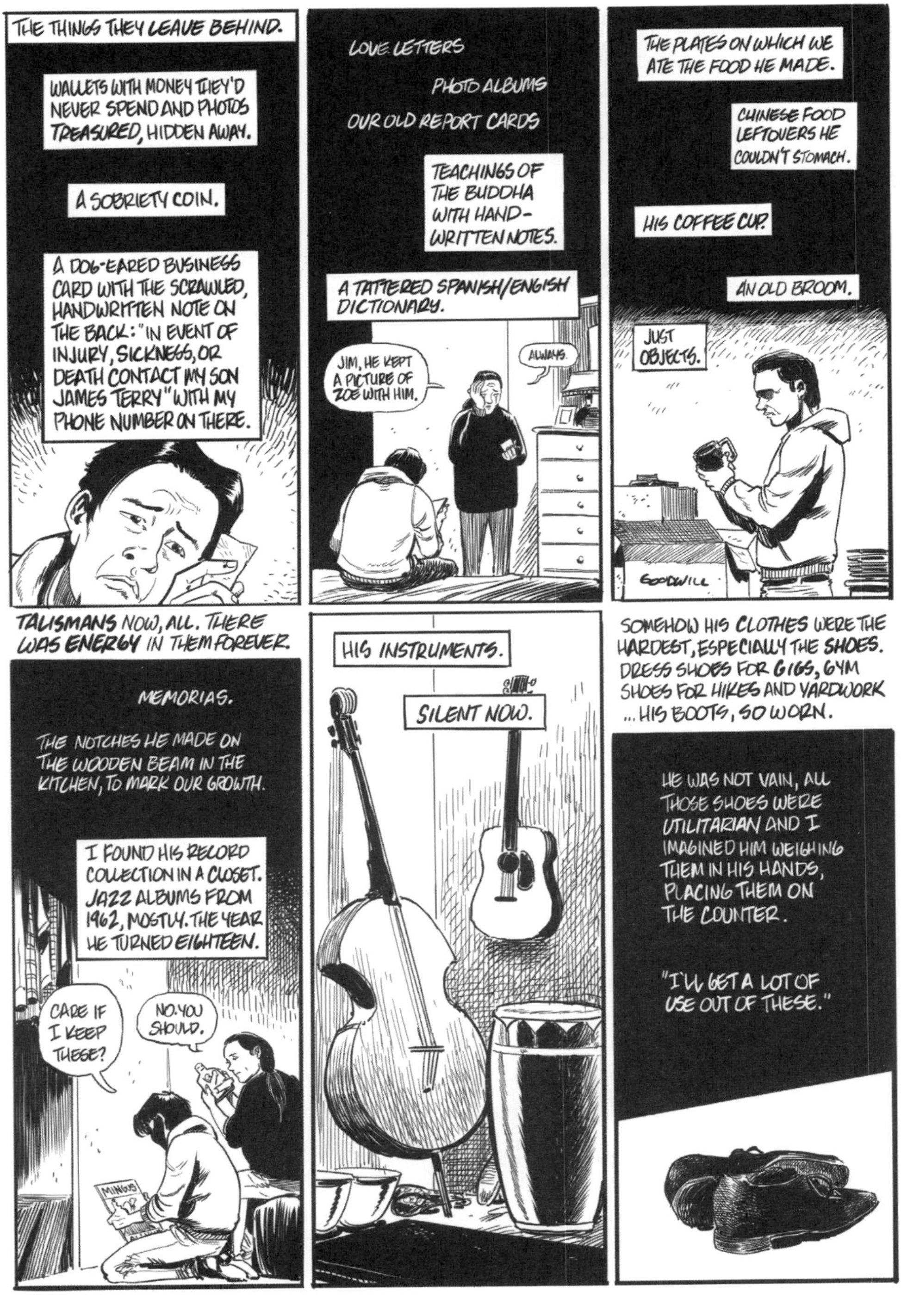
THE THINGS THEY LEAVE BEHIND.
WALLETS WITH MONEY THEY'D NEVER SPEND AND PHOTOS TREASURED, HIDDEN AWAY.
A SOBRIETY COIN.
A DOG-EARED BUSINESS CARD WITH THE SCRAWLED, HANDWRITTEN NOTE ON THE BACK: "IN EVENT OF INJURY, SICKNESS, OR DEATH CONTACT MY SON JAMES TERRY" WITH MY PHONE NUMBER ON THERE.
LOVE LETTERS
PHOTO ALBUMS
OUR OLD REPORT CARDS
TEACHINGS OF THE BUDDHA WITH HAND-WRITTEN NOTES.
A TATTERED SPANISH/ENGISH DICTIONARY.
JIM, HE KEPT A PICTURE OF ZOE WITH HIM.
ALWAYS.
THE PLATES ON WHICH WE ATE THE FOOD HE MADE.
CHINESE FOOD LEFTOVERS HE COULDN'T STOMACH.
HIS COFFEE CUP.
AN OLD BROOM.
JUST OBJECTS.
GOODWILL
TALISMANS NOW, ALL. THERE WAS ENERGY IN THEM FOREVER.
MEMORIAS.
THE NOTCHES HE MADE ON THE WOODEN BEAM IN THE KITCHEN, TO MARK OUR GROWTH.
I FOUND HIS RECORD COLLECTION IN A CLOSET. JAZZ ALBUMS FROM 1962, MOSTLY. THE YEAR HE TURNED EIGHTEEN.
CARE IF I KEEP THESE?
NO. YOU SHOULD.
MINGUS
HIS INSTRUMENTS.
SILENT NOW.
SOMEHOW HIS CLOTHES WERE THE HARDEST, ESPECIALLY THE SHOES. DRESS SHOES FOR GIGS, GYM SHOES FOR HIKES AND YARDWORK ... HIS BOOTS, SO WORN.
HE WAS NOT VAIN, ALL THOSE SHOES WERE UTILITARIAN AND I IMAGINED HIM WEIGHING THEM IN HIS HANDS, PLACING THEM ON THE COUNTER.
"I'LL GET A LOT OF USE OUT OF THESE."

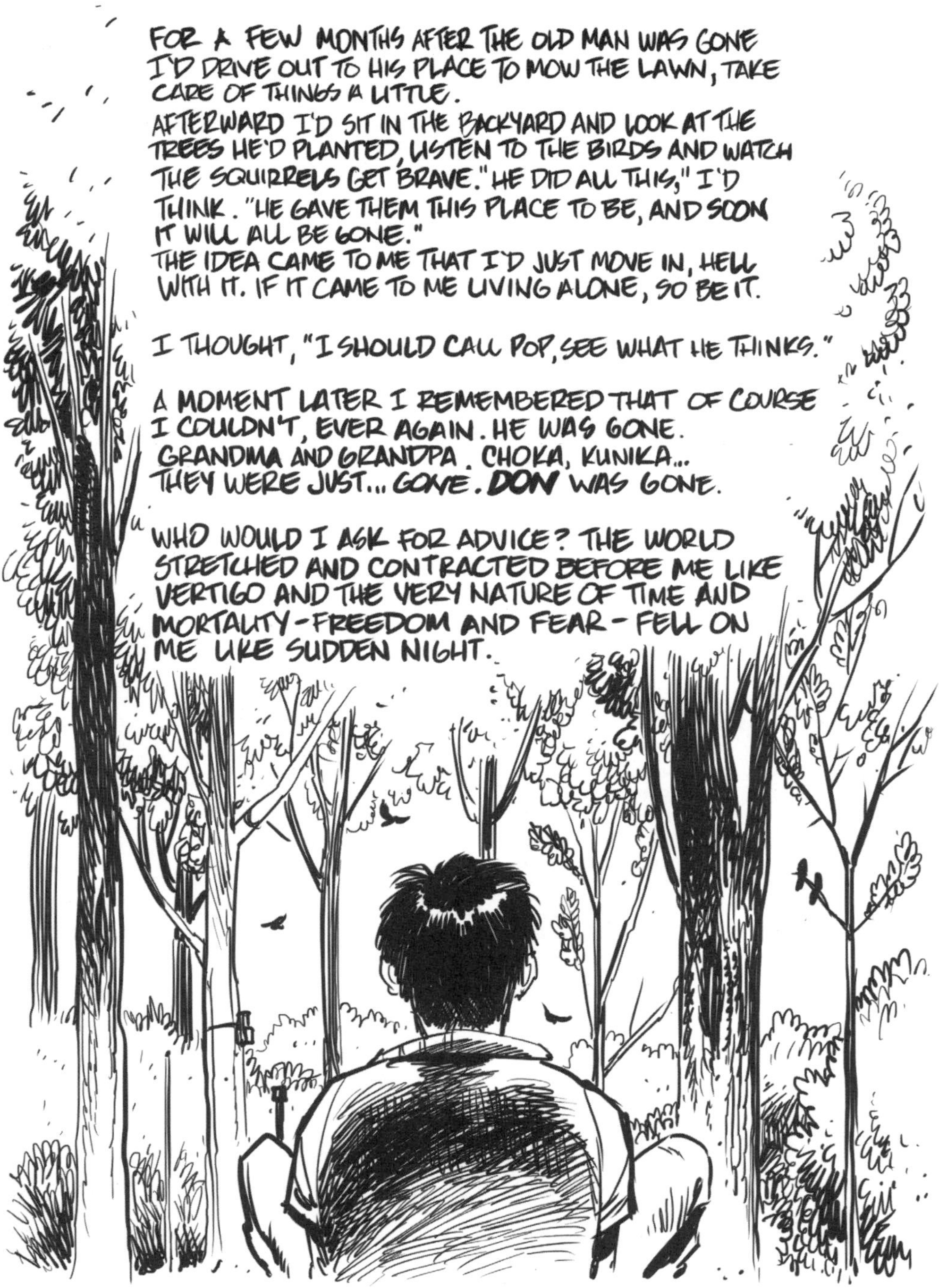
FOR A FEW MONTHS AFTER THE OLD MAN WAS GONE I'D DRIVE OUT TO HIS PLACE TO MOW THE LAWN, TAKE CARE OF THINGS A LITTLE.
AFTERWARD I'D SIT IN THE BACKYARD AND LOOK AT THE TREES HE'D PLANTED, LISTEN TO THE BIRDS AND WATCH THE SQUIRRELS GET BRAVE. "HE DID ALL THIS," I'D THINK. "HE GAVE THEM THIS PLACE TO BE, AND SOON IT WILL ALL BE GONE."
THE IDEA CAME TO ME THAT I'D JUST MOVE IN, HELL WITH IT. IF IT CAME TO ME LIVING ALONE, SO BE IT.
I THOUGHT, "I SHOULD CALL POP, SEE WHAT HE THINKS."
A MOMENT LATER I REMEMBERED THAT OF COURSE I COULDN'T, EVER AGAIN. HE WAS GONE. GRANDMA AND GRANDPA. CHOKA, KUNIKA... THEY WERE JUST... GONE. DON WAS GONE.
WHO WOULD I ASK FOR ADVICE? THE WORLD STRETCHED AND CONTRACTED BEFORE ME LIKE VERTIGO AND THE VERY NATURE OF TIME AND MORTALITY - FREEDOM AND FEAR - FELL ON ME LIKE SUDDEN NIGHT.

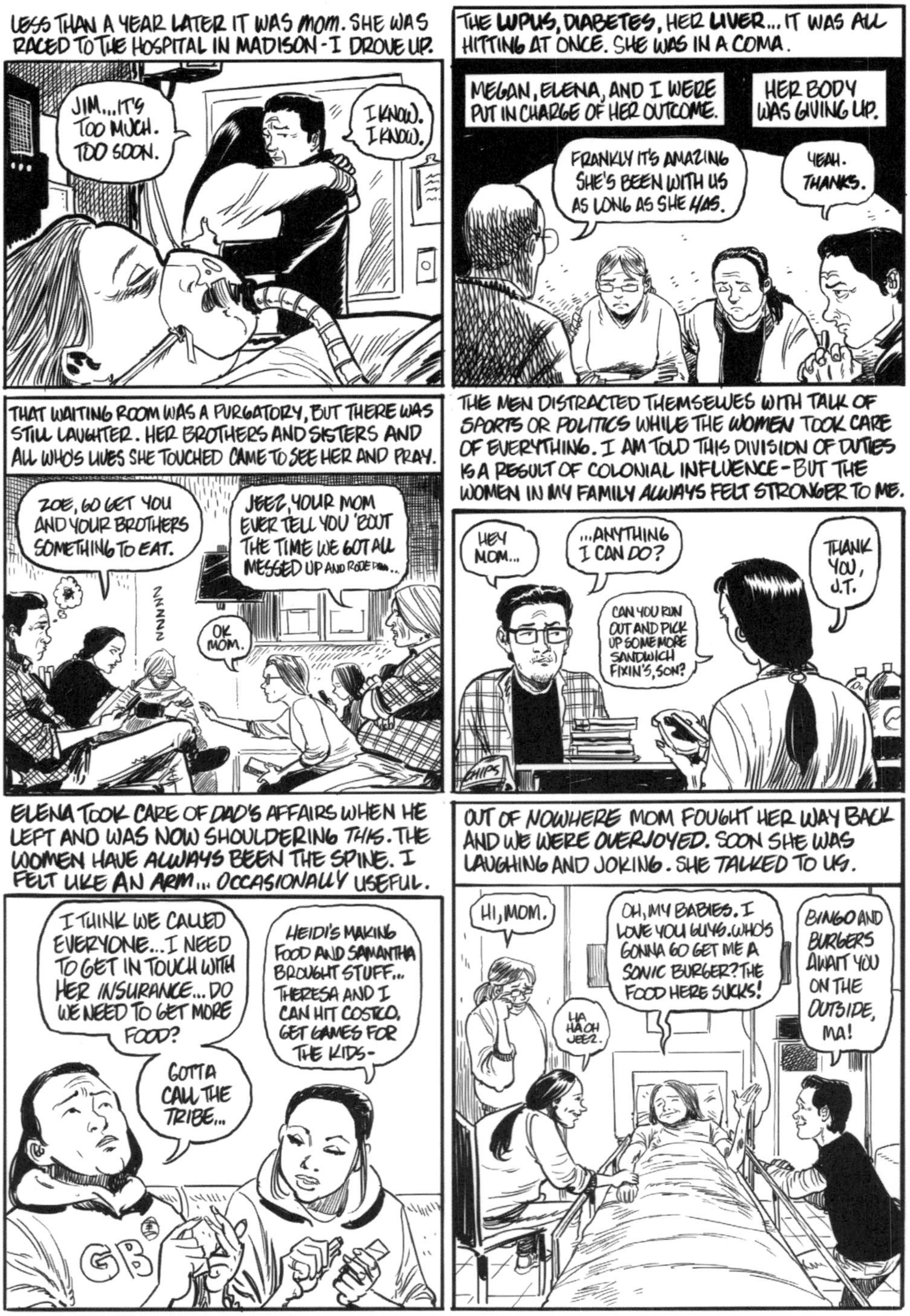
LESS THAN A YEAR LATER IT WAS MOM. SHE WAS RACED TO THE HOSPITAL IN MADISON - I DROVE UP.
JIM...IT'S TOO MUCH. TOO SOON.
I KNOW. I KNOW.
THE LUPUS, DIABETES, HER LIVER... IT WAS ALL HITTING AT ONCE. SHE WAS IN A COMA.
MEGAN, ELENA, AND I WERE PUT IN CHARGE OF HER OUTCOME.
HER BODY WAS GIVING UP.
FRANKLY IT'S AMAZING SHE'S BEEN WITH US AS LONG AS SHE HAS.
YEAH. THANKS.
THAT WAITING ROOM WAS A PURGATORY, BUT THERE WAS STILL LAUGHTER. HER BROTHERS AND SISTERS AND ALL WHO'S LIVES SHE TOUCHED CAME TO SEE HER AND PRAY.
ZOE, GO GET YOU AND YOUR BROTHERS SOMETHING TO EAT.
JEEZ, YOUR MOM EVER TELL YOU 'BOUT THE TIME WE GOT ALL MESSED UP AND RODE...
ZZZZZ
OK MOM.
THE MEN DISTRACTED THEMSELVES WITH TALK OF SPORTS OR POLITICS WHILE THE WOMEN TOOK CARE OF EVERYTHING. I AM TOLD THIS DIVISION OF DUTIES IS A RESULT OF COLONIAL INFLUENCE - BUT THE WOMEN IN MY FAMILY ALWAYS FELT STRONGER TO ME.
HEY MOM...
...ANYTHING I CAN DO?
THANK YOU, J.T.
CAN YOU RUN OUT AND PICK UP SOME MORE SANDWICH FIXIN'S, SON?
CHIPS
ELENA TOOK CARE OF DAD'S AFFAIRS WHEN HE LEFT AND WAS NOW SHOULDERING THIS. THE WOMEN HAVE ALWAYS BEEN THE SPINE. I FELT LIKE AN ARM... OCCASIONALLY USEFUL.
I THINK WE CALLED EVERYONE... I NEED TO GET IN TOUCH WITH HER INSURANCE... DO WE NEED TO GET MORE FOOD?
GOTTA CALL THE TRIBE...
HEIDI'S MAKING FOOD AND SAMANTHA BROUGHT STUFF... THERESA AND I CAN HIT COSTCO. GET GAMES FOR THE KIDS-
GB
OUT OF NOWHERE MOM FOUGHT HER WAY BACK AND WE WERE OVERJOYED. SOON SHE WAS LAUGHING AND JOKING. SHE TALKED TO US.
HI, MOM.
OH, MY BABIES. I LOVE YOU GUYS. WHO'S GONNA GO GET ME A SONIC BURGER? THE FOOD HERE SUCKS!
HA HA OH JEEZ.
BINGO AND BURGERS AWAIT YOU ON THE OUTSIDE, MA!

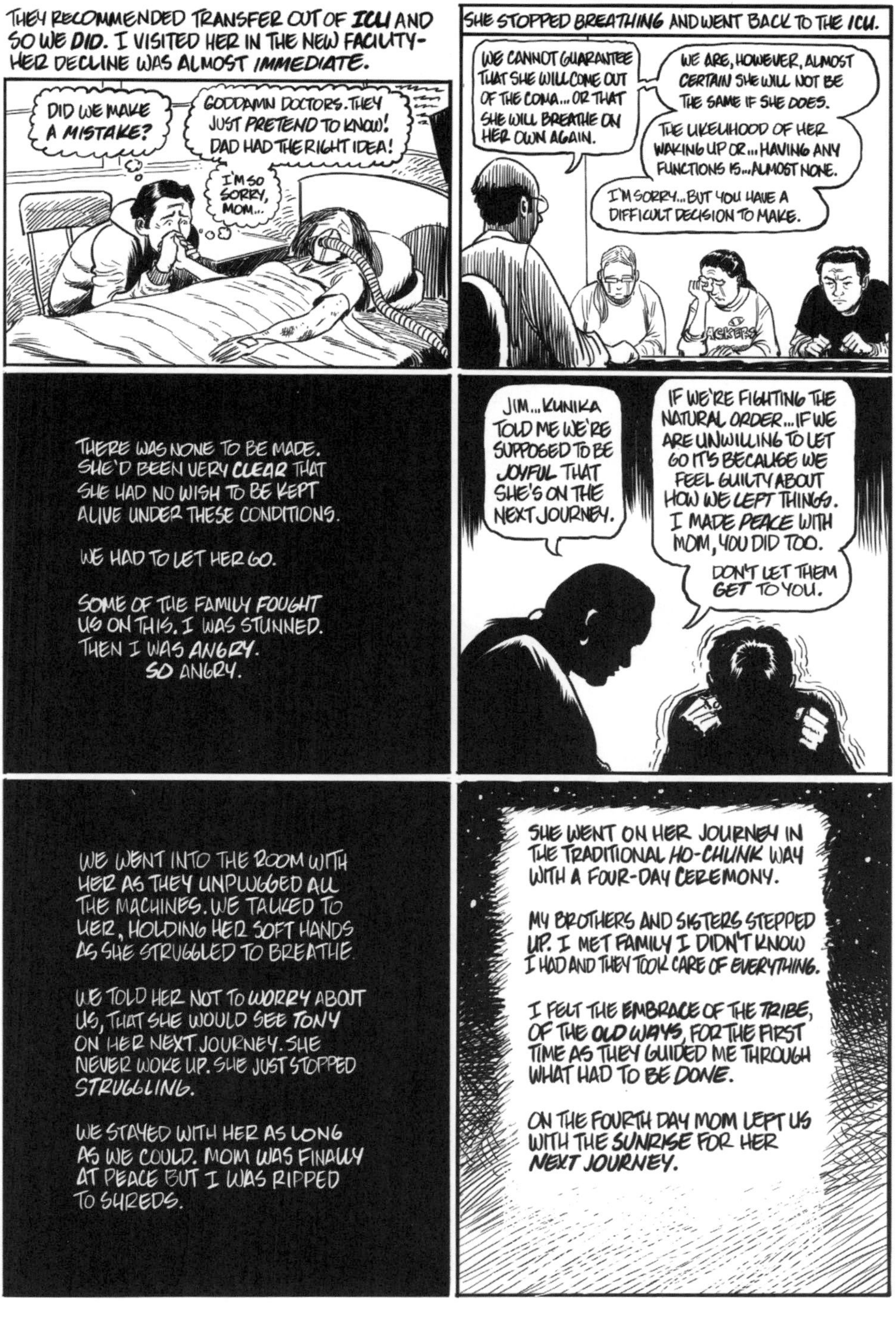
THEY RECOMMENDED TRANSFER OUT OF ICU AND SO WE DID. I VISITED HER IN THE NEW FACILITY-HER DECLINE WAS ALMOST IMMEDIATE.
DID WE MAKE A MISTAKE?
GODDAMN DOCTORS. THEY JUST PRETEND TO KNOW! DAD HAD THE RIGHT IDEA!
I'M SO SORRY, MOM...
SHE STOPPED BREATHING AND WENT BACK TO THE ICU.
WE CANNOT GUARANTEE THAT SHE WILL COME OUT OF THE COMA... OR THAT SHE WILL BREATHE ON HER OWN AGAIN.
WE ARE, HOWEVER, ALMOST CERTAIN SHE WILL NOT BE THE SAME IF SHE DOES.
THE LIKELIHOOD OF HER WAKING UP OR... HAVING ANY FUNCTIONS IS... ALMOST NONE.
I'M SORRY... BUT YOU HAVE A DIFFICULT DECISION TO MAKE.
THERE WAS NONE TO BE MADE. SHE'D BEEN VERY CLEAR THAT SHE HAD NO WISH TO BE KEPT ALIVE UNDER THESE CONDITIONS.
WE HAD TO LET HER GO.
SOME OF THE FAMILY FOUGHT US ON THIS. I WAS STUNNED. THEN I WAS ANGRY. SO ANGRY.
JIM... KUNIKA TOLD ME WE'RE SUPPOSED TO BE JOYFUL THAT SHE'S ON THE NEXT JOURNEY.
IF WE'RE FIGHTING THE NATURAL ORDER... IF WE ARE UNWILLING TO LET GO IT'S BECAUSE WE FEEL GUILTY ABOUT HOW WE LEFT THINGS. I MADE PEACE WITH MOM, YOU DID TOO.
DON'T LET THEM GET TO YOU.
WE WENT INTO THE ROOM WITH HER AS THEY UNPLUGGED ALL THE MACHINES. WE TALKED TO HER, HOLDING HER SOFT HANDS AS SHE STRUGGLED TO BREATHE.
WE TOLD HER NOT TO WORRY ABOUT US, THAT SHE WOULD SEE TONY ON HER NEXT JOURNEY. SHE NEVER WOKE UP. SHE JUST STOPPED STRUGGLING.
WE STAYED WITH HER AS LONG AS WE COULD. MOM WAS FINALLY AT PEACE BUT I WAS RIPPED TO SHREDS.
SHE WENT ON HER JOURNEY IN THE TRADITIONAL HO-CHUNK WAY WITH A FOUR-DAY CEREMONY.
MY BROTHERS AND SISTERS STEPPED UP. I MET FAMILY I DIDN'T KNOW I HAD AND THEY TOOK CARE OF EVERYTHING.
I FELT THE EMBRACE OF THE TRIBE, OF THE OLD WAYS, FOR THE FIRST TIME AS THEY GUIDED ME THROUGH WHAT HAD TO BE DONE.
ON THE FOURTH DAY MOM LEFT US WITH THE SUNRISE FOR HER NEXT JOURNEY.

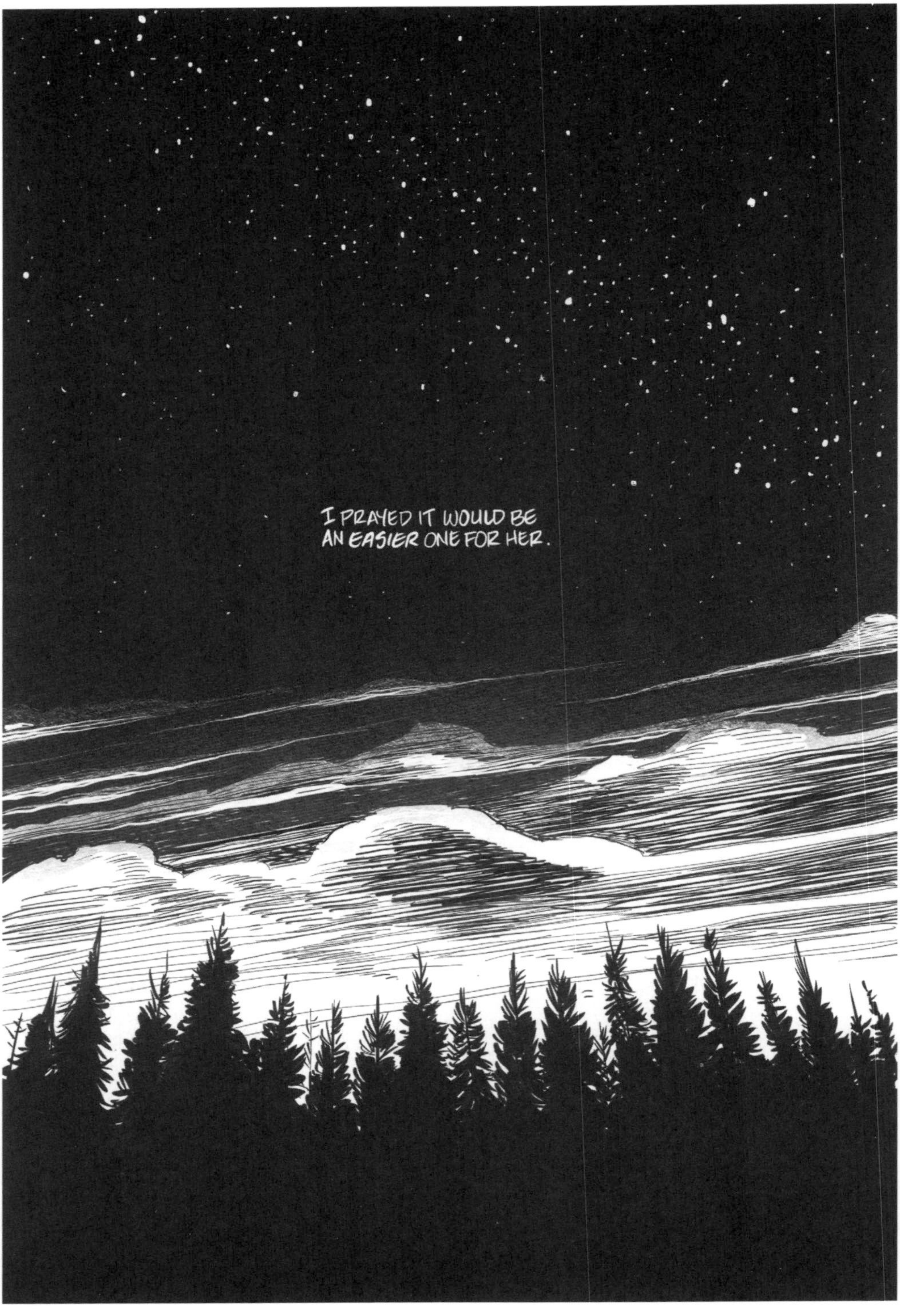
I PRAYED IT WOULD BE AN *EASIER* ONE FOR HER.

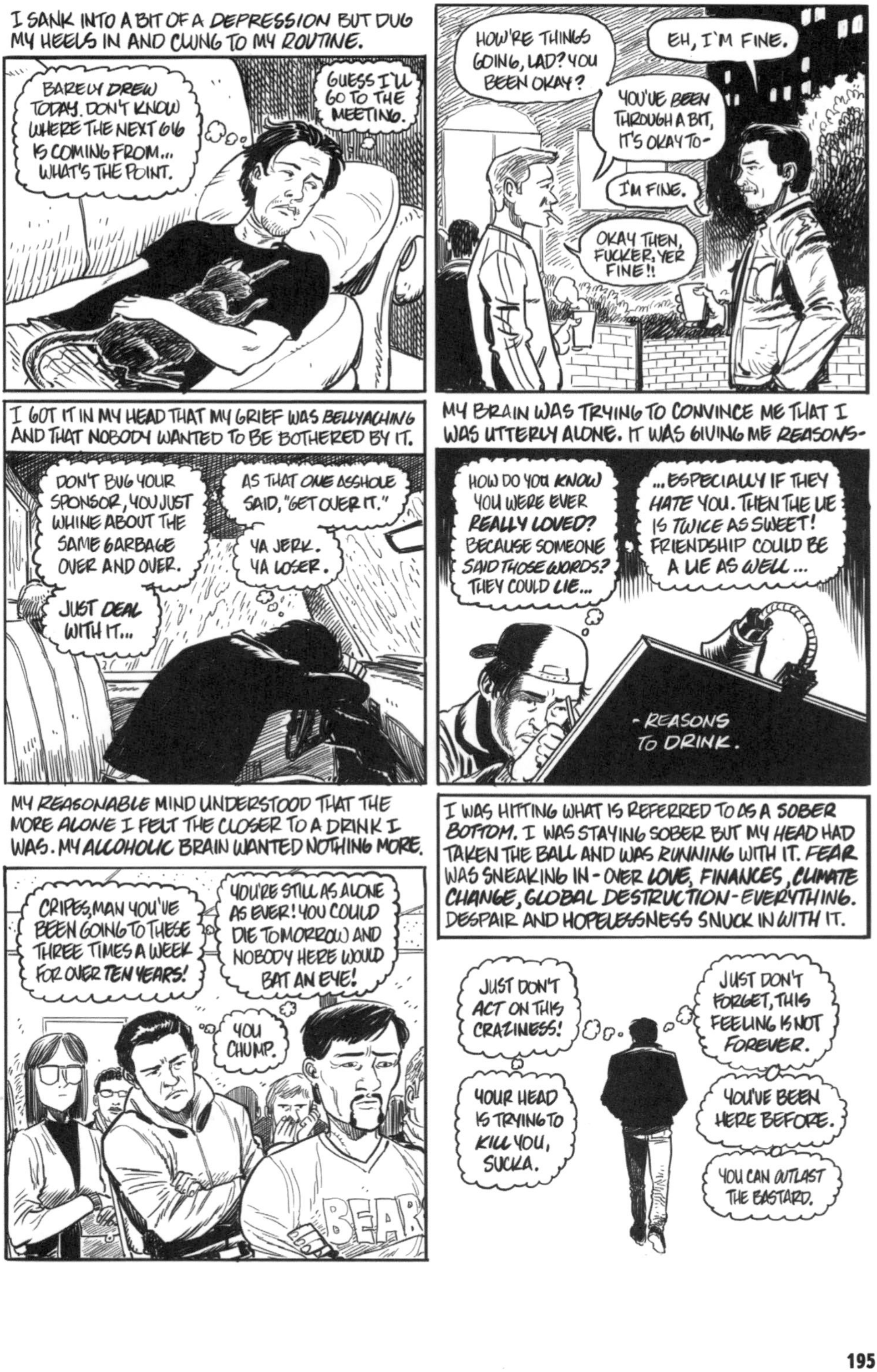

I SANK INTO A BIT OF A DEPRESSION BUT DUG MY HEELS IN AND CLUNG TO MY ROUTINE.
BARELY DREW TODAY. DON'T KNOW WHERE THE NEXT GIG IS COMING FROM... WHAT'S THE POINT.
GUESS I'LL GO TO THE MEETING.
HOW'RE THINGS GOING, LAD? YOU BEEN OKAY?
EH, I'M FINE.
YOU'VE BEEN THROUGH A BIT, IT'S OKAY TO-
I'M FINE.
OKAY THEN, FUCKER, YER FINE!!
I GOT IT IN MY HEAD THAT MY GRIEF WAS BELLYACHING AND THAT NOBODY WANTED TO BE BOTHERED BY IT.
DON'T BUG YOUR SPONSOR, YOU JUST WHINE ABOUT THE SAME GARBAGE OVER AND OVER.
AS THAT ONE ASSHOLE SAID, "GET OVER IT."
YA JERK. YA LOSER.
JUST DEAL WITH IT...
MY BRAIN WAS TRYING TO CONVINCE ME THAT I WAS UTTERLY ALONE. IT WAS GIVING ME REASONS-
HOW DO YOU KNOW YOU WERE EVER REALLY LOVED? BECAUSE SOMEONE SAID THOSE WORDS? THEY COULD LIE...
...ESPECIALLY IF THEY HATE YOU. THEN THE LIE IS TWICE AS SWEET! FRIENDSHIP COULD BE A LIE AS WELL...
-REASONS TO DRINK.
MY REASONABLE MIND UNDERSTOOD THAT THE MORE ALONE I FELT THE CLOSER TO A DRINK I WAS. MY ALCOHOLIC BRAIN WANTED NOTHING MORE.
CRIPES, MAN YOU'VE BEEN GOING TO THESE THREE TIMES A WEEK FOR OVER TEN YEARS!
YOU'RE STILL AS ALONE AS EVER! YOU COULD DIE TOMORROW AND NOBODY HERE WOULD BAT AN EYE!
YOU CHUMP.
BEAR
I WAS HITTING WHAT IS REFERRED TO AS A SOBER BOTTOM. I WAS STAYING SOBER BUT MY HEAD HAD TAKEN THE BALL AND WAS RUNNING WITH IT. FEAR WAS SNEAKING IN - OVER LOVE, FINANCES, CLIMATE CHANGE, GLOBAL DESTRUCTION - EVERYTHING. DESPAIR AND HOPELESSNESS SNUCK IN WITH IT.
JUST DON'T ACT ON THIS CRAZINESS!
YOUR HEAD IS TRYING TO KILL YOU, SUCKA.
JUST DON'T FORGET, THIS FEELING IS NOT FOREVER.
YOU'VE BEEN HERE BEFORE.
YOU CAN OUTLAST THE BASTARD.

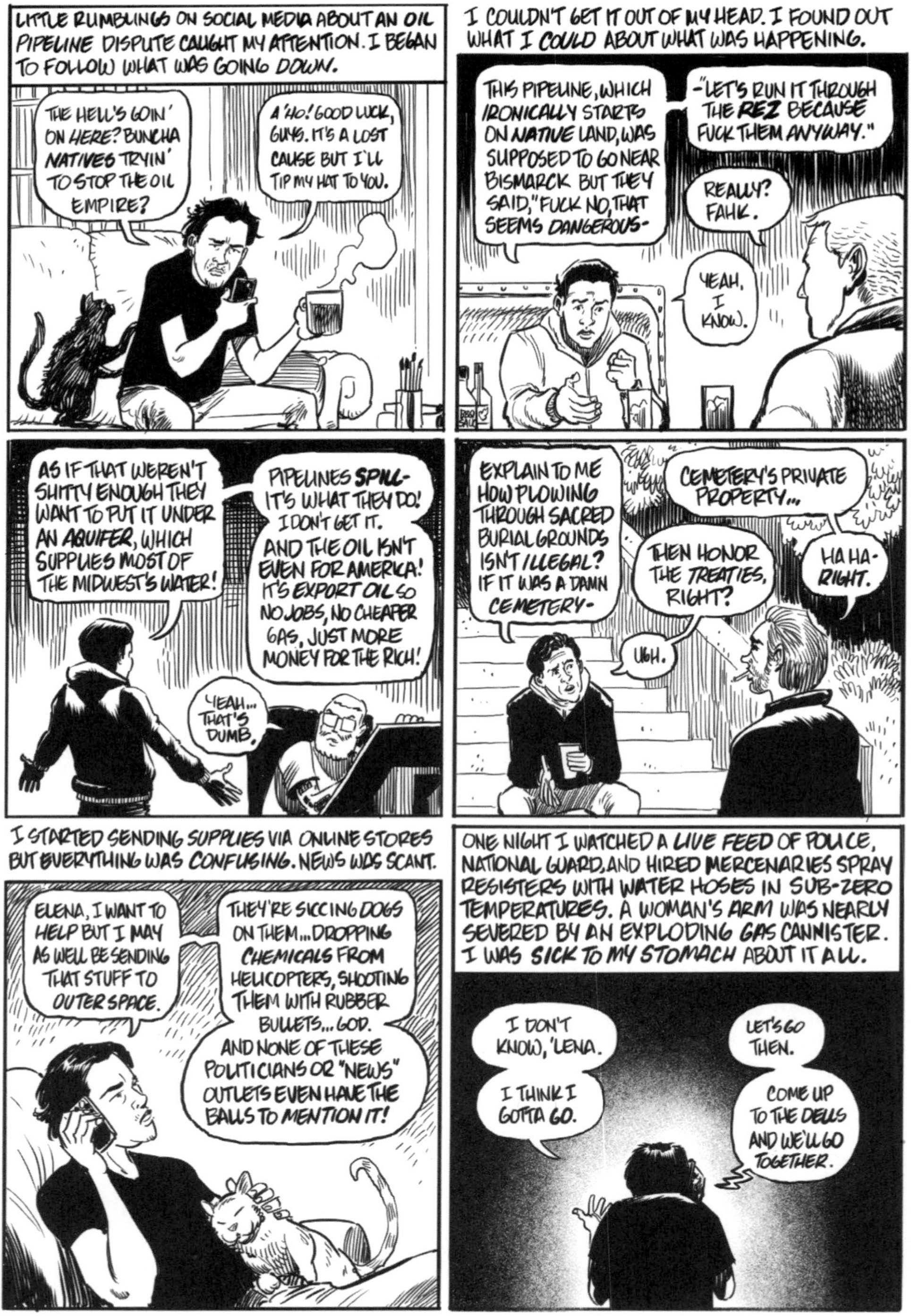
LITTLE RUMBLINGS ON SOCIAL MEDIA ABOUT AN OIL PIPELINE DISPUTE CAUGHT MY ATTENTION. I BEGAN TO FOLLOW WHAT WAS GOING DOWN.
THE HELL'S GOIN' ON HERE? BUNCHA NATIVES TRYIN' TO STOP THE OIL EMPIRE?
A'HO! GOOD LUCK, GUYS. IT'S A LOST CAUSE BUT I'LL TIP MY HAT TO YOU.
I COULDN'T GET IT OUT OF MY HEAD. I FOUND OUT WHAT I COULD ABOUT WHAT WAS HAPPENING.
THIS PIPELINE, WHICH IRONICALLY STARTS ON NATIVE LAND, WAS SUPPOSED TO GO NEAR BISMARCK BUT THEY SAID, "FUCK NO, THAT SEEMS DANGEROUS-
-"LET'S RUN IT THROUGH THE REZ BECAUSE FUCK THEM ANYWAY."
REALLY? FAHK.
YEAH, I KNOW.
AS IF THAT WEREN'T SHITTY ENOUGH THEY WANT TO PUT IT UNDER AN AQUIFER, WHICH SUPPLIES MOST OF THE MIDWEST'S WATER!
PIPELINES SPILL-IT'S WHAT THEY DO! I DON'T GET IT.
AND THE OIL ISN'T EVEN FOR AMERICA! IT'S EXPORT OIL SO NO JOBS, NO CHEAPER GAS, JUST MORE MONEY FOR THE RICH!
YEAH... THAT'S DUMB.
EXPLAIN TO ME HOW PLOWING THROUGH SACRED BURIAL GROUNDS ISN'T ILLEGAL? IF IT WAS A DAMN CEMETERY-
CEMETERY'S PRIVATE PROPERTY...
THEN HONOR THE TREATIES, RIGHT?
HA HA- RIGHT.
UGH.
I STARTED SENDING SUPPLIES VIA ONLINE STORES BUT EVERYTHING WAS CONFUSING. NEWS WAS SCANT.
ELENA, I WANT TO HELP BUT I MAY AS WELL BE SENDING THAT STUFF TO OUTER SPACE.
THEY'RE SICCING DOGS ON THEM... DROPPING CHEMICALS FROM HELICOPTERS, SHOOTING THEM WITH RUBBER BULLETS... GOD.
AND NONE OF THESE POLITICIANS OR "NEWS" OUTLETS EVEN HAVE THE BALLS TO MENTION IT!
ONE NIGHT I WATCHED A LIVE FEED OF POLICE, NATIONAL GUARD, AND HIRED MERCENARIES SPRAY RESISTERS WITH WATER HOSES IN SUB-ZERO TEMPERATURES. A WOMAN'S ARM WAS NEARLY SEVERED BY AN EXPLODING GAS CANNISTER. I WAS SICK TO MY STOMACH ABOUT IT ALL.
I DON'T KNOW, 'LENA.
I THINK I GOTTA GO.
LET'S GO THEN.
COME UP TO THE DELLS AND WE'LL GO TOGETHER.

I PACKED A FEW THINGS AND HEADED TO THE **DELLS**. ELENA WAS GETTING DONATIONS TOGETHER AND EVERYONE WANTED TO HELP.

ALL THE NATIONS WERE **COMING** TOGETHER. **COMANCHES** WERE DRIVING FIREWOOD UP THERE. DINÉ AND MOHAWK AND ALGONQUIN AND OTHERS I'D ONLY **READ** ABOUT... JOURNEYING.

IT WASN'T JUST NATIVES, EITHER. ANYONE WHO CARED ABOUT THE PLANET OR WHAT KIND OF WORLD WE WERE LEAVING FOR THE **NEXT GENERATION** WAS **WELCOME**.

WHY **NOT** THIS URBAN NATIVE? THIS HALF-BREED WHO NEVER FELT HE BELONGED ANYWHERE OR WITH ANY GROUP? THERE WAS **NOBODY LEFT** TO **DEFINE** ME.

HOME WAS NO LONGER WHERE IT'D ALWAYS BEEN. THEY BULL-DOZED POP'S HOUSE AND THE DELLS NO LONGER MEANT **MOM**.

I BEGAN THE JOURNEY UPSET AND **LONELY**. IT DIDN'T MATTER. SOON I'D BE OFF WITH MY SISTER AND COUSIN, DOING SOMETHING.

I WAS NO BRAVE WARRIOR - MY SELF-PRESERVATION INSTINCTS KEPT ME FROM HEROICS BUT I HOPED TO HELP IN **SOME** WAY, MAYBE EVEN **LEARN** A LITTLE.

MAYBE. IF THEY'D **HAVE** ME.

PART 5

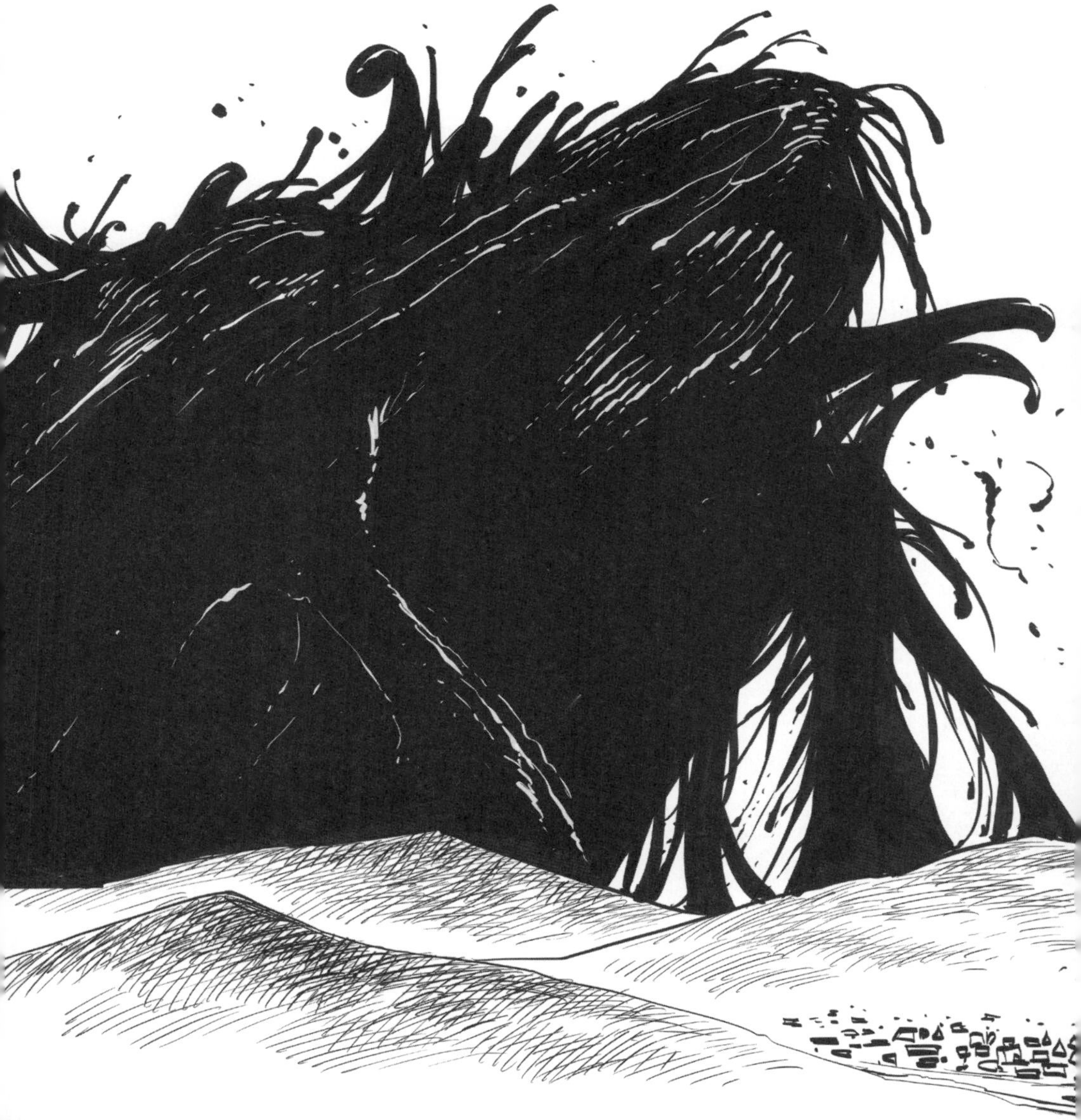

WETHA, ELENA, AND I PACKED THE JEEP WITH ANYTHING WE COULD THINK TO BRING. THERE WERE BLANKETS AND JACKETS AND **COLD WEATHER** GEAR. WE PLANNED ON SLEEPING IN A **TENT** BUT REALLY HAD NO IDEA WHAT TO EXPECT.

MANNY, WETHA'S SON, MADE HER PROMISE **NOT TO GET** *ARRESTED*. "BUT THIS IS FOR *MOTHER* NATURE, SON." SHE REASONED. "YEAH, BUT YOU'RE ***MY*** MOTHER." SO SHE PROMISED HIM.

I WAS GOING WITH TWO OF MY FAVORITE PEOPLE BUT I WAS STILL NERVOUS. SURE, I WAS WORRIED ABOUT THE *PHYSICAL DANGER*- THE VIDEOS SHOWED CLEAR *HARMFUL INTENT* AND I UNDERSTOOD THAT THE "NON-LETHAL" AMMO WAS SPECIFICALLY BEING AIMED AT ***FACES*** AND ***GROINS***. *DIRTY POKER* AND *PAINFUL*. ***CRIPPLING*** PAINFUL. TERRIFYING.

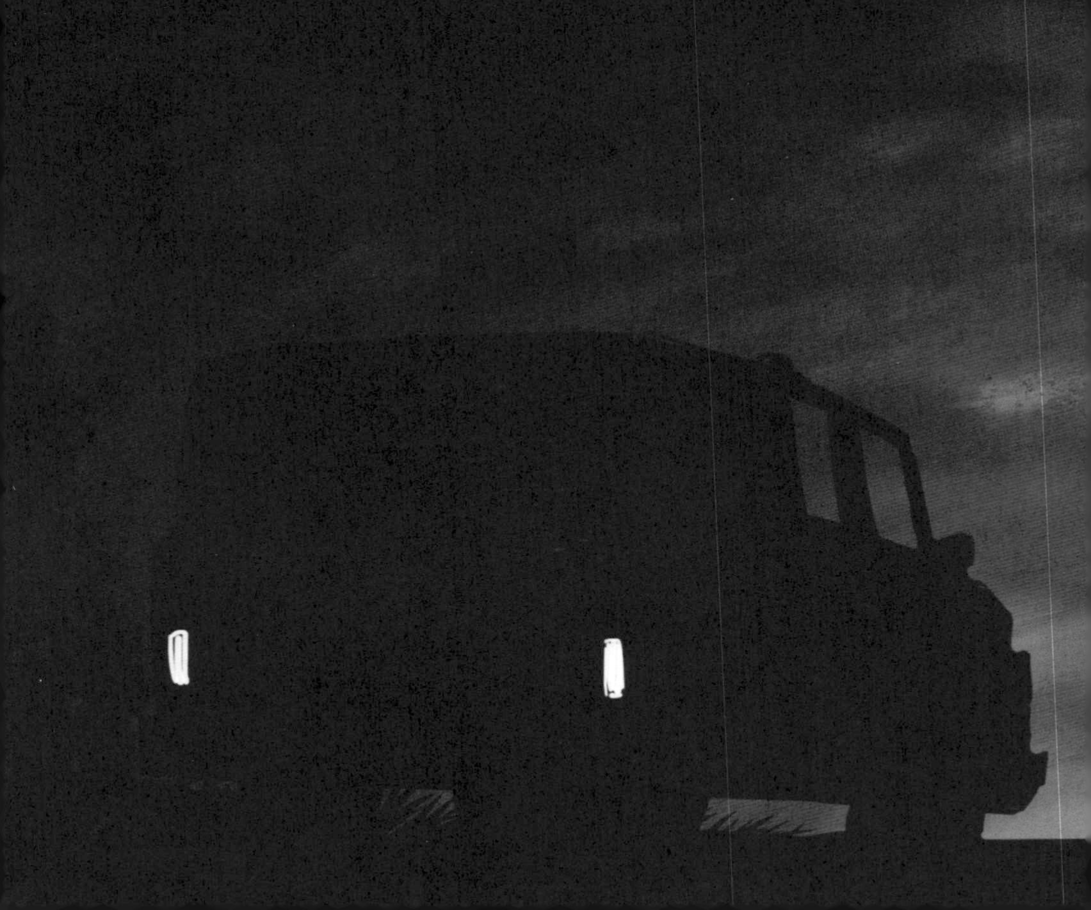

WHAT WORRIED ME *MORE* WAS THAT - UNLIKE ME - THESE WERE *REAL INDIANS*. NATIVES WHO WERE TAKING A STAND AGAINST SOMETHING *OLDER* THAN THE COUNTRY ITSELF ~ *GREED*... TO PROTECT A RESOURCE AS OLD AS *LIFE* ~ WATER...

WOULD THEY SPOT ME AS A FRAUD IMMEDIATELY? WOULD THEY KNOW THAT - ALTHOUGH MY INTENTIONS WERE TRUE - I WAS NOT QUALIFIED TO STAND ALONGSIDE THEM? THE LIFELONG FEELING OF EXCLUSION, A GENETICALLY INDUCED *IMPOSTER SYNDROME* RATTLED AT THE BACK OF MY MIND AND IN THE BASE OF MY GUT.

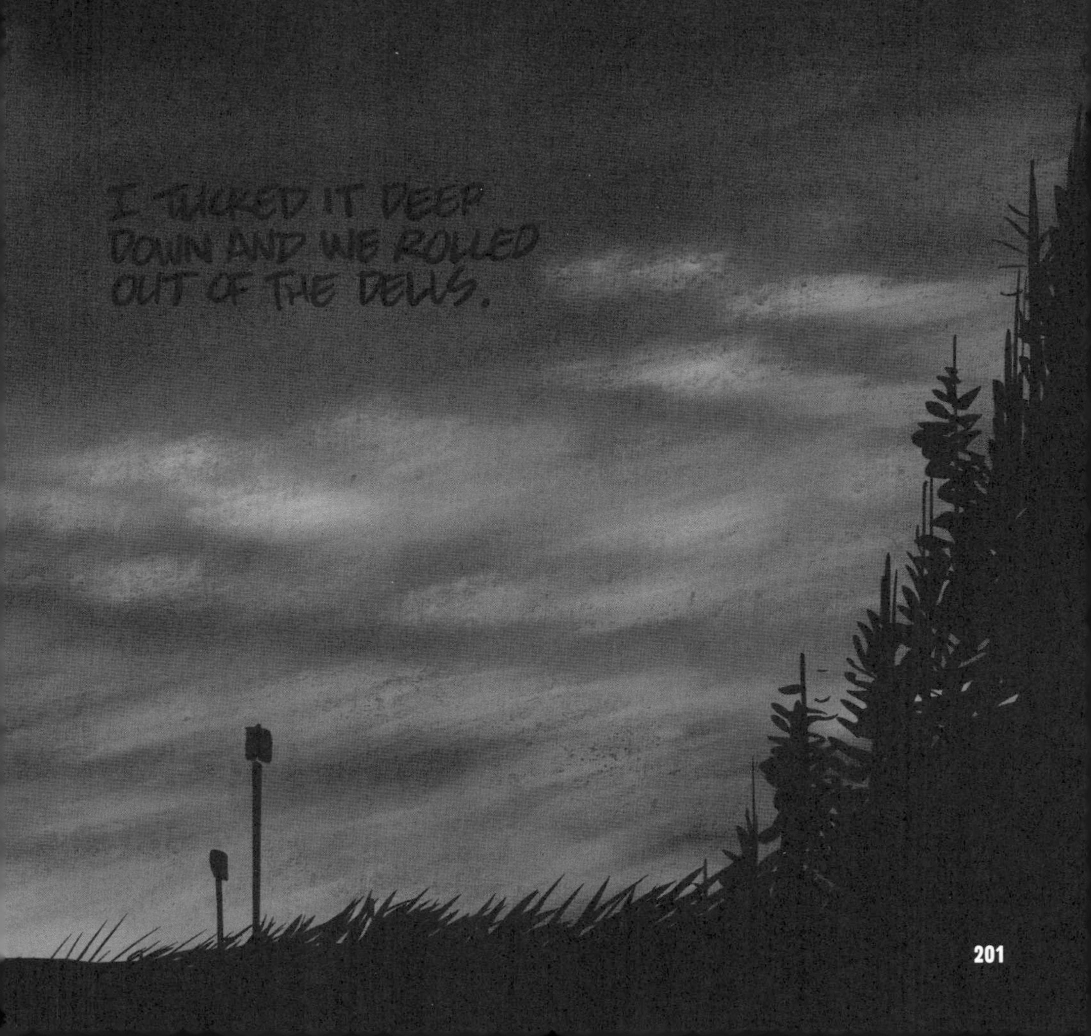
I TUCKED IT DEEP DOWN AND WE ROLLED OUT OF THE DELLS.

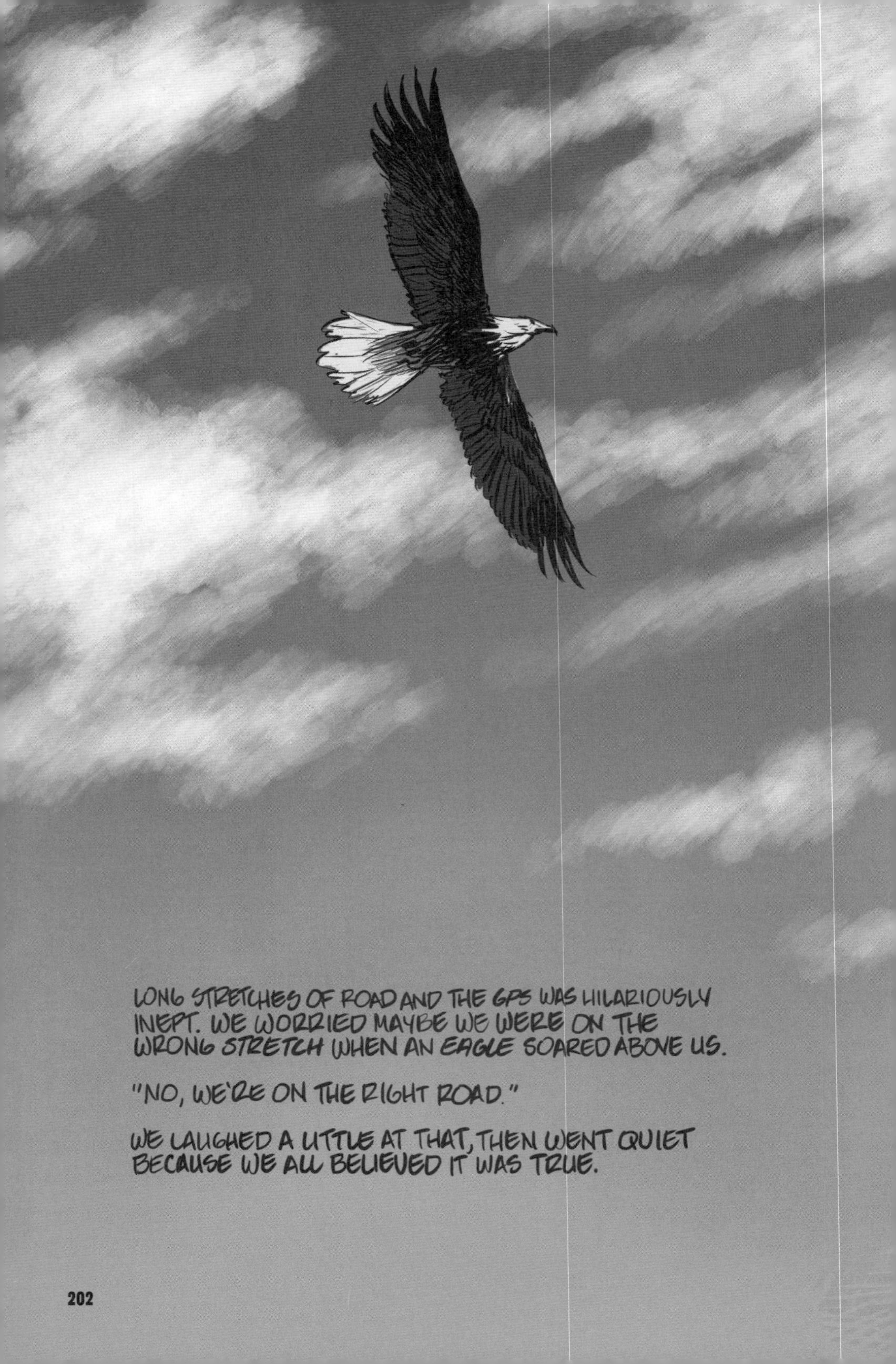
LONG STRETCHES OF ROAD AND THE GPS WAS HILARIOUSLY INEPT. WE WORRIED MAYBE WE WERE ON THE WRONG STRETCH WHEN AN EAGLE SOARED ABOVE US.
"NO, WE'RE ON THE RIGHT ROAD."
WE LAUGHED A LITTLE AT THAT, THEN WENT QUIET BECAUSE WE ALL BELIEVED IT WAS TRUE.

WE WERE TREATED TO A PRETTY SPECTACULAR MINNESOTA SUNSET AS WE PASSED THE CITY. WETHA USED TO LIVE THERE AND WE STOPPED TO EAT AT ONE OF HER OLD HAUNTS, AND I PONDERED HOW LITTLE I KEPT UP WITH MY FAMILY. SHE WENT THROUGH SOME REAL HARD TIMES TO GET TO THIS MOMENT, SAME AS ELENA DID. SAME AS ME, I SUPPOSED.

AND SO HERE WERE THREE NATIVES ALIVE IN THIS WORLD. OUR ANCESTORS WERE HUNTED AND KILLED (OR IMPRISONED IN ONE WAY OR ANOTHER) BY THE VERY GOVERNMENT WE THREE LIVED UNDER. ALCOHOL AND STRANGE, UNHEALTHY FOOD TRIED TO KILL US AS DID EVERY TEACHER, MOVIE, BOOK, AND POLITICIAN THAT TRIED TO TELL US WE WERE *NO LONGER RELEVANT.*

WE THREE WHO STUMBLED THROUGH THIS WORLD AND MADE MISTAKES AND STRUGGLED TO FIGURE WHERE WE FIT IN– WHERE WE *BELONGED*... WERE TOGETHER *NOW* IN A JEEP ON THE WAY TO THE BIGGEST INDIGENOUS RESISTANCE IN RECENT HISTORY.

WE WERE *RIGHT* WHERE
WE BELONGED.

SOMEHOW.

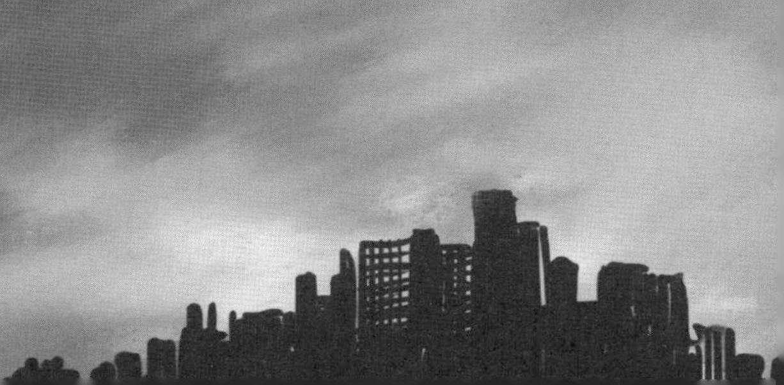

AS WE ROLLED IN TO SOUTH DAKOTA THE SUN VANISHED AND THE WORLD TURNED WAY DARKER THAN I WAS USED TO. GPS WAS WORTH-LESS BUT WE'D SEEN AN EAGLE FLYING ALONGSIDE US EARLIER AND WE TOOK IT AS A GOOD SIGN. WHAT WASN'T A GOOD SIGN WERE THE MANY *TRUMP* SIGNS WE SAW... I HAD THE SINKING DREAD THAT HE MIGHT ACTUALLY WIN, AS INSANE AS IT SEEMED - AND HE WAS NO FRIEND TO *NATIVES* OR *NATURE*. HE ALSO HAD MONEY IN THE VERY PIPELINE IN QUESTION. I PUSHED IT DOWN - OUT OF MY HANDS.

AFTER A WHILE IT WAS AS IF WE WERE ON A DISTANT PLANET, THERE WAS *NO LIGHT* SAVE OURS AND THE WORLD SEEMED TO END JUST BEYOND THE HEADLIGHTS. ELENA PUT IN *NEIL YOUNG* AND IT WAS A COMFORT TO US ALL.

I ASKED THEM IF THEY WERE NERVOUS.

ELENA BELIEVED IN WHAT WAS HAPPENING THERE AND SAW IT AS THE BEAUTIFUL, IMPORTANT THING IT WAS... WHICH PUT HER FEARS WAY IN THE BACKGROUND.

WETHA WAS EXCITED - TO BE THERE, TO HOPEFULLY SEE FAMILY AND FRIENDS SHE HADN'T FOR SOME TIME... AND TO FIGHT THE MAN IN WHATEVER WAY SHE COULD.

ME, I WAS BEGINNING TO WONDER WHY I WAS ALONG. I KEPT THAT TO MYSELF.

WE DROVE DEEPER INTO THE DARKNESS AND IT HIT ME OUT OF NOWHERE HOW **ALONE** WE THREE WERE. ALL OF OUR PARENTS WERE GONE. WETHA'S FATHER, AN ACTIVIST AND BADASS, HAD PASSED SOME TIME BEFORE AND HER MOTHER, JEAN - A LEGENDARY ACTIVIST AND ONE OF THE STRONGEST WOMEN I KNEW - WENT BACK TO THE EARTH JUST RECENTLY.

AND OF COURSE... ELENA AND I WERE ALONE NOW.

WE FELT AS THOUGH THE SPIRIT OF JEAN DAY WAS CHEERING US ON. MOM WOULD HAVE BEEN WORRIED ABOUT US. DAD? HE PROBABLY WOULD HAVE THOUGHT WE WERE *NUTS*.

BUT THEY WERE **GONE** NOW. THE MANY TIMES I THOUGHT OF CALLING THEM ONLY TO *PAUSE* AND REMEMBER. WE WERE BEHOLDEN TO NO ONE SAVE THE *NEXT GENERATION* AND THERE WASN'T ANYONE FOR US TO ASK "HOW SHOULD WE PROCEED?" IN THAT DARKNESS I BEGAN TO UNDERSTAND THE IDEA OF LIVING FOR THE *NEXT GENERATION*. THOSE WHO CAME BEFORE LEAVE, AND SOMETIMES THEY LEAVE A MESS. SOMETIMES THEY PREPARE YOU AND SOMETIMES THEY CRIPPLE YOU BUT IN THE END IT'S UP TO YOU HOW YOU LIVE AND THE ONES WHO *BENEFIT* OR *SUFFER* ARE THE *CHILDREN WE HAVE NOW*.

I THINK EVERYONE WHO WAS RESISTING AT STANDING ROCK UNDERSTOOD THAT *LONG* BEFORE I DID.

I STILL DON'T *COMPLETELY* UNDERSTAND, BUT I'M TRYING.

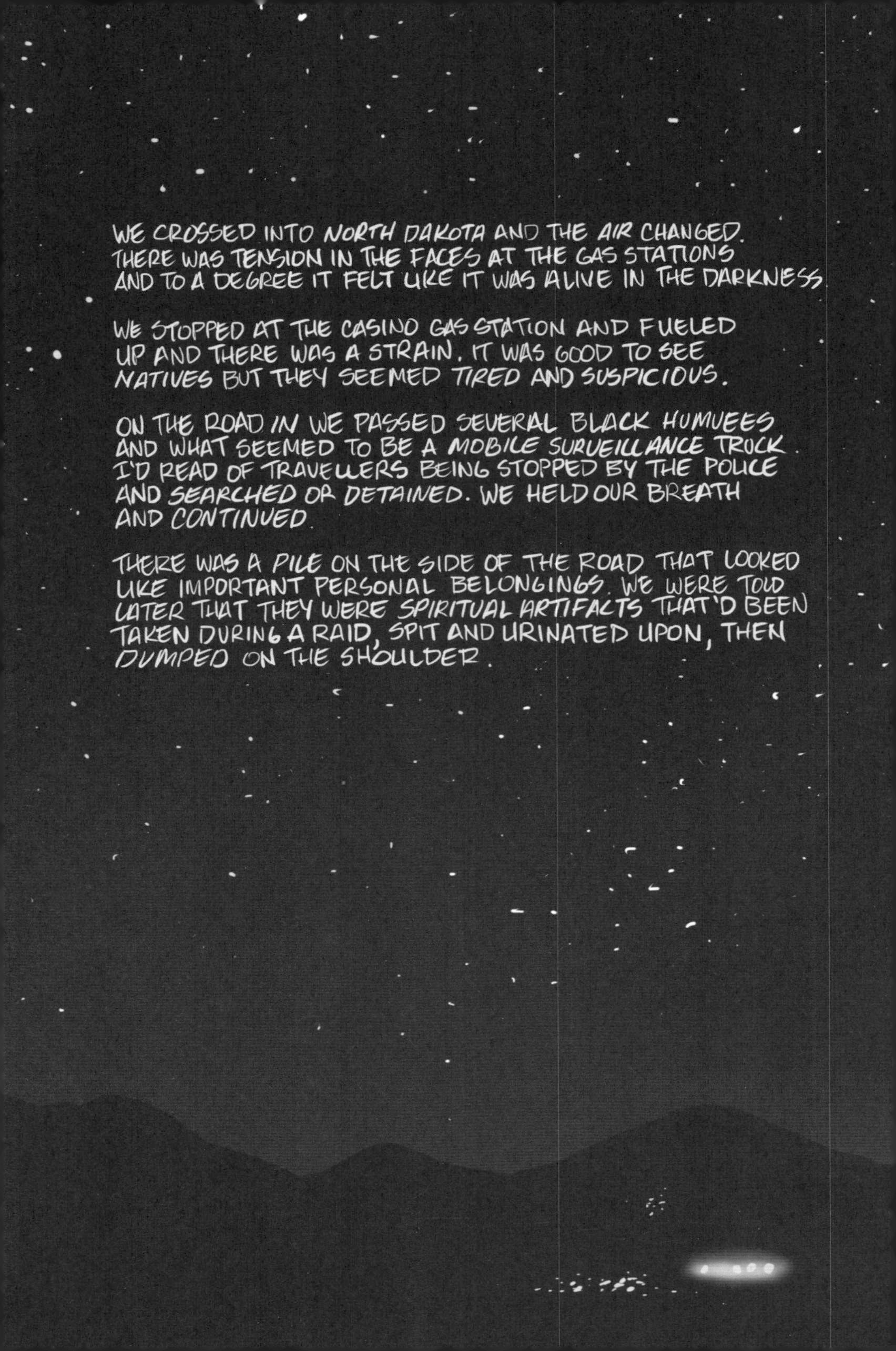
WE CROSSED INTO NORTH DAKOTA AND THE AIR CHANGED. THERE WAS TENSION IN THE FACES AT THE GAS STATIONS AND TO A DEGREE IT FELT LIKE IT WAS ALIVE IN THE DARKNESS.
WE STOPPED AT THE CASINO GAS STATION AND FUELED UP AND THERE WAS A STRAIN. IT WAS GOOD TO SEE NATIVES BUT THEY SEEMED TIRED AND SUSPICIOUS.
ON THE ROAD IN WE PASSED SEVERAL BLACK HUMVEES AND WHAT SEEMED TO BE A MOBILE SURVEILLANCE TRUCK. I'D READ OF TRAVELLERS BEING STOPPED BY THE POLICE AND SEARCHED OR DETAINED. WE HELD OUR BREATH AND CONTINUED.
THERE WAS A PILE ON THE SIDE OF THE ROAD THAT LOOKED LIKE IMPORTANT PERSONAL BELONGINGS. WE WERE TOLD LATER THAT THEY WERE SPIRITUAL ARTIFACTS THAT'D BEEN TAKEN DURING A RAID, SPIT AND URINATED UPON, THEN DUMPED ON THE SHOULDER.

EVENTUALLY WE BEGAN TO SEE LIGHTS. I'D NEVER FELT LIKE MORE OF A *TOURIST* AS WE DROVE THROUGH THE REZ. THE DARK SLEEPING HOMES OF THOSE WHO DEALT WITH THIS HOSTILITY AND OPPRESSION *EVERY DAY*. I BRISTLED AT THE IDEA OF ANY MODERN *NON-NATIVE* BEING RELOCATED AGAINST THEIR WILL AND TOLD "THIS IS WHERE YOU LIVE NOW."

THERE WERE A FEW DIFFERENT CAMPS AND WE ENDED UP AT THE LARGEST ONE, OCETI. SOMEONE MANNING THE GATE STEPPED UP AND ASKED IF WE WERE CARRYING ANY DRUGS, ALCOHOL, OR WEAPONS. WE SAID NO.

HERE, I THOUGHT, WAS WHERE I'D BE EXPOSED. YOU CAN'T COME IN HERE, FAKER, YOU'RE BARELY NATIVE. THANKS FOR YOUR CHEAP IDEALISM BUT YOU HAVEN'T EARNED THE RIGHT TO BE HERE.

HE LOOKED IN THE JEEP. "THIS YOUR FIRST TIME AT THE CAMP?"

WE TOLD HIM IT WAS AND HE SMILED AND SAID,

"WELCOME HOME."

THANKING HIM, WE ROLLED ON THROUGH PAST CONSTRUCTS STURDY AND RAMSHACKLE, TENTS AND CAMPERS AND WOOD STRUCTURES AND CARS AND *TIPIS* EXTENDING INTO THE BLACK BEYOND HEADLIGHTS OR CAMPFIRES. FIGURES WANDERED IN AND OUT OF THE LIGHT AS WE IDLED THROUGH ON THE HARD-PACKED AND FROZEN MUD PATH.

FINALLY WE CAME TO A STOP ON THE OUTSKIRTS AND SET UP OUR TENT IN THE DARKNESS, WHICH WAS NOT TOTAL. ACROSS THE RIVER ON THE *DAPL* SIDE BEAMED GREAT WHITE *FLOODLIGHTS*, ILLUMINATING THE PIPELINE'S CONSTRUCTION AREA AND KEEPING AN EYE ON THE EDGE OF CAMP.

THE EERIE MECHANICAL BUZZ OF A SMALL *AIRPLANE* CIRCLED OVER THE CAMP, A DARK AND LIGHTLESS SHADOW BLOTTING OUT THE STARS AS WE SETTLED IN. OUR PHONES WERE FUNCTIONING ODDLY, MINE HAD THE WRONG DATE AND TIME. I WAS TOLD LATER THAT THE PLANE HAD SOME KIND OF SCRAMBLER ON IT.

NAZGUL, I THOUGHT. THOSE FLOODLIGHTS ARE THE EYE OF SAURON AND WE'RE ALL ON THE EDGE OF MORDOR.

THE COLD SNAPPED ME OUT OF NERD LAND AND BACK TO THE ACTUAL SITUATION. I WORRIED ABOUT MY CATS BACK HOME. HOW BITTER I WAS THAT I'D FOUGHT WITH SOMEONE *DEAR* TO ME BEFORE I'D *LEFT.*

IT ALL SEEMED VERY FAR AWAY NOW AND THE COLD WAS *RIDICULOUS.*

WE AGREED THAT A TRIP TO BISMARCK FOR WARMER GEAR WAS IN ORDER AND I TRIED TO FIGURE A WAY TO COMPLETELY COVER MY FACE AND STILL *BREATHE.* BEFORE I FINALLY DRIFTED OFF TO AN UNEASY SLEEP I SHOT OUT MY USUAL PRAYER TO OL' *H.P.*, MY "HIGHER POWER."

THANK YOU FOR KEEPING ME SOBER TODAY. THANK YOU FOR THE DAY. THANK YOU FOR MY FAMILY AND FRIENDS. PLEASE HELP ME TO DO MORE GOOD THAN HARM. AND... LET ME BE OF SOME SERVICE HERE... THIS SITUATION SUCKS.

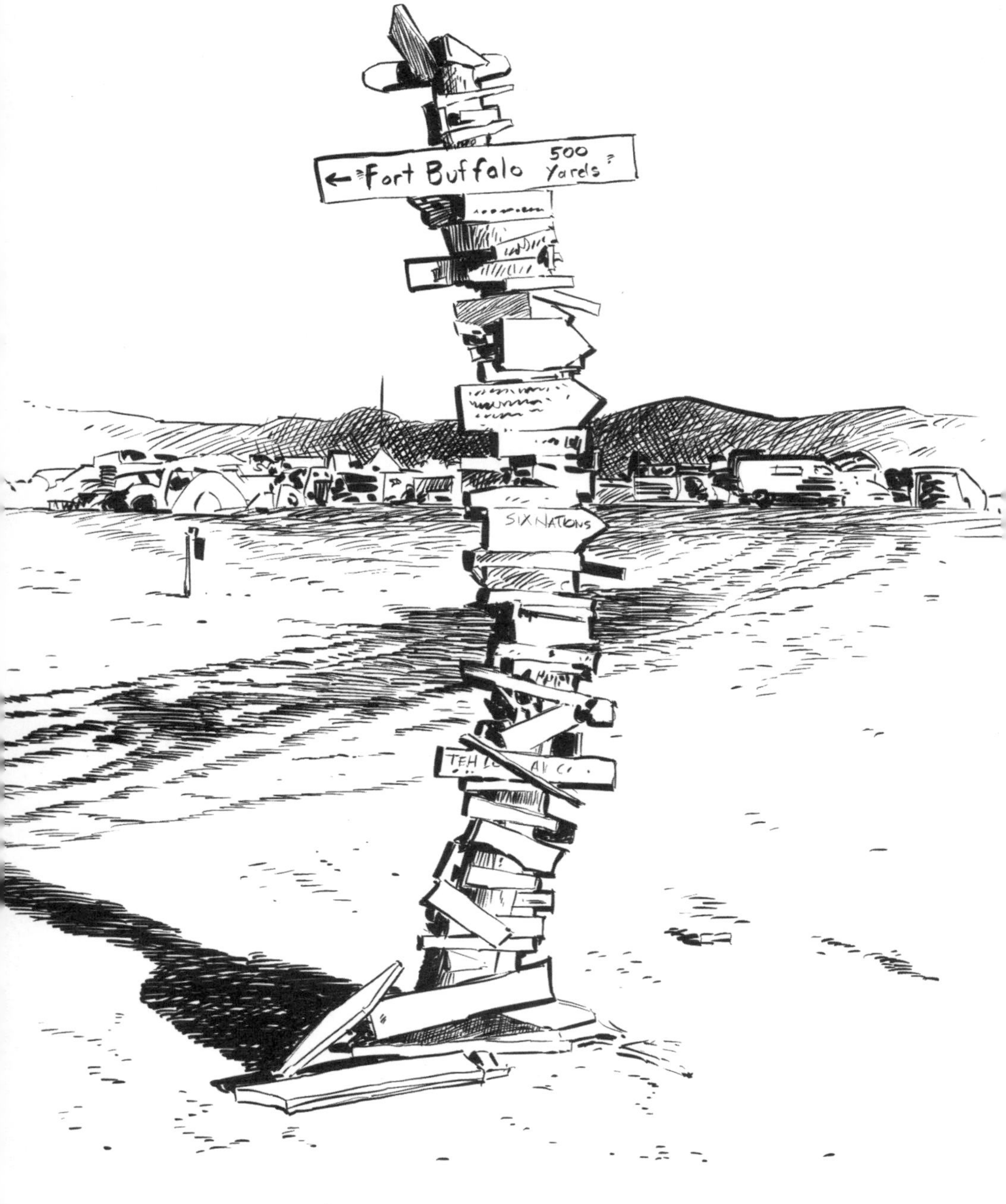

← Fort Buffalo
500 Yards
SIX NATIONS

WE WALKED AROUND A BIT THE FIRST NIGHT BUT WERE TRIPPING OVER TENT ROPES AND STUMBLING INTO DEAD ENDS. THE NEXT MORNING I WOKE UP BEFORE THE SUN, STIFF AND COLD AND IN NEED OF COFFEE. I GRABBED MY CUP AND HEADED INTO THE CHILL DARKNESS.

I MET A FELLA FROM OREGON WHO WAS MANNING A LARGE COFFEE MACHINE. HE'D BEEN THERE FOR WEEKS AND HE EXPLAINED THE GENERAL AIR OF THE CAMP, LAUGHING WHEN I OFFERED TO PAY FOR THE COFFEE. HE TOLD ME THAT AT DAWN AN ELDER SPOKE AT THE *SACRED FIRE* AND I SHOULD CHECK IT OUT FOR A MORE ACCURATE GAUGE.

AFTER FINDING OUT WHERE TO DONATE THE *GEAR* WE BROUGHT I FOLLOWED A PATH TO THE SACRED FIRE. I FOUND A SPOT TO *LEAN* AND AS THE SUN CAME UP THE P.A. SYSTEM CRACKLED TO LIFE AS THE ELDER BEGAN TO PRAY. IT WAS IN *LAKOTA* SO I DIDN'T FOLLOW, BUT IT WAS NICE TO HEAR THE LANGUAGE BEING SPOKEN. AFTER THE PRAYER HE GREETED US IN *ENGLISH*.

HE SPOKE OF THE URGENCY OF THE RESISTANCE, AND THE IMPORTANCE OF *PEACEFUL ACTS* — THE DANGER OF BEING GOADED INTO REACTION. PATIENCE AND A *SPIRITUAL STRENGTH* WERE ALLIES. VIOLENCE WAS A TRAP THAT *DAPL* WANTED THE RESISTANCE TO FALL FOR.

BEHIND HIM WERE GREAT HILLS, SCORCHED AT THEIR PEAKS TO THE DIRT. I WAS LATER TOLD THAT A *FIRE* WAS LIT THERE AND AS IT CREPT TOWARD CAMP THERE WAS LITTLE TO DO BUT PRAY, AND A *STRONG* WIND BLEW ACROSS CAMP AND UP THE HILL — PUSHING THE FLAMES BACK TOWARD FROM WHERE THEY CAME.

I'D HEARD THAT ABOUT WHATEVER THEY WERE DUMPING FROM ABOVE WITH THEIR *HELICOPTERS*... THAT A *WIND* CAME AND BLEW IT AWAY.

I BELIEVED IT.

WHY WOULDN'T I? I'D SEEN MIRACLES HAPPEN.

IN BISMARCK WE GOT A FEEL OF THE LOCAL HOSPITALITY. IT WAS LIKE EASY RIDER WHEN WE THREE STEPPED INTO THE DINER - ELENA AND WETHA LOOKED VERY NATIVE AND ANGRY EYES FOLLOWED US TO THE BOOTH.

I UNDERSTOOD THE HOSTILITY - SOMEONE'S TRYING TO LIVE A LIFE AND THAT'S HARD ENOUGH WHEN IN COME THESE TROUBLEMAKING STRAGGLERS. THESE NATIVES WHO DON'T HAVE THE DECENCY TO DIE OUT LIKE A GOOD "CONQUERED" PEOPLE OR AT LEAST STAY PUT ON THE RESERVATIONS WHERE THEIR CONTINUING SUFFERING DOESN'T HAVE TO BE SEEN.

GOTTA COME AROUND REMINDING EVERYONE THEY'RE STILL HERE AND THAT THIS GREAT NATION WAS BUILT ON A GENOCIDE PLAN. AND NOW THEY WERE DISRUPTING THINGS, BITCHING ABOUT A PIPELINE. TALKING ABOUT THE PLANET LIKE IT WASN'T A UTILITY TO BE RAPED AND ABANDONED.

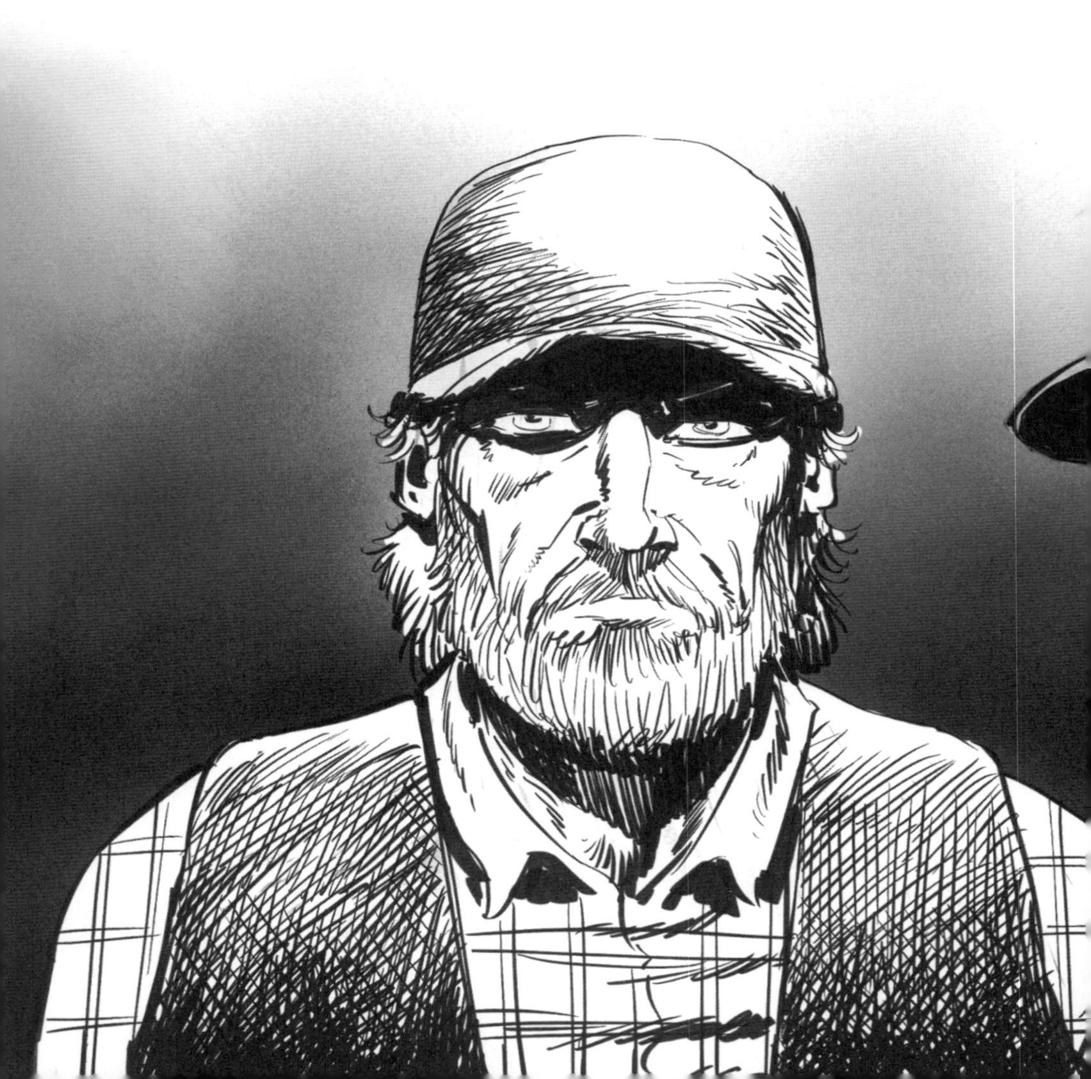

SURE, I UNDERSTOOD THE HOSTILITY.

I ALSO UNDERSTOOD WHAT THE WHITE MAN IN THE TRUMP HAT WAS DOING WHEN HE BEGAN *BOASTING* TO OUR VERY KIND, POSSIBLY GAY WAITER HOW THINGS WERE GOING TO *CHANGE* ONCE TRUMP WAS IN OFFICE.

IT WAS JUST ANOTHER BULLY. EAGER TO SHOW HIS UGLINESS, JUST WAITING TO BE TOLD IT WAS OKAY TO, LIKE A FEVERED DOG TUGGING A LEASH.

I TOLD THE WAITER HE WAS CRAZY TO LIVE UP HERE AND WE BOTH LAUGHED. WE LAUGHED LOUD ENOUGH TO BE HEARD.

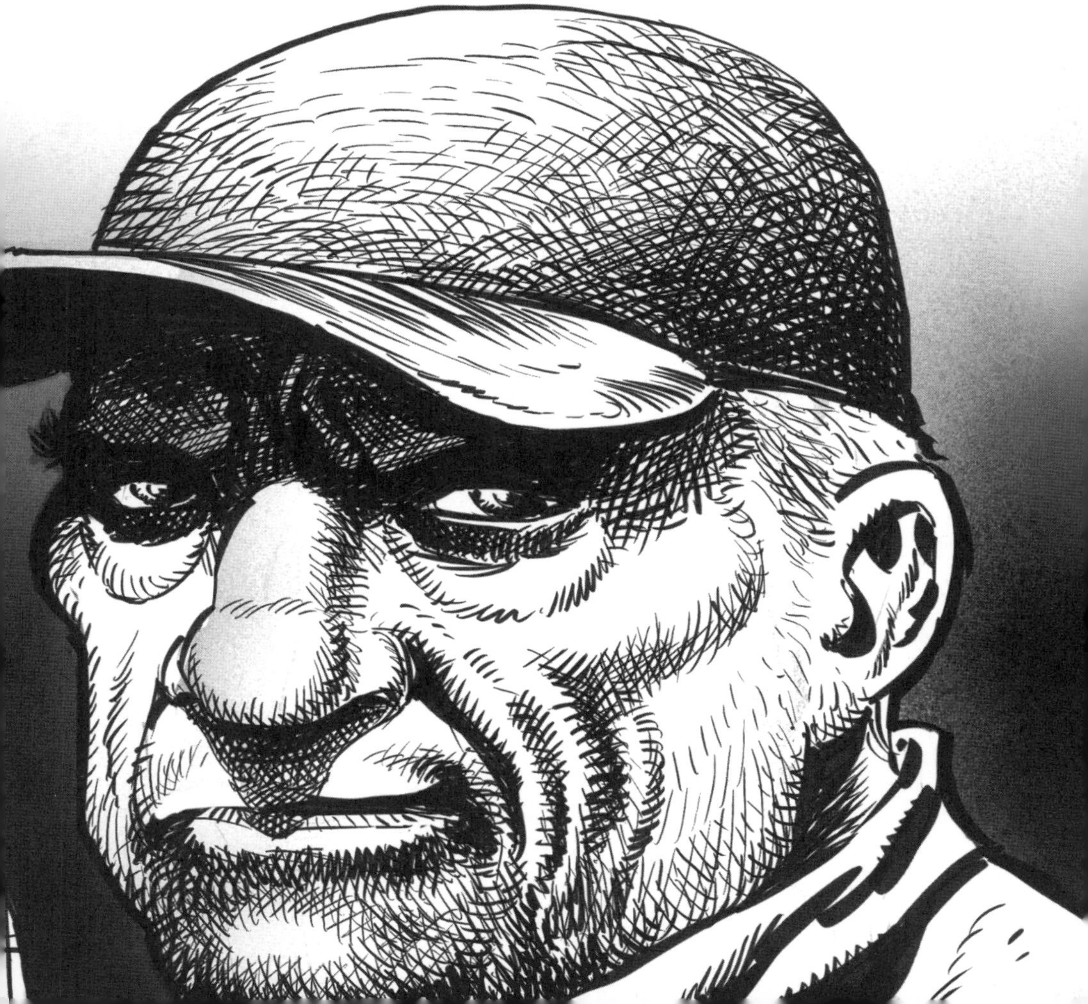

WE DECIDED TO CHECK OUT THE BRIDGE, WHERE MOST OF THE ACTION TOOK PLACE. DAPL CLAIMED THE RESISTANCE SET FIRE TO SOME VEHICLES BUT THAT MADE ZERO SENSE AND WAS LAUGHED OFF BY EVERYONE AT CAMP. THE CHARRED VEHICLES WERE CLEARLY A STRATEGIC BLOCKADE TO KEEP ANYONE FROM CROSSING, AS WAS THE RAZOR WIRE STRUNG ABOUT THEM - WHICH EXTENDED OFF THE BRIDGE AND INTO THE WATER ON EITHER SIDE

WETHA AND I WALKED TOWARD THE BRIDGE AND FOLKS WARNED US ABOUT THE SNIPERS IN THE HILLS AND ON THE VEHICLES. SHE STRODE ON CONFIDENTLY BUT I WAS SUDDENLY AWARE OF EVERY SHRUB, SOUND, AND SHIFT IN THE GENTLE BREEZE. THE SKIN ON MY FACE FELT RECEPTIVE.

WE GOT TO THE SCORCHED TRUCKS AND I NOTED THE BOILED ASPHALT AS A FEW MEN BECKONED US CLOSER. WE JOINED THEM AGAINST THE TRUCK.

"JUST STAY BEHIND THESE TRUCKS. YOU CAN PEER OVER THE SIDE IF YOU WANT BUT BE QUICK. THEY GOT PEOPLE WATCHING EVERYTHING."

I POPPED MY HEAD OVER THE HOOD AND SAW A SWAT-TYPE VEHICLE PARKED. SURE ENOUGH THERE WAS A SNIPER ON THE ROOF, AIMED RIGHT AT MY FACE. I PULLED BACK, THEN SNAPPED A PIC.

"WELL, THAT'S UNSETTLING."

"BROTHER, IT'S JUST FEAR. HE WON'T SHOOT UNLESS YOU TRY CROSSING BUT HE STAYS THERE TO KEEP YOU AFRAID."

I THOUGHT ABOUT THIS. MORE BULLIES. MORE FEAR.

HOW DOES ONE OVERCOME FEAR? FEAR USED AS A WEAPON ITSELF?

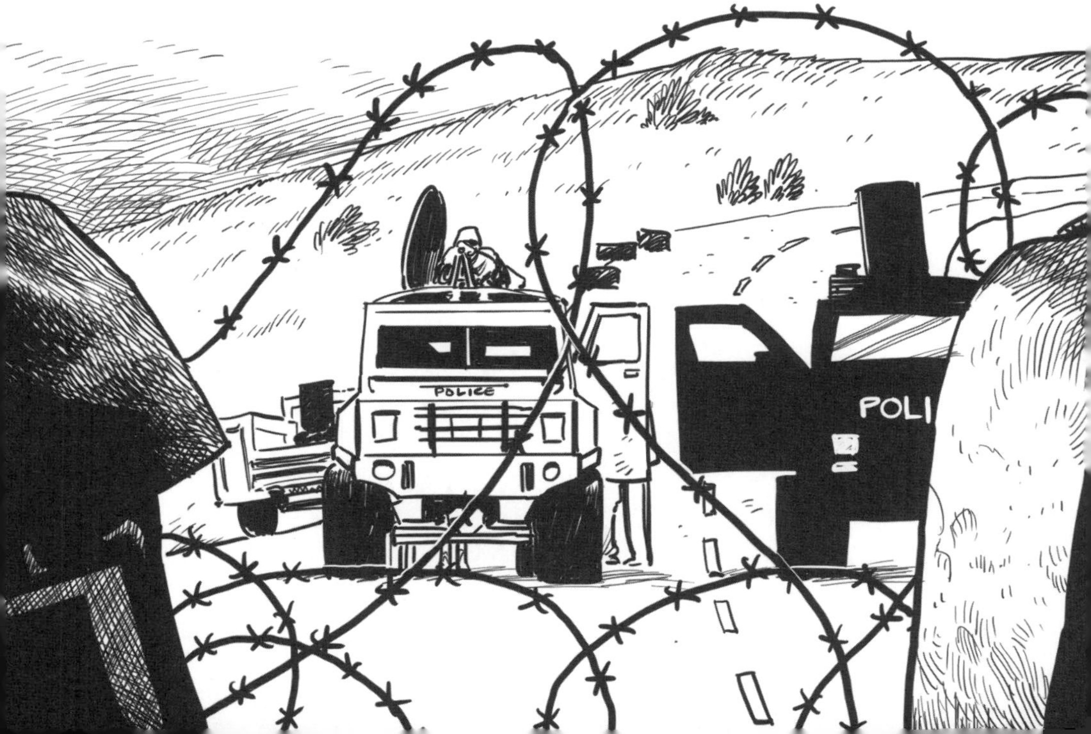
POLICE
POLI

LATER ON THERE WAS AN *ENERGY SHIFT* IN THE CAMP. MOVEMENT ALL AROUND ME AND I ASKED SOMEONE AS SHE RUSHED BY WHAT WAS UP.

"IT'S A CALL TO ACTION. WE'RE GOING TO THE FRONT LINES."

"THE BRIDGE?" ~ "NO, IT'S MOVED."

"CAN I GO? CAN I FOLLOW YOU?"

SHE WAS FRUSTRATED BUT PATIENT, ASKING IF I'D *REGISTERED* YET, WHICH I HADN'T. APPARENTLY GOING TO THE LINES WAS AN ALMOST *GUARANTEED ARREST,* AND IF YOU WEREN'T IN THE CAMP'S SYSTEM THEY COULDN'T GET YOU OUT OF JAIL. THAT MEANT THE LAW COULD TRANSFER YOU SOMEWHERE VERY FAR FROM THE ACTION AND YOU MIGHT JUST GET "LOST" IN IT ALL.

I THANKED HER AND SHE NODDED, RUSHED OFF.

THE GROUND BENEATH ME TREMBLED AND I SPUN AROUND, STEPPING BACK AS THREE TEENAGE NATIVES RODE PAST ME ON HORSES, GALLOPING BAREBACK TOWARD THE FRONT LINE.

THEY DIDN'T SEE ME, THEY WERE FOCUSED ON WHERE THEY WERE HEADED AS THOUGH IT WAS TWO HUNDRED YEARS AGO AND *DEFENSE* WAS IN NEED. IT WAS 2016 AND DEFENSE WAS NEEDED. THE LAND WAS IN DANGER. THEY WANTED TO PUT SOMETHING IN THE WATER THAT COULD *KILL ALL THE LIFE* AND THEY CHARGED FORTH TO *PROTECT* IT.

WATER PROTECTORS.

I STOOD IN A DAZE, WATCHING THEM STRIDE BY. TWO BOYS AND A GIRL, *NONE* OF THEM MORE THAN *SEVENTEEN. FEARLESS.*

STUMBLING BACK TO OUR CAMP, PROUD OF THEM BUT ASHAMED OF MYSELF, I TOLD ELENA AND WETHA WHAT I'D LEARNED.

I WANDERED THE CAMP, TALKING TO PEOPLE AND HELPING WHERE I COULD. RUNNING INTO SOME HO-CHUNKS, I HELPED SET UP THEIR CAMP. I GOT THE SAME SILENT "TOUGH GUY" TREATMENT AND FELT PRETTY UNWELCOME SO WHEN THEY OFFERED ME SOUP I DECLINED AND WANDERED OFF AGAIN.

I CHOPPED WOOD, WHICH IS THE EASIEST THING TO DO. I HELD LADDERS, I JUST WENT FROM CAMP TO CAMP ASKING IF I COULD HELP WITH ANYTHING. MY PROGRAM OF SOBRIETY TRAINED ME - WHEN I WAS *UNCOMFORTABLE*, HELP. IN ANY WAY POSSIBLE. KEEPS ME BUSY AND *OUT* OF MY HEAD.

THE WATER PROTECTORS RETURNED, THE ACTION WAS QUICK AND NOT MUCH HAPPENED. WE'D MET WITH WETHA'S AUNT *LISA*, WHO WAS THERE WITH HER DAUGHTER AND A FRIEND, ALL FROM THE SOUTHEAST CHEROKEE TERRITORY. THEY WERE WARRIORS.

THEY TOLD ME THE *WOMEN* WERE *FIRST* ON THE LINES. FRONT ROW. SOME HELD LARGE MIRRORS BEFORE THEM SO THE MERCS AND POLICE COULD SEE WHAT THEY LOOKED LIKE IN THEIR GEAR, WITH THEIR WEAPONS. THE WOMEN GOT *SHOT* FIRST, PEPPER SPRAYED, GASSED, THEY STOOD UP FRONT.

THEY SANG AND PRAYED *FOR* THOSE MEN WITH WEAPONS. THAT THEY MIGHT BE *ENLIGHTENED*. THAT THEIR HEARTS AND MINDS MIGHT OPEN UP TO A *LARGER UNDERSTANDING*.

LATER, I WAS AT THE SACRED FIRE AND THERE WAS DANCING, SINGING - PRAYER. THE MAN WITH THE *MIC* WAS *FROM* THE STANDING ROCK REZ.

"THE HOSTILITY YOU'RE FEELING, THAT YOU'VE EXPERIENCED IN THE TOWNS, THAT'S HOW WE'VE ALWAYS BEEN TREATED. THEY DON'T *WANT* US HERE AND THEY AIN'T SHY ABOUT LETTIN' US KNOW.
BUT THAT DOESN'T MEAN WE HAVE TO LET IT POISON *OUR* HEARTS.
THERE'S A *SNIPER* LOOKING AT US RIGHT NOW. LET'S *ALL* *WAVE* TO HIM."

I WAVED IN THE GENERAL DIRECTION WITH EVERYONE ELSE, GRINNING. THEN THE MAN CONTINUED:

"LET'S WAVE TO HIM SO HE KNOWS HE'S NOT *ALONE*. HE'D RATHER BE WITH HIS FAMILY, NOT OUT HERE. LET HIM KNOW WE'RE HERE *WITH* HIM, *NOT AGAINST HIM*. WE ARE DOING THIS FOR *HIS* FAMILY, TOO."

I CONTINUED WAVING BUT MY FACE CHANGED. THIS MAN'S PHILOSOPHY PIERCED MY SPIRIT AND FILLED IT WITH *LIGHT*.

THAT IS HOW YOU FIGHT FEAR.

COMPASSION. EMPATHY. LOVE.

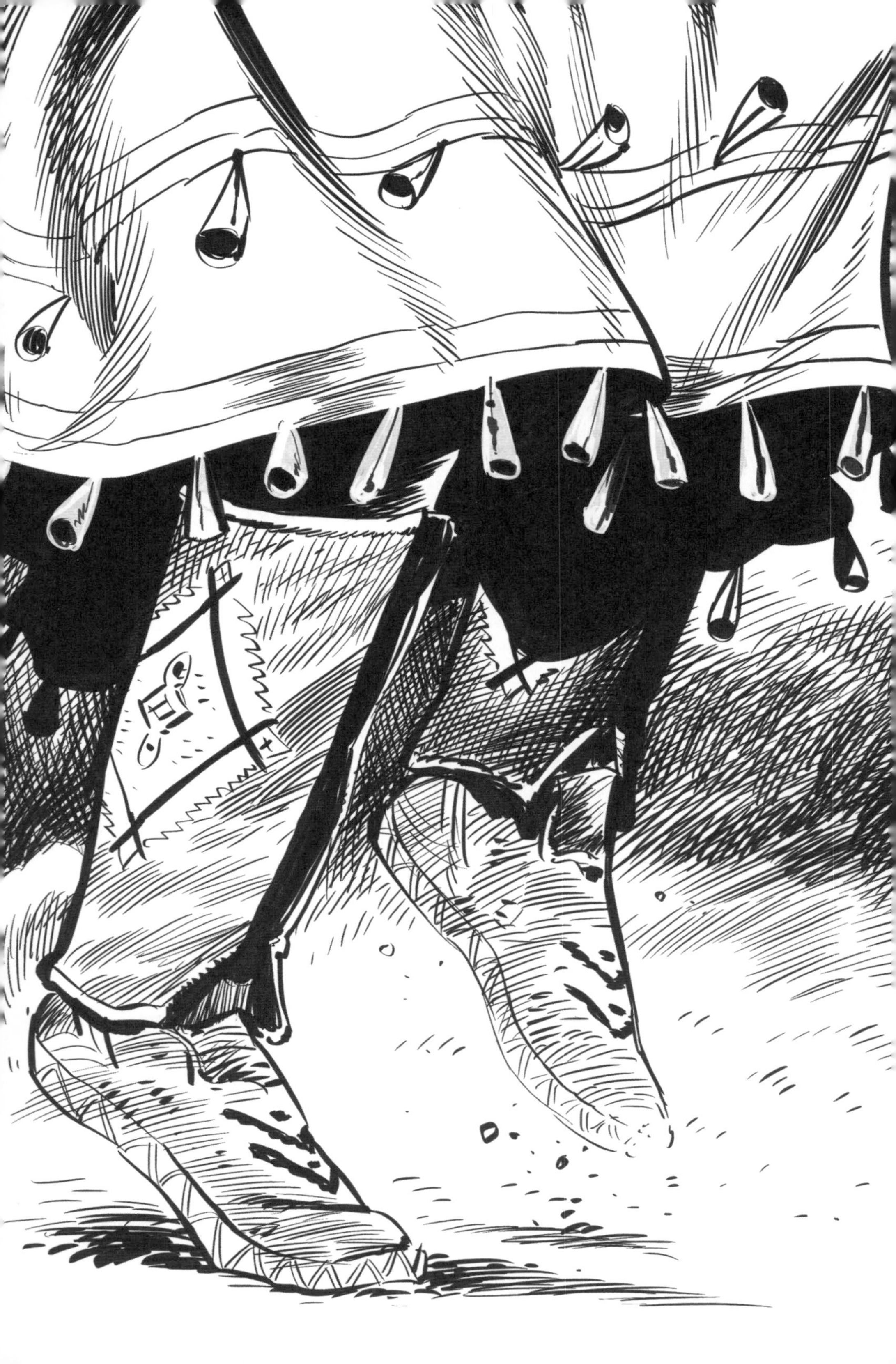

THAT IS WHAT I HEARD, THAT IS WHAT I SAW IN *ACTION*. OF COURSE THERE WERE THOSE WHO WANTED TO *FIGHT* AND THERE WAS CONFLICT BUT WHAT I SAW WAS A *PEACEFUL RESISTANCE*.

I WATCHED A WATER CEREMONY, WHICH ONLY WOMEN DO BUT ALL ARE WELCOME TO JOIN. AT THE RIVER THEY CALLED *WOMEN*, *MEN*, AND *TWO SPIRITS* TO HELP WITH THE PRAYER. THOSE WHO DIDN'T IDENTIFY AS MEN OR WOMEN, WHO WERE CONSIDERED SACRED.

THERE WAS A MOMENT OF PRAYER WHEN THE WOMEN RETURNED FROM A MARCH TO BRING AWARENESS TO MISSING AND MURDERED INDIGENOUS WOMEN. THE "MAN CAMPS," TEMPORARY RESIDENCIES FOR MEN WORKING THE PIPELINES, WERE NOTORIOUS BLACK HOLES FOR WOMEN, ESPECIALLY NATIVES.

PEACEFUL RESISTANCE. BUT NOT *NAIVE*. NOT *WEAK*.

AN ELDER TOOK THE MICROPHONE AND WARNED US ABOUT INFILTRATORS. LIKE *FIFTH COLUMNISTS*, THERE WERE **DAPL** FOLK WHO WERE ENTERING THE CAMP TO INCITE *VIOLENCE* OR *DISARRAY*. THEY WANTED THE RESISTERS TO ABANDON THE *PRAYER* AND PICK UP GUNS.

I'D HEARD ABOUT THIS AND I PAID ATTENTION. I WAS EAGER TO HEAR THE PLAN FOR *DEALING* WITH THIS.

"SO IF YOU SEE SOMEONE WHO'S ACTING LIKE THIS, OR SEEMS LIKE THEY DON'T BELONG..."

MY EARS BUZZED. REPORT THEM? ARE THERE POLICE OF SOME SORT?

HE CONTINUED. "IF YOU SEE SOMEONE LIKE THIS, *INVITE THEM TO YOUR CAMP. TALK TO THEM. HAVE COFFEE AND FEED THEM AND LET THEM KNOW WE ARE DOING THIS FOR THEIR CHILDREN TOO.*"

I WAS FLOORED. I LEANED AGAINST A POLE, IT WAS ASTONISHING AND THE OPPOSITE OF HOW I'D BEEN TRAINED BY THE *CULTURE OF FEAR*.

DON'T *FEAR* YOUR NEIGHBOR. UNDERSTAND THEM.
LOVE OVER HATE.
THIS WAS *COURAGE* OF THE SPIRIT.
I WAS ELECTRIFIED.

THEY WERE THINKING.

BIGGER THAN ALL THIS.

AND THEY HAD THE HEART TO BACK IT UP.

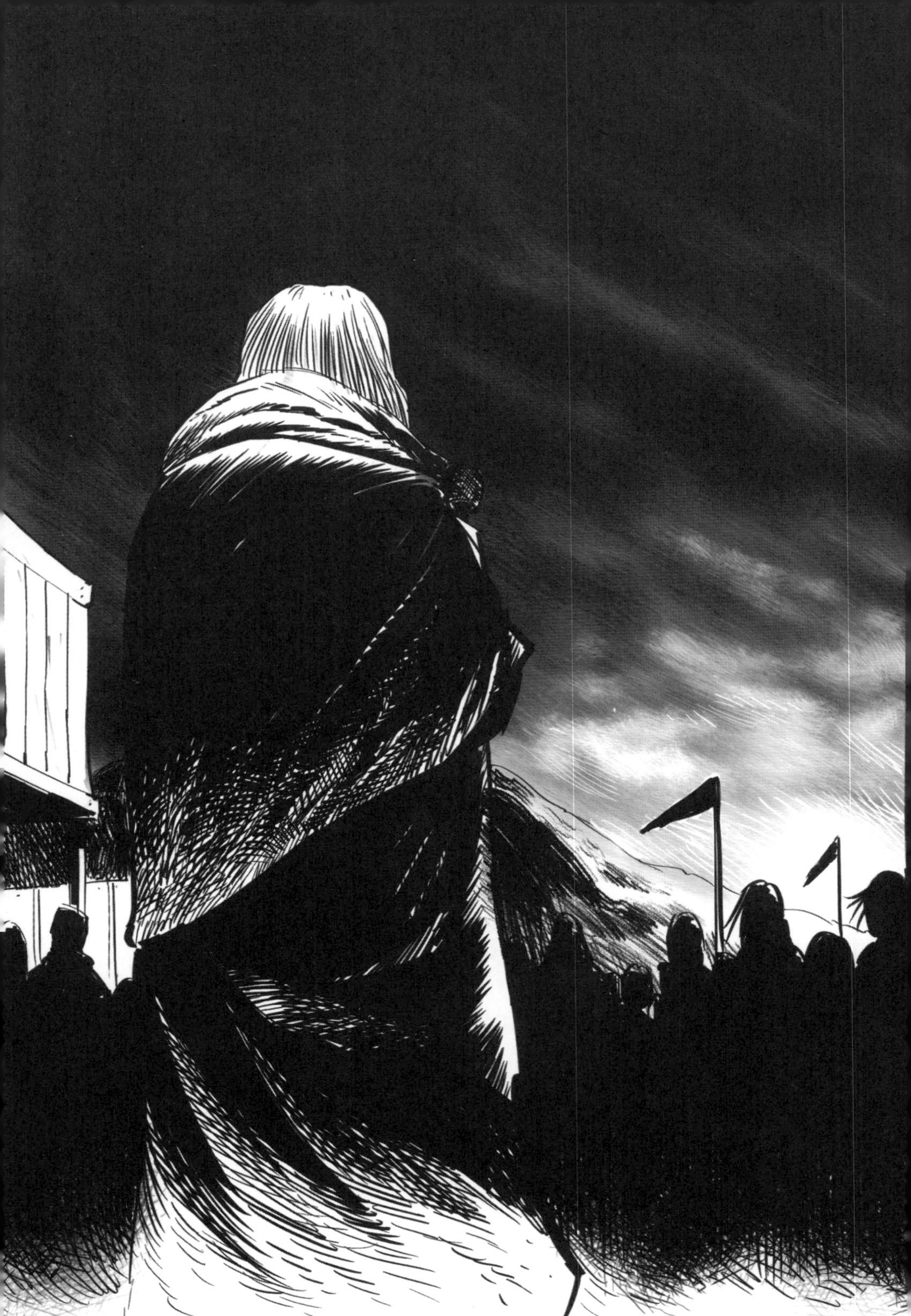

THE NIGHT OF THE ELECTIONS I HAD TERRIBLE DREAMS. I WOKE TO
COLD AND THE SOUND OF HELICOPTERS AND AIRPLANES CIRCLING
ABOVE. WHEN I FINALLY AWOKE ELENA WAS SITTING UP, LOOKING
AT HER PHONE.

"HE WON." SHE WHISPERED, HORRIFIED.

MY INSIDES CURDLED. SO THE CAMPAIGN OF HATE AND FEAR SPOKE
TO THE PEOPLE. WE FELT SICK. THE ENTIRE CAMP HAD A GLOOM.
HOPE WAS DIMINISHED. IGNORANCE AND ANGER WON... IT HARDLY
SEEMED POSSIBLE. THE FUTURE FELT CLOSED. THE BULLIES
HAD WON. STUNNED, WE HEADED FOR THE SACRED FIRE.

MANY WERE GATHERED, SOME WERE CRYING. THIS FIGHT WAS OVER...
THE LAND WOULD NOW BE GLEEFULLY RAPED AND ABANDONED,
SOLD TO THE HIGHEST BIDDER. THE RICH WOULD GET RICHER AND
THE FUTURE GENERATIONS WOULD PAY THE PRICE.

AN ELDER TOOK THE MIC AND EVERYONE LISTENED, STILL IN SHOCK.

THIS IS WHAT I HEARD.

"IT'S A BAD TIME. WHEN IT'S A TIME LIKE THIS IT'S EASY TO LOSE
HOPE, TO LOSE STRENGTH.

"JUST REMEMBER. TWO HUNDRED YEARS AGO THE APOCALYPSE
HAPPENED FOR OUR PEOPLE, FOR THE LAND. IT WAS THE END OF
ALL THINGS WHEN THE WHITE MAN CAME. THEY TOLD US ABOUT
SIN. THEY TOLD US WHEN WE DIED WE'D GO TO PARADISE. BUT
WE WERE ALREADY LIVING IN PARADISE.

"WHEN THEY CONVINCED US WE HAD SOULS... WE LOST OUR SPIRIT.

"BUT OUR ANCESTORS SURVIVED. THEY WERE HUNTED AND PUT IN PRISON
OR KILLED. JUST FOR BEIN' INDIAN. BUT THEY SURVIVED. THEY
PRAYED IN SECRET AND KEPT THE WAYS THE BEST THEY COULD.

"WE ARE THEIR GRANDCHILDREN. WE ARE HERE NOW BECAUSE
THEY SURVIVED. WE ARE NOT A MYTH. WE ARE STILL HERE.

"AND OUR GRANDCHILDREN WILL BE HERE BECAUSE WE
SURVIVED THESE TIMES. WE HAVE NOT LOST OUR SPIRITS. THEY
WILL KNOW WE FOUGHT FOR THEM. THEY WILL BE HERE
BECAUSE WE SURVIVED."

I TOOK A BREATH AND LOOKED AROUND. EVERYONE WAS
HOLDING HANDS.

THEY ALL MADE ME FEEL STRONG.

NOT LONG AFTER, WE LEFT CAMP. NONE OF US WANTED TO LEAVE BUT WE STAYED AS LONG AS WE COULD, OUR LIVES BACK HOME NEEDED ATTENTION. WE'D EXPERIENCED SOMETHING ENTIRELY *UNIQUE* AND THE ENERGY WAS *POWERFUL*.

I SAW THINGS, HEARD THINGS, FELT THINGS THAT I CANNOT PROPERLY CONVEY. *MAGIC* THINGS. THE THINGS I GREW UP BELIEVING BUT LOST SOMEWHERE - WAKING UP IN MY MIND AND MY HEART.

WITHIN A DAY I'D FORGOTTEN *FACEBOOK*, *TWITTER*, SOCIAL MEDIA IN GENERAL. I WORKED AND ATE AND LAUGHED WITH MY *FELLOWS* AND KNEW *PEACE*. IN A TIME OF GRIEF AND WOE I FOUND *HOPE* AND STRENGTH.

FOR A TIME, I WAS EXACTLY WHERE I BELONGED.

I CAME HOME BUT COULDN'T SHAKE THE CAMP. AT THANKSGIVING I WENT BACK ALONE, BUT IT HAD CHANGED.

THERE WERE MANY PEOPLE NOW, TOO MANY FOR THE MESSAGE TO STAY PURE. I WAS TURNED AWAY FROM THE TENTS I'D HELP SET UP AND SLEPT IN THE JEEP, FREEZING.

I FOUND LISA AND MY FRIENDS AND STAYED IN A TIPI WITH THEM THE NEXT NIGHT, IT WAS WARM IN THERE AND I WAS SOON ASLEEP. DEEP IN A FORGOTTEN DREAM, I WAS SHOCKED AWAKE BY A CRY IN THE CAMP. *"FIRE! FIRE!"*

RUBBING THE SLEEP FROM MY EYES I LOOKED UP AND SAW *CORLEE* RUN OUT WITH A FIRE EXTINGUISHER. A FEW MINUTES LATER SHE RETURNED. "IT'S ALL GOOD."

THE CAMP MIGHT HAVE CHANGED, BUT THEIR *WARRIORS'* HEARTS HAD NOT.

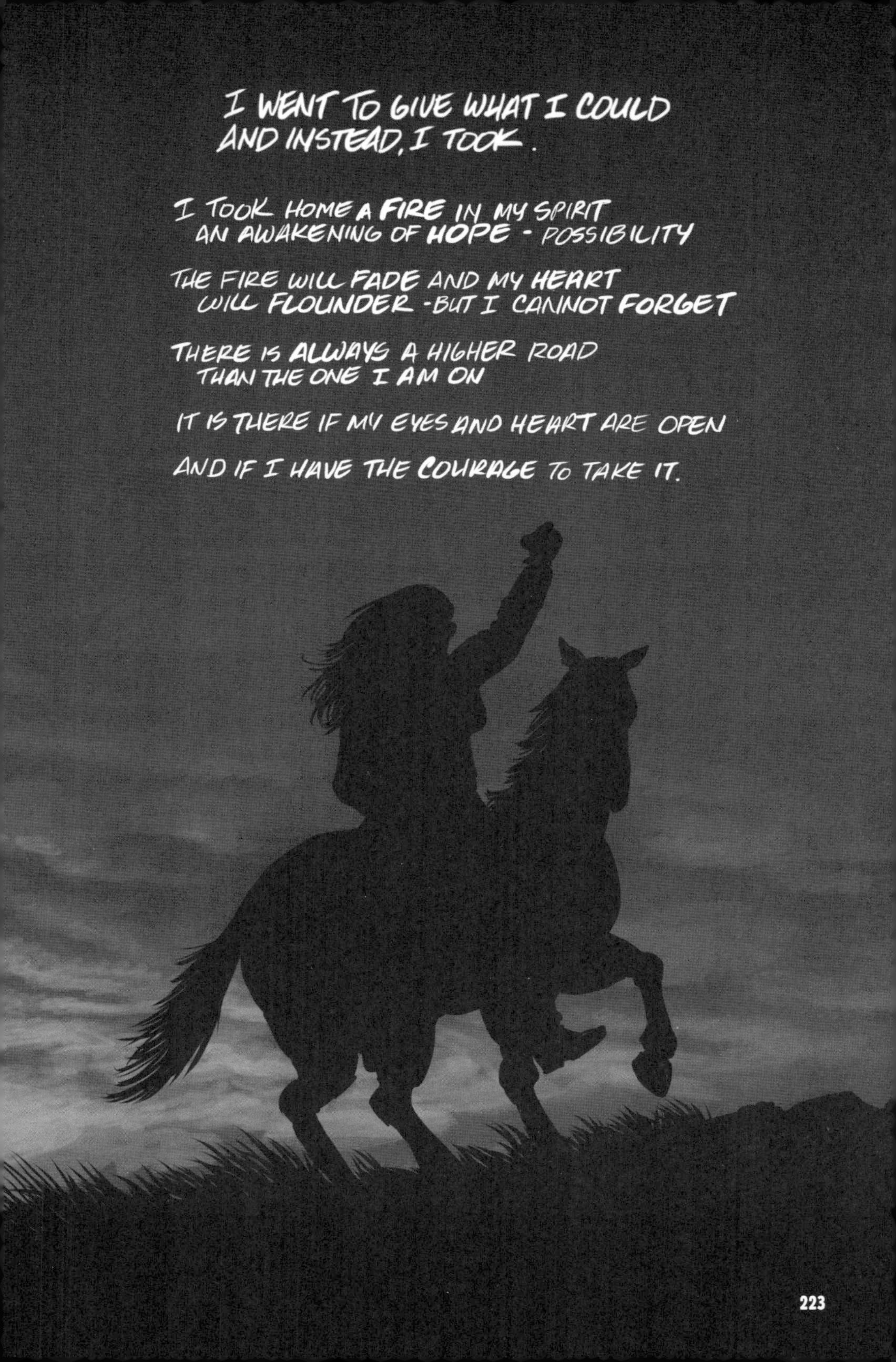
I WENT TO GIVE WHAT I COULD
AND INSTEAD, I TOOK.
I TOOK HOME A FIRE IN MY SPIRIT
AN AWAKENING OF HOPE - POSSIBILITY
THE FIRE WILL FADE AND MY HEART
WILL FLOUNDER - BUT I CANNOT FORGET
THERE IS ALWAYS A HIGHER ROAD
THAN THE ONE I AM ON
IT IS THERE IF MY EYES AND HEART ARE OPEN
AND IF I HAVE THE COURAGE TO TAKE IT.

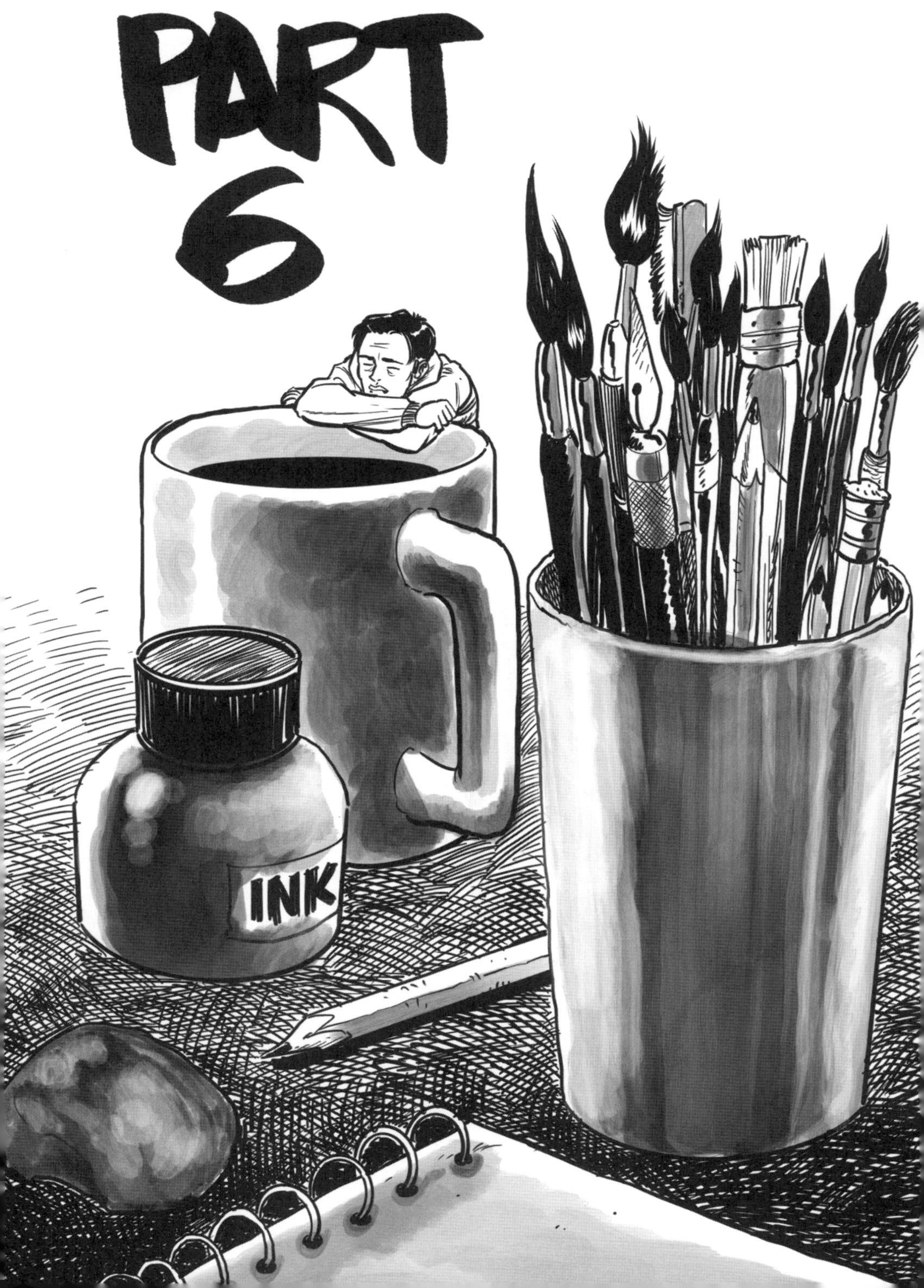
PART 6
INK

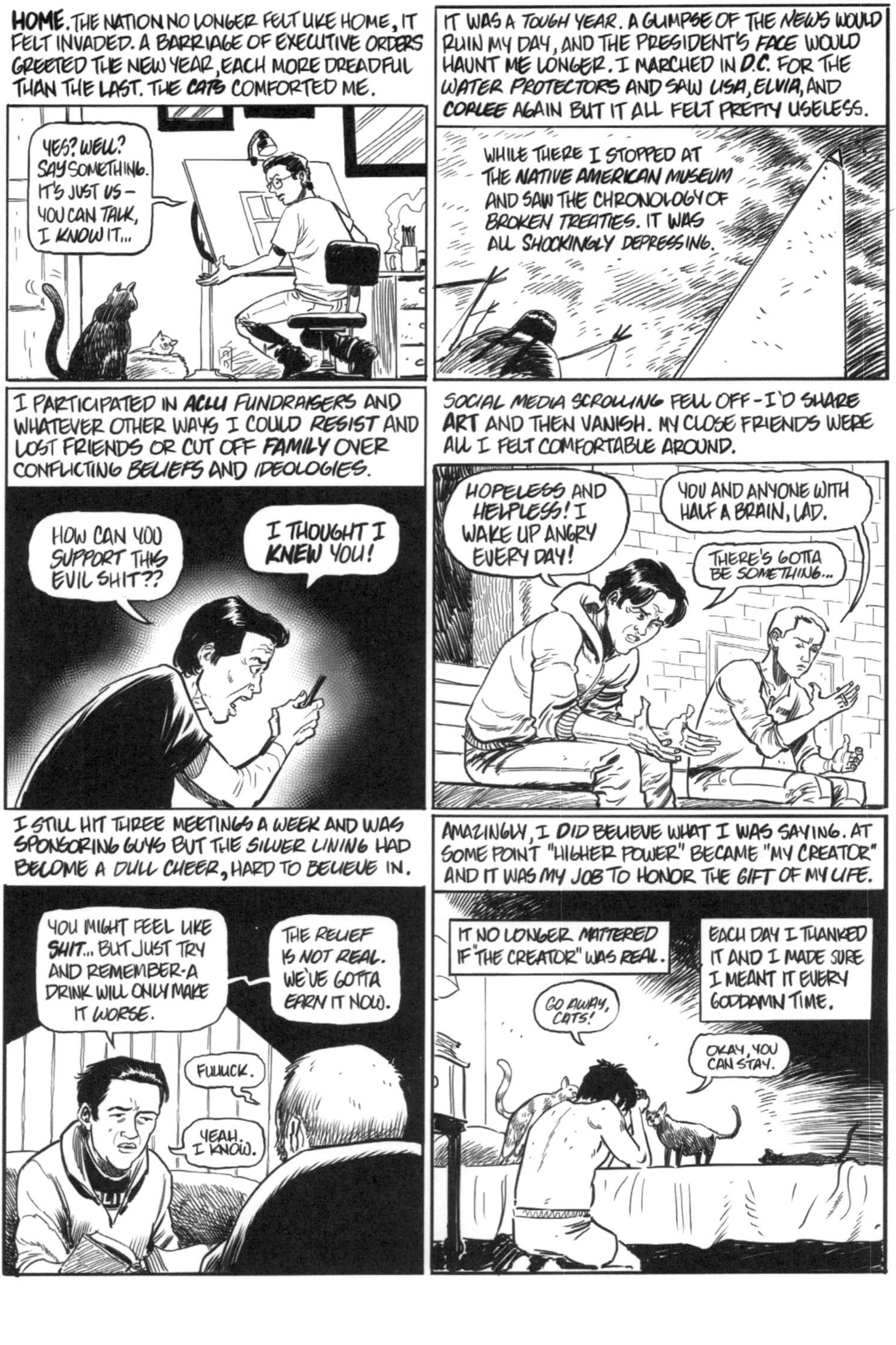
HOME. THE NATION NO LONGER FELT LIKE HOME, IT FELT INVADED. A BARRIAGE OF EXECUTIVE ORDERS GREETED THE NEW YEAR, EACH MORE DREADFUL THAN THE LAST. THE CATS COMFORTED ME.
YES? WELL? SAY SOMETHING. IT'S JUST US — YOU CAN TALK, I KNOW IT...
IT WAS A TOUGH YEAR. A GLIMPSE OF THE NEWS WOULD RUIN MY DAY, AND THE PRESIDENT'S FACE WOULD HAUNT ME LONGER. I MARCHED IN D.C. FOR THE WATER PROTECTORS AND SAW LISA, ELVIA, AND CORLEE AGAIN BUT IT ALL FELT PRETTY USELESS.
WHILE THERE I STOPPED AT THE NATIVE AMERICAN MUSEUM AND SAW THE CHRONOLOGY OF BROKEN TREATIES. IT WAS ALL SHOCKINGLY DEPRESSING.
I PARTICIPATED IN ACLU FUNDRAISERS AND WHATEVER OTHER WAYS I COULD RESIST AND LOST FRIENDS OR CUT OFF FAMILY OVER CONFLICTING BELIEFS AND IDEOLOGIES.
HOW CAN YOU SUPPORT THIS EVIL SHIT??
I THOUGHT I KNEW YOU!
SOCIAL MEDIA SCROLLING FELL OFF - I'D SHARE ART AND THEN VANISH. MY CLOSE FRIENDS WERE ALL I FELT COMFORTABLE AROUND.
HOPELESS AND HELPLESS! I WAKE UP ANGRY EVERY DAY!
YOU AND ANYONE WITH HALF A BRAIN, LAD.
THERE'S GOTTA BE SOMETHING...
I STILL HIT THREE MEETINGS A WEEK AND WAS SPONSORING GUYS BUT THE SILVER LINING HAD BECOME A DULL CHEER, HARD TO BELIEVE IN.
YOU MIGHT FEEL LIKE SHIT... BUT JUST TRY AND REMEMBER - A DRINK WILL ONLY MAKE IT WORSE.
THE RELIEF IS NOT REAL. WE'VE GOTTA EARN IT NOW.
FUUUCK.
YEAH. I KNOW.
AMAZINGLY, I DID BELIEVE WHAT I WAS SAYING. AT SOME POINT "HIGHER POWER" BECAME "MY CREATOR" AND IT WAS MY JOB TO HONOR THE GIFT OF MY LIFE.
IT NO LONGER MATTERED IF "THE CREATOR" WAS REAL.
EACH DAY I THANKED IT AND I MADE SURE I MEANT IT EVERY GODDAMN TIME.
GO AWAY, CATS!
OKAY, YOU CAN STAY.

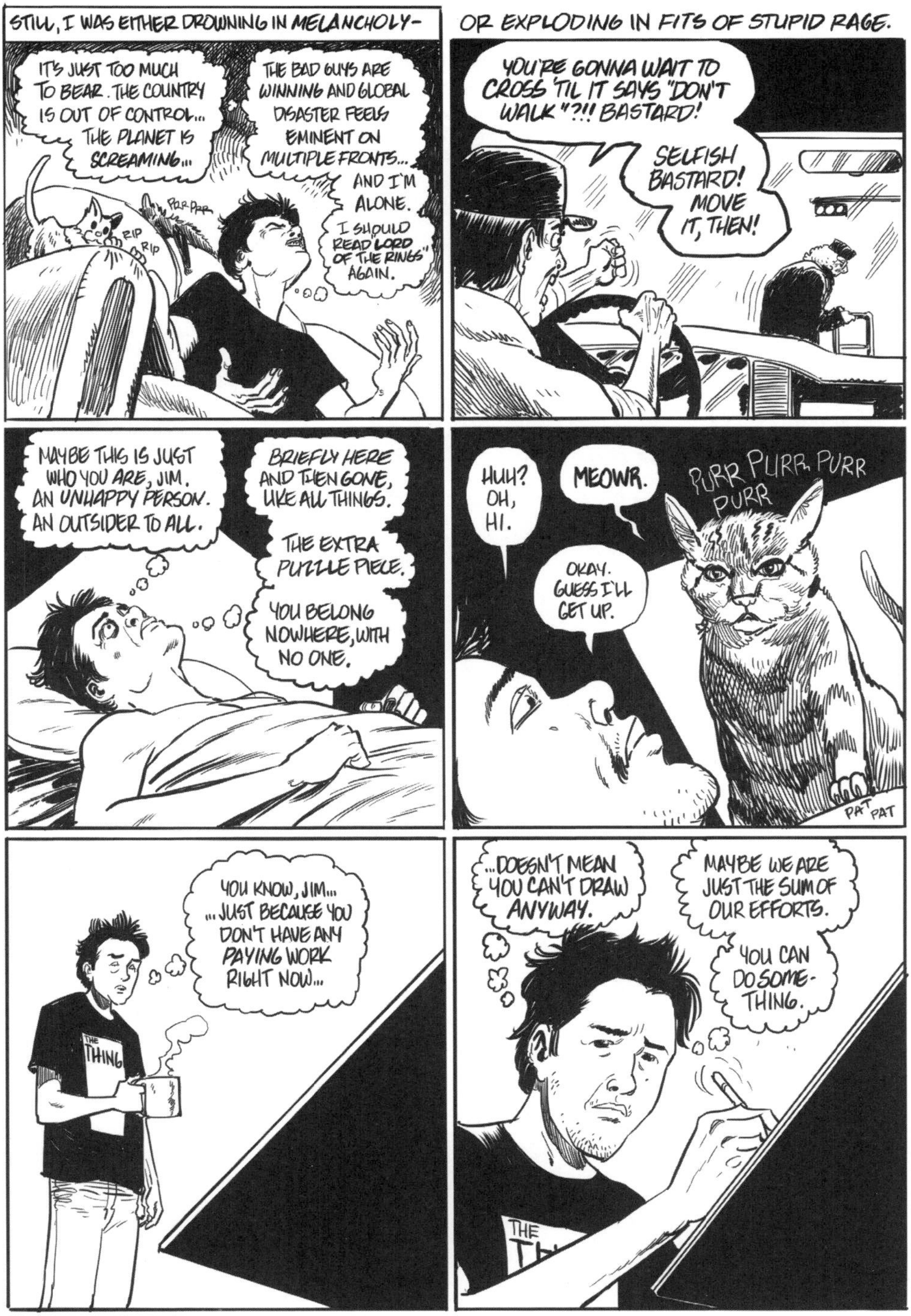
STILL, I WAS EITHER DROWNING IN MELANCHOLY-
IT'S JUST TOO MUCH TO BEAR. THE COUNTRY IS OUT OF CONTROL... THE PLANET IS SCREAMING...
THE BAD GUYS ARE WINNING AND GLOBAL DISASTER FEELS EMINENT ON MULTIPLE FRONTS...
AND I'M ALONE.
I SHOULD READ "LORD OF THE RINGS" AGAIN.
PRR PRR
RIP RIP RIP
OR EXPLODING IN FITS OF STUPID RAGE.
YOU'RE GONNA WAIT TO CROSS 'TIL IT SAYS "DON'T WALK"?!! BASTARD!
SELFISH BASTARD! MOVE IT, THEN!
MAYBE THIS IS JUST WHO YOU ARE, JIM. AN UNHAPPY PERSON. AN OUTSIDER TO ALL.
BRIEFLY HERE AND THEN GONE, LIKE ALL THINGS.
THE EXTRA PUZZLE PIECE.
YOU BELONG NOWHERE, WITH NO ONE.
HUH? OH, HI.
MEOWR.
PURR PURR PURR PURR
OKAY. GUESS I'LL GET UP.
PAT PAT
YOU KNOW, JIM... ...JUST BECAUSE YOU DON'T HAVE ANY PAYING WORK RIGHT NOW...
THE THING
...DOESN'T MEAN YOU CAN'T DRAW ANYWAY.
MAYBE WE ARE JUST THE SUM OF OUR EFFORTS.
YOU CAN DO SOMETHING.
THE TH

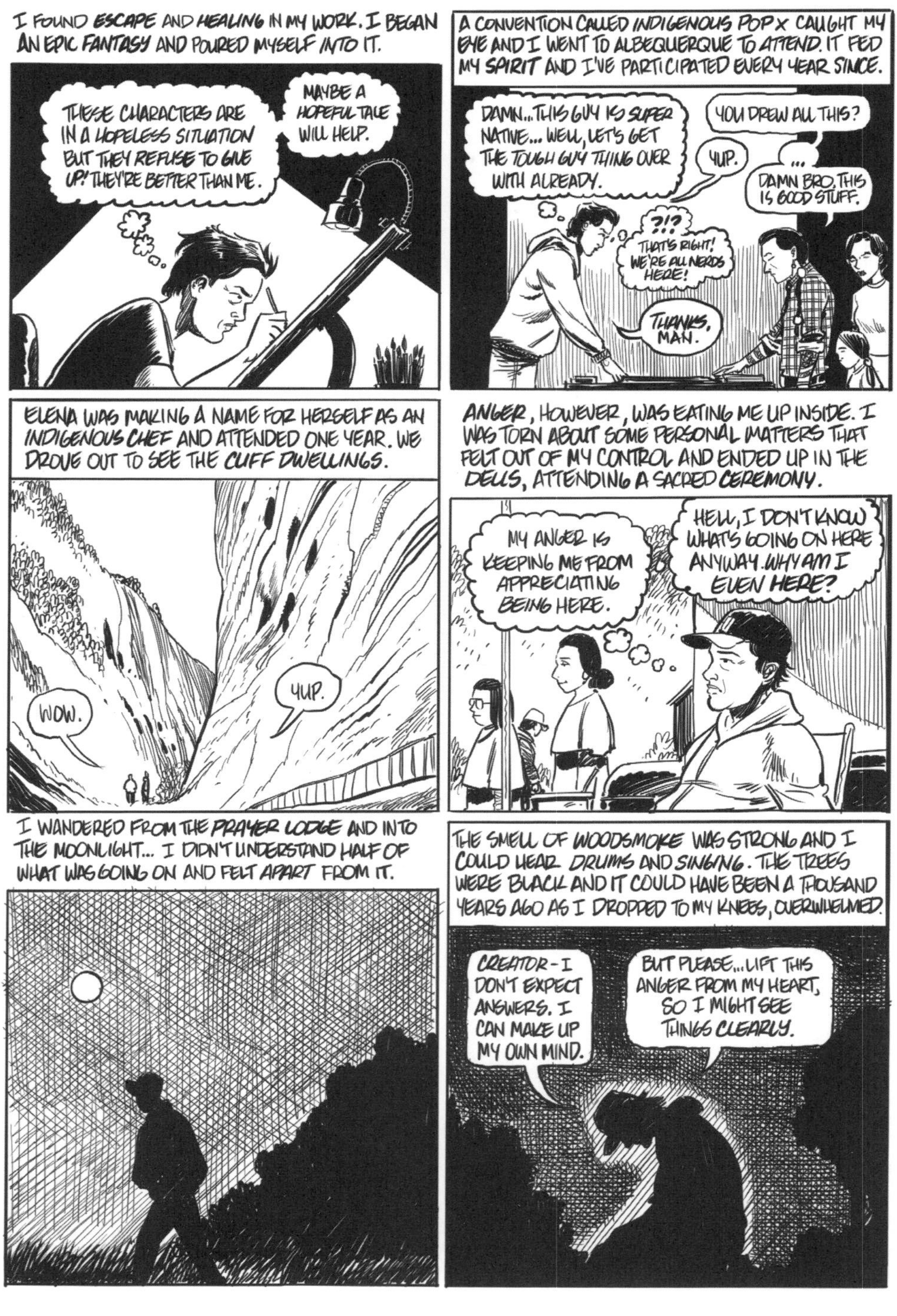
I FOUND ESCAPE AND HEALING IN MY WORK. I BEGAN AN EPIC FANTASY AND POURED MYSELF INTO IT.
THESE CHARACTERS ARE IN A HOPELESS SITUATION BUT THEY REFUSE TO GIVE UP! THEY'RE BETTER THAN ME.
MAYBE A HOPEFUL TALE WILL HELP.
A CONVENTION CALLED INDIGENOUS POP X CAUGHT MY EYE AND I WENT TO ALBEQUERQUE TO ATTEND. IT FED MY SPIRIT AND I'VE PARTICIPATED EVERY YEAR SINCE.
DAMN... THIS GUY IS SUPER NATIVE... WELL, LET'S GET THE TOUGH GUY THING OVER WITH ALREADY.
YOU DREW ALL THIS?
YUP.
... DAMN BRO. THIS IS GOOD STUFF.
?!? THAT'S RIGHT! WE'RE ALL NERDS HERE!
THANKS, MAN.
ELENA WAS MAKING A NAME FOR HERSELF AS AN INDIGENOUS CHEF AND ATTENDED ONE YEAR. WE DROVE OUT TO SEE THE CLIFF DWELLINGS.
WOW.
YUP.
ANGER, HOWEVER, WAS EATING ME UP INSIDE. I WAS TORN ABOUT SOME PERSONAL MATTERS THAT FELT OUT OF MY CONTROL AND ENDED UP IN THE DELLS, ATTENDING A SACRED CEREMONY.
MY ANGER IS KEEPING ME FROM APPRECIATING BEING HERE.
HELL, I DON'T KNOW WHAT'S GOING ON HERE ANYWAY. WHY AM I EVEN HERE?
I WANDERED FROM THE PRAYER LODGE AND INTO THE MOONLIGHT... I DIDN'T UNDERSTAND HALF OF WHAT WAS GOING ON AND FELT APART FROM IT.
THE SMELL OF WOODSMOKE WAS STRONG AND I COULD HEAR DRUMS AND SINGING. THE TREES WERE BLACK AND IT COULD HAVE BEEN A THOUSAND YEARS AGO AS I DROPPED TO MY KNEES, OVERWHELMED.
CREATOR - I DON'T EXPECT ANSWERS. I CAN MAKE UP MY OWN MIND.
BUT PLEASE... LIFT THIS ANGER FROM MY HEART, SO I MIGHT SEE THINGS CLEARLY.

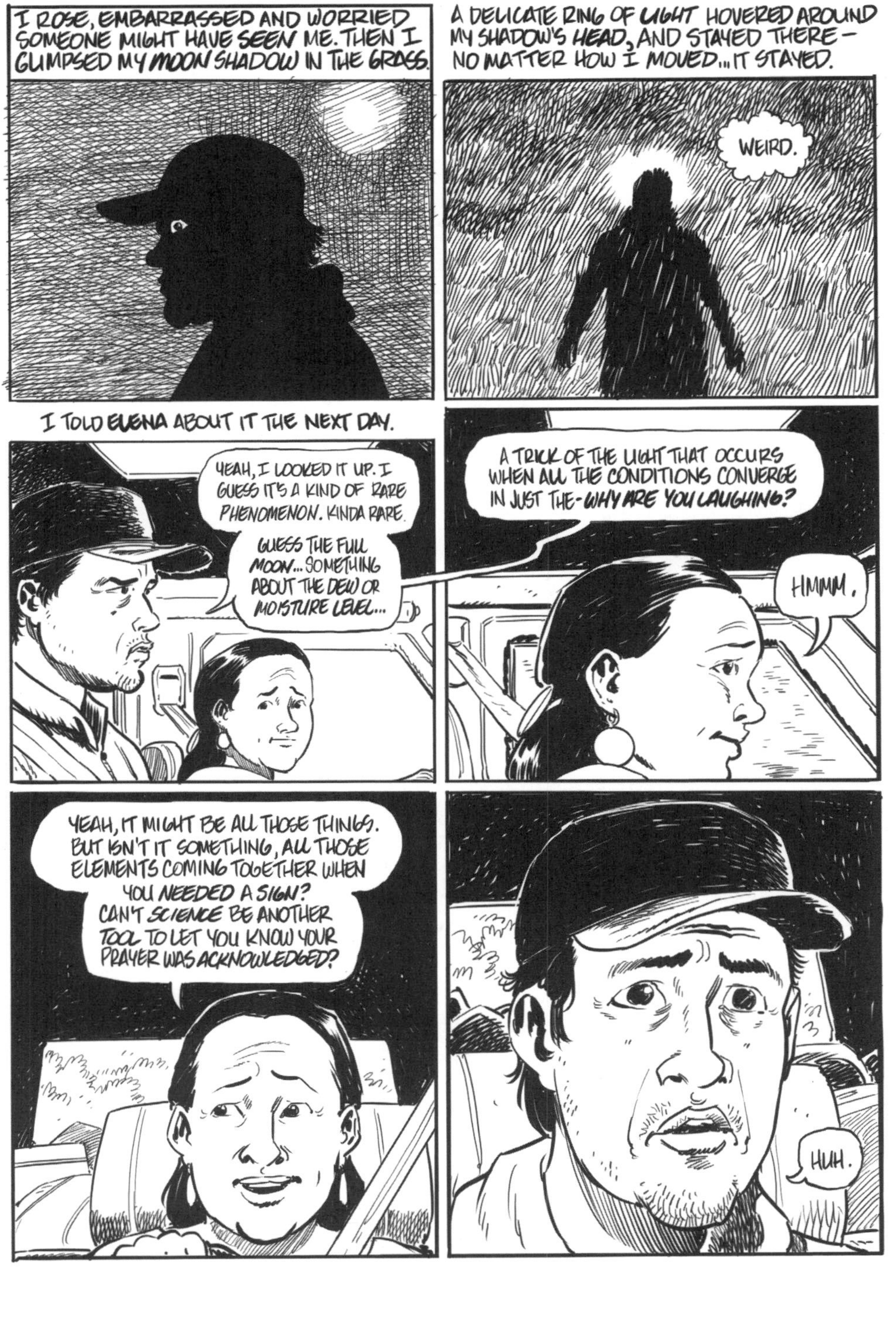
I ROSE, EMBARRASSED AND WORRIED SOMEONE MIGHT HAVE SEEN ME. THEN I GLIMPSED MY MOON SHADOW IN THE GRASS.
A DELICATE RING OF LIGHT HOVERED AROUND MY SHADOW'S HEAD, AND STAYED THERE — NO MATTER HOW I MOVED... IT STAYED.
WEIRD.
I TOLD ELENA ABOUT IT THE NEXT DAY.
YEAH, I LOOKED IT UP. I GUESS IT'S A KIND OF RARE PHENOMENON. KINDA RARE.
GUESS THE FULL MOON... SOMETHING ABOUT THE DEW OR MOISTURE LEVEL...
A TRICK OF THE LIGHT THAT OCCURS WHEN ALL THE CONDITIONS CONVERGE IN JUST THE- WHY ARE YOU LAUGHING?
HMMM.
YEAH, IT MIGHT BE ALL THOSE THINGS. BUT ISN'T IT SOMETHING, ALL THOSE ELEMENTS COMING TOGETHER WHEN YOU NEEDED A SIGN? CAN'T SCIENCE BE ANOTHER TOOL TO LET YOU KNOW YOUR PRAYER WAS ACKNOWLEDGED?
HUH.

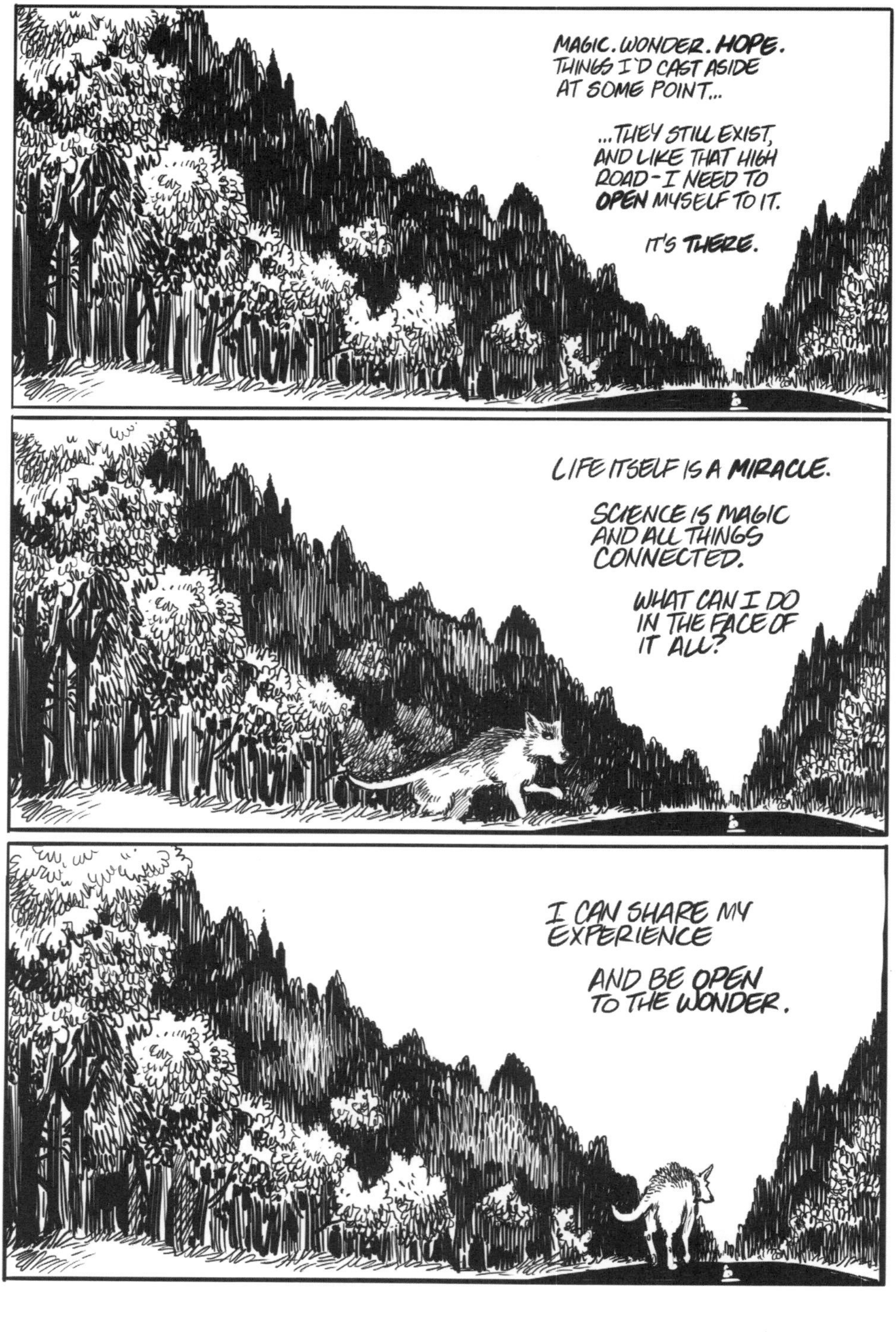
MAGIC. WONDER. HOPE. THINGS I'D CAST ASIDE AT SOME POINT...
...THEY STILL EXIST, AND LIKE THAT HIGH ROAD - I NEED TO OPEN MYSELF TO IT.
IT'S THERE.
LIFE ITSELF IS A MIRACLE.
SCIENCE IS MAGIC AND ALL THINGS CONNECTED.
WHAT CAN I DO IN THE FACE OF IT ALL?
I CAN SHARE MY EXPERIENCE
AND BE OPEN TO THE WONDER.

TO ME THAT WAS A COSMIC, MIND-BLOWING REVELATION.
THOSE INSANE, LONELY DRUNKEN NIGHTS WEREN'T FAR OFF.
EVERYTHING *DID* LEAD TO THIS MOMENT, THIS VERY MOMENT.
AS I WRITE THIS, AS YOU READ THIS.

EVERYTHING.

EVERY CHANCE TAKEN, EVERY MUSICAL NOTE,
ALL THE FRIENDS MADE AND LOST
EVERY LOVE, THE CHANCE ENCOUNTERS ON BRIDGES
IN BARS IN CLASS AT WORK OR NOT MEANING TO
RECOVERY AFTER DESPAIR, EVERY MOMENT OF DREAD

WATCHING A LOVED ONE BREATHE IN SLEEP

THE KINDESSES, A KISS, A HUG, HOLDING A HAND
STOLEN GLANCES MISSED OPPORTUNITIES REGRETS
SICKNESS AND DEATH AND EVERY FILM WATCHED
EVERY BOOK READ EVERY PAGE DRAWN EVERY MEAL
ALL THE FIGHTS LOST AND HATE ENDURED

SWEATING OUT A SICKNESS

CRAZY HORSE IN DEFIANCE RED CLOUD IN PRAYER
MY FATHER PLAYING THE BASS HIS BROTHERS DYING
CHIEF BIG FOOT CROSSING THE BADLANDS MY MOTHER
MY MOTHER CALLING ME TO TELL ME HOW OLD TONY'D BE
CHIEF BIG FOOT MURDERED AND FROZEN IN THE SNOW

STEALING GRANPA'S GLASSES

MY SISTER BECOMING A LEADER, EVERY SUNRISE
MY OTHER SISTER A MOTHER, EVERY RAINDROP
TRAGEDY HISTORY LIES TRIUMPHS LOSS
LOST CAUSES ALL REBELLION ALL OF IT
EVERY MOMENT IN TIME, TIME ITSELF

BEYOND MAN, BEYOND TIME

MIRACLES. TRAGEDIES. ALL LEADING
TO THIS MOMENT. YOU READING OPENING
YOUR MIND TO MINE. HEARING MY THOUGHTS,
HEARING MY STORY. SEEING MY WEAKNESS

MY STRENGTH

LET US OPEN OUR HEARTS AND
BE CONNECTED.

EVERYTHING HAS LED
UP TO NOW.

WHAT DO WE DO
WITH IT?

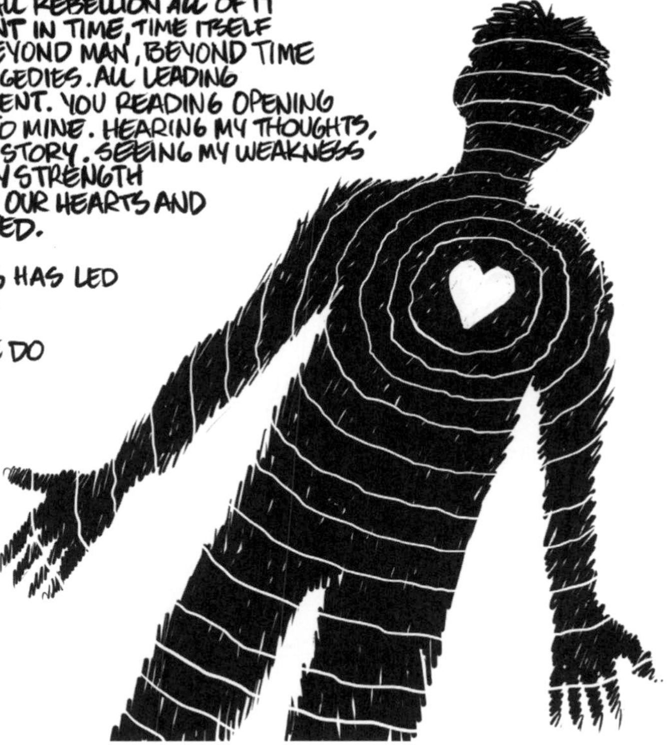

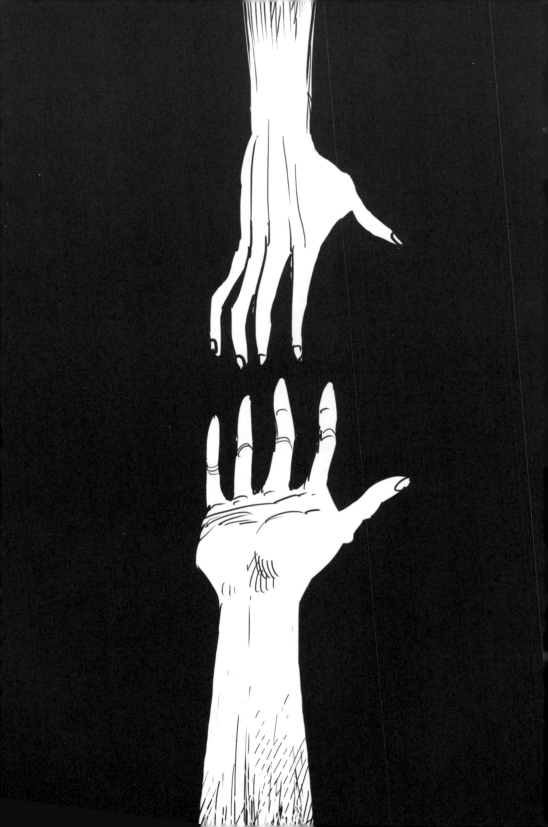

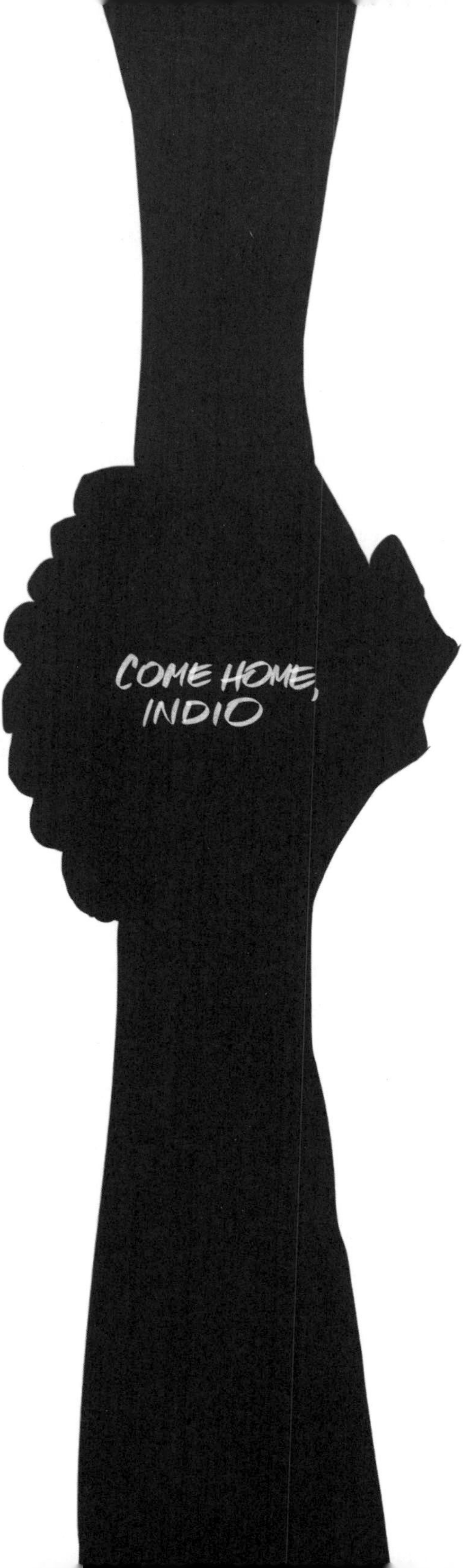
COME HOME,
INDIO

AUTHOR'S NOTE

In the creation of this book, there were a few issues I struggled with. And I'd like to take a second to share some of my thoughts on them.

As I was writing this memoir I realized some serious omissions had to be made. Significant moments and people close to me were left out, either for the sake of brevity, or because I thought those people wouldn't want to be represented in a book. Some folks told me they wanted to remain private, and I did my best to respect that. But I'd like to acknowledge that many good people were kept out of the mix, and this in no way indicates that they weren't important to me.

Another thing I want to address is the language used in the book. I realize quite a bit of it is harsh and might be triggering. In discussions with my editor, I considered changing things so as to make it less offensive. But in the end, I felt it was necessary to leave that ugliness in there, because racism and homophobia were slung about so casually by people in my life when I was growing up, that pretending this wasn't the case seems a disservice to all those who, like me, suffered from those barbs.

Finally, I take great care in my daily life, and certainly in anything I create, not to advertise or represent the specific program by which I got sober. To paraphrase a great author of horror books, however, I will say, "If you look in a phone book it'll probably be at the very front of the alphabet."

Please take care,

Jim Terry
Chicago, Illinois
June 2020